CORPS COMMANDERS
OF THE BULGE

MODERN WAR STUDIES

CORPS COMMANDERS OF THE BULGE

Six American Generals and Victory in the Ardennes

Harold R. Winton

Foreword by Dennis Showalter

University Press of Kansas

Published by the University Press of Kansas (Lawrence, Kansas 66045),
which was organized by the Kansas Board of Regents and is operated
and funded by Emporia State University, Fort Hays State University,
Kansas State University, Pittsburg State University, the University of
Kansas, and Wichita State University

ISBN-13: 978-0-7006-1508-7

Printed in the United States of America

Since we already require excellent intellectual qualities of those who are to be outstanding in the lower positions of command, and since these requirements increase with every level, it naturally follows that we have a completely different opinion than do people generally of the men who fill with distinction the second positions of an army.

Clausewitz

CONTENTS

Contents

ILLUSTRATIONS AND MAPS

Photographs

John Millikin being congratulated by Jacob L. Devers
Manton S. Eddy being decorated by George S. Patton, Jr.
Manton S. Eddy
J. Lawton Collins

Maps

FOREWORD

This work addresses, systematically and in detail, a question that until this day has remained essentially unanswered. How, exactly how, did the truncated, marginalized U.S. Army of the interwar period produce so many capable division and corps commanders by the time of the D-Day campaign of 1944–1945?

It has been said, accurately, that he who has not fought the Germans does not know war. Discussions of the army's performance during its graduation exercises tend to concentrate at the top and the bottom. At policy and strategy levels, the focus is on Anglo-American friction and the competence of Dwight Eisenhower and his army commanders. At the sharp end, the issue of American "fighting power" vis-à-vis the German adversary inspires discussion of everything from tank design to infantry replacement policies.

Without competence in the middle parts of command, however, superior generalship and battlefield virtuosity alike are likely to be wasted. Given the nature of modern war and the scale of the fighting in Northwest Europe, effectiveness at division and corps levels was crucial to performance in all of the contending armies. Here, if anywhere, the Germans might have been expected to enjoy an advantage. To a history of large armies and a widely praised system of military education, they added five years of ruthless combat: surely time enough for cream to rise to the top. Even the British army, hardly a touchstone for military preparedness during the interwar years, had possessed a structure of higher commands and a spectrum of missions that allowed senior commanders to test their ideas and try their wings.

The United States Army did not neglect what it called "the art of command." Its Command and General Staff School at Fort Leavenworth was designed to train middle-grade officers for assignment at division and corps levels. Its curriculum and ethos, however, encouraged the development of staff officers rather than commanders: problem solvers rather than battle captains. The Army War College, created in 1903, emphasized preparing its students for high command but focused largely on theory drawn from history, especially American experience in the Civil War and in World War I. Post-1918 technological developments, and their accompanying pressure for devolved authority and individual initiative, were largely neglected.

The army, moreover, had for all practical purposes no operational command structure above the regiment. Divisions and corps were paper formations. Most of the regiments, grossly undermanned and geographically dispersed, were more notional than functional. Even the major overseas garrisons, Hawaii and the Philippines, were essentially administrative entities. The exponential expansion of the army that began in 1940, and the accompanying purge of senior National Guard officers who at least had some practice handling a division, produced a network of two-star generals who essentially learned their craft on the job.

This was an unpromising matrix for final victory. Even if its best days were past by the summer of 1944, Hitler's Wehrmacht was a formidable enemy that charged a bloody tuition for its lessons. But the men who led Eisenhower's divisions and corps across Europe performed well—so well that they are seldom included in the list of America's military shortcomings compared to the Germans, the Soviets, and even the British. There were around a hundred of them. The photos that appear scattered throughout the volumes of the official history or concentrated in the illustrations of the books in the military history sections of contemporary bookstores look strangely alike under the steel helmets or the bills of dress caps. If their names may not be household words in the twenty-first century, they hold a respected place in that body of "good ordinary generals" on whose competence all armies depend no less than on the skill and wills of their ordinary soldiers.

These generals were a cohort in the most basic sense. They held the same rank: major general. The usual congressional concern for keeping budgets and egos down meant that, unlike most other armies, corps and division commanders were differentiated by appointment but not by rank. Yet paradoxically, those who held the higher post were the invisible men of the general officer corps.

The division was the army's building block. Generals are usually identified with the divisions they commanded: Terry Allen with the 1st and 104th; P. Wood with the 4th Armored; and so on. The army commanders are familiar for the most part because there were fewer of them. Corps were anonymous. Their identities were amorphous. They had no permanent structure; divisions and supporting units shifted from one to another, often with bewildering speed. Even their designation by roman numerals made it just that much more difficult to tell them apart amid the Is and the Xs.

Yet the corps was the fundamental unit of operational command in the European Theater of Operations. It was to the corps that Patton, Hodges, and their counterparts turned to run the battles that army headquarters planned. The corps was like an O-ring: easy to overlook but a vital element in the system's functioning. With no administrative responsibilities, its headquarters provided tactical direction to the flexible combinations of forces required by the modern mobile battlefield. Its command was a corresponding test of a general officer's ability, his professionalism, and not least his character.

Winton features six of the U.S. Army's best: Leonard Gerow, J. Lawton Collins, John Millikin, Matthew Ridgway, Troy Middleton, and Manton Eddy. He takes them through their prewar careers and their respective experiences in the army's educational system and then sends them into action in a critical situation: the Battle of the Bulge. His decision to focus on an operation involving an initial series of defeats is unusual—and correspondingly praiseworthy. Adversity spotlights character and ability—or their absence—more clearly and unforgivingly than victory.

Winton has been engaged in this project for years and shows an easy mastery of a broad spectrum of sources. While maintaining focus on the corps that directed the ground battle, he presents their actions in context by segueing his presentation easily from frontline battalion to army group levels. He systematically integrates the role of airpower in U.S. ground operations. He presents the German perspective of events, offering a consistent, solid analysis of command problems and command decisions on "the other side of the hill."

Winton avoids in exemplary fashion the editorializing and second-guessing that mars so much operational history. He allows his subjects' achievements—and mistakes—to tell their own stories. The result is a seminal presentation of the processes of developing senior officers from a near-vestigial professional army to command a national conscript force. It is also a model account of the Battle of the Bulge. Winton does a particularly outstanding job of challenging the still-familiar canard that the U.S. Army won its war by unsophisticated use of overwhelming materiel superiority. The German offensive was a desperate undertaking. But the Wehrmacht had five years of practice at beating long odds. In the Bulge it gave its remaining best at all levels. Victory—and victory at relatively low cost—reflected "brute force" less than it did the operational fine-tuning provided by six men: the American corps commanders.

The U.S. Army had no "right" backgrounds like Britain's Brigade of Guards or Germany's General Staff to ease the path of promising juniors. Personal qualities were correspondingly important. Carefully avoiding the temptations of psychohistory on one hand and prosopography on the other, Winton describes a half dozen different but harmonious blends of intelligence, character, and energy—the kinds that may not predict, but certainly prefigure, success in command. Connections, serendipity, a certain randomness, also helped bring these particular generals to the Ardennes in the winter of 1944. But what ultimately made them the right men at the right time was their common experience of an advanced formal, institutional education for command that combined with their individual talents and potentials in a distinctively American fashion. Winton's generals built individually upon a system that, whatever its shortcomings, provided a solid matrix for developing professional ability. Like the army in which they served, the corps commanders in the Battle of the Bulge were not found wanting when tested against the best across the battle line.

Dennis Showalter

PREFACE

The seeds for this study were sown on a cold winter day in 1985 on a small bus winding its way through the Ardennes during a battlefield tour being conducted by the U.S. Army's School of Advanced Military Studies (SAMS). The instructors were one of my faculty colleagues, Douglas V. Johnson II, and one of my students, Gregory M. Fontenot. Both were eminently qualified. Doug had taught the advanced sections of the History of the Military Art course at West Point, and Greg had produced a superb master's thesis on the 7th Armored Division in the Ardennes campaign. Greg opened his lecture on the bus with the observation that this was the largest single action fought by the U.S. Army during World War II. That statement immediately piqued my interest, simply because I had never thought of the battle in terms of its scale, but in terms of its causes, its conduct, and its consequences. But of course, I thought to myself, it *was* the largest American battle of the war. Normandy was arguably more important, because if the Allies had not gotten ashore, there simply would not have been a campaign in Northwest Europe. But the Bulge was demonstrably a larger affair, both in terms of the forces employed and in terms of the geographic area covered. It also had more than its fair share of high command drama and gripping stories of small bands of lonely soldiers fighting against terrible odds in conditions that Eric Larrabee tellingly characterizes as "indescribable repulsiveness and stress."[1] As I walked the ground that year and listened to what Doug and Greg had to say, I realized what a multifaceted undertaking this had been and how much could be learned from studying it closely. In short, I became "hooked" on the Bulge.

My fascination with the Ardennes campaign was abetted by the fact that in the following summer Doug and Greg both moved on, leaving me with responsibility for the enterprise. Over the next four years, I had the opportunity to return annually to the Ardennes to help the SAMS students develop some of the many insights one can take away from studying this epic struggle in almost every area of military art and science: leadership at all levels; the importance of small unit cohesion; the reciprocal relationships among tactics, operational art, and strategy; the influence of terrain on land combat and of weather on both land and air combat; the interplay among intelligence, operations, and logistics; the centrality of combined arms to effective tactical forms; and the interplay of moral, mental, and material factors in war. In the final stage of this experience, my colleague, then at Fort Leavenworth and now at Air University, Daniel J. Hughes, teamed up with me to convert it from a battlefield tour, in which the students have a rather passive role, into a staff ride, in which the students are active participants. I was also privileged to assist in the conduct of a command staff ride led by General Montgomery Meigs, USA, then commanding U.S. Army forces in Europe, and attended by Congressman Ike Skelton (D-Mo.), a true champion of the study of history in the armed services. And so, over the years, I came to be acquainted with many of the major aspects of this remarkable campaign.

As my appreciation for the Bulge developed, my awareness became more acute of two realities. First, it was, as Greg's opening comment had noted, immense. Nearly 30 American divisions and a like number of German divisions took part, including on both sides more than a million men, 2,300 tanks, and roughly 5,900 pieces of artillery. Additionally, the Americans were supported by some 4,000 Allied aircraft; and the German air effort, while not nearly as large, saw the last gasp of the Luftwaffe that launched a thousand planes on New Year's Day. Second, the literature of the campaign is equally vast. There is a veritable cornucopia of works published on the Bulge, ranging from the accounts of individual soldiers and small unit actions, to analyses of the strains that the campaign placed on the Anglo-American coalition, to other works that attempt to cover the entire campaign, so to speak, from the foxhole to Versailles. As I surveyed this literature, however, it appeared to me that two things were missing. First, I found it difficult to determine in any depth what role had been played by the American corps commanders who participated in the battle. Second, although I could find a great deal of material on the ground battle and some material on aerial combat, there was almost nothing that attempted to establish connections between the two. This latter concern became more personally pressing in 1990 when I took up my current position at the U.S. Air Force's School of Advanced Air and Space Studies (SAASS) and began to view my historical and theoretical studies in a more three-dimensional framework than I had previously. I thus determined it would be useful to examine the contributions to the campaign made by the six American corps commanders and to ensure that the portrayal of the larger contextual factors paid some attention to the air operations that helped influence and shape it.

One personal disclaimer is required. My father, Walter F. Winton, Jr., to whom this work is dedicated, fought in the Bulge as the G-2, or intelligence officer, of the 82nd Airborne Division. After V-E Day, he became G-2 of XVIII (Airborne) Corps, commanded by Matthew B. Ridgway. He subsequently served under Ridgway in four different assignments, perhaps most notably as his aide-de-camp in the Korean War. He was, and still is, a "Ridgway man." I believe he is so with good reason. Despite this belief, I have attempted to be as objective in my assessment of Ridgway as I have of the other protagonists of this work. It is left to the reader to determine the extent to which this effort has succeeded.

As in any work of this magnitude, many obligations must be acknowledged. Two of my superiors at SAMS, then Colonels Richard Hart Sinnreich and L. D. "Don" Holder, allowed me to return repeatedly to the Ardennes to soak up the battlefield. And two commandants of SAASS, Colonels Philip Meilinger and Thomas Griffith, staunchly supported requests for sabbaticals to get this work into gear and to bring it to completion. My SAASS colleagues graciously absorbed increased teaching and advisory loads during these absences. The Air University Foundation generously supported the acquisition of photographs and the production of maps.

Archivists, librarians, and other colleagues have been of inestimable assistance. Foremost is Dr. Timothy Nenninger, chief of modern military records at the National Archives. Tim has gone far out of his way to track down documents during and between my trips to Washington, D.C., and to College Park, Maryland; he is an important asset to the study of military history in this country and a true friend to those who practice the craft. Robin Crookson, German records specialist at the National Archives, answered many questions and facilitated acquisition of the foreign military studies collection by the Air University Library; and Holly Reed was of great assistance in the still photograph collection. David Keough, senior archivist/historian in the historical reference branch at the U.S. Army Military History Institute (MHI), Carlisle Barracks, Pennsylvania, has offered many kind suggestions and insights to facilitate my work and responded with alacrity to many email queries. Dr. Richard Sommers, head of the patron services branch in MHI's recently dedicated Ridgway Hall, graciously and efficiently eased my labors in the institute's still photo collection. John Slonaker, head of the historical reference branch at MHI, guided me through the institute's comprehensive collection of unit histories. Eric Voelz, archivist at the National Personnel Records Center, St. Louis, Missouri, was immensely helpful in locating and providing access to the personnel records of the six protagonists of this study. Bob Lane and Dr. Shirley Lassiter, successive directors of the Air University Library, Maxwell Air Force Base, Alabama, have supported without hesitation the acquisition of materials to support this work. Additional assistance from this fine institution has been provided by Sarah Vickery, chief of the technical services branch; Lynn Lonnegran, acquisitions specialist; Steve

Chun, Ron Fuller, and Joan Phillips, bibliographers; Glenda Armstrong, formerly cartographic specialist; and, especially, Edith Williams, interlibrary loan librarian. Joseph Caver and Dr. James Kitchens were unfailingly helpful and courteous in guiding me through the relevant airpower papers at the U.S. Air Force Historical Research Agency. Elaine McConnell, former archivist in the special collections at the Combined Arms Research Library, Fort Leavenworth, Kansas, provided cheerful and efficient responses to repeated requests. Diane Jacob at the Virginia Military Institute Archives in Lexington, Virginia, was extremely helpful in guiding me through the Leonard T. Gerow papers. Dr. Larry Bland and Marty Gansz provided excellent assistance at the George C. Marshall Library, also in Lexington. Dr. John P. Millikin of Phoenix, Arizona, General John Millikin's grandson, graciously allowed access to his grandfather's private papers. Z. Frank Hanner, director of the National Infantry Museum at Fort Benning, Georgia, kindly provided extracts of Manton S. Eddy's combat log. Dr. Boyd Dastrup, command historian at the U.S. Army Field Artillery Center, provided useful insights on the organization of corps artillery in World War II. And Dwight Strandberg of the Dwight D. Eisenhower Library in Abilene, Kansas, competently guided me through its collections. Michael Briggs, editor-in-chief at the University Press of Kansas, offered encouragement and a number of very helpful suggestions in the final stages of composition. Kelly Rhodes proved a wizard on the scanner and saved me many hours. Dennis Showalter reviewed the manuscript with his indomitable mixture of perspicacity, attention to detail, and verve. Jonathan House offered numerous, specific suggestions that focused the narrative and polished the presentation. Douglas Johnson asked many shrewd questions that sharpened the analysis. Together, these three scholars constituted a "Dream Team" of collegial, professional assistance that any military historian would treasure.

I would also like to thank Lieutenant Colonel Henry G. Phillips, USA, Ret., for sharing early drafts from his biography of Manton S. Eddy and providing keen insights into Eddy's character and professional competence.[2] Dr. David Hogan of the U.S. Army Center for Military History similarly provided excerpts of an early draft of his study of the First Army headquarters in World War II and has responded with grace and dispatch to a number of follow-on requests.[3] Chapter Two, "Toward an American Philosophy of Command," is a revised version of an article of the same title that appeared in the October 2000 *Journal of Military History* and is included here with the kind permission of the editor. The late Colonel John Madigan, USA, provided a very helpful critique of an early draft of that article. Material from the profile of General Ridgway found in Chapter Three originally appeared in the March-April 2002 *Assembly* under the title "'The Right Way, the Wrong Way, the Ridgway': Matthew B. Ridgway as Division Commander." It is likewise included with the editor's permission.

My wife, Barbara, who has lived with this project for far too long, provided constant encouragement, prodded when necessary, and graciously assisted in the research. She is the love of my life and enriches all that I do.

These intellectual and emotional debts are indeed significant. However, as one confronts the enormity of the Bulge, one is left with a tremendous feeling of humility in light of the incredible sacrifices made by the soldiers who fought on both sides and the manifest impossibility of ever grasping it all. It was truly an epic in both American and German history. I am thus compelled to close with the observation that, despite the generous assistance of many friends and associates, what follows represents my own work; and the aforementioned are blameless in regard to any errors of fact or infelicities of interpretation discovered by the reader.

ABBREVIATIONS

AAA	antiaircraft artillery
AAR	After-Action Report
AD	Armored Division
AEAF	Allied Expeditionary Air Force
AEF	American Expeditionary Forces
AFB	Air Force Base
AG	Army Group
AIB	Armored Infantry Battalion
AUL	Air University Library
CAFH	Center for Air Force History
CARL	Combined Arms Research Library
CBO	Combined Bomber Offensive
CCA	Combat Command A
CCB	Combat Command B
CCR	Combat Command Reserve
CG	Commanding General
CGSC	Command and General Staff College
CGSS	Command and General Staff School
CIGS	Chief of the Imperial General Staff
CMH	Center of Military History
CO	Commanding Officer
CP	Command Post
DDEL	Dwight D. Eisenhower Library
DSC	Distinguished Service Cross
DSM	Distinguished Service Medal
ETHINT	European Theater Historical Interview
ETO	European Theater of Operations
FA	Field Artillery
FEB	Führer Escort Brigade
FGB	Führer Grenadier Brigade
FMS	Foreign Military Studies
FUSA	First United States Army
G-1	General Staff-1 (personnel and administration)
G-2	General Staff-2 (intelligence)
G-3	General Staff-3 (plans, operations, and training)

G-4	General Staff-4 (logistics)
GCML	George C. Marshall Library
GIR	Glider Infantry Regiment
ID	Infantry Division
I&R	Intelligence and Reconnaissance
IR	Infantry Regiment
KIA	killed in action
LD	Line of Departure
LNO	Liaison Officer
LOI	Letter of Instructions
LSU	Louisiana State University
MHI	Military History Institute
MIA	missing in action
NAII	National Archives II
NCO	Noncommissioned Officer
NDU	National Defense University
NPRC	National Personnel Records Center
OAFH	Office of Air Force History
OB	Oberbefehlshaber (Commander-in-Chief)
OCMH	Office of the Chief of Military History
OKH	Oberkommando des Heeres (High Command of the Army)
OKW	Oberkommando der Wehrmacht (High Command of the Armed Forces)
PGD	Panzergrenadier Division
PIR	Parachute Infantry Regiment
POW	prisoner of war
Pz	panzer
RAF	Royal Air Force
RCT	Regimental Combat Team
RG	Record Group
SAASS	School of Advanced Air and Space Studies
SAMS	School of Advanced Military Studies
SGS	Secretary of the General Staff
SHAEF	Supreme Headquarters Allied Expeditionary Forces
Sitrep	Situation Report
SRH	Special Report Historical
SS	Schutzstaffeln (protection squads)
TAC	Tactical Air Command
TAF	Tactical Air Force
TD	tank destroyer

TF	Task Force
USA	United States Army
USAFHRA	United States Air Force Historical Research Agency
USAWC	United States Army War College
USMA	United States Military Academy
USMC	United States Marine Corps
USSBS	United States Strategic Bombing Survey
USSTAF	United States Strategic Air Forces in Europe
VG	Volksgrenadier
VGD	Volksgrenadier Division
VMI	Virginia Military Institute
VT	variable time
WDCSA	War Department Chief of Staff Army
WIA	wounded in action
WPD	War Plans Division

1

Introduction

EARLY ON THE AFTERNOON OF 18 DECEMBER 1944, Major General Troy H. Middleton, Commanding General (CG), VIII Corps, while in his command post at Bastogne, Belgium, received a telephone message from Colonel John H. Gilbreth, Commanding Officer (CO), Combat Command Reserve (CCR), 9th Armored Division.[1] The call requested permission either to withdraw or to reinforce Task Force (TF) Rose, a composite infantry-tank-engineer contingent of about 200 men, commanded by Captain Lawrence K. Rose. Rose's men had been defending a critical road junction ten miles northeast of Bastogne for over five hours and were being pressed on three sides by the lead regiment of the 2nd Panzer Division. We do not know precisely what Middleton was thinking as he considered this request, but we can reconstruct the major considerations that influenced him. Over the previous two days, the German XLVII Panzer Corps had blown a hole ten miles wide in the middle of the VIII Corps sector. Two other German corps had made similar, though not as dramatic, advances farther to the north; and still another two were pressing steadily in the south. German tanks were now west of the Clerf River, the last natural obstacle between VIII Corps' original front lines and Bastogne. If the Germans captured Bastogne, they would control a major road hub enabling them to sustain their offensive at least to the Meuse River, and perhaps beyond. The outlook was bleak, but help was on the way. A combat command of the 10th Armored Division was en route to Bastogne and projected to arrive that evening. Furthermore, the 101st Airborne Division was departing from Rheims, France, on its way by truck to Bastogne. Middleton did not know for certain when the Screaming Eagles would arrive, but with luck it would be sometime on the next day. The human calculus was fairly clear. If Middleton refused Colonel Gilbreth's request for either withdrawal or reinforcement, most of Captain Rose's soldiers would die or spend the rest of the war in German stalags. If he granted the withdrawal request, they could live to fight another day. But the tactical calculus was much more ambiguous. Would reinforcing TF Rose jeopardize the defense of other positions east of Bastogne? How much time could be gained by continuing to defend the road junction, versus falling back to the next position? How much time did he have to have? Could the 101st Airborne and an armored combat command actually defend Bastogne? If so, for how long and under what circumstances? How important was Bastogne anyway? How many lives was it worth? The immediate fate of TF Rose represented just one of the many decisions Middleton would have to make in the campaign that came to be known as the Battle of the Bulge, and he was just one of the six American corps commanders who fought in that campaign.[2]

This book is about those six men, the decisions they made, the actions they took, and the education and experiences that prepared them to become senior commanders. These commanders, listed in the sequence their formations became engaged in the battle, were Major Generals Leonard T. Gerow, CG, V Corps; Troy H. Middleton, CG, VIII Corps; Matthew B. Ridgway, CG, XVIII (Airborne) Corps; John Millikin, CG, III Corps; Manton S. Eddy, CG, XII Corps; and J. Lawton Collins, CG, VII Corps.[3] The book asks four major questions. What were these officers taught about command? How did they grow professionally from their precommissioning studies to the eve of the Bulge? What effect did they and their corps have on the campaign itself? And, how well did their actions and orders live up to what they had been taught?

Additionally, it investigates the contribution to the campaign of the U.S. Army command structure, in which the corps played a particular role. Organized as an intermediate tactical echelon of command subordinate to the field army and largely devoid of administrative and logistical responsibilities, the corps provided sustained tactical direction to a flexible grouping of subordinate divisions, field artillery groups, engineers, and other combat support assets whose number and composition varied with the fluctuating requirements of a dynamic battlefield. The question here is the extent to which this command structure itself influenced the conduct of the Ardennes campaign.

Finally, the book seeks to determine the ways in which airpower, particularly Allied airpower, influenced the conduct of the campaign. Here, several issues must be clarified. First, the corps was not directly involved in the planning of air operations. This function was principally executed one level above the corps, where each field army had associated with it a tactical air command whose primary mission was to provide it both close air support and relatively shallow air interdiction.[4] Thus, the primary nexus of air-ground cooperation was at the field army–tactical air command interface. There was also liaison one level higher between numbered air forces and army groups. During the Ardennes campaign, these connections were between the American Ninth Air Force and 12th Army Group and between the British 2nd Tactical Air Force and 21st Army Group. And finally, the theater headquarters,

Supreme Headquarters Allied Expeditionary Forces (SHAEF), was, under certain circumstances, able to draw upon the resources of the United States Strategic Air Forces in Europe (USSTAF) and the British Bomber Command. The Ardennes campaign represents one of these circumstances. Despite the lack of direct corps involvement in air-ground operations, this issue is being addressed for two reasons. The first is historical: to determine the extent to which the corps battles were influenced by air support. The second is historiographic: despite the abundance of literature on ground operations in the Bulge and a significantly less robust body of literature on its air operations, little has been done to make concrete connections between the two.[5]

Why should there be another study of the Bulge? The primary reason is that there simply does not exist a detailed study of the six American corps commanders who participated actively in the campaign. But to answer the question fully, we must briefly survey the relevant literature. Leaving aside the air studies and the almost-too-numerous-to-count photographic essays interlarded with text, works on the Bulge can be divided into three major categories.

The first group consists of accounts that focus on small-unit actions. They include, among others, Gerald Astor's *A Blood-Dimmed Tide*, Roscoe C. Blunt's *Inside the Battle of the Bulge*, William C. C. Cavanagh's *Krinkelt-Rocherath*, Janice Holt Giles's *The Damned Engineers*, S. L. A. Marshall's *Bastogne*, George W. Neill's *Infantry Soldier*, Robert H. Phillips's *To Save Bastogne*, Michael Reynolds's *The Devil's Adjutant*, and Stephen M. Rusiecki's *The Key to the Bulge*.[6] These are important works. They remind us of the eternal verity that after the strategists decide upon their grand designs and after their intermediate subordinates divine how best to execute these schemes, the tough, messy job of winning wars depends upon the willingness and ability of lonely individuals to put their lives on the line when all their physical senses tell them the risk is not worth the gain.

The second assortment of works about the Ardennes campaign places it in the context of coalition tension engendered by the conflicting strategic concepts and personalities of Dwight Eisenhower and Bernard Montgomery, with Omar Bradley and George Patton as deeply interested and strongly opinionated participants. This literature includes books such as David Irving's *The War between the Generals*; the memoirs of the protagonists; and such biographical studies as David Eisenhower's *Eisenhower at War*, Nigel Hamilton's *Monty: Final Years of the Field Marshal, 1944–1976*, Carlo D'Este's *Patton*, and that strange hybrid, Omar Bradley and Clay Blair's *A Soldier's Life*.[7] These books are important as they relate to the Bulge. The political center of gravity of Hitler's plan for the Ardennes offensive was fracturing Anglo-American unity. Furthermore, one of the most important decisions, and certainly the most controversial, made by Dwight Eisenhower during the campaign was to place Bernard Montgomery in command of the American First and Ninth Armies, an action whose eminent operational sense was overshadowed by the fact that it both encouraged Montgomery's already well-developed feelings of egocentrism and wounded Omar Bradley's sense of professional pride to the very quick.

The final category of works dealing with the Bulge includes those that attempt to assess the campaign comprehensively. These include, among many others, Hugh Cole, *The Ardennes*; Trevor N. Dupuy, David L. Bongard, and Charles C. Anderson, Jr., *Hitler's Last Gamble*; John S. D. Eisenhower, *The Bitter Woods*; George Forty, *The Reich's Last Gamble*; Charles B. MacDonald, *A Time for Trumpets*; Robert E. Merriam, *Dark December*; and John Toland, *Battle*.[8] Each book displays the particular qualifications of its author, ranging from Cole, whose thorough scholarship and balanced objectivity set a high standard for the writing of official history; to MacDonald, who won a Silver Star as an infantry company commander in the Bulge and later served with the army history office; to Eisenhower, whose family lineage granted him unique access to the principals and whose ability to carry a sustained narrative marked him as a most capable historian; to Dupuy, whose consulting firm created a mammoth database drawn from the Ardennes campaign for use in validating Cold War computer simulations. Each is valuable in its own right. However, they all share a common tendency—they split the story into two halves: the sharp end of the spear and the deliberations at the top. Thus, although the corps commanders are not completely neglected, they tend to get short shrift and little detailed attention.

There are, however, two works deserving of special mention. One is specifically focused on the Ardennes; the other is not. J. D. Morelock's *Generals of the Ardennes* defies categorization.[9] Morelock's method was to examine one American commander at every level from theater to combat command (in armored units, the latter was one level below the division). The choices at the first two levels were givens: Eisenhower at theater and Bradley at army group. At field army, there appeared to be two obvious choices: Courtney Hodges at First Army and George Patton at Third Army. Instead, Morelock focused on William Simpson at Ninth Army, based on the rationale that Simpson's unselfish provision of units to First Army contributed positively to the campaign. At the corps level, Morelock's subject is Middleton. This was eminently appropriate, for Middleton's VIII Corps had by far the largest frontage of any unit in the opening phase of the campaign. However, Morelock's analysis of Middleton covers only the period up to 26 December 1944, leaving out the VIII Corps commander's contributions during the remainder of the campaign. The second work that is somewhat outside the above categories is Russell Weigley's *Eisenhower's Lieutenants*.[10] Based on extensive primary source research and flowing from Weigley's broad understanding of the institutional development of the American army, this is an important and extremely useful work. And, although the Ardennes is not Weigley's sole focus, he devotes well over a hundred pages to the campaign. Weigley's judgments on individual personalities are shrewd and broadly informed. However, like the more comprehensive accounts of the Ardennes mentioned above, his analysis tends to be split between the gripping and tightly written narratives of regimental and divisional actions and the deliberations at field army, army group, and theater headquarters. Although attention to the corps level is not absent, neither is it prominent.

Why has the literature on the Bulge in particular, and World War II in general, tended to neglect the corps level of command? The most obvious reason is that corps, being flexible groupings of combat units, have no dedicated constituency. The army veterans' organizations that sprang up after World War II tend to center around either the regiment or the division. These organizations maintain membership rosters, produce newsletters, conduct reunions, and generally foster a sense of brotherhood and comradeship. There are no such organizations for corps. Why is this so? One insight into this phenomenon comes from Michael Howard's recollections of the various echelons of higher command seen from the eyes of a subaltern: "As a very young platoon commander in Italy, I knew my brigade commander. . . . I knew the name of my divisional commander, though I never clapped eyes on him. I never knew at any given moment even the name of my corps commander; and I knew about the Army commander only through the press."[11] A similar explanation came from a Charlottesville, Virginia, newspaper editor, turned World War II infantry officer, who opined similarly:

> The 29th Division did battle directly for Saint-Lô as part of XIX Corps—a point incidental to this account, for a corps headquarters was to me a vague upper sphere with which I had no contact. Often, I was forgetful of which corps was directing our devoted efforts. I am sure that to a corps staff the 2d Battalion [116th Infantry Regiment] was little more than one of the many colored pins on its operations maps. . . . In brief, XIX Corps and I were unmindful of each other as personalities.[12]

But such sentiments were not confined to junior officers. When asked what he thought was the best level of command, John W. Leonard, who commanded the 9th Armored Division from the Bulge to V-E Day and both V Corps and XVIII (Airborne) Corps after the war, replied, "A division, the largest unit that has a soul!"[13] Thus, the corps' constantly shifting organization made it difficult, if not impossible, for anyone except those who served on a corps staff for a protracted period to forge with it any sort of emotional bond.

A more speculative explanation is that there seems to be a human fascination with military history written at two levels: the very top and the very bottom. At the upper reaches, we are enthralled by the notion of great men making decisions that affect the destinies of millions, or at least hundreds of thousands. At the lower reaches of combat, we are likewise gripped by the human drama of individuals and small groups facing the lonely realities of deprivation and the always-present possibility of traumatic injury, or even death. This human tendency toward divergence of perspective has wider manifestations as well. World War II television programming on The History Channel, for example, frequently features *Battleline*, a documentary focusing on the experience of two individuals on opposite sides of a significant battle. It also airs frequent studies of the generalship of men such as Eisenhower, Montgomery, and Patton, as well as Douglas MacArthur and Erwin Rommel. Coverage of the Gulf War reflected the same trend: detailed analyses of weapons systems and crew training complemented by excerpts of General Norman Schwarzkopf's famous "Hail Mary Play" briefing. Why does this programming tend to divide itself between the very top and the very bottom? One would have to conclude that it is because the responsible television executives know this is what the viewing public wants to watch. This bifurcated tendency is also reflected in the immensely popular works of Stephen Ambrose. It is implicitly evident in all his works, but it is explicit in his coverage of the Bulge. Commenting critically on Montgomery's claim to have "taken command" of the battle on the northern shoulder, Ambrose argues:

> No one did. Once Eisenhower set the broad objectives—to hold firm along Elsenborn Ridge, to stop the Germans short of the Meuse, and to prepare a coordinated counterattack against the shoulders of the Bulge—this was not a general's battle. At Bastogne, at Elsenborn, at St.-Vith, at Trois-Ponts, it was a battalion commanders' battle, or the company commanders', or the squad leaders'.[14]

In other words, what happened at theater level was important; what happened from battalion level down was important; what happened in between was not.

Although such a division of focus is entirely understandable, it leaves significant gaps in our knowledge and understanding of military art and science. Unless we are able to appreciate the specific challenges that arise at what might be called the "middle management" of combat and the human attributes required to meet these challenges, our appreciation of what war really is will remain dangerously imperfect. And while the general population can afford to neglect these middle levels, those who have either a serious desire or a professional obligation to understand warfare as a whole simply cannot. This book is written with such readers in mind. For when one probes beneath the surface, one finds that the corps was not only an important echelon of military organization but also that its commanders required distinct capabilities and labored under several intrinsic constraints.

The basic function of the corps was to act as a flexible command module, to which the army commander could attach a variable number of maneuver divisions, artillery groups, and other combat support assets with which to fight an extended portion of a major operation in accordance with the shifting requirements of a dynamic battlefield.[15] The 1942 *Field Service Regulations* expressed its functions as follows:

> The corps is primarily a tactical unit of execution and maneuver. It consists of a headquarters, certain organic elements designated as corps troops, and a variable number of divisions allocated in accordance with the requirements of the situation. The composition of the corps will depend upon its mission, the terrain, and the situation. The flexibility of its organization permits an increase or decrease in the size of the corps, or a change in the type of divisions and other nonorganic elements constituting the corps by the attachment or detachment of divisions and reinforcing units at any time during the operations.[16]

In practical terms, corps were usually assigned from two to five divisions. These guidelines were not, however, inviolable. During Operation Cobra in July 1944, Collins had six divisions under his command. At the other end of the scale, a corps headquarters could be pulled out of the line entirely and assigned no divisions at all while it planned for a future action. The corps artillery headquarters was similarly flexible. Like the corps, it was a command shell to which a variable number of artillery groups, normally consisting of medium and heavy artillery, could be allocated from field army headquarters, again dependent upon changing battlefield dynamics. Engineer groupings were similarly flexible.

The responsibilities of corps command were naturally more comprehensive than those of a division commander. A division commander would normally direct the activities of 12,000 to 15,000 soldiers, but the corps commander could be responsible for 50,000 to 80,000, depending on the particular configuration of his organization. The corps commander also had to be a tactician on a larger scale. And he had to judge the relative capabilities of various types of divisions as well as the diverse human capabilities of the division commanders. The fluidity of the battlefield and the extended lead times required to move divisions into place meant that he had to anticipate emerging tactical requirements earlier than did his subordinates in order to create conditions for their success. In discussing his own elevation from command of the 82nd Airborne Division to that of the XVIII (Airborne) Corps, Matthew Ridgway described the mental and human dimensions of corps command as follows:

> The corps commander is almost exclusively concerned with battle tactics. He is responsible for a large sector of the battle area, and all he must worry about in that zone is fighting. He must be a man of great flexibility of mind, for he may be fighting six divisions one day and one division the next as his higher commanders transfer divisions to and from his corps. He must be a man of tremendous physical stamina, too, . . . anticipating where the hardest fighting is to come, and being there in person, ready to help his division commanders in any way he can.[17]

It was an apt description, but there was even more to it than Ridgway implied. Because of the army's rank structure in World War II, corps commanders were major generals, the same grade as the division commanders subordinate to them. Thus, their formal authority stemmed solely from their position, with no corresponding grade differential to give added force to their orders. This fact, combined with the reality that the composition of the corps was constantly shifting, created an interesting human dynamic in which division commanders could play on their relations with the army commander, at times to the corps commander's detriment. All this placed a particular premium on the ability of the corps commander to use the force of his personality and intellect to ensure his orders were wholeheartedly accepted and enthusiastically carried out and thus makes the examination of corps command of more than passing interest.

This book begins with a re-creation of what was taught about the nature of command at the U.S. Army Command and General Staff School (CGSS), which was attended by all six of the prospective corps commanders, and at the U.S. Army War College, which was attended by all but Manton Eddy. In addition to giving us insight into the interwar army's expectations of those it entrusted with the sacred responsibility of command, this analysis also provides a defensible basis for evaluating the performances of the six protagonists.[18] The next step is to examine the development of the six men as military professionals, tracing their careers from their precommissioning studies to the eve of the Bulge. The ultimate purpose of these minibiographical sketches is to answer the question, "Knowing what we know so far, what would we anticipate about this individual's performance in the forthcoming battle?" A transition is then necessary to summarize the events on both sides leading up to the Bulge, including a brief assessment of why the Americans were so stunningly surprised by the German offensive. This sets the stage for the guts of the book—analysis of the six American corps commanders in the Battle of the Bulge. Their actions are studied in three phases: the period of German initiative, 16–21 December 1944; the period of contested initiative, 22 December 1944–4 January 1945; and the period of American initiative, 5–31 January 1945.[19] Each of these segments opens with an overview of the strategic and operational situation, to include the influence of airpower on the campaign, followed by a detailed examination of each corps battle. We end by briefly tracing the post-Bulge careers of the six commanders and answering the questions outlined above.

The evidence comes from multiple sources. The philosophy of command study is based on curriculum records of the CGSS and the Army War College, supplemented by secondary studies of army education in the interwar period. The six pre-Bulge cameos are sketched from the official personnel records of each officer, located at the National Personnel Records Center (NPRC), St. Louis, Missouri; their academic records at the aforementioned educational institutions; George C. Marshall's and Dwight D. Eisenhower's papers; and, where available, biographies, memoirs, and personal papers of the protagonists themselves. The last category is rather uneven. Collins and Ridgway both published their memoirs and left extensive collections of papers at the Eisenhower Library and the U.S. Army Military History Institute (MHI), respectively.[20] Additionally, Clay Blair has written an extended treatment of the American airborne units in World War II that illuminates Ridgway's role in their training and combat employment.[21] After stepping down from the presidency of Louisiana State University, Middleton cooperated actively in the development of a biography.[22] Eddy left a copy of his combat activities log at the National Infantry Museum, and a biography was published in 2000.[23] There is no biography of Gerow, but he did leave a small collection of papers at the Virginia Military Institute. Millikin is the most obscure of the six. Except for cryptic references in the register of West Point graduates, an extremely brief obituary in the *Washington Post*, and a one-paragraph entry in a standard biographical reference, there is virtually no published material about him.[24] This void was partially offset by his grandson kindly granting access to a small collection of papers and photographs that are retained by the family. But for the crux of the study, the investigation of the campaign itself, this unevenness is overcome by reference to official records. Such records, available at the National Archives, include unit journals and message files, daily situation and intelligence reports, monthly after-action reports, unit histories, and many other relevant documents. This trove of evidence is extremely rich and constitutes the fundamental basis upon which assessments of the six commanders' battlefield performances are based. For the German side of the campaign, the most widely used sources are the interviews and reports prepared by senior German officers after the war, collectively known as the Foreign Military Studies (FMS) series. This series is available at the National Archives; and a microfiche version of the collection is also on hand at the Air University Library, Maxwell Air Force Base, Alabama. Additional material, particularly on the German side of the campaign, comes from a collection of detailed studies prepared by the U.S. Army Office of the Chief of Military History (OCMH) staff, now available at the National Archives. In sum, despite the unevenness of biographical information concerning the six protagonists, the primary and secondary sources for the study as a whole are clearly adequate and in some cases extremely robust.

Now let us discover what the rising generation of U.S. Army officers in the aftermath of World War I was taught about the nature of command.

PROLOGUE

2

Toward an American Philosophy of Command

War is a shabby, really impractical thing anyway, and it takes a genius to conduct it with any sort of economy and efficiency.[1]   *William Faulkner*

FAULKNER WAS CERTAINLY NO LOVER OF WAR, nor was he a particularly close student of it; but his experience of World War I provided him sufficient insight to realize that the proper conduct of war required a profound aptitude. He referred to the person who possessed such aptitude as a genius. The term "genius," however, can also be used in a slightly different context to describe the qualities that compose the aptitude rather than the individual who possesses it. The American army between World Wars I and II did not use the term in its approach to military leadership. Rather, it referred to the art of command. Command was defined by the *Field Service Regulations* as the legal authority a person exercised over subordinates.[2] The art of command was understood to mean the ability of the commander to direct the efforts of his unit to the accomplishment of a mission and was generally felt to require a combination of intellectual and psychological qualities particularly adapted to the conduct of war. The burden of this investigation is to discover the particular blend of such qualities articulated by the U.S. Army during the period between the wars. It does so by examining instruction in the art of command at CGSS and the Army War College during the interwar era. The immediate purpose is to determine what Gerow, Middleton, Ridgway, Millikin, Eddy, and Collins were taught about command. However, the survey also sheds light on the United States Army in a particularly formative period of its history. During the two decades between the world wars of the twentieth century, the American army was undergoing a transformation from a frontier constabulary force to the land and air warfare instrument of a major world power.[3] Thus, while the immediate focus is on our six protagonists, this investigation will also shed light on the army as a whole.

Particular attention to the issue of command was a product of the army's World War I experience. The army had clearly benefited from the creation of the General Service and Staff College at Fort Leavenworth, Kansas, in

1902, which later evolved into two institutions: the School of the Line and the General Staff College.[4] Invigorated by the work of men such as Brigadier General J. Franklin Bell and Major John F. Morrison, the schools at Leavenworth provided a cadre of men who understood how to maneuver and supply large military formations and who, just as importantly, spoke a common language about how this was done. Thus, during World War I, "Leavenworth men" dominated the staffs of the American Expeditionary Forces (AEF) and the major subordinate headquarters.[5] Eight of the twelve officers who served as General John Pershing's chiefs of staff and principal staff officers were graduates of both Leavenworth schools. Additionally, the chiefs of staff of both of the AEF's field armies and nine of the ten officers who served as corps chiefs of staff were Leavenworth graduates. While on the whole their influence was quite positive, there was also a countervailing disadvantage: the AEF's higher level commanders, who were several years senior to their principal staff officers, had not had the benefit of the rigorous education enjoyed by their juniors. There developed in the upper ranks of the AEF a distinct perception that commanders were at times willing to cede too much authority to their staffs and that staff officers were prone to intrude upon command prerogatives. Thus, one of the issues facing the army after the war was to restore the proper balance between commanders and staff officers. The need to do so was also driven by a conviction among many that the Treaty of Versailles had not settled the underlying issues that had led to World War I and that the army would again be called upon to prove its mettle in a major war. Given these circumstances, it was only natural that the art of command should be addressed in the school system.

The army's officer education system between the wars was divided into three tiers. At the first level, virtually all officers attended a basic and an advanced course specific to their assigned branch. For example, they would attend the Infantry School at Fort Benning, Georgia; the Field Artillery School at Fort Sill, Oklahoma; the Cavalry School at Fort Riley, Kansas; or the Air Corps Tactical School at Maxwell Field, Alabama. Here they were taught the tactics and techniques peculiar to their branch of service. From time to time an officer from one branch would, for purposes of broadening, attend the advanced course of a different branch; but instruction at each of these schools had a single focus. At the middle level, a much smaller number of officers would attend the CGSS at Fort Leavenworth, Kansas. The focus of this curriculum varied somewhat, depending on the years in which they attended; but its essence was the interaction of combined arms, principally at the division and corps levels, i.e., higher level tactics and at times the lower end of what is today called the operational level of war. The final tier was the

Army War College located at Washington Barracks in the national capital. The curriculum here had some overlap with that taught at Leavenworth, but its focus was broader, with attention being devoted to preparation for war and war's conduct and encompassing strategy, as well as field army and theater-level operations. In September 1920, the War Department issued a general order directing the commandants of the General Staff School and the Army War College to amplify and extend instruction in the art of command.[6] As noted above, this order appears to have flowed from analysis of wartime experience. To determine how effectively each institution carried out this directive, assessment of its command instruction will be preceded by a brief examination of its mission and general curriculum structure.

THE COMMAND AND GENERAL STAFF SCHOOL

The CGSS mission was to train middle-grade officers for command and general staff assignments at the division and corps levels.[7] This mission had four specific components: tactics and techniques of the various branches in order to ensure combined arms coordination; operations of large units up to the corps; command and staff functions at corps level; and duties of the corps area general staff within the United States. Additionally, the school was required to provide instruction in tactical principles through the use of historical research and historical examples. Significantly, graduation was required for an officer to become eligible for a general staff assignment.

The curriculum at Leavenworth evolved in four distinct phases between the wars, based on varying lengths of the course, which were dictated by the War Department's determination of requirements for general staff officers.[8] From 1919 to 1923, there were two schools at Leavenworth based on the prewar model: the School of the Line and the General Staff School, each lasting just under a year. Officers who graduated in roughly the top half of the former were selected to attend the latter as well. In 1923 the War Department directed the consolidation of these two schools into a single Command and General Staff School with a one-year course of instruction. The purpose of this consolidation, which almost doubled the number of graduates, was to provide a general staff education to the large number of officers who had entered the service during World War I. It is also noteworthy that the word "Command" was added to the school's title. Education of the surfeit of World War I officers was completed by 1928, at which point the CGSS curriculum was extended to two years. However, rather than reverting to the previous system, in which only half the officers attending the first year were selected for the second, all officers selected for CGSS under the new dispensation attended for two years. The time thus provided allowed for a thorough review of the basics of combined arms at the level of the independent brigade; a complete consideration of the various operations of a division; and an extended analysis of corps operations up to and including those of a corps acting independently within a theater of operations. The price paid for this extended study of the art of war was a reduced student output, which was affordable throughout the late 1920s and early to mid-1930s. In 1936, however, the War Department, perhaps anticipating the requirements for general staff officers in an expanding army, directed the return to a one-year curriculum, thus doubling the number of graduates. It remained a one-year course until 1940 when CGSS was suspended and a special short course in staff work was instituted to meet the demands of full mobilization.

The implications of this for the corps commanders in question are fairly significant. Three—Collins, Eddy, and Ridgway—were at Leavenworth for the extended two-year course. Of the three who attended the single-year course, two—Middleton and Millikin—remained on the faculty for four years each. Additionally, Eddy served as a faculty member for four years following graduation from the longer course. In sum, these six officers spent a total of twenty-one years at Leavenworth between the wars, either as students or as instructors. This works out to an average of three and one-half years per person.[9] Although one must be chary of drawing direct correlations between education and combat capability, it does seem fair to suggest that what was taught at Leavenworth and how it was taught at least conditioned the way in which these officers approached their professional responsibilities.

The content of the CGSS curriculum progressed from the simple to the complex.[10] It began with a review of basic military organization and lectures on how to solve tactical problems; moved on to discuss tactical techniques at a fairly low level; and progressed to the heart of the course, tactical principles, which examined in detail the relation between such subjects as attack and defense, fire and maneuver, and the employment of divisions and corps in various types of terrain. This was followed by an examination of miscellaneous subjects, including strategy, military psychology and leadership, and training methods. The teaching methods were mostly practical.[11] Map exercises, map maneuvers, and map problems, in which the student was required to arrive at a tactical decision and compose the orders required to execute that decision, took up roughly 70 percent of the instruction time. A member of the faculty closely critiqued the students' written orders. Conferences, which were really faculty-led general discussion sessions in a question-and-answer mode, constituted about 20 percent of instructional time, with the remaining 10 percent being devoted to lectures.

The fundamental basis of Leavenworth instruction in command was the *Field Service Regulations*, which laid down a straightforward statement of the commander's responsibilities and articulated simple, definite expectations of how these duties were to be carried out.[12] The commander was described as "the controlling head . . . the master mind . . . [from which] must flow the energy and impulse which are to animate all under him." He was enjoined to "keep in close touch with all subordinate units by means of personal visits and observation . . . [in order to] know from personal contact the mental, moral, and physical state of his troops, the conditions with which they are confronted, the accomplishments, their desires, their needs, and their views . . . [and to] extend help where help is needed and give every encouragement in adversity, but never hesitate to exact whatever effort is needed to attain the desired end." Unity of command was deemed "essential to success." Decision as to the course of action to be taken in any circumstance was "the responsibility of the commander and presupposes on his part an analysis of all the facts and factors bearing on the problem under consideration." The particulars of this analysis were to include consideration of the mission as set out in orders and instructions from higher authority as well as being "deduced by him from his knowledge of the situation," information pertaining to the enemy forces, the state of his own command, terrain and weather, a comparison of the various course of action open to him, and finally a decision.[13]

The manual made several definite statements concerning the responsibility of command but did not explore in depth the relationship between the commander and his staff. While personal conferences between commanders and their subordinates were deemed to be periodically advisable, the commander was specifically told that he alone was responsible for his actions and could "not share the responsibility therefore with any of his subordinates. The decision, no matter how arrived at, is his alone."[14] Furthermore, the commander could not plead the absence of orders as a rationale for inaction. "If the subordinate commander knows what the general plan—the end in view—is, lack of initiative on his part is inexcusable." The general function of the staff was to elaborate details to implement the commander's decision, with the chief of staff acting not only to supervise the staff but also to control and coordinate the actions of the subordinate units in the commander's name. The manual did not address the extent to which the staff gathered information or provided analysis and recommendations regarding the proposed course of action.

The army's doctrine of command did, however, include guidance as to the issuance of orders.[15] Clear and decisive orders were "the logical result of definite and sure decisions, and are the means of transforming the decision into action." The object of orders was "to bring about a course of action, in accordance with the intention of the leader, suited to the situation and with full cooperation between all arms and services." Commanders were instructed to issue orders in sufficient time to allow their subordinates to study the situation and issue their own instructions, with specific times established as the probable minimums required for orders to reach all subordinate units under favorable conditions; these times were one and a half hours for a regiment, three hours for a brigade, and six hours for a division. And, while details of time and place were to be carefully stated to avoid ambiguity, commanders were enjoined not to trespass on the province of subordinates by issuing orders that were overly detailed. The order "should contain everything beyond the independent authority of a subordinate, but nothing more."

The *Field Service Regulations*, while instructive in the basic way that such manuals are intended to be, clearly required elaboration. Such elaboration on the subject of command was provided by various Leavenworth senior officers. In his 1923 welcoming address to Middleton's class, Brigadier General Harry A. Smith, who had served as commandant of the Army Service Schools in France and as the AEF civil affairs officer after the Armistice, offered some brief but pointed thoughts on the subject of command.[16] Smith stated categorically that while the mission of the school was to teach both command and staff, the former would receive greater emphasis. Smith told his students that the school's applicatory method was designed specifically around the commander's need to render a "clear, simple, and complete" decision. He charged them, above all, to make their decisions definite: "A weak or wobbly decision, or one that can be read in two ways, will be unsatisfactory always."

Two years later, when Gerow and Millikin arrived at Leavenworth, they were greeted by a new commandant, Brigadier General Edward L. King, a cavalryman with a reputation as "a progressive and vigorous leader and a stern disciplinarian."[17] Drawing on his combat experience as chief of staff of the 28th Division and commanding general of an infantry brigade, King devoted his welcoming address almost entirely to the subject of command.[18] His remarks elaborated those qualities that would allow the commander "to maintain, by his own ability and personality, that prestige which his military rank confers on him." His framework consisted of three elements: the commander's personal qualities, his knowledge of his organization, and his executive ability "to make the greatest possible use of this organization."

But before warming to his main theme, the commandant offered an extended aside on the relationship between commanders and staff officers.

King hinted strongly that staff supremacy had been both an American and a German problem in World War I. The commander had to be aware of the staff's capabilities and limitations and give it clear guidance; he was free to ask for advice from the staff or not, but he alone was responsible for his decisions. Consciously or subconsciously paralleling Clausewitz's discussion of genius, King argued that command was an art and as such it "makes use of rules but it also transcends all rules."[19] The commander, like an artist, first created a mental sketch, which represented a tentative decision; after receiving more detailed information from his staff, he would be able to create a completed canvas, which represented a final decision.

King then cataloged a number of qualities he deemed essential to command.[20] Although he listed character as being the first requisite of a commander, he did not elaborate on character, per se, perhaps assuming that the relatively mature officers in his audience had sufficiently internalized its meaning. There were a number of significant adjunct qualities. First among these was Colonel G. F. R. Henderson's axiom that the art of command was essentially "the art of dealing with human nature." King went on to argue that the command of large bodies of men transcended the command of individuals. In light of this reality, strength, vigor, and self-confidence were required to inspire confidence in one's subordinates and had to be actively demonstrated. To obtain loyalty from his subordinates, a commander had to give loyalty to his superiors. Justice, directness, simplicity, and common sense were also extolled. Paralleling the Clausewitzian ideal of fusing knowledge with action, King approvingly cited an extended passage from William Tecumseh Sherman to the effect that neither knowledge nor action alone was sufficient, but that action guided by knowledge was the requisite of modern generalship. Perhaps again drawing some inspiration from Clausewitz, King declared that the ultimate proof of the effective commander was the ability of his command to respond effectively under even the most difficult conditions.[21]

There are no surviving lectures on the subject of command during the period 1931–1935 when Collins, Eddy, and Ridgway attended CGSS. However, the instructional circular for 1932–1933, when Eddy was in his first year and Collins was in his second, contains several pithy observations on the relationship between a commander and his staff. Neither was to assume the function of the other; the commander's guidance and control of the staff could become relaxed as the staff developed familiarity with the commander's methods; and as the commander's relation with his chief of staff grew from "theoretical to actual intimacy," the commander would be able to give his chief of staff greater responsibility for directing the staff, thus giving himself greater opportunity to deal with his subordinates and consider future developments.[22]

Despite the general common sense and historical awareness of the lectures by various CGSS commandants on the subject of command and the addition of the word "Command" to the school's title, one gets the fairly strong impression that its métier remained the production of well-grounded, competent staff officers. The graduates were to become problem solvers rather than visionaries and motivators. Nevertheless, it is important to note that repetitive exposure to the "Estimate of the Situation," a logical schema for the analysis of tactical and operational situations, created a mental discipline that aided future commanders as well as staff officers.[23] And finally, one must note that problem solving is the essential first skill in Lord Moran's definition of military leadership as "the capacity to frame plans which will succeed and the faculty of persuading others to carry them out in the face of death."[24]

THE ARMY WAR COLLEGE

There is much more extensive documentation of command instruction provided at the Army War College than there is of such teaching at Fort Leavenworth. This instruction generally paralleled that contained in the *Field Service Regulations* and the lectures of CGSS commandants, but its breadth and depth gave Gerow, Middleton, Ridgway, Millikin, and Collins more nuanced and substantive insights into the nature of command. This documentation also provides additional insights concerning the gradual maturation of an American philosophy of command.[25]

The Army War College was established in 1903 at Washington Barracks in the nation's capital at the instigation of Secretary of War Elihu Root as part of his program of army reforms following the Spanish-American War.[26] Its first president was one of the army's premier educators and later chief of staff, Major General Tasker H. Bliss. The college was clearly conceived as a developmental institution for the newly created army general staff and was an adjunct to it. And, although the army's mobilization and deployment in World War I encountered significant difficulties, the organization and functioning of the general staff, fed by the graduates of both the General Staff College at Leavenworth and the Army War College in Washington, allowed the army to go to war in 1917 in a much more efficient manner than it had in the debacle of 1898.[27]

The college's first postwar commandant, Major General James W. McAndrew, who had served as Pershing's chief of staff, and twenty-four faculty members, most of whom had combat experience as general staff officers, significantly revised the curriculum.[28] This group divided the course of studies into the two branches of military art outlined by Clausewitz: the preparation for war and the conduct of war.[29] While this basic structure thus had a Germanic influence, the detailed organization of each segment was clearly patterned on the French "G" system, which had been adopted by the AEF. That structure consisted of four sections: G-1 for personnel and administration; G-2 for intelligence; G-3 for plans, operations, and training; and G-4 for logistics. Thus, McAndrew's original focus was on staff duties more than command responsibilities. But the performance of those staff duties was placed in a broad educational context that investigated political, social, and economic developments as well as purely military subjects; and this broadening of curriculum focus was evident in the significant expansion of the lecture program from roughly twenty-five lectures per year to around ninety. The direct tie between the army general staff and the college was severed in that the commandant was no longer given the dual responsibility as director of war plans. The college, however, continued to analyze war plans for the general staff, and the two institutions maintained an intimate working relationship.

When Middleton arrived at the college in 1928, the curriculum still retained McAndrew's basic structure, but it had been amended to place an even more significant emphasis on command than that called for by the previously cited War Department order of 1920. This change seems to have occurred in large part due to the efforts of McAndrew's immediate successor, Brigadier General Edward F. McGlachlin, who had served as the commander of the First Army artillery in France and whose first faculty directive definitively stipulated that preparation for high command was the college's principal duty.[30] The increased emphasis on command was evident in the opening lecture to the class of 1929 given by the assistant commandant, Colonel John L. DeWitt, who had served during the war as the assistant chief of staff for supply (G-4) of the First Army.[31] Dewitt noted that the college's mission was "to fit selected officers for usefulness on the General Staff of the War Department and higher echelons of the field forces and especially, as far as their natural abilities will permit, for the command of large units."[32] Thus, DeWitt confirmed for Middleton and his classmates the Clausewitzian proposition that although intellectual development was an important and even necessary ingredient for successful command, it was clearly not sufficient.[33]

Colonel DeWitt then provided his own thoughts on the subject of high command. A commander, he said, would be judged on a number of standards: his plan of operations, his imagination, his determination to see his plan through, and "by that highest of all qualifications of a commander,— the courage of responsibility."[34] In this formulation, the chief distinction between the commander and the staff officer was that the former bore ultimate responsibility for his actions and thus had the authority to put his plan into effect, while the latter had neither the ultimate responsibility nor any authority apart from that of the commander. This nexus of responsibility and authority in the person of the commander placed on him an absolute requirement for character.

Additional instruction in command was found in the Conduct of War Course, which included a number of lectures dealing with high-level command and staff actions during World War I. These included the functioning of the First Army general staff, the operations of the Services of Supply, the strategy of the Central Powers, British naval strategy, operations of the American Air Service, and Allenby's campaign in Palestine. The latter was delivered by Colonel John Herr, a cavalryman who had served as a division chief of staff during the war and would go on to become chief of the cavalry branch.[35] Herr's lecture demonstrated an acute insight into the effect of Allenby's leadership on the campaign:

> We are impressed with the following: the rugged personality and amazing energy of Allenby; the stressing always of the morale factor; prompt decisions enabling every detail of preparation to be directed purposefully; the constant anticipation by Allenby and his staff of the problems and difficulties of the future, which could result only from an exhaustive study of the physical characteristics of the theater of war and of the conditions particular to it; the influence of supply on every phase of strategy and of operations; the outstanding role of mobility in concentration[,] in connecting groups in combat[,] and in pursuit. That although mobility is dependent on supply and the physical condition of the troops, the will of the commander is the driving factor.[36]

War College instruction in the art of command in the late 1920s was thus a useful combination of theory and practice.

When Gerow and Millikin entered the War College in 1930, instruction in command had evolved slightly from that given to Middleton two years earlier. Among the more interesting lectures was one by the noted Russian military authority and former member of the imperial army, Lieutenant General Nicholas Golovine, on the Galician campaign of 1914. In this campaign, the

Russian Southwest Army Group, after a series of initial reverses, defeated four Austrian armies commanded by General Conrad von Hotzendorf, the Austrian chief of staff.[37] Golovine attributed the leadership component of the Russian victory to the productive interaction of three factors: the intelligence of Southwestern Army Group chief of staff, General Mikhail Alexeiev, "the brains which led the armies to victory"; the staunch support of Alexeiev by his commander, General Nicholas Ivanov; and "the energetic and unyielding will" of the Grand Duke Nicholas who kept his nerve when, Golovine implied, Ivanov was on the verge of losing his. Although the Russian officer's conclusions may not have conformed to American leadership ideals, they did offer food for thought on how different personalities could interact to bring about positive results.

A number of lectures previously found in the Conduct of War course were now incorporated into a new course entitled "Analytical Studies."[38] These lectures included not only Colonel Herr's study of Allenby in Palestine, but also one by General Peyton C. March on his experiences as army chief of staff during World War I. The meat of the Analytical Studies course, however, was a series of comparative, historical studies of typical problems facing theater commanders and their staffs: theater organization and administration; embarkation and debarkation of an expeditionary force; and offensive and defensive operations under different scenarios. Although it would be too strong to say that the intent of these exercises was to develop operational "norms" in the Soviet sense of that term, they were clearly intended by their instigator, Major General William D. Connor, a former engineer officer who had served as Pershing's G-4 in the AEF and who possessed a penchant for empirical studies, to provide a series of comparative data points that would aid the future commander's judgment.[39]

The orientation for the 1930–1931 Conduct of War course also contained a robust explanation of the functions and responsibilities of command. This document stated that the commander would be judged by "his courage in accepting responsibility, his decisions, his execution, and his leadership."[40] The commander was depicted as the driving force of his organization: "From him must flow the energy and impulses which animate all under him." Although he was encouraged to use his staff, he could not "divest himself of responsibility for all plans, policies, or basic decisions which affect the employment of his command." He was enjoined to remove himself from trivial details in order to "have a clear, broad picture of the line of action he has mapped out for the accomplishment of his mission."

When Ridgway arrived at the Army War College in 1936, the basic structure of command instruction was similar to that of his predecessors; but it had been supplemented by two superb lectures on Ulysses S. Grant and Robert E. Lee delivered by Colonel Arthur L. Conger and Dr. Douglas Southall Freeman, respectively. As a preface to these and other lectures, the assistant commandant, Colonel Ned Rehkopf, who had served as a field artillery colonel in the AEF and as an instructor at Leavenworth in the early twenties, gave the students an extremely literate and insightful orientation on the subject of command and how to study it.[41] He began with the flat assertion that "to command is to make decisions." He then explored in some depth the qualities commanders needed to make good decisions in combat, arriving at the observation that "surely no man could walk with himself through thirty or fifty years of life without realizing he does not possess all those qualities desirable in a great commander." But, because commanders seldom had a second chance in war, they had to find some means of preparing themselves as best they could, for which Rehkopf cited Patrick Henry's observation that the best way to judge the future was by the past. Rehkopf's use of history, however, was not to search for rules, but to enrich the mind.

Colonel Arthur L. Conger was a Harvard graduate who had become one of the army's foremost educators and an authority on Grant, having published *The Rise of U.S. Grant* in 1931.[42] His book is packed with citations from a wide assortment of military theorists and commanders, including Clausewitz, De Saxe, Turenne, Frederick, Napoleon, and even Hindenburg. Like the book, his lecture "Grant as a Leader" was explicitly framed in a Clausewitzian paradigm that emphasized Grant's progressive development and his ability to profit from his own experience.[43] Conger began by citing nine specific qualities of Clausewitzian genius: strength of character, will power, ability to grasp a situation (he did not use the term *coup d'oeil*), ability to discriminate among information sources of varying reliability, resolution, presence of mind, physical and moral courage, a well-balanced mind, and a sense of locality.[44] After elaborating on each of these attributes, he took up his main theme, Grant's progressive development as a commander. Conger traced Grant's tactical growth from his raid on Belmont, Missouri, where he "committed the favorite sin of beginner—dispersion" and had his brigade routed as a result; to the attack on Fort Henry, where he placed himself too far back in the formation and allowed the Confederate infantry to escape; to Shiloh, where he learned "what to avoid on the rash side." He then traced Grant's strategic growth from the opening of the Mississippi, to the conquest of Tennessee, and ultimately to direction of the entire war. The overall thrust of Conger's lecture to the future commanders in his audience was very straightforward: you must grow in command.

Douglas Southall Freeman, whose Pulitzer Prize–winning, four-volume biography of Lee was published in 1934–1935, was widely recognized as America's foremost authority on the military icon of the Confederacy. His lecture on Lee to the War College Class of 1937 was his second in that forum and came as he was working on the sequel to his biography of Lee, *Lee's Lieutenants*.[45] Freeman's interpretation outlined the circumstances that conditioned Lee's leadership and his responses to the operational environment created by those circumstances. He argued that Lee operated under four specific constraints: the Confederacy's political ideal of states' rights, a smaller force operating on interior lines against a foe with command of the sea, inferior armament and equipment vis-à-vis the Union army, and the obligation to defend Richmond. In light of these circumstances, Lee had to adopt a strategy whose basis was surprise and economy of force. This strategy required four specific ingredients: superior intelligence, extensive use of field fortifications, the ability to judge with great accuracy the offensive and defensive power of a given number of men, and the maximum mobility possible with an inadequate supply of wagons and horses. One remarkable aspect of Freeman's presentation was its depiction of Lee's ability to sense and exploit the relationship between the physical and the moral factors in war. For example, during the action at Mine Run in December 1863, when Lee was told there was a danger to his right flank but that it was covered by a cavalry regiment, his immediate response was to ask who commanded the regiment. He knew that one colonel's regiment did not necessarily have the same staying power as another's. Even when one makes allowance for Freeman's obvious sympathies for Lee and the southern cause he represented, one has to conclude that Ridgway and the other members of the War College Class of 1937 received useful instruction in the art of command.

The same can be said for Collins, who immediately followed Ridgway to the War College. The curriculum for the class of 1938 was, in essence, unchanged from the previous year; but instruction in command had evolved in two ways. First, Colonel Oliver Spaulding replaced Conger as the lecturer on Grant; second, while Freeman returned as the Lee lecturer, his presentation took a completely different approach.

Spaulding was a former chief of the War Department History Branch who had worked closely with Conger in the use of military history to enhance officer education at both Leavenworth and the War College.[46] His lecture offered a comparative analysis of Washington and Grant as military commanders that assessed both their periods of military apprenticeship and their active careers in high command.[47] Spaulding emphasized Washington's serious study of military art, his development of a good military library, and his ability to learn from experience during his years as a colonial officer. He pictured Grant as a man who, unlike Washington, came to a military career almost by accident and who appeared, at best, to be capable but undistinguished at the end of the Mexican War, though growing significantly during the Civil War. Spaulding ended by reminding his listeners that there was an imponderable quality of command that lay beyond the realm of rational analysis: the leader's personal magnetism. "In infinitely varied form, he must have it, but what it is and why it is we do not know."[48]

One of the refreshing aspects of Freeman's instructional style for the historian examining it over a half a century later is that each year he came at his subject from a different angle. Freeman's lecture on Lee to the War College Class of 1938 described Lee's qualities of leadership and articulated seven strategic rules Lee followed in his campaigns.[49] The four qualities upon which Freeman elaborated were Lee's combination of an acute intellect with physical endurance, a strength of will that was never paralyzed by material inferiority, a profound belief that superior strategy was the key to victory, and a moral leadership based on the personal example of self-denial. Although this last factor came closest to explaining Lee's personal magnetism, the majority of Freeman's lecture was devoted to an exposition of his third point, Lee's strategy, which was elucidated through a series of maxims.

It is the task of military education to create an environment in which *self*-development can take place. Judged by this standard, one would have to give the Army War College high marks for its instruction in the art of command in the decade from Middleton's arrival in 1928 to Collins's graduation in 1938. The commonsensical but insightful orientations by assistant commandants Colonels DeWitt and Rehkopf; the Analytical Studies Course introduced by General Connor; and the biographical lectures by Colonels Herr, Conger, and Spaulding and Dr. Freeman presented a wide and sophisticated variety of approaches to the extremely complex subject of command in war.

SOME CLOSING OBSERVATIONS

Given this generally high quality of instruction at the Army War College, there remains one final task—to define what the United States Army's philosophy of command *was* during the interwar period. Such a formulation requires synthesis of the army's doctrinal statements on command with the instruction presented at the CGSS and the Army War College.

The most overwhelming impression one derives from such a synthesis is the centrality in the interwar military psyche of the commander as the single animating force and solely responsible agent of and for his command. This notion was evident in the *Field Service Regulations* themselves, in thoughts on command given at Leavenworth by Generals Smith and King, in orientations at the Army War College by Colonel DeWitt, and even in printed material for the War College's Conduct of War course. Elaborations on the staff's responsibility to assist the commander in the discharge of his duties only served to reinforce the basic point of command responsibility. The European notion of a collective responsibility shared between a commander and his chief of staff, evident in partnerships such as those between Scharnhorst and Gneisenau, Hindenburg and Ludendorff, and Alexeiev and Ivanov, was distinctly antipathetic to the American philosophy of command.

This philosophy also emphasized the strength of the commander's will as one of the important, if not the cardinal, attributes of a commander. This was evident in the *Field Service Regulations*; but it was prominent as well in Colonel Herr's portrait of Allenby, in Colonel Conger's depiction of Grant, and in Dr. Freeman's analysis of Lee. The importance of strength of will as a determinant of command was, of course, shared by many European command philosophies; but it was also deeply rooted in the American character. For example, one could argue that from the formation of the original colonies, to the expansion across the Alleghenies, to the domestication of the Midwestern Plains, and ultimately to the taming of the West, the history of America had been one of willpower and determination triumphing over physical obstacles.

Another factor that stood out in American instruction on command was a type of mental acuity that rapidly and accurately captured the essence of complex situations. Again, this quality was mentioned in the *Field Service Regulations* and figured prominently in Conger's study of Grant, in Spaulding's analysis of Washington, and in Freeman's portrait of Lee. Although generally parallel to the European notion of *coup d'oeil*, articulators of the American version did not seem to care whether this shrewd sense, raised to a high pitch, had been developed by formal education and study, by personal experience, or by a combination of the two. The important thing was that the commander possessed it, not how he got it. Here, too, we see a reflection of the American experience where the self-made man who could figure things out for himself has more often than not been seen as being at least on a par with those whose intelligence had been derived from formal education.

Closely allied to this situational awareness was knowledge of terrain and its influence on all military operations. Again, the *Field Service Regulations* emphasized the point; and it was driven home by the numerous map exercises at Leavenworth and the War College. It also featured prominently in Herr's lecture on Allenby and Freeman's 1938 presentation on Lee. This trait was so universally a factor of tactical and operational acumen, however, that it would be dangerous to ascribe to it some sort of particular Americanism. Nevertheless, one can see, at least through the latter part of the nineteenth century and perhaps into the early twentieth, how American society's closeness to the soil gave this quality a cultural connection as well as a professional imperative.

Care for one's subordinates was another vital component of the American commander. This quality was evident in the *Field Service Regulations*, in General King's address on command at Leavenworth, in Colonel Herr's study of Allenby, and particularly in Dr. Freeman's analysis of Lee. Again, this factor was found in the leadership literature of many other armies, but it seemed to have very definite ties to the American psyche. Although the American commander could and should be tough and demanding (Freeman commented parenthetically on Thomas Jackson's extremely insistent march discipline) and although mission accomplishment remained the paramount consideration, the commander of soldiers who were also citizens of a great democracy simply could not be indifferent to their welfare.

Celerity of action was another frequently expressed ideal for the American commander. This was reflected in Herr's study of Allenby, in Conger's analysis of Grant, and very strikingly in Freeman's exegesis of Lee. There was also something about this quality that resonated with the notion of the impatient American, be he a businessman for whom time was money or a citizen for whom war was an unwelcome interruption of normal life that should be brought to a successful conclusion as rapidly as possible.

And, finally, in parallel with another Clausewitzian criterion, there was recognition that the commander was required to endure physical privation.[50] This quality was emphasized in both Conger's analysis of Grant and in Freeman's study of Lee. And again, although not unique to the American ideal of command, it did reflect the toughness of the American spirit that had endured the rigors of a severe economic depression.

The qualities outlined above were the themes most frequently emphasized in written field regulations and in command instruction presented at Leavenworth and the Army War College during the years between World Wars I and II.

There are several noteworthy omissions. Given the very significant, one could almost say horrendous, effect of new inventions on the conduct of war evident in World War I, it is surprising that virtually nowhere is an appreciation for the potential of new technology discussed as a command desideratum. One can partially explain this lacuna by arguing that such developments were studied as part of tactics, not as part of command, which was fundamentally a human activity. Nevertheless, the virtual exclusion from the army's instruction in command of the new pace of decision making that would be dictated by mechanized and aerial warfare and facilitated by significant improvements in the range and reliability of radios does raise at least some questions about the adequacy of that instruction. Another topic largely neglected was the Moltkean ideal of giving one's subordinates sufficient freedom of action to allow them to take action in war's fluid environment that was responsive both to the dictates of the immediate situation and the framework of the higher commander's will. The *Field Service Regulations* hinted at this ideal when they informed commanders not to include in their orders material that was not beyond the subordinates' independent authority and when they stated that a subordinate's failure to act in the absence of orders was inexcusable if he was aware of the general end in view. General King also addressed it very briefly in his lecture on command at Leavenworth. It was not, however, part of the fabric of the American leadership philosophy.

Clausewitz's observation that hunger for glory was the most potent of all command motivators was also conspicuous by its absence from the American command construct.[51] Spaulding mentioned the subject of ambition at the end of his lecture on Washington and Grant. He was not, however, able to relate this quality to either of his protagonists, each of whom consciously eschewed the trappings of public renown. Instead, he mentioned it almost as an afterthought in the context of Alexander, Genghis Khan, and Napoleon where it seemed to fit more clearly.[52] Spaulding's willingness to raise the issue of personal ambition in the commander's makeup perhaps indicates that he believed it to be important but realized that for an American audience, the subject had to be dealt with obliquely.

In sum, it is apparent that in the years between the world wars, the American army actively strove to develop a concept of command that it believed would help equip it for another contest with a major adversary. Given the episodic nature of the American military experience, this articulation not surprisingly took much of its inspiration from contemplation of the past. The two main sources for this study were the American Civil War and a wide range of national experiences of World War I. There is also a combination of direct and indirect evidence that certain of Clausewitz's observations on military genius had been consciously or subconsciously assimilated by several of those who took part in this effort. The resulting product was a reasonably coherent, though not fully mature, command philosophy.

These observations lead indirectly to two related questions. To what extent was the philosophy of command hammered out by the army between the wars distinctively American? And to what extent was it intended to be distinctly American? The evidence on both questions is mixed. As indicated above, the philosophy itself was eclectic—borrowing from not only American experience but also from a wide range of European experiences during World War I. Here, one would have to conclude that those who offered their thoughts on the art of command were primarily pragmatists: they realized that the army required a coherent doctrine of command to be effective in future war, and they cast their net widely to develop it. This observation is directly related to the question of motivation. It is tempting to see in this story the army as a reflection of a society that was acutely aware of its distinctiveness and that prided itself on its separation from, one might even say superiority to, the tired old societies of the Continent. And certainly this notion was very much at the forefront of Pershing's handling of the AEF in World War I.[53] Furthermore, many of the officers in positions of influence at CGSS and the War College between the wars had been closely associated with Pershing. But this evidence is merely suggestive. In the actual speeches and lectures given at both institutions during the interwar era, there is very little evidence to substantiate the interpretation that these officers were consciously attempting to develop a distinctively American philosophy of command. Rather, one is led to conclude that the result was a philosophy that shared much with those of many other armies but that also had some particular resonance with the American spirit simply because the men who developed it *were* Americans.

These broadly interpretive questions serve to put the command education of our six protagonists into the context of a maturing American army, and they take us into a wider ambit than we can travel for any great distance. To bring us back to the task at hand, one can conclude that Gerow, Middleton, Ridgway, Millikin, Eddy, and Collins were exposed to a reasonably coherent body of thought concerning the nature of command during their years in the army school system. The chief canons of this philosophy were assumption of sole responsibility, strength of will, mental acuity, appreciation of terrain, care for subordinates, celerity of action, and ability to endure privation. These criteria provide a useful analytical framework for the ultimate assessment of our subjects, but leadership is not a product of knowledge alone. Knowledge must be combined with talent and experience. To see that combination in action, let us now trace the careers of these six men from their precommissioning studies to the eve of the Bulge to determine what kinds of soldiers they were and what command actions and orders we might anticipate from them in the coming battle.

3

The Making of Six Corps Commanders

> How a soldier makes use of the active service that does come his way makes all
> the difference between his success or failure as a commander when he reaches
> the climax of his career. In other words, the creation of sound military judgment
> is the work of a lifetime and depends on an officer's own efforts.[1]
>
> W. G. F. Jackson

THE DEVELOPMENT OF A SENIOR MILITARY COMMANDER is a complex
undertaking that requires both institutional processes and individual effort.
Having assayed the former, we should now examine the latter. We shall trace
each future corps commander's professional development from the time of
his precommissioning studies to the eve of the Ardennes campaign. Three
issues are addressed: the nature of the experiences themselves; the officers'
use of and growth from these experiences; and the noteworthy qualities of
character, temperament, and intellect that were germane to their command
effectiveness. The object is to anticipate, to the extent possible, what their
development up to 15 December 1944 suggests as to how they would deal
with the significant challenges of the coming campaign. To maintain parallel-
ism with the story that follows, we shall consider them in the sequence their
various corps were committed to battle, i.e., Gerow, Middleton, Ridgway,
Millikin, Eddy, and Collins.

LEONARD T. GEROW

Leonard Gerow was born in Petersburg, Virginia, on 13 July 1888. He entered the Virginia Military Institute (VMI) in the summer of 1907 and there
accumulated a solid record.[2] He graduated twelfth in a class of fifty-two,
commanded one of the six cadet companies, and was elected class valedic-
torian.[3] Shortly after graduation, he received a commission in the Regular
Army as a second lieutenant of infantry. After a normal series of infantry
assignments in various regiments, he was detailed to the signal corps.[4] April
1918 found him in Brest, France, where he served as executive officer to the
AEF chief signal officer. He was soon promoted to major and transferred to

Paris, where he was responsible for purchasing, and later disposing of, the AEF's signal equipment. He excelled in these duties, receiving both American and French decorations.[5]

In mid-1920, Gerow was ordered to Washington to serve in the chief of infantry office and later the War Plans and Organization office of the War Department. In September 1924, he left Washington to attend the infantry officers' advanced course at Fort Benning, where he earned top honors.[6] He was then assigned to CGSS. Leavenworth was another significant point in Gerow's life, for there he solidified his relationship with an infantry major four years his junior, Dwight D. Eisenhower.[7] Gerow and Eisenhower formed a two-man study team to foster their mastery of the curriculum.[8] Their collaboration paid off, with Eisenhower graduating first in the class of 245 and Gerow eleventh.[9] Both earned the designation of honor graduate, given to the top 10 percent of the class.

From Leavenworth, Gerow returned to high-level staff duty, this time serving for four years as assistant executive officer for the assistant secretary of war, following which he was selected for the Army War College. When he left the War College in the summer of 1931, Gerow got his first chance for troop duty since his brief stint as a signal battalion commander in 1920, serving with the 31st Infantry until May 1934, first in the Philippines and then in Shanghai. This time he commanded two different infantry battalions. In command, he received high marks from Major General E. E. Booth, the Philippine Department commander.[10] When he returned to the United States in December 1934 for duty on the 9th Corps Area staff at the Presidio of San Francisco, he found waiting for him a letter from the VMI superintendent, Major General John A. Lejeune, USMC, Ret., inviting him to be detailed as the VMI commandant. Though tempted by the offer, Gerow demurred in order to keep his career on track.[11] After two very brief stateside assignments, Gerow reported to the War Plans Division (WPD) of the War Department in April 1935, where he was promoted to lieutenant colonel in August of the same year and appointed as the division's executive officer in May 1936. Here, Gerow worked closely with some of the army's best minds, including then brigadier generals Walter Krueger and George Marshall. Both rated him highly.[12] After two years away from Washington, he was promoted to brigadier general in October 1940; two months later, he became head of WPD. When Gerow reported to Marshall on 16 December 1940, the chief handed him a sheaf of papers with red tags marked "urgent" and cryptically told him, "You'd better go to work right now."[13] For the next fourteen months, Gerow handled a plethora of important assignments in what was arguably the most responsible brigadier general position in the army. As relations with

Japan deteriorated in late 1941, Gerow, like other senior American planners, sought means to deter Japanese aggression in the Far East.

But Gerow's greatest contribution to the eventual Allied victory in World War II was probably his prolonged campaign to get Eisenhower assigned to WPD. These efforts began even before Gerow arrived in Washington. On 18 November 1940, Gerow sent Eisenhower, then commanding a battalion of the 15th Infantry Regiment at Fort Lewis, Washington, and slated to become the 3rd Infantry Division (ID) chief of staff, a telegram saying that he needed him in WPD, asking him if he objected, and requesting an immediate reply.[14] Eisenhower replied immediately and emphatically—in the negative. In a three-page, single-spaced, typewritten letter, he bared his soul to Gerow, telling him that he had been away from troops for so long that he simply could not afford to return to staff duty at this delicate juncture in his career, adding in a postscript, "If war starts I expect to see you raise the roof to get a command, and *I go along*! [emphasis in original]"[15] Gerow withdrew the request but reopened the bidding in a letter of 2 January 1941, inviting Eisenhower to come to WPD as his executive officer.[16] Eisenhower again begged off.[17] But five days after the Japanese attack on Pearl Harbor, Eisenhower, by now promoted to brigadier general, received a call from Washington conveying Marshall's orders for him to report immediately to the War Department.[18] Two days later, he was in Marshall's office being told, as Gerow's deputy and heir apparent, to develop a strategy for the Pacific.[19] This set the stage for Ike's meteoric rise to high command. It also signaled a reversal of roles between Eisenhower and Gerow, who for some time had been designated to assume command of the 29th ID. Soon, Eisenhower would become the sponsor and Gerow the protégé, rather than vice versa.

Gerow excelled as a division commander. The 29th acquitted itself well during the Carolina maneuvers of August 1942. In September, Eisenhower, by now commander of the European Theater of Operations (ETO), attempted to get Gerow, whose division was en route to England, assigned as his deputy; but Marshall demurred.[20] Eisenhower withdrew the request; but he kept in touch with Gerow, passing on to him insights gained from his North African campaign and the Kasserine Pass debacle.[21] Thus, it should have come as no surprise to Gerow when in July 1943 he was instructed to take over V Corps, which had command of all field troops then in England and, of significantly greater importance, responsibility for tactical planning of the Normandy invasion. Gerow spent the next eleven months preparing for the invasion by supervising training and constantly refining tactical plans.

As the original U.S. Army corps designated for Normandy, V Corps was assigned the toughest nut to crack—Omaha Beach.[22] The steep hills immediately inland, the undetected presence of the German 352nd Division, and the low cloud cover that prevented accurate bombing of the coastal fortifications conspired to bring about all the worst fears imagined by the Allied planners: troops pinned down on the shore, corpses bobbing in the waves, and chaos on the beaches and aboard ships as one element of the plan after another went badly awry. Ultimately, a few resolute leaders took charge and organized a determined push inland that narrowly averted disaster. Gerow, of course, had little control over this; but he kept his nerve and a cool head, which was probably the most important thing for him to do. Russell Weigley's commentary on him at Normandy is instructive: "Gerow [was] studiously calm under pressure—he held to the old style of gentlemanly self-control in leadership."[23] Gerow's leadership in the subsequent tough, grinding fight through the Norman hedgerows was similarly described by Charles B. MacDonald as "calm, almost implacable, painstaking, dependable."[24] After Patton's breakout at Avranches, V Corps headquarters was pulled out of the line, instructed to assume command of three divisions, and ordered to close the Falaise-Argentan Pocket behind the nearly encircled German Seventh Army. There followed the liberation of Paris, in which Gerow had to contend with a subordinate French commander whose national interests clashed sharply with Gerow's tactical priorities and the almost impossible task of governing a newly liberated city while continuing the momentum of an ongoing offensive. Despite these frustrations, Gerow handled himself creditably and was awarded a Silver Star for moving into Paris under hostile fire.[25]

The Siegfried Line campaign severely tested Gerow's leadership. This effort, which began in mid-September 1944 and ended only when the Germans launched their counterattack in the Ardennes, can best be described as the autumn of Allied discontent.[26] Having outpaced the ability of the logistic structure to keep them supplied, faced by a hastily reorganized but extremely effective German defense, and encumbered by inhospitable weather that seriously degraded the effectiveness of airpower, American ground forces found themselves locked in a series of bloody battles of attrition. In the early weeks of the campaign, Gerow was called back to the United States to testify before a War Department panel investigating lack of preparedness for the attack on Pearl Harbor.[27] Gerow's testimony before this panel was evasive, seeking to minimize his responsibility for misunderstandings between the War Department and the army commander in Hawaii, General Walter C. Short, in the period leading up to the attack.

Gerow returned to the ETO for the bloody battles of the Hürtgen Forest. This operation conducted by the First Army, now under the command of

Lieutenant General Courtney H. Hodges, was not particularly controversial at the time; but it has become so since subjected to historical scrutiny.[28] In the Hürtgen, the offensive to capture the town of Schmidt in early November 1944 represented the nadir of V Corps' tactical competence.[29] Gerow directed Major General Norman D. (Dutch) Cota to attack with the three regiments of his 28th ID on diverging axes, thus dissipating the force of the main effort; he ordered the posting of one battalion to an exposed ridge, subjecting it to devastating artillery fire observed by the Germans from dominating high ground; and he either failed to appreciate or overlooked the virtual impassability of the Kall River gorge to wheeled and tracked vehicles, which left the 112th Infantry Regiment almost totally unsupported when counterattacked by German armor. Even more egregiously, he allowed Cota, who had performed magnificently at Normandy as assistant commander of Gerow's old 29th Division but whose actions at Schmidt were strangely lethargic, to absorb all the blame for the attack's dismal and bloody failure.[30] It was clearly not Gerow's finest hour.

Despite the debacle at Schmidt, in late November 1944 Gerow was designated to assume command of the soon-to-be-activated Fifteenth Army, whose duties would be largely administrative in nature, supervising the occupation of German territory and inspecting the training of newly arrived divisions.[31] One must suspect that Gerow's selection for this post was due in no small part to his long, intimate relationship with Eisenhower.[32] The change was to take effect in mid-January 1945. In the meantime, Major General Clarence R. Huebner, the irascible but effective commander of the 1st ID, was assigned as deputy V Corps commander to understudy Gerow.[33] Operationally after Schmidt, V Corps continued offensive operations to seize control of the Roer River dams, with the 2nd ID attacking on 13 December 1944 to capture the town of Wahlerscheid, just north of the Losheim Gap.[34]

This attack kicked off with a feeling of cautious optimism. But had one been aware of the impending German onslaught that was to strike V Corps with incredible fury on 16 December, one would have wanted to ask the somewhat obvious question, "Which Gerow will show up for the coming battle, the Gerow of Omaha Beach, or the Gerow of Schmidt?"

TROY H. MIDDLETON

Troy Middleton was born on 12 October 1889 in Copiah County, Mississippi.[35] He left home at age fourteen to become a preparatory student at Mississippi A&M College in Starkville. Shortly before his graduation in

1910, he received an alternate appointment to West Point; but the principal appointee did not relinquish his position. After graduation, Middleton therefore enlisted in the army, banking on his ability to obtain a direct commission. This estimate proved to be correct, and he was commissioned in early 1913.

When America entered the war in April 1917, he was a captain commanding a company in the 1st Battalion, 47th Infantry Regiment, of the 4th Division.[36] Middleton's war record was distinguished. On 7 June, he was promoted to major and elevated to battalion command. From 28 to 30 July, his unit successfully attacked a strongly contested German position in the Forêt de Nesles along the Ourcq River. On 26 September, his battalion, with now Lieutenant Colonel Middleton in command, led the 4th Division's attack through the Bois de Fays as part of the Meuse-Argonne offensive. Middleton's unit punched through the German defenses and advanced five miles, after which he was elevated to regimental executive officer. When the commander and senior staff of the 39th Infantry Regiment were gassed on 10 October, the division commander unhesitatingly selected Middleton to take over this unit. He arrived at the regimental headquarters only hours before its attack into the Bois de Forêt the next morning. Middleton was promoted to colonel on 14 October, making him, at two days past his twenty-ninth birthday, both the youngest colonel and youngest regimental commander in the AEF. For his actions in the Bois de Fays and the Bois de Forêt, he was subsequently awarded the Distinguished Service Medal (DSM), his brigade commander calling him "the best all around officer, on and off the field, that I have been privileged to observe in the A.E.F."[37]

Middleton used the next eighteen years to reflect upon his war experience, study new methods and techniques of combat, and pass the insights thus developed on to other officers of his generation. After occupation duty in Germany, he was selected to be on the initial faculty of the newly forming Infantry School at Camp Benning, Georgia.[38] Like many other officers, Middleton was reduced in rank following the postwar demobilization, so he reported to Benning as a captain. By July 1920 he had regained the grade of major. Here he served on the Infantry Board, which examined the technical capabilities and field worthiness of new weapons; and he attended the infantry officers' advanced course, from which he graduated in first place. While at Benning, he put down in writing some of the more important lessons he had garnered from his World War I experience. On 7 March 1923, at the invitation of the Chief of Infantry, Major General C. S. Farnsworth, Middleton presented a lecture at the Army War College, "Infantry and its

Weapons."[39] Middleton's lecture was an elegant, effectively delivered synthesis of technical capability, tactical knowledge, martial spirit, leadership, and principles of military instruction. It was thus not surprising that General Farnsworth informed Middleton before his return to Benning that he would soon be attending the CGSS.[40]

Middleton arrived at Leavenworth in the summer of 1923. He graduated eighth in a class of 248, thus earning, together with his classmate and confidant Major George S. Patton, Jr., who graduated seventeen places below him at twenty-fifth, the designation as an honor graduate.[41] Middleton's academic performance, his combat record, and his previous instructor experience made him a highly attractive candidate for service on the CGSS faculty, a position he held from 1924 to 1928. The list of Middleton's students reads like a Who's Who of World War II. It includes Dwight Eisenhower; Jacob Devers, six army commanders—Courtney Hodges, Alexander Patch, Robert Eichelberger, William Simpson, Simon Buckner, and Leonard Gerow—and ten corps commanders.[42] Middleton found Eisenhower a particularly engaging student, recalling years later that Ike would come into his office, sit on a corner of his desk, and quiz him earnestly and practically about what it was like to command troops in combat.[43]

At the completion of Middleton's tour as a Leavenworth instructor, he was sent to the Army War College, still in the grade of major. Here again, he excelled, though in this case the evidence is somewhat more circumstantial because unlike the CGSS, the Army War College did not maintain class standings.[44] Middleton's accomplishments must therefore be inferred from the assignments he was given in the various class requirements. He chaired an important student study project and served in significant positions on both a military history study problem and the culminating command post exercise.

Upon graduation in 1929, Middleton was posted to the 29th Infantry at Fort Benning, where he served as a battalion executive officer. In the summer of 1930, he was ordered to Louisiana State University (LSU).[45] After six years at the university, during which he served for several years as the dean of men in addition to his military duties, Middleton, now a lieutenant colonel, was assigned to the Philippines. While there, he received an offer from LSU to become dean of administration with an annual salary of $5,400. Eisenhower, who was serving as MacArthur's aide at the time, advised him to decline, telling him that a war was sure to come and Middleton was bound to become a general. Middleton, however, considered his prospects for advancement bleak and the offer simply too good to reject. His request for retirement of August 1937 was approved effective that October. In the aftermath of Pearl Harbor, Middleton returned to active duty and, thanks partly to Marshall's acute awareness of his capabilities, rose quickly to command of the 45th ID, with promotion to major general.[46] The division was subsequently alerted for duty in the Mediterranean theater, having earned high marks from Marshall and others for its training and discipline.[47]

Middleton soon proved that he could handle a division in combat as well as he could in training. In July 1943, the 45th deployed directly from the United States to assault a hostile shore in Sicily. Despite the reservations of Omar Bradley, Middleton's corps commander, concerning the ability of an untested unit to undertake such a mission, the 45th performed well, quickly seizing its initial objectives and executing a difficult change of front when Bradley's right flank was cramped by a boundary change between Patton's and Montgomery's armies.[48] The 45th continued a rapid advance across the island and was the first American unit to reach Sicily's north shore, a fact that Middleton attributed to the division's extensive night training.[49] Eisenhower called Middleton's performance in the early phases of the Sicily campaign "superior."[50] Shortly thereafter, he mentioned Middleton to Marshall as one of three potential corps commanders.[51] The 45th's next major operation was the amphibious assault at Salerno. When the Germans launched a resolute counterattack and the Fifth Army commander, Mark Clark, was actively considering an evacuation of the beachhead, Middleton communicated his own resolution both up and down the chain of command. He told Clark to leave ammunition and supplies on the beach because the 45th was staying; and he told his staff that there was not going to be another Dunkirk in Italy.[52] As the 45th advanced toward the Volturno, however, a knee injury sustained during training in the United States began acting up; and Middleton found himself unable to sustain the physical rigors of mountain warfare. He therefore requested and was granted relief from command.[53]

Middleton's knee was evaluated at Walter Reed in mid-February 1944 as being mildly arthritic. He was judged qualified for duty, though an orthopedic consultant recommended no marching, walking over rough terrain, or climbing.[54] There followed a rapid series of messages between Eisenhower, by then in England preparing for Overlord and desperate for corps commanders with combat experience, and Marshall, in which Marshall informed Eisenhower that he could have Middleton if he was willing to take a chance on his knee.[55] When Eisenhower replied that he was "quite willing to take a chance on Middleton's arthritis," Marshall immediately cabled approval.[56] By 4 March Middleton was in England and had assumed command of VIII Corps.[57]

Middleton's combat experience during the early campaigns in Europe demonstrated that he could command a corps competently in difficult situations. VIII Corps' initial mission was to secure the base of the Cotentin Peninsula while Collins's VII Corps captured Cherbourg. Marshlike terrain and a well-developed German resistance, which had been aided by a severe storm that destroyed an artificial port and significantly delayed the delivery of ammunition to the American forces in France, conspired to blunt the initial VIII Corps offensive of 3 July. When Bradley was finally able to orchestrate a breakout from the Normandy bridgehead, VIII Corps was given an important supporting role on the west coast of the Cotentin Peninsula and passed to the control of Patton's Third Army.[58] Middleton used the 4th and 6th Armored Divisions (AD) to capture Avranches, which opened up the interior of France for Patton's much-heralded exploitation. As Patton's lead elements were racing across the French countryside, VIII Corps received the less glamorous task of securing the ports of Brittany. This mission involved controlling two infantry and two armored divisions dispersed over a distance of roughly 200 miles and cracking the tough defenses at Brest.[59] In this prolonged operation, Patton, whose focus was fixed clearly to the east, became impatient with Middleton's requests for additional ammunition and support. Ultimately, however, the staunchness of the German resistance and Bradley's insistence that the port be taken as a sign of American determination vindicated Middleton's tactical judgment.[60] For the final stages of the siege, control of VIII Corps was passed to William Simpson's newly activated Ninth Army. Following the fall of Brest on 20 September, VIII Corps, still under the command of Ninth Army, was moved to the east where it was given an economy of force mission to defend an eighty-mile front in the Ardennes Forest between First and Third Armies. In early November, Bradley shifted Simpson's headquarters to the north.[61] This placed Middleton's corps under the control of First Army, now commanded by Courtney Hodges. Thus, 15 December 1944 found Middleton with his corps headquarters in Bastogne, Belgium, having been given a mission that required him to remain relatively static for nearly three months while the remainder of the First Army units continued their frustrating drive toward Cologne and Patton's units to the south prepared for an offensive in the Saar Basin.

Had one known at this juncture about the impending German counteroffensive, one would have anticipated that Middleton, who was, next to Marshall, the consummate American infantryman of the interwar era and a now-proven division and corps commander, would deal with it competently and unflappably.

MATTHEW B. RIDGWAY

Matthew Ridgway was born on 3 March 1895 at Fort Monroe, Virginia, the son of a Regular Army field artillery officer.[62] He entered West Point in the summer of 1913.

He compiled an unremarkable academic record at the academy, graduating 56th in a class of 139. His military and extracurricular accomplishments as cadet adjutant, then the second-ranking position in the corps, and manager of the varsity football team, however, earned him wide respect.[63] America's entry into World War I in April of 1917 caused Ridgway's class to graduate two months early. After a short tour on the Mexican border, he was ordered back to the academy to teach foreign languages, where he developed fluency in Spanish.[64] After the war, Douglas MacArthur, the newly appointed superintendent, assigned Captain Ridgway to be the director of athletics. This was a significant responsibility for a junior officer; but Ridgway quickly won the superintendent's trust and confidence, MacArthur referring to him as "one of the finest officers I have ever known."[65]

In 1922 Ridgway received orders to attend the company-grade officers' course at Fort Benning.[66] He was then assigned to the 15th Infantry Regiment in Tientsin, China, commanded by Lieutenant Colonel George C. Marshall. In late 1927 he accompanied General Frank McCoy on the American mission to supervise the elections in Nicaragua. His service as temporary secretary general of the Nicaraguan Electoral Commission not only earned the admiration of McCoy, who became an important mentor and patron, but also of Nicaraguan president Adolfo Díaz, who penned a glowing letter to the American ambassador commending Ridgway's effectiveness in his dealings with the Nicaraguan National Guard.[67] He had the good fortune to return to Benning during Marshall's tour as assistant commandant of the infantry school. He also graduated at the top of his advanced course class and earned a special accolade from Marshall, who noted his "dramatic talent."[68]

In 1933 he reported to Leavenworth to attend CGSS, from which he graduated a relatively undistinguished 46th in a class of 118.[69] From Leavenworth, he was posted to Chicago as G-3 of the Second Army and Sixth Corps Area, commanded by General McCoy. Here, Ridgway not only established a reputation as an effective operational planner, he also cemented his already solid relationship with Marshall.[70] Ridgway entered the Army War College in the summer of 1936. Late that year, Major General George S. Simonds, commander of the Fourth Army in San Francisco, listed Ridgway as the top pick to become his G-3 in the summer of 1937.[71]

Simonds got his wish, and Ridgway was duly posted to Fourth Army upon graduation. Here, Ridgway performed the normal operations functions of directing army maneuvers; but he also maintained his close relationship with Marshall, who was selected as the army's deputy chief of staff in October 1938.[72] In May 1939, Marshall was selected to conduct a military-diplomatic mission to Brazil to open negotiations for the construction of a series of airfields across the northern portion of that country.[73] Marshall had Ridgway, still a major, detailed from the Fourth Army staff to accompany him on this sensitive and important mission. During the cruise to Rio de Janeiro aboard the U.S.S. *Nashville*, Marshall and Ridgway had long conversations on the foredeck in which Marshall, who had just been designated as Malin Craig's successor as chief of staff, discussed his plans for rebuilding the American army, thus drawing Ridgway even more deeply into his circle of confidants. Shortly thereafter, Ridgway received orders to report to the War Plans Division in Washington, with primary responsibility for Latin America. Here, in line with others of his generation on the eve of an approaching war, he was rapidly promoted to lieutenant colonel and colonel. With the outbreak of hostilities in December 1941 came the additional duty of serving as Marshall's daily operational briefer, and Ridgway began to despair of ever being able to leave the War Department.[74] His redemption was not long in coming, for in January 1942 Marshall detailed him to be Bradley's assistant commander of the newly forming 82nd ID at Camp Claiborne, Louisiana.

Bradley and Ridgway made an excellent command team, but two developments significantly altered Ridgway's career.[75] The first was Marshall's decision to transfer Bradley to command the 28th ID, which the chief felt needed an infusion of aggressive leadership. This gave Ridgway command of the 82nd.[76] The second development was even more far-reaching—to convert the 82nd into an airborne division.[77] The original design of the airborne division included one parachute regiment, two glider regiments, divisional artillery, and a light complement of support organizations. The plan for the 82nd was to add to it the 504th Parachute Infantry Regiment (PIR) and convert the remaining infantry units into the two glider regiments. Just as the 82nd was gelling as an airborne division, it was ordered to provide the nucleus for formation of the 101st Airborne Division. Ridgway gulped; but to be equitable, he produced two rosters with cadres of roughly equal competence and literally flipped a coin with Major General Bill Lee, prospective commander of the 101st, to determine who got which group. The organizational tables were then altered to include two parachute regiments and one of gliders, instead of vice versa. Ridgway was fortunate to draw Colonel James M. Gavin's tough and highly regarded 505th PIR as his second airdrop unit.

In March 1943 Ridgway was summoned to Washington for a conversation with Marshall concerning the conduct of airborne operations in support of the invasion of Sicily. The chief then ordered him to North Africa for conversations with Eisenhower's planners.[78] The 82nd's experience in Sicily was traumatic. Because there were only sufficient transports for a single airborne regiment, Gavin's 505th and Colonel Reuben H. Tucker's 504th came in on two separate nights. Most of Gavin's regiment was misdropped and badly dispersed over a wide area of southern Sicily.[79] Tucker's experience was even worse.[80] Despite strenuous efforts by Ridgway to warn all ground and naval units of the 504th's night drop, American land-and-sea–based antiaircraft artillery mistook the American transports for German aircraft and opened a murderous fire, downing twenty-three airplanes and damaging another thirty-seven, resulting in over 300 casualties. Despite these setbacks, Bradley, who was commanding the II Corps under Patton during the invasion of Sicily, judged the airborne operations to have been successful, both for the confusion they sowed in the Axis command structure and for the singular contribution of Gavin's 505th in stopping the Hermann Göring Division from reaching the American landing beaches.[81] Given these generally positive results for the first large-scale airborne operation in American history, Ridgway was awarded the DSM for his role in its planning and implementation.[82] After brief participation in the Italian campaign, the 82nd was deployed to the United Kingdom to prepare for the Normandy invasion.

The final D-Day plan called for two American airborne divisions, the 82nd and the 101st, to land behind Utah Beach and protect the west flank of the invasion force from German counterattack. Air Chief Marshal Trafford Leigh-Mallory, commander of allied tactical air forces, developed the gloomy prognostication that at least half the transports would be shot down. Based on this estimate, he attempted on several occasions, right up to the eve of D-Day, to convince Eisenhower to cancel the operation.[83] Ridgway, however, was convinced that the risks, while real, were manageable and that the requirement to protect the landing force justified their acceptance. He was strongly supported by Bradley, now elevated to command of the American ground forces; and Eisenhower ultimately agreed. In the event, very few transports were shot down; but both the 82nd and the 101st missed the bulk of their drop zones. Nevertheless, they accomplished their missions. The 82nd, though, had a number of harrowing engagements, particularly in forcing a crossing of the Merderet causeway in order to open the door for J. Lawton Collins's VII Corps to seal the base of the Cotentin Peninsula.[84]

Here Ridgway and Gavin confirmed their reputations as combat leaders of exceptional toughness; and when the 82nd was withdrawn to England to prepare for future operations, Ridgway was elevated to command the newly formed XVIII (Airborne) Corps while Gavin was given command of the division.

In September 1944, Eisenhower ordered XVIII (Airborne) Corps' superior headquarters, First Allied Airborne Army, to conduct a three-division airborne drop into Holland to capture the bridge at Arnhem over the lower Rhine and give Montgomery's Twelfth Army Group access to the North German Plain. Code-named Market-Garden, it was a bold, risky attempt to accelerate the end of the war in Europe.[85] Although the Americans provided two of the three divisions for this operation, command of the airborne forces went to Ridgway's old nemesis, Frederick A. "Boy" Browning. The reasons for this are unclear, but the most likely explanation is that because the operation was in support of Montgomery's army group and because close liaison would be required between the airborne forces and the advancing British ground forces, Eisenhower wanted a British officer in command at the corps level. In the event, the operation failed. Although the 101st and the 82nd eventually captured their bridges after some stiff German resistance, the British 1st Airborne Division units at Arnhem were defeated before British ground forces reached them. Market-Garden remains one of the most controversial episodes of World War II, and there was no single factor that brought about its failure. However, at least two historians have been tempted to speculate that with Ridgway in command of the airborne forces, things might have turned out differently.[86] What is incontrovertible is that what could have been Ridgway's first opportunity to see combat as a corps commander turned out instead to be a deep disappointment.[87]

After Market-Garden, the 82nd and 101st were, as they had been on previous operations, left in the line to fight as conventional infantry.[88] From mid-November to the end of the month, they were withdrawn and quartered in the vicinity of Rheims, France, with a small forward element of the XVIII (Airborne) Corps headquarters. The main portion of the corps headquarters remained in England, where it planned for future operations and supervised the arrival of new airborne units into the theater. Meanwhile, Ridgway continued to carry on an extended correspondence with Marshall arguing for the assignment of more robust combat support units to airborne divisions.[89] In early December, frustrated over the continued success of Army Ground Forces headquarters in blocking adoption of his proposals, he dispatched Major General Maxwell D. Taylor, who had assumed command of the 101st just before D-Day, back to Washington to argue the case in person.[90]

Thus, by the eve of the Bulge, Ridgway had established a reputation as a sound and aggressive division commander, but his ability to command a corps in combat had not been tested. Therefore, the operative question on the eve of the coming German attack was, "Will he be able to make the transition from division to corps command?"

JOHN MILLIKIN

John Millikin was born on 7 January 1888 in Danville, Indiana; his father, Horace F. Millikin, was a barber.[91] The younger Millikin entered the Military Academy in June 1906. His record at West Point was one of only moderate distinction. Although he captained the basketball team his senior year, he earned no cadet rank and graduated in 1910, 38th in a class of 82.[92] His first posting was as a regimental officer with the 5th Cavalry, initially at Schofield Barracks, Hawaii. In 1914, after occasional duty in Arizona, his regiment was transferred to Fort Myer, Virginia. In November 1917, he married Mildred March, eldest daughter of the Army Chief of Staff, General Peyton C. March.[93] Thus, Millikin was propelled by marriage into the inner circles of army political life. In early 1918, he was assigned as the executive officer of the newly established General Staff School in Langres, France.[94] Following the Armistice, promotion to lieutenant colonel led to his assignment as chief of the military police corps and deputy provost marshal for the AEF.[95] Millikin handled his responsibilities with close care and attention to detail. When his duties were completed in the summer of 1919, he was awarded a DSM and commended by the AEF provost marshal.[96]

When he returned to the United States, he was assigned to the G-3 division of the army general staff, with a number of additional duties: acting aide to the army chief of staff and secretary of war, assistant chief of staff to the commander of army troops in the District of Columbia, and provost marshal of the District of Columbia.[97] In the summer of 1919, racial tensions in Washington boiled over.[98] Millikin played a large part in calming this rapidly brewing storm. Acting in close concert with District Commissioner Louis Brownlow, the metropolitan police, and U.S. Marines dispatched from Quantico, he deployed several hundred cavalrymen into the city, interposing them between the largest groups of African Americans and whites. His prompt action significantly reduced the level of violence and won him high praise from Brownlow, his commanding officer, Secretary of War Newton Baker, and his father-in-law.[99]

Millikin's service as March's aide gave him both a number of perks and insight into one of the turbulent periods of army history. The former included accompanying the general on an inspection trip to Europe and the opening of the Panama Canal; watching his wife christen the launch of the army transport ship, *Argonne*; visiting various installations in the United States; and participating in the whirl of Washington social events.[100] The latter included the headaches of demobilization, a growing tension between March and Pershing as the star of the former waned and the latter waxed, and an almighty row over the future size and shape of the army between March and Baker on one side and Congress on the other.[101] With General John J. Pershing's appointment as chief of staff in 1921, Millikin became a "March man" in a Pershing army.

From 1921 to 1924, Millikin served as the G-4 and later the G-2 of the Hawaiian Division at Schofield Barracks. In 1924, he was selected to attend the Cavalry Officers' Advanced Course at Fort Riley, Kansas. Millikin's early record at Riley was mixed. His efficiency report, prepared by the school commandant, Brigadier General Edward L. King, described him as "keen, impressive, has latent ability, self satisfied."[102] In his academic report, the assistant commandant noted: "Good staff man. Active. Requires pushing at times."[103] The total picture that emerges from the two reports is one of an efficient, capable officer with at least a touch of reserve and aloofness.

Despite these reservations concerning his demeanor, Millikin's career was clearly on track as he was selected to attend CGSS in 1925. He did well, graduating thirtieth in a class of 245, just below the cutoff for honor graduate.[104] Millikin remained on the Leavenworth faculty for four years. Not surprisingly, his duties revolved primarily around cavalry instruction.[105] He led numerous conferences on his branch's role in reconnaissance, counter-reconnaissance, and flank security. But he also offered instruction in wider subjects such as corps and army organization, operations of a detached corps, and army-level logistics. Selection for attendance at the Army War College from 1930 to 1931 indicated Millikin was still progressing nicely. He graduated with an overall "superior" rating, the highest in the reporting lexicon, and was recommended for command of a brigade in peacetime or a division in combat.[106] The commandant, Major General W. D. Connor, characterized him as bright, capable, and energetic.

Following graduation from the War College, Millikin returned to the Cavalry School at Fort Riley where he moved steadily up the ladder of academic responsibility. He served for two years as head of the tactics department; one year as director of instruction; and two years as executive of the academic division, making him the assistant commandant's right-hand man. From 1934 to 1936, he worked for Colonel Jonathan M. Wainwright, son of an "Old Army" cavalryman, first captain of the corps of cadets at West Point, and a widely respected, thoughtful cavalryman.[107] Millikin's positions at Fort Riley gave him an excellent vantage point from which to assess the debate in his branch as to its future in the light of ongoing mechanization. During his five-year tenure, articles such as "Cavalry in Future War," "Mechanized Forces," and "The Cavalry and Mechanization, 1936" were standard fare in the *Cavalry Journal*.[108] Additionally, the 1st Cavalry Brigade (Mechanized) came to Fort Riley for maneuvers in the late spring of 1934.[109] But the truest indicator of his service at Riley was that Wainwright, having been designated to command the 3rd Cavalry Regiment at Fort Myer in 1936, requested that Millikin, who had been promoted to lieutenant colonel a year earlier, be assigned as his executive officer.[110]

Millikin's return to troop duty began a long, steady rise to corps command. In the summer of 1938, Millikin commanded a composite force from the 3rd and 10th Cavalry Regiments on an extended march. He continued to get high marks for the performance of his duties. Wainwright called him "a brilliant officer with an unusually active mind."[111] But in a follow-on report, the regimental commander captured aspects of Millikin's personality previously only adumbrated: "A very forceful, level headed man, cold and stern but conscientious. An efficient officer, better liked by his superiors than his subordinates but respected by all."[112] The following year, Wainwright softened the implicit critique in the middle clause of the last sentence, noting that Millikin was "loyal to his superiors and subordinates alike."[113] Millikin's next assignment was as G-3, First Corps Area. In the summer of 1939, while still on the First Corps Area staff, he was promoted to colonel. He was designated as chief of staff of the provisional corps in the First Army maneuvers. These exercises, also known as the Plattsburg maneuvers for their location in upstate New York, were designed to prepare the army to conduct large-scale operations. Millikin came through with flying colors, earning an official commendation for his work in directing the efforts of the corps staff and assisting the corps commander, Major General J. A. Woodruff.[114] The trials also allowed Millikin to witness operations of the 7th Cavalry Brigade, the significantly expanded and much more powerful successor to the 1st Cavalry Regiment (Mechanized).[115]

In April 1940, he assumed command of the newly created and experimental 6th Cavalry Regiment (Horse and Mechanized), stationed at Fort Oglethorpe, Georgia, which was designated as a corps reconnaissance regiment. This unit was field tested in the initial phase of the Third Army maneuvers, immediately after Millikin's arrival.[116] He earned his spurs in the field. The Red Force commander, Brigadier General R. O. Van Horn, informed the chief of cavalry that the 6th Cavalry was always on top of things and that Millikin was "the man for the job."[117] His corps area commander, Lieutenant General S. D. Embick, called his performance in the field "alert, intelligent, zealous, and enthusiastic."[118] And perhaps most significantly, the Blue Force commander, Major General Walter Short, wrote Chief of Staff George Marshall that the 6th Cavalry "got better results than any other cavalry unit at the maneuvers."[119]

With these good reports, it is not surprising that Millikin was selected to command the 1st Cavalry Brigade at Fort Bliss, Texas, a subordinate unit of the First Cavalry Division, and promoted to brigadier general in October 1940. Over the next three years, he received a succession of general officer troop duty assignments as the army rapidly expanded. He remained at Fort Bliss for only seven months but earned high marks from his division commander, Major General Innis P. Swift, for the imagination he showed in developing training exercises.[120] He was given command of the newly formed 2nd Cavalry Division at Camp Funston, Kansas, in April 1941 and promoted to major general in July. The 2nd Cavalry would eventually be deployed to North Africa in 1943 but was inactivated and its soldiers used as logistical support troops.[121] Thus, it was fortuitous that in August 1942 Millikin was placed in command of an even newer unit, the 33rd Infantry Division.[122] After deployment of the division to Fort Shafter, Hawaii, Millikin received orders in September 1943 instructing him to assume command of the III Corps at Fort McPherson, Georgia.[123]

The reasons behind Millikin's elevation to corps command are difficult to determine. He had received a series of positive reports for his actions as a division commander of two different divisions. But as late as January 1943, Lieutenant General Lesley McNair, commander of Army Ground Forces and the man who, short of Marshall, held the keys to the kingdom for general officer advancement in those forces, noted that he was insufficiently acquainted with Millikin to add any substantive comments to his efficiency report.[124] Nevertheless, eight months later, McNair recommended to Marshall that Millikin be given command of III Corps.[125] One is therefore driven to speculate that the expanding army required formation of another corps headquarters and that Millikin's troop-duty record since his assumption of command of the 6th Cavalry had been sufficiently impressive to overcome the fact that he was, to both McNair and Marshall, something of an unknown quantity.

Over the next year, McNair's opinion was to change. III Corps moved from Fort McPherson to the Presidio of Monterey, California, where it took on the thankless but necessary task of evaluating the training status of both divisions and nondivisional units in preparation for overseas deployment.[126] Based on McNair's periodic inspection visits to III Corps and more frequent contact by telephone and written communication, he judged Millikin to be *"well balanced, physically and mentally, active and aggressive"* (emphasis in original), just the qualities he and Marshall sought in the commanders to be sent overseas.[127] Thus, when III Corps embarked for Europe in September 1944, it had at its helm a man who had progressed steadily through the army's professional development system for three decades and found to be, as well as peacetime preparation could tell, capable of command in war.

In the period leading up to the Bulge, however, Millikin remained almost utterly innocent of the realities of combat.[128] III Corps initially served under Ninth Army command in Normandy, where it oversaw the arrival of new units into the theater. On 10 October it was placed under Third Army control and shifted east to Étain. In early December, it moved to Metz, where it became operational, and directed the 26th Infantry Division in forcing the capitulation of the German garrison at the nearby Fort Jeanne d'Arc. Thus, the real question about Millikin when the Germans launched their offensive into the Ardennes on 16 December was whether his clearly adequate peacetime preparation would be able to overcome his almost total lack of combat experience.

MANTON S. EDDY

Manton Eddy was born in Chicago on 16 May 1892. His father, George M. Eddy, was a successful insurance man.[129] Manton, or "Matt," as he came to be known, attended a preparatory school, Shattuck Military Academy, in Faribault, Minnesota. Upon graduation in 1913, he returned to Chicago and began selling insurance. Lack of success in this arena led his father to suggest that he use his honor graduate designation from Shattuck to obtain a Regular Army commission. Seeing the wisdom of his father's advice, Matt was sworn in as a first lieutenant on 29 November 1916.

Eddy soon found himself in France with the 4th Division, commanding a machine-gun company of the 39th Infantry Regiment in a state of equipment chaos and doctrinal void.[130] He and his fellow soldiers were sorely tested in the Aisne-Marne operation. The regiment failed dismally in its effort to cross the Vesle River and suffered high casualties in the process. During a subsequent, partially successful attempt to force the river, German artillery was brought to bear on one of Eddy's machine-gun positions. Eddy quickly moved to the gun and cradled in his arms a young soldier nicknamed "Sister" McKey. McKey looked at his commander and said plaintively, "Captain, don't let me die; you got me into this."[131] He then expired. At this moment, the crushing responsibility of command seared Eddy's soul with feelings of guilt over his own ignorance. It was a defining event in his professional life. Wounded in the knee shortly after McKey's death, Eddy convalesced until early October.[132] Upon his return to duty, he was appointed battalion executive officer and acting battalion commander of the 1st Battalion, 39th Infantry, serving briefly in that capacity during the Meuse-Argonne offensive. In late October, he was given command of the 11th Machinegun Battalion. After routine postwar assignments, he reported to Fort Benning for the company commanders' course in the beginning of 1921.

At Benning, Eddy began to display some potential for advancement in the service. But despite diligent studies, he graduated with a nonremarkable rating, being described by the assistant commandant as "an average officer of good presence, manners, and personality."[133] He remained at Benning for three years, serving on the Infantry Board and commanding a company of the 29th Infantry Regiment. He left Benning in 1925 to become professor of military science at Riverside Military Academy in Gainesville, Georgia, where he served for four years. When he left Gainesville in 1929 for the infantry officers' advanced course, Eddy received glowing testimonials from the mayor, the chamber of commerce, and the academy superintendent for his energetic support of civic activities.[134]

Eddy's return to Benning was fruitful. He arrived at the beginning of Marshall's reforming tenure as assistant commandant, and the opportunity to reflect on his combat experience not only helped him put that experience into a wider context, but may have also brought him to the particular attention of the future chief of staff. He based his required research monograph on his own combat experience. The paper was ponderously titled and awkwardly written.[135] But what it lacked in grace, it made up for in passion and analysis. The fire came from Eddy's heartfelt depiction of a microcosm of the American army being thrown into a conflagration for which it was glaringly ill prepared, punctuated by the dramatic account of "Sister" McKey's dying in his arms. Marshall had instructed his faculty to bring to his attention any student monographs that showed a flash of inspiration. Eddy's biographer asserts that the report was so forwarded.[136] The evidence to that effect is circumstantial. Nevertheless, Marshall's narrative remarks on Eddy's efficiency report referred to him as a "superior type, a natural leader."[137] Marshall doled out such praise sparingly, and one can infer from this pithy summary a high opinion.

While in Hawaii from 1931 to 1932, Eddy commanded a battalion of the 21st Infantry for six months, followed by service as the assistant departmental G-3 for just under a year and a half. He earned particularly high marks in the latter billet, which may have been instrumental in his selection for CGSS.[138] He reported to Leavenworth in the summer of 1932. His overall record was mixed, graduating in the middle of the class and failing to be judged "especially qualified" for duties as a corps chief of staff.[139] But the commandant, Major General Stuart Heintzelman, detected promise in Eddy, which led to a selection for faculty duty. Over the next four years of teaching subjects such as infantry organization and weapons; brigade, division, and corps operations; and historical illustrations of various tactical maneuvers, Eddy mastered the discipline of higher-level tactics.[140] In a sense, the six years at Leavenworth allowed him to make up in professional education what he lacked in civil education.

After Leavenworth, Eddy rose quickly through the ranks as a commander and staff officer, but he was disappointed in not being selected to attend the Army War College. He was promoted to lieutenant colonel in August 1938, just before taking up duties as the executive officer of the 10th Infantry Regiment at Fort Thomas, Kentucky. Over the next two years, he dealt with the routine details of unit and garrison administration and won high marks from his regimental commander for his performance of duty, contact with civilians, and potential for future service.[141] But the stress of regimental duty took a physical toll, significantly elevating his blood pressure.[142] Although this condition responded favorably to rest, it had to be closely monitored. Nevertheless, Eddy's solid performance as a regimental officer was sufficient to garner him advancement to higher level staff duty. In July 1940, Eddy moved to Baltimore to take up duties as the G-2 of the Third Corps Area. He continued to impress his superiors with his efficiency, initiative, and zeal, earning promotion to colonel in October 1941.[143]

Eddy's star rose quickly. In the Carolina Maneuvers held in November 1941, he was given command of the 113th Infantry Regiment of the 44th Division, which was detailed to perform antiairborne operations, reporting directly to the First Army commander, Lieutenant General Hugh Drum. Eddy got high marks for the unit's work and by March 1942 received a recommendation for promotion to brigadier general.[144] In mid-1942, he assumed command of the 9th ID and soon pinned on his second star. The reasons Marshall picked Eddy to command the 9th are obscure. Perhaps a vague recollection of Eddy's advanced course monograph had something to do with it. More likely, it was the more mundane process of screening Eddy's efficiency reports and consulting with senior officers such as McNair, whose judgment Marshall trusted. It was a good call. Despite not having attended the War College, Eddy was a well-schooled and experienced tactician. He also had the common touch. Ernie Pyle would later describe him as "old-shoe."[145] Thus, to a man like Marshall, who so clearly understood that the great challenge facing him and his subordinates was to mobilize, train, and lead into combat a *citizen* army, Eddy was a natural.[146]

The 9th ID's commitment to combat was something of an anticlimax. The division's three infantry regiments were parceled out to three different landing elements in Operation Torch, thus relegating Eddy to the nontactical role of deputy commander of Patton's Western Task Force. The division was not reunited until March 1943 when, in the wake of the debacle at Kasserine Pass, it was committed in the II Corps offensive east of El Guettar.[147] It was a rough baptism of fire. The division's next major operation was the attack to seize Bizerte as part of the final Allied drive on Tunis.[148] The 9th performed credibly in this operation, despite having to attack over very tricky terrain and contend with a large gap on its eastern flank.

The 9th ID had a limited role in the Sicily campaign, arriving on the island for only the final two weeks of operations, as the German units were evacuating to the Italian mainland.[149] Nevertheless, Eddy's division had performed credibly enough to be selected for the Normandy invasion. Assigned to Collins's VII Corps, its initial mission was to follow the 4th Infantry ashore at Utah Beach and move west to cut the Cotentin Peninsula. It performed this task with alacrity and quickly wheeled toward Cherbourg. The garrison was rapidly seized, and Eddy's leadership from the front garnered him a DSC. After capturing Cherbourg, the 9th ID continued its operations with VII Corps during the Cobra breakout and the repulse of the Mortain counterattack. Eddy's stock rose steadily. Thus, when Major General Gilbert Cook, commander of the XII Corps in Patton's recently activated Third Army, developed acute hypertension, Eddy got the nod as his replacement.[150]

Eddy assumed command in the heady days of late August as the Third Army was knifing its way through the French interior. Assigned the role of guarding Third Army's right flank, Eddy asked Patton how nervous he should be about the fact that there was no one but Germans to his south. Patton replied that this depended on Eddy's own constitution.[151] In reality, there were two good reasons for Eddy not to be unduly concerned: the active operations of Brigadier General O. P. Weyland's XIX Tactical Air Command and Patton's shrewd reading of Ultra intelligence.[152] In Eddy's defense, he was unaware of the latter, as Ultra information was not passed below field army level.

Eddy soon found that commanding a corps was not all that easy. After the Third Army reached the Seine and priority of effort in the theater shifted to the north, XII Corps found itself involved in heavy slugging against a determined enemy at the end of a tenuous line of communication. After forcing multiple crossings of the Moselle and conducting an artful double-envelopment of Nancy, Eddy endured two crises of command.[153] The first came on 30 September when he ordered the withdrawal of two regiments of the 35th ID from positions in the Forêt de Grémecey, east of the Seille River.[154] This action incurred Patton's immediate and stinging wrath. Patton's anger was, as usual, fleeting, and Eddy soon found himself being recommended for a DSM for his conduct of the drive to the Seine and the continuation of the attack east of the Moselle.

He encountered a second major challenge in late November.[155] It centered on the deteriorating relationship between himself and the commander of the 4th AD, Major General John "P" Wood.[156] The matter was complicated by the fact that Wood was a West Point classmate of Patton's and one of the army commander's closest confidants. He was also a superb tactician, who has been hailed by historians as an "American Rommel" and "one of the best of the [American] division commanders—perhaps the very best."[157] But the rigors of the Lorraine campaign had taken a heavy toll. The attrition in warfare as well as in spirit had transformed Wood into an irritable and difficult subordinate. After Eddy complained to Patton that "P" was moving too slowly and was "almost insubordinate," the army commander intervened with a letter hand delivered by his chief of staff, Major General Hugh J. Gaffey, telling Wood to follow orders or risk relief.[158] After another incident less than two weeks later, Patton relieved Wood at Eddy's request, replacing him with Gaffey.[159] Being forced to choose between the bold and brilliant but erratic Wood or the stable and dependable but cautious Eddy, Patton chose Eddy.[160]

By mid-December, XII Corps had reached the out-works of the German West Wall. It was conducting a slow, grinding attack against skillful opposition. No one at the corps headquarters had any hint of the coming German offensive in the Ardennes. But if they had, they probably would have had confidence that their commander of the past four months, a steady, combat-experienced achiever who had survived two crises in command, was now well in the saddle; though he played his cards close to his vest, he would be able to lead them effectively through the coming campaign.

J. LAWTON COLLINS

Joseph Lawton Collins was born on 1 May 1896 in New Orleans as the tenth of eleven children.[161] His family was supported by the revenues from his father's shop in Algiers, Louisiana. In 1913, he followed his older brother, James, to the banks of the Hudson. At West Point, he graduated in the top quarter of his class and earned a reputation that was to stick with him the rest of his life as a man of quick decision and rapid action.[162] Like other members of the class of April 1917, Collins did not see active service in World War I.[163] Assigned to the 22nd Infantry at Fort Jay, Governor's Island, New York, he was soon promoted to major and placed in command of a battalion. Shortly after the war ended, he reverted to the rank of captain and was posted to occupation duty in Coblenz, Germany. After serving for just over a year as a company commander, he was assigned as the assistant G-3 of the army occupation forces. He returned to West Point in the summer of 1921 for instructional duty in the department of chemistry. He received positive marks from his superiors for his enthusiasm in the classroom and attention to detail in the preparation of his lessons.[164] While at West Point, he also took official action to have his name entered in the Army Register as "J. Lawton Collins," rather than "Joseph L. Collins," in order to avoid confusion between himself and James, whose middle initial was also L.[165]

After four years at the academy, it was on to Benning where he attended the company officers' course. Based on his performance there, the assistant commandant made the laconic observation, "He gets results," and selected him for faculty duty after attendance at the field artillery advanced course.[166] Collins returned to Benning in the summer of 1927. Later that year, Marshall became the assistant commandant, and Collins immediately came to his attention. Marshall's characterization of him was effusive: "Has a bright mind and a natural aptitude for logical and constructive thinking. A superior type."[167] Marshall drew Collins into the inner circle of officers that met at his quarters to discuss the military implications of current books on politics, economics, and sociology.[168] Collins left Benning in 1931 to become a student at CGSS. He graduated twenty-second in a class of 125.[169] He was then ordered to troop duty in the Philippines as executive officer of the 23rd Infantry Brigade, Philippine Scouts, arriving in August 1933.

After less than a year of troop duty, he was assigned as the G-2/G-3 of the Philippine Department, where he served for the next two years.[170] A mix-up in the Chief of Infantry's office resulted in his attending the Army Industrial College for a year before going on to the War College in 1937.[171] Collins's record at the War College was impressive. In the school's major command post exercise, he drew plum assignments as deputy chief umpire during the first phase and as the field army chief of staff in the second.[172] The commandant characterized him as being "broadminded; original independent thinker, with active imagination."[173] Solid performance as a student led to selection for instructional duty. As a War College faculty member, Collins lectured on the concentration and offensive operations of field armies and army groups.[174]

With Marshall rising to become chief of staff in September 1939, Collins soon found himself detailed to the General Staff secretariat. Promotion came quickly as he prepared position papers for Marshall, boiling the essence of complex issues down to pithy two-page summaries. In January 1941, Marshall struck out the assistant chief of staff's endorsement of Collins's efficiency report, replaced it with the handwritten observation, "Colonel Collins is outstanding in the Army," and released his protégé to become the chief of staff of VII Corps in Birmingham, Alabama.[175] Collins was the first man in his class to pin on eagles.[176] The corps chief of staff position allowed him to help prepare the army for a war he was certain was coming but for which he knew it was painfully unprepared. The Japanese attack on Pearl Harbor dramatically altered Collins's career.[177] VII Corps was immediately dispatched from Alabama to California to defend the West Coast. Almost immediately after arriving in San Francisco, he was posted to Hawaii as chief of staff of the Hawaiian Department. In the aftermath of the Japanese attack, his commander, Major General Delos C. Emmons, an Army Air Forces officer, concentrated on air defense and internal security matters and gave Collins principal responsibility for ground defenses.[178] Collins was promoted to brigadier general in February 1942. Two months later, Eisenhower cabled Emmons to see if he would concur with Collins's assuming command of the 25th ID. Emmons assented, also recommending Collins's promotion to major general and, subsequently, award of a DSM.[179] Collins trained the division for combined arms operations and demonstrated its effectiveness in defense of the islands with his usual imagination and flair. In October, the division left Hawaii, ostensibly for assignment to the Southwest Pacific Theater, but it was diverted to Guadalcanal.

Here, Collins operated under XIV Corps, commanded by Major General Alexander M. Patch, to eliminate the Japanese forces on Guadalcanal.[180] The 25th drew a tough assignment. Its zone of operations south of the 2nd Marine Division was covered by triple canopy jungle, cut by severely broken and very well-defended terrain, and divided into three distinct sectors that made coordinated division action almost impossible. Collins's plan was based on sound terrain analysis, good tactical sense, and an ingenious logistical support concept.[181] When the attack kicked off on 10 January 1943, Collins led from the front, spending most of his time at regimental command posts but frequently moving forward to battalion level as well. By the end of January, Japanese resistance had been crushed. Collins's detailed after-action report highlighted the need for improved communications gear in jungle terrain, more Japanese-language interrogators, and the mental toughness but lack of mental agility of the Japanese soldier.[182] On 26 January 1943, Collins wrote Marshall with a summary of the 25th ID's accomplishments, attributing much of its success to the tactical ideas promulgated by Marshall at Benning.[183] The chief forwarded an extract of this letter to President Roosevelt with the notation, "General Collins is one of our youngest Division [*sic*] commanders and one of the brilliant officers in our Army."[184]

Both the results of the Guadalcanal operation and the favorable reviews Collins received suggest that the action marked a most successful start to Collins's combat career. But there was trouble beneath the surface. Although General Patch recommended Collins for award of a second DSM for his actions in the campaign, his May 1943 efficiency report suggested distinct reservations about his subordinate's command persona.[185] He lauded Collins for aggressiveness and industry but also noted that the 25th ID commander was "opinionated to a pronounced degree and has a strong tendency to tell everyone not only what to do but how to do it. He does not encourage his juniors to feel free to voice their opinions."[186] Six months later, Patch's successor, Major General Oscar W. Griswold, echoed these sentiments in two efficiency reports rendered in late 1943, the latter of which stated explicitly that Collins was "not recommended for Corps Command [*sic*]."[187] For the first time in his career, Collins's chances for advancement were, at best, problematic.

It therefore came as a stroke of very good fortune when, in December 1943, Collins was authorized to take leave in Washington to visit his family.[188] Soon after arriving home, he paid a visit to Marshall, during which he unabashedly lobbied the chief for command of a corps. Marshall replied that he had discussed the issue with MacArthur, but the theater commander had responded that Collins was too young. As Collins was leaving Marshall's office, he said he would like to try for a command in Europe. "Maybe you will," the chief replied.[189] Marshall was as good as his word. Collins was soon en route to England to be screened by Bradley and Eisenhower as the prospective commander of VII Corps, which would be one of the two American corps landing at Normandy on D-Day. Although Collins was not Ike's first choice, he got the nod.[190]

Collins took firm hold of VII Corps.[191] He closely supervised training. He moved the operational portions of the corps command post to Plymouth to facilitate planning with the navy. And he delivered a compelling presentation on the VII Corps plan for the assault that favorably impressed the landing force commander, General Bernard L. Montgomery. He was similarly decisive in the invasion itself; and the nickname "Lightning Joe," which had been given to him by his troops in the Pacific, soon became attached to him in Europe as well.[192] At Bradley's direction, VII Corps moved to seal off the Cotentin Peninsula. Collins then quickly reorganized the forces under his command and drove the 4th, 79th, and 9th IDs toward Cherbourg. Collins pressed hard; and by 27 June Cherbourg was in Allied hands, becoming the first French city to rehoist the tricolor.

Collins's most significant contribution to the Allied cause came a month later when VII Corps led the First Army breakout in Operation Cobra.[193] The Germans had contained the offensive along a line that ran from Caen, through St. Lô, to the Gulf of St. Malo. The tough hedgerow fighting augured poorly for a breakout into the interior of France. As Bradley fretfully paced his command tent, he gradually developed a concept to break the stalemate. He would make a classic penetration with the concentration of three divisions on a narrow front, supported by heavy bombers to inundate a large area immediately in front of the attacking force with high explosive bombs. To lead the ground assault, Bradley chose "the nervy and ambitious Collins."[194] Collins refined Bradley's plan, requesting two additional divisions, one armored and one motorized infantry.[195]

Collins made good use of all the assets Bradley gave him.[196] At the end of the first day of the assault on 25 July, the three infantry divisions had not gained the maneuver space Collins originally thought would be necessary to commit his armored formations. This created a dilemma. If the tank and motorized units were committed too early, they could get bogged down in a slugging match and not be able to make the breakthrough. If they were committed too late, the Germans might move sufficient reserves into the area to block their penetration. In either event, Bradley's grand scheme for a breakout would come to naugh—the Germans would have the Allies contained. It all came down to Collins's assessment of the coherence of the German defense. Late on the afternoon of the 25th, he sensed that the Germans were reacting sluggishly. Based on this perception, he committed two mobile columns the next morning. It was a very nicely calculated decision.[197] By the 27th, the 2nd and 3rd ADs were in open country, moving quickly south; the German defenses had begun to disintegrate.

After Cobra, VII Corps blunted the German counterattack at Mortain and provided the one element of dash in an otherwise rather plodding First Army advance to the German border. Collins's performance in the Hürtgen was no more inspired than that of any other senior American commander, though it did not reach the nadir of Gerow's at Schmidt.[198] Thus, by late 1944, Collins had staked out a reputation as one of the most effective, and perhaps the most effective, corps commanders in the European theater. December 1944 found VII Corps advancing slowly on the V Corps left flank, north of the impending German offensive. Unforeseen events would eventually bring VII Corps into the battle. Given Collins's combat record to that point in the war, one would expect that participation to be characterized by sound decision and quick action.

SOME CLOSING OBSERVATIONS

This composite portrait of our six protagonists prior to the Bulge has examined three issues: the nature of their experiences; how they used and grew from these experiences; and significant qualities of character, temperament, and intellect that were germane to their command effectiveness.

Their various assignments can be classified into five categories: professional schooling, instructor duty, staff duty, noncombat troop duty, and combat experience.[199]

In addition to their branch schools, all six attended CGSS and all but Eddy attended the Army War College. The only objective measure of their relative academic performance is thus their class standing at CGSS. If one computes their graduating percentiles in terms of class standing and class size, they emerge in the following order: Middleton (97th), Gerow (96th), Millikin (88th), Collins (82nd), Ridgway (61st), and Eddy (58th).[200] Academic accomplishment is certainly no indicator of combat success, but it is interesting to note that none finished below the middle of his class and four of the six were in the top 20 percent of their CGSS contemporaries.

The interwar army gave extensive opportunities for instruction, and such experience was looked upon with great favor for two reasons. First, it was considered the next best thing to troop duty for learning one's profession; second, the peacetime army recognized that educating future leaders demanded instructors who combined a degree of intellectual attainment with well-honed soldiering skills. Four of the six had extensive instructional experience. Middleton, Collins, Millikin, and Eddy spent twelve, eleven, ten, and eight years, respectively, teaching. Ridgway spent three years "on the platform," while Gerow spent only six months in an instructional capacity.

The picture on staff duty is almost a direct obverse. Gerow and Ridgway each spent twelve years as staff officers, while Millikin, Eddy, Collins, and Middleton spent eight, five, four, and two, respectively.

In terms of noncombat troop duty, Gerow, Millikin, Middleton, and Ridgway were the most experienced, with thirteen, twelve, eight and one-half, and eight years, respectively. Eddy had seven years of such service, while Collins had only five and one-half. In terms of combat experience, which for our purposes includes only time engaged in actual operations against a hostile force, Eddy and Middleton, who had both seen combat in World War I, led the pack with eighteen and fifteen months, respectively. Collins was next with eight and one-half months, while Gerow and Ridgway had six and one-half and five months, respectively. Millikin had only two weeks of combat experience when III Corps was committed to the Bulge.

How did they use these experiences? Generally, quite well. Gerow squeezed all he could from his assignments, parlaying his top spot at the infantry officers' advanced course into positions of steadily increasing responsibility in the War Department. And he remained true to his own plan for professional development, eschewing the opportunity presented in 1934 to return to VMI to become the commandant of cadets in order to serve on a corps area staff. Middleton was a seeming natural, but one who also grew. He found a way to synthesize his experience with his learning, particularly while teaching at Benning and Leavenworth, in order to prepare himself systematically for high command. When he came out of five years of retirement in 1942 and quickly rose to division command, it seemed as though he had not missed a beat. Ridgway, who in 1928 was offered the opportunity to serve on a diplomatic mission to Nicaragua with General Frank McCoy, correctly recognized it for the career broadening opportunity it was. This experience and the subsequent effort to resolve tensions between Bolivia and Paraguay gave him insight into Latin American politics that proved invaluable to Marshall in the early days of World War II. When the 82nd was converted into an airborne division, Ridgway threw himself wholeheartedly into mastering this new form of warfare. Millikin developed steadily as well, though his light seems to have been hidden under a bushel during the long period between the retirement of his patron, General Peyton C. March, in 1921 and his assignment as a regimental executive officer in 1936. From then until his elevation to corps command in 1943, he demonstrated at each level of responsibility that he was prepared for the next. Eddy must be reckoned as having grown the most. Starting with only the most rudimentary military education, he steadily advanced up the chain, proving himself competent at each new level of responsibility. In contemporary vernacular, he was a "Plugger," and the four years of instructor duty at CGSS seem to have been particularly important in his professional development. Collins, too, grew steadily as he progressed through the ranks. His extensive personal reading, his wide-ranging travels, and his habit of systematically recording and analyzing his experiences, evident in the detailed after-action review of the 25th ID's operations in Guadalcanal, all purposely contributed to the progressive development of a refined military mind. In short, while each of the six had a different mix of the experiences available to officers of their generation, each found a way to profit from the hand he was dealt or, in several cases, to draw the card he felt he needed.

When we examine these experiences for commonality, we discover both the lack of an early common denominator and the existence of certain roughly congruent patterns. Unlike the British army, in which a commission in the Brigade of Guards or an upper-crust regiment such as the Rifle Brigade significantly aided one's chances of advancement, the U.S. Army had no inside track to high command. Even in an age in which the Regular Army officer corps was predominantly populated by USMA graduates, only three of our six subjects were West Point men. There were, however, slightly congruent patterns. Five of the six were infantrymen; the sixth was cavalry. This is a slightly skewed sample. Of the thirty-four officers who served as corps commanders in World War II, twenty-two were commissioned in the infantry, nine in the cavalry, and three in the field artillery.[201] All attended CGSS; all but Eddy attended the Army War College. Four of the six had extensive instructor experience. The one common denominator was successful division command, but even here there was a distinction. Gerow and Millikin were both elevated to corps command based on their peacetime training of a division. These appointments were driven by the fact that the requirement for corps commanders exceeded the availability of suitable, combat-experienced division commanders. But Collins, Ridgway, Middleton, and Eddy all earned their corps command by demonstrating they could handle a division well in combat. To be sure, this was on-the-job training—the greater complexities of corps command rendered the results uncertain. But the episodic nature of war makes learning by doing almost inevitable.

Experiential pattern analysis is necessary to understand the commanders with whom we deal, but it is not sufficient because different people react differently to the same circumstances. This raises the question of how well before the Bulge these men had measured up to the army's desiderata of command, which were articulated as traits of character and intellect. In terms of sole acceptance of the responsibility of command, Ridgway, Collins, and Middleton were the strongest exemplars. No one in their organizations had any doubt as to who was in command. Eddy, under Patton's rough tutelage, had made measurable strides in this regard. Gerow's avoidance of responsibility for the Schmidt debacle calls him into question here, while Millikin's lack of combat experience leaves the issue open. Ridgway, Collins, Middleton, and Eddy were also well noted for significant strength of will demonstrated at Normandy, Guadalcanal, Salerno, and Cherbourg, respectively. Gerow demonstrated this quality at Normandy, and perhaps somewhat to excess in the Hürtgen. Again, Millikin was insufficiently tested to make a judgment. In terms of mental acuity, Collins clearly stands out: his instinct in the Cobra breakout operation helped rescue the badly bogged-down First Army. But Middleton, Ridgway, and Eddy were no slouches either. Middleton's performance in Brittany, Ridgway's at Normandy, and Eddy's in the capture of Cherbourg all indicated clear, flexible military minds that rapidly and accurately read complex situations. Gerow's performance in the Hürtgen raises questions here, while Millikin's solid record in peacetime maneuvers is suggestive but inconclusive. All six had demonstrated in both peacetime and combat an informed appreciation of terrain, though Gerow's analysis of the ground in the attack on Schmidt was woefully inadequate. Their care for subordinates is difficult to judge. Eddy was clearly the most empathetic with the citizen soldiery of the American army; Ridgway fought a long, hard, bureaucratic battle to obtain hazardous duty pay for his soldiers in the glider regiments; and Middleton's request of relief from division command when he discovered that his bad knee would not let him keep up with his advancing troops was a significant indicator of selflessness. Patch's and Griswold's comments on Collins's egotism insert a question mark here, and Gerow and Millikin each had aloof personalities that did not convey the milk of human kindness coursing through their veins. But one must be careful not to infer too much from this. In war, raw professional competence is a much better harbinger of concern for one's subordinates than is either humility or approachability. In celerity of action, Collins was clearly at the head of the pack. He was known as "Lightning Joe," and he moved quickly enough to justify it. Within the constraints of an airborne command, Ridgway was equally quick. Millikin's peacetime commands and his cavalry training indicated that he was capable of rapid action. Middleton frequently drew important, secondary assignments in which speed was not of the essence, making this characteristic hard to judge. Both Bradley and Patton saw Eddy as a solid, reliable commander who liked to line up his ducks before he acted. And Gerow's command of V Corps up to the Bulge was more reminiscent of Meade than of Jackson.[202] In terms of the physical stamina required to endure privation, Ridgway was the clear standout. He was as tough physically as he was mentally—command of an airborne division in combat demanded it. Collins and Millikin were about equal in this regard. Collins was relatively young and had a strong constitution, while Millikin was fresh. There were questions about the other three. Middleton had a bad knee. Eddy had a history of hypertension, and he was fighting nerves and insomnia with sedatives and alcohol.[203] Gerow conveys the impression of being exhausted by the strain of the fall campaign.

So at the end of the day, who was best prepared to command a corps in the Bulge? Middleton and Collins were clearly at the top. Both were superb tacticians and had demonstrated over the course of almost the entire European campaign that they could handle a corps effectively. Eddy came next: he was sound, but he did not yet have the depth of experience of the other two. Ridgway's solid record as the commander of the 82nd Airborne Division augured well for his success, but his lack of corps experience raised a question mark. Gerow had the experience, but his performance at Schmidt raised doubts. Millikin was an unknown.

One final consideration must be addressed: how closely were they connected with the army's senior leaders, Marshall and Eisenhower? With Marshall, Collins and Ridgway were clearly the most intimate. When Collins's prospects for advancement in the Pacific appeared dim, Marshall transferred him to Europe. Ridgway felt close enough to Marshall to maintain a very regular correspondence with him while in division command. Marshall had nothing but respect for Middleton, suggesting him to Eisenhower as a potential corps commander despite his bad knee and even arranging for Middleton to have a physical therapist assigned to VIII Corps to mitigate the injury's effects.[204] Gerow had been in the inner circle as chief of WPD. Marshall's opinion of Gerow may have been dimmed by the events leading up to Pearl Harbor, but he approved Gerow's elevation to corps and army command. Eddy was known to Marshall, though he was not part of the inner ring of confidants. Millikin was a "March man." It is instructive of Marshall's objectivity that Millikin had been given a corps, but he was definitely not close to the chief.

With Eisenhower, things were a bit different. His close, personal relationship with Gerow undoubtedly accounts for the fact that Gerow had been designated to assume command of Fifteenth Army in early 1945. Eisenhower had been impressed by Collins's speedy capture of Cherbourg and key role in the Cobra breakout. His relationship with Middleton went back to Leavenworth, where Middleton was a highly regarded tactics instructor and Ike a star pupil; and Eisenhower had enthusiastically accepted him to command VIII Corps when Marshall made the offer. He had also carefully monitored the performance of division commanders in the Normandy campaign and elevated Ridgway and Eddy to corps command based on their strong showings. But Millikin, whose name he uncharacteristically misspelled as "Milliken," was virtually a complete unknown to him.[205]

Having surveyed the development of our six main characters, it is now appropriate to see how the stage was set for the coming drama.

Gerow, head of the War Plans Division, posing with Marshall and other members of the Army General Staff in Marshall's office, November 1941. Courtesy Virginia Military Institute Archives.

Middleton, Commanding General, 45th Infantry Division, talking tactics with Patton and Bradley near Messina, 25 July 1943. Courtesy Dwight D. Eisenhower Library.

Middleton in earnest conversation with Eisenhower at St. Vith, 9 November 1944. National Archives.

Ridgway, Commanding General, 82nd Airborne Division, probably in Cherbourg, ca. July 1944. National Archives.

Millikin in his office at III Corps headquarters, Fort McPherson, Georgia, 30 November 1943. U.S. Army Military History Institute.

Millikin talking training with Leslie J. McNair, Commanding General, Army Ground Forces, and Charles S. Kilburn, Commanding General, 11th Armored Division, at Camp Cooke, California, April 1944. Courtesy Millikin family.

Eddy, Commanding General, 9th Infantry Division, visiting the front in Tunisia with his assistant division commander, Donald A. Stroh, 8 May 1943. U.S. Army Military History Institute.

Eddy, Commanding General, 9th Infantry Division, with a captured German officer at Cherbourg, 28 June 1944. U.S. Army Military History Institute.

Eisenhower congratulating Collins after awarding him the Oak Leaf Cluster to his Distinguished Service Medal for success of the VII Corps D-Day landings, somewhere in France, 26 July 1944. Onlookers Bradley and Gerow were similarly decorated. Bettmann/Corbis.

4

The Coming of the Bulge

The bleaker the situation, with everything concentrating on a single, desperate attempt, the more readily cunning is joined to daring. Released from all future considerations, and liberated from thoughts of future retribution, boldness and cunning will be free to augment each other to the point of concentrating a faint glimmer of hope into a single beam of light which may yet kindle a flame.[1]   *Carl von Clausewitz*

To UNDERSTAND HOW THE BATTLE OF THE BULGE UNFOLDED, we must examine its antecedents. But because those origins are, for the most part, already fairly well known and have been studied in great depth in other works, their treatment here can be relatively brief.[2] Accordingly, this chapter will but sketch the salient features of German planning and preparation for the offensive, Allied ground and air operations in Northwest Europe preceding the Bulge, the Anglo-American failure to anticipate the German attack, the state of the ground and air forces on each side, and the terrain and weather that affected the operation.

GERMAN PLANNING AND PREPARATION

Well over a century before Hitler made his fateful decision to strike into the Ardennes in a desperate attempt to reverse Germany's fortunes on the Western Front and split the Anglo-American alliance, Clausewitz's thoughts noted above had perfectly articulated the underlying logic of his thinking. This does not imply that Hitler was some sort of military genius. Clearly, he was not; his failure to account for the disparity between his ends and his means on a grand-strategic level made him distinctly anti-Clausewitzian. But Hitler, like Clausewitz, realized that desperate times called for desperate measures. And once the Americans and British had established a successful lodgment in Northwest Europe in June 1944, Germany was in desperate straits. This desperation was compounded by the nearly simultaneous massive and sophisticated Russian offensive in the east known as Operation

Bagration that virtually obliterated Army Group Center, destroying some thirty divisions and inflicting over 400,000 German casualties.[3]

On 31 July 1944, Hitler conducted an extended conference, during which he announced his conclusion that the western theater would demand strategic priority in Germany's defensive efforts.[4] This determination was made, not coincidentally, just as Patton's Third Army was breaking through at Avranches and was poised to debouch into the interior of France. Between the end of July and 19 August, the Führer decided to regain the initiative in the west by launching a major offensive sometime in November when the weather would inhibit the use of Allied airpower.[5] But the location still had not been determined. By mid-to-end September, Hitler announced he had reached the "momentous decision" to launch the offensive through the Ardennes, with the ultimate geographical objective of Antwerp.[6] The primary considerations underlying this location were the thinness of the Allied lines in that sector of the front and the availability of a concealed staging area in the forests of the Eifel region east of the Ardennes. Field Marshal Wilhelm Keitel, Oberkommando der Wehrmacht (OKW) (High Command of the Armed Forces) chief of staff, and General Alfred Jodl, Oberkommando des Heeres (OKH) (High Command of the Army) chief of staff, were told to work out the details and report back to Hitler.

On 11 October, Keitel and Jodl presented a draft plan to Hitler that outlined an attack with Sixth SS and Fifth Panzer Armies arrayed along a sixty-kilometer front from Monschau in the north to the confluence of the Our and Sauer Rivers in the south.[7] Sixth SS Panzer Army was to constitute the main effort, crossing the Meuse near Liège and moving swiftly to Antwerp; Fifth Panzer Army was to make a strong supporting attack that also carried the Meuse early in the operation. They estimated that under the most favorable conditions, Antwerp could be gained in a week. But they concluded with a number of "prerequisites for success," including destruction of the estimated five divisions in the Allied strategic reserve; stability along the Western Front when the offensive was launched; retention of Holland; mobilization of manpower and materiel; and, of transcendent importance, ten to fourteen days of cloud cover to prevent the Allied air forces from halting the offensive. Hitler accepted the general outline of the plan but wanted the base of the offensive broadened to reduce the likelihood of a successful Allied riposte from the flanks. He also approved the recommendation that Field Marshal Walter Model's Army Group B be the directing operational headquarters.

There ensued a long tug of war between Hitler and his subordinate military commanders that revolved around a classic ends-means mismatch.

From Hitler's perspective, the only worthwhile strategic result was an Anglo-American defeat of such magnitude that a negotiated peace on the Western Front was at least plausible. This meant not only the destruction of twenty-five to thirty Allied divisions, but also the capture of Antwerp. If Germany's reserves of manpower and materiel were to be husbanded for one last roll of the iron dice, Hitler's was the only *political* goal that made sense. But such an outcome appeared to be well beyond Germany's *military* grasp. Operational success, i.e., an offensive that could destroy a significant number of Allied formations and seriously delay the American, British, and Canadian armies, was eminently practicable. And the Wehrmacht had in Field Marshal Gerd von Rundstedt, Oberbefehlshaber (OB) (Commander-in-Chief) West; Model; and General Hasso von Manteuffel, commander of the Fifth Panzer Army, experienced combat leaders thoroughly proficient in the conduct of large-scale military operations.[8] The fourth major player, General Sepp Dietrich, commander of the Sixth SS Panzer Army, had come up through the ranks of the Waffen-SS. Although he lacked the higher level military skills of his Wehrmacht counterparts, he was a realist and a savvy tactician.

We now know that the German onslaught in the Ardennes ultimately came to naught. In fact, it probably hastened the downfall of the Third Reich. But in prospect, this result was not so clear. Even the eternally optimistic Patton dryly noted in his diary on 4 January 1945, "We can still lose this war."[9] Furthermore, the Ardennes offensive was, in Hitler's mind, to be complemented by a resurgence of U-boat attacks in the North Atlantic using new, sophisticated submarines for which neither the Americans nor the British had an effective antidote. Thus, the Ardennes offensive represented merely one of two prongs in Hitler's overall plan to bring the western Allies to their knees.[10]

Generals Siegfried Westphal and Hans Krebs, chiefs of staff of OB West and Army Group B, respectively, were summoned to Hitler's headquarters in East Prussia on 22 October, sworn to secrecy, and briefed on the operation plan now code-named Wacht am Rhein (Watch on the Rhine), a designation designed to convey a defensive intent in the event it was intercepted by the Allies.[11] The only major change from the previously briefed concept was the addition of Seventh Army to the initial attacking force, which Army Group B was to use in a limited offensive role to protect the southern flank of Manteuffel's Fifth Panzer Army. The generals were instructed to have all preparations in place by 20 November for an attack date of 25 November. They were also told to expect a total of twenty-one divisions from the strategic reserve but that nine more would have to be taken from OB West. Hitler assured them they would have significant reinforcements of antiaircraft,

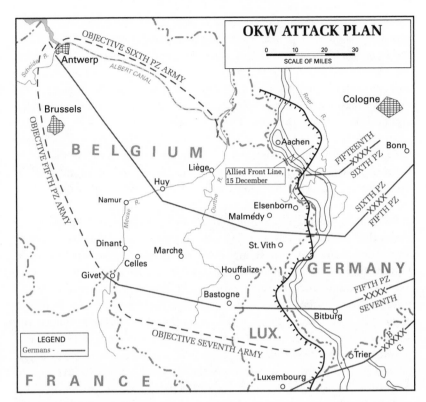

Map 1. OKW Attack Plan

artillery, and rocket forces as well as 1,500 fighters to support the offensive; and Keitel pledged over four million gallons of fuel and an additional fifty trainloads of ammunition.

Though diverse in their temperaments and military gifts, all four principal subordinate commanders, Rundstedt, Model, Manteuffel, and Dietrich, were united in their opposition to the OKW plan, which they saw as overly ambitious.[12] Rundstedt was a sixty-nine-year-old icon—an aloof, impersonal, but brilliant strategist who had been relieved as OB West in early July and reinstated in early September. Model was in his early fifties, extremely vigorous, and accustomed to leading from the front. His daring, driving ability to respond effectively to operational emergencies on the Eastern Front had earned him the nickname "the Führer's Fireman," and he was one of the few Wehrmacht generals whom Hitler appeared to trust.[13] Manteuffel, still in his forties, was the wunderkind of the German panzer corps. Diminutive in stature, powerful in intellect, and forceful in bearing, he was perhaps the ideal choice to handle a major tank formation on a difficult assignment. Dietrich came from a much different mold than the other three. A rough, coarse, hard-drinking Bavarian with no general staff training who had come up through the ranks, he was tolerated by his fellow generals for only two reasons: in a tough fight he had the instincts of a barroom brawler, and he was a Hitler confidant. When Westphal, Model, and the two army commanders gathered on 2 November at Model's headquarters to discuss their task, they unanimously agreed that the seizure of Antwerp, the crown jewel of Hitler's concept, was unattainable. Model and Manteuffel developed a much less ambitious alternative, known as the "small slam," which the Führer adamantly rejected.

But Hitler's steadfast determination could not overcome the physical realities that frustrated and impeded assembly of the attacking force. Allied airpower was one of the most important factors in this delay. The American Eighth Air Force and the Royal Air Force (RAF) Bomber Command had made systematic and debilitating attacks on the German oil industry and transportation system since the success of the Normandy invasion had been assured in July 1944. Although there was a tremendous fight among the strategic air commanders and their advisors as to which target, oil or transportation, was more significant, the effects felt on the ground were synergistic and created tremendous friction in the Germans' efforts to prepare and concentrate their forces.[14] The shortage of fuel deprived the panzer divisions and the supply services of the wherewithal they needed for adequate training. Many tank drivers, recently brought into the armor from the infantry, would not, therefore, possess either the technical or tactical skill needed to drive well in close terrain. The lack of fuel also dictated that new truck drivers, many of whom had also been recently requisitioned from the infantry, would have to negotiate the winding, snow-covered roads of the Eifel and the Ardennes with only the most rudimentary training.[15] This problem was exacerbated by the long road marches necessitated by a rail net that was functioning at less than full capacity.[16]

Air attacks on the rail net, though designed for the strategic effect of crippling the German economy, also had the operational effect of badly complicating the German force concentration. Manteuffel complained bitterly that throughout November and early December his senior logistician had to trace every supply issue from its request until arrival at its final destination because the adaptations and delays induced by air strikes had rendered the entire supply system unreliable.[17] Equally vexing, Manteuffel frequently had to dispatch senior staff officers to track down units that were supposed to have arrived in their concentration areas but were instead still aboard trains frequently discovered to be hiding in tunnels. The accumulated effects delayed the start of the offensive from 25 November to 16 December.[18] This meant that the Germans would enjoy only seven days of marginal weather, rather than the ten to fourteen that they had originally anticipated.[19]

The vicious fighting in the Hürtgen Forest, referred to by the Germans as the Roer region, also inhibited the strategic concentration. To the Americans, this bloody meat grinder seemed reminiscent of the dark days of World War I: high casualties and little to show for it. But it was also exerting a remorseless attrition on the Wehrmacht and placing tremendous pressure on OB West and OKW to divert units and supplies from building up for the impending offensive to holding the existing front.[20] Although these pressures were by and large resisted and replenishments were provided wherever possible, the American obstinacy in the Hürtgen disrupted both the timing of the Ardennes offensive and the forces committed to it. As a result, instead of having thirty divisions planned for the offensive, Army Group B could muster only twenty, not all of which were in position on 16 December.[21] Five more divisions were en route or on alert, and an additional five were included in the OKW reserve but of doubtful availability.[22]

On the whole, the assembly of the Fifth Panzer Army went more smoothly than that of its northern counterpart. Sixth SS Panzer Army headquarters had only been formed in October. It was composed of two-thirds Wehrmacht officers and enlisted men, the other third coming from the Waffen-SS.[23] Its subordinate formations included two SS panzer corps and one Wehrmacht corps. Although the SS units were ferocious fighters, they were not known for their staff acumen. In light of this and Dietrich's own lack of general staff training, the highly regarded Major General Fritz Kraemer had been assigned as the Sixth SS Panzer Army chief of staff in mid-November; but at least in the eyes of the OKW historian, this support was not adequate compensation.[24] One must also note that Sixth SS Panzer Army's concentration problems may have been due to the fact that, having the northern portion of the attack, it was closer to the bloody fighting in the Hürtgen than was the Fifth.

Nevertheless, the entire force planned and implemented extremely effective operational security measures. These measures included the aforementioned operational code name of Wacht am Rhein; delayed and only very limited distribution of the plan to subordinate headquarters; a written oath of secrecy from all those included in the planning process, with a death penalty for breach thereof; the use of couriers, rather than radio, telephone, or teletype, to transmit orders; prohibitions against forward reconnaissance; extensive camouflage of the forces deployed into the Eifel area; severe noise and light restrictions; and portrayal of a bogus assembly of the Sixth SS Panzer Army near Cologne, supported by fake radio messages and daylight troop movements.[25] Furthermore, to reduce the likelihood of desertion, soldiers from Alsace, Lorraine, and Luxembourg were excluded from the attacking units.

ALLIED GROUND OPERATIONS AFTER THE BREAKOUT FROM NORMANDY

Allied ground operations after the Normandy breakout were guided by Eisenhower's "broad front" strategy. It was dubbed "broad front" for two reasons: first, Eisenhower believed that two major thrusts, one north of the Ruhr directed by Montgomery's 21st Army Group, and one south of the Ruhr directed by Bradley's 12th Army Group, would become the primary instruments of German defeat in the west; second, this concept stood in contradistinction to a notion put forward by Montgomery that envisioned a single, more narrow thrust, under his command, being directed at Berlin.[26] Eisenhower's plan has been criticized for being essentially political in nature, i.e., being based on the perceived unwillingness of the American people to see the lion's share of credit for victory go to a British commander.[27] This explanation of Eisenhower's decision is valid, but only partially so.

Ike's strategy was also buttressed by sound military logic.[28] Strategic muscle hangs on a logistical skeleton. As Eisenhower surveyed Western Europe, he found Antwerp and Marseilles to be the two major ports through which his forces would have to be supplied.[29] The Channel ports would be important adjuncts early on in the campaign, but they simply did not have the capacity of the crown jewels—Antwerp and Marseilles. The distance between these two ports meant that the southern wing of the Ruhr encirclement would have to remain in touch with a force that, at a minimum, covered the supply lines coming north from Marseilles. Additionally, the broad front concept played to overall Allied strength and German inferiority because it kept pressure on a number of points, thus denying the Wehrmacht the ability to amass sufficient reserves to defeat the Anglo-American advance. Montgomery's single thrust, though possessing the theoretical advantage of concentration of force and seeming decisiveness, put this advance at risk.[30] Ironically, a number of analysts have argued that the Ardennes offensive proves the bankruptcy of the broad front strategy.[31] In fact, it demonstrates exactly the opposite. First Army pressure along the Roer River vastly complicated the German task of assembling the striking force for Hitler's offensive. And as the story unfolds, it will become evident that the overall balance of Eisenhower's dispositions, despite the gaping vulnerability in the VIII Corps sector, allowed relatively unengaged forces both north and south of the German penetration to be directed against it beginning 17 December. Montgomery's idea would have 1) allowed the Germans to amass a much more formidable counteroffensive force; 2) not provided an easy opportunity to strike it from two directions; and 3) potentially placed the outcome of the campaign, and thus the war, in the strategically most important theater hostage to the results of a single, decisive operation.[32] In short, while Eisenhower undoubtedly had a legitimate political rationale for resisting Montgomery's ideas, he also had a well-reasoned military logic supporting his own concept.

Nevertheless, in late August, Eisenhower faced a classic strategy-logistics dilemma.[33] In the wake of the near destruction of the Seventh Panzer Army, Hitler finally authorized a general German withdrawal east of the Seine. Military logic said to pursue the Wehrmacht and not allow it to reestablish a defense. But this logic had to be weighed against the restrained ability to supply the pursuing force. In late August and early September, Eisenhower made two critical decisions. The first was to continue the pursuit east of the Seine. The second was to give priority between his two principal thrusts to Montgomery's 21st Army Group. This decision was driven by two considerations: first, the logistical consequences resulting from forgoing an operational pause demanded that one or the other of the major advances receive priority; second, the northern route both threatened the North German Plain, the easiest avenue into the heart of Germany, and included the vital port of Antwerp. Thus, although Eisenhower was continuing to play out his broad front strategy, he was tilting it to the northeast, rather than the east.

No sooner had he made this decision, however, than he deviated from it by throwing all his eggs into the northern basket. On 10 September at a conference in Brussels, Eisenhower authorized Montgomery to launch a massive airborne operation to seize a bridgehead over the Rhine in the Dutch city of Arnhem.[34] Breathtaking in its audacity, this offensive, code-named Market-Garden, is one of the most controversial episodes of World War II.[35] The plan called for the American 101st and 82nd Airborne Divisions and the British 1st Airborne Division to lay down a sixty-mile carpet and capture critical bridges from Eindhoven, through Nijmegen, to Arnhem, with the British XXX Corps, commanded by Lieutenant General Brian Horrocks, then attacking along this corridor to relieve the British airborne forces and reinforce the Rhine River crossing at the far end. From its heart-throbbingly promising beginning to its devastatingly tragic end, Market-Garden was bedeviled by friction in both planning and execution. The main effects of this high-payoff, high-risk operation were to commit the strategic reserve with no appreciable gain and to halt Bradley's 12th Army Group while logistical priority was given almost exclusively to Montgomery's 21st. Whether or not the potential early entrée to the North German Plain was worth the casualties incurred and other opportunities lost is still being debated. But in the aftermath of Market-Garden, one thing was crystal clear: contrary to some exhilarating expectations in the heady days of August, the war was *not* going to be over by Christmas.

There followed a grim, logistically constrained campaign of pushing up to the German border, most of which has already been described. There were, however, two additional major elements of this phase of the war. The first was Montgomery's long, arduous, and palpably reluctant operation to clear the Schelde estuary. German forces were finally cleared from the banks by 8 November; the channel was then swept of mines; and the first ship docked in Antwerp on 29 November, nearly three months after the port's capture.[36] The second was the linkup of American and French units coming up the Rhone valley with the remainder of the Allied force.[37] This juncture occurred in mid-September and occasioned the formation of 6th Army Group under General Jacob Devers. Devers's command included Patch's Seventh Army and de Lattre de Tassigny's First French Army. Although clearly the tertiary force in the campaign, 6th Army Group covered the lines of communication from Marseilles and, in bitter fighting of its own, wheeled east into the inhospitable Vosges Mountains to engage the German Nineteenth Army and begin the liberation of Alsace. In late November, the French 2nd AD, operating under Seventh Army, captured Strasbourg. In early December, Patch began a push to the Siegfried Line intended to support Patton's offensive in the Saar; but the Germans retained a sizeable toehold west of the Rhine, referred to as the "Colmar Pocket."

Thus, on 16 December the Allied ground forces were arrayed over four hundred miles in three army groups from the North Sea to the Franco-Swiss border. Montgomery's 21st Army Group covered a front from the entrance of the Maas River into the North Sea, then east to roughly Nijmegen, then south to the Roer River, some twenty miles east of Maastricht. Along this line were deployed the First Canadian Army, under General Henry Crerar, and the Second British Army, under General Miles Dempsey. Bradley's 12th Army Group extended from his junction with Montgomery's 21st to roughly the German city of Bitche, some thirty miles southeast of Saarbrücken. His major formations were Lieutenant General William Simpson's Ninth Army, Hodges's First Army, and Patton's Third Army. Middleton's VIII Corps in the Ardennes, under Hodges's command, occupied the most lightly held portion of this front. Devers's 6th Army Group ran from its junction with Bradley's to the Franco-Swiss border, with Patch's Seventh Army in the north and de Lattre de Tassigny's First French Army in the south.

ANGLO-AMERICAN AIR OPERATIONS IN EUROPE

In the air, Germany had to contend with a two-front war against the USSR in the east and the Anglo-American coalition in the west; on the Western Front it also had to contend with two allies who were each forcing it to fight a different kind of two-front war—against both strategic attack into the German heartland and robust support of ground formations advancing relentlessly, if somewhat episodically, toward the German border.[38] In point of fact, however, these two themes of the British-American air onslaught were played with varying levels of intensity depending on the requirements and capabilities of any given phase of the overall European campaign. From the evacuation of British and French forces from the Channel ports in the summer of 1940 until the end of March 1944, the Allied air effort against the Continent grew from weak demonstrations, whose main purpose seemed to be to stimulate British morale, into a formidable force, inexorably wearing down the Luftwaffe.

From April to June 1944, the major air objective was to prepare for Overlord. This involved two tasks: achieving air superiority over the skies of Western Europe and interdicting the road and rail communications from the interior of France to both the actual invasion beaches in Normandy and the deception beaches at Pas de Calais. Because it was clear that these two missions were vital to the invasion's success, Eisenhower insisted that he be given authority over the employment of the strategic air forces as well as the Allied Expeditionary Air Force (AEAF), commanded by Air Marshal Trafford Leigh-Mallory.[39] Realizing that the success of the global grand strategy of "Germany First" hinged on the success of the invasion, the Combined Chiefs of Staff granted Eisenhower's request. With the effort thus focused and with additional air reinforcements pouring into England, good things continued to happen. The air war against the Luftwaffe continued apace.

The air support to D-Day was massive.[40] A vast armada of American and British cargo aircraft transported three divisions of paratroopers and gliders to the flanks of the landing beaches. P-38s of the Eighth and Ninth Air Forces formed a virtually impenetrable umbrella over the invasion force. RAF Bomber Command pummeled coastal batteries. And B-17s of the

Eighth Air Force attacked German formations just inland from the beaches. As already indicated, heavy air support was instrumental in the VII Corps breakthrough in Operation Cobra. Thereafter, the main locus of American air action was the relationship between the tactical air commands subordinate to Ninth Air Force, each of which worked in close conjunction with a field army. And the main locus of British air action was similar in the relationship that existed between the two air groups of the Second Tactical Air Force, which was commanded by Air Marshal Arthur Coningham, and the First Canadian and Second British Armies operating under Montgomery. In early August, Major General Hoyt S. Vandenberg replaced Lewis Brereton as commander of the Ninth Air Force.[41] Shortly thereafter he and Coningham combined to redeem partially the ground commanders' failure to close the Falaise-Argentan gap by using masses of rocket-firing Typhoons and bombing/strafing P-47s to inflict great carnage on the Seventh Panzer Army.[42]

In mid-September, direction of the RAF Bomber Command and the Eighth Air Force reverted from Eisenhower to the Combined Chiefs of Staff, with the caveat that Ike's requirements would have priority over all other missions if he requested support.[43] This caveat would become significant in the Bulge. In mid-October, the AEAF headquarters was abolished, its operational functions were moved to the newly created SHAEF Air Staff, and administrative supervision of the American Ninth Air Force was given to the USSTAF.[44] Although this move theoretically left Eisenhower without a coalition air commander, in reality, his deputy, Air Marshal Arthur Tedder, filled that function admirably. And, as would become evident in the Ardennes campaign, effective cooperation between Vandenberg and Coningham prevented the development of an artificial "seam" between the two national air forces.

Furthermore, with air superiority over the battle area assured, the robust tactical air formations of both countries could devote themselves almost exclusively to support of the ground units. Airpower was employed operationally to screen the Third Army southern flank—allowing Patton to take risks there, which were further mitigated by accurate awareness of German unit strengths and locations—and to halt, harass, and impede the movement of large formations.[45] It was used tactically in a variety of ways: as scouts to spot enemy units for his advancing armor spearheads, as roving patrols to attack enemy units maneuvering on or near the battlefield, and as flying artillery for units in contact. With Army Air Force engineers working strenuously to refurbish captured bases and construct new ones where required, the tactical air formations not only provided superb support—they also fundamentally altered the battle calculus to the Wehrmacht's detriment. It is not too strong to say that the ground formations enjoying such superb support became quite accustomed to it and even dependent upon it. And, as already noted, this tactical and operational dependence had strategic consequences in the German planning for the Ardennes offensive.

THE ALLIED FAILURE TO ANTICIPATE THE BULGE

In the annals of American military history, the German strategic surprise in the Ardennes offensive of December 1944 is equaled only by the Japanese attack on Pearl Harbor in December 1941 and the Chinese Communist invasion of Korea in December 1950. As in all cases of surprise, it had two essential ingredients. The first was what the attacker did to conceal his efforts and mislead his adversary. The second was why the surprised force either failed to detect signs of impending action and/or misinterpreted the signs that were detected. The considerable German efforts of cover and deception have already been noted. It is therefore time to turn our attention to the Allied side. Before proceeding, however, several comments are in order. First, because of the magnitude of the surprise and the fact that it led to the largest battle the U.S. Army fought in World War II, the literature on it is vast.[46] Thus, it will be possible here only to skim the surface. Second, these phenomena are often referred to as "intelligence failures." To the extent that intelligence resources failed to discover the essential facts of the impending enemy action or that intelligence officers misjudged these facts, this label may be accurate. But it is also incomplete. Commanders are responsible for correctly divining enemy capabilities and intentions. And they are also responsible for establishing a command climate in which bad news is not rewarded by shooting the messenger. Furthermore, commanders, by their very personalities and natures, establish an overall psychological climate within which exists the range of expectations of probable enemy action. Thus, in almost every case of strategic surprise and certainly in the case of the Bulge, the term "command failure" is at least as apropos as is the term "intelligence failure." Third, it is important to recognize that divining the future, especially when one has a foe that is actively attempting to conceal and mislead, is as intrinsically difficult and problematic in the military sphere as it is in all other activities of life. Inference and intuition are vital because virtually everything in war is shrouded with uncertainty—shades of gray color the landscape of strategy much more than blacks and whites.[47]

In the clear light of hindsight, there were numerous indicators of an impending German offensive, despite the draconian security measures imposed

by Hitler and OKW. Ultra had detected the formation of the Sixth Panzer Army as early as mid-September and by mid-November had assessed
its force composition.[48] In mid-to-late November, aerial reconnaissance,
though limited by overcast weather, detected numerous train movements
across the Rhine; these movements were confirmed by Ultra intercepts of
messages from the German State Railway System and requests from Model's
Army Group B to the Luftwaffe for aerial cover over troop debarkations.[49]
During this same period, Ultra detected a significant reinforcement of Luftwaffe formations in the western portions of Germany.[50] In early December,
German U-boats operating in the North Atlantic were given urgent instructions to provide weather information to support the battle on land and in
the air.[51] Throughout the early days of December, ground units were also
known to be moving into the Eifel area opposite VIII Corps.[52] In the final
days before the offensive, several POWs spoke of an upcoming attack; and
a German woman who came across the lines reported a significant buildup
of German forces and the forward movement of bridging equipment from
Bitburg.[53]

    There are multiple reasons these indications of an offensive did not lead
to the anticipation of an all-out German counteroffensive in the minds of
Allied commanders. But the dominant explanation goes something like
this: aware of German significant economic challenges brought about by
the Combined Bomber Offensive (CBO) and knowing Hitler was fighting a
two-front war, senior allied leaders took it as a given that Germany's task
was to conduct the best possible defense; this defense could, and probably
would, involve the husbanding of reserves; but these reserves would most
likely be used to parry and blunt Allied attacks, particularly in the Roer
region north of the Ardennes, where the American forces were most densely
concentrated.[54] There were, however, several significant variations on this
theme, which are reflected in both the general tone and specific comments of
intelligence estimates at various headquarters in the run-up to the Bulge.

    SHAEF clearly accepted the dominant explanation mentioned above;
but in early December its G-2, British Major General Kenneth Strong,
pointed out an attack in the Ardennes as one of three possibilities for a reforming panzer army.[55] Based on this appreciation, the SHAEF chief of
staff, Lieutenant General Walter Beddell "Beetle" Smith, dispatched Strong
to Bradley's headquarters. Strong had an extended conversation with Bradley during which the 12th Army Group commander said he appreciated
the danger but had designated certain divisions to move to the Ardennes if
needed. If Bradley was cautiously optimistic, his chief of intelligence, Brigadier General Edwin Sibert, was positively effusive. In a condescending and

hauntingly inaccurate estimate published on 12 December, he stated baldly: "It is now certain that attrition is steadily sapping the strength of German forces on the western front and the crust of defenses is thinner, more brittle and more vulnerable than it appears on our G-2 maps or to the troops in the line."[56] Montgomery's G-2 was singing a similar tune. The 21st Army Group intelligence estimate of 3 December noted that Rundstedt was conducting a conservative, by-the-book defense, "obviously without benefit of higher intuition" (an oblique reference to Hitler's supposed noninvolvement in operational matters) and that any attempt to take Antwerp "is just not within his potential."[57]

At army level, however, there were somewhat more accurate prognostications. The most famous, perhaps notorious, of these was that formed by Colonel Benjamin A. "Monk" Dickson, First Army G-2.[58] Dickson was a 1918 West Pointer who had left the army shortly after World War I to become a mechanical engineer but had retained a reserve commission. Conversant in both French and German, he was a natural to become an intelligence officer when World War II broke out. Dickson worked his way up from G-2 of II Corps in North Africa and Sicily to G-2 of First Army as one of the many staff officers who rode Bradley's coattails. Befitting a good intelligence officer, he was something of a pessimist; but his occasionally prickly personality did not fit well in a headquarters dominated by the icy temperaments of its commander, Lieutenant General Courtney H. Hodges, and chief of staff, Major General William B. Kean.[59] Furthermore, Dickson, no shrinking violet, held a low opinion of G-2s further up the chain who did not possess his language skills, most notably Sibert at 12th Army Group. On 10 December, he published what has become a famous document in the story of the Bulge, First Army Intelligence Estimate 37. This appreciation foreshadowed "the all-out application of every weapon at the focal point and the correct time to achieve defense of the Reich west of the Rhine by inflicting as great a defeat on the Allies as possible."[60] But the prescience of this insightful estimate was vitiated by what followed. The locus of the attack, in keeping with the bulk of the high priority targets indicated in Dickson's analysis of armor reserves, was indicated as being north of the Ardennes; and the timing was in response to the First Army's crossing of the Roer River.[61] In other words, Dickson, while sensing more accurately than most the scale of the coming attack, like the rest of the Allied establishment couched his forecast in the framework of a German response to American initiative. There is an anticlimactic and ironic twist to this story. At an evening briefing to Hodges and his staff on 14 December, Dickson, after reading the VIII Corps report of the German female line-crosser mentioned above, dramatically slapped the map and exclaimed, "It's the Ardennes!"[62] The next morning, he departed for leave in Paris!

Further to the south in Nancy and somewhat earlier than Dickson, the Third Army G-2, Colonel Oscar W. Koch, came to a similar conclusion.[63] Because of the vagaries of basing, XIX Tactical Air Command (TAC), which supported Third Army, was in a better position to observe the area of the Eifel than was IX TAC, which supported First Army. Based on this aerial reconnaissance, Koch had spotted the large number of trains moving into and out of this area. But, for some reason not entirely clear, he did not put these movements into the framework adopted in VIII Corps and First Army, i.e., that the Germans were shuttling new units in and out of the Eifel to give them a modicum of combat experience in a quiet sector before using them elsewhere. This, of course, is precisely how the Americans were using the Ardennes, so it was a subtle but inaccurate inferential leap to deduce that the Wehrmacht was employing the same technique. On 9 December, Koch held a special briefing for Patton in which he called attention to the troop buildup on Third Army's northern flank. Koch listed several capabilities for this force, which he estimated at nine divisions. It could shuttle north or south to meet advances of First or Third Armies; it could remain stationary and divert reinforcements meant for coming offensives; or it could launch a spoiling attack. This last capability signified Koch's apprehension that the force he identified could make a preemptive move to disrupt Third Army's impending Saar offensive. Thus, Koch's estimate was more accurate than Dickson's analysis of 10 December in two respects. First, it correctly pointed to the major buildup as being in the Eifel. Second, it indicated a degree of German initiative not previously foreshadowed. However, in common with all the Allied estimates, it did not warn of a massive counteroffensive whose purpose was not the mere delay of the advancing Allied force, but a significant defeat with strategic consequences. Nevertheless, Koch had given his commander credible warning of an enemy capability that could affect his future plans. Patton, who, despite his mercurial temperament and his well-deserved reputation for bluster, was a very attentive listener to well-reasoned intelligence, then did the sensible thing.[64] He told his staff to continue to prepare for the Saar offensive but also to begin contingency planning in case Koch's forecast proved accurate. One can only speculate as to why he did not pass his G-2's assessment either to Bradley, his immediate superior, or to Hodges, his lateral counterpart.

There are almost as many interpretations of why the Allies failed to anticipate the German counteroffensive as there are analysts. The absence of Ultra information is partially valid.[65] Hitler's almost paranoiac security paid off, and the senior Allied commanders did not receive intercepts of any OKW–OB West–Army Group B radio traffic related to the upcoming offensive—because there was none. (The extent to which this absence of traffic should have raised antennae and generated intense efforts to gain information through conventional means has, of course, been hotly debated.[66]) But there were, in fact, leaks in the system, particularly in Luftwaffe and railway traffic.[67] Obscuring cloud cover also played a part, but it did not entirely prevent aerial reconnaissance. Credit must also be given the discipline of the German soldier in reducing significantly the visual signatures of significant troop movements after leaving the railheads. Nevertheless, in the final analysis, the easiest deception to perpetrate is one that induces the enemy to accept as true that which he already believes or is predisposed to believe.[68] And on this point, one cannot but agree with Hugh Cole, the official American historian of the Bulge, who ended his version of this sad story with the poignant observation that "Americans and British had looked in a mirror for the enemy and seen there only the reflection of their own intentions."[69]

There is, however, one more important question to address: did senior American commanders take a consciously calculated risk to accept the possibility of a German offensive in the Ardennes? The short answer is a qualified "yes." Given the length of the front and the number of divisions available, Eisenhower could not be strong everywhere.[70] Continuing the offensive during the winter of 1944–1945 dictated concentration in some areas and dispersion in others. As he and Bradley examined the possibility of a German counterstroke in the Ardennes, they concluded that it was poor terrain for an attack, that it threatened no strategic objective, and that forces from the flanks should be able to contain any offensive the Germans were capable of mounting. In a phrase, Ike and Bradley deemed the risks manageable; furthermore, they were justified by the necessity to retain the initiative. In a sense, they were correct. The Ardennes in winter was a poor place to attack; there was no immediate strategic objective threatened; and the German offensive was ultimately contained by forces attacking from the flanks. But both commanders failed in prospect to comprehend three things: the size of the attacking force, the audacity of the strategic concept that lay behind it, and the profound psychological impact this offensive would have on the American army. Of the two, Bradley is more culpable than Eisenhower.[71] He was closer to the situation and thus bears the more direct responsibility. Despite his apologia of having calculated the risks, he neither focused special intelligence collection efforts on the Eifel region, where any attacking force would have to assemble, nor instructed his staff to prepare contingency plans to deal with an Ardennes offensive, both of which would have flowed from serious contemplation of an enemy capability. These omissions indicate that, although Bradley indeed considered the risks and, with a somewhat generous interpretation, can even be given credit for having calculated them, his calculations were not nearly as thorough as they should have been.[72]

THE CONTENDING FORCES

In mid-December 1944, the fighting acumen of American divisions was still uneven; but having been tested by the diverse demands of the fighting across Europe, the mean capability was noticeably higher than it had been six months earlier at Normandy.[73] This was largely due to a widespread but decentralized learning process, usually focused at divisional level. In fighting through the Norman hedgerows, various units experimented with different tactical techniques and technical improvisations that eventually produced effective means for gaining ground against skillful German resistance. As the army's units rolled into the villages and cities of interior France, they discovered that the direct application of heavy firepower, combined with the adroit use of engineers, set conditions that, if promptly exploited by well-positioned infantry, could neutralize German attempts to defend the urban areas that controlled the road networks. Attacks against German fortified positions, particularly in the Siegfried Line, demonstrated that decentralized adaptation had its limits. Although the army eventually breached this string of prepared fortifications, the lack of specialized equipment made the success more costly than it should have been. But crossings of the Seine, Meuse, and Moselle Rivers again showcased an adaptive force that could adjust an imperfect doctrine on the fly and come up with effective techniques. The Hürtgen represented the one significant failure in an otherwise generally successful experience. In this dark, damp, depressing, and seemingly endless forest, the Americans never found an effective way to counter the well-sited German defenses. The result was a significant bloodletting, only partially redeemed by the fact that the Germans bled as well. Nevertheless, taken as a whole, the American army had shown in its drive across Europe the ability to learn while it fought; by mid-December 1944, it had become a force with which to be reckoned.

In assessing the underlying strengths and weaknesses of various American army divisions, both common and variable factors must be considered. The four common factors include the army's organizational philosophy, its excellent logistical support, its system of individual replacements, and its weapons. The variable factors were combat experience, leadership, how various divisions coped with the individual replacement system, the types of divisions, and the attachments they received from the field army and corps to augment their organic combat power.

The army's organizational philosophy was a product of pre–World War II analysis of its World War I experience, results of late 1930s maneuvers, and the strongly held ideas of Lesley J. McNair.[74] The army came out of World War I with a "square" division, i.e., one containing four infantry regiments organized into two brigades of two regiments each. The strength of this scheme was its staying power—a division had sufficient strength in raw manpower to be left in the front lines for an intermediate period. But it had two drawbacks that were theoretically visible throughout the interwar period and practically manifested in exercises conducted in 1937 and 1939. Its strength of roughly 20,000 men made it unwieldy, and the presence of a brigade echelon of command between the division and regimental echelons made it unresponsive. Thus, in October 1940, Marshall implemented the long-anticipated decision to change the organization of the infantry division to a "triangular" one, containing three regiments with no intervening brigade headquarters. McNair strongly supported this shift and further stipulated that the division should contain only those assets it would normally require—other units it would need only periodically should be pooled at the field army to be distributed according to circumstances.[75] Thus, the infantry division organization would include a reasonable, though not robust, artillery establishment with fifty-four 105-mm and twelve 155-mm howitzers; but it would not contain tank, tank destroyer, or air defense units.[76]

The two other types of divisions that fought in the ETO were airborne and armored. Airborne divisions were organized similarly to infantry divisions, though with a variable mix of parachute and glider regiments and fewer specialized troops to buttress the infantry. The airborne division artillery was also lighter than its infantry counterpart, consisting of a 75-mm pack howitzer battalion for each parachute regiment; a jeep-towed, short-barreled 105-mm howitzer battalion to support each glider regiment; and a similar battalion for general support of the division.[77] By 1943, armored divisions were organized to facilitate the changing tactical realities of combat that demanded a more or less continuous flux in tactical organization. Each division was assigned three armored infantry battalions and three tank battalions as well as three battalions of artillery. But there was no fixed organization immediately below the division level. Instead, the division had three "combat command" headquarters, designated A, B, and R (for Reserve), R being noticeably less robust than the other two. To these headquarters, the division commander would assign a variable number of armored infantry and tank battalions as his analysis of the situation dictated.

To keep these relatively lean divisions fighting, the army's ground forces relied on a productive and populous America to supply them with materiel and men. But in addition to raw production, the army's logistics system required energy, manpower, a genius for organization, a network for distribution, and time. By the end of 1944, all these factors had come to bear in Europe. The vital ports of Antwerp and Marseilles were open; Patch's attack from southern France had linked up with Montgomery's and Bradley's drive from Normandy; rail lines were repaired; and a series of depots had been established behind the advancing forces that contained almost all the impedimenta of war an industrialized and mass agricultural society could produce: ammunition, fuel, rations, clothing, spare parts, field hospitals, repair facilities, and a communications network to make it all work. The one exception to this generally positive picture was a significant shortage of 105-mm and 155-mm howitzer ammunition that by November–December 1944 was beginning to crimp American offensive planning.[78] Finally, it should be noted that the vast fleets of trucks used to transport supplies from the depots to the front lines were also perfectly capable of moving troops when the situation demanded it. This capability, which was a direct reflection of Marshall's and McNair's organizational philosophy, gave the American army a substantial advantage in tactical and operational mobility over its German adversary.[79]

Replacements, particularly infantry replacements, however, were an entirely different matter. The problem here was fourfold. First, the grand strategy of the war was based in large part on America's serving as the arsenal of democracy. This meant that many skilled, able-bodied males were just as important working a lathe as they were carrying a rifle. It also meant the establishment of a global logistical network that required millions of men. Second, the military strategy of the war, while fully recognizing the vital significance of a ground advance into the heart of Germany, also demanded very substantial naval and air components. The confluence of these realities produced a decision, taken in June 1943, to limit the army's total mobilization to 88 divisions, rather than the 120-odd that had been anticipated in early 1943 and the nearly 200 envisioned in Major Albert Wedemeyer's 1941 "Victory Program."[80] Thus, by the end of 1944, there were only 44 American divisions in the ETO, a number that precluded creation of a significant strategic reserve.[81] The third factor was the army's system of feeding replacements individually into divisions as casualties were suffered, which in many cases precluded effective integration of this new blood.[82] The final factor, of course, was the magnitude of the casualties themselves, particularly during the bloody fighting in the Hürtgen. To meet projected and actual requirements for Europe, between April and September of 1944, the War Department took over 91,000 men from divisions in the United States and converted them into individual replacements.[83] But even this infusion was insufficient; and by late 1944, the European theater was combing its logistical structure for soldiers to retrain as infantry and converting air defense units to infantry in a desperate attempt to make good the deficiency in frontline strength.[84] Thus, the Bulge came at a time when the American army was seriously depleted of its most necessary human asset: the experienced combat infantryman.

American weapons ranged from the very good to the barely adequate. The M-1 Garand rifle was one of the best infantry weapons of World War II; the water-cooled .30 caliber light machine gun was reliable but cumbersome; the heavier .50 caliber machine gun, which was mounted on trucks and tanks, was deadly when it could be brought into action. The M4 Sherman tank, the workhorse of both armored divisions and separate tank battalions, was mechanically reliable but decidedly undergunned. Those armed with a 75-mm gun were inferior in firepower to almost all German tanks, while those armed with the recently fielded high-velocity 76-mm gun were only marginally more capable.[85] The M-10 self-propelled tank destroyer was deliberately designed with inadequate protection; but when used skillfully in conjunction with tanks and infantry, it could add an important element to the battle calculus.[86] Finally, the 105-mm and 155-mm howitzers, which were the staples of divisional and corps artillery, respectively, were both accurate and reliable. The real secrets of American artillery, however, were its centralized system of fire control and its well-trained and ubiquitous forward observers that together allowed commanders from company to corps to concentrate massive amounts of accurate fire at places and times of their choosing with minimal warning to the enemy.[87] Artillery was the biggest killer on the battlefield, and it would be employed on multiple occasions with devastating effect during the Bulge.

Despite the generally even capability of American army divisions, especially when compared to that of their German counterparts, battle performance varied based on combat experience, leadership, type of unit, and attachments. Experience was the most significant variable, ranging from that of the completely green 106th ID, which arrived in France on 6 December and occupied the northern portion of the VIII Corps front on 11 December, to battle-hardened units such as the 1st ID, which fought its way ashore at Omaha Beach on D-Day, and the 2nd ID, which followed right behind it.

But there was difference in leadership capability as well, with the division and regimental commanders and the divisional staffs being the key players. Again, the 106th proved to be almost inept, while units such as the 1st and 2nd IDs and the 4th and 7th ADs performed with a combat efficiency that any army would envy. Part of this leadership involved how commanders worked to overcome the vagaries of the individual replacement system by establishing divisional training schools for new arrivals that not only imparted essential combat craft, but also fostered the development of esprit de corps.[88] There was one type of division that almost always stood out— the airborne. These formations had distinct advantages: the excitement of jumping out of airplanes and the lure of airborne pay attracted into them a particularly aggressive type of soldier, noncommissioned officer, and officer. Furthermore, although they had been kept in the line after both D-Day and Market-Garden longer than their commanders would have liked, the fact that they were withdrawn from combat to prepare for future operations gave them the opportunity to retrain, refit, and integrate replacements that no other combat units in the ETO ever received. On the other side of the ledger, airborne divisional artillery, while well configured for its mission, was patently inadequate for sustained ground combat and always required significant reinforcement. This made their commitment to the Bulge risky. The final variable was attachments. Those infantry divisions that had an attached tank battalion had a huge advantage over those that did not. In this respect, McNair proved to be incorrect: combined arms of infantry, artillery, *and* tanks were the norm, not the exception.

In contrast to the American army's generally even capability, with local allowances made for experience, leadership, and attachments, the German army of December 1944 was a heterogeneous conglomeration of widely varying units with extremely diverse capabilities. But the German ground forces also possessed some underlying strengths and weaknesses that were fairly common across the board.

The diverse units included the Waffen-SS, the Wehrmacht panzer troops; the newly raised volksgrenadier divisions (VGD), or "people's infantry"; two specialized brigades; and a special operations detachment formed exclusively for the Ardennes offensive.

The Waffen-SS were Hitler's elite.[89] Growing out of the protection squads (Schutzstaffeln) that guarded the Führer and other Nazi leaders in the early years of the National Socialist movement, they were formally recognized as an independent armed force in August 1938. Deeply, perhaps even fanatically, loyal to the Nazi regime, the Waffen-SS expanded throughout the war, developing a well-deserved reputation for ruthlessness and brutality in combat and draconian occupation practices. After the abortive assassination attempt of 20 July, Hitler turned increasingly to what he saw as the only trustworthy military organization under his command. And desirous that the coming victory be perceived by the German people as having been "won by the SS, the Party, and himself," it is not at all surprising that the Waffen-SS would be given the central role in the coming offensive.[90] Dietrich's Sixth SS Panzer Army was designated the Schwerpunkt, or force of main effort, for Hitler's grand plan. It was to break through the American front lines, move rapidly and audaciously to seize the Meuse River bridges north and south of Liège, then drive to Antwerp. To perform this vital task, it was given priority in both resources and time. The resources consisted mainly of two SS panzer corps, containing four SS panzer divisions and two VGDs, and one additional corps with two VGDs.[91] The SS panzer divisions together with the Panzer Lehr (Training) Division, which was subsequently transferred to Manteuffel's Fifth Panzer Army, were withdrawn from the West Wall in October and assembled in Westphalia, where they were infused with replacements, issued 250 new tanks, given parts to overhaul those already on hand, and trained in offensive tactics under the watchful eyes of the Sixth SS Panzer Army staff.[92] The two-month period allowed for this refitting was, by far, more generous than that afforded to any of the other attacking formations.

The Wehrmacht panzer troops enjoyed a special place in the World War II German army by virtue of their central role in the blitzkrieg concept. But, by late 1944, they had been worn down by both the undermining effect of the tremendous losses on the Eastern Front and the similarly remorseless advance of the Anglo-American ground-air team. Nevertheless, infused with reserves of men and materiel husbanded for the Ardennes offensive, they represented a capable and potent striking force, particularly in the hands of a master tactician such as Hasso von Manteuffel. They consisted of two primary types of divisions: panzer and panzergrenadier divisions. By the eve of the Bulge, the distinction between the two was not as significant as it had been in 1940, owing primarily to the dilution of tank strength in the panzer divisions. By December 1944, a typical panzer division contained one tank regiment of two battalions, two armored infantry regiments, a self-propelled artillery regiment, and various divisional troops. A panzergrenadier division was similarly organized but had only a single tank battalion, which was frequently equipped with assault guns rather than tanks.[93]

The VGDs were essentially light infantry divisions. They consisted of three infantry regiments of two battalions each, an artillery regiment, an antitank battalion, and a modicum of support troops.[94] Their artillery was horse-drawn, as was the bulk of their logistical support, a typical division having a complement of just over 3,000 horses.[95] The term "grenadier" was, in long Prussian/German tradition, an honorific granted to units that had distinguished themselves in combat.[96] Perhaps Hitler hoped that this appellation, combined with the reference to the German Volk, would add prestige to units whose soldiers were culled from the flotsam and jetsam of the 1944 military establishment: the navy, Luftwaffe ground organizations, and rear echelon formations. The new age bracket of military service, extending from sixteen to sixty, provided additional manpower to the volksgrenadiers. Together, these measures produced roughly 250,000 new combat soldiers. But the key questions would be training and cohesion. Although all but one of the VGDs taking part in the offensive were withdrawn from the front lines for training and integration of the new men and although the German NCOs and veterans were a solid core around which to build, the results were sure to be uneven. Thus, at least in some cases, one would have to assume a lower level of tactical flexibility and initiative from the VGDs than had characterized German infantry earlier in the war.

Two specialized brigades also deserve mention: the Führer Begleit (Escort) Brigade (FEB) and the Führer Grenadier Brigade (FGB). Both were essentially miniature divisions and both were held in OKW reserve, i.e., under Hitler's control, to be used as exploitation forces when a significant opportunity occurred such as a major weakness in the Allied lines that would facilitate ultimate accomplishment of the offensive mission. Alternatively, they could be used to counter a significant threat to the attacking forces, thus allowing the advance to continue unimpeded. The FEB had heretofore served as Hitler's military escort; thus its commitment to the Ardennes offensive represented both its baptism of fire and an earnest of the Führer's determination to prevail.[97] Its organization had been expanded to include a panzergrenadier regiment; an additional independent grenadier battalion; a reinforced panzer battalion; artillery and antitank battalions; an attached assault gun brigade; and, perhaps most remarkably, a complete Luftwaffe flak regiment.[98] In short, it had a remarkable array of firepower. The FGB was almost as formidable. It consisted of a panzergrenadier regiment, a tank battalion, artillery and engineer battalions, a flak battalion, and an attached assault gun brigade.[99]

The most unusual unit in this offensive juggernaut was the 150th Brigade.[100] It was Hitler's personal brainchild; and to command it he chose one of his favorite soldiers, Otto Skorzeny, the daring commando who had, among his many other exploits, liberated Mussolini from a mountaintop prison in Italy and prevented the Hungarian government from surrendering to the Allies.[101] On 21 October, Hitler called Skorzeny to his East Prussian headquarters, promoted him to lieutenant colonel in the Waffen-SS, delivered an extended harangue, and briefed him on "perhaps the most important job of your life."[102] Dressed in British and American uniforms and equipped with Allied materiel, Skorzeny's men were to dash forward and seize at least one bridge over the Meuse. Although this operation now seems somewhat far-fetched, a similar deception had been used with some effect in 1940 when German soldiers posing as tourists on bicycles and motorcycles had entered Luxembourg several days before the offensive to disrupt communications and otherwise facilitate Guderian's impending attack through the Ardennes.[103] Nevertheless, Skorzeny balked, protesting that preparation time was inadequate. But Hitler insisted, and Skorzeny was duly passed on to General Heinz Guderian, chief of OKH, and then to Jodl, who informed him of the Sixth SS Panzer Army attack plan, which he would support. Skorzeny's operation, code-named Grief, developed into two parts. The seizure of the Meuse Bridges was to be carried out by a relatively conventional armored-infantry brigade, albeit one camouflaged to the extent possible as American. To complement this force, a special operations company of nine teams fluent in English and the American idiom would fan out to sow confusion in the enemy ranks. Despite significant shortfalls in both captured American equipment and linguistically capable Germans, Skorzeny's unit represented an ingenious addition to the overall attack plan that was destined to produce widespread results.

If the capabilities of these formations varied significantly, there were also some underlying commonalities of logistics, a highly competent general staff, a territorially based replacement system, and very effective weapons.

Logistical support of the offensive was a subject of great moment. By and large, the economic efficiencies wrought by Albert Speer's rationalization of the German war industry had, despite the adverse effects of heavy, sustained Anglo-American air offensive, produced most of the wherewithal required for the attack.[104] Food was no problem at all.[105] Ammunition supply was similarly adequate—fifty trainloads were required, and fifty trainloads were delivered to ammunition dumps west and east of the Rhine. Even gasoline, which was in extremely short supply, was adequate for the advance to the Meuse. Just over four million gallons were required; and these, too, were refined and stockpiled. The problem was distribution. Moving gasoline forward was complicated by several factors: the shortage of transport vehicles, the necessity to move only at night, and the inadequate road net west of the Rhine. Thus, by the eve of the attack, only some two million gallons had reached the Eifel area, with the reminder languishing in storage facilities further to the east. As the offensive moved west, the problem would only get worse.

The progenitors of the German General Staff date back to the earliest days of Brandenburg-Prussia, but its development as a formidable military institution began under the direction of the legendary Helmuth von Moltke in the mid-nineteenth century.[106] Its performance in World War I was marked by operational brilliance offset by strategic maladroitness and a dysfunctional tendency to interfere in policy and politics. After the war, Hans von Seeckt made it the intellectual epicenter of the new and reformed Reichswehr; but after assuming power in 1933, Hitler gradually brought it to heel in matters of strategy.[107] Nevertheless, throughout World War II it retained high standards of admission and sufficient practical and formal education to make it an effective instrument in developing and implementing plans for units and formations ranging from the division to the theater of war.[108] Although SS units tended to have fewer general staff officers than their Wehrmacht counterparts, the general staff system worked generally throughout the German army to multiply its combat effectiveness.

Another significant strength enjoyed by the Germans was a territorially based replacement system.[109] This system was organized around thirteen Wehrkreise (military districts), each of which provided units to designated divisions and corps. This established a regional affiliation between the members of each division. A soldier from Bavaria, for instance, would find himself in a unit made up almost exclusively of other Bavarians. In a country in which customs and dialects varied significantly from one region to the next, this affiliation constituted a definite advantage. Furthermore, upon completion of training, soldiers were not sent individually to the front. They were formed into battalions and marched to their divisions. There, the battalion would be greeted by the division commander, dissolved, and its soldiers forwarded to the division replacement training battalion. This unit was organized into companies representing each regiment in the division. Thus, the replacements' final training was provided by NCOs and officers who had a vested interest in their combat performance because they might soon return to the regiment as well. It was a system explicitly based on the fundamental truth that soldiers in combat fight first and foremost for the respect and mutual protection of their comrades, and it served the German army extremely well throughout most of World War II. As the Ardennes offensive progressed, the difficulties of getting to the front were to undermine this system, but up to mid-December 1944 it functioned quite effectively.

German weapons were, on the whole, extremely effective, though SS units were equipped with newer models and more ample quantities than the Wehrmacht.[110] Infantry companies had a large complement of automatic weapons, and the infantry regiments had either a company or platoon of direct-fire 150-mm guns. The workhorse Mark IV H, which represented roughly half of the tanks committed to the Ardennes, was superior to the Shermans equipped with the 75-mm main gun, though not those armed with the high-velocity 76-mm. The Mark V Panther, which had been designed in 1942 and produced in 1943 to counter the Russian T-34, had undergone a number of technical improvements. By late 1944, the G variant was a formidable weapon featuring well-sloped armor and a 75-mm high-velocity gun. Because the Germans had improved all three elements of their tank fleet: protection, firepower, and mobility, while the Americans had adjusted only the latter two, the Panther was more than a match for even the up-gunned Sherman. Rundstedt had roughly 450 Panthers at his disposal. The most feared tank was the Mark VI Tiger. Its 88-mm gun and its 100 mm of armor made it lethal and nearly invincible; even an individual Tiger, when well supported by infantry, could wreak havoc in both attack and defense. Its Achilles heel, however, was its lack of mechanical reliability; and its weight of over sixty tons made it awkward to employ in the thickly forested, hilly Ardennes. The Germans also fielded an impressive antitank capability, ranging from the very handy panzerfaust, an ingenious shoulder-mounted launcher that fired a small rocket tipped with an armor-penetrating warhead, to a wide array of towed and self-propelled antitank guns. Furthermore, both the much-dreaded 88-mm and the less ubiquitous 105-mm antiaircraft guns were frequently employed against tanks and other ground targets with devastating effect. German divisional artillery was comparable to the American with roughly fifty pieces of light and medium howitzers. Nondivisional artillery had heavier calibers and a large complement of multibarreled rockets known as nebelwerfers (smoke throwers). But the German artillerists had neither the sophisticated fire direction system, the numerous corps of forward observers, the motorized transport, nor the singular advantage of aerial observation enjoyed by their American counterparts. Offsetting these disadvantages was a significant number of self-propelled assault guns, frequently mistaken by GIs for tanks, that added a strong punch to infantry and armor attacks. It was the presence of this wide variety of general and special purpose weapons that led Russell Weigley to conclude correctly that, taken as a whole, the U.S. Army, while more mobile than its German adversary in 1944, possessed noticeably less firepower.[111] The one exception, of course, was the American artillery, whose superior control and mobility significantly magnified its rough numerical equality.

In sum, when one considers a number of diverse indicators, including combat experience, organization, logistics, replacement systems, and weapons, one can conclude that there was a rough qualitative equality between the German and American ground forces.[112] Advantages of one side were offset by countervailing advantages on the other. Such was not the case, however, for the air forces. Here, the American superiority was overwhelming.

The tactical forces were particularly impressive. Vandenberg's Ninth Air Force alone had some 1,000 medium and light bombers and roughly 1,700 fighters, mostly P-47 Thunderbolts.[113] The P-47's robust air-cooled engine, sturdy air frame, and substantial weapons-carrying capacity made it the fighter most loved by American pilots and GIs alike and most dreaded by the German soldiers, who referred to it as the "Jagbo," short for "Jagdbomber," or hunter-bomber.[114] Coningham's 2nd TAF was also formidable. His arsenal of nearly 1,300 planes, consisting of sturdy and capable Wellington medium bombers, fast, maneuverable Spitfire fighters, and rocket-firing Typhoon fighter-bombers made it a force to be reckoned with.[115]

Although the strategic air forces had been released from Eisenhower's command, both Spaatz and Air Chief Marshal Arthur "Bomber" Harris would respond with alacrity to his calls for assistance. By December 1944, USSTAF strength had reached some 3,700 B-17s and B-24s.[116] Bomber Command had similarly grown to a strength of roughly 1,900 Lancasters and Halifaxes.[117] Furthermore, there was a growing disparity in pilot experience. By late 1944, American pilots were entering combat with an average of over 300 hours of flying experience, 170 of which had been in combat aircraft, while their German counterparts had averaged only 170 hours of total air experience, merely 40 of which had been in operational aircraft.[118]

The Luftwaffe was but an eviscerated caricature of its former self. By the fall of 1944, it had regrouped east of the Rhine, reestablished its chain of command, and begun to put into place a semifunctional flight-support infrastructure.[119] Surging fighter production in the closing months of the year and dissolution of the bomber force allowed some 2,300 aircraft to be scraped together for the newly established Luftwaffe West.[120] But there was more shadow than substance in this organization. The dearth of available fuel severely curtailed pilot training. The systematic Allied attacks on the German rail network delayed the delivery of both aircraft and spare parts to the widely dispersed fighter bases. And most significantly, a fractured German high command undermined its direction. The inspector of pilots, Major General Adolf Galland, envisioned husbanding the fighters for a "Great Blow" against the Allied bombers. Hitler, on the other hand, wanted them preserved to support the coming land offensive.[121] Additionally, the remorseless attrition of fighter pilots in the month leading up to the offensive both drained operational effectiveness and precipitated a crisis of confidence between the cockpit force and the Luftwaffe high command.[122] In sum, despite its strength measured in terms of "rubber on the ramp," the Luftwaffe on the eve of the Ardennes assault was a nearly spent force, capable of at most one final, desperate effort. And here, one must also note an inherent anomaly in German operational planning: the huge disparity between the Allied air forces and the Luftwaffe demanded the attack be launched during a period of severely reduced visibility. Under such conditions, the German air arm could not hope to make a significant contribution.

TERRAIN AND WEATHER

The Ardennes is a geographic term given to a largely forested region of eastern Belgium, northern France, and the western half of Luxembourg.[123] To its east, it blends into a more heavily forested region of the German Rhineland known as the Eifel. The Ardennes roughly resembles a large right triangle with its apex pointed to the southwest. The eastern base runs along a line about ninety miles in length extending from the German town of Monschau in the north to the city of Luxembourg in the south. Its southern border lies along an eighty-mile, generally east-west line from Luxembourg to the French town of Mézières. From there, its western/northwestern boundary follows the line of the Meuse north to Namur, then bends with the river northeast to Liège.

The Germans faced several problems in attacking through this region. First, the road network, while fairly extensive due to recognition of the region's tourist potential after World War I, runs generally northeast-southwest, i.e., perpendicular to the German line of attack, which was from southeast to northwest. Second, most of the roads are quite narrow, and many follow meandering streams with steep banks. Thus, the destruction or disabling of a single vehicle could seriously impede an attack's progress. And behind the front lines there would emerge multiple, competing demands for the utilization of this precious road space, ranging from horse-drawn logistical support for the frontline forces, to similarly horse-drawn artillery units attempting to displace forward, to reserve formations being ordered up to support attacks that were making insufficient progress. This constricted road network also converted each tiny hamlet and village into a rallying point for the American defenders. And it made major road junctions such as St. Vith, Bastogne, and Baraque de Fraiture (intersection point of the north-south N15 and east-west N28 highways and one of the highest places in the Ardennes) objectives of higher tactical, if not operational and strategic, importance.

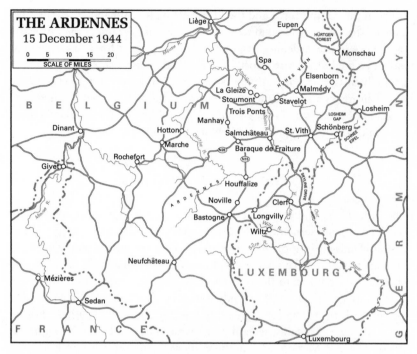

Map 2. The Ardennes, 15 December 1944

Major terrain features along the eastern border of the Ardennes included, from north to south, the following: the high ground around the Belgian town of Elsenborn, which became known as the Elsenborn Ridge; the Losheim Gap, through which Rommel's 7th Panzer Division had passed on its way to the Meuse in 1940; the Schnee Eifel, a large, forested plateau directly south of Losheim; and an extended, open plateau running southwest and then south from the Schnee Eifel that was called "Skyline Drive" by the GIs. Just west of the Schnee Eifel and east of the Skyline Drive is the Our River, which gains depth and obstacle value as it flows south into Luxembourg. The Clerf River, which flows from north to south thorough the Luxembourgian town of the same name (since renamed Clervaux), forms a moderate obstacle to east-west movement. The Sûre River originates southwest of Bastogne and flows generally east until it reaches the confluence of the Our; it then flows southeast and south toward the Moselle, continuing Luxembourg's eastern border. This branch of the river is frequently referred to by its German spelling, Sauer, and is so indicated on maps.

Dietrich and Manteuffel faced countervailing advantages and disadvantages in attacking across this terrain.[124] Dietrich had the shorter distance to travel from his jumping-off point to the Meuse, it being only some fifty miles from Losheim to Liège. But he would have to get through the marshy forests east of the Elsenborn Ridge and capture the high ground itself before his attack could pick up speed. Manteuffel had nearly ninety miles to go from his attack positions just east of Clerf to Dinant on the Meuse. But once his armored formations cleared the Clerf River, they would break into open country that was, comparatively speaking, a tanker's paradise. However, about ten miles west of Bastogne, the Fifth Panzer Army would have to contend with the difficult Ourthe River and then two wide bands of forested hills before reaching the Meuse.

The weather was cold and predominantly overcast. At Stavelot in the northern Ardennes, there are freezing temperatures 112 days a year; at Bastogne in the southern Ardennes, that figure is 145.[125] Exposure to this winter weather represented a constant combat readiness challenge as commanders sought to ward off trench foot, frostbite, and other cold-weather injuries and illnesses. Overcast conditions made Allied reconnaissance flights impossible for one-third of the month leading up to the German offensive; and for the remainder, conditions were only marginal.[126] But lying on the boundary between weather patterns coming from the west off the Atlantic and from the east out of Russia, weather in the Ardennes could also be variable.[127] Thus, from 23 to 27 December, when a strong Russian high pressure system moved into the region, temperatures dropped precipitously; the ground froze, aiding cross-country mobility; and the skies cleared, allowing the fearsome Allied air armada to make its force felt on the battlefield.[128]

SOME CLOSING OBSERVATIONS

An objective, retrospective assessment of the situation on the eve of the Bulge leads one to conclude that Rundstedt, Model, Dietrich, and Manteuffel were right—the offensive would probably fail. But as Clausewitz's cogent observation noted above so clearly articulates, desperation leads to daring and daring can produce results significantly out of proportion to the material investment. Looked at in prospect, one should not underestimate the impact of doing the unexpected on a grand scale—such action frequently carries with it the potential to unhinge the opponent. Lee's audacious attack at Chancellorsville and Guderian's stunning breakthrough at Sedan are but two instructive examples. With a little bit of luck and a few critical American mistakes, the bold German attempt to rend asunder the Western Allies and free Germany to deal exclusively with the Russian advance from the east might *just* have succeeded. The grand drama of Germany's final, desperate bid to win the war would also prove interesting on an intermediate level. Here, it tested the mettle of Generals Gerow, Middleton, Ridgway, Millikin, Eddy, and Collins. How well would these men meet the challenge of corps command in conditions they could have scarcely imagined?

PHASE I: GERMAN INITIATIVE IN ACTION

5

The Germans Attack, the Allies React

Soldiers of the West Front!! Your great hour has arrived. Large attacking armies have started against the Anglo-Americans. I do not have to tell you anything more than that. You feel it yourself: WE GAMBLE EVERYTHING! You carry with you the holy obligation to achieve things beyond human possibilities for our Fatherland and our Führer![1]   *Gerd von Rundstedt, 16 December 1944*

IT WAS SATURDAY, just nine days before Christmas; things were pretty relaxed at the various Allied headquarters that were about to be caught up in the huge German offensive. In the Belgian resort of Spa, where people of means had come for centuries to take the warm water cure, Hodges had established the First Army command post in a comfortable hotel.[2] In addition to the previously noted absence of the G-2, who was on leave in Paris, the G-3, G-4, and chiefs of section for artillery, ordnance, and antiaircraft were all in England.[3] Further to the south, Bradley had positioned his 12th Army Group headquarters well forward in recently liberated Luxembourg City. He spent most of the day motoring to Versailles with his aide, Lieutenant Colonel Chester Hansen. The purpose of the trip was to confer with Eisenhower on the growing crisis in infantry replacements. But there was a social context as well: the Supreme Allied Commander had just received notice that President Roosevelt had nominated him for his fifth star.[4] Montgomery, who the day before had petitioned Ike for permission to hop across the Channel and visit his son for Christmas, was feeling in need of some recreation.[5] To satisfy that craving, he flew from his forward headquarters in Zonhoven, Holland, to play golf in Eindhoven with the accomplished British professional, Dai Rees. At Versailles, Eisenhower was not only celebrating his coming promotion, he was also toasting the wedding of his orderly to a Women's Army Corps driver.[6] Despite the chill of the raw, winter weather, it seemed to be a wonderful day indeed.

REACTION ON THE GROUND

Early that evening, Ike and Bradley received their first indication that 16 December 1944 would go down in history as something profoundly different.[7] During the course of a routine conference in the SHAEF war room, Major General Strong was called out by the American deputy G-2, Brigadier General Thomas J. Betts. When Strong returned, he informed the assembled group of fragmentary reports indicating multiple German penetrations into the First Army sector, particularly in the Ardennes area occupied by Middleton's VIII Corps. Reaction was mixed. Bradley thought it was designed to preempt Patton's impending Saar offensive. Eisenhower, however, had a much different take. Reasoning that there was nothing in the Ardennes of any strategic value and recalling the recent reports of enemy buildup in the Eifel, he correctly divined that it was "no spoiling attack."[8] Although Eisenhower clearly did not appreciate the full magnitude of the offensive at this juncture, he was sufficiently concerned to instruct Bradley to get Middleton some help by moving to the Ardennes the 10th Armored Division from Patton's Third Army and the 7th Armored Division from Simpson's Ninth Army. When Bradley countered that Patton would object to the disruption of his forthcoming attack, Eisenhower retorted curtly, "Tell him that Ike is running this damn war."[9] Bradley dutifully complied, calling Patton personally but letting his chief of staff, Major General Leven C. Allen, pass the instructions on to Simpson.[10] Thus, acting on scanty information but excellent instinct, Eisenhower made the first American move to counter the German attack—less than one full day into the operation, Hitler and the OKW's assumption of a week's delay in the movement of Allied reserves to the threatened area had been proven demonstrably false. Furthermore, Eisenhower's willingness to overrule Bradley, his most trusted subordinate, not only indicated that he was capable of acting decisively on his own convictions, it also foreshadowed a coming rift between the top two American commanders in the ETO, a rift that was, however, to act against the Germans, rather than for them. But it was not all work and no play. As they stayed up into the night waiting for reports to come in, Eisenhower and Bradley passed the time by playing five rubbers of bridge and watering down Ike's coming elevation to five-star status with champagne and whiskey.[11]

The next morning Bradley left for Luxembourg, while Eisenhower conferred with his staff. Given the lack of robust American ground strength and Eisenhower's conscious decision to keep pressure on the Wehrmacht on multiple fronts, reserves were slim. The only forces of any consequence on the Continent were the 82nd and 101st Airborne Divisions at Rheims, refitting after nearly two months in the line following Market-Garden. As reports of German advances continued to come into SHAEF, Eisenhower quickly decided to release these two divisions to Bradley, but he wanted his staff to determine the optimal location.[12] Smith, Strong, and the British deputy G-3, Major General John Whiteley, gathered in Smith's office. They first attempted to divine the German intention, which they took to be a variant of the "small slam," an advance to the Meuse to split the 12th and 21st Army Groups. They then deliberated how best to thwart this effort. Studying the map of the Ardennes, they settled on Bastogne. Smith pressed Brigadier General Royal B. Lord, chief of staff of the Communications Zone, for an estimated arrival time. Lord gave him a time that was good enough, and shortly before midnight Smith issued the requisite orders.[13] Although the original SHAEF concept of employing both divisions at Bastogne would be modified by subsequent events, the Allies had again begun to make up time on OKW by deciding to commit their strategic reserve on the second day of the battle and by aiming it in generally the right direction. Anticipating that additional troops would probably be needed to stem the tide, the SHAEF staff then took preliminary measures to hasten the movement of the 11th Armored, 17th Airborne, and 87th Infantry Divisions from England to the Continent.[14]

Neither Bradley's 12th Army Group nor Hodges's First Army was functioning as effectively. On the 17th, despite the declarative statement from Eisenhower to the contrary, Bradley still conceived of the German assault as a spoiling attack, confiding to Hansen, "This fellow aims to lighten the pressure in our pushes of the First and Third Armies. . . . if he can force us to pull our strength out of there to stop his counter attack, he will achieve his primary purpose."[15] When Hansen raised the issue of alerting the headquarters for a possible withdrawal, Bradley replied, "I will never move backwards with a headquarters. There is too much prestige at stake."[16] When Bradley returned to his headquarters late that afternoon and was briefed on the significant enemy buildup, he exclaimed, "Pardon my French—I think the situation justifies it—but where in the hell has this son of a bitch gotten all his strength?"[17] By the next morning, 12th Army Group "scrambled wildly to redispose our divisions and stop them [the German drives] before the advances could gain too significant a headway."[18] Bradley had originally planned to drive to Spa to confer with Hodges but was dissuaded when Hodges's aide, Major William C. Sylvan, called to suggest travel by air to Liège, thence by escort to Spa, in light of German airborne drops between Malmédy and Eupen on the 17th. Shortly thereafter, he canceled the trip entirely to confer with Patton. This was the first significant indication that Bradley's ability to meet face-to-face with Hodges was becoming tenuous.

And from the 16th to the 18th of December, Hodges clearly could have used some moral support from his army group commander. What happened to Hodges during these three critical days is still something of a mystery.[19]

During the 16th, his staff had debated the significance of the offensive, the G-2 representatives making the case for an all-out offensive, while the G-3 section felt it was designed to disrupt the ongoing advance on the Roer. Hodges apparently sided with the latter, for when Gerow called for authorization to halt the 2nd ID's attack toward Wahlerscheid, the army commander refused. The mood turned much more sour on the 17th. As the day wore on, the army staff learned of a major breakthrough by an armored column in the Losheim Gap, the surrounding of two regiments of the 106th ID on the Schnee Eifel, and the massacre of a large number of American prisoners near Malmédy. Even worse, Hodges was clearly incapacitated. Accounts vary as to the source and depth of this lapse. His aide recorded that he spent all morning in the G-3 section. His deputy chief of staff said that he was suffering from influenza and "feeling very badly because of what had happened."[20] His chief of staff said that he was "confined to his bed, barely conscious with viral pneumonia."[21] And strangest of all, the chief of staff's military secretary said that on the morning of the 17th he discovered Hodges, "sitting with his arms folded on his desk and his head in his arms. . . . General Hodges spent the entire day there at his desk seeing no one and taking no calls."[22] Whatever the cause and whatever the precise condition, by the morning of the 18th, Hodges, though still weary, had recovered sufficiently to order Major General James Gavin, acting commander of XVIII (Airborne) Corps, to deploy the 82nd Airborne Division to the southwest of Spa at Werbomont, rather than its original destination of Bastogne. In mid-afternoon, concerned by continuing reports of German armor near the command post, he ordered the evacuation of the First Army headquarters to Chaudfontaine, roughly halfway between Spa and Liège.

In the meantime, with the Germans also cracking through the thin crust of the 28th ID along the Skyline Drive and racing headlong toward Bastogne, Eisenhower continued to monitor the situation and to ponder a theater-level response to the ever-deepening attack. By the evening of the 18th, he felt he had a sufficiently coherent concept to call for a meeting of all major commanders at Verdun on the 19th.

At this gathering, attended by Tedder, Strong, SHAEF G-3 Major General Harold R. Bull, Bradley, Devers, Spaatz, Patton, and Major General Francis de Guingand, Montgomery's chief of staff, Eisenhower had essentially two tasks to test his mettle as a commander. The first was intellectual—to propound a feasible concept for halting the German attack and eventually eliminating the salient. The second was moral—to convince those in attendance that it not only *could* be done, but that it *would* be done. He began with the second and more important of the two. Although clearly tired, even haggard, he opened the meeting with the declaration, "The present situation is to be regarded as one of opportunity for us and not of disaster. There will be only cheerful faces at this conference table."[23] When Patton suggested that even more opportunity could be created by allowing the Germans to go all the way to Paris, Ike countered, "George . . . the enemy must never be allowed to cross the Meuse."[24] This clear guidance reflected appreciations Eisenhower had formed with his staff on the 17th and 18th, indicating a "must-hold" line that ran north of Luxembourg City and Sedan in the south, then followed the Meuse on its western extremity, and swung south of Liège in the north.[25] The military rationale for this line was obvious: if German forces got west of the Meuse, they would seriously disrupt Allied logistical installations, drive a deep wedge between the British and Americans, and perhaps even threaten Hitler's ultimate objective of Antwerp. But there was a deeper, political rationale to Eisenhower's calculations as well. As long as German forces were contained by the Meuse and major population centers were not captured, Eisenhower would be given a relatively free hand to deal with the situation as he saw fit. But should it appear that the SHAEF forces were incapable of stopping the German assault, the political cohesion of the alliance might be jeopardized; of necessity, Eisenhower's own prerogatives as Supreme Allied Commander could be called into question by the Combined Chiefs of Staff.

Eisenhower's plan to counter the attack, which reflected classic doctrinal thinking, had three major components.[26] First, hold the "shoulders" of the penetration. This would prevent the expansion of the base of the attack and direct its force into the center. At the time of the Verdun meeting, the shoulders were being tenuously held by V Corps in the north and by the 4th ID in the south; but both efforts had to be reinforced to ensure success. Second, attack the penetration. Eisenhower's general concept for such attacks was to thin out the lines north and south of the Bulge and direct forces toward it from both sides. In the north, Hodges's situation was so fluid that definite guidance could not yet be laid down for how this was to be accomplished. In the south, however, Patton's dispositions and foresight created a real opportunity.[27] Taking advantage of Koch's early anticipation of a German attack into the Ardennes and responding to Bradley's order of the 18th to be prepared to attack into the southern flank of the penetration, the Third Army commander had instructed his staff to develop three variants. Thus, when Ike asked him what he could do, Patton calmly replied that he could attack with three divisions on 21 December. This was perhaps the greatest moment of Patton's career; but Eisenhower derisively snapped, "Don't be fatuous, George," and admonished him not to attack before the 22nd in order to avoid the piecemeal commitment of his forces.[28] While Eisenhower's cautions would prove justified, he was also the fortunate beneficiary of Patton and his staff's thorough preparation. But Patton's attack would also require assistance from Devers's 6th Army Group on Third Army's southern flank. Devers's flexibility was limited by the fact that the Germans held the Colmar Pocket; nevertheless, Eisenhower shifted the 12th/6th Army Group boundary north into the Saar region, freeing Patton to focus exclusively on the battle in the Ardennes.[29]

The third element of the SHAEF concept for halting the offensive, which was not addressed in detail at the Verdun conference, was to create a backstop at the Meuse.[30] This safety net was very tenuous. It consisted of preparing the river's major bridges for demolition and positioning whatever forces could be scraped together from the Communications Zone for their security. At a time when tremendous demands were being placed on the logistical system to move large combat formations, to replenish vast quantities of fuel and ammunition, to displace threatened logistical installations to the rear, and to treat the mounting numbers of sick and wounded, this was not an easy task. Nor were its results certain. Eisenhower's concern for the Meuse bridges on the evening of the 19th was reflected in an "eyes only" message he sent to Bradley, Montgomery, and Lieutenant General John C. H. Lee, commander of the Communications Zone, shortly after his return to Versailles, reminding them "of the vital importance of insuring that no repeat no Meuse bridges fall into enemy hands intact."[31]

While Eisenhower was at Verdun, Whiteley, who was considered by many Americans to be the most competent British staff officer on the SHAEF staff, was visiting Montgomery in Holland.[32] Monty, concerned that the enemy advances in the First Army zone constituted a threat to his own rear area, had already begun to take precautions by ordering the British XXX Corps to occupy a blocking position west of the Meuse. But he also told Whiteley that the larger solution would be to put him in charge of the northern shoulder of the Ardennes. This would allow him to command both the Ninth and First U.S. Armies, leaving Bradley with command of only Patton's Third Army. Upon Whiteley's return to Versailles on the evening of the 19th, he raised the matter with Strong, who, by midnight, became convinced that they must both confer immediately with Smith. Their case to the SHAEF chief of staff rested primarily on the loss of communication between Bradley and Hodges and the likelihood that this condition would get worse over the next few days; but it was buttressed by reports Whiteley had received of significant confusion in the First Army rear area. Smith was not receptive. He excoriated them both as disloyal allies, overly quick to advance British interests at the first sign of American trouble, and he threatened them with expulsion from the SHAEF staff. But over the next few hours, Smith underwent a profound change of heart. As he turned over the events of the last few days in his mind, including a recommendation from an American, Brigadier General Thomas J. Betts, that Hodges be relieved, he began to see the wisdom of the proposal; but he clearly had to check with Bradley. When Smith called him, Bradley questioned the necessity of the action but accepted its operational logic, though noting that he was concerned about the political implications of a British commander's being placed in charge of so many American soldiers. When Smith learned that Bradley had seen neither Hodges nor Simpson since the battle had begun, the rearrangement of the command structure became, in his mind, "an open and shut case."[33]

Accordingly, on the morning of the 20th, Smith informed Whiteley and Strong that he would put the idea to Eisenhower as his own. He then laid out the argument. Eisenhower, having earlier that morning failed to get a firm estimate from Bradley on where he could hold, bought it and phoned Bradley to inform him of the pending change. Now faced with the reality of losing two-thirds of his command, Bradley objected strenuously, at one point saying he could not take responsibility for such an action and would be forced to resign. Eisenhower finally terminated the conversation with, "Well, Brad, those are my orders."[34] It was gut-wrenching for Ike. His long, intimate friendship with Bradley went back over thirty years to their days on the Plain at West Point; on the other side of the coin, the decision clearly had the potential to accentuate Monty's well-developed egocentrism and feed his deeply held desire for control of as many American ground troops as he could get.[35] It would be second-guessed by the senior American commanders in Europe and perhaps in Washington as well.[36] But given the overwhelming need to halt the German advance, it was clearly the right thing to do. By making the Bulge an *Allied* battle, rather than a purely (though mostly) American one, Ike not only created increased assurance that Monty would continue to protect the Meuse with the British XXX Corps and perhaps commit some more British troops as well, he also ensured that Hodges would have command supervision from the army group level. And, *most significantly*, he had dealt a decisive blow to Hitler's political goal of driving a wedge between the Americans and the British. It was Eisenhower's finest moment in the Bulge.

Montgomery moved quickly to take control over the southern portion of his area of operations, which now extended south to an east-west line from

Givet on the Meuse to Prüm, just inside Germany. His approach was to use the forces in contact to delay the German advance, form a reserve with which to counterattack when the impetus of the offensive had sufficiently diminished, and use the XXX Corps as a safety net west of the Meuse. Although his phrase used to describe this concept, "tidying up the battlefield," infuriated many Americans, as a grand-tactical construct, it made a good deal of sense. There is conflicting evidence about the attitude with which Montgomery's tactics were put into place. In the first conference with Hodges and Simpson, held at Hodges's headquarters in the early afternoon of the 20th, one of Monty's aides said the field marshal strode in "like Christ come to cleanse the temple."[37] De Guingand, however, paints a picture of a much more businesslike meeting.[38] Monty's immediate orders were to shift Simpson's boundary to the south so that Hodges could concentrate on eliminating the penetration and to direct that Collins's VII Corps headquarters be pulled out of line, given three divisions, and assembled between the Belgian city of Marche and the Meuse, but not to become immediately engaged.[39] Monty quickly judged Hodges to be too tired to exercise effective command and contacted Smith to request that SHAEF appoint a new First Army commander.[40] Smith asked for twenty-four hours, and on the 22nd Ike wrote Monty expressing his confidence in Hodges's ability to rebound but inviting the field marshal to "inform me instantly if any change needs to be made on the United States side."[41] Monty replied that night that while Hodges was "a bit shaken early on and needed moral support," he was "doing better now."[42] Given Ike's support for Hodges, Monty apparently concluded that it was better to work with the First Army commander than to precipitate a crisis. He also sensed that he could compensate for whatever deficiencies he detected in Hodges by meeting with him frequently and dealing directly with the corps commanders.[43]

To the south, Patton was busy as well.[44] Before he left Verdun on the 19th, he called the Third Army chief of staff, Major General Hobart R. Gay, with instructions for two divisions to move to the III Corps assembly area at Arlon and for one to move to Luxembourg City. On the 20th, he drove to Bradley's headquarters, made arrangements to move his command post to Luxembourg City, then drove to Arlon to meet with Middleton; Millikin; Major General Hugh J. Gaffey, commander of the 4th AD; and Major General Willard S. Paul, commander of the 26th ID. On the 21st, he held a major conference at Third Army headquarters to coordinate the details of the III Corps attack that would be launched on the morrow. He closed his diary that night with the plea, "Give us victory, Lord."[45]

REACTION IN THE AIR

The air situation was bleak. While the German spearheads were advancing rapidly westward and Eisenhower's last reserves were moving through the literal as well as the figurative fog of war to engage them, the weather was almost exactly what OKW had hoped for. From 16 to 18 December it was marginal, characterized by very low clouds, variable but generally low visibility, and light rain.[46] From 19 to 21 December, however, it was absolutely atrocious. A deep, heavy fog hung over the entire Ninth Air Force, reducing visibility to less than a hundred yards.[47] Ninth Air Force was able to drop over 400 tons of bombs on Trier and Duren in interdiction missions on 17 December, and on the 18th it put up over 600 aircraft in the area ranging from Kaiserslautern to Malmédy and Stavelot.[48] IX TAC P-47s, operating under conditions of low ceiling and visibility, attacked the spearhead column for the 1st SS Panzer Division, commanded by Lieutenant Colonel Joachim Peiper.[49] On the night of 19/20 December, however, Ninth Air Force got up only two sorties; no tactical operations at all were conducted on the 20th or the night of 20/21 December.[50]

Here we must consider the extremely significant, though generally overlooked, air implications of Ike's decision to shift the 21st/12th Army Group boundary to the south. The most immediate was the transfer of IX and XXIX TACs, which supported First and Ninth armies, respectively, from Vandenberg's Ninth Air Force to Coningham's 2nd TAF. Because this left Ninth Air Force with only XIX TAC and IX Bomber Division and because Vandenberg knew IX TAC would be backed up by aircraft from 2nd TAF, he transferred three fighter groups from IX to XIX TAC. Spaatz also boosted Ninth Air Force's combat power by placing under its control a P-51 Group and the entire 2nd Bomber Division from the Eighth Air Force.[51] But the most far-reaching air implication of Eisenhower's decision was to bring the entire RAF into the battle. For 2nd TAF, this would be no problem at all: Coningham had already demonstrated that his sympathies lay much more with Eisenhower than with Montgomery. Furthermore, the 2nd TAF commander got along famously with both Vandenberg and the IX TAC commander, Major General Elwood "Pete" Quesada. Thus, Coningham dispatched his signal officer quickly to IX and XXIX TACs to ensure they were integrated into his command system and took control of these forces, secure in the knowledge that the TAC commanders could do their jobs and that Vandenberg would not resent his exercise of authority over them.[52] Even Harris, who had previously resisted any diversion from his ongoing efforts to "de-house" German factory workers, joined in enthusiastically. One of the few bright spots in this otherwise gloomy period was an attack on 19 December by RAF Bomber Command against Trier, a key road junction east of the Ardennes. The attack, which was carried out in spite of heavy fog conditions over both the bases and the target, earned Harris a congratulatory telegram that Tedder dispatched at Eisenhower's request. When Harris replied that SHAEF could count on Bomber Command "in any weather short of the impossible," Eisenhower noted to Tedder on the incoming message, "they have already achieved the impossible."[53]

The operational concept worked out to provide air support to the ground forces was very straightforward. Fighter-bombers would provide their normal close support to the armies as weather permitted; fighter-bombers and medium bombers would interdict the movement of troop units and supply columns out to an inner ring of targets that followed the Rhine to Bingen, and then swung west to Saarburg. The role of the heavy bombers would be to extend interdiction to targets beyond the Rhine and southeast to Saarbrücken, while also being available to strike at closer targets as needed.[54]

The operative phrase for the tactical air support was "as weather permitted," and its prolonged lack of permission caused Eisenhower "a special concern, even anxiety."[55] He was not alone. When the air briefer at 12th Army Group informed Bradley on 19 December that weather was "hampering and preventing air operations," Hansen reported that his boss "shook his head sadly."[56] The next day, Bradley's aide noted: "Air would seem to be the pivotal center of our counterattacking force. . . . So far the air contribution has been negligible. All because of the weather. The German appears to have picked his time for a strike carefully and once again weather is fighting on his side."[57] At First Army headquarters, Hodges's aide penned a similar lament on the 21st: "The third successive day that the weather is bad. With good weather we could stop this. . . . If only a break would come."[58]

SUMMARY

By the evening of the 21st, the Germans, having failed to gain the Meuse, were clearly behind their original timetable. But largely because of the absence of Allied air, they were continuing to exercise the overall initiative. St. Vith had fallen. Bastogne was encircled. Between these two major road junctions in the northern and southern zones of the salient, the Germans were racing to the west, with three panzer divisions in the breach and one armored spearhead past Ortheuville, some twelve miles west of Houffalize.[59] Although the Allies had taken appropriate measures to deal with the offensive, the Germans still held the upper hand.

But to appreciate fully how this all transpired, we must now consider the actions of the six corps. V and VIII Corps were engaged immediately on 16 December, and XVIII (Airborne) Corps became operational at Werbomont three days later. Meanwhile, III, XII, and VII Corps prepared to enter the fray.

6

V Corps Halts the German Schwerpunkt

But the action of the 2d and 99th divisions on the northern shoulder could well be considered the most decisive of the Ardennes campaign.[1]

John S. D. Eisenhower

THE ATTACK OF THE SIXTH SS PANZER ARMY embraced a portion of the V Corps sector ranging from Monschau in the north to a point just north of Losheim in the south, a distance of some twenty miles. This was a much narrower attack than that with which Middleton's VIII Corps had to contend, facing both the Fifth Panzer and Seventh Armies along a front of some sixty miles. Gerow's task was thus simpler than Middleton's, but his corps had a more important role. In fact, one could argue that V Corps had *the* most important role in the Battle of the Bulge. If Dietrich's Sixth SS Panzer Army were to break through quickly, there was little behind the thin forward crust to stop it from reaching the Meuse. And if the SS panzers made it to the Meuse rapidly and in good order, all of Hitler's best hopes and all of Eisenhower's worst fears could possibly be realized. Fortunately for Gerow, the Germans made some critical mistakes; and the soldiers under him, with only a few exceptions, fought well and gallantly. Nevertheless, it was his job to establish the conditions for their success; the six days from 16 to 21 December 1944 would prove to be the most important of his life.

THE INITIAL SITUATION

Gerow was fortunate to have Huebner as his deputy. Although deputy corps commanders were appointed from time to time, the position was not authorized.[2] As noted earlier, Huebner's presence was based on his designation as Gerow's successor, to be effective when the latter assumed command of Fifteenth Army. Huebner was an infantryman's infantryman. After graduating from a Nebraska business college in 1909, he enlisted in the army and served with the 18th IR.[3] He received his commission in 1916 and served with the 1st Division in World War I. His interwar assignments included three years as an instructor at Fort Benning and four years on the CGSS faculty. Huebner was looked upon as a strict disciplinarian and a knowledgeable tactician. Years later, the novelist Anton Myrer, whose book Once an Eagle became an unofficial leadership manual for the U.S. Army, used Huebner as one source for the composite of the novel's hero, Sam Damon.[4] Most recently, however, Huebner had proven himself as a division commander, having come ashore with the 1st ID on D-Day and led it all the way across France and into Belgium. He was to prove a valuable adjunct to Gerow's command during the first, critical phase of the campaign.

The terrain in the V Corps sector favored the defense.[5] The area from Monschau to Losheim was thickly wooded, restricting movement of vehicles to forest trails and roads. To the immediate west of this band of forest lays a stretch of undulating, generally open high ground known as the Elsenborn Ridge. Charles B. MacDonald described it as "a high ridgeline on the German [east] side of the town of Elsenborn and nearby Camp Elsenborn. It is shaped like a boomerang, with the highest point, at just over two thousand feet between Elsenborn and the village of Wirtzfeld, forming the southern prong of the boomerang and its slopes dropping off sharply to a reservoir, the Lac de Butgenbach."[6] It was on the eastern and southern faces of this terrain feature that Gerow would anchor the V Corps defense. The major road in the sector runs east-west from Losheim through Losheimergraben to Büllingen, Butgenbach, Waimes, and Malmédy, then bends southwest to Stavelot and Trois Ponts. Just west of Malmédy, there is a branch leading northwest to Spa, location of First Army headquarters. There is also a decent network of trafficable trails and secondary roads. To the north of the Losheimergraben-Büllingen road, a trail through the Honsfelder Wald leads from Udenbreth, Germany, through Mürringen, to Büllingen, where it connects with the main road.[7] Further to the north, another trail from Hollerath, Germany, cuts through a wetland forest to the almost-joined villages of Rocherath on the north and Krinkelt on the south. From these twin villages, there proceeds a secondary road through Wirtzfeld to Elsenborn and points west in the Hohes Venn, a high, largely uninhabited marshland between the Elsenborn Ridge and the Meuse, which stretches to the north as far as Eupen. Another secondary road runs north-south from Wahlerscheid, a German custom post, to Rocherath.[8]

On the morning of 16 December, V Corps was arrayed from north-south with the 8th and 78th Divisions north of Monschau, the 102nd Cavalry Group screening immediately west of Monschau, and the 99th ID (-) holding the line from Höfen, just south of Monschau, to a point just north of Losheim. The 2nd ID, supported by the bulk of the 395th IR of the 99th ID, was continuing an attack through the 99th on a north-south axis along and paralleling the Rocherath-Wahlerscheid road. This attack represented the southern prong of the V Corps/ First Army effort to seize the Roer River dams by an envelopment around the Monschau Forest.

The 99th was thus to bear the brunt of the Sixth SS Panzer Army attack. It was new to the theater, having arrived in early November and begun moving into position between the 9th and the 14th of the month.[9] It was commanded by Major General Walter E. Lauer, who had been commissioned from ROTC and fought in the AEF in World War I. He had served as a division chief of staff and assistant division commander in North Africa before assuming command of the 99th.[10] North of the 2nd ID's attack corridor, the 99th was disposed with the 3rd Battalion, 395th Infantry, near Höfen and the divisional reconnaissance squadron to its south near Kalterherberg.[11] South of the 2nd ID's zone, the 1st and 3rd Battalions of the 393rd were in the forest east of Krinkelt, the regiment's 2nd Battalion having been attached to the 395th to support the 2nd ID's attack. Further south, the 394th Infantry held just west of the Belgian-German border, its 1st Battalion guarding the critical Losheim-Losheimergraben-Büllingen road. Concerned about the openness of his right flank, which butted up against the VIII Corps' 14th Cavalry Group in the Losheim Gap, Lauer took prudent action to guard it by designating 3rd Battalion, 394th Infantry, as the division reserve and positioning it at Buchholz Station, roughly a mile-and-a-half west of Losheimergraben.

Unlike the 99th, the 2nd ID was a veteran outfit. Known as the "Indianhead Division" for the prominent depiction of an American Indian on its large shoulder patch, the 2nd traced its proud combat lineage back to Belleau Wood. In the European campaign, it came ashore at Omaha Beach on 7 June; captured the vital Hill 192 in the battle for St. Lô; and repeated the feat by seizing Hill 92, which controlled the approaches to Brest.[12] The 2nd was commanded by Major General Walter M. Robertson. A 1912 Military Academy graduate, Robertson had served with the inspector general department of the AEF in World War I and taught for three years at both CGSS and the Army War College between the wars. Beginning in late 1940, he made a steady rise from command of the 9th IR, to assistant commander of the 2nd ID, to its commander in 1944.[13] Robertson's offensive plan to get to the Roer dams called for the 9th and 38th IRs to attack in column along the Rocherath-Wahlerscheid road, with the 99th's 395th Infantry supporting on the east and his own 23rd Infantry in reserve at Camp Elsenborn.[14] By the morning of the 16th, his lead regiment had reached Wahlerscheid.

Sixth SS Panzer Army's attack plan, which would virtually bypass Robertson's division, was a classic armor concept.[15] Dietrich arranged in echelon

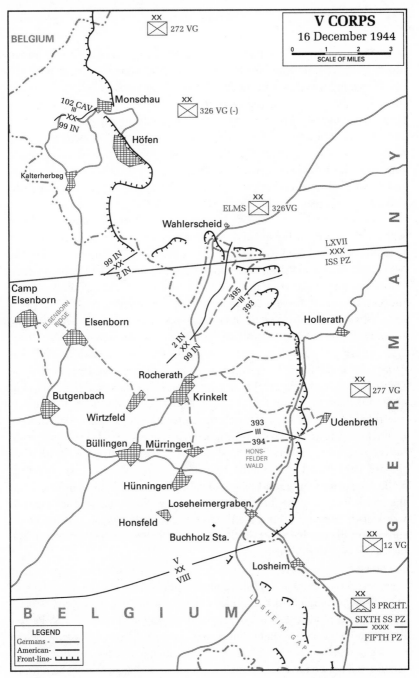

Map 3. V Corps, 16 December 1944

two SS panzer corps, the I and II, respectively, to make the main attack along a twelve-mile front from just south of Wahlerscheid to Krewinkel, about two miles south of Losheim. The lead corps was to conduct a break-in, make a breakthrough, and carry the Meuse; the II SS Panzer Corps was to pass through the first echelon corps and continue the attack on order, presumably at or about the line of the Meuse, then conduct an exploitation to Antwerp. Meanwhile, the LXVII Corps would make a supporting attack on the northern flank along the Monschau-Eupen axis. The entire effort was to be preceded with a massive artillery bombardment to stun the American defenders and create conditions for the break-in.

I SS Panzer Corps was clearly the Schwerpunkt of the Schwerpunkt; it was amply equipped for its mission, containing two SS panzer divisions, a parachute division, and two VGDs. It was led by Lieutenant General of the Waffen-SS Hermann Priess, who had assumed command in October 1944.[16] Priess had joined the army in 1919, later leaving it for the Nazi Party and the SS. He rose to division commander on the Eastern Front and was commended by Manteuffel for his counterattacks against the Russians in the summer of 1943. Known as a man of few words and strong action, Priess was probably the ideal leader to command this key formation. The plan of attack for the I SS Panzer Corps was, however, beyond Priess's control. Dietrich, reasoning that the infantry would not have sufficient power to penetrate the main lines, wanted to lead with the panzer divisions. But he was overruled by Model, who followed the conventional rationale that infantry broke in, while armor broke through.[17] Thus constrained, Priess arranged his corps in two echelons. The break-in force consisted from south-north of the 3rd Parachute Division attacking through the Losheim Gap, the 12th VGD advancing along the Losheim-Losheimergraben-Büllingen road, and the 277th VGD moving through the Honsfelder Wald and the forest east of Krinkelt-Rocherath. Behind them, the 1st SS Panzer Division would break through in the southern half of the sector, while the 12th SS Panzer Division broke through in the north.

The 1st SS Panzer Division was of special interest because of its particular organization for combat. Its lead kampfgruppe was commanded by Lieutenant Colonel Joachim Peiper, a ruthless, driving officer whose bravery, ferocity in combat, and tactical skill had earned him command of the 1st SS Panzer Regiment at age twenty-eight, while only a major.[18] Peiper's force, which in today's parlance would be called an advance guard, was big and powerful.[19] It consisted of two tank battalions—with a mixed force of seventy-two Mark IVs and Panthers in one and forty-five Tiger IIs in the other—a panzergrenadier battalion, a 150-mm gun company, an artillery battalion, engineer and antiaircraft companies, and a Luftwaffe flak battalion. In all, Peiper commanded just under 5,000 soldiers and some 800 vehicles. His objective was simple: race to the Meuse and capture the bridges. The man and the mission were made for each other.

The westward movement of the panzer divisions was controlled by five Rollbahnen, or movement routes, designated alphabetically from north to south.[20] Route A moved from Hollerath, Germany, through Krinkelt and Elsenborn, into the Hohes Venn, and on to Liège; Route B originated in Udenbreth, Germany, moving south of Krinkelt to Butgenbach, Malmédy, and Spa. Both were designed to protect the 12th SS Panzer's north flank. Route C, the 12th SS Panzer's major axis of advance, utilized the main road from Losheim to Losheimergraben and Büllingen, and then continued west to Butgenbach, Waimes, and Malmédy. Route D, which indicated the 1st SS Panzer's main attack line, advanced from Losheim through Honsfeld, then cut across country to Möderscheid and Schoppen before picking up the road to Ligneuville and Wanne. Route E, which lay in the VIII Corps sector and protected the southern flank of the 1st SS Panzer's advance, originated in Manderfeld, then proceeded to Andler, Born, and Recht, crossing the Salm River at Vielsalm.

There has been some controversy about the rigidity of these routes. On the eve of the offensive, Hitler called Model and told him in no uncertain terms that there would be "no deviation by the Panzer units east of the Maas [Meuse] toward the north" and that Dietrich must keep his orientation to the west, not becoming encumbered with fighting on his right flank.[21] Hitler's clear intent here was to head off either a conscious or unintended drift toward the "small slam." Later that night, Model called Hitler back, informing him that his instructions had been relayed to Dietrich, who presumably passed them on to Priess. Viewed literally, Hitler's "no deviation" admonition would mean that the Rollbahnen were inviolate and that to infringe upon one's neighbor's march route was to risk the Führer's wrath.[22] However, both Kraemer and Priess indicated in postwar interviews that the routes were actually much less constricting.[23] Kraemer stated categorically that in the Sixth SS Panzer Army concept, the Rollbahnen were intended to control generally the advance as far as the north-south line Verviers-Spa-Stavelot. After that line was reached, new orders would be given as the situation required. And Priess stated equally explicitly that division commanders were free to choose alternate routes. In fact, the German practice of indicating march routes for two exploiting divisions in a corps area, rather than the American practice of establishing boundaries, in and of itself, suggests a certain amount of flexibility. In sum, the overall direction of the I SS

Panzer Corps had to be directly west to the Meuse; the Rollbahnen indicated assigned routes of advance for the panzer divisions; but local deviations were authorized as long as the western thrust of the attack was not compromised.

The LXVII Corps, commanded by Lieutenant General Otto Hitzfeld, figured much less prominently in the Sixth SS Panzer Army plan, but it was not without significance.[24] With two VGDs, the 326th and the 272nd, it was to attack through Höfen, Monschau, and points north, then move into the Hohes Venn where it would protect Dietrich's right flank. This effort was to be abetted by an airborne landing in the area of Eupen. Of some note, Hitzfeld forbade an artillery preparation on the Monschau itself, reasoning that it would be of little effect on the well-dug-in Americans.[25]

Several conclusions emerge from this survey. First, time would be everything. If the Germans could quickly break in, then quickly break through, all would be lost for V Corps; the 1944 I SS Panzer Corps breakthrough at Losheim-Elsenborn would go down in history with the XIX Panzer Corps 1940 breakthrough at Sedan. Second, terrain would dictate the battle. The major east-west routes and the key choke points of Büllingen, Butgenbach, and Krinkelt-Rocherath would focus combat power at these locations based on the Germans' absolute need to seize them to continue their attack to the west and the Americans' similarly desperate requirement to hold them in order to establish a viable defense.

SENSING AND SHAPING THE BATTLEFIELD, 16–17 DECEMBER

The Sixth SS Panzer Army attack opened at 0530 with a heavy artillery barrage all along the front. It was of mixed effect. Damage to troops was negligible, an advantage of the Americans having had just enough time to establish positions with overhead cover. But damage to communications was considerable. Telephone contact from the regimental level down was noticeably disrupted, and radios did not offer a satisfactory substitute. As a result, headquarters above battalion were not entirely in the picture most of the day and artillery support to the defenders was erratic.

In the sector of the 394th IR, commanded by Colonel Don Riley, two battalions of the 48th Regiment of the 12th VGD, attacking through the woods northeast of Losheimergraben, found an opening in the 1st Battalion's sector; but as daylight ended, the rest of the battalion held firm in and around Losheimergraben.[26] During the course of the battle, the battalion captured a copy of Rundstedt's order of the day, cited above.[27] This document, which was passed quickly up the chain of command, provided an early indicator of a large-scale offensive. About a mile west at Buchholz Station, the 3rd Battalion was hit by the lead echelon of the 12th VGD's 27th Regiment. The opposing commanders both brought up reinforcements, but at the end of the day the Germans had still not gained control of the station. Nevertheless, Lauer's slim division reserve was already engaged. On the extreme south flank and actually several hundred yards into the VIII Corps sector, Colonel Riley had prudently positioned the Intelligence and Reconnaissance (I&R) Platoon in the wood line northwest of Lanzerath. This gallant platoon held off a battalion of the 3rd Parachute Division for the entire day.[28] As the sun set on the 16th, the 394th had taken some hard knocks; but its positions were generally intact.

The 393rd IR, immediately to its north and commanded by Lieutenant Colonel Jean D. Scott, was more roughly handled. Scott's regiment, minus a battalion attached to the 395th IR supporting the 2nd IR attack, occupied the Krinkelter Wald out to just beyond the German border. A major north-south road known as the International Highway ran along the southern two-thirds of his front. Two trails led from the International Highway into his sector. The northernmost entered roughly center sector and ran due west to Rocherath. The second entered near his boundary with the 394th IR and angled northwest until it joined the first trail about a mile east of Rocherath. The 277th VGD hit Scott's two battalions hard.[29] One company of the 3rd Battalion, positioned where the northernmost trail intersected the International Highway, was overrun by a force six times its strength. When the battalion commander organized a second line of resistance, Priess, already becoming impatient with the delay, gave the 277th a battalion of SS panzer-grenadiers. Lauer released a company of the 394th to help the 393rd, and by nightfall both attackers and defenders were reorganizing after heavy losses. To the south, the 1st Battalion fared better initially; but when the 277th VGD commander, Colonel Wilhelm Viebig, committed his division reserve, the power of numbers prevailed. Despite several spirited counterattacks, the 3rd Battalion was forced to fall back into the woods. When darkness came, the Germans sent out patrols to probe the gaps rent in the 393rd Infantry's defenses. Thus, although the 99th ID's lines had held in the center, their prospects of doing so on the morrow rested primarily with the Germans.

In the north, the situation was much more sanguine.[30] Hitzfeld's LXVII Corps was seriously short of troops. The 272nd VGD was fighting hard to hold off the 78th ID, which was attacking as part of the northern pincer against the Roer dams. And the 326th VGD could muster just under a regiment for its attack on Monschau. This assault was handily repulsed by troops of the 38th Cavalry Squadron. Although late in the day they sensed the impending arrival of German reinforcements, by evening the cavalrymen were themselves augmented with an engineer company. Just to their south at Höfen, the 3rd Battalion, 395th Infantry, had similar results. Attacked shortly after the German artillery lifted, the battalion mowed down hundreds of 326th VGD assaulters. Although the front line was penetrated, the enemy salient was quickly reduced. And like the cavalry to the north, the battalion's casualties were remarkably light.[31] These fortunate results and the absence of any German offensive capacity north of Monschau allowed Gerow to concentrate all his energies and attention on the south and center of the V Corps front.

In the late morning of 16 December, as the 2nd ID was continuing its attack at Wahlerscheid, the Division Artillery commander, Brigadier General John H. Hinds, received a call from a captain on Lauer's staff requesting that some tank destroyers attached to the 2nd ID be transferred to the 99th.[32] Hinds was disquieted by this request. When he confided his unease to Robertson, the latter decided that he and Hinds should pay a visit to Lauer's headquarters. There they were further disturbed by an apparent lack of organization and the discovery of Lauer playing a piano in a corner of the building that housed his command post. Lauer informed Robertson that his front units had been attacked but the situation seemed well in hand. Robertson, however, was sufficiently concerned by his division's precarious position along the Rocherath-Wahlerscheid road that he ordered the 23rd IR in division reserve to move forward from Camp Elsenborn to the woods north of Rocherath.

As the fighting developed during the 16th, Gerow worked to grasp the situation. The extent of his early sensing that something serious was going on was evident in the fact that at about 1100 he called Hodges, requesting permission to halt the 2nd ID's attack.[33] Hodges, loath to forsake the effort to capture the Roer dams, refused. On the other hand, the army commander responded positively to Middleton's request for return of CCB, 9th AD, which had been designated as the V Corps reserve for the Roer attack, from V Corps to VIII Corps.[34] This left Gerow in the difficult position of having to continue the 2nd ID attack without an armored reserve either to exploit that attack or fend off the German assault. At 1200, Gerow's headquarters reported to First Army that "enemy counterattacks in the zones of the 3rd Bn, 395th Inf[,] 1st Bn 393rd Inf, and 1st Bn 394th Inf made some penetrations, but all were repulsed and positions restored without loss of ground."[35] Nevertheless, by mid-afternoon, Lauer had become sufficiently concerned about his situation to request two battalions from the 2nd ID as reinforcements.[36] Accordingly, Gerow directed the transfer of 1st and 3rd Battalions of the 23rd Infantry, i.e., two-thirds of Robertson's reserve, to the 99th. Lauer then ordered the 1st Battalion, which was truck-mounted and reinforced with both tank and tank destroyer companies, to Hünningen, a small town northwest of Losheimergraben in which defensive positions had prudently been prepared, to back up the 394th Infantry. The 3rd Battalion was ordered to move into the woods east of Krinkelt and prepare to attack on the next morning to restore the lines of the 393rd Infantry.

These were prudent moves, but they did not solve the basic problem—the 2nd ID was stuck out like a finger waiting to be cut off, having unknowingly attacked right into the seam between the right wing of the I SS Panzer Corps and the left wing of the LXVII Corps. Thus, it was extremely fortunate that Huebner visited Robertson on the evening of the 16th for a serious discussion of the events of the day.[37] The deputy corps commander assuredly briefed the 2nd ID commander on what was known at that time—that the 99th had been hit across its front. He may also have given him the gist of Rundstedt's captured order. These two seasoned professionals perhaps also inferred from First Army's transfer of CCB, 9th AD, to VIII Corps that Middleton's situation was worrisome as well. Whatever the specifics of their deliberations, it all added up to trouble. Huebner's parting admonition was chilling: "Go slow and watch your step; the overall situation is not good."[38] Reacting with alacrity, Robertson instructed his chief of staff to develop a division withdrawal plan. And on his own initiative, he ordered Colonels Chester J. Hirschfelder and Francis H. Boos, commanding the 9th and 38th IRs, respectively, to make no further advances that night.

While Huebner was dealing face-to-face with Robertson, Gerow was working the phone to First Army. This effort paid off. Responding positively to Gerow's request for reinforcements, Hodges directed that the 1st ID's 26th Infantry be transferred from VII Corps, on Gerow's left flank, to V Corps. The order for this movement was sent out from First Army headquarters just before midnight, and trucks full of reinforcements were soon rolling south toward Camp Elsenborn.[39] Gerow would assign this unit to the 99th to extend its right flank and begin to establish a defense along the southern face of the Elsenborn Ridge. Though it was probably not yet formulated in Gerow's mind, from this action we can begin to detect the early outlines of an overall corps plan.

Gerow's last significant act on the 16th was a phone conversation with Lauer around midnight. Lauer related that "all my front line units had reported in, that my entire front was practically reestablished on its original line—that the situation was in hand and all quiet—but that my right flank had me considerably worried."[40] In one sense, Lauer was right—his inexperienced division had acquitted itself well, in several cases extremely well. But Lauer's rather upbeat assessment was questionable in three respects. First, there is no indication that Lauer had left his command post during the entire day; his report thus appears to have been made on the results of reports from the front lines, which were fragmentary owing to the cut telephone lines, rather than on his personal sense of the sights and sounds of the battle. Second, having placed the 3rd Battalion, 23rd Infantry, behind his own 393rd Infantry, Lauer should have had at least some concerns about his center as well as his right. And finally, his account of the battle indicates he was definitely aware of the Rundstedt order on the 16th.[41] What Gerow made of Lauer's estimate is not recorded, but he could not help but remember it when events of the next day proved it decidedly optimistic.

17 December started badly for the soldiers of V Corps, and it got worse as it went along.

Joachim Peiper spent the 16th in Losheim, seething at the delay of the 3rd Parachute Division in clearing the woods beyond Lanzerath, which were staunchly defended by the 394th Infantry's tiny I&R Platoon, and by the inability of the 12th VGD to capture either Buchholz Station or Losheimergraben.[42] Finally, at about midnight, he moved forward to Lanzerath, where he encountered Colonel Helmüt von Hoffman, commanding the 9th Parachute Regiment. Hoffman, a Luftwaffe officer, was no match for his ruthless SS junior. Peiper, apparently with the authorization of Priess, demanded the attachment of one of Hoffman's battalions and immediately ordered his kampfgruppe to advance. Although forced to contend with narrow, winding roads, scarcely better than improved trails, it blew through Buchholz Station, overrunning two companies of the 3rd Battalion, 393rd Infantry, and soon reached Honsfeld, where it likewise overwhelmed a small detachment of the 14th Cavalry Group. From there, Peiper's route lay along a secondary road to Mödersheid. But this road was in terrible shape, and Peiper now needed gas. So he moved north to Büllingen, where he had learned there was a gasoline dump.

Büllingen served as a major service area for both the 2nd and the 99th IDs. It was defended only by the 245th Combat Engineer Battalion, which V Corps had released to the 99th ID shortly before midnight on the 16th, and a few other small tank destroyer units. With the engineers spread thin attempting to cover all the major approaches into Büllingen, the lead elements of Peiper's force had only to deal with a single company, recently arrived in position. The engineers were quickly forced back. Peiper thus not only got his gas—his unit significantly disrupted the support services for the two V Corps divisions doing the main fighting, captured a large number of troops, and overran both divisions' airfields.

Gerow and the V Corps then got a major reprieve. Instead of attacking northwest from Büllingen in the direction of Butgenbach, Peiper moved southwest toward Möderscheid to get back on Route B. An advance to Butgenbach would have unhinged the entire southern face of the V Corps defense, thus creating a vacuum in the rear of the 2nd and 99th IDs, which in turn would have significantly aided the advance of the right wing of the I SS Panzer Corps. A northern swing from Butgenbach to Elsenborn would have compounded the effect. Had Priess been given perfect knowledge of the situation and been able to foresee the bitter fighting on the eastern face of the Elsenborn Ridge that would rage for the next three days, he might have been tempted to order Peiper to make a temporary diversion to the northwest or even north. But such knowledge and prescience were not available to either commander, and "*immer west*" was the order of the day. Thus was V Corps spared a potential disaster.

As Peiper's troops were filling their tanks in Büllingen, Gerow was again on the phone to Hodges, imploring him to authorize cessation of the 2nd ID's attack on the Roer River. Hodges was slow to be talked out of continuing the attack; but he finally relented, authorizing Gerow to handle things as he deemed best.[43] This was all the clearance Gerow needed. He immediately contacted Robertson, instructing him to get his division back to the twin villages. Gerow's persistence with Hodges early on the 17th was extremely fortunate for several reasons. It put into action, just in the nick of time, the extrication of the 2nd ID from a position in which its only escape route was about to be completely severed. Furthermore, had the 2nd not been able to occupy the Krinkelt-Rocherath complex, the 99th would have had no tangible means of support as it withdrew later in the day. This would have given the 12th SS Panzer Division a clear shot at the northern three Rollbahnen and opened its way to the Meuse.

Robertson had stayed up most of the night of the 16th/17th, refining the withdrawal plan begun after Huebner's visit and moving north along the Rocherath-Wahlerscheid road to brief Colonels Hirschfelder and Boos on its particulars.[44] It was an ingenious and savvy concept. The easy thing to do would have been, in effect, to order the division to execute a march to the rear, with the 38th Infantry leading and the 9th Infantry fighting a rearguard action. However, such an order would have magnified the normal tendency of withdrawals, which is to have the troops most distant from the enemy hurry their advance toward safety and disregard the plight of their less fortunate comrades still in contact. Robertson's plan was, instead, an inside-out withdrawal, i.e., the 38th Infantry would hold in place while the 9th fought through it, then the 9th would hold in place as the 38th withdrew. In addition to extricating these two regiments, Robertson also had to block the potential threat from the southeast and secure the road back to the Elsenborn Ridge. For the former, he placed the 3rd Battalion, 38th Infantry, on the southern edge of Krinkelt; for the latter, he dispatched the 2nd Battalion, 23rd Infantry, to Wirtzfeld. And again acting on his own authority, he attached Lauer's 395th Infantry, which had been supporting his attack, to the 2nd Division. Upon withdrawal, the 9th Infantry, which had already taken heavy casualties in the attack on Wahlerscheid, was to move to Wirtzfeld and Krinkelt, while the 38th was to defend Rocherath.

As the 2nd ID plan was being implemented, the 99th was under heavy pressure.[45] In the south, the 1st Battalion, 394th, fended off multiple infantry attacks, though with depleted stocks of ammunition and steadily mounting casualties. Late in the day, German engineers finally repaired a destroyed bridge that had prevented the commitment of tanks thus far in the battle. The resulting pressure was too much; shortly thereafter, Lauer authorized Colonel Riley's 394th to withdraw to Mürringen, where, together with the 1st Battalion, 23rd Infantry, at Hünningen, commanded by Lieutenant Colonel John M. Hightower, it was to establish a defense along the southern approaches to the twin villages. But with Germans infiltrating through the woods, this order was more easily given than implemented. Similar problems faced the 2nd Battalion, 394th ID, as it fought its way back through the Honsfelder Wald toward Mürringen, and the 3rd Battalion, now down to a single company, as it withdrew as well. Thus, as night fell, Riley had but fragments of a regiment in Mürringen. Arriving at Hünningen, the 27th Regiment, 12th VGD, made a series of attacks, heavily supported by artillery, against Hightower's battalion. These repeated assaults were repulsed, but German infiltration around both Hünningen and Mürringen continued. Just before midnight, Hightower, now attached to Hirschfelder's 9th Infantry, was ordered to withdraw to Krinkelt. Hightower demurred, pleading the need for his withdrawal to be made simultaneously with that of Riley's reorganizing 394th Infantry in Mürringen. But his and Riley's ability to hold was now clearly measured in hours.

Things were no better east of the twin villages.[46] There, the 277th VGD, reinforced by both panzergrenadiers and tanks of the 12th SS Panzer Division, forced Colonel Scott's 393rd Infantry to withdraw. Scott's plan was for his 1st and 3rd Battalions to pull back through the 3rd Battalion, 23rd Infantry, now defending in the woods east of Krinkelt-Rocherath; reorganize; and then extend that battalion's flanks to the south and north, respectively. The 3rd Battalion, 23rd Infantry, was heavily engaged before either of the 393rd Infantry's battalions could regroup. On its northern flank, the lines were held against successive infantry assaults; but when supported by tanks, these attacks prevailed.[47] The 3rd Battalion's defense then progressively unraveled, and all organized resistance east of the twin villages ceased. As night was falling, soldiers of the 393rd Infantry and the 3rd Battalion, 23rd Infantry, were streaming back into the twin villages.

Fortunately, the 2nd ID had established a sufficient force there to constitute something of an anchor.[48] Robertson spent the entire day moving up and down the Rocherath-Wahlerscheid road encouraging and admonishing his soldiers and giving orders to units to deal with a kaleidoscopically changing situation, all the time enduring the indignity of German artillery. The 395th Infantry was withdrawn into Rocherath in relatively good order by late afternoon and was dispatched to block the northern and northeastern approaches to the village.[49] The 38th Infantry had a harrowing fight. Finding that its intended positions east of Rocherath were occupied by the Germans, Colonel Boos directed the regiment to move into the eastern edges of the twin villages. The 277th VGD and elements of the 12th SS Panzer Division mounted several attacks against the 1st Battalion, 9th Infantry, commanded by Lieutenant Colonel William D. McKinley, which had staunchly covered the 38th Infantry's withdrawal. Although these efforts were largely repulsed with a combination of bazookas, mines, and artillery, the tide could not be completely stemmed; and mixed groups of tanks and infantry slipped into Rocherath. Further south, similar events were happening along the 38th Infantry's just-established front.

Gerow and Robertson conferred in the early evening.[50] Robertson informed the corps commander that he could hold Krinkelt-Rocherath long enough for the remaining units of the 99th Division to pass through, then withdraw to the Elsenborn Ridge. There, he believed a credible stand could be made. Gerow accepted this counsel and so ordered. With the arrival of the 26th IR in the late morning and its movement into position in and around Butgenbach by early afternoon, the corps situation was showing early signs that disaster might be averted. Additionally, the remainder of the 1st ID had been released from VII Corps to V Corps.

Despite this good news, Gerow knew that he had failed in one respect: he had been unable to defend the V Corps/VIII Corps boundary. At 1730, he discussed the situation with Middleton, who informed him that he had his hands full trying to save the exposed infantry regiments of the 106th ID east of St. Vith.[51] They mutually concluded that neither had the resources to close the growing gap between their corps.

But Gerow was soon to get reinforcement that he thought might help him redress the issue. Lieutenant General William H. Simpson, commander of the Ninth Army, had generously offered to First Army his 30th ID, which First Army had further assigned to V Corps at 2025.[52] Gerow's original intention was to order the 30th to move directly to Malmédy, from which it would attack southeast "as early as possible to close the gap between V Corps and VIII Corps."[53] 1st ID was to conduct a supporting attack on the 30th ID's left flank. Neither of these offensive activities proved feasible, but the additional strength would allow Gerow to extend his southern flank further to the west.

Although the attacks against the 2nd and 99th IDs were the main issues of the day, Gerow also had to deal with a German airborne operation in the corps rear area. Originally scheduled for the early hours of 16 December, this drop had been postponed for lack of transport to move the troops to the departure airfield.[54] When it was made early on the 17th, it was plagued with additional friction: several hundred men were dropped around Bonn, most of the rest were badly scattered, and less than one-tenth of the force was delivered to its drop zone in the Hohes Venn between Malmédy and Eupen. The commander, Colonel Friedrich von der Heydte, was able to gather only a handful of men. Thus, the operation did not constitute a significant threat. But combined with knowledge of Skorzeny's troops operating in the American rear, Gerow had to devote the 18th Infantry from the 1st ID and a conglomeration of corps and division rear area troops to contain the threat.[55]

One other event in the corps rear was to have profound implications for the entire American army in the days ahead as the defense continued, particularly against the SS units that were being increasingly thrown into the V Corps battle.[56] As Kampfgruppe Peiper continued its attack west from Möderscheid and Schoppen, it came to the Baugnez crossroads, about four miles south and a bit east of Malmédy. Here it encountered Battery B, 285th Field Artillery Observation Battalion, which was moving south to St. Vith to support the 7th AD. After a brief and very uneven firefight, 113 survivors, including several men from other units at the crossroads, were rounded up in a field. As they stood there shivering in the cold, a German soldier began firing into the crowd; others soon took it up. After this firing continued for several minutes, other SS soldiers moved through the now stricken mass, killing anyone found alive with small arms at close range. Of the 113 men,

67 were killed in the field or within 200 meters thereof; 46 managed to escape, though 4 of these subsequently died of wounds. Later that afternoon, Lieutenant Colonel David Pegrin, commanding the 295th Combat Engineer Battalion defending Malmédy, encountered several survivors, who quickly related to him what had just transpired. Pegrin immediately notified First Army, which dispatched investigators to his headquarters. Details of this atrocity, which became known as the Malmédy Massacre, soon spread like wildfire throughout the American forces, stiffening the resolve of every GI and significantly reducing the opportunities provided to SS troops to surrender, in the unlikely event they attempted to do so.

By the end of the second day of the German offensive, Gerow had sensed its nature, magnitude, and implications just in time to make an opening response. And he had barely begun to shape the battlefield for what lay ahead. But his boundary with VIII Corps had been torn asunder by the 1st SS Panzer Division, and powerful forces in the shape of the 12th SS Panzer Division were gathering east of Krinkelt-Rocherath to shatter his still-fragile defenses. For Priess knew full well that if this formation did not get onto the three northern Rollbahnen quickly, I SS Panzer Corps' maneuver room would be restricted to the narrow avenue opened by Kampfgruppe Peiper; this was far too slim to sustain a general advance to the Meuse. Much would therefore hinge on the fighting of the next two days.

STAVING OFF DEFEAT AND ESTABLISHING A FRAMEWORK FOR VICTORY, 18–19 DECEMBER

The tale of this fighting is not easily told. For purposes of simplicity and comprehension, it is arranged into times, areas, and units. But by midnight of 17/18 December, confusion and chaos ranged on both sides, particularly the American. Individual soldiers, small bands of comrades, and remnants of units had been out of touch with their neighbors and higher headquarters as the various withdrawals of the 17th played out. Supply troops, messengers, medics, and other noncombat soldiers whose duties required them to move about the battlefield swelled their numbers. To invoke a naval simile, the sea in and around Krinkelt-Rocherath had a number of ships on both sides maneuvering to gain position for the next phase of the battle; but it also had the flotsam and jetsam of shattered vessels bobbing aimlessly on the surface.

The opening action was the withdrawal of the remnants of the 394th Infantry and 1st Battalion, 23rd Infantry, from Mürringen and Hünningen.[57] Riley's direct support artillery battalion was out of ammunition, and he had just received withdrawal authorization from Lauer. Despite periodic German artillery fire along the Mürringen-Krinkelt road, most of the surviving 394th soldiers made it through to safety. But as one of Riley's battalions approached Krinkelt, it detected Germans in the village, abandoned its vehicles, and moved across country to Wirtzfeld. Other soldiers from the 394th came upon the deserted vehicles and drove them without incident through Krinkelt and on to Wirtzfeld. The artillery, however, was unable to drag many of its guns through the heavy snow and was forced to abandon all but five of its pieces. Hightower's battalion followed a similar route to Wirtzfeld but, being more heavily engaged than the 394th, lost the bulk of one company in the withdrawal.

Recognizing the importance of defending Krinkelt-Rocherath and that he could not afford to focus on it exclusively, Robertson assigned his assistant division commander, Colonel John H. Stokes, to command the disparate elements of every 2nd ID regiment plus the 395th Infantry now occupied in the twin villages.[58] The 38th and the 395th IRs constituted the bulk of the defending force in the villages themselves, while Colonel McKinley's 1st Battalion, 9th Infantry, guarded the eastern approach covering the exit from the Krinkelter Wald. These units were reinforced with a tank battalion and just over a battalion of tank destroyers and were backed up by the combined artillery units of the 9th and 2nd IDs, which were reinforced by several battalions of corps artillery. To the east, the Germans had assembled a regiment of the 277th VGD, the entire 25th Panzergrenadier Regiment of the 12th SS Panzer Division, one tank battalion, and a second that would join the fight during the day.[59]

The first blow fell on McKinley's unit.[60] Infantry wave attacks were successively repulsed, but tanks ultimately carried the day. Nevertheless, armed with a few bazookas and some well-placed mines, McKinley's soldiers knocked out several tanks and slowed down the rest. The toll was heavy. Gathering in the town after passing through the 38th Infantry, McKinley counted just over 200 officers and men of the 600 he had taken into battle.[61] Many units covered themselves with glory in the desperate fighting in and around Krinkelt-Rocherath, but none more so than the 2nd Battalion, 9th Infantry. Colonel Boos told McKinley unequivocally, "You have saved my regiment."[62]

In the villages themselves, the odds were much more even than they had been in the woods. American infantrymen armed with bazookas got close-in shots that in some cases penetrated the armor; many others disabled the panzers, which could then be finished off by tanks and tank destroyers. In other cases, more desperate measures were required: pouring gas on tanks and setting them ablaze, or jamming rifles into sprockets. The battle that raged throughout Krinkelt-Rocherath on the 17th was a microcosm of Stalingrad. Soldiers fought street-by-street, house-by-house. On several occasions, the front line would stabilize with Germans on one side of a street, Americans on the other. But one thing was unequivocal at the end of the day: although the Germans had made numerous penetrations *into* the village, the determined defenders of the 2nd and 99th IDs had stopped them from getting *through* the village.

A major reason for this was incredible artillery support. By a combination of the accidents of topography and conscious design, Elsenborn Ridge was being transformed into an elevated artillery park, ringed by infantry, tanks, tank destroyers, and engineers, for whom the artillery became their first line of defense. Here, the 1st, 2nd, and 99th Division Artilleries, augmented by several corps units, occupied a rectangle roughly four miles wide and six miles long.[63] And despite the earlier interruption to the supplies from Büllingen, ammunition was again flowing forward. On the 18th, the 38th Field Artillery Battalion of the 2nd ID alone fired 5,000 rounds![64]

Early that evening, Gerow made the unprecedented decision to attach the entire 99th ID to the 2nd.[65] Robertson was designated the commander of the combined force, with Lauer as his deputy; but clearly the former would be calling the shots for both divisions. Gerow never recorded his reasoning for the decision, but informed speculation can shed some light on the issue. Elements of the two divisions were closely intertwined in Krinkelt. The divisions would soon be withdrawing to the Elsenborn Ridge, where they would have to establish a unitary defense. Between the two of them they could barely muster a division's worth of combat power. It would also be useful to integrate the efforts of their artillery arms. Beyond the exigencies of the situation, however, was the human equation. Robertson had just pulled off a textbook example of how to conduct a withdrawal under pressure. He had been foresighted, calm, and direct, never losing his composure under extremely trying circumstances. Lauer, on the other hand, while demonstrating unquestionable competence before the battle, had not shown a similarly deft touch during it. Perhaps most significantly from the V Corps perspective, the move simplified Gerow's command situation on the east flank of the Elsenborn Ridge, giving him one commander to deal with there, rather than two.

Fortunately, things further north were well in hand.[66] At Höfen, the 326th VGD made repeated assaults against the 3rd Battalion, 395th Infantry, and its attached tank destroyers. A predawn attack carried the village, but the Germans were beaten off at daybreak. A second advance, this time supported by tanks, came several hours later. It was disrupted even before it started by a barrage of a thousand rounds of 4.5-inch rockets fired by the 18th Field Artillery Battalion.[67] The tanks were kept away by accurate fire from the tank destroyers. When the infantry penetrated the front line, the battalion commander, Lieutenant Colonel McClernand Butler, called for multiple artillery concentrations on his own positions. These and a small but spirited counterattack broke the back of the German effort, and Butler's lines were restored shortly after midday. A final attack, which was beaten back after dark, constituted the last significant threat to the Höfen-Monschau sector.

To the west, Peiper had passed through the town of Stavelot along the Amblève River on the morning of the 18th; left a small detachment to guard its vital bridge; and proceeded west to Trois Ponts at the junction of the Amblève and the Salm Rivers, where his effort to cross the Salm was frustrated by an alert and very gutsy engineer company that blew the bridges over both rivers on the north side of the town.[68] His only westward choice was thus along the north bank of the Amblève to La Gleize, from which a secondary road led to another bridge in the hamlet of Cheneux.

Meanwhile, the 30th ID, commanded by Major General Leland S. Hobbs, was arriving in the V Corps area. Hobbs was a member of the 1915 Military Academy "class that stars fell on" and a graduate of both the Army and Naval War Colleges, who had commanded the 30th since late 1942.[69] With Peiper on the loose, Hobbs was receiving conflicting orders from First Army and V Corps, so he sensibly drove to Spa to get definitive instructions. Hodges, who was preparing his headquarters to move to the rear, instructed Hobbs to split his 119th IR, sending half to Werbomont and half along the Amblève Valley to head off Peiper.[70] Meanwhile, Hobbs had already ordered the 117th Infantry to cover north of the Amblève from Stavelot to Malmédy, while the 120th Infantry would extend the division's lines to Waimes to link up with the 1st ID. Although unsupported by artillery, Lieutenant Colonel Ernest Frankland, commander of the 1st Battalion, 117th Infantry, dismounted his troops north of Stavelot and assaulted the town.[71] There it fought a sharp action with Peiper's rear guard but was unable to reach the bridge. Fortunately, when tanks from Peiper's main body came back to deal with this threat to their rear, they were held off by fighters from the 365th Fighter Group that were using the few breaks in the cloud cover to harass Peiper's advance.

Gerow's southern flank now extended west to Werbomont. It was weak at that extremity; but help was on the way in the form of the 82nd Airborne Division, which was assembling there on the evening of the 18th.[72] Another note of assurance was the arrival of CCA, 3rd AD, shortly before midnight, which gave Gerow a welcome corps reserve.[73] Additionally, First Army had greatly simplified his command situation by transferring control of the 8th and 78th IDs on his northern flank to VII Corps.[74] Thus, late on the 18th, it appeared to Gerow that with Krinkelt-Rocherath in his hands and the beginning of defenses being established on the eastern face of the Elsenborn Ridge, he might just be able to hold on. But he had no certain idea of what the Germans were going to throw at him next.

Just then he got another major break. The failure of the 12th SS Panzer Division to break through Krinkelt-Rocherath on the 18th, the third day of the offensive, was apparent on German situation boards all the way up to OKW. Drastic measures were called for, and drastic measures would be taken. Dietrich directed that the 12th SS Panzer Division be pulled out of the Krinkelt-Rocherath area, to be replaced by the 3rd SS Panzergrenadier Division (PGD), and sent around to the south.[75] The original attack axis was to flow from Büllingen to Möderscheid, then to Schoppen, and on to Waimes; but the Büllingen-Möderscheid road was judged by I SS Panzer Corps too mired for tanks, and permission was granted to attack on the Büllingen-Butgenbach axis instead. Additionally, Dietrich concluded that a single corps could not both continue to attempt a breakthrough on the Krinkelt-Rocherath front and control the offensive from Büllingen to points west. Hence, Priess was left with the former, less promising task, while the reinvigoration of the offensive was passed to the II SS Panzer Corps commanded by Lieutenant General of the Waffen-SS, Wilhelm Bittrich.[76] Bittrich was a long-standing member of the SS, having joined in 1932. He had risen through the ranks and been cited multiple times for bravery, assuming command of the II SS Panzer Corps in late June 1944. Whether he could accomplish what Priess had not remained to be seen. But one thing was certain: the Sixth SS Panzer Army's attack was entering new and uncharted waters. This major reorganization on the German side gave V Corps something of a breather on the 19th.

An early morning probe against the 38th Infantry was beaten off by artillery; but the Germans took desperate measures to extract whatever tanks they could, even sending forward spare crews to man those immobilized by American fire or mechanical breakdown.[77] Later in the afternoon, the 277th VGD, 3rd PGD, and 12th VGD attacked Rocherath, Krinkelt, and Wirtzfeld, respectively; but again heavy artillery support gave the Americans breathing room. Robertson's plan of withdrawal was flexible.[78] It called for the 395th and 38th IRs, under the direction of Colonel Stokes, to peel away first and move to blocking positions near Wirtzfeld. The 9th Infantry would "probably hold tonight," then either move to the newly established defense on the east face of the Elsenborn Ridge or cover the Krinkelt-Wirtzfeld road. Meanwhile, the bulk of the 23rd Infantry would continue to organize the new line of defense. This "movement to a new position" began at 1730 and was complete by 0200 on the 20th, with no significant pressure from the Germans.[79]

XVIII (Airborne) Corps was activated the morning of the 19th and given the mission of blocking any enemy advances between the Amblève River and La Roche, some twelve miles to the southwest. It thus became the gap filler between V Corps and VIII Corps, and at 1455 V Corps released to XVIII (Airborne) Corps both the 82nd Airborne Division and the 119th IR of the 30th ID.[80] The other two regiments of Hobbs's division would follow over the next several days. But on the 19th, one of those regiments, the 117th Infantry, made a significant contribution to the American cause when its 1st Battalion destroyed the bridge over the Amblève at Stavelot, thus isolating Peiper from his logistical support and placing his kampfgruppe in a very precarious position.[81] But for now, the activation of the XVIII (Airborne) Corps meant that Gerow could devote virtually all his energies to defending the Elsenborn Ridge.

Fortunately for him and the soldiers of V Corps, 12th SS Panzer Division was experiencing great difficulty disengaging from Krinkelt-Rocherath and swinging around to the south for an attack on the Büllingen-Butgenbach axis. The causes were fourfold.[82] First, the road net in the area was constricted. Second, there was tremendous competition for this limited road space: logistical vehicles, artillery units, and second echelon forces being fed into the battle created an immense traffic jam in and around the Losheim-Losheimergraben-Manderfeld triangle that seriously impeded both Dietrich's advance and the attack of Manteuffel's right wing against St. Vith. Third, all this heavy traffic had made the secondary roads difficult to travel on and the cross-country trails almost impossible. Finally, the 1st Division Artillery shelled Büllingen heavily, thus reducing its value as a staging area.[83] Thus, German actions against the Butgenbach area on the 19th amounted to little more than probes.[84]

All the while, the V Corps situation was continuing to improve. The 16th Infantry, which had come in shortly after the 26th Infantry on December 17, now extended the corps front to Waimes. Additionally, the 18th Infantry, which Gerow had released from antiairborne duties, was now en route to bolster the defense; the 9th ID, less one regiment, had moved into the Monschau sector to provide additional assurance in the north.[85] Thus, by midnight on the 19th, Gerow had two regiments of the 1st ID arrayed from Waimes to the eastern tip of Lac de Butgenbach; the hard-hit but consolidated 2nd/99th Division moving in to establish new positions from north-west of Wirtzfeld around the eastern face of the Elsenborn Ridge; and two-thirds of a fresh division in the north. He may have sensed that the lack of significant pressure in the Krinkelt-Rocherath sector during the day presaged action elsewhere on the morrow, but he was well prepared for wherever the Germans struck.

REAPING THE FRUITS OF FORESIGHT, 20–21 DECEMBER

Napoleon is said to have expressed a preference for lucky generals. On 20 December Gerow was a lucky general, for the 12th SS Panzer Division's at-tack went right into the teeth of V Corps' greatest strength. The 12th SS Pan-zer Division was commanded by Lieutenant Colonel of the Waffen-SS Hugo Kraas.[86] Despite his junior rank, Kraas was highly regarded. Joining the SS in 1935, he was commissioned through the officer training school in 1938; rose steadily up the ranks; was decorated for bravery for his hard fighting in Russia; and after recovering from wounds, was raised to division command in the fall of 1944. During the night of the 19th/20th, Kraas's division was still gathering in Büllingen, with no coordinated attack plan yet formed.

But on the American side, things were well in order. Having had three days to establish its positions, the 26th Infantry, commanded by Colonel F. R. Seitz, was defending from a position of strength.[87] It occupied the high ground on about a four-mile front, its left resting on the eastern end of Lac de Butgenbach and its right about a mile west of Butgenbach. To take ad-vantage of the flow of the ground, the regimental center jutted south onto a promontory known as the Dom Butgenbach, frequently referred to as the Dom B. Between the Dom B and Büllingen, roughly at the same elevation as the former, was another piece of high ground known as the Schwarzen-bückel.[88] Thus, if the attack came from Büllingen, both the Schwarzenbückel and the Dom B would have to be taken before Butgenbach itself could be as-saulted. This central portion of the line was defended by the 26th Infantry's 2nd Battalion, commanded by Lieutenant Colonel Derrill M. Daniel. Craft-ing a reverse-slope defense with outposts along the high ground, Daniel had assembled his company commanders on the evening of the 17th and told them, "We fight and die here."[89] Daniel's moral steel was reinforced by good positions with overhead cover, a platoon of Shermans, four tank destroyers, and a wealth of artillery. By the morning of the 20th, General Hinds had been authorized by V Corps Artillery to orchestrate the fires of the 1st, 2nd, and 99th Division Artilleries and corps units in the immediate area. This arsenal comprised "348 pieces, including 16 divisional and 7 corps artillery battalions plus several tank destroyer and antiaircraft artillery battalions."[90] Hinds was also authorized to use variable-time (VT) fuzes, which caused the shells to explode above the ground, greatly adding to their destructive power.

The fighting on the 20th was confused. At midnight on the 19th/20th, the 1st SS Panzer Regiment of the 12th SS Panzer Division was still not closed into Büllingen. Nevertheless, the regimental commander, Herbert Kuhlmann, decided to launch a night attack with infantry and tank destroyers, the latter of which were particularly unsuited for the task. Conflicting reports of the attack prohibit a definitive account, but several features are common to all the accounts. This assault was launched against both the Schwarzenbückel and the Dom B; it made several penetrations into Daniel's lines, one to the edge of the manor house at the Dom B; and it was eventually beaten off with infantry, tanks, tank destroyers, and liberal doses of artillery.[91]

Shortly after noon on the 20th, Gerow issued a directive that succinctly stated the corps' mission, accurately summed up the situation, and offered a bit of a pep talk to his hard-fighting soldiers. The mission was to "stabilize the line immediately on positions now held . . . prevent further penetrations, mop up all infiltrations of the lines, and prepare to resume the offensive."[92] He added, "Friendly reinforcements are constantly arriving and supplies are adequate. Our situation improves each day." And he directed that "every man act with spirit and aggressiveness to inflict a crushing defeat on the enemy."

During the night of 20/21 December, Bittrich directed Kraas to make another attempt to break the American lines.[93] By then, the bulk of the 12th SS Panzer Division was well in hand. But rather than trying again on the Büllingen–Dom B–Butgenbach axis, Kraas decided to flank the Dom B and strike Butgenbach directly from the south. The need to avoid enfilading fire from the Dom B demanded that this attack be made at night. Kraas formed his division into two parallel columns. But when one battalion failed to arrive in the assembly area, he changed the entire plan, deciding instead to assault the Dom B itself from the south and east. This assault sorely pressed Colonel Daniel's battalion. It opened with a heavy artillery preparation from German howitzers and nebelwerfers. Tanks broke through on the west flank, moving up and down the foxhole line, killing infantrymen at point-blank range and firing directly into the battalion command post. But a platoon of 90-mm tank destroyers came through from Butgenbach to repulse the German armor. Additionally, the advancing tanks from the east suffered from antitank mines emplaced during the night. Again, the artillery was devastating. At least nine different battalions answered Daniel's repeated calls for fire, pumping out an incredible 10,000 rounds.[94] The German infantry were decimated. Around noon, Kraas realized he had failed and broke off the attack. Shortly before his death in 1990, Kraas called 21 December 1944 "the darkest day in his military life."[95] And well he might. In a count soon after the attack, an American graves registration unit located 782 German bodies.[96] The 12th SS Panzer Division had indeed suffered a "crushing defeat." Gerow's soldiers had held the Elsenborn Ridge; by holding it, they had seriously frustrated the plans of the Sixth SS Panzer Army to reach the Meuse.

SOME CLOSING OBSERVATIONS

Neither defeat nor victory has a single cause, and this battle was no exception.

On the defeat side, the Germans made a number of mistakes. Model's overriding of Dietrich's desire to put his armored formations in the initial wave was the first. Although Peiper's decision to stay on Rollbahn D, rather than swinging to the northwest or even north, was justified by what he knew on that fateful morning of the 17th, in retrospect it represented a significant lost opportunity. Dietrich's decision to shift the main axis of the attack on the evening of the 18th is debatable. On the one hand, one more hard push against the 2nd and 99th IDs in Krinkelt-Rocherath might have punched through. On the other, the tenacity of the American defense on the 18th could not have given him high confidence in this option. What is indisputable is that the disengagement and reengagement of the 12th SS Panzer Division took far longer than he calculated. By the time a coordinated attack could be made on the morning of the 21st, the 26th IR, backed by a corps' worth of artillery, was virtually impregnable. This raises the question, why not bypass the Büllingen-Butgenbach axis and swing around through Schoppen and Malmédy toward Spa? The simple answer may lie in the terrible condition of the roads. But one other suggests itself. Unlike the Wehrmacht armor units that made a high art of finding weak spots and exploiting them, the SS seems to have taken a sort of perverse pride in being able to conquer any obstacle it encountered. If there is any validity to this line of argument, the tendency proved fortunate for the V Corps.

On the American side, Gerow was fortunate in whom he had fighting for him. Despite Lauer's somewhat tentative leadership during the battle, his division fought credibly, especially for a unit thrust into such a fiery furnace for its first major engagement. It bent and even chipped in places, but it did not break.[97] The 2nd ID was simply magnificent. Led by an old pro, it responded like the veteran unit it was. And the 26th Infantry, which absorbed the brunt of the 12th SS Panzer Division's attention on December 20 and 21, likewise fought both heroically and intelligently. The integration of combined arms was one of the big secrets of V Corps' success. Infantry, armor, tank destroyer, artillery, and engineers were knit together into a cohesive whole.

But Gerow deserves credit as well. Like any good commander should, he established conditions that allowed his subordinates to succeed. His early transfer of two battalions of the 23rd Infantry from Robertson to Lauer gave the 99th ID commander the ability to back up his right and his center, which later proved key in slowing the German advance while the 2nd Division became established in Krinkelt-Rocherath. Perhaps Gerow's most significant contribution was persisting in his conversation with Hodges on the morning of the 17th for authority to withdraw the 2nd ID from its attack on Wahlerscheid. A twelve-hour delay would have been very costly; twenty-four hours could well have been disastrous. His decision to attach the 99th ID to the 2nd was unprecedented and controversial but clearly justified. Finally, by about the evening of the 17th he had developed an overall concept to fight the battle: keep the Germans at bay with a credible infantry shield and build up sufficient artillery on the Elsenborn Ridge to make the defense thereof almost guaranteed.[98] In sum, while the outcome on the Elsenborn Ridge was an important and impressive victory for the soldiers of V Corps, their commander must also receive a share of the credit.

7

VIII Corps Slows the Flood

We can't hold Bastogne if we keep falling back.[1]
Troy H. Middleton, 19 December 1944

TROY MIDDLETON'S VIII CORPS SECTOR WAS HUGE.[2] Its front extended some eighty-five miles, from the V/VIII Corps boundary slightly north of Losheim, along the eastern edge of the Schnee Eifel, then along the Our and Sauer Rivers on the eastern border of Luxembourg until it reached the First/Third Army boundary where the Moselle River crosses the Franco-German border, just past the southeast corner of Luxembourg. Defending the sixty miles of this front attacked by the Fifth Panzer and Seventh Armies would be impossible. Merely delaying these forces would demand consummate skill from Middleton and incredible bravery on the part of his soldiers. Neither of these ingredients was provided in full measure; but both were available in sufficient quantity to allow VIII Corps to accomplish its important mission.

THE INITIAL SITUATION

The terrain in Middleton's sector, like that of Gerow's to the north, generally favored the defense. Comprising roughly the southern three-quarters of the Ardennes, it was hilly, generally wooded, crossed by numerous rivers and streams, and with a sparely developed road network. The latter factor accentuated the significance of the villages and towns that occupied its major intersections. Six of these were of major importance: St. Vith and Baraque de Fraiture in the north; Houffalize, La Roche, and Marche in the center; and Bastogne in the south. In this phase of the campaign, two would occupy Middleton's principal attention: St. Vith and Bastogne, the latter being the locus of the VIII Corps headquarters. In addition to the Schnee Eifel, the major obstacles to east-west movement were the Our, Clerf, and Sauer Rivers, previously described; the Salm River, which flows north toward the Amblève, some ten miles west of St. Vith; and the Ourthe River, which originates southwest of Bastogne and flows north, then northwest until it reaches the Meuse at Liège. The latter was a particularly significant obstacle, whose importance Manteuffel pointedly appreciated.[3]

Middleton's extended front was occupied by three infantry divisions and a portion of one armored division. The northernmost unit was the 106th ID, commanded by Major General Alan W. Jones and augmented by the attached 14th Cavalry Group, commanded by Colonel Mark Devine. It occupied roughly twenty-one miles of front, stretching from the corps' northern boundary, south to the German village of Lützkampfen, just north of the junction of the Belgian, Luxembourgian, and German borders. Jones's headquarters was in St. Vith, which lay in the northern portion of the division sector, about twelve miles west of the Schnee Eifel. The 106th had relieved the 2nd ID and assumed responsibility for its sector on the evening of 11 December. It was, thus, the former of the two types of prototypical units in VIII Corps—the untested and the exhausted. Furthermore, after having completed the full Army Ground Forces series of training exercises and participating in Second Army maneuvers, it had been levied for overseas replacements, losing over 7,000 of its 13,000 officers and men in the four-month period from April to August of 1943. Although brought to full strength before overseas deployment, this personnel turbulence undoubtedly affected its internal cohesion.[4] To the south of the 106th was the 28th ID, commanded by Major General Norman D. "Dutch" Cota.[5] The 28th ID was in the second of the two categories mentioned above, having taken over 6,000 casualties in the bloody November fighting in the Hürtgen.[6] Although its ranks had been filled with an infusion of replacements, like the 106th, one would have to wonder how effectively these new men had been integrated into the organization. Unlike the 106th, however, it did have a cadre of combat-experienced officers and noncommissioned officers to provide firm direction in times of crisis. The 28th's sector was also wide, reaching some twenty-five miles from Lützkampfen in the north to a point opposite the German village of Wallendorf, where the Our flows into the Sauer. Cota's command post was in Wiltz, a small town on the river of the same name, generally in the southern portion of the division sector and roughly ten miles west of the division's frontline trace. To the south of the 28th was the newly arrived 9th AD, commanded by Major General John W. Leonard. Its narrow sector of four miles, from Wallendorf in the north to just past Dillingen in the south, was only occupied by the 60th Armored Infantry Battalion (AIB). The division's CCB had been ordered north to V Corps to support the 2nd ID's attack toward the Roer dams, and its CCR had been held back by Middleton in corps reserve. Middleton's southernmost unit was the 4th ID, commanded by Major General Raymond O. "Tubby" Barton. The 4th was one of the most experienced infantry divisions in the ETO, having come ashore on Utah Beach at D-Day and fought its way across France and Belgium, into the western portions of Germany. Like the 28th, it had suffered heavily in the Hürtgen, with over 7,000 battle and nonbattle casualties; but unlike the Keystone Division, it had not yet received its full complement of replacements and was still seriously short of infantrymen.[7] Barton's front of some thirty-five miles ran from Dillingen in the north to the First/Third Army boundary in the south. The 4th ID was also the most newly arrived unit in the VIII Corps area, having replaced the 83rd ID on 13 December. Middleton's meager reserve consisted of the aforementioned CCR, 9th AD, which he positioned in Trois Vierges, about nine miles east of Houffalize on the Bastogne–St. Vith road; four corps engineer battalions; and, with First Army release, an additional three battalions of army engineers operating in the corps area.[8]

Fortunately for Middleton, the Germans did not have the strength to attack his entire front. The combined zones of the Fifth Panzer and Seventh Armies extended from a line roughly contiguous with the American V/VIII Corps boundary in the north, south to a point on the Moselle due east of Luxembourg City and south of Trier. But General Erich Brandenberger's Seventh Army had only four divisions capable of attacking, which limited its offensive effort to the northern half of its area, whose southernmost point was just east of the Luxembourgian village of Dickweiler. This meant that Middleton had to defend only about sixty miles of his eighty-five-mile front. Furthermore, all Brandenberger's formations were foot-bound, consisting of one parachute division and three VGDs. Thus, the VIII Corps commander would be able to concentrate the bulk of his attention on the thirty-five miles of front being assaulted by the Fifth Panzer Army.

But this was still no easy task. For unlike Gerow, who had the tactically challenged Sepp Dietrich as his major opponent, Middleton was faced with one of the Wehrmacht's most savvy tacticians, Hasso von Manteuffel. The descendant of a Prussian family that traced its aristocratic origins to the thirteenth century and prided itself on military service, Manteuffel, an award-winning equestrian, was attracted to the panzer troops in the late 1930s.[9] With superb service on the Eastern Front, he soon became a Hitler favorite and was given command of the Fifth Panzer Army in September 1944 at the age of forty-seven. Manteuffel's plan was grounded in his extensive experience and personal reconnaissance of the assault area, sound in its overall considerations, and brilliant in its minor details. In late November, he went to the Eifel region disguised in the uniform of an infantry colonel.[10] There, he pointedly quizzed commanders on the habits of the American defenders.

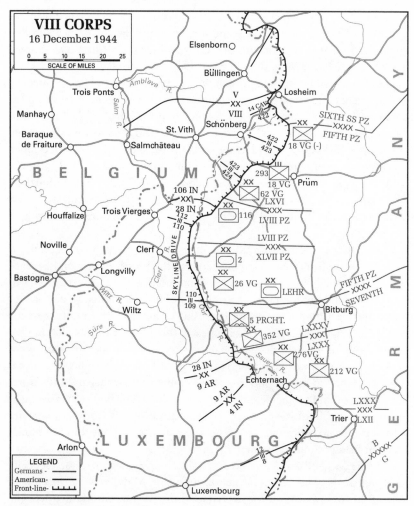

Map 4. VIII Corps, 16 December 1944

From these inquiries, he detected an interesting pattern: "Until midnight the enemy was vigilant and alert, and his reconnaissance patrols were lively until early in the morning. But from four or five o'clock their alertness and care decreased considerably. The activity of the artillery was until now limited to harassing fire and to occasional sudden concentrations. From all this we could draw the conclusion that the enemy felt pretty safe."[11]

Manteuffel also reasoned that it would be absurd to begin his offensive with the long artillery bombardment stipulated in the OKW plan.[12] Instead, it would be better to infiltrate heavily armed assault detachments into the American front lines and have them attack at about 0530 while a simultaneous artillery barrage was directed against targets further in the rear. It took some doing to convince Hitler to approve these deviations from the OKW concept; but with Model's support and some persuasive arguments on his part, he pulled it off. Two other features distinguished Manteuffel's concept from Dietrich's. First, in the sector of the 28th ID where he would attack with his two panzer corps, he would lead with his panzer divisions rather than with the VGDs. He reasoned that, despite the thinness of the American lines, the VGDs did not have the training, experience, or firepower to ensure the early breakthrough so vital to success of the whole enterprise. And second, instead of attacking with his two panzer corps in echelon as was done in Sixth SS Panzer Army, he would put them abreast. This disposition was based on the sound thinking that "if we knocked on 10 doors, we would find several open."[13]

Manteuffel's ideas for attacking in the north with infantry were even more ingenious.[14] He recognized that even if bypassed, the two regiments on the Schnee Eifel would be able to interfere with his supply lines and disrupt the momentum of the offensive. Therefore, they had to be eliminated quickly and decisively. The Schnee Eifel is a seven-mile-long plateau running parallel to the Our River, some four miles to its west. To its north is the Losheim Gap; to its south is a secondary road leading from Prüm, through the village of Bleialf, to the town of Schönberg on the Our. Roughly two miles northeast of Schönberg along the Our is the village of Andler. With the exception of a bridge at Steinbrück, further to the southwest, the bridges at these two villages control all communication between the Schnee Eifel and points west. Manteuffel quickly recognized that early capture of Schönberg and Andler would allow him to encircle whatever American forces were posted on the Schnee Eifel and open the door to St. Vith. Accordingly, he dictated a plan to the commander of the 18th VGD to envelop the Schnee Eifel from the north and south.

Manteuffel's overall disposition for the attack had three corps arrayed from north to south.[15] The LXVI Corps, commanded by General Walter Lucht, included two VGDs, the 18th and the 62nd. It was lined up against the 106th ID. The LVIII Panzer Corps, commanded by General Walter Krüger, comprised the 116th Panzer Division and the 560th VGD. Its attack zone was the northern third of the 28th ID's sector. The XLVII Panzer

Corps, commanded by General Heinrich von Lüttwitz, consisted of the 2nd Panzer Division, the Panzer Lehr Division, and the 26th VGD. It was to attack the center of the 28th ID's line. Manteuffel had personally requested from Rundstedt that Krüger and Lüttwitz, whom he considered "the most suitable Pz leaders in the western theater of war," be assigned as his principal armored lieutenants; he had somewhat less confidence in the sixty-two-year-old Lucht, whom he regarded as "rather old."[16]

Time was the most important ingredient of Manteuffel's plan.[17] In the south and the center, he anticipated seizing the major villages along the Skyline Drive by noon on the 16th. This would allow the panzer division commanders to commit their armor across the Our in the early afternoon of the 16th and arrive along the line Houffalize-Bastogne by the evening of the 17th. On the 18th, he envisioned the army's advance elements at Marche, with a continuation of the attack to and across the Meuse on the 20th. In the north, he expected the infantry corps to capture St. Vith on the 16th and advance to the Salm on the 17th. There, it would either continue the attack to the west or move to the south to protect against an American counterattack from that flank. This timetable was extremely ambitious, but it had to be. Manteuffel knew that if it took a week to ten days to get *to* the Meuse, it would be virtually impossible to get *across* the Meuse.

Brandenberger's plan for the attack of the Seventh Army was significantly constrained by the composition of his force.[18] With but four foot-mobile divisions, the best he could do was to instruct his northernmost corps, LXXXV, commanded by General Baptist Kniess, to advance to the west as far as possible to protect Manteuffel's southern flank. The two divisions of this corps would generally attack the southern third of the 28th ID. The center corps, LXXX, commanded by General Franz Beyer, would launch a holding attack against the slim sector of the 9th AD and the northern third of the 4th ID.

Given the relative strength ratios at the start gate, particularly in the center of the 28th ID, there would inevitably be both a break-in and a breakthrough. Middleton's chief tasks would be to buy as much time as he could; to limit the depth of the penetration to the extent possible; and, thereby, to set generally favorable conditions for future success.

SENSING THE BATTLEFIELD, 16–17 DECEMBER

If the German attack on the Schnee Eifel had been a football play with Manteuffel as the coach, one could say that it was run almost exactly as it had been diagrammed, though at slightly slower speed. To put this effort in context, we must examine the dispositions of the 106th ID, with its attached 14th Cavalry Group, and a bit of immediate background.[19] The cavalry unit was employed in a classic economy-of-force role, occupying the four-mile front between the V/VIII Corps boundary and the northern extremity of the Schnee Eifel. The promontory itself was occupied, from north to south, by two of the division's regiments, the 422nd Infantry, commanded by Colonel George L. Descheneaux, Jr., and the 423rd Infantry, commanded by Colonel Charles C. Cavender. The area south and somewhat west of the 423rd was defended by the 424th Infantry, commanded by Colonel Alexander D. Reid. General Jones, demonstrating prudent concern for an attack through the Losheim Gap, had positioned the 3rd Battalion, 423rd Infantry, as a division reserve, about four miles northwest of St. Vith in the village of Born. Before these dispositions were adopted, Middleton had authorized a withdrawal of the southern part of the 2nd ID's sector, now occupied by the 424th Infantry, from a more advanced position along the West Wall and had petitioned First Army for permission to withdraw from the Schnee Eifel as well. Hodges, anticipating a future attack in the direction of Bonn, was unwilling to surrender hard-earned ground and denied Middleton's request, a judgment with which the corps commander later concurred.[20] Middleton's concern for the Losheim Gap/Schnee Eifel sector was also indicated by his positioning of nine battalions of corps artillery in the area, one, the 275th, supporting the 14th Cavalry Group.

The German artillery preparation that opened at 0530 hours on 16 December attacked various targets.[21] Close to the V/VIII Corps boundary, it was focused on the scattered outposts of the 14th Cavalry Group, which was attacked by the 3rd Parachute Division, the southernmost element of Dietrich's Sixth SS Panzer Army. In the southern portion of the Losheim Gap, there was no artillery at all, as troops of the 18th VGD had found a mile-wide opening that Manteuffel wanted quickly exploited. In the remainder of the sector, the artillery concentrated on battalion and regimental command posts, adroitly located by 18th VGD patrols before the attack. Devine's command was put under heavy pressure, and by early evening the 14th Cavalry Group had been forced back some four miles. Meanwhile, a battalion of the 18th VGD, supported by assault guns, had captured Kobscheid and Auw, two villages northwest of the Schnee Eifel. Thus, by the end of the first day, Jones's left flank had been driven well back; except for a small cavalry force at the village of Andler, the northern route to Schönberg was open. Along the Schnee Eifel, the overall effect was just what Manteuffel wanted: a demonstration by the 18th VGD's replacement battalion was handily repulsed, but the American defenders rested on their laurels.[22] On the southern extremity of the ridge, more initiative was shown when Colonel Cavender organized a scratch reserve force and recaptured the key village of Bleialf after it had been seized by the southern prong of the 18th VGD's attack. The soldiers of the 424th acquitted themselves well; but the assault of the 62nd VGD forced them out of the town of Eigelscheid, thus opening the southeastern approach to St. Vith. The big picture that emerged for the 106th at the end of the day was that there was strong pressure on both flanks but the center was holding firm.

Here we must briefly consider the man whose decisions would significantly affect the fate of the Golden Lions of the 106th ID, Major General Alan W. Jones. He had the seemingly perfect career for a division commander. Commissioned from the University of Washington in 1917, Jones served at Fort Benning during Marshall's tenure as assistant commandant of the Infantry School; graduated from CGSS in 1936 and the War College in 1938; served on the Army G-3 staff in 1941; was promoted to brigadier general and made assistant division commander of the 90th ID in 1942; and was given command of the 106th in 1943.[23] But his baptism in battle would reveal two character flaws that gave lie to the résumé: he was unwilling to communicate bad news to his superiors, and he was paralyzingly indecisive. Truth to tell, however, he did not do all that badly on the 16th.[24] Early in the fight, he refused Colonel Cavender's request for commitment of the division reserve to retake Bleialf, judging that it was too early in the battle to play his one big chip; but after sending the reserve commander, Lieutenant Colonel Joseph P. Pruett, forward to reconnoiter and report back, he committed it that evening to help extricate two hard-pressed artillery battalions east of the Our.[25] Given his limited options, it was not a bad move.

But when Jones contemplated the events of the morrow, his inexperience began to show and his decision making began to deteriorate. Middleton was partially culpable as well, as two closely related issues surfaced. The first was what to do about the 422nd and 423rd, whose exposed position on the Schnee Eifel clearly put them in jeopardy. Early in the evening, Middleton called Jones to suggest that he withdraw the two exposed regiments. Jones demurred, expressing confidence that they could hold their positions. Close to midnight, the two commanders conferred again by phone. Middleton informed Jones that the 7th AD had been committed to VIII Corps and that its lead unit, CCB, should arrive on the 17th. Jones expressed concern about the 422nd and 423rd; Middleton told him to do as he saw fit, apparently feeling that Jones would probably withdraw them.[26] Here we enter an area of controversy, for part of Jones's subsequent decision to leave the regiments in place was based on the time on the 17th that Middleton told him to expect CCB, 7th AD, to arrive. According to the VIII Corps assistant G-2, Lieutenant Colonel W. M. Slayden, who had been detailed by Middleton to help Jones and his staff get acclimated to their first combat assignment, Jones related that the corps commander had told him the unit would begin arriving at 0700 the next morning.[27] Based on his knowledge of the 7th AD's position far to the north in the Ninth Army area, this struck Slayden as highly improbable; but he was reluctant to question Middleton's authority.

The second issue was what Jones should do with CCB, 9th AD, which Hodges, at Middleton's entreaty, had released to VIII Corps late in the morning and Middleton had subsequently assigned to Jones.[28] The commander of this formation, Brigadier General William H. Hoge, reported to Jones for instructions early in the evening. The division commander considered two possibilities: to protect the southeast approach to St. Vith along the Eigelscheid-Winterspelt-Steinbrück axis; or to commit it to the center of the sector at Schönberg, which would not only blunt the converging wings of the 18th VGD attack but also hold open the door for a possible withdrawal of the two regiments on the Schnee Eifel.[29] It was a tough call: guard the most dangerous approach to St. Vith or backstop the most threatened two-thirds of his command. Early the morning of the 17th, Jones ordered Hoge to attack toward Winterspelt.[30] Jones's defenders have argued that given what he knew at the time, this decision made eminent sense—an argument that has a good deal of merit. But in the clear light of hindsight, Jones's decision can be critiqued at two levels. First, if the decision was contingent upon the early arrival of the 7th AD, Jones should have asked Middleton some pointed questions about his level of confidence in the projected arrival time. Second, to hedge against the possibility of an uncertain assumption, he could have explored with Hoge the advisability of dividing his command into two groups, one covering each axis. But Alan Jones simply did not have the confidence, the tactical reasoning skills, or the imagination to challenge his corps commander, to question his own assumptions, or to develop unorthodox solutions.

But, again, Middleton muddied the water. Shortly before 2100 on the 16th, he issued a directive with two stipulations.[31] The first was general in nature: "Troops will be withdrawn from present positions only repeat only if positions become completely untenable." Middleton's wording here was undoubtedly intended to convey that he wanted the corps to conduct a grudging defense, rather than a delay; but it put a good deal of onus on subordinate commanders to define what was meant by the phrase, "completely untenable." In the inexperienced mind of Alan Jones, this was asking a lot;

it also created a disincentive for him to order the withdrawal of the 422nd and 423rd, notwithstanding Middleton's earlier suggestion that he do so. The second part of the order was to hold "at all costs" a line along the high ground just west of the Our. This stipulation would allow Jones to withdraw his two exposed regiments, but he still had to comply with the first provision of Middleton's order. The events of the 17th were to prove that the corps commander's intention to hold well forward in the corps sector did not yet appreciate the full magnitude of the German offensive.

As happened in the V Corps sector, the 106th's situation deteriorated rapidly on the 17th.[32] The two keys to Schönberg, Andler and Bleialf, were held respectively by a single troop of cavalry and Colonel Cavender's ad hoc reserve. The former succumbed to an accident of war—a battalion of Tiger tanks from Dietrich's Sixth Panzer Army wandered south of the interarmy boundary and came through Andler looking for a good route to the west. With Andler overrun, the northern, and stronger, wing of the 18th VGD reached Schönberg and the vital bridge over the Our at 0845. The southern wing of the 18th VGD recaptured Bleialf early in the morning. Although it did not reach Schönberg until dusk, the capture of the bridge by the northern blade of the scissors had barred the door even if it had not completed the encirclement. In the meantime, a confused welter of units, most of them corps and divisional artillery, streamed to the rear. But two divisional artillery battalions, elements of three corps artillery battalions, assorted support units, and two infantry regiments—altogether some 8,000 to 9,000 men—were trapped east of the Our. In mid-morning, Jones instructed the two infantry regiments as follows: "Expect to clear out area west of you this afternoon with reinforcements. Withdraw from present positions if they become untenable. Save all transportation possible."[33] This order indicated that Jones was unaware that the exposed regiments' positions had become not only untenable but indeed dire, and its effect was vitiated by its not being transmitted from division headquarters until early afternoon.[34] Thus, the two regimental commanders, who had limited contact with each other and even more limited contact with their commanding general, remained largely passive during the day as the noose around their necks was gradually but inexorably tightened by the 18th VGD.

The first tangible indicator of the 7th AD arrived at Jones's headquarters at roughly 1030 in the person of Brigadier General Bruce C. Clarke, commander of the division's CCB.[35] Clarke had earlier reported to Middleton; been dispatched north to help Jones; and advised his division commander, Brigadier General Robert W. Hasbrouck, to assemble the division at Vielsalm, from whence it could support the 106th. In their conversation, Hasbrouck informed Clarke that delays in receiving route clearances from First Army had postponed the departure of CCB's lead elements until 0500.[36] Thus, when Jones told Clarke to attack east as soon as possible to assist his beleaguered regiments on the Schnee Eifel, the latter was painfully embarrassed to admit that it would be some time before he would have any troops with which to execute the order. As the afternoon wore on, Jones, whose anxiety for his two forward regiments was made even more acute by the fact that his only son, Lieutenant Alan W. Jones, Jr., was assigned to the 423rd Infantry, became increasingly agitated, and his mood began to swing precipitously.[37] At one point, he ruefully observed to Clarke that he had "lost a division quicker than any other division commander in the U.S. Army." Shortly thereafter, he cheerfully told Middleton, "Don't worry about us, General. We'll be in good shape. Clarke's troops will be here soon."[38] Meanwhile, the fate of St. Vith hung on the outcome of a race between the 62nd VGD forces attacking west out of Schönberg and CCB, 7th AD, moving south to Vielsalm, then east to St. Vith. The former were impeded by a last-ditch division reserve built around the engineer battalion; the latter was significantly hampered by the flotsam and jetsam of artillery and service units withdrawing to the west of St. Vith, some under orders to do so, others in headlong retreat that bordered on panic.[39] In the event, Clarke's troops arrived just in time to stiffen Jones's engineers. As they did, Jones handed over the defense of St. Vith to Clarke.

That night, as units of CCB dribbled into St. Vith, Manteuffel, who had expected to seize the town on the 16th, moved up to Schönberg to exhort the 62nd VGD commander to press the attack with greater vigor on the morrow. En route, he dismounted to avoid a traffic jam and encountered Model, who was conducting his own reconnaissance in the congested area. After the two exchanged pleasantries, Model inquired, "And how is your situation, Baron?"[40] "Mostly good," Manteuffel replied. "So? I got the impression you were lagging in the St. Vith sector," rejoined the army group commander. "Yes, but we'll take it tomorrow," said Manteuffel. "I expect you to. And so that you'll take it quicker, tomorrow I'm letting you use the Führer Escort Brigade," Model pointedly responded. The two senior commanders, whose instincts had led them both to the same point on an immense battlefield, then drifted off on their separate ways.[41]

By the evening of the 17th, Middleton had an even more serious problem: in the sector of the 28th ID, Manteuffel's two panzer corps had achieved a clean breakthrough and were headed to the west. Cota's division was arrayed from north to south, with the 112th Infantry defending a five-mile front from the boundary with the 106th at Lützkampfen to just north of

Kalborn, the 110th Infantry defending a ten-mile front from Kalborn to Stelzembourg, and the 109th Infantry defending an additional nine miles from Stelzembourg to the boundary with the 9th AD opposite Wallendorf.[42] The commanders of these formations were Colonel Gustin M. Nelson, Colonel Hurley E. Fuller, and Lieutenant Colonel James E. Rudder, respectively. Cota held the 2nd Battalion of the 110th in division reserve at Donnange, roughly five miles west of the Skyline Drive and generally in the center of the 110th's sector. This meant that Fuller would have to man his extended front with only two battalions. Cota was something of an enigma. His first twenty-seven years of service had been superb.[43] Commissioned from West Point in 1917 with Ridgway and Collins, he graduated from CGSS in 1931 and the War College in 1936. As assistant division commander of the 29th ID, he won a DSC for his actions on Omaha Beach. Thus, he seemed a natural to take over the 28th ID in August 1944. But Cota's leadership in the battles of the Hürtgen was no more inspired than Gerow's.[44] Although the fighting conditions there were deplorable, one had to suspect at this juncture that Cota might have been promoted one level too far. He would soon have the opportunity to demonstrate whether he had deserved his elevation to division command. Over the next six days, his thinly stretched lines along the Our would be assaulted by three panzer divisions and four VGDs, constituting arguably the most severe test to which any American division in the ETO was subjected during the entire course of the war.

Colonel Nelson's 112th Infantry was well dug in and, for the most part, vigilant on the morning of the 16th.[45] Panzergrenadiers of the 116th Panzer Division infiltrated the 1st Battalion's lines near Lützkampfen; but as they moved further to the west, they were brought under effective fire and all but eliminated. When reinforced by the division's panzers, the Germans did little better. Over fourteen tanks were knocked out by tank destroyers supporting the 424th Infantry to the north; several more fell victim to mines. Farther south at Ouren, Nelson's men acquitted themselves equally well. There, the soldiers of the 560th VGD stormed across a bridge only to be mowed down by well-directed small arms fire from the 3rd Battalion. By nightfall, General Krüger had to live with the unhappy reality that his corps attack had been repulsed by a single regiment.

Having been relieved as a regimental commander in the 2nd ID, Colonel Hurley J. Fuller was in some ways an improbable personage to be placed at the epicenter of the Keystone Division's trial by fire. His story was closely bound up with Middleton.[46] As a junior officer in the Argonne, he had tasted heavy fighting early in life, but he had a difficult personality and a sharp, unbridled tongue. These qualities may have contributed to General Robertson's decision to relieve him during the Normandy campaign. Fuller then appealed to Middleton, with whom he had had previous association, for a second chance. Middleton vouched for Fuller's fighting qualities to Bradley, and Bradley offered him up to Cota when the 112th was in need of a regimental commander in late November. Fuller established his headquarters at the Hotel Claravallis in the picturesque town of Clerf.[47] The town is situated at a sharp bend of the river bearing the same name, with precipitous drops on both sides, especially from the east. The bridge over the Clerf River at this point had great tactical significance, for when one comes out of the town to the west, there is open country and a hard-surfaced road leading to the N-12 highway that connects St. Vith and Bastogne. Between Clerf and Bastogne are only a few scattered crossroads that offer any defensive capability at all. With a ten-mile front and but two battalions to man them, Fuller had no choice but to place platoon and company-sized outposts along the Skyline Drive, send reconnaissance patrols to the Our, and run contact patrols between his outposts. The three main points of defense were Heinerscheid and Marnach in the 1st Battalion sector and Hosingen in the 3rd Battalion area. Marnach was of particular importance, for it lay along the east-west route from Dasburg, on the east bank of the Our and at the primary crossing point for the 2nd Panzer Division, to Clerf. But Hosingen, too, was a major concern, for although the road connecting it to Bastogne was significantly poorer than the road through Clerf, it was also more direct.

On the morning of the 16th, all hell broke loose in Fuller's sector.[48] Artillery was accurately directed against positions on the Skyline Drive and in Clerf. Panzergrenadiers from the 2nd Panzer Division and infantrymen from the 26th VGD infiltrated in strong groups up and down the Skyline Drive. Company B at Marnach was particularly hard pressed. The 1st Battalion commander, Lieutenant Colonel Donald Paul, attempted to help it by sending a strong contingent south from Heinerscheid; but the detachment ran into trouble and was forced back to its original position. About mid-morning, Fuller petitioned Cota for commitment of the 2nd Battalion; Cota refused, telling Fuller it was too early in the battle. But Cota did release to Fuller two companies of the attached 707th Tank Battalion. Fuller divided this force into penny packets, sending two platoons to Marnach via a northeasterly approach from Münshausen, keeping one platoon in reserve at Clerf, and directing others to various artillery units under attack along the western slope of the Skyline Drive. Confusion abounded in the force dispatched to Marnach, but the gallant defenders held on against desperate odds. The Germans had reached the Skyline Drive, but they had failed to secure a single major crossroads along it. Furthermore, the installation of bridges at Dasburg and Gemund, the latter being the crossing site for Panzer Lehr, had taken longer than expected. Lüttwitz was clearly behind schedule; but the weight of force available for the morrow boded ill for the soldiers of the 110th Infantry, despite the fact that at around 2100 Cota had released all but one company of the 2nd Battalion to Fuller for an early-morning counterattack toward Marnach.

Like the 110th Infantry, the 109th had a new regimental commander. He was junior to Fuller but a certified American hero, Lieutenant Colonel James E. Rudder, who had won a DSC on D-Day when his intrepid 2nd Ranger Battalion assaulted the 100-foot cliffs at Pointe du Hoc.[49] Rudder's handling of the 109th on 16 December was both cool and professional.[50] The recent arrival of the 9th AD in the VIII Corps area shortened his front and allowed him to constitute his 1st Battalion as a regimental reserve; he was also fortunate to have a company of the 707th Tank Battalion and a company of tank destroyers. Despite the width of his front, he was additionally aided by the steep banks of the Our in his sector. Each of his frontline battalions was opposed by a full division: the 2nd Battalion in the north faced the 5th Parachute Division, and the 3rd Battalion in the south was opposed by the 352nd VGD. The German paratroopers made good progress, threatening the 2nd Battalion's headquarters at Brandenburg; but Rudder committed one infantry company from the reserve to help it out. The volksgrenadiers in the south presented a thornier problem because when they attacked into a wide gap south of Company E's position in Führen, they threatened the main supply route of the 3rd Battalion, positioned in the corner formed by the Our River and the Sûre River, which flows into the Our from the west. Into this gap Rudder committed the two additional companies of his infantry reserve, supported by a platoon of tanks. Although Company E remained isolated at Führen, Rudder considered the situation well in hand and was confident that he could handle things on the next day.

Cota also handled himself well. Although his initial dispositions were faulty—he accepted far too much risk in the center of his sector and the initial reports flowing to VIII Corps were overly optimistic—he maintained his composure throughout the day and did not commit his reserve until he was sure that the situation in Fuller's sector justified it.[51] Like Middleton, he sensed the vital importance of holding on to the line immediately west of the Our and frequently adjured his subordinates to do so. Unlike Jones, Cota was not burdened with a position like the Schnee Eifel that became untenable as soon as the Germans attacked. Furthermore, for the critical center of Cota's sector there was little defensible terrain to which to withdraw. It would be possible for the 112th to fold back to the northwest and for the

109th to conduct a similar withdrawal to the southwest. But for most of the hard-pressed soldiers of the 110th, there was simply no place to hide.

Early on the morning of the 17th, Colonel Nelson's soldiers heard the ominous sounds of Mark V Panthers assembling in Lützkampfen in preparation for a renewed assault on Ouren.[52] The 112th put up a spirited defense, aided by a platoon of tank destroyers from CCR, 9th AD, that Middleton had released to Cota and Cota to Nelson, as well as by several flights of tactical aircraft that braved the marginal weather to support VIII Corps. But the weight of the attack was too great to endure, and in mid-afternoon Nelson sent his second in command to Wiltz to render a personal report on the situation to Cota and to petition for permission to withdraw the 1st and 3rd Battalions, which were positioned east of the Our. Cota had already obtained such authorization from Middleton, with two provisos: that the bridges over the Our be destroyed and that positions west of the river be such as to deny the Germans the ability to cross. In the event, the 116th Panzer Division captured Ouren before the bridges could be destroyed, and Nelson lost a portion of his regimental headquarters before it could be withdrawn from that village. But with a little bit of luck and some quick thinking, the two battalions were extricated, and Nelson was able to establish a new defensive line on the high ground about a mile-and-a-half west of the Our.[53] In the meantime, the 116th Panzer Division had discovered that the crossing sites at Ouren were unsuitable for tanks. Therefore Krüger ordered the unit to proceed south to Dasburg to follow in the wake of the 2nd Panzer Division and then move north back to its original route.[54] The shift of the 116th to the south would take time, and time was every major commander's most precious commodity.

In the center, the soldiers of Colonel Fuller's regiment had a much tougher day.[55] Along the Skyline Drive from Heinerscheid to Hosingen, men of the 110th Infantry would be attacked not only by the 2nd Panzer Division and 26th VGD that had been committed against them on the previous day, they would also face advance elements of the 116th Panzer Division and Panzer Lehr, proving just how important this piece of real estate had become. During the night of the 16th, Fuller ordered Lieutenant Colonel James R. Hughes, his 2nd Battalion commander, to counterattack to Marnach. Maneuvering to the north of Clerf through the small village of Reuler, Hughes ran into a tank-infantry force from the 2nd Panzer Division. The Americans forced the Germans to give some ground, but they were heavily outnumbered and getting to Marnach was clearly beyond the realm of possibility. To complicate Fuller's problems, Colonel Meinard von Lauchert, commanding the 2nd Panzer Division, had dispatched troops to the north where they discovered another route into Clerf.[56] This force outflanked Hughes's 2nd Battalion and made it into the northern reaches of Clerf, near Fuller's headquarters. Early the next morning, perilously low on ammunition and bereft of all outside support, the defenders of Hosingen surrendered. At the other end of the regimental sector, Heinerscheid was overrun sometime after noon by the reconnaissance battalion of the 116th Panzer Division.

Meanwhile in Clerf, Fuller was given a welcome infusion of strength. Middleton had attached a task force of CCR, 9th AD, to the 28th ID. Cota, however, was not to employ it without Middleton's permission. Notwithstanding this injunction, by midday Cota felt that the situation of the 110th was so dire that he exceeded his authority and dispatched a company of tanks to Fuller. Fuller ordered one platoon to Heinerscheid, one to Colonel Hughes, and one into the melee in the eastern edges of Clerf itself. The first arrived just as Company A was putting up its last resistance and meeting its demise soon thereafter; the second was all but wiped out by Lauchert's relentlessly advancing panzers; the third withdrew without authority after losing two tanks. By late afternoon, Fuller had thrown in everything he had to the defense of Clerf. His 1st Battalion had virtually ceased to exist, his 2nd Battalion was cut off by the twin prongs of Lauchert's advance toward the town, and only remnants of his 3rd Battalion would live to fight another day. Shortly after dark, one of the Mark Vs roaming through Clerf began pouring shots into the Hotel Claravallis. Fuller barely managed to escape but was captured shortly thereafter. For all practical purposes, the 110th Infantry Regiment had ceased to exist as an effective fighting force. Lüttwitz's corps had blown open a ten-mile-wide hole in the center of Middleton's lines, but Fuller's valiant soldiers had bought the VIII Corps commander twenty-four to thirty-six precious hours.[57]

Further south, the situation was not nearly as bad.[58] Colonel Rudder attempted to relieve his Company E, isolated at Führen the day before, but the position was overrun by soldiers of the 352nd VGD. Additional pressure threatened to cut off his 3rd Battalion, but the unit held on despite a large number of infiltrators in its rear. In the 9th AD sector, the 60th AIB, now placed under the command of CCA, received a strong attack from soldiers of the 276th VGD, many of whom had filtered into its lines the night before. By the end of the day, they were behind all the battalion's frontline companies; but the CCA commander, Colonel Thomas L. Harrold, had a sizeable force in hand with which to attempt a relief on the 18th. In the 4th ID sector, the 12th Infantry held its own. Middleton, who was fully aware of the imperative to hold the shoulders of the penetration and concerned about the German drive toward Luxembourg City where Bradley's 12th Army Group was headquartered, had decided that with 10th AD moving into the VIII Corps area from the south, he would commit its lead element, CCA, in Barton's sector on the morrow. Given how tense things were to become in the center of his sector, this represented a very fine judgment on his part.

On the evening of the 17th, Middleton's biggest problem was clearly in a quadrilateral drawn from Bastogne to Noville, a village five miles north along the road to Houffalize; to Clerf; to Hosingen; then back to Bastogne. Within this area, he would have to fight a significant delaying action with precious few assets. At 1535, he issued verbal instructions to General Leonard for CCR, 9th AD, to move the bulk of the command from Trois Vierges to Oberwampach.[59] This positioned his reserve five miles east of Bastogne. At 1950 a message came in from the 28th ID G-3 to the effect that Fuller's headquarters had been overrun by tanks; about the same time, Cota personally rendered a similar report to Middleton.[60] Two hours later, Middleton ordered CCR, 9th AD, now under corps control, to establish two strong roadblocks along the N-12 highway leading into Bastogne from the northeast "without delay."[61] With the exception of a few engineers still at his disposal, he had played all his chips. Over the next two days, the race for Bastogne would play out. But shortly after dark, as Lauchert's tanks were probing their way across the Clerf, it is important to remember that SHAEF had still not released the 82nd and 101st Airborne Divisions to Bradley. Thus, when Middleton committed CCR, 9th AD, to block the northeastern approach to Bastogne, he had nothing left with which to defend the vital hub itself. And with Panzer Lehr also breaking through at Hosingen, a betting man would have been wise to wager that Lüttwitz would win the race.

TRADING LIVES FOR TIME, 18–19 DECEMBER

The doctrinal description of a delay is trading space for time. Over the next two days, Middleton would do so. But more importantly, he would be trading *lives* for time. In a sense, he had been doing this already. But with the Germans pressing hard upon St. Vith and the door to Bastogne flung wide open, the consciousness and poignancy of the tradeoff became much more acute. Middleton was making value judgments that some men's lives would have to be expended so other men's lives could be spared. And these value judgments were bound up in a geometric calculus: in the north, retention of St. Vith would both stymie the attack of Manteuffel's northern wing and constrict the maneuver room available on Dietrich's southern flank; in the center, Bastogne's defense would slow the impetus of Manteuffel's

southern attack; and in the south, retention of the shoulder would both protect Bradley's headquarters and limit the ability of the offensive as a whole to
expand its base. All three were important, but it remained to be seen on the
morning of the 18th which could actually be accomplished. We shall again
survey the VIII Corps battle from north to south, but two observations are
in order. First, with Houffalize undefended and the 116th and 2nd Panzer
Divisions moving ever west, Middleton experienced increasing difficulty in
exercising control over the events in St. Vith; second, once CCA of the 10th
AD was committed to the battle in the south, the situation in that sector became sufficiently stabilized that he could leave the bulk of the fighting there
to Generals Leonard and Barton. But in the center, things were desperate,
and in attempting to keep the XLVII Panzer Corps at bay along the tenuously held approaches to Bastogne, Middleton's command mettle would be
sorely tested.

During the night of 17/18 December, Middleton grasped that he was dealing with a full-blown counteroffensive and further divined that the main effort of this offensive was in the north along the V/VIII Corps boundary.[62] In
that area, he was given some breathing room by Lucht's inability to mount
a major offensive against St. Vith and by the initiative of Hasbrouck, who
struggled mightily to organize a coherent defense of the town and its envi-
rons, despite the lack of unifying command authority. For reasons not entirely clear, Middleton did not appoint a single commander for the St. Vith
sector, trusting instead to Hasbrouck's and Jones's ability to work things out
on the ground. By causing Jones and Hasbrouck to cooperate and coordinate, rather than allowing one of them to *decide*, Middleton jeopardized the
defense of St. Vith. Admittedly, he had a tricky problem. Hasbrouck, though
only recently appointed as division commander, had the preponderance of
combat power and was clearly the more competent of the two; but Jones
was the senior in rank.[63] The correct decision would have been to ignore the
canons of military protocol and give the sole responsibility to Hasbrouck by
attaching the 106th ID to the 7th AD, as Gerow attached the 99th ID to the
2nd ID. But Middleton did not make the call.

Nevertheless, Hasbrouck and Jones, along with Clarke and Hoge, managed to work things out relatively well.[64] Hasbrouck emerged as the principal architect of the defense of the entire St. Vith sector, particularly to the
north and south, while Clarke was the dominant personality in the town
itself; Hoge carried a big stick on the southeastern portion of the perimeter.
The various defenders of St. Vith were given something of a respite on the
third day of the offensive. The 18th VGD, having been checked to the east
of St. Vith by Clarke's hastily arranged defenses the night before, probed

the northeastern approaches to the town; but this effort was beaten back by tanks and antiaircraft artillery hurriedly appropriated from Hoge's command. Meanwhile, the FEB, promised to Manteuffel by Model the night before, was well to the rear and not formally released to Lucht until late on the 18th.[65] The 62nd VGD gained a tenuous foothold across the Our, but it made little headway against the 424th Infantry and CCB, 9th AD. Nevertheless, Hoge convinced Jones to allow him to give ground to the northwest in order to tie in with Clarke on his left. This movement began the formation of a horseshoe defense arrayed from the northeast to the southeast quadrants of St. Vith. Hasbrouck, concerned with the northern approaches to the town and anxious to secure its lifeline to the west, which ran through the intersection at Poteau to his division headquarters at Vielsalm, ordered his CCA to secure Poteau, while CCR protected the division's left flank north of Vielsalm. CCA secured the majority of Poteau by late in the day, though a few Germans remained in the village's northern edge. To the south, Hasbrouck dispatched small forces that could at most give early warning of approaching enemy formations. Thus, by the evening of the 17th, a patchwork defense of St. Vith was beginning to fall into place. But the German pressure had been sufficient to cancel a hoped-for attack east from the town to secure the Schönberg bridge and rescue the two trapped regiments on the Schnee Eifel. Efforts to provide the surrounded soldiers with aerial-delivered supplies proved futile, and Jones's final instructions to them were so divorced from reality as to be truly tragic.[66]

In the center of the corps sector, Colonel Joseph H. Gilbreth's CCR, 9th AD, was disposed along the N-12 highway from the road junction leading to Clerf, southwest to Mageret, some three miles northeast of Bastogne.[67] From front to rear, he positioned TF Rose, consisting of a company of tanks, a company of armored infantry, and a platoon of engineers to defend the road junction itself; TF Harper (named for Lieutenant Colonel Ralph S. Harper), similarly constituted, about three miles to the southwest at an intersection just outside the village of Allerborn; and Team Booth, an assortment of infantry, tank destroyers, and light tanks, north of Allerborn to protect TF Harper's left flank. Gilbreth's headquarters was in Longvilly, about a mile-and-a-half southwest of Allerborn, with an artillery battalion in Mageret. Given what little he had to work with and the fact that the Germans would be largely road-bound, these arrangements made a good deal of sense.

But they broke down badly in execution, partially caused by Middleton's conscious decision to sacrifice TF Rose, partially caused by the disintegration of TF Harper, partially caused by Gilbreth's indecision at a critical moment, and partially caused by the plain fact that two panzer divisions and a VGD were converging on Bastogne.[68] At about first light, the 2nd Panzer Division's reconnaissance battalion began probing Captain Rose's positions. Well supported by artillery, Rose gamely held his ground; but as the day wore on, the Germans built up their strength, eventually bringing up their Panthers and all but encircling Rose's small contingent. At 1405, Gilbreth put in a call to VIII Corps headquarters requesting authority either to withdraw the task force or to reinforce it.[69] Middleton, desperate for time and unwilling to jeopardize the delay potential of the units closer to Bastogne, refused both entreaties. At 1430 Gilbreth reported that TF Rose was completely cut off, and at 1525 his executive officer notified the corps headquarters that the task force had been overrun roughly an hour earlier.[70]

Middleton had two very specific reasons for needing more time. Most immediately, he was awaiting the arrival of CCB, 10th AD, en route from Luxembourg City. Its commander, Colonel William Roberts, arrived in Bastogne at 1600. Of even greater significance, Middleton had been alerted early on the morning of the 18th that both the 82nd and 101st Airborne Divisions were coming to his corps.[71] Hodges's subsequent decision to employ the 82nd in the north against Kampfgruppe Peiper meant that Middleton would only get the 101st. Still, he reasoned, with one more armored combat command arriving the evening of the 18th and at least one division coming in sometime on the 19th, Bastogne just *might* be held—and if it might be held, every hour, nay, every minute needed to get Roberts's combat command and the airborne troopers into position was worth the blood taken to buy it. Nevertheless, Bradley insisted that Middleton displace the VIII Corps headquarters to the rear, and Middleton dutifully dispatched a party to Neufchâteau to make the necessary arrangements.

As all this was going on, CCR, 9th AD, was being roughly handled. For some inexplicable reason, given the fact that they had clearly heard the battle noise associated with TF Rose's battle to the northeast, Harper's troops were taken unawares. In the ensuing fight, the Americans took heavy casualties, the task force commander was killed, and the survivors retreated in noticeable disorder to Longvilly. Colonel Gilbreth's effort to stem the flow was only partially successful, and large groups of stragglers continued down the road to Mageret. There, however, they found no respite, for the advance guard of Panzer Lehr captured this village just three miles northeast of Bastogne at about 1900. Gilbreth then attempted to effect a breakout with his command post, some security units, and stragglers from TF Harper. But after one contingent of his headquarters made it out at about midnight, he postponed the departure of the rest of his group until the following morning when he hoped to have the effort better organized.

Given this unfolding debacle, Middleton's instructions to Roberts, now operating directly under corps control, were crystal clear: "CCB [10th AD] will move without delay in three teams to the following positions to counter enemy threats. One team to the southeast to Wardin; one team to the vicinity of Longvilly; and one team to the vicinity of Noville. Move with the utmost speed. Hold these positions at all costs."[72] In compliance with these instructions, Roberts constituted three task forces, each commanded by a field grade officer. TF O'Hara, named for Lieutenant Colonel James O'Hara, was dispatched to Wardin; TF Cherry, named for Lieutenant Colonel Henry T. Cherry, was sent to Longvilly; and TF Desobry, named for Major William R. Desobry, was ordered to Noville. The latter two were en route to their positions by 1845, while the former began moving shortly thereafter.[73] Each task force contained a mixture of medium tanks, infantry, and engineers, with TF Desobry being marginally the strongest, having two infantry companies, rather than the one assigned to the other two task forces.[74]

Fortunately for Middleton, Lauchert's route took him west, rather than southwest, and the 2nd Panzer Division did not pursue its drive down the N-12 highway from Longvilly to Bastogne. He got a similar break when the very experienced panzer leader and commander of Panzer Lehr, General Fritz Bayerlein, reached Niederwampach, six miles due east of Bastogne, and decided to attack Bastogne via Mageret, rather than cutting southwest through Wardin to the well-surfaced road that led into Bastogne south of the Wiltz River.[75] As he discovered to his dismay during the night of 18/19 December, the route to Mageret deteriorated into little more than a pasture trail, significantly slowing his advance.

There was also relatively positive news in the south.[76] Though the 109th Infantry's headquarters was forced to fall back to the village of Diekirch, the majority of the regiment was still well in hand. CCA, 9th AD's counter-attack to restore the positions of the 60th AIB ran into staunch resistance from the 276th VGD and was forced to withdraw, but roughly half of the isolated infantrymen were able to break out to friendly lines over the next several days. The attack of CCA, 10th AD, in the 12th Infantry's sector jumped off at 0800; less than two hours later, a report from a staff officer at 4th ID came into the corps headquarters with the cheerful comment, "Our positions are in good shape."[77] This observation turned out to be slightly premature, for during the day two battalions of the 212th VGD mounted an attack through a gap in the 12th Infantry's line that threatened to unravel much of the regiment's position. But the Germans lacked the force to exploit this opportunity; and while the counterattack of CCA did not make substantial progress, its infusion of strength stabilized the situation for the time being and forced Brandenberger to release his slim Seventh Army reserve.

Thus, at the end of the long and trying day of the 18th, Middleton was faced with two major questions for the next: how would the defenders of St. Vith fare against the steadily mounting German pressure, and would CCB, 10th AD, be able to hold off Lüttwitz's XLVII Panzer Corps long enough for the 101st Airborne to get into the fight for Bastogne?

The answer to the first question was better than expected.[78] The Germans wanted St. Vith very badly, at this point even more than they wanted Bastogne. Its continued retention by the Americans was constricting the maneuver room of Dietrich's Sixth SS Panzer Army and preventing Manteuffel from aiding the advance of the German Schwerpunkt. Accordingly, Model, Manteuffel, and Lucht gathered for another conference at the 18th VGD headquarters, two miles northeast of St. Vith. Lucht was ordered to envelop the town to the north and south on the 20th. These instructions looked good on paper, but the LXVI Corps commander was facing the tyranny of the congested Ardennes road network, regular encroachments into his area by Dietrich's units, and the hampering effects of destruction of the bridge at Steinbrück by Hoge's engineers. Accordingly, the best he could do was arrest a few offending parties from the north, move his infantry and artillery forward incrementally, emplace a tactical bridge at Steinbrück, and plan for a (hopefully) coordinated attack the following day. Nevertheless, Hasbrouck and Jones still had their problems. The 9th SS Panzer Division, following hard on the heels of the 1st, mounted a sharp attack on Poteau. CCA held this effort at bay but was virtually a prisoner in its own position. The 7th AD trains, which Hasbrouck had prudently moved west of Vielsalm to La Roche, were beginning to be harassed by elements of the 116th Panzer Division.

But predictably and catastrophically, the 422nd and 423rd, cut off from all outside support and surrounded by a ring of German steel, finally capitulated, thus allowing Lucht to focus solely on his challenge at St. Vith. Soon thereafter, a German lieutenant in the area captured the scene: "Endless columns of prisoners pass; at first about a hundred; half of them negroes [presumably from the corps artillery units], later another thousand. Our car gets stuck on the road. I get out and walk. Generalfeldmarschall Model himself directs traffic. (He's a little undistinguished looking man with a monocle.) Now the thing is going. The roads are littered with destroyed American vehicles, cars and tanks. Another column of prisoners passes. I count over a thousand men."[79]

Meanwhile, Middleton was becoming progressively less able to influence events at St. Vith as his communications with Hasbrouck and Jones became ever more tenuous. A report Hasbrouck dispatched by messenger that reached the VIII Corps headquarters at 1800 on the 19th read as follows: "7th AD still holds positions shown on overlay. No friendly troops known to be on our north. CCB, 9th AD, 424th Inf and 112th Inf on our south. Am protecting my flanks as far west as L'Ourthe River as best I can with miscellaneous units. Request you establish communication with me."[80] Hasbrouck's request was eminently reasonable, as army doctrine stipulated it was the responsibility of the higher headquarters to maintain communication with subordinate echelons. But with the direct road from Bastogne to St. Vith occupied in force and the more westerly route through Houffalize also cut, there was little Middleton could do but dispatch a return message to Hasbrouck saying, "You are doing a grand job. Hold your positions and we will do the same."[81] Shortly thereafter, he provided as much material support as he could by assigning the 356th FA Group to support the 7th AD.[82] The position at St. Vith was also strengthened by the arrival of Colonel Nelson's 112th Infantry, with its supporting artillery battalion, south of the town. The regiment was promptly attached by Jones to the 106th ID with Middleton's and Cota's concurrence.[83] In sum, the situation at St. Vith on the evening of the 19th was becoming precarious—the flanks were in increasing danger, it was being progressively cut off from VIII Corps control, and it was about to receive a significant attack on the 20th.

In Wiltz, Cota's headquarters had been hit a glancing blow by Panzer Lehr and had received a more substantial attack by the 26th VGD on the 18th.[84] Under this pressure, Cota began to displace his command post to Sibret, four miles southwest of Bastogne, though he remained in Wiltz to organize its defense until the morning of the 19th. After his departure, a regiment of the 5th Parachute Division added its weight to the attack of the volksgrenadiers. The resulting encirclement captured the town and most of its defenders.

The situation at Bastogne was significantly improved by the arrival of the 101st Airborne Division at an assembly area on the west side of the town during the night of 18/19 December. Middleton remained in Bastogne during the night to orient Brigadier General Anthony C. McAuliffe, the acting division commander, and Ridgway, who passed through Bastogne en route to Werbomont, before departing for Neufchâteau on the morning of the 19th.[85] Having advised Bradley that his last reserves were committed and that the 101st would be left largely to its own devices, he unambiguously instructed McAuliffe to "hold Bastogne."[86] With CCB, 10th AD, deployed on the three most likely German routes into Bastogne (and the remnants of CCR, 9th AD, on the center of them), McAuliffe had a fighting chance to get his men into position for a defense of the town. Nevertheless, as

Marlborough famously remarked about Waterloo, the race for Bastogne would be a near-run thing.

Fortunately for McAuliffe and Roberts, Lüttwitz lacked the force required to seize Bastogne *and* to continue the attack to the west. This was a reflection at the corps level of the larger problem of inadequate force for the entire offensive, but it was also a consequence of the Germans' inaccurate appreciation of how rapidly Eisenhower would react and how flexibly the American transportation system could respond in an emergency.[87] The 101st had stolen a march on the 26th VGD, whose reconnaissance detachment had only arrived at Oberwampach, some six miles east of Bastogne, at 2000 on the 18th, with its main fighting force between Oberwampach and Draufelt, a further six miles distant.[88] Lüttwitz's plan was straightforward in some respects, curious in others. Lauchert was to continue the attack to the west. Bayerlein, having put his division on the road to Mageret, had no choice but to attack into Bastogne along the Mageret-Neffe axis. The 26th VGD commander, General Heinz Kokott, was directed to circle north of Bastogne and attack through Foy, which lies between Bastogne and Noville.[89] This would take him directly through Longvilly, still occupied by the remnants of CCR, 9th AD. Additionally, with his division exhausted from its game effort to stay up with the two panzer divisions and having to cut across the rear of Panzer Lehr to get to its objective, Kokott had a very tall order.

Noville was squarely in Lauchert's path.[90] Accordingly, TF Desobry, which had occupied positions in, north, and east of the village, was in for a sharp fight. Neither Major Desobry nor Colonel Roberts knew that Lauchert's desire for Noville was not motivated by a desire to attack Bastogne, but they could not afford to take the chance. Early in the morning, Lauchert launched a probe that drove in Desobry's outposts. A follow-on attack in regimental strength was sufficient to cause Desobry to seek Roberts's permission to withdraw two miles to Foy, which he deemed significantly more defensible. Roberts advised him to stay put but provided a platoon of tank destroyers, which Desobry used as a mobile reserve. Additionally, the Noville garrison was reinforced by the 1st Battalion, 506th PIR, commanded by Lieutenant Colonel James L. LaPrade. A joint American attack northeast from Noville jumped off at 1400 but ran headlong into a strong attack mounted by the 2nd Panzers. LaPrade and Desobry withdrew their force back to Noville. In subsequent heavy fire directed at their mutual command post, LaPrade was killed and Desobry was seriously wounded. The Germans continued to press vigorously. Both Brigadier General Gerald J. Higgins, the 101st's assistant division commander, and Colonel Robert F. Sink, commander of the 506th PIR, felt that further resistance at Noville was fruitless and so advised McAuliffe. McAuliffe sought permission from the corps commander to withdraw; but Middleton replied unambiguously, "You can't do it. We can't hold Bastogne if we keep falling back."[91] So instructed, McAuliffe ordered the garrison to hold on.

The fight at Longvilly went much worse.[92] During the night of the 18th, Colonel Cherry had sent an advance guard forward to Longvilly, leaving the main body a thousand yards to the west. When Cherry went to the rear to report on the situation to Colonel Roberts, he became cut off from his command by Bayerlein's reconnaissance battalion in Mageret. He then ordered Captain William F. Ryerson, left in command of the main body, to attack Mageret from the northeast and reestablish the line of communication. After due reconnaissance, Ryerson reported that this task was beyond his means. There were now three units behind German lines northeast of Bastogne—the remnants of CCR, 9th AD, Cherry's advance guard, and the main body of TF Cherry, now, effectively, Team Ryerson. Cherry established his command post at Neffe. At about mid-morning on the 19th, the advance guard, with help from CCR, 9th AD, held off an attack by a single regiment of the 26th VGD. Later in the day, after some dabbling by Lüttwitz in Kokott's business, a larger attack was mounted with strong support from 2nd Panzer Division. In the ensuing fight, Cherry's advance guard was all but wiped out, as were the various units of CCR, 9th AD, trapped between Longvilly and Mageret. Although small numbers of stragglers and infiltrators from both units made it to Bastogne, virtually all of their equipment was either destroyed or abandoned. Team Ryerson also took heavy casualties but managed to fight its way into Mageret; by midnight it had occupied a portion of the village but had been unable to dislodge the Germans. Meanwhile, in Neffe, Colonel Cherry put up a very good show against Bayerlein's tanks and panzergrenadiers. A reconnaissance platoon outposting the hamlet was driven back into Bastogne; but Cherry and his small command contingent, fighting against long odds, remained operational in a chateau until late in the day.

Further to the south, there was a significant breakdown of coordination between the 101st and CCB, 10th AD.[93] Moving along the road leading out of Bastogne toward Wiltz, Colonel O'Hara, apparently with Roberts's concurrence, decided that the most dangerous threat lay directly along this road. Accordingly, he ignored Wardin itself and placed his force where it could block the main road. Thus, when Company I of the 501st PIR occupied Wardin, it was without support. During the day, troops of Panzer Lehr outflanked O'Hara's position and moved toward Wardin. A regimental attack to gain the village scattered the greatly outnumbered airborne troopers and inflicted heavy casualties. When apprised of this development, Colonel

O'Hara petitioned CCB for permission to pull back toward Marvie, two miles to the west. Roberts initially refused but assented soon thereafter when made aware of the complete situation by O'Hara's operations officer.

Despite this gaffe, at the end of the day, the "Race for Bastogne" was clearly won by the 101st. There had been multiple antecedents of this success, several of which have already been mentioned. Foremost was Eisenhower's early decision to release the 101st and 82nd and the implementing instructions of his staff to launch them toward Bastogne. The American logistical system also played a part. The defense mounted by the 28th ID, particularly the heroic resistance of Colonel Fuller's 110th Infantry, was indispensable. Although CCR, 9th AD, did not provide the delay that Middleton had hoped for, it was a sufficient enough nuisance on the 18th and the 19th to occupy part of the 2nd Panzer Division and the bulk of the 26th VGD, thus providing vital breathing room for Lieutenant Colonel Julian J. Ewell's 501st PIR. The same can be said for TF Cherry, notwithstanding the fact that its commander was physically isolated from the action. And here one must point to the vital contribution of CCB, 10th AD. For despite the miscommunication with TF O'Hara on the southern flank, without this armored command to its front, the 101st would have been fighting in the streets of Bastogne, rather than in its outlying villages.

But we must also include Middleton's actions and orders. He intuitively sensed the importance of Bastogne and how to hold it. He committed CCR, 9th AD, to exactly the right place at exactly the right time. He parceled out his engineer battalions judiciously to delay the attack toward the town.[94] Finally, he committed CCB, 10th AD, to exactly the right *places*. Much has been made of Middleton's lack of dogmatism in violating the canon of concentration when he instructed Roberts to form three teams and defend three isolated locations, rather than employing his command as a single entity.[95] But it was not simply flexibility for which Middleton should be commended here. Rather, it was his ability to see the whole situation as it *actually* was and to take the *appropriate* action. As Clausewitz succinctly observed, the mark of a refined military mind is to have one's appreciations not conflict with objective reality.[96] Closely allied to this overall comprehension and decisiveness was Middleton's ability to remain calm in the face of great danger to his command and to issue precise, well-reasoned instructions.[97] Other people were losing their heads, Alan Jones being merely the most conspicuous. Middleton kept his. It was his finest hour.

But every hero has feet of clay. Middleton seriously complicated matters at Bastogne by repeating the mistake of St. Vith—not designating an overall commander. It was clearly called for. The isolation of the garrison was eminently predictable. Roberts's and McAuliffe's forces were, by Middleton's design, inextricably intertwined. There was also tension between Roberts, who doubted the ability of an artilleryman to employ armor properly, and McAuliffe, who pointed out the patent absurdity of attaching a division to a combat command.[98] All of this called for a single, authoritative voice in Bastogne; but Middleton instead asked for cooperation. He also issued another general "no withdrawal" order that bore little resemblance to reality. In a letter of instructions dated the 19th, he directed all corps units—now comprising the 4th, 28th, and 106th IDs; the 7th, 9th, and 10th ADs; and the 101st Airborne Division—to hold along a line that ran from a point on the V/VIII Corps boundary near the village of Recht, southeast to St. Vith, west to a line east of the Bastogne-Liège highway, then south to Bastogne and southeast to Breitweiler in the 4th ID sector.[99] The final paragraph read, "There will be no withdrawal. Units whose front lines are now west of the line to be stabilized will regain lost ground." Perhaps this last sentence indicated that Middleton realized the stabilization line had been violated, as indeed it had—the 116th Panzer Division having already reached Houffalize. Furthermore, there was simply no way for VIII Corps to halt the westward flow. As he admitted to Bradley, he had no corps reserves—the 7th AD and the remnants of the 106th were barely hanging on at St. Vith; the 28th ID was a division in name only; and the 101st and CCB of the 10th AD would have their hands full merely defending Bastogne, much less stopping the 2nd Panzer Division and Panzer Lehr from moving to the west. The only place that Middleton's order was capable of being executed was on the southern shoulder.

Things there were relatively sanguine. The 109th Infantry at Diekirch was pummeled by artillery brought up by the 352nd VGD, and although the infantry attack was not mounted in great strength, Rudder's cumulative losses and huge expenditure of ammunition forced him to ask Cota for permission to retire.[100] Cota consulted Middleton, who assented; Rudder withdrew in good order to the west. In the 9th AD sector, a welcome but unexpected reprieve came when the new commander of the 276th VGD felt that the division required a day of rest and reorganization before pursuing the attack.[101] CCA used this break to good advantage, stiffening its lines with obstacles and constituting a small reserve. Nevertheless, General Leonard remained concerned about the sizeable left-flank gap between his unit and Rudder's regiment. At 1730 the 10th AD reported that the western and center columns attacking in the 4th ID sector were "making slow progress against strong eny [enemy] resistance" and that the eastern column had reached the outskirts of Echternach.[102]

In sum, by the evening of the 19th, it was clear that Middleton's grand tactical delay had been successful. While his overall performance as corps commander on the 18th and 19th had not been perfect, it had been good enough to accomplish VIII Corps' three most essential tasks: the defense of St. Vith, Bastogne, and the southern shoulder. In terms of immediate tactical command, retention of St. Vith was more creditable to Hasbrouck, Clarke, and Hoge than it was to Middleton; but the corps commander deserves credit for being sufficiently aware of the town's importance to direct both CCB, 9th AD, and the entire 7th AD to buttress the hard-pressed 106th. Middleton's overall handling of his command responsibilities in this extremely important two-day period of the Battle of the Bulge was extremely commendable.

HOLDING ON FOR DEAR LIFE, 20–21 DECEMBER

Over the next two days, Middleton's task became greatly simplified by the reorganization of the theater brought about by Eisenhower's decision to give Montgomery control over the northern half of the penetration and by Patton's recognition that the battle for the southern shoulder required a dedicated focus. The new 12th /21st Army Group boundary, effective on the 20th, ran along a west-east line from Givet to Prüm, intersecting the Bastogne-Liège highway near Houffalize. This put all forces in St. Vith under First Army control and Middleton's VIII Corps under Patton's Third Army. Patton would soon put the battle for the southern shoulder under control of Eddy's XII Corps. But until it could be moved into position from the Saar, he established a provisional corps commanded by Major General William H. H. Morris, commander of the 10th AD, to direct the actions of the 9th AD, to which was attached Rudder's 109th Infantry, the 4th ID, and his own 10th AD, whose CCA was operating in Barton's sector.[103] In other words, effective 20 December, other than monitoring reconstitution of Cota's shattered 28th ID, Middleton's sole focus was the defense of Bastogne.

There were, however, a few loose strands in this theoretically scalpel-like division of forces. Although the change went into effect at 1200, the lack of communication between Middleton and the 7th AD/106th ID tandem headquartered at Vielsalm caused a period of uncertainty as to command arrangements.[104] At 1515 on the 21st, a message was sent from 7th AD to VIII Corps plaintively inquiring, "Is this unit still a part of that corps?"[105] Almost as bizarre, on the morning of the 20th, Middleton sent a message to Hasbrouck asking him to ask Jones to mount an attack from the south with a battalion of the 112th Infantry located near Gouvy to take pressure off Bastogne, "if it is not engaged."[106] Jones duly ordered a company of the 112th to the south, but it had little effect.[107] In the meantime, the indispensable Colonel Slayden, dispatched to Middleton at Jones's behest, returned with the word that both divisions would be assigned to First Army, with further attachment to XVIII (Airborne) Corps at Werbomont.[108] Late that night, the situation seemed to be further clarified when 7th AD received a message from First Army attaching it to Ridgway's corps "when communication is established."[109] But the cold reality was that as early as the morning of the 20th, and perhaps even earlier, the battle at St. Vith had been beyond Middleton's control.

In Middleton's immediate area, both Manteuffel and Lüttwitz were noticeably discomfited by the failure to take Bastogne on the 19th and also at odds about how to proceed. The XLVII Panzer Corps commander, who had raised the issue of Bastogne with Manteuffel in a preattack map exercise, wanted to make a significant effort to take the town, apparently reasoning that it was a case of "pay me now or pay me later."[110] He was strongly supported in this sentiment by Bayerlein. Manteuffel, however, was more concerned with the need for speed in the now-delayed dash to the Meuse. A compromise emerged. 2nd Panzer would drive to the west; 26th VGD would continue its attack into Bastogne, though coming in from the northeast, rather than through Foy as intended the day before; Panzer Lehr would also assault Bastogne but would hold forces in reserve to swing south of the town, and then head west.

Before considering the results of this effort, we should briefly take stock of the Bastogne situation as a whole. The German side has already been sketched—Lüttwitz had three divisions at his disposal, and their strength could only grow as their field and antiaircraft artillery moved up and their supply lines made more secure. Furthermore, the 5th Parachute Division, though under control of a different army headquarters and moving slowly westward, would provide some degree of protection on the southern flank. Offsetting all this was the fact that Lüttwitz did not have the authority to employ the corps as he wished—the dictates of the larger plan overrode his own desires. On the American side of the ledger, there was the obvious disadvantage of being cut off from replenishment by land. This would prove to be particularly pressing in two areas: artillery ammunition and medical supplies, the latter compounded by capture of the 101st's medical company. There was also the psychological disadvantage of isolation, but this was offset in the case of the airborne soldiers by the obvious truth that their very raison d'être called for them to fight behind enemy lines. Although there was a finite limit to how long they could hold out, the notion itself was not foreign. Furthermore, the division's strength was significantly augmented by CCB, 10th AD; the 705th Tank Destroyer (TD) Battalion; two battalions of corps 155-mm artillery; and the battered remnants of CCR, 9th AD.[111] Additionally, there was the promise of relief from Patton's coming attack from the south. Thus, Middleton had some justification for telling McAuliffe, as he left Bastogne for Neufchâteau on the morning of the 19th, to be of good cheer.[112] Such counsel was, of course, easier to give than to receive; but there were objective reasons for cautious optimism. Middleton also did something constructive to help McAuliffe—early on the afternoon of the 20th he attached all units in Bastogne to the 101st, thereby effecting the unity of command the town's successful defense clearly required.[113]

Despite the significant attachments to the 101st and the now-established unity of command, the defense of Bastogne would have to be conducted well and valiantly to be won. It was.[114] Roberts and McAuliffe developed a constructive relationship that produced an effective pattern of tank-infantry cooperation to hold the Germans at bay.[115] McAuliffe, Roberts, and the 101st's regimental commanders were able to shift reserves around within Bastogne and repel the multiple attacks mounted by Lüttwitz's corps. But tactical technique alone was not enough. Spirit was also required. And, as will be subsequently demonstrated, such spirit was present in ample quantity.

The most intense action on the 20th came at Noville. Lauchert was absolutely determined to seize the outlying crossroads in order to continue his march to the west.[116] Early in the morning, the village was pounded with the entire complement of the 2nd Panzer's artillery and assaulted by panzergrenadiers supported by small packets of tanks. When the defenders of Noville radioed in that the situation was critical, McAuliffe, this time without reference to Middleton, ordered a fighting withdrawal. It was complicated by the German seizure of Foy the night before. Nevertheless, McAuliffe mounted a counterattack to retake Foy; so supported, amid some considerable confusion, and with significant casualties, the remnants of TF Desobry and the 1st Battalion, 506th PIR, fought their way back into Bastogne by nightfall. With Noville in German hands shortly before darkness, having taken roughly thirty-six hours to capture, Lauchert jumped command lines and radioed Krüger, commander of the adjacent LVIII Panzer Corps, for permission to drive south into Bastogne. Krüger's reply was prompt, definite, and empathically negative: "Forget Bastogne and head for the Meuse!"[117] To the east, a regiment of the 26th VGD placed under Bayerlein's control probed along the rail line running from Bastogne to Bourcy, but no appreciable gains were made.[118] A panzergrenadier regimental attack from Panzer Lehr against Neffe was repulsed by the 501st PIR. The lead echelon of Bayerlein's other panzergrenadier regiment attempted to gain Marvie but was easily beaten back by TF O'Hara. These three abortive efforts established a pattern that was to persist for the next several days: German infantry, scantily supported by armor and artillery, could not prevail against a well-conducted infantry-tank-artillery defense.

As McAuliffe's and Roberts's troops were credibly handling the second day of the Bastogne defense, Middleton traveled to Arlon where Patton held a conference to plan the III Corps attack, which was to kick off on the 22nd. Patton greeted him with typical bombast: "Troy, of all the goddamned crazy things I've ever heard of, leaving the 101st Airborne to be surrounded in Bastogne is the worst!"[119] Middleton, who had graduated seventeen places higher than Patton at CGSS, was fazed neither by the Third Army commander's profanity nor by the challenge to his tactical judgment. "George," he replied, "just look at that map with all the roads converging on Bastogne. Bastogne is the hub of the wheel. If we let the Boche take it, they will be at the Meuse in a day." With that issue behind them, Patton next sought Middleton's counsel as to the best axis for the 4th AD, which would be the westernmost unit of the impending attack—should it be the due south-north route from Arlon, or should it lay along the southwest-northeast approach coming in from Neufchâteau? Middleton replied that he would use both roads for the 4th Armored, with the weight on the Neufchâteau road, which offered the shortest route to the 101st, though the weight of the III Corps attack as a whole would have to be further east. Patton agreed with Middleton on the latter provision but ultimately chose to keep III Corps concentrated and put the 4th Armored on a single axis north from Arlon. Patton did not have sufficient force to maintain a unified front along even the narrower corridor that he chose, and the Germans proved extremely adept at infiltrating units between the gaps in his advancing columns. Nevertheless, this issue became controversial.[120]

When Middleton returned to his command post, he asked McAuliffe to report to him in Neufchâteau "if the situation will not be jeopardized."[121] McAuliffe complied, and while not minimizing the risks to his command, his overall demeanor in the ensuing conference was calm and confident.[122] When Middleton asked him how long he believed he could hold out if surrounded, McAuliffe's estimate was "at least 48 hours and maybe longer." When the corps commander warned him that the 116th Panzer Division might be committed to the battle, McAuliffe replied, "I think we can take care of them."[123] Middleton, sensing he was dealing with a solid commander and recognizing the realities of the situation, gave McAuliffe authority to act as he saw fit in the event communications were severed. Although there is no formal record of the conversation, Middleton undoubtedly apprised the 101st commander of the details of the impending IIII Corps attack and might have even given him a prognosis of its likely progress. Reflecting a bit less optimism than earlier indicated, he opined that he deeply wanted to hold Bastogne but was not sure the existing conditions would allow it. McAuliffe was much more worried about the consequences of a withdrawal, and rightfully so. In Bastogne, he had the advantage of defending a built-up area. In a withdrawal, his paratroopers would "be chewed to pieces."[124] In parting, Middleton attempted to make light of the very somber situation by enjoining McAuliffe, "Now, Tony, don't get yourself surrounded."[125]

McAuliffe made it safely back to Bastogne, but just barely. During the night of the 20th/21st, Lüttwitz sent the 26th VGD's reconnaissance battalion, supported by a contingent of Bayerlein's tanks, against Sibret. This force, combined with a battalion of the 5th Parachute Division, also desirous of capturing Sibret, clearly outmatched the slim remnants of Cota's 28th ID. The resulting action forced Cota to displace his command post to Vaux-lez-Rosières and, by the morning of the 21st, severed the main artery leading into Bastogne from the southwest.[126] This movement reflected a reversion on the part of Manteuffel and Lüttwitz to their original plan: send the panzers west and leave the problem of Bastogne to the 26th VGD. The 101st now had the clear advantage, and the best that Kokott could do on the 21st was mount one heavy attack along the Bastogne-Bourcy railroad.[127] This effort slipped behind the right flank of the 506th PIR; but a counterattack by the survivors of the regiment's 1st Battalion, the valiant defenders of Noville, eliminated the penetration and captured numerous prisoners.

In sum, on the evening of the 21st, the 101st and its attached units were surrounded but not sorely pressed. In the two days since leaving Bastogne, Middleton had done the best he could to ensure that these soldiers would be able to hold out. He had, albeit with some delay, established a unified command structure in the town. He had given Patton his best counsel as to how best to effect the garrison's relief. And he had conferred personally with McAuliffe to offer what moral encouragement he could, to apprise him of the entire situation, and to make sure that he understood that he had full authority to act as he saw fit in the event communications were severed.[128] Until the III Corps attack that would kick off on the next day broke through to Bastogne, there would be little that he could do but act as McAuliffe's main point of contact with the rest of the American army. In the meantime, with Sibret in enemy hands and the belt of German control around Bastogne likely to expand, Middleton prudently withdrew his headquarters to Florenville, just over ten miles southwest of Neufchâteau.[129]

SOME CLOSING OBSERVATIONS

The situation in the original VIII Corps sector after the first six days of battle was mixed. It resembled a dike, pounded by a massive wave, that had broken in some places but held fast in others. Predictably, the major breaks were where the forces had been distributed most thinly—along the V/VIII Corps boundary and in the center of the corps sector. In both places, major German forces were still flowing to the west, though those in the north were noticeably constricted by the thin peninsula of resistance west of St. Vith, while those in the center were running free, though on their southern flank impeded by the island of resistance at Bastogne. The area south of Bastogne was still fluid; the far south of the original corps sector had bent but not been cracked.

The German situation was the product of several factors. The overall superiority against VIII Corps brought to bear by Manteuffel's Fifth Panzer Army and Brandenberger's Seventh Army was virtually guaranteed to produce a major breakthrough. The potential of the former had been significantly enhanced by Manteuffel's shrewd plan for encirclement of the troops on the Schnee Eifel and by his well-conceived infiltration tactics in the sector of the 28th ID. Brandenberger's progress, while not as substantial as had been hoped for, was probably as good as could have been realistically expected. Lucht's problems at St. Vith and Lüttwitz's consternation at Bastogne were both due to a combination of inadequate means, poor road nets, and American reinforcements arriving much more rapidly than anticipated. Krüger's free run in the center was the result of the Americans' having run out of forces. When Middleton thought he would be getting both the 101st and the 82nd Airborne Divisions, he planned to put the latter at Houffalize.[130] But Hodges required the 82nd much more urgently at Werbomont, leaving Houffalize and points west free for the taking.

On the American side, Middleton's immediate subordinates ranged from Hasbrouck, Roberts, and McAuliffe, who performed magnificently; to Cota who performed very well under extremely intense pressure; to Barton and Leonard who performed competently under much less pressure; to Gilbreth, the disintegration of whose combat command was at least partially his fault; to Jones, perhaps the most tragic figure in the Bulge. The soldiers of VIII

Corps were also a mixed bag. On one hand, there was the incredible bravery displayed by the defenders of St. Vith, Marnach, Hosingen, Clerf, Wiltz, Noville, and many little crossroads whose importance was significant but beneath the purview of this study.[131] At the other end of the spectrum were the panicked troops of the 106th Division Artillery headquarters and TF Harper, CCR, 9th AD.

What about Middleton himself? There, too, there is evidence on both sides of the ledger. His most substantial contribution came on 18 and 19 December, when, after a ten-mile gap had been blown wide open in the center of the corps and with but scant reserves to hold the tide, he saw exactly how best to employ each little scrap of force at his disposal; issued clear, concise orders; and kept his head even in moments of great crisis. The result, combined with the extra day bought by the 110th Infantry's heroic defense east of the Clerf, was that Ewell's 501st PIR met Bayerlein's Panzer Lehr Division on the *east* side of Bastogne, rather than the *west*. Although it was not within Middleton's ultimate authority to hold Bastogne, he was the first to develop the mental calculus that it *could* be held. Furthermore, his decision to commit the lead combat command of 10th AD to reinforce Barton's 4th ID on the southern shoulder when the bottom had dropped out in the center, indicates perhaps better than anything else he did that he grasped the big picture and would accept risk where it was less important in order to have insurance where it was more important.

On the other side of the coin, his most egregious failure was not issuing a preemptory order to Jones on the evening of the 16th to withdraw the 422nd and 423rd Infantry Regiments from the Schnee Eifel. Although Jones bore the more immediate *command* responsibility to do so, Middleton bore the *moral* responsibility for this decision.[132] Having been in the area much longer than Jones, he understood the vulnerability of the position far better than the division commander, even to the point of previously petitioning First Army for authority to withdraw from it when there were absolutely *no* indications of German offensive intentions. By perhaps noon on the 16th, and certainly by nightfall, the Schnee Eifel had, to use the words of Middleton's LOI of the 17th, become "completely untenable." If Jones did not have the sense to realize this and act accordingly, Middleton should have. His failure to establish unity of command in St. Vith and his initial disinclination to do so in Bastogne also detracted from the conduct of the corps defense. Finally, his order on the 17th to hold initial positions until "completely untenable" and to retain the high ground west of the Our "at all costs" and his similar order on the 19th for "no withdrawal" west of the Bastogne-Liège highway were simply beyond the realm of possibility. The latter probably did little damage, but the first stipulation of the former contributed to Jones's hesitation to withdraw the 422nd and 423rd.

But taken as a whole, the VIII Corps commander has to get high marks. Although his failure to withdraw the two exposed regiments promptly from the Schnee Eifel was truly regrettable, by holding St. Vith as long as it was under VIII Corps control and by retaining Bastogne and the southern shoulder, he established many of the important conditions that would later allow the U.S. Army to reverse the tide. And he did so against very long odds. Middleton's contribution in the first phase of the Bulge was nicely articulated by Matt Eddy, who encountered the VIII Corps commander at Third Army headquarters on 2 January. That night, Eddy noted in his diary, "I don't think we could have picked a better Corps [*sic*] for the Germans to attack."[133]

8

XVIII (Airborne) Corps Stands in the Breach

> If a man hits you a surprise blow and knocks you sprawling, you've got to get
> up off the ground at once, and flatten him, or you are beaten.[1]
>
> *Matthew B. Ridgway*

THE ROLE OF RIDGWAY'S XVIII (AIRBORNE) CORPS in the opening
phase of the Battle of the Bulge was even more complex than that of Middleton's VIII Corps. The bulk of the corps headquarters staff flew to France
from England, where they had been supervising training of the 6th and 17th
Airborne Divisions and preparing for future operations, and then moved by
truck from Rheims to Werbomont, where the headquarters became operational at 1200 on the 19th, slightly less than thirty-six hours after receiving
notice of its commitment from SHAEF.[2] Thus, Ridgway and his staff had to
absorb on the fly all the basic ingredients of military decision making: the
terrain, the capabilities and limitations of friendly forces, the personalities of
commanders, and the enemy situation. Furthermore, the corps headquarters
had never been in combat before. Ridgway had brought with him, from the
82nd, "Doc" Eaton as his chief of staff and several of the staff principals.[3]
But for the vast majority of soldiers on the corps staff, including Lieutenant
Colonel Alexander Day Surles, the corps G-3, the Ardennes campaign would
be their first taste of combat.[4] The fact that they were untested did not entitle
them to an easy task on which to cut their teeth. The First Army concept was
to use Ridgway's corps as the seed around which to build a force that would
perform multiple missions: contain, then eliminate Kampfgruppe Peiper,
whose lead elements were in Stoumont (on the north bank of the Amblève
about four miles northwest of Trois Ponts); prevent reinforcements from the
main body of the 1st SS Panzer Division from reaching Peiper; make contact with and support the 7th AD and 106th ID in the St. Vith salient; halt
whatever additional enemy forces were thrust into the battle; and cover the
concentration of Collins's VII Corps. With enemy strength steadily building
in the XVIII (Airborne) Corps sector and with only the most scattered of
any other American resistance between Werbomont and Bastogne, these missions would stretch Ridgway and his corps to the limit. Very fine judgments

would have to be made as to how aggressively to push back the intruders, what ground could be held, and what ground would have to be ceded to the enemy. These judgments were not always made perfectly. Nevertheless, by midnight on 21 December, the situation in the corps sector, though still quite dicey in places, was more stable than it had been two-and-a-half days earlier.

GETTING ORIENTED, 19 DECEMBER

The terrain in what became the XVIII (Airborne) Corps sector covered a wide swath of the north-central Ardennes. As almost everywhere in the region, the keys were rivers, villages, highways, and road junctions. The defensive capacity of the Salm decreases from north to south, while La Roche and Hotton constitute important points at which to cross the major obstacle of the Ourthe. The dominant highways in the area are the north-south N-15 and the east-west N-28, which cross at the summit of Baraque de Fraiture. This intersection figured importantly in the corps battle, though Ridgway was stretched far too thinly to afford it much protection. Between this junction and La Roche is the village of Samrée; it was also of some value because of a road leading from it to the northwest that connects to the east-west route joining Manhay with Erezée, Hotton, and Marche. The latter is the most significant junction in the central Ardennes, with major highways leading from it to Liège, Namur, and Givet.

Ridgway left Bastogne on the morning of 19 December. His initial inclination had been to depart for Werbomont during the previous night; but Middleton convinced him that a few hours of sleep would be a good idea.[5] The most direct route was through Houffalize, but Ridgway wisely chose the more westerly approach through Marche, thereby missing what would have been a very unpleasant encounter with the 116th Panzer Division.[6] After establishing his command post in a two-story farmhouse, one of the few habitable buildings in Werbomont, he proceeded immediately to Hodges's headquarters at Chaudfontaine. There he conferred with Hodges and Kean. Hodges had specifically requested that Ridgway's headquarters, rather than Major General John B. Anderson's XVI Corps, be assigned to First Army to plug the widening gap between V Corps and VIII Corps.[7] The order issued after this conference indicated that the First Army commander and chief of staff envisioned a progressive series of missions for Ridgway as his corps gained force.[8] For the 19th, he was assigned only Gavin's 82nd; the 119th Regimental Combat Team (RCT) of the 30th ID; and the 3rd AD, minus its CCA, which was still in V Corps reserve. Furthermore, Hodges had already

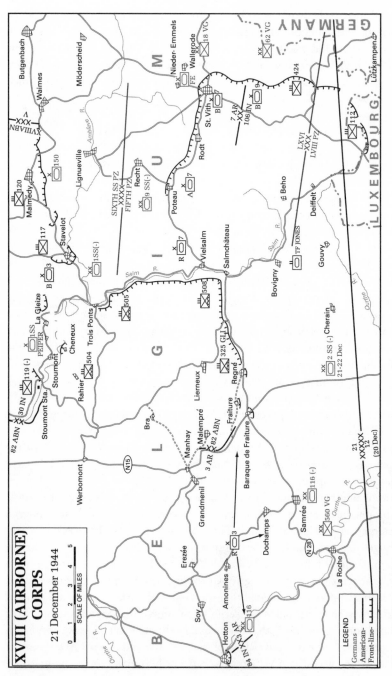

Map 5. XVIII (Airborne) Corps, 21 December 1944

decided that CCB, 3rd AD, would attack south to block advances west of Stavelot and "be prepared" to assist the 119th RCT in the capture of both Stoumont and La Gleize, where Kampfgruppe Peiper had been halted. This meant that the rump of the 3rd AD, consisting only of CCR and a reconnaissance battalion, would be the sole force available to screen the corps' wide-open right flank. Nevertheless, Ridgway was instructed to block any further advances west of a line that ran from east of Stavelot, north of the Amblève, to about Trois Ponts, then south to Houffalize and west to La Roche and Hotton.[9] The army order further stipulated that when the situation stabilized, "it is intended to give the remainder of the 30th Inf Div to XVIII Airborne Corps and give XVIII Airborne Corps a zone of action between V and VIII Corps." With the scant forces at his disposal, Ridgway was to hold a line some thirty-six miles long and "annihilate" any German forces west of that line; and in a day or two when he received control over the rest of the 30th ID, which was already fully engaged attempting to hold the line from Malmédy to Stoumont, he was to reach out to Middleton at Bastogne.[10] It was a tall order.

Although assigned to XVIII (Airborne) Corps, the rump of the 3rd AD was still en route on the 19th. Thus, Ridgway was only responsible for two scenes of action on his initial day in combat as a corps commander: the 119th RCT at Stoumont and the movement to contact the 82nd in multiple directions from Werbomont.

The 3rd Battalion, 119th Infantry, commanded by Lieutenant Colonel Roy C. Fitzgerald and supported by eight tank destroyers and two antiaircraft guns but without any field artillery within range, had occupied Stoumont on the evening of the 18th.[11] In the early hours of the 19th, Peiper launched a strong panzergrenadier attack against Stoumont, supported by Panthers and Tigers. As the battle raged on in the eastern edge of the village, Fitzgerald's men, reinforced by ten Shermans, put up a game defense; but they were ultimately forced to withdraw by German superiority in both numbers and firepower. The SS soldiers did not, however, reach the bridge across the Amblève that Peiper coveted. Their advance was checked just west of Stoumont at Stoumont Station when the 119th regimental commander, Colonel Edwin M. Sutherland, committed his reserve, supported by tanks and self-propelled artillery. That evening, Peiper, with his fuel running precariously low and almost completely cut off from outside support, requested permission to withdraw. But the 1st SS Panzer Division commander, Colonel Wilhelm Mohnke, refused, telling him to hold on until the main body, now just east of the Salm, broke through to him to continue the advance to the west. Peiper was checked, but eliminating his robust force would prove to be much more difficult.

The 82nd continued to pour into Werbomont as the day wore on, and Gavin pushed the division out in almost all directions of the compass to develop the situation.[12] The 504th PIR, commanded by Colonel Reuben H. Tucker III, moved northeast in the direction of La Gleize, reaching the hamlet of Rahier. Colonel William E. Ekman's 505th PIR headed due east toward Trois Ponts, stopping at Haute Bodeux. The 508th PIR, under Colonel Roy E. Lindquist, struck out southeast toward the 7th AD's and 106th ID's headquarters at Vielsalm, arriving at Bra. The majority of the 325th Glider Infantry Regiment (GIR), commanded by Colonel Charles Billingslea, was held in division reserve; but its 3rd Battalion outposted Barvaux and Manhay. By the end of the day, Gavin had established a strong protective arc around Werbomont and placed his troops in position either to engage the enemy, to make contact with the westernmost units in the St. Vith salient, or to screen the vulnerable southwest flank, as circumstances would dictate on the next day.

EXPANDING THE CORPS SECTOR, 20 DECEMBER

On its second day of battle, the role of XVIII (Airborne) Corps was significantly expanded. In the north, it assumed control of the entire 30th ID, whose sector ran north of the Amblève from east of Malmédy to west of Stoumont Station; in the center, it picked up control of the St. Vith salient; and to the southwest, it assumed command over both CCR, 3rd AD, screening in the "V" formed by the N-15 highway and the Ourthe northwest of Houffalize, and the 84th ID, which arrived at Marche in the early evening. It was now responsible for a front of roughly eighty-five miles, and almost the entire front was active.[13]

On the morning of the 20th, Ridgway dispatched a note to Major General Leland S. Hobbs, commander of the 30th ID, whom he thought would be upset about the detachment of his 119th RCT to XVIII (Airborne) Corps.[14] Hobbs had graduated from West Point in 1915 with both Bradley and Eisenhower and had been a stand-out on the Army football team.[15] Thus, he and Ridgway had known each other for a long time. Although Ridgway admired Hobbs in many respects, he also thought him something of a whiner, who frequently asked for more attachments to his division than were justified.[16] Shortly after drafting the missive to Hobbs, Ridgway received a call from General Truman C. Thorson, First Army G-3, asking him to report to Chaudfontaine. Ridgway arrived at approximately 1130; Hodges informed him that the addition of the remainder of the 30th ID to his corps, adumbrated on the 19th, would be effective later on the 20th.

Additionally, he would command the 7th AD and 106th ID when contact was made with the forces in the St. Vith area. Ridgway then outlined an ambitious plan "to pivot on MALMEDY, advancing vigorously to the SE and E . . . ; destroy or drive back all enemy forces in zone; reestablish contact with isolated elements of the 7th Armored and 106th Divisions; and be prepared for further offensive action."[17] Hodges and Kean were in full agreement, but Ridgway's plans would be altered by two circumstances. The accumulating strength of the enemy offensive would render it impossible to continue the corps attack to the southeast after linking up with the 7th AD; the more conservative tendencies of Montgomery, who would assume direction over First Army that afternoon, would also restrain and modify Ridgway's desire to remain on the offensive. Ridgway returned to Werbomont forthwith to outline his concept to Gavin, Hobbs, and Major General Maurice Rose, commander of the 3rd AD. As these plans were being fleshed out, a fair amount of fighting was developing in the corps area.

CCB, 3rd AD, commanded by Brigadier General Truman E. Boudinot, was committed against Peiper from the north.[18] Boudinot divided his command into three task forces arrayed from east to west. The eastern force blocked the road between Stavelot and Trois Ponts, which had been used for the past two days to push modest amounts of supplies and reinforcements forward to Peiper. CCB's attack virtually ended Peiper's tenuous contact with the 1st SS Panzer Division's main body. The center task force was repulsed north of La Gleize, and the western force was also halted north of Stoumont. Peiper was now penned in but, like a cornered tiger, still dangerous.

Just how dangerous was evident in the attempt by the 119th Infantry, reinforced by a company of medium tanks, to take Stoumont from the west. Stoumont sits above the north edge of the Amblève, with a steep bank to its south and an equally steep and heavily wooded hill to its north.[19] The only approach from the west is along the winding valley road that runs uphill from Targnon, a hamlet on the road between Stoumont and Stoumont Station. This road was mined and protected by SS panzergrenadiers, who occupied the high ground to the north as well as a large sanatorium on the west edge of the village. In short, Stoumont was a wonderful place to defend and a horrible place to attack. Nevertheless, two companies of the 1st Battalion, 119th Infantry, recaptured the sanatorium shortly after dark.[20] Shortly before midnight, Peiper's men mounted a strong tank-infantry counterattack that drove the Americans from the building. As the fight raged on during the night, the SS soldiers attempted vainly to press further to the west, while the men of the Old Hickory Division clung tenaciously to the ground just outside the sanatorium.

Colonel Tucker's troopers of the 504th PIR also found that Peiper's men still had some sting.[21] Slightly less than two miles southwest of La Gleize, a small bridge crosses the Amblève, leading almost immediately to the hamlet of Cheneux, and thence to Rahier, Werbomont, and points west. Though the bridge was incapable of supporting large vehicles, its precise capacity was probably unknown to the Americans; furthermore, one always had to worry about the ability of German engineers to reinforce such structures, as they had further to the east. Peiper had outposted Cheneux with infantry supported by a large contingent of mobile 20-mm antiaircraft guns, known in the GI vernacular as flak wagons. Gavin believed that capture of the bridge was "imperative."[22] Accordingly, he told Colonel Tucker to seize it, which first required the capture of Cheneux. Tucker ordered his 1st Battalion, commanded by Lieutenant Colonel Willard E. Harrison, to make the assault. With an afternoon mist denying artillery support and their attack impeded by barbed wire fences across the open fields, Harrison's men were chewed up, driven to ground, and thrown back by withering fire from the flak wagons. Tucker ordered another try, which, supported by two tank destroyers, miraculously but barely carried the outskirts of Cheneux. At the end of the day, Harrison's airborne troopers clung precariously to the edge of the hamlet, but his two assault companies had suffered twenty-three killed and over two hundred wounded.[23] Meanwhile, the 505th and 508th PIRs reached the Salm, the latter linking up with patrols from the 7th AD. When the two divisions made contact, conditions were met to bring the soldiers in the St. Vith Pocket into the ambit of the XVIII (Airborne) Corps. To understand how those conditions evolved, we must jump back several hours and enter the mind of the 7th AD commander.

On the morning of the 20th, feeling increasingly isolated from Middleton, now displaced to Neufchâteau, Hasbrouck sent a messenger to First Army to provide information on the situation in the St. Vith area and to clarify the command situation. The messenger carried a letter addressed to General Kean, which read as follows:

Dear Bill:
I am out of touch with VIII Corps and understand XVIII Corps is moving in.
My division is defending the line St. Vith–Poteau both inclusive. CCB, 9th AD, the 424th Inf Regt of the 106th Div and the 112th Regt of the 28th Div are on my right and hold from St. Vith (excl) to Holdingen. Both infantry regiments are in bad shape. My right flank is wide open except for some reconnaissance elements, TDs and stragglers we

have collected and organized into defense teams as far back as Cheram [Chérain] inclusive. Two German Divisions, 116 Pz and 560 VG, are just starting to attack NW from their right on Gouvy. I can delay them the rest of today *maybe* but will be cut off by tomorrow. VIII Corps has ordered me to hold and will do so but need help. An attack from Bastogne to the NE will relieve the situation and in turn cut off the bastards in the rear. I also need plenty of air support. Am out of contact with VIII Corps so am sending this to you. Understand the 82AB is coming up on my north and the north flank is not critical.

BOB HASBROUCK[24]

This electrifying message clarified the deteriorating situation at St. Vith and, with its request for an attack out of Bastogne, indicated just how cut off from VIII Corps Hasbrouck had indeed become. Hodges's response, dispatched at 1230 while Ridgway was still at the First Army command post, informed Hasbrouck that help was en route, and that he would come under Ridgway's command "when communication is established." He also stipulated, "You retain under your command following units: 106th Inf Div, RCT 112 [of the 28th ID], and CCB, 9th AD."[25] Hodges had finally appointed a single commander in the St. Vith salient and made that commander Hasbrouck, who was not only more competent than Jones but also had the bulk of the combat power.[26]

The German pressure on St. Vith during the 20th was intermittent. The most serious attack came from the north, mounted by a lone tank company of Colonel Otto Remer's FEB.[27] Remer's tanks were handily dispatched by a nifty bit of defensive work on the part of the 31st Tank Battalion, augmented by a platoon of tank destroyers in hull defilade position and well supported by pre-planned artillery.[28] Although Remer had additional reinforcements close at hand, this bloody nose caused him to postpone a major attack until the next day when his entire brigade would arrive at St. Vith.[29] From Wallerode on the northeast side of town, a regimental attack by the 18th VGD that attempted to carry the railway station was beaten back by Clarke's men, magnificently supported by divisional artillery that "threw everything at Wallerode but the shoes on their feet."[30] But much more ominously for Hasbrouck and the other embattled defenders of St. Vith, Lucht used the 20th profitably to push forward his corps artillery. Furthermore, the 7th AD's tenuous lines of supply were interdicted by the 116th Panzer Division, marauding to the southwest.

On that front, some modest stability was supplied by CCR, 3rd AD, and the 84th ID. Although the bulk of his command was elsewhere, General

Rose knew that his division's main scene of action would become the central Ardennes on the XVIII (Airborne) Corps' right flank. Accordingly, he moved his command post to Erezée, some five miles east of Hotton, and dispatched three combined arms columns to develop the situation. With the broken terrain of this area, dividing one's forces in the face of the enemy was a risky proposition; but Rose thrived on risk.[31] Like Eddy, he was one of the few senior American officers who was not a college graduate; even more distinctively among this group, he was Jewish. This heritage may have given him a particular zeal in the fight against Nazism. His naturally offensive inclinations and his study of tank warfare under George Patton made him an ideal armored commander. At the head of CCA, 2nd AD, he had been a stalwart in both the Normandy campaign and the Cobra breakout. He assumed command of the 3rd AD on August 7th.[32] Ridgway called him "one of the most gallant soldiers I have ever known."[33] Two of Rose's columns made contact with lead elements of the 116th Panzer Division, supported by the 560th VGD, giving early warning of an attack that was to develop in greater strength on the following day.[34] In the meantime, the 84th ID, commanded by Brigadier General Alexander R. Bolling, began arriving at Marche during the night, from which it would reach out to join with the 3rd AD and protect the Hotton-Marche road.[35]

At the end of the day on the 20th, XVIII (Airborne) Corps could chalk up some modest but noteworthy accomplishments. In the north, the combined actions of CCB, 3rd AD; the 119th RCT; and the 504th PIR had begun to close the net on Kampfgruppe Peiper. In the center, a defensive shield had been established along the Salm and contact had been gained with the St. Vith defenders. In the southwest, a thin screen had been thrown out as far as Marche to guard the vulnerable right flank. Nevertheless, there would be no resting on laurels, for a combination of staunch resistance by and heavy pressure from forces of both the Sixth SS Panzer and Fifth Panzer Armies would sorely test Ridgway and his now significantly expanded corps on the following day.

ATTACKING WHERE POSSIBLE, HOLDING WHERE POSSIBLE, 21 DECEMBER

The pressure began with an unexpected, last-ditch German effort to break through to Malmédy.[36] Despite its signal success in sowing alarm and confusion behind the American lines, Otto Skorzeny's 150th Panzer Brigade had failed to secure any crossing sites over the Meuse. Skorzeny wanted one more chance for glory, and he petitioned Dietrich to give him a conventional combat mission that would make a noteworthy contribution to Sixth SS Panzer Army. The resulting assignment was the seizure of Malmédy, which lay along Rollbahn C, originally the attack route of the 12th SS Panzer Division. With Malmédy in German hands, Dietrich would, at long last, have some maneuver room north of the Amblève. On the 20th, Skorzeny assembled his variegated force, an odd assortment of German and American vehicles, complemented by panzer mock-ups made to resemble American tanks, in Ligneuville, four miles south of Malmédy. His two-prong attack, east and west of the objective, kicked off on the morning of the 21st. The right wing got almost nowhere, summarily halted by the well-dug-in 120th Infantry and devastating artillery. The left wing fared marginally better, penetrating in small force along the seam between the 120th and 117th IRs. But this threat was also quickly eliminated and with it the last threat to Malmédy and the role of the 150th Panzer Brigade in Hitler's Ardennes offensive. To add injury to insult, Skorzeny was wounded by American artillery late in the day, almost losing his right eye.

Meanwhile, on the west flank of the 30th ID, the combat team formed around the 119th Infantry had been designated TF Harrison, so named for the assistant division commander, Brigadier General William K. Harrison, who assumed direct control of the operation to recapture Stoumont.[37] Harrison was a quiet man of deep spiritual convictions and accustomed to leading from the front, having been wounded and briefly hospitalized in September when his jeep was struck by German 75-mm fire. At Stoumont, however, he was dealing with a very tough tactical problem and a resourceful adversary.[38] Before dawn Peiper launched a tank-infantry attack out of Stoumont that was ultimately repulsed but which spoiled an assault that Harrison had planned for early in the morning. An attack later in the day recaptured a portion of the sanatorium; but in close fighting reminiscent of Krinkelt-Rocherath, the Panthers and Tigers shelled the building so heavily that no further advance was possible. A flanking movement north of Stoumont by the regiment's 2nd Battalion worked its way between that village and La Gleize, but it was brought under heavy fire from both locations and the battalion commander captured. Even before learning of the latter development, Harrison withdrew this unit, reasoning that its continued exposure served little purpose, absent success from the west.

At Cheneux, Colonel Tucker sent his 3rd Battalion on a march around the hamlet.[39] This action, combined with a push by Lieutenant Colonel Harrison's now-reinforced 1st Battalion, cleared the village and forced Peiper's outpost to withdraw north of the Amblève, leaving behind fourteen flak wagons, a battery of artillery, many other odd vehicles, and piles of bodies. Thus, on at least one flank, Peiper was being forced to pull in his horns. Further to the east at Trois Ponts, Colonel Ekman's 2nd Battalion, commanded by the redoubtable Lieutenant Colonel Benjamin H. Vandervoort, had a tremendous fight on its hands to prevent the main body of the 1st SS Panzer Division from linking up with Peiper.[40] From this pivotal position, Vandervoort had sent one company to the east bank of the Salm on the 20th; but heavy pressure from Mohnke's SS panzers and panzergrenadiers forced him to withdraw it to the west bank on the 21st.[41] Ridgway had told Gavin in no uncertain terms that the 82nd had to hold along the Salm in order to extricate the forces in the St. Vith Salient.[42] Gavin went to Trois Ponts to see things for himself. Impressed by the obstacle value of the river and the grit of Vandervoort's paratroopers, he left Trois Ponts convinced that the position would hold; it did.

The fight at St. Vith was clearly the most critical in the corps sector.[43] On the northern edge of the town, Remer was still having problems getting his tanks up, but he sent out a strong patrol west of Rodt that temporarily interdicted the Vielsalm–St. Vith lifeline. More ominously, General Lucht, with his corps artillery in position, launched a determined infantry assault from the east and northeast. Pummeled by large-caliber artillery and nebelwerfers and assaulted by two regiments of the 18th VGD, Clarke's gallant soldiers, who had fought a classic mobile defense of St. Vith for four straight days, could finally bear no more.[44] By around 2200 they withdrew to a holding position just west of the town. This movement was conducted in extremely good order despite the confusion inherent in any night retrograde operation and the weight of the German attack.[45] Nevertheless, Clarke's withdrawal and additional pressure from a regiment of the 62nd VGD forced Hoge's CCB, 9th AD, to pull back as well. Shortly before midnight, the Germans entered St. Vith; but their ability to exploit this gain was significantly hampered by the long, punishing fight it had taken them to gain it.

Ridgway's handling of the situation at St. Vith on the 21st was firm and foresighted in some respects but uncharacteristically tentative in others. As noted above, his instructions to Gavin to hold the line of the Salm as a precondition for withdrawing the increasingly threatened forces east of the river were uncompromising and unambiguous. But he undid the good work Hodges had done to establish unity of command in the salient by discontinuing the attachment of the 106th ID to the 7th AD, thus making Jones and Hasbrouck again coequal actors.[46] This action was in response to two separate communications from Hasbrouck who, after Jones had objected to the First Army stipulation, said he preferred to cooperate with the 106th ID commander, rather than exercise command over his forces.[47] Hasbrouck's feelings on this issue notwithstanding, Ridgway's reversal complicated command arrangements in the St. Vith area. When Ridgway was advised by Hasbrouck that St. Vith had fallen, he gave the 7th AD commander leave to adjust his lines as he felt necessary but did not authorize a full withdrawal.[48] At ten minutes before midnight, he called Kean, telling him that with additional pressure from the south being brought by the 2nd SS Panzer Division, he did not think Hasbrouck's soldiers could continue to hold and "would like to authorize their withdrawal back to the 82nd area tonight."[49] Kean replied that previous instructions issued directly to the 7th AD commander made it clear he was not expected to sacrifice his command. Ridgway revealed in a side comment what was probably at the root of his indecisiveness, telling the First Army chief of staff, "I don't know the ground out there." For although he had been forward to Vielsalm to confer with Hasbrouck that afternoon and had received a generally optimistic report, he had not yet ventured into the salient itself to see with his own eyes and hear with his own ears the sights and sounds of the battlefield. He would rectify this condition on the following day; but at this juncture, the best he could do was send his assistant chief of staff to Vielsalm with instructions to authorize Hasbrouck and Jones to withdraw if they felt it necessary.

Pressure was also building on the southwest flank, further threatening the forces in St. Vith as well as the concentration of VII Corps, which Ridgway was obligated to protect. At Baraque de Fraiture, now referred to as "Parker's Crossroads," Major Arthur C. Parker III, the executive officer of the 589th FA Battalion, collected an assortment of defenders built around the unit's three remaining howitzers.[50] The position had been probed since the 19th by elements of the 560th VGD, but the 2nd SS Panzer Division mounted a major attack on the 21st. Parker's outfit was temporarily aided by tanks from the 3rd AD attempting to retake Samrée, and the scratch unit staunchly held on despite the wounding and evacuation of its namesake. Nevertheless, one had to wonder how long this vulnerable seam between the 82nd and the 3rd AD could be held with both units being sorely pressed on several fronts. Further west, the slim forces at Hotton held on by their fingernails against a strong probe by a kampfgruppe of the 116th Panzer Division.[51] They were aided in this effort by a counterattack from Soy mounted by Colonel Howze's CCR, 3rd AD, and by the threat from Rose's task forces northeast of the Ourthe that forced the 116th Panzer Division to protect its right flank as it moved toward Hotton. But pressure from the 560th VGD forced the 7th AD trains to displace from La Roche to Marche, removing them even farther from the scene of action, and trapped Rose's right-flank task force north of the Ourthe between La Roche and Hotton. The 84th ID patrolled south of the Marche-Hotton line without significant enemy contact.[52]

The good news on the evening of the 21st was that General Krüger, having been repulsed at Hotton, became unwilling to force the issue and decided to reroute the 116th Panzer Division back to La Roche to cross the Ourthe, thus slowing the impetus of the LVIII Panzer Corps advance.[53] These intentions were not, of course, known in Werbomont; it was becoming clear that Rose's slim force could not hold out much longer by itself. Thus, Ridgway, now augmented with five parachute infantry battalions that had participated in Operation Dragoon, assigned two of these units to the 3rd AD.[54] Another was sent to Hobbs, who was instructed to eliminate all resistance in his zone, "as rapidly as possible, with all your drive behind it."[55] Ridgway's intent was to comply with First Army instructions to restore the line from Malmédy to St. Vith. This would prove to be manifestly impossible in the near term; but the elimination of Peiper's force would allow CCB, 3rd AD, to be committed to the corps right flank, where Ridgway sensed the greatest danger was mounting. The final two parachute battalions were used to constitute a small corps reserve. Another action taken by Ridgway on the night of the 21st indicated he was acutely aware that his extremely wide corps sector and the heavy pressure coming at his troops from multiple directions were straining his ability to remain on top of the entire situation. In a message to his administrative superior, Lieutenant General Lewis H. Brereton, commander of the First Allied Airborne Army, he requested that Brigadier General Floyd L. Parks, an old friend who was serving as Brereton's chief of staff, be sent forward temporarily to act as his deputy.[56]

SOME CLOSING OBSERVATIONS

The overall situation on the night of the 21st was somewhat more promising than it had been on the 19th. Peiper had been clearly checked, and the net around his force was tightening. Skorzeny's advance on Malmédy had been repulsed, as had Krüger's much more significant drive on Hotton. And the 84th ID had been able to occupy its defensive line with virtually no enemy interference. In sum, there were considerably more forces in the gap between V and VIII Corps than there had been two-and-a-half days earlier, and there was at least some degree of cohesion among these forces. But St. Vith had been lost, and the units in the salient to its west were under intense pressure. Equally worrisome, the long, thin line from Salmchâteau to Hotton was clearly vulnerable. Ridgway and his soldiers still had a great deal of work cut out for them— they were facing continuing advances by the 1st and 2nd SS Panzer Divisions; the 116th Panzer Division; the 18th, 62nd, and 560th VGDs; and the FEB. The "glass half full" had been aided by the immense traffic jam and mired roads east of St. Vith that had for several days prevented Lucht from bringing the full weight of his corps to bear on the vital road hub. It had also been materially helped by the fact that Peiper's supply line had been previously cut and that Krüger was indecisive and nervous in his advance to the west.

On the friendly side, the 30th ID had been staunch in the defense, though less redoubtable in the offense, albeit acting under very tough conditions. The 82nd had proven that it could both attack and defend against even SS panzer troops. The 7th AD and the 106th ID, the latter strengthened by CCB, 9th AD, and the 112th Infantry, 28th ID, had acquitted themselves well in the short time they had been under XVIII (Airborne) Corps control. Their retention of St. Vith had seriously complicated the entire German offensive and, combined with the staunch defense of the Elsenborn Ridge by Gerow's soldiers, had effectively choked its main effort. Rose's soldiers likewise handled themselves with distinction; in one of those accidents of history that no one could possibly anticipate, Major Parker had provided a shining example of what a single, inspired individual can do to help turn the tide of a large battle.

Ridgway's strengths were his fierce determination, his aggressive inclinations, and his unbounded energy. He was also calm. Many another commander faced with the daunting mission he had might well have wilted under the pressure; Ridgway was both unfazed and unperturbed, never doubting for a moment that he could stem the German tide. He grasped the corps mission as a whole, understanding the vital necessity of establishing a blocking force down from the northern shoulder of the German penetration that could eventually be used to reach an arm back toward the southern shoulder. His biggest mistakes both had to do with the St. Vith salient. The first was undoing Hodges's establishment of unity of command under Hasbrouck. Although the 7th AD commander's reluctance to assume this role is partially exculpatory, the correct action at this juncture would have been to tell Hasbrouck to grasp the nettle. He was also slow to perceive how dire the situation at St. Vith actually was. Again, Hasbrouck's positive assessment when Ridgway visited him at Vielsalm on the afternoon of the 21st offers a partial explanation. But had he gone farther forward and talked to the commanders more directly who were exposed to the German onslaught, he might have judged things differently. His instincts for doing so would kick in on the next day, and by the afternoon and evening of the 22nd his customary decisiveness would return. That story must wait until we consider the second phase of the campaign, but we still must judge Ridgway's overall contribution during XVIII (Airborne) Corps' first three days of battle to have been positive and constructive. Given the difficulty of the assigned tasks and the conditions under which they had to be accomplished, that was a lot.

9

III, XII, *and* VII Corps Prepare *for Battle*

But even the man who planned the operation and now sees it being carried out may well lose confidence in his earlier judgment. . . . War has a way of masking the stage with scenery crudely daubed with fearsome apparitions. Once this is cleared away, and the horizon becomes unobstructed, developments will confirm his earlier convictions—this is one of the great chasms between *planning and execution*.[1]   *Carl von Clausewitz*

WE SHALL NOW BRIEFLY CONSIDER the activities of Millikin's III Corps, Eddy's XII Corps, and Collins's VII Corps as they prepared to enter the fray. Each commander entered the battle under different circumstances. By being initially outside the zone of the German offensive, they all had at least some time to make ready for the tasks that lay ahead. Nevertheless, decisions for their participation all arrived with a certain amount of unexpectedness, putting a premium on flexibility, balance, and retention of mental composure.

III CORPS PREPARES TO ATTACK THE SOUTHERN FLANK AND RELIEVE BASTOGNE

On 16 December, Third Army was operating to the south of the penetration with its headquarters in Nancy, in the final phases of planning an offensive to penetrate the Siegfried Line in the Saar region. III Corps, then mopping up at Metz, was to be in reserve. Patton recognized that although Millikin was untried, he was also fresh, not having been through the rugged fighting of the Lorraine campaign.[2] He met with Millikin on the 17th to discuss the possibility that III Corps would be used to command an attack into the southern flank of the German advance. The Third Army historian, Martin Blumenson, noted that the meeting was chilly and speculated that Patton's reserve was based on Millikin's relationship by marriage to Peyton C. March, Patton being a longtime devotee of John J. Pershing.[3] This is plausible, but Patton may have simply been uncomfortable putting a major army action in the hands of an untested corps commander. Despite whatever reservations he may have harbored, he sensibly told Millikin to study the terrain south of the Ardennes. On the morning of 18 December, Patton met with Bradley and later told General Gay to alert the 80th ID and 4th AD to prepare for movement to the north.[4] That evening, Millikin and his principal staff officers met with Patton and his staff at Nancy and were directed to move the corps headquarters to Longwy, some thirty-five miles south of Bastogne.

On the 19th, Millikin and his staff went to Luxembourg City to meet with the 12th Army Group chief of staff, Lev Allen, per Bradley's instructions of the night before.[5] As his corps headquarters was arriving at Longwy, it learned that, contrary to previous expectations, III Corps was to command the 9th and 10th ADs and locate its headquarters in Luxembourg City.[6] This was based on a decision by Bradley, made on the 18th but apparently not communicated to Patton, to use III Corps to attack north of Luxembourg City.[7] The corps headquarters duly displaced to Luxembourg, but at 1600 Allen told Millikin to revert to the mission that Patton had outlined earlier and move the III Corps headquarters to Arlon.[8] The reason for the change is unclear. Patton and Bradley presumably discussed the issue at the Verdun conference earlier in the day, and the Third Army commander's views on the III Corps role prevailed.[9] Despite the marching and countermarching of his headquarters, Millikin and his staff were waiting at Luxembourg City upon Bradley's return from Verdun. Bradley's aide recorded an initial impression of Millikin as a "sharp eyed man, quite professional on the build of a professional cavalry officer."[10] With the commitment of his corps now resolved, Millikin conferred briefly with Bradley and departed for Arlon. On the 20th, as lead elements of the III Corps headquarters were arriving in that town, Patton met there with Millikin, Middleton, Gaffey, and Major General Willard S. Paul, commander of the 26th ID.[11] Patton accepted Middleton's estimate that Bastogne could and should be held. Thus was set what would become the most important element of the III Corps offensive mission—the relief of Bastogne. Patton directed that the attack be launched the morning of 22 December. III Corps would have assigned the 4th AD and the 26th and 80th IDs. The Third Army commander also stipulated that the main axis of the 4th AD's attack was to be due north from Arlon, rather than northeast through Neufchâteau.

The corps sector covered roughly thirty miles from the Alzette River in the east to approximately Neufchâteau in the west. The left flank was completely open, VIII Corps having no effective forces at its disposal save those at Bastogne.[12] The terrain over which III Corps was to attack was marked by a number of cross compartments, dense woods, occasional open fields, and small villages and medium-sized towns that controlled tactically significant road junctions. Additionally, the steep approaches to and limited crossing sites over the Sûre River formed a significant obstacle in the eastern three-quarters of the corps sector. The lack of air support added to the challenge. Enemy forces in the sector were believed to consist of four divisions of the Seventh Army. These included the 5th Parachute Division and three VGDs, the 212th, 276th, and 352nd. The sudden change of direction, tough terrain, bad weather, capable adversary, and force of only three divisions to attack on a wide front gave Millikin a formidable challenge.

Like the XVIII (Airborne) Corps staff, the III Corps staff was new to combat. Nevertheless, it jumped into action and issued a corps order on 21 December.[13] This order stipulated that the three divisions would attack abreast—with the 80th ID, commanded by Major General Horace L. McBride, in the east, the 26th ID in the center, and the 4th AD in the west. Eddy's XII Corps would be on the right flank. Each division was reinforced by two or three battalions of corps artillery, an ample allocation. Although the 6th Cavalry Group, previously assigned to the corps, had been detached, Millikin, the old cavalryman, was not about to leave his left flank unguarded. Accordingly, he composed a "Task Force Lion," consisting of a reinforced corps engineer battalion, to screen the west side of the attack. It was not much, but it would provide him with at least some early warning of a threat from the west. By the evening of 21 December, Millikin had done everything he could to ensure that III Corps would be ready for its important mission of attacking the southern flank of the German penetration and relieving the now-surrounded defenders of Bastogne. The dawn would bring the beginning of his first day in combat.

XII CORPS MOVES NORTH FROM LORRAINE

During the first several days of the German attack, it appeared that XII Corps would play no significant role in the campaign. In fact, on the first day of the offensive, Patton considered sending Eddy, whom he described as "depressed and nervous," back to the rear for a rest. He refrained, however, because he sensed that the order might have just the opposite of its intended effect.[14] Eddy's most pressing problem at the moment was the high rate of trench foot in the recently assigned 87th ID.[15] After ten days of increasing incidence of this condition, he had just decided, with Patton's concurrence, to relieve the commander, Brigadier General Frank L. Culin. He notified Culin of his prospective relief on the afternoon of the 19th; but before he could designate a successor, he received a call from Patton late in the evening alerting him to future movement north to assume command of the 4th ID and 10th AD on the southern shoulder. Major General Wade H. "Ham" Haislip's XV Corps would probably take over the XII Corps sector, and Eddy told Culin to disregard his orders concerning relief, apparently not wanting to burden Haislip with the turmoil of replacing a division commander.[16]

Eddy spent the 20th conferring with his division commanders and Haislip.[17] In another development that was to have some future bearing on the fighting in the Bulge, he learned from Patton that over the next two days Major General Paul W. Baade's 35th ID, which was seriously under strength after over five months of continuous frontline combat, would receive some 1,600 replacements. The 35th ID would be sent to Metz to conduct refresher training.[18] The confirming call from Patton came at around 1750, instructing Eddy to move his command post to Luxembourg City, now the location of both 12th Army Group's and Third Army's tactical headquarters, and informing him that his existing corps sector would be split between Major General Walton H. "Johnnie" Walker's XX Corps in the north and Haislip's XV Corps in the south.

Eddy left on the morning of the 21st for Luxembourg City, arriving at 1000.[19] There ensued a round of meetings to get the lay of the land, receive instructions from Patton, meet his new subordinates, and develop a sense of the possible. At Bradley's headquarters, he talked to Lev Allen. Patton's G-3, Brigadier General Halley G. Maddox, then escorted him to the Third Army command post only a few blocks away, where he conferred with Generals Barton and Morris. He also learned that the 5th ID, commanded by Major General Stafford L. "Red" Irwin, then moving into position behind the 4th ID, would be assigned to XII Corps. Patton told him he had to go on the offensive the next day. Eddy quickly realized that the only way he could comply with this order was to attack with a single regiment of the 5th ID. After discussing the matter with Barton, Morris, and Irwin later in the evening, he decided that that regiment would be the 10th Infantry, which he would attach to Barton. Having been advised by Patton that Barton might need a rest, he talked privately to Brigadier General James S. Rodwell and Colonel Richard S. Marr, assistant division commander and chief of staff of the 4th ID, respectively, to get a feel for Barton's stamina. Both officers vouched for their division commander, confirming Eddy's own assessment, "I thought Tubby looked allright too."[20] Having had a very long day and done what little he could to satisfy Patton's demand for a supporting attack on the III Corps right flank, Eddy retired for the night. Meanwhile, his staff worked feverishly to push the XII Corps command post forward from Lorraine on winding, treacherous roads under intermittent Luftwaffe attack. These roads were choked with scores of convoys carrying shivering soldiers, multifarious weapons, and all manner of supplies north to engage the German onslaught.[21]

VII CORPS PREPARES TO BLUNT THE PENETRATION

During the first four days of the German offensive, Collins's VII Corps played a supporting role, sending units to the south to help Gerow's embattled V Corps, shifting its boundary to the south, and rounding up a few of von der Heydte's scattered paratroopers. At midnight on the 16th, the entire 1st ID was placed on alert for movement, and the 26th Infantry Regiment was dispatched immediately to Camp Elsenborn.[22] On the next day, the corps accounted for forty-six German paratroopers, killing sixteen, wounding one, and capturing twenty-nine; it also sent the remainder of the 1st ID to V Corps.[23] On the 18th, VII Corps assumed responsibility for the northern half of Gerow's sector, with the 8th and 78th IDs and the 102nd Cavalry Group now falling under its command. It also released elements of the 9th ID and CCA, 3rd AD, to V Corps. On the 19th, the remainder of Rose's division was attached to V Corps, although CCR, 3rd AD, would soon move on to Ridgway's XVIII (Airborne) Corps. By detaching units and moving its right-flank boundary farther south, Collins's unthreatened VII Corps had served as a reservoir of troops that paid the bill for Hodges to put additional combat power in Gerow's hands and for Gerow to focus all his attention on the vital battles at Krinkelt-Rocherath and the Dom Butgenbach, where such attention was sorely needed. Collins had, in short, been a good neighbor.

This relatively passive role changed dramatically on 20 December shortly after Montgomery arrived at First Army headquarters. Monty knew that he would have to mount a multidivision counterattack against the penetration; he also knew that a corps headquarters would be required to direct this effort. Having closely followed and highly regarded Collins in both the capture of Cherbourg and the Cobra breakout, there was no doubt in the 21st Army Group commander's mind that Lightning Joe was his man for this mission.[24] Hodges notified Collins of his new assignment on the afternoon of the 20th, setting off a whirlwind of activity.[25] Collins's first order of business was to coordinate with Simpson and Major General Raymond S. McLain, whose XIX Corps would take over the VII Corps sector. Here it was important to organize a phased extraction of the corps troops, particularly the artillery, in such a way as to avoid alerting the Germans to the redisposition of the headquarters. This coordination was accomplished by the early morning hours of the 21st.

Collins then hit the road. His first stop was Chaudfontaine, where Hodges's command post was in the process of displacing across the Meuse to Tongres. Hodges gave him the basics: he would command the 84th ID, at the time deploying around Marche; the freshly arrived 75th ID, commanded by Major General Fay B. Prickett; and the 2nd AD, commanded by Major General Ernest N. Harmon and coming in from Ninth Army the following day. The First Army commander also told him that Bolling's 84th ID would remain under XVIII (Airborne) Corps control until about 23 December and that he might later pick up some or all of Rose's 3rd AD. On the 23rd, he was to take command of a sector reaching from Marche to Dinant and be prepared to attack on order in any one of several different directions. In the meantime, Ridgway would cover his concentration. So instructed, Collins went to Marche to get the lay of the land and a feel for how much protection he could expect from Bolling's men. He found the 84th ID commander directing his regiments into position along the Marche-Hotton road, relaxed and certain that he could hold. Collins then drove nine miles due north to Méan, where his chief of staff had located the new headquarters. With much done, yet much still to do to assemble his arriving divisions and prepare for an attack in a yet-to-be-determined direction, he called it a day.

SOME CLOSING OBSERVATIONS

At this juncture, we should briefly consider the role played by the corps itself as a flexible echelon of command during the opening phase of the campaign. Put simply, it functioned exactly as it had been designed. The modular corps structure allowed Hodges to shift forces gradually from Collins's quiet front to Gerow's that was anything but. It also allowed him, in less than three days, to expand Ridgway's slim force from a division and a single regiment to a five-division command stretching from Malmédy to Marche. Even more significantly, the First Army commander added three divisions to VIII Corps, putting a total of seven divisions under Middleton's command by 19 December. Patton was also the beneficiary of this system. He quickly realized that Middleton's focus had become overstretched and established a provisional corps to take over the southern shoulder, later bringing XII Corps up from Lorraine to assume that role. And most notably, by adding two divisions also hurried up from the south, he converted Millikin's III Corps from a rear area mop-up echelon with a prospective reserve mission into a full-scale counterattack force. Furthermore, within the limits of time and space, the corps structure also allowed senior commanders to choose the specific corps commander they wanted for a particular role. Patton probably would have preferred that Eddy, rather than Millikin, command the Third Army attack toward Bastogne; but XII Corps was simply too far away from the scene of action for that to transpire. Nevertheless, he was able to get his most reliable corps commander into the second-most-important action on the southern shoulder. And, perhaps most notably, the pull-and-plug corps system allowed Montgomery to put his impending counterattack in the capable hands of Joe Collins.

The remarkable Allied capability to react positively to the massive and unexpected German counteroffensive launched on 16 December 1944 was attributable, at least in part, to the command capabilities of the six American corps commanders directly involved in the action or preparing soon to become so. It also owed a good deal to the doctrine and the organizational system that had clearly recognized the requirement for such flexibility. Even though the Wehrmacht still held the initiative on the evening of 21 December, the forces now in place or soon arriving would allow the U.S. Army to contest that initiative over the next two weeks.

Gerow, presumably at V Corps headquarters in Eupen, Belgium, ca. December 1944. Courtesy Virginia Military Institute Archives.

Middleton inspecting the VIII Corps front, 28 January 1945. National Archives.

Ridgway with Montgomery at XVIII (Airborne) Corps headquarters near Harzé, Belgium, 12 January 1945. When Ridgway captioned this photograph for his memoirs, he noted of Monty, "Later he was to be my deputy at SHAPE." Matthew Ridgway Collection at U.S. Army Military History Institute.

Ridgway and Gavin in serious conversation, somewhere in Belgium, 20 January 1945. Clay Blair Collection at U.S. Army Military History Institute.

Collins, Montgomery, and Ridgway gather at VII Corps headquarters, Méan, Belgium, 26 December 1944, to begin planning for elimination of the Bulge. The absence of Courtney Hodges, Commanding General, First Army, is indicative of Monty's direct involvement in managing the northern half of the German penetration. Matthew Ridgway Collection at U.S. Army Military History Institute.

Collins gesturing in battle, perhaps in the Bulge, winter 1944/1945. U.S. Army Military History Institute.

This frame from a captured German film depicts an SS NCO beside a disabled American half-track signaling his unit to move forward. Many of the sequences in this film were staged after a clash between the elements of the 1st SS Panzer Division and the 14th Cavalry Group on 18 December near Poteau, Belgium. National Archives.

Private Adam H. Davis and Technical Sergeant Milford A. Sillars, two weary survivors of the 110th Infantry Regiment, 28th Infantry Division, which staunchly delayed the German XLVII Panzer Corps but was ultimately overrun, stand together in Bastogne on 19 December 1944. Sergeant Sillars's sunken eyes and his lack of a weapon speak eloquently of the regiment's travail. National Archives.

A destroyed German Panzer Mark IV near Bastogne. This tank was one of several that were engaged by bazooka fire from paratroopers of the 101st Airborne Division and tank destroyers of the 705th TD Battalion during a Christmas Day attack by the 115th Panzergrenadier Regiment. National Archives.

MEMORANDUM RECEIPT
VIII CORPS

DATE 18 JAN 1945

RECEIVED FROM THE 101ST AIRBORNE DIVISION

THE TOWN OF BASTOGNE, LUXEMBOURG PROVINCE, BELGIUM

CONDITION: USED BUT SERVICEABLE, KRAUT DISINFECTED

SIGNED Troy H. Middleton

TROY H. MIDDLETON
MAJ GENERAL USA
COMMANDING

Memorandum of receipt from the 101st Airborne Division that Middleton signed for a "Kraut disinfected" Bastogne on 18 January 1945. Courtesy Dwight D. Eisenhower Library.

Bodies of American soldiers killed by soldiers of Kampfgruppe Peiper, 1st SS Panzer Division, on 17 December 1944 in what became known as the Malmédy Massacre. News of the atrocity spread like wildfire through the American units in the Bulge. This photograph was taken on 16 January 1945, three days after the nearby Baugnez crossroads were recaptured by soldiers of the 30th Infantry Division. National Archives.

Soldiers of the 48th Armored Infantry Battalion, 7th Armored Division, dropping to the ground as German shells fall near them, outside St. Vith, 24 January 1945. The heavy damage to the buildings came both from the vicious fighting in and around the town and from an attack by nearly 300 planes of RAF Bomber Command on 26 December 1944. National Archives.

Soldiers of the 290th Infantry Regiment, 75th Infantry Division, taking up positions near Amonines, Belgium, 4 January 1945. The heavy snowfall evident in this picture significantly complicated elimination of the German penetration. National Archives.

The war goes on. Soldiers of the 504th Parachute Infantry Regiment, 82nd Airborne Division, moving up to Heersbach, Belgium, in preparation for their attack into the Siegfried Line, 28 January 1945. National Archives.

PHASE II:
INITIATIVE IN FLUX

10

The Struggle for Initiative: Tension in the Allied Camp

I do not think Third U.S. Army will be strong enough to do what is needed. If my forecast proves true then I shall have to deal unaided with both 5 and 6 Panzer Armies.[1]   *Bernard L. Montgomery, 22 December 1944*

I wish Ike were more of a gambler, but he is certainly a lion compared to Montgomery.[2]   *George S. Patton Jr., 27 December 1944*

FROM 22 DECEMBER 1944 TO 4 JANUARY 1945, there occurred an intense struggle for initiative, which until 21 December had belonged strictly to the Germans. During these two weeks, the outcome of the Bulge hung in the balance. The III Corps offensive from the south began on 22 December. VII Corps' Christmas Day halting of the 2nd Panzer Division only four miles from the Meuse dealt another serious blow to the German effort. But neither of these events signified that OKW was without recourse. As late as 31 December, both Hitler and Model believed that a new attack toward Liège and Aachen could still be mounted *if* they captured Bastogne.[3] Thus, Bastogne became the new Schwerpunkt; on 3 January, a last, desperate attack was launched to capture it. By the evening of the 4th, this effort had achieved its final gain, with only modest success. Thereafter, the Germans seized no additional territory in the Ardennes, and the initiative passed wholly to the Americans. It is to this pivotal "swing" period in the Battle of the Bulge that we now turn our attention.

ALLIED GROUND PLANNING IN THE TRANSITION PHASE

There were four broad options for dealing with the Ardennes penetration. The first was to cut it off behind its base, with an attack from the south toward Prüm, along a major highway dubbed by the Third Army staff as the "Honeymoon Trail." It was Patton's much-preferred course of action, but it required a concomitant northern attack aimed in the same direction from

Gerow's base at the Elsenborn Ridge.[4] This made Patton's plan a nonstarter because there was no analogous road leading from the northern shoulder into the Eifel and, as the abortive efforts of Sixth SS Panzer Army had convincingly demonstrated during the preceding six days, the roads in and around the Losheim Gap were incapable of sustaining major troop movements, much less their follow-on supplies. Theoretically, there was the option of cutting off the German attack at its base. This would entail an attack south from Malmédy, through St. Vith to Weiswampach, then east across the Our, complemented by an attack from the south along the Skyline Drive. Collins proposed the former, but its logistical supportability was questionable. Regarding the southern pincer, the Skyline Drive did have a well-surfaced road along its entire length; but the maneuver space was barely sufficient for a regiment, much less a corps. Such a small force would have absolutely no chance of fighting its way through to close the trap, and the idea was never seriously proposed by anyone on the southern side of the penetration. That left two possibilities: to join forces at the waist, with converging attacks on Houffalize, or to squeeze out the forces in the Bulge by direct pressure, much as one squeezes toothpaste from a tube. What was eventually adopted was a combination of these two approaches.

The result was driven by the interplay of the minds and egos of Eisenhower, Bradley, and Montgomery. Eisenhower's decision to divide the Bulge into two halves had, on the surface, solidified the Anglo-American Alliance and made it impervious to Hitler's attack on the political center of gravity. But beneath the surface, tensions still ran deeply. Montgomery began to envision command of two American armies as a prelude of even greater things to come when the Bulge would be eradicated.[5] Bradley was desperate to get both First and Ninth Armies back under his control as quickly as possible so he could eliminate the Bulge and then mount a major offensive up to the Rhine, across the Rhine, and south of the Ruhr.[6] Eisenhower had to resolve these tensions and harness the competing energies in a way that would benefit the Alliance as a whole, and he was willing to entertain a certain amount of compromise. As he confided to his chauffeur, Kay Summersby, "If I can keep the team together, anything's worth it."[7] On the other hand, Eisenhower could not compromise to the extent that he jeopardized either his broad front strategy or his own overall command of the land effort. Thus, devising an offensive prescription for eliminating the Bulge was important in and of itself, but it was also important as a prelude to larger issues of theater strategy in follow-on operations.

Both these themes were evident in a tense meeting between Montgomery and Bradley at the 21st AG tactical headquarters in Zonhoven on Christmas Day. Four days earlier, the British Chief of the Imperial General Staff (CIGS), Field Marshal Alan Brooke, had warned his temperamental subordinate that he "should not even in the slightest degree rub this undoubted fact [the wisdom of Monty's commanding two American armies] in to anyone at SHAEF or elsewhere."[8] But this sound counsel fell on deaf ears. Montgomery was riding a high horse, and he was not about to let anyone forget it. In a thirty-minute private conference, he unloaded on Bradley with both barrels. He said that the Germans had given them a "bloody nose," that this was primarily the fault of Eisenhower's strategy of wanting to be strong both north and south of the Ardennes, and that the only thing to do now was to draw back everywhere south of the Meuse in order to allow for a strong thrust in the north under Monty's direction.[9] Bradley said virtually nothing; Monty interpreted this silence as acquiescence, which it certainly was not.[10] When Bradley recounted the incident years later, he said that Monty "began by lecturing and scolding me like a schoolboy" and that "never in my life had I been so enraged and utterly exasperated."[11] He claimed that he held his tongue out of considerations of Allied unity. Bradley was indeed an Eisenhower devotee, and he may well have wanted to avoid disappointing his commander by engaging in an altercation with Montgomery. Whatever the explanation for Bradley's silence, he left Zonhoven determined to regain control of First and Ninth Armies as quickly as possible.[12]

Accordingly, he repaired to Luxembourg City and crafted a plan to do just that. On the 27th, he briefed his concept to Eisenhower at SHAEF.[13] To close the Bulge, Bradley envisioned a two-pronged attack at the waist, with the southern blade being an attack by Patton directed at both Houffalize and St. Vith and the northern blade being an attack by Hodges, using VII Corps to meet up with Patton's forces at Houffalize and XVIII (Airborne) Corps to cover Collins's left flank. Despite the obvious passion of Bradley's presentation, Ike bought almost none of it. He said he would make no tactical decisions on handling the Bulge until he talked to Monty, but that Bradley would not regain command of First Army until a linkup was effected between the forces north and south of the penetration. As for the long term, he was determined that future advances would be methodical and "risk no more Bulges."[14] The most he granted Bradley was provisional authority to press to the Rhine as quickly as circumstances warranted after the German salient had been eliminated.

Ike's next move was to confer with Montgomery. This meeting took place on the 28th in Eisenhower's command train at Hasselt, Belgium. Monty pointedly excluded de Guingand from the session. Concerned about residual German strength in the penetration and wanting to preserve XXX Corps for

Operation Veritable, his planned offensive by General Henry Crerar's First Canadian Army to close on the Rhine, he resisted setting a definite date for an attack to eliminate the Bulge.[15] Ike finally wrung a concession from Montgomery that if no additional German attacks occurred, the northern riposte would be launched by 3 January.[16] But Monty could not resist berating Eisenhower much as he had Bradley three days earlier. He charged that the German attack had been the direct result of Ike's flawed strategy. He insisted that all Allied attacking power be dedicated to an offensive into northern Germany and that "one man must have powers of operational control and coordination over the whole northern thrust."[17] In other words, it was to be Monty's strategy with Monty in control. Although Montgomery told Ike he was willing to serve under Bradley, rather than vice versa, coming after his session with Bradley on Christmas Day it could hardly have been a serious offer; and Ike told Monty he had no intention of giving Bradley such a role.[18] How much of this Eisenhower agreed to is a matter of some disagreement. Monty told both Brooke and General Frank Simpson, Director of Military Operations at the War Office, that he had bought it all.[19] But Brigadier E. T. Williams, a member of Monty's staff, characterized Ike after the meeting as having been merely exasperated at how frequently he had to keep explaining the basics of his strategy to Montgomery, hardly the attitude of a commander who had just caved in to his subordinate.[20] Brooke's reading of the 21st AG commander's account of the conversation also sensed trouble, the CIGS noting in his diary: "Monty has had another interview with Ike. I do not like the account of it. It looks to me as if Monty, with his usual lack of tact, has been rubbing into Ike the results of not having listened to Monty's advice!"[21]

Brooke's premonitions were well-founded, and things came to a head on 30 December when Montgomery dispatched de Guingand to SHAEF with a letter rearticulating the points made at Hasselt. Harking back to a previous meeting on 7 December at which he had suggested but not insisted that he should have operational control of 12th AG as well as his own, Monty said, "I therefore consider it will be necessary for you to be very firm on the subject, and any loosely worded statements will be quite useless."[22] He went on to say that Eisenhower could not possibly direct the efforts of the two main army groups himself. Finally, he "suggested" that the forthcoming SHAEF directive conclude with the sentence, "From now onwards full operational direction, control, and co-ordination of these operations is vested in the C-in-C 21 Army Group, subject to such instructions as may be issued from time to time."[23] In other words, Eisenhower was to abdicate control of the land battle to Monty. Whether it was the tone of the communication or the realization that Montgomery simply would not desist from discussing the subject, Eisenhower found it deeply disturbing. He simply could not tolerate that sort of insubordination in an official communication.

At this juncture, he also received a radiogram from Marshall. The army chief of staff was disturbed by British press reports that parlayed Eisenhower's decision to give Montgomery command of the northern half of the Bulge into another opportunity to plump for the appointment of a land force commander subordinate to Eisenhower, with Monty being the front-row candidate. He adjured Ike, "My feeling is that under no circumstances make any concessions of any kind whatsoever. You not only have our complete confidence but there would be a terrific resentment in this country following such action. . . . You are doing a grand job and go on and give them hell."[24] Assured of the chief's full support, Ike decided to bring matters to a head and drafted a letter through Marshall to the Combined Chiefs of Staff outlining the profound differences between himself and Montgomery on the subject of command and proposing that either he or Monty be relieved.[25] If the latter, he mentioned Field Marshal Harold Alexander, the Allied commander in the Mediterranean theater, as a possible replacement at 21st AG.[26] When de Guingand got wind of this message, he petitioned Eisenhower for a twenty-four-hour stay of execution. "Beetle" Smith, perhaps recalling the twenty-four-hour reprieve granted by Montgomery when Hodges's fate had hung in the balance, supported de Guingand, and Ike relented. De Guingand then hurried to Zonhoven, where he forthrightly told his chief that unless he backed down quickly he would be sacked. With the Americans carrying the lion's share of the war in Northwest Europe, any choice between Eisenhower and Montgomery would inevitably be made in the former's favor. Monty was particularly nonplussed that Alexander, whom he regarded with utter disdain, would be nominated to replace him; he finally realized that he had pushed too hard.[27] De Guingand, loyal supporter and ever-efficient staff officer, had already drafted a sincere and direct message of apology that Monty used as the basis of his signal to Eisenhower. The message read:

Dear IKE,
Have seen Freddie and understand you are greatly worried by many considerations in these difficult days. I have given you my frank views because I have felt you like this. I am sure there are many factors which may have a bearing quite beyond anything I realize. Whatever your decision may be you can rely on me one hundred percent to make it work

and I know BRAD will do the same. Very distressed that my letter may
have upset you and I would ask you to tear it up.

Your very devoted subordinate,

MONTY[28]

Eisenhower accepted Monty's apology and cabled Marshall that he had no
intentions of appointing a land forces deputy.[29] Later that evening, after
having received Hodges, Monty also fell into line with Eisenhower's desire
for 3 January as the start date for the northern offensive to kick off against
the Bulge and, as a bonus, pushed one division of XXX Corps across the
Meuse.[30] His plan, which closely resembled Bradley's concept, had Collins's
VII Corps making the main effort in the direction of Houffalize and Ridgway's XVIII (Airborne) Corps conducting a supporting attack on the left in
the direction of St. Vith.

Thus, the final Allied plan for eliminating the Bulge was a compromise.
Patton, under Bradley's command, would fight to cut the penetration at the
waist by attacking due north from Bastogne to Houffalize. Hodges, under
Montgomery's command, would apply direct pressure, with Collins's and
Ridgway's corps attacking southeast toward Houffalize and due east toward
St. Vith, respectively. This was about the best that could have been expected.
Contrary to the opinion of Patton and his apologists, there was simply no
feasible way to bag all the Germans in the Bulge.[31]

THE GERMANS SHIFT THEIR GAZE TO BASTOGNE

On the German side, the fundamental problem was one of tension between
continuing the attack to the west and securing Bastogne. The first indication
that the latter was to take priority over the former came on 26 December.
As Millikin's III Corps was on the verge of breaking through to the encircled
101st, Model directed Manteuffel to disengage the FEB, which was supporting a critical advance of the 116th Panzer Division near Hotton, and send it
forthwith to Bastogne.[32] Manteuffel dutifully complied, recognizing that the
situation on his southern flank now represented "the greater danger."[33]

But this was just the beginning. With St. Vith in German hands and Manteuffel's forces obviously making greater progress than Dietrich's, Bastogne
was now attracting attention at OKW as well. Even before the 26th, Manteuffel had been given the XXXIX Corps headquarters from OKW reserve,
commanded by the "experienced, prudent, and determined" General Karl
Decker, to oversee operations at Bastogne.[34] At this juncture in the campaign,

Major Percy Schramm, the OKW historian, referred to the southern hub as "the point of main difficulty" and opined, "Obviously the enemy command also recognized that Bastogne had a decisive meaning for the success or failure of the offensive."[35] On 1 January, Hitler and his confidants took stock of the offensive. They recognized that the grandiose objectives set for it had not been achieved, but they took some comfort in having at least temporarily regained the initiative for the first time since the Normandy landings.[36] This realization led Hitler to continue hatching plans for an offensive into Alsace, coded-named "Nordwind."[37] But the concomitant requirement for the success of this lesser effort was to keep as many American forces as possible engaged in the Ardennes. To do that, something vital had to be threatened. Accordingly, Hitler, who had even earlier insisted that Bastogne be captured, reiterated that intent in a directive of 3 January.[38] Thus, by the end of the second phase of the campaign, the German Schwerpunkt in the Ardennes had shifted twice. The first was from Dietrich's northern attack across the Elsenborn Ridge to Manteuffel's advance in the center to gain the Meuse. The second was from the drive on the Meuse to the seizure of Bastogne. Both these adjustments were made in response to failure, rather than to the exploitation of unanticipated opportunities. Thus, the defeat of the final attempt to capture Bastogne would be proof positive that the initiative in the Ardennes had been irretrievably lost.

THE AIRPOWER EQUATION

Despite the limited ground options for eradicating the Bulge, the Allied air effort contributed substantially to the reversal of German fortunes in the transition phase of the campaign. On 23 December, an eastern high pressure area, known as a "Russian High," moved to the west over the Ardennes, providing nearly picture-perfect flying conditions for the next five days.[39] This resulted in both the Allied air forces and the Luftwaffe surging to their full capacities. Given the disparities in strengths, however, good flying weather provided the British and American forces a substantial advantage that helped shift the tactical and operational initiative to the Americans.

The first manifestation of this shift was resupply of the beleaguered Bastogne defenders.[40] On 21 December the 101st Airborne Division G-4 sent an urgent request for aerial replenishment of artillery ammunition to VIII Corps. This request was relayed through Third Army and SHAEF to IX Troop Carrier Command. Bad weather on the 22nd prevented the mission from being flown; the troops in Bastogne began to wonder who was going to get into Bastogne first—the aerial resupply, Millikin's III Corps, or the Germans. When the weather broke on the 23rd, the answer became the resupply. U.S. Air Force pathfinders landed in mid-morning and quickly established liaison with the G-4. Before noon, 21 C-47s put their loads squarely onto the 101st drop zone.[41] By the end of the day, 249 C-47 loads had been dropped, providing the surrounded garrison with 230 tons of ammunition, medical supplies, and rations. Eight planes were lost to enemy action. On the 24th, the division received some 240 tons dropped by 160 aircraft. Christmas Day, however, was bleak. Bad weather in England grounded the transports; artillery ammunition for the 155-mm howitzers was almost depleted; small arms ammunition was a problem as well—in one battalion, most of the frontline soldiers were down to a single bandolier; medical supplies were reaching critical levels as the number of casualties escalated from determined German attacks; and Millikin's relief forces were discovering the German resistance to be very tough indeed.[42]

The 26th, however, was a *dies mirabilis*. The weather over England broke, and the airflow provided a veritable cornucopia to the GIs on the ground. One glider landed with surgeons and medics, and others brought in nearly 3,000 gallons of gasoline. This manna was supplemented by 169 tons of supplies delivered by 269 C-47s. And the best news of all was that a tank-infantry task force from the 4th AD, aided by timely and well-coordinated assistance of P-47s from XIX TAC, broke through to Bastogne.[43] On the 27th, the narrow corridor leading into Bastogne was widened sufficiently for a truck convoy to get through, and the last day of aerial resupply brought in another 126 tons of ammunition, with a number of the gliders delivering ammunition directly to the 155-mm howitzer firing positions. Though the heaviest fighting for Bastogne was still to come, it was no longer an isolated outpost.

While the relief of Bastogne caught the world's attention, the skies over and beyond the Ardennes were filled with Allied aircraft.[44] On 24 December, Eighth Air Force put up over 1,800 bombers and nearly 800 fighter escorts to bomb communication centers in the tactical area. On the 28th, it launched nearly 1,200 bombers, escorted by over 500 fighters, to pound marshaling yards and railways again. RAF Bomber Command participated in this effort as well. On the night of 22/23 December, it attacked marshaling yards at Coblenz and Bingen with 283 aircraft. And on 26 December, it delivered a devastating attack on St. Vith with 274 Lancasters. Ninth Bomber Division attacked transportation centers on the inner ring with 670 mediums on the 23rd and 814 more on Christmas Day. On 23 December, XIX TAC flew 374 missions in direct support to corps, fighter sweeps, and armed reconnaissance and another 109 directed against the Bonn airfields and Prüm. The British tactical air forces also participated, with 2nd TAF flying 91 sorties over the northern sector of the Bulge on the night of 24/25 December and another 294 on the 27th.

This onslaught of Anglo-American airpower produced several effects. The first was the establishment of air superiority over the battlefield. In the first period of the battle, the Luftwaffe had been very aggressive despite the adverse weather. Although this aggressiveness had not significantly aided the German advance or contributed to the dissolution of the ground defense along the American front, it had, particularly on 16 and 17 December, forced American pilots to jettison their bombs and go after the Luftwaffe.[45] On the 23rd, when the weather broke, the Luftwaffe launched 900 sorties but was forced to allot roughly half of them to defending its own forces. The overall number of sorties declined steadily, until by the 30th Luftwaffe West was able to get up only 200 aircraft. The over 4,000 tactical and strategic sorties launched by the American and British air forces that day made it abundantly clear that the Allies were masters of the skies.

The second effect was to impede the forward flow of German fuel and ammunition. This is an issue of some complexity because many forces were acting in concert to degrade the German supply effort. The huge traffic jams on the northern shoulder, which took place in and behind the narrow corridor between the Elsenborn Ridge and St. Vith, had a very significant impact on the critical opening days of the battle. With the lead elements of I SS Panzer Corps confined to this constricted area, the motorized impedimenta of artillery, engineers, other support troops, and supply columns constipated the already inadequate road network from the assembly areas to the line of contact. The snow and rough terrain that had delayed the strategic concentration remained significant factors in impeding a supply effort that had now had to meet the greatly increased demands of a large-scale offensive.

Nevertheless, the Allied air threat acted in three significant ways to slow both the movements of combat formations and their requisite sustenance. First, it confined road and rail movement to the hours of darkness, roughly 4:30 p.m. to 8:30 a.m., of which several hours per night were frequently required for snow removal.[46] Second, the attacks on the German rail system east of the Rhine, especially along the line from Cologne to Karlsruhe, significantly degraded the ability of the Reichsbahn to support the advancing armies.[47] Finally, the air attacks on towns west of the Rhine slowed the operational redeployment of units, degraded tactical mobility, and impeded supply movements.

The effects of bombing significant road junctions are clearly illustrated in the attacks on Bitburg, St. Vith, and Houffalize. In its postbattle assessment of German unit movement by road into the Ardennes, the USSTAF A-2 determined that Bitburg was the point with the highest volume of traffic.[48] It was attacked by B-17s of the Eighth Air Force on 23 December, 2nd TAF aircraft on the night of 24/25 December, and B-26s of the IX Bomber Division on Christmas Day.[49] According to General Brandenberger, traffic through the city was delayed for a week following these attacks.[50] In the wake of the withdrawal of the 7th AD and 106th ID from the St. Vith salient, medium bombers from the IX Bomber Division attacked the city on 25 December with 137 tons of bombs.[51] This attack merely slowed traffic for a few hours, but things soon got much worse. On the day after Christmas, nearly 300 Bomber Command Lancasters and Halifaxes plastered St. Vith with 1,140 tons of heavy bombs, making rubble of virtually the entire city and blocking all its major roads. This apocalyptic destruction completely halted traffic for three days, reduced the town's throughput capacity by 50 percent following the repairs, and required the construction of major detours along unimproved roads and across fields.[52] Farther south, Houffalize was attacked four times by medium bombers of IX Bomber Division and twice by Bomber Command Lancasters and Mosquitoes. Traffic was completely blocked for two days, and capacity was reduced by roughly 25 percent. Manteuffel noted that they "greatly disorganized the march forward as the damage had been done all in one place at a spot where a detour was impossible."[53]

Although it is difficult to assess relative values to disruption of German supply produced by ground defense, clogged roads, terrible weather, close terrain, and air attacks, the cumulative effects were noted by almost all major German participants in the battle. And airpower was frequently mentioned as probably the catalytic ingredient in the supply friction formula. Jodl said, "The crushing attacks on transport installations . . . had the consequence that the difficult transportation situation which had been in existence already for a long time could not be improved in spite of every kind of auxiliary service and repair and restoration work."[54] Manteuffel declared that the activity of enemy air "controlled the supply routes, railways, and roads completely. . . . There was not enough room for road transportation. Continuous breakdowns by air attacks increased this lack, which industry could not make up any more to an adequate extent."[55]

Lieutenant General Karl Thoholte, Model's senior artillery advisor for the Ardennes offensive, painted a virtual tapestry of ways in which Allied airpower inhibited German artillery support.[56] The Allied air forces negated the use of German rail artillery; seriously impeded the forward movement of ammunition and fuel to support the artillery battle; prevented the artillery from determining the depth of American defenses beyond the immediate line of contact; provided the American artillery a significant advantage in target location, which was particularly important in the counter-battery duel; and reduced the effectiveness of German artillery to 50 or 60 percent of its potential. These effects, he maintained, were particularly felt in the lack of artillery support for the attacks against the Elsenborn Ridge and Bastogne.

Tactical air forces directly contributed to defeat of the German offensive on 25 and 26 December.[57] On the 24th, reconnaissance elements of the 2nd Panzer Division had arrived at Celles, a small town four miles east of the Meuse, virtually out of gas and cut off from the remainder of the division. They were met the next day by Harmon's 2nd AD. While the almost continuous coverage of American Thunderbolts prevented the 2nd Panzer Division main body from advancing to join its forward unit, the lead combat command of the 2nd AD attacked into Celles. In one engagement en route to the village, American tanks were engaged by German tanks concealed near a farm. The P-47s then rolled in and flushed four Panthers into the open, where they were engaged and destroyed by tanks and tank destroyers. On the morning of the 26th, a German relief force that had moved up to the outskirts of Celles during the night was attacked by British rocket-firing Typhoons directed in by an American artillery spotter. A follow-on group from Panzer Lehr met the same fate.

As the battle for the Meuse reached its denouement, 1,100 sorties of C-47s augmented Eisenhower's strategic reserve by shuttling the newly arrived 17th Airborne Division from England to Rheims in just six days.[58] From this staging area, the division was trucked to a position just west of Bastogne where it was quickly thrown into the fray. On the return trips, the Gooney Birds evacuated over 5,000 casualties to hospitals in England.

The only sour note of the period was two incidents involving friendly air attacks on American soldiers and Belgian civilians at Malmédy on 23 and 25 December.[59] On 23 December, six B-26s of the 322nd Bomber Group, IX Bomber Division, mistakenly dropped their eighty-six-bomb load of 250-pounders on Malmédy, some thirty-three miles short of the intended target. On 25 December, four B-26s from the 387th Bomber Group dropped sixty-eight 250-pound bombs on Malmédy in lieu of St. Vith, about twelve miles to the south. These erroneous attacks, which occurred in conditions of good-to-excellent visibility, were verified by IX Bomber Division photographic reconnaissance. According to the U.S. Army official history, they killed thirty-seven soldiers of the 120th IR and nearly panicked the town's civilian population.[60]

To welcome in the new year, the Germans demonstrated they had one more surprise in store. Galland's idea of the "Great Blow" was to make itself manifest, but in a completely different form than he had intended. Toward the end of December, Major General Dietrich Peltz, commander of Jagdkorps II, was told to prepare plans for a massive attack on Allied airfields with all available daylight aircraft.[61] Code-named Operation Bodenplatte, or "Baseplate," the objective of this attack was to create conditions that would allow the Luftwaffe to fight the Allied bombers on a more even footing and thus be able to mount an effective defense of German airspace. In order to catch the British and Americans by surprise, which was the sine qua non of the attack, the plan called for all fighter formations to maintain complete radio silence and fly at treetop level under Allied radar coverage, guided by Ju-88 night fighters along their routes up to the German front lines. To make this attack, the Germans were able to assemble nearly 800 fighters organized into 33 groups from 10 different Jagdgeschwader. Everything looked good on paper, and there was a feeling of confidence among many of the pilots as they prepared for takeoff on the morning of 1 January 1945.

Bodenplatte broke down badly in execution. The stringent security arrangements taken to protect the secret of the attack led to late, incomplete, and inadequate briefings that ranged from sparse details to heroic exhortations. The information that Luftwaffe planes would be flying at low level over the German front lines was received by only very few of the antiaircraft batteries. Although there are no firm figures for how many German planes were downed by their own flak, estimates run up to 100, or 12.5 percent of the force. Furthermore, the radio silence, while superb for security, created all sorts of doubts in the minds of inexperienced pilots in formations whose internal cohesion was problematic at best. Thus, when squadron leaders were shot down or disappeared from view, the formations became scattered and disoriented. In a few cases, Allied aircraft were already airborne and able to break up the German formations before they reached their targets. And, of course, Allied antiaircraft weapons played a role in blunting the attack.

As a result, of the some seventeen Allied (predominantly British) airfields targeted, only four were attacked successfully. Five were bombed with moderate success; three were struck intermittently or not at all; and five were either hit by mistake or as targets of opportunity, with no effect. Altogether, the Germans destroyed some 120 RAF and 30 American aircraft. Figures on the German losses vary wildly; the most probable number is about 300, or an adverse ratio of 2:1. Bodenplatte's worst effect on the German fighter force was the devastating toll on its pilots: 214 total losses, with 151 killed or reported as missing and 63 taken prisoner. It was a blow from which the

Luftwaffe never recovered, and it ceded to the Anglo-American coalition absolute and total command of the air.

After the relatively clear conditions of 1 January, fog and snow again blanketed the Ardennes. On 3 January, for example, conditions in the battle area were limited to ceilings of 200 to 300 feet and visibility from 50 to 1,500 yards, with similar conditions obtaining on the next day as well.[62] This effectively shut down the Allied air effort. But the cumulative support given during the brief period of flyable weather had helped significantly to turn the tide. Furthermore, unlike the ground action, which was almost entirely American, the air effort during the transition phase of the Bulge was clearly Allied, with the British fully participating in an integrated air effort.

11

III, VIII, *and* XII *Corps Fight for Initiative in the South*

The relief of Bastogne is the most brilliant operation we have thus far performed and is in my opinion the outstanding achievement of this war.[1]
George S. Patton Jr., 29 December 1944

WITH THE BULGE EFFECTIVELY DIVIDED IN HALF by the German push beyond the Ourthe River, it is now possible to examine the campaign from the perspectives of the three corps fighting the southern battle and the three corps fighting the northern battle. Given that the initial surge for American initiative came from the south, we shall start there with consideration of Millikin's III Corps, Middleton's VIII Corps, and Eddy's XII Corps.

III CORPS ATTACKS FROM THE SOUTH

The thrust of III Corps into the southern flank of the German penetration was broader and more complex than simply the effort to relieve Bastogne, but that relief was clearly the most significant aspect of the attack. Thus, the story of the offensive cannot be intelligibly told without also relating the German attacks against the town and the staunch resistance its defenders offered. It will therefore be necessary to relate the events of the III Corps attack from 22 to 26 December in parallel with the events in and around Bastogne, even though the units therein were under VIII Corps control.

Launching the Attack, 22–23 December

The III Corps attack that kicked off on 22 December 1944 was no ordinary operation. The effort to move Millikin's corps headquarters up from Metz and the even more prodigious effort to concentrate three divisions along a line from Arlon to Luxembourg City in three days had required a good deal of foresight, flexibility, and logistical wherewithal. But it was different in another aspect as well. Patton, who normally gave his corps commanders fairly wide latitude (except when it came to postponing attacks), meddled and hectored constantly during this operation. On the day before the attack, he made it known that he favored the III Corps divisions attacking in "column of regiments or in any case lots of depth."[2] The obvious purpose of this preference was to provide for speed. But it ignored two realities: first, III Corps was attacking on a front of roughly twenty-five miles; second, the Germans, who were moving from east to west, would be easily able to infiltrate the widely separated columns that following this guidance would entail.[3] Millikin dealt with the situation properly. He informed his division commanders of Patton's desires but stipulated that he would not dictate their formations. In the event, none of them followed the Third Army commander's guidance. Given the widths of their attacking fronts, they simply could not.

Millikin's three division commanders were all solid and competent. But among this group, Hugh Gaffey was a special case.[4] Commissioned in the field artillery in 1917, he served as a regimental artillery officer in the AEF. A 1936 CGSS graduate, he served with Patton at the Desert Training Center and in North Africa, rising to command of the 2nd AD. When Patton was pressured by Eisenhower to remove Major General Hobart R. "Hap" Gay as his chief of staff during preparation for the Normandy landings, he reached out to Gaffey. Gaffey was later Patton's personal choice to assume command of the 4th AD in early December when Eddy's patience ran out with "P" Wood. He was thus experienced but new to the division. Millikin was acutely aware of Gaffey's close association with Patton and of the fact that Patton kept watch over the 4th AD with proprietary interest. Willard Paul had a prototypical infantry career.[5] Commissioned in 1917, he served for three years as an instructor at Fort Benning in the early 1930s, graduating from CGSS in 1935 and the War College in 1937. He commanded the 75th ID for a short while before assuming command of the 26th ID during its stateside training. He was highly regarded by both Bradley and "Beetle" Smith. Horace McBride was a 1916 USMA graduate commissioned in the field artillery, who, like Gaffey, had combat experience in the AEF.[6] He graduated from CGSS in 1928 and the War College in 1936. He joined the 80th ID as the division artillery commander in 1942 and assumed command of the division in 1943.

Gaffey clearly realized that the task of the 4th AD was not just to make a thin, pencil-like thrust into Bastogne.[7] Rather, it was to establish a corridor sufficiently wide to withstand German counterattack and to permit the use of Bastogne itself as a base of future operations to the northeast. His scheme of maneuver was simple: CCA, commanded by Brigadier General Herbert L. Earnest, would advance on the right, along the main road toward Martelange

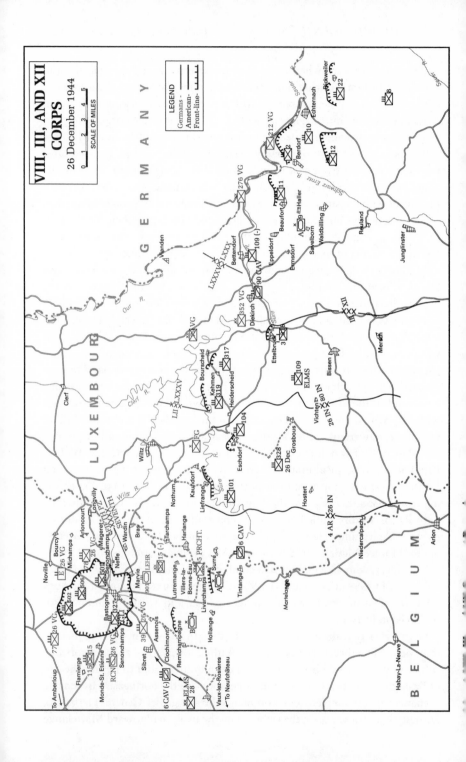

on the Sûre; Dager's CCB would attack on a web of secondary roads to the west in the direction of Burnon. On 22 December, CCA encountered a series of obstacles on the road created by VIII Corps engineers to keep the Germans from continuing their attack to the south. Indeed, so abysmal was the cross-corps communication and so great was the apprehension of continued German advances, that the 4th AD reconnaissance squadron was forced to dissuade incredulous VIII Corps engineers from creating additional obstacles as the attack progressed. Despite these difficulties, CCA assaulted Martelange. The battle was still in progress at midnight. To the west, CCB, being beyond the headwaters of the Sûre and facing no appreciable German forces, had a virtual cakewalk. It reached Burnon in a few hours and encountered only sporadic resistance. After a temporary halt, it continued its advance to the north; and in an over-eager moment of optimism, III Corps informed VIII Corps that it anticipated contact with the 101st by that evening.[8] Millikin, acting on instructions from Patton, told Gaffey to continue the attack.

In the center, Paul's troops had a slightly rougher go.[9] The 26th ID attacked in the typical Leavenworth "two up, one back" formation. The 104th Infantry was on the right; the 318th was on the left; and the 101st, minus just over one battalion, was in reserve. The 104th advanced easily through dense woods until about noon when it was attacked vigorously by several hundred men from the head of a regiment of the 352nd VGD. This attack threw one company of the 104th back almost three-quarters of a mile. Heavy artillery fire forced the Germans to withdraw to Grosbous. There, the 104th continued to apply pressure throughout the day. This action protected the right flank of the 318th Infantry and gave it a clear shot well to the north. After advancing about six miles with no enemy in sight, the 318th ran into strong resistance at Rambrouch, which was occupied by a battalion of the FGB.[10] This battalion's combat effectiveness had been undermined when its commander was killed by American artillery fire on the evening of the 22nd.[11] Nevertheless, given the strength of the resistance, the 26th ID halted to regroup. Shortly before midnight, its two forward regiments continued the attack in accordance with Millikin's orders; neither made significant gains.

In the eastern portion of the corps sector, the 80th ID attacked on a five-and-one-half-mile front with the Alzette River on the right and the village of Useldange on the left.[12] McBride's soldiers were well rested and well oriented when they kicked off at 0600 across the Arlon-Mersch road. The 318th and 319th IRs advanced abreast from right to left, with the 317th IR in reserve. To their north, the 352nd VGD, commanded by Major General

Erich Schmidt, was advancing from east to west, apparently oblivious to the American presence. On the right flank, the 318th advanced up a narrow defile to Ettelbruck, where it encountered a regiment of the 352nd that had just occupied the village. Although their supporting artillery was driven back to Diekirch, the Germans held onto Ettelbruck, while the Americans occupied the heights to the west and the south. On the division's left flank, the 3rd Battalion of the 319th Infantry dispersed the trains and regimental artillery of the southernmost of Schmidt's lead regiments. By the end of the day, the Blue Ridge soldiers had advanced some eight miles and had significantly disrupted the westward progress of the 352nd VGD. But there was no respite. Millikin ordered McBride to advance to the line of the Wiltz River and seize crossings in the sector.[13]

Despite the fact that the 4th AD did not break through to Bastogne, the first day had been relatively encouraging. In each division zone, the right-flank unit had encountered some resistance, but the left-flank unit had made good progress. The 80th ID had noticeably interrupted the progress of the 352nd VGD. The 26th ID, despite running into the FGB, had advanced some six miles. And most encouraging of all, the 4th AD had reached the Sûre and, on its left flank, advanced well over half the distance to Bastogne.

Patton kept up the verbal pressure all day. Shortly before noon, he called Colonel James H. Phillips, Millikin's diligent chief of staff, and "directed that we drive like hell. That we keep on attacking tonight," adding, "This is their last struggle and we have an opportunity of winning the war."[14] Late in the afternoon, he came to III Corps headquarters to lay down detailed tank tactics for Gaffey.[15] Patton's guidance was based on the brutal experience of the Lorraine campaign, in which the Sherman's vulnerability to the Panther had been painfully evident. He wanted the enhanced-armored Shermans, which were in very short supply, used wherever possible. He also prohibited shallow envelopments that would expose the Sherman to enfilade fire, insisting that all flanking actions start one or one-and-a-half miles before reaching the enemy. Though sound advice for open country, it would be difficult to implement in the close terrain through which Gaffey would be fighting. Patton also gave Millikin the gratuitous counsel to "go up and hear them [the shells and bullets] whistle."[16] Despite the concerned tone of these various instructions and exhortations, the generally satisfactory advances of the 22nd caused the III Corps commander to rise at least marginally in Patton's estimate. The latter confided that night in a letter to his wife, "John Millikin is doing better than I feared."[17]

In what was undoubtedly the largest German psychological blunder of the campaign, Lüttwitz sent an emissary to McAuliffe seeking surrender of the Bastogne garrison and threatening to "annihilate" the defenders with an artillery corps and six flak battalions if the demand were not met.[18] He was obviously motivated by the thought that a victory on the cheap would resolve the tension between continuing the attack toward the west and capturing the transport nexus necessary to support that offensive. And he was encouraged by the surrender of the two regiments of the 106th on the Schnee Eifel to hope that he might pull off a similar coup.[19] But he utterly misread the mood of McAuliffe, who had absolutely no intention of surrendering and probably realized as much as the XLVII Panzer Corps commander did that, all things considered, the defenders of Bastogne had the upper hand.[20] McAuliffe's reply, a laconic "Nuts!" was both an emphatic rejection of Lütt-witz's ill-considered démarche and a moral fillip to the "Battered Bastards of the Bastion of Bastogne," to the troops coming to their relief, and to the GIs throughout the Bulge.[21]

23 December brought distinct disappointment to the hopes for an early relief and the advance in general.[22] Worried about CCB, 4th AD's advance from Burnon toward Chaumont, General Kokott, the 26th VGD commander, alertly reinforced elements of the 5th Parachute Division with four Tiger tanks, about a dozen assault guns, and supporting infantry. About a mile south of Chaumont, the 5th Parachute Division, stiffened by Kokott's reinforcements, conducted an aggressive and well-organized counterattack that knocked out eleven tanks in a fierce fight and set CCB back on its heels. CCA experienced similar trouble to the east. Although it captured Mar-telange, it was delayed by the time-consuming requirement to construct a Bailey bridge over the Sûre. After advancing several miles to the north, the Americans encountered strong opposition from elements of the 5th Para-chute Division that infiltrated through woods behind their leading echelon, forcing them to withdraw to the southwest of Warnach. On the division's far right, Gaffey committed CCR with one battalion each of tanks and infantry in hopes of closing the gap between the 4th AD and 26th ID. This force ran into a sharp engagement with the FGB just south of Bigonville. Things did not go well to the east either. The 26th ID pushed forward a few miles in the right portion of its sector against stubborn resistance. The 80th ID, though advancing steadily on the Sûre, had to contend with reserves that Seventh Army was feeding into the battle.

Patton fulminated as usual. At 1100 he again called Colonel Phillips with the following message:

> The thing wasn't going so good [as] yesterday. I am unhappy about it. I want to emphasize that this is a land battle and we must move forward.

Get them to bypass towns and go forward. I want a definite report at 1315 today on the situation. I want Bastogne by 1350. I have to give it to my boss at that time. Get those boys going. Tell Millikin to get them going if he has to go down to the front line platoon and move them.[23]

Millikin took this mixture of bromide, impractical guidance, impossible demands, and patently ridiculous justifications all in stride. That night, he sensibly told Paul, whose division was lagging behind the neighbors on both flanks, that he should push patrols up to the line of the Sûre but hold back the main strength of his infantry regiments until he had developed the situation.[24]

Things in Bastogne were beginning to get worrisome. In the morning, the 101st, intensely interested in the progress of the 4th AD, requested that VIII Corps pass on hourly reports of the location of friendly units.[25] In the early evening, Millikin received a message from the VIII Corps liaison officer that tanks had penetrated the 101st's perimeter.[26] This news came at the end of a hard day. Kokott struck at three places around the circumference. The heaviest assault was at Marvie in the southeast corner.[27] Here, the 901st Panzergrenadier Regiment, supported by tanks, gained a toehold in the village. Marvie was tenaciously defended by soldiers of the 327th GIR, reinforced by two Shermans and a company from the adjacent 501st PIR. Shortly after this engagement started, Lieutenant Colonel Harry W. O. Kinnard, the division G-3, opined to Colonel Harry G. Mewshaw, the VIII Corps G-3, "It's getting pretty sticky around here."[28] And at midnight, while the desperate fighting still raged on the perimeter, a wag at division headquarters sent a pointed message to the 4th AD reminding Gaffey's tankers that there was only one shopping day left until Christmas![29]

Delivering a Belated Christmas Present, 24–26 December

Over the next three days, Millikin began to focus combat power where it was needed most: Bastogne. He transferred two infantry battalions from the 80th ID to the 4th AD.[30] When the 6th Cavalry Group was returned to III Corps control on 24 December, Millikin devised a sensible and partially unorthodox plan to employ it. The conventional part of the plan was to use the bulk of the group to protect the corps' left flank and assist the 4th AD in its attack toward Bastogne.[31] The unconventional part of the plan was to detach the 6th Cavalry Squadron from the group and insert it, under corps control, into the seam between the 4th AD and the 26th ID, where the Germans had been particularly pesky since the beginning of the attack.

Early on the 24th, Gaffey was frustrated by the fact that neither CCA nor CCB could make any headway against the stiff German resistance they encountered at Warnach and Chaumont, respectively.[32] With his right flank to be at least partially protected by the insertion of the 6th Cavalry Squadron, he moved CCR to the division's left flank, to attack along the Neufchâteau-Bastogne axis. CCR pulled out of Bigonville, which it captured shortly before noon, and during the night of 24/25 December road-marched to Neufchâteau. We must give Gaffey primary credit for this decision, but we must also give Millikin credit for establishing the tactical conditions that allowed Gaffey to make it. During the day, CCB remained south of Chaumont, reorganizing after the bloody nose it had received from the 5th Parachute Division, while CCA made a modest advance in the direction of Tintange.[33] If there was any hope for relief of Bastogne in the near future, it probably lay with CCR.

Meanwhile, Millikin's two infantry divisions did what they could to advance to the north. In Paul's sector, it became apparent that the village of Eschdorf, two miles south of the Sûre, was being used by Seventh Army as a nexus from which to dispatch reinforcements from the FGB into the 26th ID's attack zone.[34] Accordingly, a tank-infantry task force organized around Lieutenant Colonel Paul Hamilton's 2nd Battalion, 328th Infantry, was formed to capture it. Hamilton's troops, now the vanguard of the division attack, ran into a buzz saw, taking heavy fire from a battalion of the FGB supported by tanks and 88-mm guns. After firing four basic loads of mortar ammunition and receiving help from division and corps artillery and tactical air support, the task force reached a position from which to assault Eschdorf shortly after midnight. The steep ravines and thick woods made any advance excruciatingly slow. No sooner would an area be cleared than the resourceful Germans would seep back in to disrupt the supply lines of the forward echelons and generally wreak havoc.[35] Furthermore, Millikin's conscious decision to use McBride's division as the bill payer for Gaffey's advance on Bastogne reduced the 318th Infantry to a single battalion, thereby limiting the pressure that could be placed on Ettelbruck; neither of the other two regiments made significant advances.

Things were fairly quiet at Bastogne. Lüttwitz regrouped for a major attack on Christmas Day.[36] McAuliffe used this lull to implement a plan drafted by Kinnard that reorganized the defenses by shortening the lines and providing a small armored team to each of the four regiments manning the perimeter. In the southeast corner, this consolidation entailed pulling back to just north of Marvie, which, reminiscent of the fighting at Krinkelt-Rocherath, had been bitterly contested by the 327th GIR and the 901st

Panzergrenadier Regiment since the attack of the previous day. Strong tactical air support from XIX TAC and continued air resupply also boosted the defenders' morale.[37] Patton, attempting to do likewise, prematurely signaled, "Xmas Eve present coming up. Hold on."[38] The Luftwaffe worked to convince McAuliffe's men to the contrary.[39] In a particularly heavy attack, it set numerous buildings on fire and scored direct hits on both Team Cherry's command post and a makeshift military hospital.[40] That evening, on the phone to Middleton, McAuliffe informed his boss that "the finest Christmas present the 101st could get would be a relief tomorrow."[41] Middleton replied empathetically, "I know, boy. I know."[42]

On the evening of the 24th, Millikin issued orders to all his divisions, instructing them to "stabilize lines with all-around defense and active patrolling. . . . Troops will be rested as much as possible. . . . Attack will be resumed just before daylight 25 December."[43] Perhaps this was the result of Patton's finally realizing that his orders for continuous day and night attack in the conditions under which III Corps was operating simply could not be sustained. As he noted in his diary that night,

> This has been a very bad Christmas Eve. All along our line we have received violent counterattacks, one of which forced . . . the 4th Armored back some miles with the loss of ten tanks [here, he appears to be referring to the action south of Chaumont, which actually occurred on the 23rd]. This was probably my fault, because I had been insisting on day and night attacks.[44]

On Christmas Day, the presence of the 6th Cavalry Group on the left flank of CCR, 4th AD, helped it in its attack toward Bastogne. The lead element of the command was a task force led by Lieutenant Colonel Creighton W. Abrams, which advanced from Neufchâteau to Remonville.[45] It encountered no substantial opposition en route and, upon arrival, all but wiped out a battalion of the 5th Parachute Division. But a crater north of the village stopped Abrams for the night. Fortified by infantry from the 80th ID, CCB and CCA now had the wherewithal to advance through the heavy woods south of Bastogne, albeit cautiously.[46] CCB's attack led off with an infantry assault into the Lambay Chenet Forest; then it was on to Chaumont. To the east, CCA moved forward cautiously but inexorably, capturing both Tintange and Hollange, the latter just over five miles south of Bastogne on the west side of the Arlon-Bastogne road.

Further to the east, both infantry divisions made but incremental progress. After being repulsed in a night attack, two companies from TF Hamilton stormed into Eschdorf.[47] By nightfall, the 104th Infantry pushed up a battalion to relieve Hamilton's badly battered men, and Paul's division now had a clear shot at the Sûre. In the 80th ID area, the Germans still clung stubbornly to Kehmen and Ettelbruck.[48] The best that McBride's soldiers could do was clear the southern banks of the Sûre in the zone of the 319th Infantry.

Patton continued to needle. On Christmas morning, his G-3 called the III Corps staff, reminding them that the Third Army commander was "very much interested in your people's progress" and instructing them to provide a special report on progress at 0800 each morning.[49] Two hours later, however, Patton gave Millikin a real Christmas present.[50] After an extended debate with Gay, he decided to insert the 35th ID, which was refitting at Metz, into the battle between the 26th ID and the 4th AD. Gay had objected because he felt that the 35th, having just come out of the line in Lorraine, had received insufficient time to integrate its several thousand replacements.[51] Patton was sympathetic with this argument to a point and had delayed his decision for a good two days. But the hard realities of battle demanded greater troop density on Millikin's front. The best way to get such concentration was to put another division into the line, and the 35th ID was available at Metz. As a bonus to Millikin, Patton also directed that when this went into effect on the next day, McBride's Blue Ridge soldiers would be assigned to Eddy's XII Corps, thus narrowing Millikin's focus more narrowly on Bastogne.

Bastogne's defenders had a harrowing Christmas.[52] On Christmas Eve, Kokott had received reinforcement from a regiment of the 15th Panzergrenadier Division, supported by about eighteen Mark IVs. Although it was much less force than he wanted and clearly much less than he needed to take and hold the town, he organized a significant predawn attack against the hamlet of Champs, on the northwest corner of the defensive circle at the junction between the 502nd PIR and the 327th GIR. The Germans penetrated the 327th's lines just southwest of Champs. At that point, the panzers, festooned with infantry, broke into two columns. One struck out toward Champs and was all but wiped out by rifle and bazooka fire from two companies of the 502nd and by tank destroyers of the 705th TD Battalion. The other column, heading southeast toward Bastogne, ran into a virtual hornet's nest. It, too, was decimated. Colonel Kinnard's plan of the day before to position tank destroyers and tanks close to the perimeter was clearly vindicated.

But with a second armored penetration of the Bastogne defenses in two days, pressure for a breakthrough by the 4th AD was becoming palpable. What happened to effect that breakthrough was well beyond Millikin's control. But, as noted earlier, he is entitled to at least some of the credit for CCR, 4th AD's having been placed on southwesterly approach into Bastogne, from which the relief did occur.[53] On the evening of the 25th, CCR's plan had been for Abrams to attack through Remichampagne and Clochimont, then northwest to Sibret. But on the afternoon of the 26th, having reached Clochimont, Abrams consulted with Lieutenant Colonel George Jaques, commander of the 53rd AIB, on the advisability of heading directly for Bastogne. With enfilading fire from Sibret a very real threat, this plan entailed a fair amount of risk. But Abrams was moved by the sight of C-47s dropping much-needed supplies to the Bastogne garrison being plastered by German flak. "Well," he said, "if those fellows can take that, we're going in right now."[54] Hastily arranging a coordinated salvo from four artillery battalions, Abrams ordered his lead tank-infantry team forward and told Captain William Dwight, the battalion S-3, to lead it into Bastogne. Catching the 26th VGD and 5th Parachute Division soldiers in Assenois completely by surprise, Dwight's men roared into the village just as the last artillery rounds were falling. Most of them made it through. Shortly before 1700, the lead tank made contact with the 326th Airborne Engineer Battalion on the southwest quadrant of the Bastogne perimeter. Soon thereafter, Captain Dwight reported with a salute to McAuliffe, who had been observing the attack from a nearby hilltop. "How are you, General?" the captain asked.[55] "Gee, I am mighty glad to see you," McAuliffe replied.

Later that evening, Patton's transfer of the 80th ID, on the III Corps right flank, to Eddy's XII Corps allowed Millikin to focus on the problem of widening the tenuous lifeline into Bastogne.[56]

Widening the Bastogne Corridor and Regrouping, 27–29 December

During the night of 26/27 December, some close combat was required to secure the narrow corridor.[57] First, the Assenois-Bastogne road was cleared of German infantry. Next, Abrams's task force repulsed a counterattack from Sibret. In desperation, the Germans used direct-fire artillery to interdict the road, but it too was silenced. By 0500 on the 27th, a convoy of seventy ambulances and forty supply trucks was escorted through to Bastogne. That afternoon, General Taylor, still outfitted in service dress uniform but sensibly topping it off with a steel helmet, made a run into Bastogne in a jeep.[58] After surveying the division's strength and finding that it had over 10,000 effectives, he informed Millikin, to whose III Corps the 101st was temporarily attached, that the division was prepared to attack on order.[59] Over the next two days, III Corps widened the corridor.[60] Patton shifted CCA, 9th AD, from XII Corps to III Corps; Millikin attached it to 4th AD. CCA, 9th AD, captured Sibret and Villeroux on the 27th, eliminating the left-flank threat to the Neufchâteau-Bastogne road. In the late morning of the next day, CCB, 4th AD, linked up with McAuliffe's soldiers due south of Bastogne. The lifeline to Bastogne was secure from any immediate threat, and none too soon.

To the east, General Baade's 35th ID came in on 27 December to fill the gap between the 4th AD and the 26th ID. At fifty-five, Baade was one of the oldest division commanders in the ETO.[61] Commissioned from USMA into the infantry in 1911, he gave III Corps yet another World War I combat veteran. After graduating from CGSS in 1924 and the War College in 1929, he commanded the 16th Infantry before becoming assistant division commander of the Santa Fe Division in 1942, later rising to division command. For its push south of Bastogne, Millikin assigned the division a narrow front of only five miles.[62] The attack jumped off at 0800, with the 35th ID soldiers moving through dense woods covered with six inches of snow.[63] On the division's left flank, the 137th Infantry easily crossed the Sûre near Tintange; but it encountered stiff resistance at Surré and did not secure that village until nightfall.[64] On the right flank, the 320th Infantry advanced across the Sûre in the face of heavy automatic weapons fire. By late in the day, it had secured the villages of Boulaide and Baschleiden, relieving the 6th Cavalry Squadron. At the end of the day, Baade's soldiers had managed gains of two-to-four miles.

North of the 26th ID at Wiltz, where Brandenberger located his headquarters, the Seventh Army commander was bringing new units in as fast as OKW would feed them to him.[65] The latest unit to arrive was the 9th VGD, which had been shifted south on bicycles from Denmark. Its lead elements were thrust in south of Wiltz to support the FGB. Despite these opposing reinforcements, Paul's soldiers secured the bridgehead over the Sûre that had been tenuously gained the previous day.

South and east of Bastogne, the 28th was almost a carbon copy of the 27th, with one important exception—air support.[66] With the weather closing down, XIX TAC was grounded. CCA, 4th AD, committed a battalion given over from the 35th ID and its own armored infantrymen but could not break through to the Bastogne perimeter south of Remonfosse. The 35th had a similarly tough time. On the left flank, the 137th Infantry was repulsed at Villers-la-Bonne-Eau. On the right, the 320th Infantry was halted after advancing less than a mile. Farther to the east, the 26th ID advanced steadily to within two miles of Wiltz. But a disturbing pattern was beginning to develop. As the left flank of the 35th ID moved gradually north and the right flank became almost stationary, the lead regiments formed an "echelon right." And with the 26th ID to the east moving slowly but steadily forward, a strong pocket of resistance was beginning to form in front of the right flank of the 35th ID, centered on the village of Harlange.

The 29th was a day of small gains along most of the III Corps front. The 101st Airborne, which had by now evacuated its wounded and been amply resupplied, made a limited attack to expand the perimeter to the southeast, with the 327th GIR recapturing Marvie.[67] Shortly before noon, CCA, 4th AD, secured Remonfosse and made contact with the Bastogne defenders.[68] The 35th ID broke through to Marvie from the south, widening the corridor even further.[69] It also pushed troops into Lutrebois and Villers-la-Bonne-Eau, though without completely dislodging the Germans from either position; the Harlange front remained stalemated.[70] The 26th ID, advancing cautiously with both flanks exposed, pushed a single battalion forward to the southern bank of the Wiltz River.[71]

At this juncture, we must outline the German plans to retake Bastogne and the Third Army plan to use the hard-won town as a springboard for offensive operations. The clash of these mutually contradictory intentions produced some of the heaviest fighting of the campaign.

By the night of 29/30 December, Manteuffel and Brandenberger had concentrated the equivalent of roughly eight divisions around the Bastogne perimeter.[72] But they failed to exploit this strength, and the attacks on Bastogne over the next week emerged as a series of expedients as one after another resulted either in outright failure or limited gains made at very heavy expense. In aggregate, however, they were sufficiently powerful to prevent Patton from breaking out of the Bastogne perimeter for over a week. The first assault, launched on 30 December, was a two-pronged effort by Manteuffel to cut the Neufchâteau-Bastogne road. As the western wing came in the area of Middleton's VIII Corps, we shall deal here only with the eastern assault. The second major attack in the III Corps sector came on 3 January when the 12th SS Panzer Division struck against the 6th AD occupying Mageret.

Patton issued a typically ambitious attack order on the 28th.[73] Millikin's III Corps was instructed to assume command of the 6th AD, release the 101st Airborne to VIII Corps and the 4th AD to XII Corps, attack northeast toward St. Vith, then seize crossings of the Rhine near Bonn. Middleton's VIII Corps was to continue its defense of the Meuse and attack to secure Houffalize. Eddy's XII Corps was to cross the Sauer in the direction of Echternach and attack up the Prüm Valley in the direction of Bonn. No date was given for the attack in the published order, but that night Patton instructed Middleton to attack on the 30th and Millikin on the 31st.[74]

Defending and Attacking, 30 December–4 January

Manteuffel entrusted the eastern wing of his attack against the Bastogne corridor to Decker's XXXIX Corps, to which he assigned the 167th VGD, commanded by Lieutenant General Hans-Kurt Hoecker, and the 1st SS Panzer Division.[75] The 1st SS was seriously under strength, bringing to the battle roughly fifty tanks and about two full battalions of panzergrenadiers. Although the 167th was at nearly full strength, it had experienced some difficulty in its march from its detraining points on and east of the Rhine. Decker planned to use Mohnke's SS troopers to make the main effort along the Lutrebois-Assenois axis, while the 167th made a supporting attack toward Remonfosse. This latter assault was easily repulsed. But the SS troopers attacked with a vengeance, setting the 35th ID back sharply, capturing Lutrebois, surrounding two companies of the 137th Infantry in Villers-la-Bonne-Eau, and pressing their forward elements almost to the eastern edge of the Arlon-Bastogne road. Fortunately, General Earnest's CCA, 4th AD, quickly backed up Baade's men.[76] This alertness, combined with desperate resistance from the 137th Infantry and timely air support from XIX TAC, prevented the severing of the eastern artery into Bastogne. Nevertheless, the assault caused a great deal of anxiety, for there was now a two-mile-wide and two-mile-deep salient driven into the left flank of the 35th ID, and its right flank was still making virtually no progress southeast of Harlange. It was effectively off the board until it could regain the lost ground. The midwestern men who made up the bulk of the Santa Fe Division had paid a heavy price, but Patton's insistence on inserting them into the III Corps front was clearly vindicated. Had they not been there, Mohnke's SS soldiers would have surely cut the Arlon-Bastogne highway. As it was, III Corps received a mid-afternoon message from 4th AD indicating that while things were looking up, the division "had a pretty good scare so far."[77]

Major General Robert W. Grow, commanding the 6th AD, was, like Gaffey, a longtime Patton associate.[78] He had entered federal service as an infantry officer from the Minnesota National Guard in 1916, later transferring to the cavalry. In the early 1930s, he became one of the armored pioneers, serving in the Mechanized Force at Fort Eustis and later the Armored Force at Fort Knox. He had been Patton's G-3 in the 2nd AD. When they again came together in England, Patton considered Grow's 6th AD a standard setter, right up there with Wood's 4th Armored. Grow, however, became somewhat quarrelsome during the fighting in Europe, frequently preoccupied with and critical of the support he was receiving from other division commanders.

Over the next two days, this aspect of Grow's personality simmered beneath the surface as massive amounts of friction inhibited the 6th AD's attack out of Bastogne.[79] The first issue was who would support this effort. Patton's initial inclination had been to use the 4th AD to attack on the left; but Gaffey convinced Colonel Paul D. Harkins, Patton's deputy chief of staff, that his division simply was not up to it. The next scheme was to use the 11th AD to attack out of Bastogne on Grow's left flank, but by the 30th it became apparent that the 11th AD would be needed further to the west. By the evening of the same day, it was also clear that there would be no support from the 35th ID on Grow's right flank. Thus, the 6th AD was destined to make a solitary attack from the northeast quadrant of the Bastogne perimeter. It had a hard time getting there.[80] On the night of the 30th, CCA, commanded by Colonel John L. Hines, Jr., got into Bastogne in relatively good order. CCB, commanded by Colonel George Read, was coming up the Neufchâteau-Bastogne road to take up a position on Hines's left. This artery was blocked by a march unit of the 11th AD and sheeted with ice. The resulting traffic jam so impeded Read's progress that Grow directed him to occupy an assembly area near Assenois and wait until the 11th AD had cleared the road, which took much longer than expected. In the meantime, Grow went back to Bastogne, where he instructed Hines to make a shallow attack through Neffe to seize the high ground southwest of Mageret.

The III Corps attack from Bastogne was now effectively reduced to a single combat command. Hines jumped off at about noon on the 31st.[81] Foul weather prevented air support, but the attack was backed up with ample artillery. Even so, after the Americans gained Neffe and a bit of ground to the southeast, the Germans began nipping at CCA's flanks and pounding Hines's armored infantry with artillery, which now included the entire I SS Panzer Corps' heavy guns and a nebelwerfer brigade. Bereft of help on either side, Hines decided not to press far beyond Neffe. For the next day's advance, which would be mounted with both CCB and CCA, Grow wanted support on his left from the 101st; but Taylor demurred, pointing out that he was assigned to VIII Corps and obliged to support the attack of the 11th AD.[82] Millikin told Grow to continue the attack anyway. A phone call from Patton shortly after noon indicated that the heavy fighting in and around Bastogne had finally made a significant impression. Abandoning for the moment his long-held infatuation with conquering territory, he told Colonel Phillips that "he didn't care how much ground to the Northeast [sic] Bob [Grow] gained today—to fan out and kill Germans."[83] Patton now recognized that the campaign had devolved into a struggle of attrition and that until large numbers of Germans were dead, he would be unable to gain the ground he coveted. This was an important realization.

The road running from Longvilly, through Mageret, to Benonchamps, then on to Bras was a desirable tactical objective because its capture would sever the supply line that supported the German units still pressing against the Arlon-Bastogne highway.[84] Cutting this road would allow more Germans to be killed by assuring the supply of all the units within the Bastogne perimeter, particularly those of the 6th AD's artillery and its supporting corps artillery.[85] The capture of Mageret cut this road, but the village was seized somewhat by accident.[86] On the morning of 1 January, as the 68th Tank Battalion, part of CCB, moved through Bizory in the direction of Arloncourt, it began to receive heavy, direct fire from Mageret on its right flank. Swerving to eliminate this threat, it captured the village by midafternoon, thereafter turning it over to its sister battalion, the 69th, under CCA. By nightfall the division as a whole had gained between one and two miles, expanding the Bastogne perimeter and severing the German supply route, despite receiving several sharp counterattacks. Patton called Millikin's headquarters shortly after noon and told Colonel Phillips to have the 6th AD start turning to the right, to begin an encirclement of the Harlange Pocket from the north.[87] The III Corps chief of staff assured Patton that Millikin had already instructed Grow to plan accordingly.[88]

On the evening of the 1st, Millikin instructed Grow to advance to the high ground west of Longvilly and extended the 6th AD's right-flank boundary to include the Bastogne-Bras road.[89] The wider sector led Grow to commit CCR into the fray, leaving him almost no reserves.[90] Shortly after midnight, the 6th AD fired concentrations from nine artillery battalions into Benonchamps, and CCB repulsed the Luftwaffe-supported attack against Mageret that ensued shortly thereafter.[91] The attack of 2 January was a desperate affair.[92] On the left, Task Force Wall, built around Lieutenant Colonel Arnold R. Wall's 50th AIB, reached Michamps; but it was so heavily pummeled with German artillery and machine-gun fire that it withdrew when a counterattack threatened. The 68th Tank Battalion sallied from Mageret against Arloncourt. It was bushwhacked by a semicircle of well-concealed assault guns, lost eight tanks, and escaped only with the assistance of prodigious artillery support. On the southern front, three battalions attacked toward Wardin; although they advanced about a mile, they could not establish a permanent presence in the village. By the end of the day, Grow had committed everything he had.

In the wake of the German failure to sever the main roads leading into Bastogne, OKW wanted a second effort along the same two axes. But

Model objected, citing the difficult terrain south of Bastogne and the much better tank country on the northeastern face of the perimeter. Hitler uncharacteristically relented and allowed Model to attack Bastogne as he wished.[93] To conduct this assault, Priess's I SS Panzer Corps headquarters was brought down from the north. In addition to the 26th VGD already in place, it was to command the 12th SS Panzer Division and the 340th VGD, the latter hurrying south from Aachen. The 9th SS Panzer Division was also placed under Priess. Manteuffel wanted to attack on 2 January; but Model, sensitive to delays in movement of the reinforcing divisions, postponed the assault until the 3rd.[94]

Priess's plan was to send the 9th SS Panzer and two regiments of the 340th VGD astride the Noville-Bastogne road, the former on the west, the latter on the east. This portion of the volksgrenadier attack would be just beyond Grow's left flank.[95] The 12th SS Panzer was to attack from the Bois Jacques to the southeast, along the road running from Michamps to Arloncourt, then on to Mageret. On the morning of 3 January, two battalions of the 501st PIR advanced into the Bois Jacques to give the 6th AD the left-flank protection it had wanted for the past three days. This advance caught two regiments of the 340th VGD marshaling for their own attack; but the volksgrenadiers quickly recovered and forced the American paratroopers back to their start line. Slightly to the east, the 12th SS Panzers advanced as far as Arloncourt, checking the efforts of TF Wall to link up with the advancing paratroopers.

4 January 1945 was a bad day for the 6th AD.[96] It began with an attack by the right half of the 12th SS Panzer Division south from the Foy-Mageret road. This tank-infantry assault, heavily supported by artillery, forced the withdrawal of TF Wall and the medical evacuation of the task force commander. The CCB commander, Colonel Read, devoid of additional infantry, withdrew to a line that extended his regiment and the 501st PIR along a line running from Foy, east to Bizory, terminating just west of Mageret. The left flank of the 12th SS Panzer attack was halted by a tremendous pounding from American artillery after only a short advance. But an attack by the third regiment of the 340th VGD against the 44th AIB, positioned along the Bastogne-Bras road, caused one company to panic and, when ordered to withdraw, flee all the way to Bastogne. This headlong retreat on the far right, coupled with the only somewhat more orderly withdrawal on the far left, led to considerable confusion all along the line. By mid-afternoon, one task force of CCA still held Mageret, but it was forced to withdraw to the high ground to the west. At the end of the day, the 6th AD had been forced back to a line anchored on Bizory in the north and Marvie in the south, with

a slight easterly bow in the middle that encompassed the ridgeline separating Neffe and Mageret. In other words, on the evening of 4 January, the net advance since 31 December had been a two-mile protrusion in the middle, with no gain on either flank. Grow, who admitted to Millikin that night that his infantry battalions "had been considerably chewed up," was uncertain about his ability to hold.[97] He need not have worried—the 1st SS Panzer Corps was utterly spent and in no shape to follow up its attack. Model and Manteuffel had thrown in their last chips and come up short.

Early January continued to be very tough for the 35th ID as well.[98] The 134th Infantry gained a toehold on the western edge of Lutrebois on New Year's Day, but it took several more days to gain control of the entire village. On 31 December, Colonel William S. Murray, commanding the 137th Infantry, desperately attempted to break through to his two surrounded companies in Villers-la-Bonne-Eau. His efforts were all repulsed, and further relief attempts subsequently abandoned.[99] But Villers-la-Bonne-Eau was important, and on 1 January Millikin committed the 6th Cavalry Group to support the 35th ID's efforts to recapture it.[100] Despite this assistance, the village was still held by the Germans three days later, with little sign of their imminent dislodgement. And to the east, the 320th Infantry was still stalemated short of Harlange.

On the III Corps right flank, General Paul's soldiers were conducting an almost independent operation to take Wiltz. With the 35th ID on its left strung out in an arc from south of Harlange, west to the edge of the Arlon-Bastogne road, then north and east to Marvie, and the 80th ID on its right attacking directly north, the northwesterly advance of the 26th ID kept its flanks permanently exposed. The division's progress was also slowed by Brandenberger's move to put the FGB in Seventh Army reserve and replace it with the fresh 9th VGD. In the five days since it had crossed the Sûre on 27 December, the 26th had been contained by a sharp series of counterattacks that kept it bottled up in the vicinity of Kaundorf. On 1 January, Millikin told Paul to continue the attack north to cut the Wiltz-Bastogne road. Paul's effort gained enough ground to worry Brandenberger that the entire 5th Parachute Division might be cut off in the Harlange Pocket. He appealed to Model for permission to withdraw. But Model refused, pointing out to the Seventh Army commander that the Wehrmacht was now involved in a battle of attrition. Model and Patton had thus come to precisely the same conclusion at almost exactly the same point in the campaign. They were *both* involved in a battle of attrition. On 3 January, the 26th ID inched forward, but on the next day Brandenberger counterattacked twice and forced Paul to halt and reorganize.[101]

By the night of 4 January, III Corps had made only incremental progress since the breakthrough to Bastogne on 26 December. On the northeast corner of the Bastogne perimeter, the 6th AD had pushed out a small salient past Neffe, but it had not been able to hold Mageret. The 35th ID had been thrown back two miles and was attempting to recover lost ground. The 26th ID had crossed the Sûre, but its advance on Wiltz was being bitterly contested. In a tactical sense, these meager results were extremely disappointing. But when looked at from an operational perspective, the picture brightens considerably. By relieving Bastogne, Millikin's III Corps had not only provided material comfort to the town's beleaguered defenders, it had also, over a period of nine days, attracted every spare force at Model's disposal. Bastogne had become a magnet for uncommitted German forces. By 2 January, German forces around the perimeter included the 1st, 9th, and 12th SS Panzer Divisions; the 3rd Panzergrenadier Division; the 26th, 167th, and 340th VGDs; and a panzergrenadier regiment from Panzer Lehr.[102] Millikin's attack, combined with the offensive efforts by a revived VIII Corps, drew forces away from the northern half of the Bulge and materially aided Montgomery's 3 January offensive.

Analysis

During the transition phase of the Ardennes campaign, III Corps played a key role in wresting the initiative from the Germans. Its attack was the first large-scale offensive effort the Americans mounted. By breaking through to Bastogne, it not only provided succor to the soldiers who had defended the vital road junction for eight long days, it also provided a key component of the combat power necessary to continue the town's defense when its capture became the main object of German attention. In the attacks against the reorganized perimeter around Bastogne on 3 and 4 January, Model's last gasp was directed against both VIII Corps and III Corps; but the latter received the heaviest blow. Thus, III Corps deserves a good deal of credit in the defense as well as in the attack.

What about Millikin's role in all of this? Patton's mercurial temperament, particularly evident in the first five days of the operation, imposed a tension almost as difficult to deal with as the tough terrain, bad weather, and determined German resistance. But Millikin did not wilt under this pressure. Instead, he issued commonsense guidance to his division commanders and pushed them only as far as circumstances allowed. His role in setting up Gaffey's transfer of CCR, 4th AD, from the division's east flank to the Neufchâteau-Bastogne road, which put TF Abrams in position to break through to the 101st on 26 December, has never been properly appreciated. And when he could have wobbled after the attack against the Arlon-Bastogne road by the 1st SS Panzer Division, he remained calm and steady, sensibly reinforcing the 35th ID with the 6th Cavalry Group. This same quiet competence was evident in his discussions with his division commanders on the night of 4 January after absorbing all that the 1st SS Panzer Corps could throw at him. He was assisted by an efficient staff, personified by Colonel Phillips, whose timely memoranda on the developing situation kept key players on the corps staff informed of what was going on in Millikin's mind as well as how the unfolding battle looked at both higher and subordinate headquarters. In sum, after two weeks of battle, a green commander and a green staff had performed credibly, competently, and with a nice touch of imagination in what was clearly the most visible, and perhaps the most significant, action during this phase of the campaign.

VIII CORPS REGROUPS AND ATTACKS

On the morning of 22 December, VIII Corps was, with the exception of the encircled units in Bastogne, a spent force. But there could be little rest for the weary. It would have to pick itself up and get back in the battle. It would also have to give Eisenhower and Bradley some assurance that the Meuse would not be penetrated south of Givet. Its activities during this phase of the campaign divide fairly distinctly into a period of regrouping and a period of attacking.

Regrouping, 22–29 December

Middleton's first concern was to reestablish the 28th ID as an effective fighting force. It was an uphill battle. The 110th Infantry was shattered, its erstwhile commander a German prisoner. From 15 to 23 December, its officer strength had fallen from 150 to 55 and its enlisted strength from 2,923 to 730.[103] The 112th Infantry was near St. Vith, now attached to the 106th ID, and the 109th Infantry was strung out west of Luxembourg City.[104] The only organic artillery battalion at hand was the direct support unit for the 110th Infantry, down to four of its eighteen howitzers.[105] On 24 December, while attempting to organize a defense of Neufchâteau, the G-3 reported that the division's combat efficiency was "unknown." There was little Middleton could do to help, but he did what he could. He and his staff pestered Third Army for return of the 109th Infantry, eventually securing its release to VIII

Corps on the 27th.[106] On the same day, he also attached the 7th Tank De-stroyer Group, now reduced to roughly a battalion, to Cota's division, giving it at least a modicum of direct fire power.[107]

Middleton was required to defend the Meuse from Givet to Verdun.[108] For this mission, he was assigned four engineer regiments and six French infantry battalions, already in place, as well as the 11th AD, immediately south of Givet. The 11th AD was soon to be relieved by the 17th Airborne Division, arriving in Rheims by air, and become a mobile reserve west of the Meuse to back up the static defenses. The VIII Corps sector of the Meuse was never seriously threatened, but the requirement to defend it gave Middleton one more thing to consider in his total calculations.

Middleton also acted to accomplish an implied task—gaining contact with XVIII (Airborne) Corps. He initially attempted to do so with the 4th French Parachute Battalion, Special Air Service, assigned to VIII Corps on 24 December, instructing it to operate in an elongated area northwest of Neufchâteau.[109] He later formed a small composite force, drawn from a dozen different units, most belonging to the 9th AD, to assume this mis-sion.[110] This group of four officers and just over one hundred soldiers was designated Task Force W, in honor of its commander, a Captain Wortham, and placed under corps control. Its formation and constitution indicated just how deeply in the barrel Middleton had to scrape to generate useable bits of combat power. Ridgway directed Bolling's 84th ID to extend a counter-reconnaissance screen from Marche to Beauaraing.[111] There, roughly eigh-teen miles southwest of Marche and thirty miles northwest of Neufchâteau, the two corps established a tenuous link shortly before midnight on Christ-mas Day.[112]

Bradley's plan to get to Houffalize depended largely on VIII Corps' clear-ing out the German forces west of Bastogne before it launched a major at-tack to the north. To this end, Third Army gradually increased its combat power. On 25 December, VIII Corps received the headquarters and recon-naissance elements of the 9th AD. Additionally, the 11th Armored and 87th Infantry Divisions were, at Bradley's direction, given to Middleton to use west of Bastogne to gain a stepping stone to Houffalize.[113]

The 11th AD was new to the ETO.[114] It departed the United States in late September and, after roughly six weeks of final training and equipping in Britain, arrived in Normandy in early December. When the Germans at-tacked, it was ordered into SHAEF reserve to backstop the Meuse. On 27 December, it was relieved in place along the Meuse by the 17th Airborne Division.[115] Its commander was Brigadier General Charles S. Kilburn, a West Point classmate of Ridgway and Collins, who took his commission in the cavalry.[116] Kilburn served as an aide to seven different generals in his first fourteen years of active duty, the last being General Malin Craig, who went on to become army chief of staff. After graduation from CGSS in 1935 and the War College in 1937, he served in the Chief of Cavalry's office and then joined the 1st Cavalry Division. He was assigned as assistant division commander of the 11th AD in 1942, later rising to become its commanding general. In sum, the 11th AD was an inexperienced outfit, commanded by an officer with precious little troop experience.

The 87th ID had a similar history.[117] It departed the United States in October, had a relatively brief training period in England, and arrived in Normandy in late November. The division was committed in the Saar Region in mid-December. It was then pulled out of the line and arrived near Rheims on 27 December. Its commander was Brigadier General Frank L. Culin, Jr.[118] A 1915 graduate of the University of Arizona, Culin participated in the Pershing Expedition and served for two years in the Philippines before completing a series of assignments as an ROTC and National Guard instructor. After graduating from CGSS in 1935 and the War College in 1940, he commanded the 32nd Infantry Regiment. He was promoted to brigadier general in 1943 and assumed command of the 87th ID in 1944. Thus, like Kilburn, he had only a modest amount of troop duty.

The VIII Corps mission given in the Third Army order of 28 December was fairly straightforward: seize the high ground near Houffalize and secure the Houffalize road net, while protecting the army's left flank.[119] Realizing that the prospective linkup between VIII Corps and VII Corps at Houffalize would bring with it the return of First Army to Bradley's control and, therewith, the end of his period of acute embarrassment, Patton would, over the next three weeks, go to extraordinary lengths to bring it about.[120] Middleton would thus experience some of the same impatient harassment from Patton that Millikin had received during the drive on Bastogne.

Middleton's scheme of maneuver was simple.[121] On the right, the 11th AD would attack on a front of just over five miles, its right flank at Sibret and its left flank west of the Bois de Haies de Magery, Middleton insisting that Kilburn's armor remain in contact with Culin's infantry. On the corps left flank, the 87th ID attacked on a front of just under six miles, extending from its boundary with the 11th AD to the north-south road running from Recogne to St. Hubert. The initial objective was the road leading from St. Hubert, southeast through Morhet, and on to the Neufchâteau-Bastogne road. The next goal was the parallel road at some five miles greater distance, which connects Bastogne with Ortheuville and Marche. With six regimental equivalents attacking on a front of roughly eleven miles, the prospects for success appeared at least reasonable; but timing was a problem. After publishing the Third Army order, Patton told Middleton to attack on the 30th. Just before midnight on the 28th, Middleton issued movement orders to the 11th AD and the 87th ID to assemble southwest of Bastogne, requiring them to make road marches of roughly eighty-five and one hundred miles, respectively.[122] Both divisions had to contend with icy roads.[123] Concerned by the difficulties encountered in assembling his forces, Middleton called Patton on the afternoon of the 29th to request a postponement.[124] Patton insisted that the attack be made on schedule, despite the fact that both divisions would have to attack without prior reconnaissance.

On the other side of the hill, Manteuffel developed a three-phase concept for seizing Bastogne: cut it off from outside assistance; shove the Americans, i.e., VIII Corps and III Corps, to the south; and capture the town with a direct attack.[125] All was dependent on successful accomplishment of the first task. The assault from the east was mounted by the 1st SS Panzer Division and the 167th VGD, with results already noted. The western thrust was made by Major General Walter Denkert's 3rd Panzergrenadier Division (PGD), to which the FEB was now attached. Jump-off time was planned for 0730 on the morning of the 30th. The general direction of attack was northwest-southeast, beginning on a three-mile front extending from Mande–St. Étienne to Hubermont, toward and beyond the Neufchâteau-Bastogne road, with the tiny village of Hompré set as the linkup point with the 1st SS Panzer Division. The 3rd PGD would attack on the left, angling through the Bois de Fagotte toward Villeroux, while the FEB, on the right, struck Sibret. With Middleton also setting 0730 as the time to cross the line of departure, the stage was set for a significant meeting engagement.[126]

Attacking, 30 December–4 January

And so it developed.[127] On the far right flank, CCB, 11th AD, commanded by Colonel Wesley W. Yale, attacked toward Chenogne. During the approach march, its lead task force was struck by German artillery paving the way for Colonel Remer's FEB. The task force resumed its northward drive but lost seven tanks just south of its objective. Nevertheless, it spoiled the FEB's attempt to gain Sibret. To the west, CCA, commanded by Brigadier General Willard A. Holbrook, advanced without incident to Remagne. There it encountered the eastern extremity of Panzer Lehr, and Kilburn's combat innocents proved no match for Bayerlein's hardened veterans. When the lead task force crested a ridge, "all hell broke loose."[128] A deadly mixture of German heavy weapons and small arms fire took out two tanks and rendered one hundred infantrymen hors de combat. The block was so effective and the damage so debilitating, that Kilburn persuaded Middleton to abandon the idea of attacking along a solid front, instead allowing the 11th AD to attack on the next day solely in the eastern half of the division zone. This meant forgoing all idea of mutual support between the 11th AD and the 87th ID.

Culin's soldiers were marginally more successful. The division attacked with the 345th Infantry, commanded by Colonel Douglas Sugg, making the main effort on the right toward Moircy. Despite fairly stiff resistance from Panzer Lehr, the village was captured late in the day. A sharp tank-infantry counterattack at 2100 forced its evacuation, but heavy American artillery fire convinced the Germans that holding onto it was not worth the candle. In the meantime, Denkert's 3rd PGD attack was neutralized by liberal doses of artillery from the 4th AD and VIII Corps artillery.

At the end of the day, the results were a rough standoff. From Middleton's point of view, the most encouraging development was that the Germans had been frustrated in their attempt to carry the Neufchâteau-Bastogne road. Manteuffel's effort to choke the twin lifelines into Bastogne was definitively checked. This led to a major reevaluation on Model's part, resulting in a shift in the local Schwerpunkt to the northeast corner of the Bastogne perimeter. Patton crowed that he had been right to order Middleton to attack on the 30th.[129] There were, however, two offsetting considerations. First, little ground had been gained. Although CCB, 11th AD, was just south of Chenogne and the 345th Infantry was poised similarly short of Moircy, not a single significantly habited area had changed hands. Furthermore, the rough handling at the hands of the Germans had come as a rude shock to both divisions. There were significant costs involved in giving up the advantages of the defense.

Kilburn regrouped his division for a drive north along the mile-wide valley separating the Bois de Fagotte and the Bois de Haies de Magery.[130] His staff proudly informed the Screaming Eagles that the 11th AD would take Mande–St. Étienne, which lays just north of the Bastogne-Marche road, by 1200 on New Year's Eve. The Germans had other ideas. CCB, operating on the right flank, captured Chenogne in the afternoon but was forcibly evicted by a composite force from the 26th VGD, the 3rd PGD, and the FEB. In the center, CCB reached the hamlet of Rechrival at the northern terminus of the valley but could advance no farther and took considerable losses. On the left flank, CCR, commanded by Colonel Virgil Bell, moved through Magerotte but was denied the village of Pinsamont. Yale's CCB finally secured Mande–St. Étienne in vicious house-to-house fighting early in the morning of 3 January. But by the night of the 1st, Middleton had become so disenchanted with the 11th AD's lack of combat effectiveness and the ineptness of its commander that he called for its relief in place by the 17th Airborne Division.[131] When the relief was effected on the 3rd, Kilburn's division had taken well over 600 casualties and lost 42 Sherman tanks and 12 lights.

The 87th ID experienced similarly tough fighting.[132] The 345th Infantry pushed forward on the 31st, but two days of offensive operations against Panzer Lehr took their toll. On New Year's Day, Culin committed the fresh 347th, commanded by Colonel Sevier R. Tupper, to maintain the modest momentum. By the night of 2 January, Tupper's men had taken noticeable casualties; but they had captured Bonnerue, a small village just over a mile north of Moircy. Although the Germans split the regiment by holding out in Pironpré, slightly to the southeast of Bonnerue, the capture of the latter represented something of a moral and tactical victory for the Golden Acorn soldiers, who had now effected a minor penetration across the Bastogne–St. Hubert road. It was not an auspicious baptism of fire for Culin's soldiers, but it was at least credible. And in these circumstances, being credible was probably all that Middleton or anyone else could expect.

Another piece of good news came from CCA, 9th AD. On 1 January, it secured Senonchamps in the face of a staunch and prolonged German defense.[133] This modest gain in territory was not, however, without significance. For, coupled with the 11th AD's capture of Mande–St. Étienne two days later, it indicated that VIII Corps was beginning to peel the German defenses away from the western face of the Bastogne perimeter, potentially opening up the road north to Houffalize. But more momentum was clearly required—hence Middleton's call for the fresh 17th Airborne to replace the spent 11th AD.

The 17th Airborne Division was activated in April 1943 and had trained in the United States until August 1944 and then spent just over four months training in England before it was dispatched by air to Rheims.[134] After being trucked to the VIII Corps area, it completed its relief of the 11th AD at 1800 on 3 January.[135] Its commander, Major General William M. "Bud" Miley, was a 1918 USMA graduate who became one of the U.S. Army's most noted airborne pioneers.[136] In 1940, he assumed command of the first organized parachute unit, the 501st Parachute Battalion, while only a major. He then rose quickly to two-star rank, which he reached in early 1943, and took command of the 17th Airborne two days after its activation.

Middleton's plan for the renewed attack was issued on the evening of 2 January. It called for the 17th Airborne to make the main effort to reach the line of the Ourthe River, with the 101st making a supporting attack on the east to secure Noville, while the 87th ID moved north to protect the corps' left flank.[137] The original order called for Miley's airborne troopers and Culin's infantrymen to attack on the 3rd, while Taylor's men attacked "on order," presumably later. However, on the 3rd, Middleton delayed the attack until the 4th.[138]

Manteuffel had originally hoped to mount a two-plus division attack along the axis from Mande–St. Étienne to Bastogne, but the slow movements of reinforcements into the Bastogne sector and their weakened condition upon arrival did not permit this luxury.[139] Nevertheless, Lüttwitz's XLVII Panzer Corps still had plenty of defense left in it, and his soldiers were ever eager to counterattack after losing even the smallest chunk of Belgian territory.

Thus, the 17th Airborne, like the two divisions that had to attack without proper reconnaissance five days earlier, was in for a rough initiation.[140] Miley, with four regiments assigned, attacked with the 513th PIR, commanded by Colonel James W. Coutts, and the 194th GIR, commanded by Colonel James R. Pierce, in the lead, the other two regiments in reserve. Although the paratroopers, attacking on the right, carried Cochleval and struck hard into the woods north of Mande–St. Étienne, a determined counterattack forced them back nearly to their starting point. The glidermen fared little better. They seized Hubermont, some three miles west of Mande–St. Étienne. Then, pummeled by German artillery and tanks, they too were driven back from whence they came.[141] The next day, while relating the results of this painful experience to General Gay, then visiting the 17th Airborne Division headquarters, Colonel Pierce lamented, "God, how green we are," adding hopefully, "but we are learning fast and the next time we will beat them."[142]

The Germans were similarly alert in the 87th ID zone, throwing the 147th Infantry back to its starting positions along a three-mile front.[143] That night, despondent over the repeated rebuffs of his offensive efforts, vividly impressed by the strength of the German artillery around Bastogne, and chilled to the bone by the harsh winter weather, Patton glumly noted in his diary, "We can still lose this war."[144]

Analysis

Middleton was also uncharacteristically discouraged by the abject failure of his attempt to renew the offensive. He had thrown in his last fresh troops, had practically nothing to show for it, and was becoming jittery about even holding on to what he had.[145] Unbeknownst to him, similar discouragement was also setting in on the other side. With the failure of the 3–4 January assault on Bastogne, most of which was directed against III Corps, continuing attacks from VIII Corps, and a long-anticipated attack from VII Corps and XVIII (Airborne) Corps having begun in the north, Manteuffel realized the jig was up. He now saw but dim prospects for holding back the oncoming American tide and petitioned Model for permission to begin withdrawing troops from the western reaches of the Bulge.[146] Model and Rundstedt had similar inclinations, but all were turned down by OKW. Nevertheless, the last-ditch German effort to regain the initiative by seizing Bastogne had clearly failed.

Weariness had now set in on both sides. It would take awhile for VIII Corps to pull itself back together again and jump-start its drive on Houffalize. When it did so, the Germans would no longer be attempting to reset the terms of battle. Instead, they would be striving merely to delay the inevitable. Such a realization would have been small consolation for Middleton on the night of 4 January 1945. But consolation for corps commanders in the Bulge frequently came only in the very smallest of doses.

XII CORPS PRESSES THE SOUTHERN SHOULDER

The situation facing XII Corps in the second phase of the Bulge was almost the same as that encountered by the German LXXX and LXXXV Corps in the first phase. The heavily wooded and broken Luxembourgian terrain west of the Sauer and south of the Sûre was easy to defend and hard to attack.[147] The many valleys and draws running at odd angles allowed the defender to slip in between advancing columns and wreak havoc. These features also complicated air support and increased the likelihood of accidental bombing and strafing of friendly forces.[148] The requirement to ford or advance along the numerous small streams cutting across the area meant soldiers' feet would frequently be wet, which led to steady wastage from immersion foot. And like the attacking corps of the German Seventh Army, Eddy's XII Corps would be at the bottom of the totem pole for resources. Nevertheless, Patton was insistent on attacking, both to support the III Corps attack and to establish conditions for future offensive operations. Thus, Eddy would have to do the best he could with what he had.

Attacking with Minimal Force, 22–23 December

As Gerow had demonstrated at Schmidt, the prospects of ordering a single regiment to attack on a corps front were rarely auspicious. But Eddy had little choice in the matter. He had been ordered by Patton to attack, the 4th ID and CCA of the 9th AD were exhausted from their stubborn defense, the 10th AD was still getting oriented, and the 5th ID was just coming into the corps sector. Thus, attaching Irwin's 10th Infantry Regiment to the 4th ID and telling Barton to use it offensively was the best he could do. Barton's plan for the use of these fresh legs was sound.[149] He directed the regimental commander, Colonel Robert P. Bell, to attack toward Echternach, the largest village in Luxembourg under German control. The axis of advance was along the road from the hamlet of Michelshof, some three miles to the south. At noon on the 22nd, the regiment deployed just short of its line of departure (LD). As it reached the LD, it ran right into a German assault force. The German effort was well supported with cannon artillery and nebelwerfers; several of the American attacking companies became misoriented in the close terrain; and at the end of the day, the 10th Infantry counted itself lucky to be digging in short of its intended jump-off point. Reports informed Eddy that evening that the regiment had "killed a lot of Germans," but there were no illusions that any territory had been gained.[150]

On the morning of the 23rd, Eddy convened a meeting of Generals Barton, Irwin, and Morris to review the corps plan for the assault to clear the Germans from the Sauer River bridgehead.[151] The idea was for the 5th ID to make the main attack through the 4th ID to close on the Sauer, with the latter supporting by fire.[152] On the left, the 10th AD would conduct a supporting attack to close on the Sûre. After reviewing the plan with those charged with execution, Eddy briefed it to Patton, who pronounced himself satisfied.[153]

In the meantime, Colonel Bell's soldiers fought gamely to advance on Echternach. Supported by six battalions of artillery, the 2nd Battalion, 10th Infantry, attacked into the woods northeast of Michelshof, where it cleared out one German foxhole line. German artillery rained down on the 10th Infantry soldiers, but they pressed on, only to be engaged with heavy small arms fire and a spirited infantry flank attack. The determination of the German resistance was evident when a number of gritty volksgrenadiers tenaciously dug into the snow-covered forest ground and called in more artillery, forcing the battalion again to withdraw to its original positions.

To Regain the Sauer, 24–28 December

Eddy knew better than to expect spectacular results. He was painfully aware of the problems in foxhole strength that were evident before the German onslaught and knew that, given the casualties suffered in the initial phase, frontline units were now dangerously depleted and soldiers were becoming exhausted, junior officers being a particular concern.[154] But he sensed that the Germans on the southern shoulder were on their last legs as well. Hence, there was no particular requirement for haste. Rather, the situation called for conservatism in the best sense of the word. He would gain the ground that had to be gained; but he would do so in a manner designed to preserve, to the extent possible, the fighting capability of his formations. This sensible caution had two practical manifestations. First, it meant careful tactics: steady advances and ample support from both direct and indirect fire. Second, it meant ensuring that division commanders and their subordinates were doing everything they could to preserve the fighting strength: practicing proper security, digging in with overhead cover, moving hot meals forward, and rotating troops out of the line at every possible opportunity.[155] These were the themes he harped on as he made his daily rounds to visit division and regimental commanders. In short, Eddy found himself in a situation that was a perfect fit with his natural inclinations.[156]

The 5th ID, Eddy's principal offensive instrument, was formed in October 1939, deployed to Iceland in August 1943, and came ashore at Utah Beach in July 1944.[157] Its commander, Major General "Red" Irwin, was the son of an Old Army general and another of the many members of the West Point class of 1915 to reach flag rank.[158] After taking a commission in the cavalry, he transferred to the field artillery, graduating from CGSS in 1927 and the War College in 1937. His service as the Division Artillery commander in the 9th ID put him on intimate terms with Eddy, who had good reason to think highly of him. He was subsequently promoted to major general and assumed command of the 5th ID in July 1943.[159] Eddy had given his old friend a tough nut to crack. The 5th ID's attack zone was split by the Schwarz Erntz River, which flows north into the Sauer, about four miles west of Echternach. The precipitous heights on each side made it a definite impediment to east-west movement and a wonderful place for small groups of Germans to hide. Given this obstacle and the width of his sector, which extended four miles west of the Schwarz Erntz, Irwin had little choice but to attack with all three regiments abreast. He arrayed them from right to left with the 10th Infantry, already committed; the 2nd Infantry; and the 11th Infantry. Irwin's men were up against two German divisions, the 212th VGD east of the Schwarz Erntz and the 276th VGD to its west. Both units were seriously under strength.

The 5th ID's attack kicked off at 1100 on the 24th, with the XII Corps Artillery firing over 21,000 rounds and the 5th Division Artillery adding another 5,000.[160] The 10th Infantry had mixed success in its third attempt to advance toward Echternach. The 1st Battalion, trying to make headway past Michelshof on the east side of the road, found that the Germans were tenaciously defending this approach.[161] This time, however, the 2nd Battalion was attacking on the west, over slightly more hospitable ground. By the end of the day, it had captured Hill 313, a prominent terrain feature roughly two miles southwest of Echternach. The 2nd Infantry, commanded by Colonel A. Worrell Rolfe, had the Schwarz Erntz on its left flank. Rolfe unwisely sent his 2nd Battalion up the gorge. The two attacking companies, while attempting merely to get to the floor of the defile, suffered heavy casualties from Germans skillfully concealed in its craggy outcroppings. The regimental commander thereupon stuck to the high ground and ordered his men to fight their way out of the hornet's nest on the following morning. The 3rd Battalion, attacking on the right, also ran into a buzz saw; at the end of the day, it had gained only several hundred yards. The 11th Infantry, commanded by Colonel Paul J. Black, had results similar to those of the 10th Infantry. The right-flank battalion was stymied by strong German resistance in the village of Waldbillig and flanking fire coming from a draw leading down into the Schwarz Ernst. But the left-flank battalion found a seam between two defending battalions and advanced some two miles to a piece of key, elevated terrain just southwest of Haller. At the end of the day, Irwin's soldiers had been largely blocked in the center but had made mildly encouraging results on both flanks. The pressure east of the Schwarz Ernst induced the 212th VGD commander to withdraw his front line to an arc around Berdorf and Echternach that provided the latter a bridgehead less than two miles deep.

The 10th AD, making the supporting attack, was activated at Fort Benning in July 1942.[162] It arrived in Europe in late September 1944 and received its baptism of fire in mid-November while operating under Walker's XX Corps in the encirclement of Metz, shortly thereafter crossing into Germany. Its commander, William H. H. Morris, Jr., was among the older division commanders in World War II, having graduated from West Point in 1911.[163] Like Irwin, an artillerist, he had served in the AEF in World War I, graduating from CGSS in 1925 and the War College in 1930. He had previously commanded the 6th AD and in July 1944 was commanding the XVIII Corps at Fort Dupont, Delaware, when he received news that the commander of the 10th AD, had died. Morris immediately contacted Marshall and requested relief from corps command, with assignment to the 10th AD. Both Walker and Patton were high on him, recommending him for a DSM, principally for his actions in the Metz campaign.

Morris's own CCB was in Bastogne, but the division was buttressed by CCA, 9th AD (temporarily designated CCX to avoid confusion), and two battalions of Colonel Rudder's 109th Infantry. The latter were at less than half strength, but they gave Morris what every armored division commander involved in close fighting most coveted—more infantry.[164] Furthermore, the terrain in his sector south of the Sûre was not as treacherous as that farther to the east. Morris took full advantage of these favorable auguries, attacking with a tank-heavy task force on the right and Rudder's 109th on the left.[165] The right-hand column advanced to the northwest of Eppeldorf against scattered resistance, and its success was reinforced with a task force from CCX. Rudder's soldiers encountered even less resistance and secured the south bank of the Sûre from Gilsdorf in the west, to near Moestroff in the east.

The 10th AD's attack, combined with the progress on Irwin's left flank, split the 276th and 212th VGDs. Thus, General Franz Beyer could no longer fight a coordinated corps defense, and his forces were subject to defeat in detail. Eddy, who visited all three divisions during the day, read the situation correctly and was particularly optimistic about the 10th AD's prospects for reaching the Sûre.[166]

On Christmas Day, the 5th ID continued to hammer and the German resistance showed signs of coming unglued.[167] The right flank of the 10th Infantry pulled even with the left-hand regiment of the 4th ID, while the left-flank battalion, having gained Hill 313, was checked by the seemingly impenetrable Leimerdelt draw. The 3rd Battalion, 2nd Infantry, followed up an all-night artillery barrage with a spirited tank-infantry attack that made solid gains, while the 2nd Battalion extricated itself from the Schwarz Erntz defile. West of the gorge, the 11th Infantry attacked with smoke cover and excellent armor support, surrounding Waldbillig by noon and capturing the village of Haller by the end of the day.[168] While visiting Irwin's command post, Eddy picked up an interrogation report that two captured German runners were delivering orders to withdraw.[169]

It was more of the same on the 26th, with the principal action being provided by the 10th Infantry.[170] The 1st Battalion advanced to within 800 yards of Echternach, while the soldiers of the 3rd Battalion charged into the Leimerdelt draw, killing, capturing, or routing every defender in their path. By mid-afternoon, they had reached the heights west of Echternach. The eyes of the artillery now had direct observation of the 212th VGD's crossing point on the Sauer. What followed was a dream come true for the American gunners and a scene from Dante for the desperate Germans. As battalion salvo after battalion salvo of VT fuze artillery burst murderously over the river, small groups of volksgrenadiers tried any possible means of escape. Some sought refuge across a small footbridge; others paddled frantically in rubber boats; still others braved the frigid waters and strong current, swimming furiously to gain the far shore.

The GIs felt little pity for enemy soldiers frantically attempting to reach the safety of German soil. A prisoner report had indicated that survivors from Company E, 12th Infantry, cut off in Echternach during the German attack, might still be in the town.[171] Patrols sent in to search for them on the night of the 26th proved the information to be unfounded.[172] Two days later, the 4th ID personnel officer reported that he was dropping the missing three officers and 117 enlisted soldiers of Company E from the division's rolls.[173] Here it is important to note that soldiers of the XII Corps were the first to fight over ground that their American comrades had previously defended. In fact, the Bulge was the only campaign in the European war in which this would be true on a large scale. And the experience of discovering the bodies of dead Americans in their path imparted a realization of the cruel realities of combat and a resolve to see the war through to a successful conclusion, all the way down the chain of command to the lowest private.[174] Eddy and Irwin conferred on the evening of the 26th and concluded that the objective had been essentially achieved but that several more days would be required to clear the last vestiges of German resistance from west of the Sauer. This was accomplished by the evening of 28 December.[175]

In the meantime, Eddy's corps took on a new configuration, assuming control of McBride's 80th ID from Millikin's III Corps; transferring the 109th Infantry and CCA, 9th AD, to VIII Corps; and receiving Grow's 6th AD in return for Morris's 10th AD, which was pulled out of the line and sent to Metz. There was also an unpleasant but necessary command duty. On 26 December, Eddy informed Barton that he thought the time had come for him to take a break. Barton concurred, and Brigadier General Harold W. Blakeley, the 4th ID Artillery commander, was appointed in his stead.[176] When Barton reported to Eddy to take his leave, the corps commander praised him for his good work, gave him a letter testifying thereto, and awarded him a Bronze Star.[177] Eddy's action came only two days before Marshall dispatched a message to Eisenhower mentioning the 4th ID commander as one of several experienced infantry leaders he would like to bring back to the United States to help with training. Eisenhower immediately notified Marshall of his willingness to release Barton, noting positively, "He has done a fine job but his health is now such that he can not be expected to continue for long in command of a division in the front."[178] Eddy did not have to worry about his replacement. Blakeley was a well-rounded soldier, having commanded the 5th AD Artillery and CCA, 5th AD, before coming to the Ivy Division.[179]

Planning for Future Operations, 29 December–4 January

Having gained the Sauer, Eddy and his staff began to focus on continuing the offensive when XII Corps would have the resources to do so. Events on other portions of the Third Army front would postpone that eventuality until 18 January, but in late December a delay of that length could not be clearly foreseen. Patton's initial inclination was to use Grow's 6th AD as part of whatever attack Eddy undertook. But Eddy suggested that the terrain on the southern shoulder was not suitable for armor and that the 6th AD might be more profitably employed breaking out northeast from Bastogne, reversing the axis that the 2nd Panzer Division had followed on 18 and 19 December.[180] Patton saw the wisdom of this counsel. The 6th AD was released for movement to III Corps, leaving Eddy with command of the 4th, 5th, and 80th IDs and the 2nd Cavalry Group.[181] Eddy's next venture in planning was more visionary—resuscitating Patton's fondness for a drive from the southern shoulder, northeast to Bitburg. The result was XII Corps Attack Plan A, published on 1 January 1945.[182] The mission was succinctly, if somewhat grandly, stated, "XII Corps atks D Day H Hr across SAUER R, penetrates SIEGFRIED LINE and advances N on BITBURG, prepared for further adv in direction of BONN." Elaborate air support from heavy and medium bombers of Eighth and Ninth Air Forces as well as the fighter-bombers of XIX TAC was envisioned to isolate the battle area, protect the corps flanks, and support the advancing ground columns. The scheme of maneuver called for three infantry divisions to make the main attack, with two forcing crossings of the Sauer, while the third protected the corps left flank. One armored division, provisionally identified as Patton's favorite, the 4th, would constitute the corps reserve for several contingencies: attacking through either of the infantry division's bridgeheads east of the Sauer, attacking to seize Bitburg, or continuing the attack north toward Bonn. This plan never came to fruition, but it is typical of the types of activities corps headquarters are called upon to pursue in periods of operational idleness.

Outside the headquarters, things were quiet. The corps AAR cryptically noted that, for 3 and 4 January, "no major events or changes occurred" anywhere in the corps sector.[183] Nevertheless, XII Corps had performed the important function of clearing the enemy from a significant swath of Luxembourgian territory and, thereby, paving the way for future operations. And thanks, in part, to Eddy's careful tactics and sound battle management, it had done so under very difficult circumstances, without paying an exorbitant cost in American lives.[184]

SOME CLOSING OBSERVATIONS

In the slightly less than two weeks from 22 December 1944–4 January 1945, III, VIII, and XII Corps each made material contributions toward shifting the initiative from the Germans to the Americans. III Corps was clearly the most influential in this enterprise. Its attack to relieve Bastogne was crucial to the implementation of Eisenhower's plan for regaining the initiative, but the bright light of Patton's dynamic personality placed the important part played by Millikin and his able staff in a shadow that has endured for three generations. Millikin's composure during the ferocious German assaults on the east side of Bastogne after its relief also adds to his credit. Middleton will always be most highly regarded for his determination to save Bastogne when a man of lesser constitution might well have given it up. Few people, however, are aware of the stamina he showed in clawing away at the Germans on Bastogne's western face as his corps fought desperately to get on the road to Houffalize, while the Germans sought equally desperately to reencircle the vital hub. He was physically and mentally drained by this effort. But in war, endurance counts for a lot, and Middleton endured. Eddy's role in closing to the Sauer was one of accompaniment, much like that of the pianist at a violin recital. It is also true of war that those who play secondary roles competently are highly valued—and Eddy was competent.

12

XVIII (Airborne), VII, and V Corps Fight for Initiative in the North

When the time comes to pass over to the offensive with 7 Corps my present idea is to direct it south-eastwards towards the road centre of HOUFFALIZE about eight miles north of BASTOGNE. I am not yet clear as to when I shall be able to begin this movement and hope to be able to let you know further on this point tomorrow night when the intention of 6 and 5 Panzer Armies may have become clearer.[1]   *Bernard L. Montgomery, 23 December 1944*

As PATTON WAS THE OPERATIONAL ARCHITECT of the battle on the southern side of the Bulge, Montgomery was in the north. But where Patton's impulse had been to seek the initiative aggressively and attack even when conditions were not propitious, Montgomery's animating spirit was precisely the opposite—caution. He generally preferred to meet German offensives with a steady recoil, followed by a well-prepared attack. It was a sensible approach, though it could be pushed too far. Given the strength and depth of the German advance into the Ardennes (which led him to signal to Brooke on 22 December, "RUNDSTEDT is fighting a good battle"), the paucity of Allied reserves, and the depletion of the American infantry divisions, Monty wanted to be absolutely sure that this offensive had fully run its course before he committed himself to attacking.[2] As late as 28 December, he was convinced that the Germans intended to make one more major push toward the Meuse, an estimate with which Eisenhower concurred.[3] The end-of-December attacks against Bastogne were, in fact, made to establish the essential precondition for just such an advance. But here Montgomery erred in mistaking intent for capability. Although not nearly as pusillanimous as suggested by his critics, Montgomery's efforts during this phase of the campaign were cautious, prudent, and divergent from the aggressive instincts of both Ridgway and Collins.[4]

XVIII (AIRBORNE) CORPS HALTS THE II SS PANZER CORPS

XVIII (Airborne) Corps played a pivotal role in the northern battle of transition. With the Sixth SS Panzer Army's failure to gain the Elsenborn Ridge clearly evident and Model's Schwerpunkt having shifted to Fifth Panzer Army's drive on the Meuse, Dietrich was now performing Manteuffel's original task—protecting the flank of the main effort.[5] The geographic objective of this mission was the Marche plateau, a band of high ground north and west of the line Marche-Hotton-Manhay. If this extended piece of elevated terrain could be captured, Manteuffel's advance could be shielded from the divisions Montgomery was assembling for Collins's counterstroke. Dietrich's instrument for this job was Bittrich's II SS Panzer Corps. Initially, the only force standing between Bittrich and the Marche plateau was XVIII (Airborne) Corps.

Withdrawal from the St. Vith Salient, 22–23 December

Throughout the early morning hours of 22 December, Ridgway and his staff continued to wrestle with what to do about the sorely pressed forces between the Salm and St. Vith. Ridgway's attitude toward a withdrawal was not as clearly negative as many analysts argue.[6] It is true that his pugnacious temperament made him loath to cede anything to anybody, particularly the Germans, whose National Socialist ideology he detested with a fiery passion.[7] His experience as an airborne division commander further imbued in him the necessity of holding ground. But in his conversation with General Kean shortly before midnight on the 21st, he had learned that First Army was not averse to a withdrawal of the 7th AD and had informed Kean that he had sent his assistant chief of staff forward to assess the situation and to give Hasbrouck discretionary authority to order a withdrawal. Nevertheless, two messages emanating from Ridgway's headquarters during the early morning hours of 22 December indicate that contemplating a withdrawal was one thing, ordering it was something quite different.

The first of these messages explicitly gave Hasbrouck authority to decide upon a withdrawal; but it attached the 7th AD to the 106th ID, effectively making him subordinate to Jones. Ridgway's written confirmation, dated 220635 December, read as follows:

> 1. The following msg. sent to you at 0100 is repeated for your information: "Confirming phone message to you, decision is yours. Will approve whatever you decide. Inform Jones he is to conform.

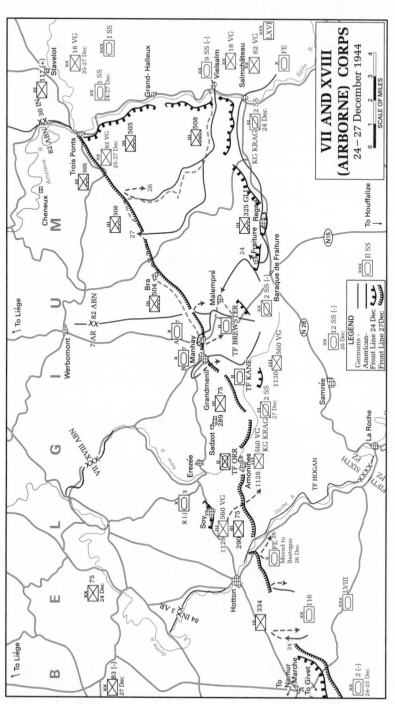

Map 7. VII and XVIII (Airborne) Corps, 24–27 December 1944

2. In addition to his force, Major General A. W. Jones will command 7th AD effective receipt of this message."[8]

This was a very confusing order. Hasbrouck was to make the call on the withdrawal, and Jones was to conform to his movements; but Jones was to command Hasbrouck. The elder Dupuy referred to it as "puzzling double-talk," which was not far off the mark.[9] It all stemmed from Ridgway's failure to come to grips with the same dilemma that had bedeviled Middleton about command at St. Vith: Hasbrouck had the preponderance of force and was vastly the more competent of the two division commanders, but Jones was senior. First Army had solved this for Ridgway by placing Hasbrouck in overall command. But both men had objected. Ridgway had heeded their protests and separated their commands, but now it came back to haunt him. He knew that during a withdrawal one man had to be in charge; but his strict sense of good order and discipline would not allow him to subordinate a major general to a brigadier general. That meant Jones had to command. But Hasbrouck clearly had both the greater force in the salient and the much more acute grasp of the situation. That meant Hasbrouck had to make the decision as to when to withdraw and have the primary consideration for movement routes, passage times, and so on. The result was a muddle.[10]

The second source of consternation was a proposal for Hasbrouck to consider establishing a "fortified goose-egg" east of the Salm. The concept was for the forces in this oblong perimeter to be resupplied by air, as the 101st was at Bastogne, and hold out for some unspecified period until XVIII (Airborne) Corps could mount a major attack to relieve them. Ridgway's staff sent forward an overlay of the proposed positions with the notation "XVIII Corps (Airborne) order for the final defense of area 21 December 1944" hastily scrawled on the bottom.[11] As a logistical and tactical idea, it had significant drawbacks: armored divisions require much heavier daily tonnages to continue fighting than do airborne divisions, and the room for maneuver within the "goose egg" was marginal.[12] As Clarke ruefully observed to Hasbrouck, it appeared that the corps commander was proposing "Custer's Last Stand."[13] Although Ridgway very quickly shelved the idea, the very act of proposing it called into question the soundness of his tactical reasoning.[14]

The situation in the salient during the night of 21/22 December was rapidly deteriorating.[15] Remer's FEB had brought the bulk of its armor up and mounted a combined arms attack on Rodt. This tiny village lay along the east-west supply route leading from Vielsalm to St. Vith that constituted the main lifeline of CCB, 7th AD. Attacking through snow-covered woods west of the road leading into Rodt from the northeast, Remer's men came within sight of the village just as daylight was breaking. The first attack on Rodt was handily repulsed, but soon enemy superiority in both men and firepower prevailed. The FEB's success forced Clarke to pull back to Hinderhausen and Combach. From these two positions, a network of small trails wove through the woods back to the Salm, but they were in miserable condition. Clarke's jeep became so badly stuck in the mud west of Hinderhausen that it took a dozen men to get it out.[16] There was also bad news in Hoge's sector, where a rifle company from the 62nd VGD found a seam between CCB, 7th AD, and CCB, 9th AD, and captured Neubrück, roughly two miles southwest of St. Vith. The supply situation was also deteriorating. Marauding panzers to the southwest and the frequent displacement of the 7th AD trains inhibited the flow of supplies *to* the division, and the mired roads east of the Salm complicated the distribution of supplies *within* the division. As a result, some soldiers were running out of food, and several artillery batteries were down to eight rounds per tube.[17]

This heavy pressure from the north and east, combined with the 2nd SS Panzer's approach from the south, led Hasbrouck to communicate directly with Ridgway in the late morning. Hasbrouck laid out an objective assessment of his division's condition and made a well-supported recommendation.

22 December 1944

TO: Commanding General, XVIII Corps

Some sort of build up north of our present position is indicated as artillery fire is being received in VIELSALM from the north or northeast.

Unless assistance is promptly forthcoming I believe our present position may become serious for several reasons, namely:

a, Our supplies must come in through a bottleneck over a bridge near VIELSALM.

b, We may become subjected to enemy artillery fire from practically any direction.

c, The road net within our position is totally inadequate to the troops and vehicles concentrated therein. The map shows many roads, but on the ground, the majority of these are mere tracks on which even a jeep bogs down if more than two or three travel in it.

d, If the 2d SS Pz Division attack should succeed in driving back the two RCT's of the 82d AB Division now between SALMCHATEAU and HERBRONVAL even as little as 3000 yards we will be completely severed from any source of supplies.

Since the chances of assistance in the immediate future do not seem bright, I would like to suggest that consideration be given to withdrawal of the 7th Arm'd and 106th Divisions to a position on the right (west) of the 82d Airborne Division where they may be of assistance in halting a possible advance north by the 2nd SS Panzer. . . . I don't think we can prevent a complete breakthrough if another all-out attack comes against CC "B" tonight due largely to the fact that our original three infantry battalions have at present melted to the equivalent of only two very tired battalions.

R. W. HASBROUCK   Brigadier General, U.S.A.
Commanding

221112

P.S. A strong attack has just developed against Clarke again. He is being outflanked and is retiring west another 2000 yards refusing both flanks. I am throwing in my last chips to help him. Hoge has just reported an attack. In my opinion if we don't get out of here and move up north of the 82d before night, we will not have a 7th Armored Division left.

RWH[18]

Hasbrouck's memorandum, which arrived at 1150, galvanized Ridgway into action. At 1225, he dispatched a message to Jones, informing him that Hasbrouck's request was approved, that movement of trains should be expedited, and that all gasoline not necessary to transport troops out of the salient was to be destroyed.[19] At 1400, he received a phone call from Kean indicating that Hodges was directing the withdrawal of 7th AD and that Montgomery, who was present with the army commander, "approved."[20] This order was actually issued at Montgomery's instigation—and the field marshal endeared himself forever to the soldiers of the 7th AD by adding the generous tribute, "They can come back with all honor."[21]

Soon thereafter, Ridgway arrived in Vielsalm to inspect the pocket. As he told Kean later that night, he met with "the principal bigwigs" in the defensive area; but the most important was his old friend Bill Hoge, whom he knew to be "calm, courageous, imperturbable."[22] He arranged a rendezvous with Hoge not far from the front lines.[23] Ridgway told Hoge he would get him out. Hoge replied, "How can you?" and in that moment revealed to Ridgway the true desperation of the situation. Ridgway answered, "Bill, we can, and we will." After leaving the CCB, 9th AD, commander, Ridgway returned to Vielsalm, where he relieved Jones of his command, appointed him as an assistant to the corps commander, and attached the 106th ID to the 7th

AD, putting Hasbrouck in charge of the withdrawal.[24] The scales had now fallen from Ridgway's eyes, and he saw the situation in the St. Vith Pocket clearly. It not only demanded withdrawing the forces therein, a realization he had reached shortly after noon, but also dictated finding a new commander for the 106th ID and putting Hasbrouck in charge of the combined force. After five torturous days of either divided command or nominal command under an incompetent, the soldiers of the two divisions in the St. Vith area had a single commander worthy of the title.[25]

Hasbrouck's plan for the withdrawal was to collapse the pocket from the flanks, with the units in the center pulling out first and those on the side folding in behind them.[26] He designated three withdrawal routes. The northern route, which followed the road from Poteau to Vielsalm, was to be used by CCR and CCA. The central route, which ran along an unimproved road from Commanster to Vielsalm, was designated for CCB and the 424th Infantry. Colonel Nelson's 112th Infantry would use the southern route, which ran from Maldingen to Beho, thence west and north along the valley of the Salm to the second bridge over the river, at Salmchâteau. Hasbrouck's plan was substantially aided by the arrival of the Siberian high, which dropped temperatures to well below freezing, significantly easing cross-country mobility.

In the fighting on the night of the 21st and the day of the 22nd, the forces in the pocket had also been helped by the considerable confusion that reigned in St. Vith as German soldiers from numerous units streamed into the town, creating a massive traffic jam. It was so bad that Model again found himself having to dismount to move forward for a command conference.[27] But by the night of the 22nd and the day of the 23rd, commanders had begun to restore discipline and to direct the attention of their soldiers toward the Americans to the west. As a result, Hasbrouck's desire to begin the withdrawal at 0200 on the 23rd could not be implemented. Hoge was heavily engaged; Clarke, also engaged, was still working furiously to reestablish unit integrity. But at 0500, Hasbrouck radioed his subordinates that it was, in effect, now or never.[28] Hoge's men were able to shake free, and, after running a minor gauntlet at Braunlauf, left the Germans in their wake and escaped almost unscathed across the Salm, as did the 424th Infantry. The bulk of CCB also made it out, though the division's mobile covering force, which it provided, was engaged for most of the day. CCA and CCR were also able to disengage with relative ease and cross the Vielsalm bridge just as the sun was disappearing in the west. The only untoward developments came in the south. There, the 440th Armored Field Artillery Battalion and the covering force of the 112th Infantry were trapped east of Salmchâteau by the convergence of a kampfgruppe from the 2nd SS Panzer Division and the lead elements of the FEB. Learning that Salmchâteau was in enemy hands, the artillerymen boldly struck out for the north, with their .50-caliber machine guns blasting at every German in their path. These brave soldiers made it to Vielsalm and across the bridge, virtually intact. Nelson's rear guard was not so lucky. An undisclosed number were trapped in the German pincers and either killed or captured. Despite this loss, the withdrawal as a whole was amazingly successful.

This was due primarily to Hasbrouck. He had the moral courage to tell Ridgway forthrightly that the evidence favoring a withdrawal was becoming overwhelming and the sophistication to do so in a manner completely loyal to the corps commander's prerogatives. He also showed himself willing to communicate with Ridgway directly, thus jumping the command channel through Jones that Ridgway had just established. He was thorough in his planning for the withdrawal and properly insistent when it came to execution. His subordinate leaders also performed well, particularly Clarke and Hoge, whose two combat commands were at the eastern extremity of the salient. But the castigation Ridgway received from Clarke and his apologists, an enterprise in which Hasbrouck never joined, is undeserved. In the clear light of hindsight, Ridgway should have ordered the withdrawal on the evening of the 21st when he went forward to visit Hasbrouck in Vielsalm, for execution on the night of the 22nd. This would have also been the appropriate time to relieve Jones. He was off by roughly eighteen hours on the former and twenty-four on the latter. But given the only marginal differential between the results that might have transpired under this optimal scenario and the events that actually took place, these errors fell within a zone of reasonable tolerance.

Halting the II SS Panzer Corps, 23–28 December

There would be precious little time for the defenders of St. Vith to rest their bodies, rejuvenate their spirits, and restore their equipment. For as Hasbrouck had told Ridgway, beyond simple considerations of humanity, the most compelling rationale for withdrawing the 7th AD was the opportunity to use it against the impending attack of the 2nd SS Panzer Division. In the pressing events of the next four to five days, emotions would run high and tempers would flare. But if the II SS Panzer Corps could be checked, an important nail could be driven in the coffin of the German offensive.

Even before the 7th AD withdrawal began, both Ridgway and Gavin realized that Bittrich's next big push would be directed at Baraque de Fraiture, the most important intersection in the north-central Ardennes. Its capture could lead to Manhay and perhaps even Werbomont, whose seizure would unhinge the entire XVIII (Airborne) Corps defense. If it were to continue on to Liège, First Army itself would be in jeopardy. Accordingly, Gavin began to accept risk on his left flank, where Peiper's kampfgruppe was still bottled up at La Gleize, and to beef up his right, where he accurately sensed the hammer was about to fall.[29] On 22 December, he released the division reserve, consisting of 2nd Battalion, 325th GIR, to its parent regiment, which was now covering the division's western flank, centered on Regné, about two miles east the junction. He further ordered Colonel Billingslea to place this battalion at the village of Fraiture, about a mile northeast of the intersection, and to augment the ad hoc defense forces at Parker's crossroads with a single company.

On 23 December, Lieutenant General of the Waffen-SS Heinz Lammerding, commander of the 2nd SS Panzer Division, positioned a panzergrenadier regiment for an assault on Baraque de Fraiture.[30] A surprise predawn raid by a single battalion was beaten back by a spirited defense. The Germans then proceeded to pound the road junction systematically with artillery and mortars. Late in the afternoon came a full regimental assault, supported by two companies of Mark IV's. The defending airborne company withdrew, bringing out just over forty men.[31] That evening, as the SS troops systematically consolidated their hold on the bleak, wind-swept hilltop, what few survivors there were of Major Parker's scratch force could find little solace. But with neither orders nor a parent unit to call their own, they had gamely held the vital road junction for upwards of four days. The cost was heavy. But by holding the 2nd SS Panzer Division four miles south of Manhay until the night of the 23rd, these few men had given Ridgway's XVIII (Airborne) Corps just barely enough time to reconstitute a semicredible defense.

The loss of Parker's crossroads was exacerbated by the fact that on the afternoon of 23 December, Rose's 3rd AD was transferred from XVIII (Airborne) Corps to VII Corps.[32] Although this made sense from the point of view of covering Collins's concentration, it placed the corps boundary just west of Manhay, which allowed Lammerding's subsequent advance to come right along a vulnerable corps seam. A more prudent course of action would have been to assign General Hickey's CCA, 3rd AD, to XVIII (Airborne) Corps, thus giving Ridgway command of the forces immediately west of Manhay. Hodges's placement of the corps boundary less than a mile west of the Manhay-Werbomont road quickly became a source of great consternation.

Gavin was livid over the loss of Baraque de Fraiture and particularly angry at the 3rd AD, which he felt had let him down.[33] But Rose was having challenges of his own. Heavy pressure from the 116th Panzer and the 560th VGD at Soy and Hotton was focusing his attention in the right and center portions of his sector, and there was little help he could offer to the 82nd Airborne. Gavin, fearing his right flank could now be rolled up by German armor running amok in his rear, went to the corps command post in search of whatever help he could get, particularly armor. With the 7th AD still conducting its withdrawal, there was no armor to give; and, in Ridgway's absence, Eaton would not release to Gavin any of the slim corps reserve. Gavin subsequently criticized Eaton for his lack of willingness to make a decision in Ridgway's absence, and John S. D. Eisenhower used this incident to criticize Ridgway for an overbearing command style.[34] Admittedly, with Ridgway spending most of the day away from the headquarters, his reluctance to delegate significant authority to his chief of staff was bound to induce delayed decisions. But with the corps reserve consisting of roughly a battalion and multiple threats on many fronts, commitment of the reserve was properly reserved to the corps commander. Ridgway soon returned to the command post where, after a short phone conversation with Gavin, he dealt promptly with the emerging threat.[35] He extended the 82nd Airborne's boundary west to Tri-le-Cheslaing, he informed Gavin he would have help farther to the west on the next day from the 7th AD, he directed the corps artillery to begin planning to halt an offensive from the south, and he ordered the corps engineer to place obstacles along the Manhay-Werbomont road.[36] The next morning, he positioned Hoge's CCB, 9th AD, at Malempré and attached it to the 82nd Airborne Division.[37]

But the key portion of Ridgway's response would be positioning a major component of the 7th AD along the Manhay-Werbomont road. He so ordered, and Hasbrouck gave the nod to Colonel Dwight A. Rosebaum's CCA.[38] Accordingly, the bone-weary men of CCA were rounded up on the morning of 24 December and dispatched to hold off the 2nd SS Panzer Division between Manhay and Baraque de Fraiture.[39]

With all this in place or moving into place, Ridgway was supremely confident that his corps would hold. At 0610, he called the First Army G-3 and reported that the situation in the south was "normal and quite satisfactory."[40] Thirty-five minutes later, he called Brigadier General Herbert T. Perrin, who had replaced Jones as commander of the 106th ID; Hasbrouck; and Hobbs with a line-in-the-sand exhortation:

> In my opinion this is the last dying gasp of the German Army. He is putting everything he has into this fight. We are going to smash that final drive here today in this Corps Zone. This command is the command

that will smash the German offensive spirit for this war. . . . Impress every man in your division with that spirit. We are going to lick the German here today.[41]

And at 0900 he asked Kean to convey to Hodges "my complete assurance about my position."[42]

Later that day, Montgomery came to Werbomont. He dealt with Ridgway deftly, congratulating him on his fine work to date: "The corps has fought with distinction."[43] But this was merely a pleasant smoke screen. Monty's real mission was to "suggest" that Ridgway withdraw the XVIII (Airborne) Corps to a more defensible position. The existing disposition resembled a right triangle, with the 82nd Airborne occupying the vertical leg and most of the horizontal leg, both of which were subject to very heavy pressure. These two legs ran from just west of Trois Ponts, south generally west of the Salm to near Salmchâteau, then due west to Fraiture and slightly northwest to Tri-le-Cheslaing. Monty's idea was to pull the 82nd back to the hypotenuse, which ran directly from Trois Ponts to Tri-le-Cheslaing, shortening Gavin's front from roughly eighteen miles to only eight. To conform to this scheme, CCA, 7th AD, would also have to pull back from south of Manhay to the high ground immediately to its north.[44] Giving up ground was anathema to Ridgway; but in his phone conversation with Kean just as Monty was departing, he related, "He's coming back [to First Army headquarters] with a very important suggestion, which originated with him, and which, in view of the picture he gave me, I entirely agree with."[45] What convinced Ridgway was Montgomery's depiction of the Germans as having the power for one more major push. Years later, he would lament that the anticipated surge never came; in fact, it did not.[46] But despite the protestations of both Ridgway and Gavin that giving up ground was detrimental to the morale of airborne soldiers, Montgomery's proposal, which was implemented after his confirming visit to First Army, made eminent sense.[47]

On the night of 24 December, there occurred an untoward confluence of circumstances that almost cracked the corps defense at Manhay, its most vulnerable point.[48] Lammerding deployed two panzergrenadier regiments north of Baraque de Fraiture, each supported by armor. The 560th VGD struck the 3rd AD positions west of Manhay, while to the east, Remer's FEB drove a platoon of the 325th GIR out of Regné. These two actions provided valuable maneuver room for the 2nd SS Panzer Division. As Rosebaum was deploying CCA, 7th AD, south of Manhay late in the day, he received orders to pull back to the north in accordance with Montgomery's instructions to Ridgway. The withdrawal was to begin 242230 December, which, as bad luck would have it, was just one and one-half hours after the start of the German attack. The Germans deceptively led their advance with a captured American Sherman. In the confusion of commanders being called back to the rear for orders, an enemy column got into the 7th AD positions south of Manhay and opened fire. As the tanks rolled into the village, they again achieved surprise. At this point, CCA, 7th AD, almost disintegrated, with scared and confused soldiers streaming north toward Werbomont. The situation was only saved by two developments. The commander of the 23rd AIB, Lieutenant Colonel Robert L. Rhea, aided by Hasbrouck and other troops from CCB, 7th AD, mounted a bare-bones defense about a mile north of the village. And the German high command had other ideas. Bittrich was now more interested in using Manhay as a gateway to the west, from which he could threaten Collins's defense of the Meuse directly, than he was in a drive north toward Liège. Accordingly, he ordered Lammerding to move west on the morrow.

But with Manhay in German hands on the morning of Christmas Day, no one in the American chain of command was willing to trust his luck to enemy intentions. Hodges bombarded XVIII (Airborne) Corps, now headquartered in a more commodious setting at a chateau near Harzé, with orders to recapture Manhay, despite Montgomery's establishment of a defensive line to its north.[49] Ridgway, having just displayed to all and sundry total confidence in his ability to hold, was furiously determined to comply. He ordered Hasbrouck unambiguously to retake Manhay "by dark tonight."[50] He also arranged with Collins for CCA, 3rd AD, and the 289th Infantry Regiment of the recently committed 75th ID to recapture Grandménil, about a mile west of Manhay.[51] Hasbrouck now had no choice but to commit Clarke's battered CCB. This effort was, in the characterization of one 7th AD historian, "stillborn." Clarke had only two tank companies to commit, and one of these mustered only six tanks. Mines laid by the 3rd AD and an abatis set up either by the 3rd AD or by the retreating soldiers of CCA, 7th AD, soon blocked their progress.[52] Foot soldiers from the attached 424th Infantry were finally able to reach Manhay, but they were repulsed. Ridgway moved to the front where the German artillery was falling hot and heavy in an attempt to will the attack to victory.[53] He relieved a lieutenant withdrawing from Manhay, placed a sergeant in charge of the patrol, and dispatched it back to try again. After attempting unsuccessfully to steady the nerves of an NCO panicked by some too-close-for-comfort direct heavy weapons fire, he placed him under arrest and sent him to the rear under the guard of his driver. But it was to no avail. Manhay was simply beyond the reach of flesh and blood, or at least beyond the reach of flesh and blood drained by a week of heavy fighting.

On the next day, Ridgway committed his corps reserve, the relatively fresh 3rd Battalion, 517th PIR, commanded by Lieutenant Colonel Forrest S. Paxton.[54] He told Paxton to "take Manhay at any cost" and backed him up with eight battalions of artillery that fired over 8,000 rounds. With this prodigious support, the gritty paratroopers dislodged the 2nd SS Panzer Division and, by 0400 on the 27th, restored Manhay to control of the XVIII (Airborne) Corps. Ridgway was finally vindicated. His southern front had cracked, causing some very anxious moments, but it had now been resealed.

Just how raw nerves had become in these days of high drama was evident in an altercation between Ridgway and Clarke.[55] Shortly after the 7th AD's withdrawal behind the Salm, a surgeon noted Clarke's exhaustion and suggested he get some rest. When Clarke replied that he was unable to sleep, the doctor gave him a sedative that knocked him out "like a sack of sand." In the early morning hours of 24 December, Ridgway sent word that he wanted to see Clarke. Efforts to awake him were fruitless, but he stirred sufficiently to mutter, "The hell with it." Word of this unflattering reply got back to an incensed Ridgway. When Clarke reported later in the day, the corps commander told him quite pointedly he was not accustomed to having brigadier generals decline his summons. Clarke, no shrinking violet himself, explained the circumstances and admitted he might have said, "The hell with it," but had no recollection thereof. As Ridgway admonished him about matters of military protocol, Clarke responded with some strong words of his own about having come from Third Army with multiple decorations and being glad to go back at any time. According to Clarke's biographers, Ridgway relented somewhat at this juncture and terminated the interview by telling Clarke, "Well, just don't let it happen again." This confrontation led Clarke to harbor ill feelings toward Ridgway for the remainder of his career.

Ridgway also found it necessary to replace his corps artillery commander. While working in England planning for possible airborne operations, he began to sense that Brigadier General Theodore Buechler was not providing "that degree of conspicuously superior and instant response, in the planning field, that I regarded as essential."[56] During the early days of the Ardennes battle, Ridgway continued to have misgivings about the quality of artillery support being provided to his subordinate divisions.[57] When the defensive crisis was at its height, he decided he could no longer continue to limp along. Accordingly, he relieved Buechler and obtained the services of Colonel Lemuel Matthewson, who was serving as deputy commander of the VII Corps Artillery. This was but one of the many examples of the close cooperation between Ridgway and Collins during the Bulge; it was a great relief for Ridgway, who found the improvement in the corps artillery "almost incredible."[58] Within days of Matthewson's appointment, Ridgway recommended him to Hodges for immediate, temporary promotion to brigadier general.[59]

Meanwhile, Gavin transferred the bulk of Tucker's 504th PIR to his right flank, leaving a single battalion on a five-mile front from Trois Ponts to just beyond La Gleize to contain Peiper.[60] On Christmas Eve, the 82nd Airborne executed a textbook withdrawal, marked by a very unusual occurrence. As the rearward movement began, there were several isolated reports of Germans in the division's rear. Gavin caught wind of the situation and went to the 505th PIR's command post to sort things out. He and Ekman could not at first credit a large German force being behind the front lines, but the indicators were unmistakable. With 505th's small covering force along the Salm under noticeable pressure, Gavin decided that the movement to the new position was the overriding priority and instructed Ekman to continue the withdrawal rather than giving chase to the enemy. This mysterious band was, in fact, the remnants of Peiper's now dismounted kampfgruppe, some 800 men moving stealthily to rejoin their comrades of the 1st SS Panzer Division. Not long before dawn, Peiper's group collided with one of Ekman's covering platoons. Gavin later said of the whole affair, "On December 25th we realized that we had just succeeded in withdrawing through a hostile withdrawing force, which was a rather novel maneuver."[61]

On Christmas Day, the airborne soldiers immediately began to establish their new positions, digging foxholes and gun emplacements, laying mines, and establishing communications.[62] It was well they did, for that night the 9th SS Panzer Division's 19th Panzergrenadier Regiment, an elite unit composed of men brought into the Waffen-SS from the Black Sea region, hit the 508th's left flank with about two battalions. They were soon beaten off. But two days later, Bittrich, long delayed in bringing about a coordinated corps attack, finally moved up the much-battered 62nd VGD and the significantly fresher and more determined 9th SS Panzer Division to assault the 82nd. The volksgrenadiers struck Gavin's northern flank but were easily beaten back. The 9th SS Panzer, attacking in the center, gave a much better account of itself, completely engulfing the 3rd Battalion, 508th PIR. The attack was checked by punishing salvoes from two artillery battalions. When the sun arose the next morning, the battalion commander, Lieutenant Colonel Louis G. Mendez, pressed into service the reserve company from a neighboring battalion and counterattacked to restore his lines. The artillery and the infantry had both done good work. Gavin reported that sixty-two German bodies were recovered from a single field, and the 19th SS Panzergrenadier Regiment's report of the action noted that the unit had been "cut to pieces."

On the morning of 28 December, Bittrich had no more chips to throw into the pot. XVIII (Airborne) Corps was standing firm, and there was nothing he could do to dislodge it. Ridgway could, therefore, as he had put it to the First Army Chief of Staff four days earlier, start thinking about going the other way.[63]

Preparing to Attack, 28 December–2 January

The first two issues that had to be settled for a resumption of the offensive were the direction of the main advance and the start date. On 29 December, Ridgway met with Hodges and Collins at the VII Corps command post to discuss plans for the impending transition.[64] Hodges opened the meeting by noting that Montgomery was very much in charge and would make his decisions based on his read of the enemy situation, which still anticipated a major German drive toward Liège. This meant that the direction of the attack would most likely be Houffalize, but the timing was still uncertain. Hodges declared himself in sympathy with Montgomery's inclinations. Ridgway and Collins remonstrated strongly. They argued that St. Vith, not Houffalize, was the decisive objective. Ridgway stated that XVIII (Airborne) Corps was stronger than the Germans in every area of combat power. He further opined that "we were losing one of the decisive opportunities of the war" and told Hodges unambiguously that he would be ready to attack by 31 December. In the end, Hodges directed Collins to prepare three plans—all directed toward Houffalize—and Ridgway to prepare two plans—one toward Houffalize and one toward St. Vith. But the decisions were clearly in Monty's hands.

On the following day, Montgomery came to the VII Corps command post for a meeting with Ridgway and Collins.[65] He confirmed Hodges's previous day's précis of his estimate of German intentions, which envisioned a concerted effort by Manteuffel's right wing and Dietrich's left wing to push northwest toward the Meuse. With this in mind, he would slip his reserves to the northwest and prepare to take the offensive when he was "sure the enemy momentum has been lost and his advance has been definitely halted." Regarding the objective of the offensive, Monty stated that while he wanted it to be "as far east as practicable," Houffalize was as far as he was willing to go. When Ridgway and Collins argued for St. Vith to be the objective, Montgomery replied that the time had not yet come. Montgomery also laid out his concept for the attack—VII Corps would make the main effort with four divisions to seize Houffalize, while XVIII (Airborne) Corps would make

a supporting attack to protect the VII Corps left flank. This plan was ultimately adopted, with an attack date set for 3 January 1945.

Ridgway's instructions to Gavin, whose 82nd Airborne would be making
the main corps effort, were unambiguous:

> I feel sure you appreciate that the pending operation is in no sense simi-
> lar to the race across France. We can expect and I am sure we will get
> a violent and prolonged reaction. We must, therefore, be coordinated
> throughout the operation, with emphasis on the exploitation of the
> full power of our overwhelming artillery superiority. . . . The situation
> does not justify extended isolated thrusts. On the contrary, it calls for
> cohesive divisional action at all times, until such time as a break-up
> begins.[66]

He clearly foresaw a slugging match, in which ground would be gained incrementally at minimal cost in blood. It would be frustrating guidance for
Gavin to follow—and it would, from time to time, mean forgoing opportunities that might otherwise have been exploited. But in the larger scheme of
things, Ridgway's strictures recognized the reality: the offensive phase of the
Bulge would be much more a battle of attrition than it would be a contest
of maneuver.

Ridgway also used the interregnum to find a deputy. He had learned on
the 22nd that Brereton was unwilling to part with his chief of staff, Floyd
Parks, whose services as deputy commander Ridgway had requested on a
temporary basis.[67] He therefore turned to his old friend Bill Hoge, whom he
summarily appropriated from command of CCB, 9th AD. He had already
moved Hoge into a key position by designating him as Hasbrouck's assistant
division commander on the evening of the 23rd when he had relieved Jones
and placed Hasbrouck in command of all the forces in the St. Vith salient.
With the Germans checked, he could pull Hoge into his inner circle. It was
a savvy move. First, it gave him an additional pair of eyes and ears to cover
the extended corps front.[68] It also gave him an experienced armor officer in
whom he had great trust to expand his counsel should such expansion be
required. Finally, by placing such an officer near the epicenter of decision
making, it gave the corps headquarters expertise in both tank and infantry
combat. Relations with the 7th AD were also improved by the appointment
of Colonel William S. Triplet to command CCA, in lieu of Rosebaum, whom
Hasbrouck relieved in the wake of the Manhay debacle. Triplet became a
staunch admirer of Ridgway, later commenting: "He was a fighter, the best

I've known. . . . Clarke's statement that Ridgway knew nothing of armored warfare still irks me. I will venture that Ridgway knew as much—or more—than Clarke. *My tankers* liked Ridgway and his paratroopers."[69]

Ridgway also used the relatively calm period from 28 December to 2 January to catch up on routine administration, much of it dealing with XVIII (Airborne) Corps business on other fronts. He gave Brereton a general update on the corps' activities.[70] He congratulated McAuliffe on his fine stand at Bastogne.[71] He welcomed Taylor back to the 101st.[72] And, making sure to touch all the bases, he inquired of Brigadier General Harold L. Clark, commander of the 52nd Wing, Troop Carrier Command, as to casualties incurred in support of the 101st.[73] His engagement with these individuals indicates that leading XVIII (Airborne) Corps imposed an additional responsibility on its commander. For although, when committed, it functioned just as any other corps with a flexible organization, it also had units that were permanently assigned or in support during periods of preparation for future operations. Thus, Ridgway had to stay abreast of things that affected these units and to maintain relations with their commanders, even when they were not directly involved in his immediate activities.

Two days before the offensive, his focus was directly on the task at hand. On 2 January, he sent a motivational message to his commanders, reprising the corps' operations since 19 December and looking forward to the future. "Now," he said, "with what we are confident is an overwhelming adequacy of means, we propose to attack, attack, and attack, until a final decision is reached on the Western Front. His reaction, we may expect, will be violent. Ours will over-match it."[74] It was pure Ridgway: implacably aggressive.

XVIII (Airborne) Corps Attacks, 3–4 January

With his corps in a definite supporting role, Ridgway had little with which to attack.[75] The 7th AD, 106th ID, and CCB, 9th AD, were in no shape for offensive operations and thus relegated to corps reserve. The 75th ID, initially minus two regiments, had been committed on the corps' western boundary after the battle at Manhay; however, in accordance with First Army instructions, it was to revert to army reserve after VII Corps passed through it on 3 January. That left only the 82nd Airborne and the 30th ID. But Hodges's concept was for the attack to be conducted like a long gate, extending from the XVIII (Airborne) Corps' easternmost position at Stavelot to the VII Corps westernmost position near Marche, swinging shut from west to east with Stavelot as its hinge.[76] Under this scheme, the 30th ID's initial role was limited to active patrolling, and the army commander denied

Ridgway's request for its participation in the attack. This meant that the corps would attack with a single division, the 82nd Airborne.

The corps intelligence estimate issued during the night of 2 January correctly divined that "the enemy is believed to be politically committed by HITLER, HIMMLER, et als [*sic*], to hold the salient. He has tactically committed himself to the defensive line on the N side of the salient pending a favorable determination of the situation on the S side of the salient."[77] It further noted, again accurately, that the SS panzer units had been withdrawn from contact and that the immediate force opposing the attack was composed entirely of VGDs, of which four were identified along the corps front.[78] Nevertheless, it judged the SS units to be capable of counterattacking in up to division strength. In sum, Ridgway and Gavin had a pretty good idea of what would be facing them—an infantry crust supported by organic or attached tank destroyers and assault guns, backed up by an armored reserve.

The men of the 82nd kicked off on the morning of 3 January at 0830, wading though deep snow in an attack Gavin called "the most arduous in the Division's history."[79] The 82nd was now reinforced by the 517th PIR, commanded by Colonel Rupert Graves. It had participated in Operation Dragoon in southern France but had not received the battle hardening experience of Normandy and Market-Garden.[80] Nevertheless, Gavin now had the luxury of commanding five regiments. They were arrayed with Graves's 517th PIR, Ekman's 505th PIR, and Billingslea's 325th GIR from right to left, with Tucker's 504th PIR and Lindquist's 508th PIR held in reserve. The general line of attack was south and southeast, to the west of the Salm River.[81] On 3 January, the 517th captured Trois Ponts, the 505th seized Fosse, about two miles to the south, and the 325th took Amcomont. On the next day, the 517th reached Bergeval and patrolled east to the Salm; the 505th took the high ground southeast of Fosse, thus gaining observation of the river crossings near Grand-Halleux, some four miles south of Trois Ponts; and the 325th captured Hierlot. These were noteworthy gains, but Gavin would soon become frustrated by the fact that the 82nd had to wait for progress from Collins's VII Corps before it could continue the advance.[82] Ridgway, impatient as ever, called First Army headquarters twice, urging Hodges to release the 30th ID for the attack.[83]

Analysis

Ridgway's performance in this phase of the campaign began uncertainly but ended strongly. His hesitation in ordering the withdrawal of the forces in the St. Vith salient indicated that in making the transition from division to corps command, he would have to learn to read battle situations through the senses and reports of other men as well as through his personal reconnaissances. For a man accustomed to smelling the battlefield in his own nostrils, this would require some mental recalibration.[84] But his error had been at the margins and not fundamental. And in a strange twist of fortune, the delayed decision allowed the forces east of the Salm to begin their withdrawal after the Siberian high had frozen the ground and given them much better cross-country mobility than they would have had a day earlier. In the eleven days that followed, Ridgway showed himself adept at the higher-level coordination of infantry, armor, artillery, and engineers in both defense and attack. And his fierce willpower was a critical ingredient in staunching the wound at Manhay and halting the II SS Panzer Corps. His appointment of Hoge as his deputy, although it would obviously expire when CCB, 9th AD, was returned to its parent unit, was a mature recognition that he was being stretched and could use assistance. In short, Ridgway was solidly on his way to becoming a well-rounded corps commander.

VII CORPS HALTS THE MEUSE OFFENSIVE

Ridgway's defense against the II SS Panzer Corps was absolutely necessary to take the energy and momentum out of the German offensive and to protect the VII Corps left flank. But in the larger scheme of things, it constituted an important auxiliary function—the vital action on the north side of the Bulge was stopping the drive of the 5th Panzer Army on the Meuse. Thus, to understand what VII Corps accomplished in the coming battle, we must briefly consider the situation through the eyes of Hasso von Manteuffel.

December 22nd was pivotal for 5th Panzer Army.[85] On the evening of the 21st, Krüger, commanding the LVIII Panzer Corps, had already ordered the 116th Panzer Division, commanded by Major General Siegfried von Waldenburg, to disengage from its abortive effort to force the Ourthe at Hotton and make a new assault in the area from Ménil to Verdenne. Sensing increasing resistance in the north, poignantly aware of the fatigue of his own soldiers, and with Patton's attack from the south becoming a source of "constant anxiety," Manteuffel understood by the evening of the 22nd that "it was quite certain that our plans could not any more be realized."[86] But there was still cause for hope, albeit on a lesser scale. Some useful strategic result could still be achieved if the point of the spear could be sufficiently advanced and widened. This represented a conscious reversion to the "small solution" of destroying a significant number of American formations east of the Meuse. It was a realistic read of the failure of Hitler's grand attempt to march on Antwerp, but it was also a savvy realization of what might yet be accomplished. Manteuffel's plan required an advance to the Meuse by the 2nd Panzer and Panzer Lehr Divisions, a breakthrough beyond Marche by the 116th Panzer Division, then a wheel of the two panzer corps to the northeast to join up with the LXVI Corps and Dietrich's Sixth SS Panzer Army. Such a maneuver would have dire consequences for both Collins's VII Corps and Ridgway's XVIII (Airborne) Corps. By the end of the day on 22 December, Manteuffel had recognized that the grand design for the Ardennes offensive had failed; but he still hoped to wring out all that he could from having made the attempt.

Collins, of course, had no precise idea of Manteuffel's innermost thoughts; but he did know that the Germans' general intention was to gain ground and that his mission was to prevent their doing so. Complicating this basic estimate, however, was the fact that Montgomery's instincts were much more cautious than his, both in terms of how much ground could be given up and in how and when to return to the offensive.

Preparing for Battle, 22–23 December

Collins spent the 22nd and the 23rd touring the front and coordinating with XVIII (Airborne) Corps and First Army prior to assuming command of his sector on the afternoon of the 23rd.[87] While at Hodges's headquarters on the 22nd, he voiced concern over the movement of the 2nd Panzer Division south of Marche. This prompted Hodges to instruct Ridgway to extend a counter-reconnaissance screen from Marche to Rochefort and beyond, an assignment that went, of necessity, to Bolling's 84th ID. Shortly thereafter, Montgomery arrived and told Collins not to become involved in any defensive operations and to prepare to attack on the 24th. On the next morning, Collins went to see Ridgway at Werbomont, finding his classmate "in fine fettle, as dynamic as ever."[88] Learning that the 3rd AD, which would revert to his control later in the day, was having a rough time holding off the 116th Panzer Division and the 560th VGD and that Ridgway had already given it all the infantry he could spare, Collins loaned Ridgway a battalion each of infantry and artillery from Major General Fay B. Prickett's 75th ID, which was moving into a reserve position north of Hotton, to support Rose's fight. He then returned to Méan, where he conferred with Hodges and Horrocks and asked the British XXX Corps commander for artillery support. When informed by Hodges that his attack was to be postponed until the 25th, he noted that with reports arriving of substantial engagements by the 84th

ID, he would probably have to order the 2nd AD, commanded by Major General Ernest N. Harmon, to stop the Germans east of Dinant.[89] All of this demonstrated a sure grasp of the friendly and enemy situations and a keen sense of anticipation for the locus of the coming main action.

Halting the Drive on the Meuse, 23–27 December

When Collins assumed command of the VII Corps sector at 1630 on the 23rd, all the pieces were in place for a successful defensive stand. The 84th ID had been in position just long enough to have staying power. The 2nd AD was fresh and itching for a fight. Moreover, in Harmon, it had a seasoned officer, who had commanded the 1st AD in North Africa and then returned to the United States to command a corps and whose services as commander of the 2nd AD had been explicitly requested by Eisenhower in the fall of 1944.[90] As Gavin later noted, "Harmon had tasted battle and found it to his liking."[91] VII Corps artillery was taking up its firing positions.[92] A British armored brigade had 150 tanks on the west bank of the Meuse as a backstop.[93] And the skies were clear, giving free rein to Quesada's IX TAC and Coningham's 2nd TAF. On the other side of the hill, the situation was much more desperate.[94] Bayerlein was short an entire panzergrenadier regiment; much of his division was protecting the corps left flank; and his lead kampfgruppe was temporarily checked at Rochefort. Colonel Lauchert's 2nd Panzer was cut in half. Its most advanced force, consisting of the division reconnaissance battalion, a battalion of Mark Vs, one panzergrenadier regiment, and a considerable amount of flak and artillery, was closing in on Celles, only four miles from the Meuse; but it was perilously low on fuel. The rump of the division was southeast of Marche, guarding Lüttwitz's right flank. Farther to the east, the bulk of Waldenburg's 116th Panzer was still moving through La Roche, in preparation to attack the 84th ID west of the Ourthe. And the Luftwaffe was nowhere to be seen.

When Collins assumed command of the units in his sector, Harmon had already dispatched his CCA, commanded by Brigadier General John "Pee Wee" Collier, to Ciney, based on an erroneous report that Germans had reached that village.[95] Collins felt that he could no longer stay disengaged and ordered Harmon to secure Buissonville, relieve elements of the 84th ID in Rochefort, and generally assume a position as a westward extension of Bolling's division. With the 84th ID being hard pressed, Collins provided help on its east flank as well by attaching to it TF Doan, CCA, 3rd AD, commanded by Lieutenant Colonel Leander A. Doan. Although this move was clearly justified in the context of defending the Meuse, it further complicated

Rose's ability to maintain a solid front along the VII Corps/XVIII (Airborne) Corps boundary at Manhay. Meanwhile, Collier's troops pressed forward; by midnight on the 23rd, they had secured Leignon, two miles south of Ciney, and were continuing on toward Buissonville.[96]

24 December was a day of high drama for Collins.[97] Knowing he would be out of communication while touring his extended front, he explicitly instructed Brigadier General Williston B. Palmer, the VII Corps Artillery commander, to remain at the corps headquarters and make whatever decisions were required in his absence. After visits with Generals Rose and Prickett, he went on to Marche to check in on Bolling, who informed Collins that he indeed welcomed the help from both the 2nd and 3rd ADs. He then pressed on to Harmon's command post north of Celles.

As Collins made his peripatetic tour of the VII Corps front, events at higher headquarters took a significant turn. They began with a visit by Montgomery to First Army headquarters. Monty had by now decided that he was willing, if need be, to allow the Germans to move to the north, while they were still east of the Meuse.[98] With the British XXX Corps firmly set on the west bank, Collins's VII Corps likewise well established on the east side, and the air literally cleared for action, the 21st AG commander felt that any German thrust to the north was bound to fail. Thus, he told Hodges to rescind the orders for Collins to attack and give him discretion to refuse his right wing by withdrawing to a line from Hotton to Andenne on the Meuse. The scale of such a withdrawal is indicated by the fact that Andenne was over twenty-two miles *north* of the 2nd AD's southernmost troops, who by early afternoon on the 24th had secured Buissonville.[99] What transpired after these instructions were given to Hodges is a case study in misunderstood communication, followed by perfectly understood communication, followed by creative insubordination.

Harmon called Palmer at VII Corps headquarters, seeking permission to launch his CCB into an attack.[100] Palmer, knowing that FUSA still had not given Collins full leeway to employ the 2nd AD, demurred. Harmon called again, even more emphatically requesting to be released and correctly noting that the German 2nd Panzer Division was virtually out of fuel. Palmer again refused, but he did authorize Harmon to prepare to attack and told him to discuss the matter with Collins, whom he felt would soon be arriving at the 2nd AD command post. Not much later, General Kean called from First Army. He told Palmer that all units in VII Corps were released to Collins's discretion; but when it came to the issue of the withdrawal to the Meuse, he attempted to conceal the location of the terminal point by telling Palmer to look at the map. The gist of this call, as Palmer understood it, is best recounted in the note he sent to Collins via the 2nd AD liaison officer because the phone lines to Harmon's headquarters had gone dead:

241530 December

Gen Collins,

Bill Kean just called. . . . Bill was extremely guarded but indicated strongly that new dispositions would call for you to secure your west flank by preventing hostile movement to north on east side of Meuse, mentioning a "pivoting move" and inviting attention to an "H" and an "A" (Le Houisse and Achene [*sic*]?). . . . Commitment of 2d Armd Div for purpose of anchoring flank appeared to be what he was driving at.

    Palmer

Telephone to Ernie out[101]

The two hamlets Palmer mistakenly mentioned in his note were three miles southwest of Ciney, exactly in the area that Harmon wanted to attack. So it is not terribly surprising that Kean's ambiguous and cryptic references to "H" and "A" were misunderstood.

  The First Army chief of staff may have had a sixth sense that his intent had been misconstrued, for he called Palmer back just after the fateful note had been typed and put on the road. This time, he was much more explicit concerning the direction of the pivot: "Now listen. I am only going to say this once, so listen carefully. Roll with the punch."[102] At these words, Palmer cast his eyes on the map northward and there discovered the much more prominent names, Huy and Andenne.[103] As he told an interviewer almost three decades later, "I was never so aghast in my life."[104] He had just passed to Collins a message conveying precisely the opposite intention of the army and army group commanders. With the phone to the 2nd AD still out, he had no recourse but to dispatch another messenger, this time his aide-de-camp. Hastily grabbing the carbon copy of the first note, he penciled in a very legible addendum: "He meant pull *back*. You can use Ernie anyway you need but roll with the punch. Bolling says positive dope [information] he gets socked tomorrow on his weak left. You better come home!"[105]

The first message got to Collins not long after he arrived at the 2nd AD command post, and he approved Harmon's plan to attack with CCB but wanted it held until Christmas Day because light was fast running out.[106] When the second message arrived shortly thereafter, he told Harmon to hold for the time being but that if he heard nothing else, to go ahead with the attack on the morrow. Collins then repaired to his command post, where he rehearsed the entire matter with his staff. No one, and he least of all, was inclined to withdraw. Colonel Russell F. "Red" Akers, Jr., Assistant G-3, First Army, came to Collins's headquarters and rendered a full account of Montgomery's intentions. Collins listened to it all and then sensibly asked Akers to put the instructions in writing. Akers complied and produced the following written order:

HEADQUARTERS FIRST U.S. ARMY
A.P.O. # 230, U.S. Army
24 December 1944
SUBJECT: Confirmation of Oral Instructions
TO: Commanding General, VII Corps, APO # 307, United States Army

1. In compliance with instructions received from Field Marshal Montgomery, C-in-C 21st Army Group, Commanding General, First United States Army, is endeavoring to shorten the line now held by First Army units to halt the advance of the enemy and stabilize the line.

2. For the time being, the VII Corps is released from all offensive missions and will go on the defensive with the objective of stabilizing the right flank of the First United States Army. Commanding General, VII Corps, is hereby authorized to use all force at his disposal to accomplish this job. Commanding General, VII Corps, is authorized, whenever in his opinion he considers it necessary, to drop back to the general line: Andenne-Hotton-Monhay [sic]. In the event that the line drops back this far, the bridge at Andenne will be secured. Firm contact on the left will be maintained with XVIII Corps in the vicinity of Monhay [sic].

By command of Lieutenant General HODGES:
R.F. AKERS, JR.,
Colonel, G.S.C.,
G-3 (Ops)[107]

As Akers was delivering the verbal version of this order, Collins's mind flashed back to lectures he had given on the World War I First Battle of the Marne to reserve officers, while he was assigned as an instructor at Fort Benning.[108] At a critical juncture in that fight, Moltke the younger sent an emissary to General Alexander von Kluck, commanding the German First Army, telling him to pull back, just after he had crossed the Marne. Although the necessity for the withdrawal has been debated by historians for years, it did cede the initiative to the French and help bring about a more general retirement, dashing German hopes for victory in the opening campaign of the war. Collins had an eerie feeling of historical connection with von Kluck: he was on the extreme right flank, he was being asked to withdraw by a higher headquarters that was not as in touch with the actual situation as he was, decisive victory seemed to lie within his grasp, and extremely adverse consequences could flow from compliance with his instructions.[109] The situations were not precisely analogous, but they were close enough in the VII Corps commander's mind to steel his resolve to continue the 2nd AD's attack. Collins also perceptively noted that the instructions allowed him some wiggle room. Although it was Montgomery's clear intention that he pull back, he had not been directed to do so. More precisely, he had been told to defend; but he had not been told *how* to defend.[110] Furthermore, despite the fact that he had been "released from all offensive missions," he had not been prohibited from attacking. He thus decided to violate the spirit of the order, if not its letter, and attack. When he called Harmon with authorization to release CCB, the Hell on Wheels commander exulted, "The bastards are in the bag!"[111]

As these deliberations were taking place, the battle continued to be joined between the center and western portions of VII Corps and Manteuffel's two panzer corps. The 116th Panzer Division attacked at Verdenne.[112] The German intent was to break through to the vital Marche-Hotton road, swing west, capture Marche, then drive on Buissonville to link up with the 2nd Panzer Division, thus welding together the tip of Manteuffel's spear. It was a tall order, for Waldenburg's gas trucks had not come up, and he was forced to attack with infantry alone. Just as this force was assembling, Bolling launched a spoiling attack with one infantry battalion and three tank platoons. The panzergrenadiers broke and ran. But the Germans soon came up with five Mark Vs and in bitter house-to-house fighting, forced the Americans out of Verdenne. At midnight, the GIs were still clinging tenaciously to the southern edge of the Marche-Hotton artery and preparing to retake Verdenne in a night attack. On Bolling's far right flank, the 3rd Battalion, 333rd Infantry, at Rochefort was finally forced from the village by a major push from Panzer Lehr, but not until having imposed a significant delay that Bayerlein rated equal in valor and consequence to the defense of Bastogne.[113]

Meanwhile, Harmon was doing all he could within his limited authority. Throughout the day, numerous indicators drifted into his command post of the presence of a major force at Celles. Multiple tanks were sighted, British patrols were pushed to the west, and P-51s from IX TAC were engaged by the heavy concentration of flak in Lauchert's lead kampfgruppe.[114] CCA secured Buissonville by mid-afternoon, severing contact between Lauchert's main body and the spearhead at Celles.[115] Then, like a chess master shoving forward a rook to set up a checkmate, Harmon ordered CCB, commanded by Brigadier General Isaac D. White, south to Ciney, where it would be poised to pounce on Celles when Collins gave the green light.

Over the next three days, the American 2nd AD went through the German 2nd Panzer Division like a meat grinder through tender liver.[116] Lauchert's advance kampfgruppe was cut off and split in half. The main part of the group was assembled in the woods just east of Celles. This force was the target of a classic double envelopment conducted on Christmas Day by CCB. Task Force A was the north arm of the pincer, moving from Ciney, through Achêne, to the north side of Celles. Task Force B encircled the woods from the south. Several sharp engagements were fought along the way, but most went in favor of the Americans, who were aided by pressure against Foy–Notre Dame from the British 29th Armoured Brigade and several well-timed tactical air strikes. About 200 prisoners were rounded up in and around Celles itself; but more importantly, the main portion of the 2nd Panzer Division's lead element was solidly bagged. That evening, Collins called Hodges and reported that VII Corps had had "a crackerjack day."[117]

More were to follow. Over the next two days, the soldiers of CCB systematically reduced the pocket. They divided it into segments, pounded each section with artillery and air, and then moved in for the kill with armor and/ or infantry. About 600 German soldiers slipped out of the net; but several hundred were killed or captured, and all the equipment was abandoned. This included every vehicle and major weapon that remained from the division reconnaissance battalion, an entire panzergrenadier regiment, one tank battalion, three artillery battalions, and two-thirds of the division flak. As a symbol of the sweet victory, the commander of Task Force A established his command post in the elegant Chateau d'Ardennes, where, on the evening of the 27th, he and General White were appropriately served dinner by the hotel's tuxedo-clad waiters.[118]

CCA had work of its own.[119] On Christmas Day, Bayerlein mounted an attack to eject Collier's soldiers from Buissonville and open the lifeline to the 2nd Panzer Division's spearhead at Celles. This effort overran a cavalry outpost at Humain and penetrated to the outskirts of Buissonville but was soon driven back. CCA's counterattack gained Havrenne, but the cavalry could not dislodge Panzer Lehr from Humain. On the 26th, Panzer Lehr was relieved at Humain by the 9th Panzer Division, freshly arrived from Holland and commanded by Brigadier General Harald Freiherr von Elverfeldt. Lüttwitz ordered Elverfeldt to take up where Bayerlein had left off and take Buissonville, still the thumb at the windpipe of 2nd Panzer. It was not a fair fight. CCA had ample support from division and corps artillery, and Elverfeldt's guns were still coming up. Thus, when the Germans debouched from Humain, Harmon ordered the village drenched with artillery, separating 9th Panzer's lead elements from their reinforcements. Furthermore, Elverfeldt was instructed to extend his left wing to Rochefort, bifurcating his focus. Thus, his attack petered out at Havrenne. During the night of the 26th, American artillery continued to rain down on Humain. And to give Collier some extra punch, Harmon attached Colonel Sidney R. Hinds's entire CCR to CCA. On the 27th, Collier sent Hinds to capture Humain, while CCA proper drove toward Rochefort. Hinds had the tougher fight, but he reached Humain by noon and secured it two hours before midnight.

Except for some minor mopping up, the immediate battle before the Meuse was over.[120] In four days of tough combat, the 2nd Armored Division had captured 1,200 prisoners and captured or destroyed over 80 tanks, a similar number of guns, and more than 400 vehicles. Some of these were undoubtedly taken out of action by Quesada's IX TAC and Coningham's 2nd TAF. Nevertheless, it was an impressive achievement. Friendly casualties were mercifully moderate: 17 killed, 26 missing, a shade over 200 wounded, and but 5 light tanks and 22 mediums destroyed. On the other side of the lines, Lüttwitz was instructed to leave a thin covering force in place and again turn his face toward Bastogne.[121]

Meanwhile, on Christmas Day, a coordinated attack by the 84th ID retook Verdenne, spoiling any enemy hopes of reaching the Marche-Hotton road.[122] On the 26th, a pesky pocket of Germans holed up in a depression between Verdenne and Bourdon was reduced by accurate fire from 8-inch and 155-mm artillery. On the 27th, Waldenburg was ordered to take up the defensive. The German drive on the Meuse was now completely halted.

Collins's role in all this was pivotal. Just as he had at the critical juncture of Operation Cobra, he sensed that the Germans were weak and would crack in the face of a determined offensive. Bradley later called the 2nd AD's attack "one of the most brilliantly conducted operations of the war," but it would never have been launched without Collins's approval.[123] And though Montgomery was miffed at having his plans upset by what he considered to be premature engagement, he held no grudge against Collins, whose "aggressive spirit" he still admired.[124] Collins also demonstrated moral courage in explicitly choosing to defy his higher commanders' intent and in implicitly being willing to accept responsibility for the adverse results, should Harmon's attack go awry. The mechanics of his decision making were sound as well. Realizing that important things could well transpire on the 24th and that he would be out of communication, he deputized General Palmer to act in his stead at the corps command post.[125] Although Collins was inclined to take the offensive, he canvassed his principal advisors to learn of contrary opinions. Recognizing the significance of his decision and, perforce, of the instructions he received from Colonel Akers, he properly insisted that the latter be documented. In short, we see in this pivotal decision not only the mental acuity to perceive the situation correctly and come to an appropriate judgment, we also see the moral fortitude to do so under conditions of significant stress and the farseeing realization that it would judged by the inevitable audit of time and historical perspective. These are all hallmarks of a refined and balanced military mind. And, as Clausewitz sagely noted, "strength of character does not consist solely in having powerful feelings, but in maintaining one's balance in spite of them."[126]

Action on the Corps' Left Flank, 23–29 December

The defense in the sector of the 3rd AD was ultimately successful but not without some fairly rough edges. Collins had begun his tour of the corps front on 24 December at Rose's command post, where he found the division, still without CCB, sorely pressed and woefully short of infantry. His solution was to attach two regiments of Prickett's 75th ID to the 3rd AD.[127] Prickett had experienced a prototypical successful career, which included active service in World War I.[128] He graduated from West Point in 1916, served with the Pershing Expedition, and commanded a field artillery battalion during the St. Mihiel and Meuse-Argonne offensives. After graduating from CGSS in 1930 and the War College in 1933, he served for four years in War Plans Division, later commanding the 4th Division Artillery until assuming command of the 75th ID in 1943. The 75th had arrived in France on 13 December.[129] It was the epitome of an inexperienced division. Collins intimates that it was this lack of experience that led him to attach the 289th and 290th Infantry Regiments to the 3rd AD, rather than committing them under their parent division.[130]

By 24 December, Rose's sector comprised some nine miles of the VII Corps front, from the eastern side of Hotton, through Soy, Erezée, and Briscol, to Grandménil, the eastern terminus about a mile west of Manhay.[131] The front lines lay along an arc generally one to three miles south of the road connecting these villages, except on the far left flank, where the Germans were pressing heavily on Grandménil itself. A critical three-mile portion of this sector was centered on the village of Amonines, just over two miles south of

Erezée.[132] It was defended by TF Orr, named for Lieutenant Colonel William R. Orr. On Christmas Eve, about a battalion of the 560th VGD launched a dozen attacks to penetrate Orr's lines. Orr threw every soldier he could scrape up into the battle. With solid artillery support, the GIs held on, piling up mounds of German bodies in front of their lines.

More tough times lay ahead for the Spearhead soldiers and their attached brethren from the 75th ID.[133] On Christmas morning, just after the fall of Manhay to the Germans, Brigadier General Doyle Hickey, commanding CCA, 3rd AD, ordered the 3rd Battalion, 289th Infantry, to block the main road from Grandménil to Erezée. A resolute GI halted an attacking German column with a single bazooka round, advantageously disabling a Panther at a narrow spot in the road. The battalion then moved off toward Grandménil, while the remainder of the regiment moved south into the valley of the Aisne River. At this juncture, help arrived from a two-company task force of CCB, just released back to Rose's control and thence passed to Hickey. This unit seized Grandménil but was promptly ejected by a German counterattack. Nevertheless, Rose's and Prickett's soldiers had kept a plug in the bottle just west of Grandménil, thus denying to Lammerding's 2nd SS Panzer Division the maneuver room it needed to roll down the Manhay-Hotton road.

Two days later, Dietrich ordered the 12th SS Panzer Division to take another shot west of Grandménil, this time aiming the dart at Erezée, in a last, desperate effort to gain the Marche plateau.[134] But massive friction, induced by Allied air, low fuel supplies, cramped roads, and the new strategic priority of seizing Bastogne, conspired to limit this attack to the division reconnaissance battalion, a battalion of assault guns, and two infantry companies. It was fortunate this was so. The inexperienced 289th Infantry, now deployed south and southeast of Erezée, had allowed a 1,000-yard gap to develop between its 1st and 2nd Battalions. This gap was due south of Briscol and the minuscule hamlet of Sadzot. The Germans, who attacked shortly after midnight on the 28th, stumbled into this opening and made it all the way to Sadzot without being challenged. Hickey ordered in the 509th PIB, but it ran into the Germans as soon as it deployed into battle formation. After daybreak, the paratroopers called in their guns and recaptured Sadzot shortly before noon. Hickey then ordered the 1st Battalion of the 112th Infantry to seal the gap between the two battalions of the 289th Infantry. This effort missed the mark, allowing the Germans to move in reinforcements that blunted an attack by the 509th coming out of Sadzot. All seemed chaos and confusion. Finally, Hickey was able to restore a modicum of order and work out a coordinated plan to seal the gap and expel the Germans, both of which were effected by daylight on 29 December. This "Sad Sack Affair," so dubbed because of its proximity to the hamlet of Sadzot and its abundant miscues, covered no one on the American side with any particular glory. But like the final twitches of a beheaded chicken, it signified the dying gasp of Sixth SS Panzer Army's offensive in the Ardennes.

Preparing to Attack, 27 December–2 January

Collins, ever bright, imaginative, audacious, and ambitious, attempted to play a leading role in the formulation of plans to launch the American riposte on the north side of the Bulge. But his more aggressive instincts were ultimately constrained by Montgomery's conservatism, aided and abetted by similar inclinations on the part of Hodges and some inconvenient realities of terrain that complicated the development of a plan to cut the salient at its base.

On 27 December, Collins sent a two-page letter to Hodges proposing three different plans for the impending offensive.[135] The first was a straightforward push from the northwest quadrant of the penetration, southeast to Houffalize, then on to St. Vith, to be conducted with the 2nd and 3rd ADs and the 83rd and 84th IDs. Collins felt its chief advantages were the secure left flank and the fact that Houffalize laid "well within our grasp," but correctly noted its chief disadvantage was that "it pushes the enemy out of the bottom of the pocket instead of trapping him." The second option was a north-south push from Malmédy through St. Vith to Weiswampach, then east across the Our, executed by the 2nd and 3rd ADs, augmented by the 1st and 2nd IDs, then assigned to V Corps. This plan could, in Collins's estimate, potentially trap both the 5th and 6th Panzer Armies; but it exposed both flanks and would require a concomitant drive by Third Army north along the Skyline Drive. The third was a variant of the first and, one suspects, a throw-away option. It ran west-east but farther south than the first, aiming for Houffalize and Bastogne and requiring a forcing of the Ourthe River. Its disadvantages were exposed flanks and the fact that it had to negotiate very difficult terrain, with few countervailing advantages. As one would suspect, Collins's recommendations were for the second, first, and third options, in that order.

His bold proposal fell on deaf ears. Hodges's aide recorded that his chief "has had enough of exposed flanks for the past two weeks" and accurately prognosticated, "It is thought that the most conservative of the three plans will be the one finally adopted."[136] On 28 December, Hodges went to 21st AG headquarters for a long conference with Montgomery on the timing and location of the offensive.[137] It is likely that he at least mentioned Collins's plans, particularly the first and second options. Regarding the latter, Montgomery had significant reservations about attempting to support a four-division attack along the road that ran from Liège, through Malmédy, to St. Vith, later telling Collins, "Joe, you can't supply a corps over a single road."[138] Collins brashly replied, "Well Monty, maybe you British can't but we can." Years later, Collins noted wryly, "As always happens in such cases, the umpire, Monty, won that argument." Collins's preferred plan would have assumed a significant amount of logistical risk, particularly with both flanks of the attack being exposed to German ripostes. But the fundamental reason for this option's being rejected had nothing to do with either its logistical feasibility or its insecure flanks. Its primary deficiency was operational: it was totally dependent on a mirror-image drive from the south along the Skyline Drive, for which there was clearly insufficient maneuver space.

Collins's first option became the approved solution for the northern attack. This was ratified in a meeting among Montgomery, Collins, and Ridgway at VII Corps headquarters on 30 December.[139] Each corps commander briefed his situation and plans based on oral instructions received from Hodges on 29 December. Although Montgomery expressed a faint hope for attacking the salient further to the east, he felt that the attack "must be" aimed at Houffalize. He stated that he would not order any attack "until after the projected attack between HOTTON and GRANDMENIL had definitely expended itself." By this juncture, Montgomery should have been aware that the German Schwerpunkt had shifted to Bastogne and that the attack in the north had run its course, but he was still playing his cards very close to his vest; it must also be noted that the First Army G-2, Monk Dickson, agreed with him on the likelihood of another major German push in the north.[140] Collins planned to lead the attack with his two armored divisions from right to left, Harmon's 2nd and Rose's 3rd, each augmented by an infantry regiment. Two infantry divisions, Bolling's 84th and Major General Robert C. Macon's newly arrived 83rd, would follow behind the 2nd and 3rd ADs, respectively.

On 31 December, Collins and Ridgway went to First Army headquarters to meet with Hodges, Kean, and Thorson to arrange support for the impending offensive.[141] Army assistance to both corps was prodigious, with the weight going to VII Corps. Collins received fifteen field artillery battalions, four tank battalions, six tank destroyer battalions, and eight antiaircraft battalions, as well as the bulk of the available artillery ammunition. That evening, Hodges took the final plans to Montgomery's headquarters and learned that the field marshal now approved launching the attack on 3 January.[142]

VII Corps Attacks, 3–4 January

As Monty had predicted, the going was tough.[143] Harmon's attack had Collier's CCA on the right and White's CCB on the left, with a total of five task forces in the lead echelon. On 3 January, CCA experienced severe problems with the ice, snow, snipers, and nebelwerfer fire. Toward the end of the day when about seventeen tanks were discovered to its front, Collins ordered it to hold up, with little ground gained. CCB had it even worse. It encountered extremely heavy resistance from German artillery, small infantry units, and well-directed antitank fire, also making only negligible gains. Things went little better in Rose's zone, where Budinot's CCB on the right and Hickey's CCA on the left each attacked with two task forces. Despite tenacious opposition from well-emplaced infantry, mortar, and artillery fire, CCB secured Malempré by the end of the day. The advance of Hickey's western task force was impeded by more dug-in infantry and heavy artillery. His eastern force made modest gains after experiencing similarly heavy resistance, augmented by a well-protected minefield. Not much better progress was made on the 4th. At the end of the day, the best the 2nd AD could report was that it was engaged in a heavy fight to capture Odeigne, roughly two miles southeast of its jump-off point, while the 3rd AD, faring marginally better, had secured a 400-yard bridgehead beyond the Lienne River.

This fighting, much like that to the east in the XVIII (Airborne) Corps sector, set the pattern for much of what was to follow: painstaking, incremental gains against a stiff German defense that was maddeningly augmented by lousy weather and terrible terrain.

Analysis

Collins had fully justified Monty's faith in him. He had watched the developing situation closely, alerting Hodges and Ridgway to problems that he foresaw developing before he assumed command of his sector. He had been aggressive in ordering Harmon to attack on Christmas morning, and his permissibly insubordinate violation of Montgomery's and Hodges's intent was clearly justified by its outcome. The 2nd AD's attack against the 2nd Panzer Division was clearly instrumental in the dramatic reversal of German fortunes. Collins's audacious plan to seal the penetration at its base bore no chance of implementation—but the major reason therefore was well beyond his ken, and he deserves some approbation for formally proposing it. It clearly demonstrated a vision of the battlefield beyond that of a corps commander. Collins's performance during the transition phase of the Bulge not only offered an exemplary study in effective corps command, it also demonstrated his distinct potential to command at higher echelons.

V CORPS HOLDS ON

Except for a final paroxysm of German offensive activity on 22 December and a faint obbligato of an attack on the 28th, activities in the V Corps sector during the transition phase of the Bulge were relatively quiescent.

On the morning of 22 December, the 26th SS Panzergrenadier Regiment of the 12th SS Panzer Division launched an attack southwest of Butgenbach against the 1st ID's 26th Infantry Regiment.[144] The assault created a gap in the regimental front some 200 yards deep and 800 yards wide; but by the morning of the 23rd, a counterattack ejected the Germans and restored the lines. Two attacks were also made on the 22nd against the 9th ID near Monschau. The first was handily beaten off with artillery. The second created a penetration to a depth of 500 yards, which was quickly closed by GIs attacking from the flanks.

There followed a pause of some six days as both sides licked their wounds from the bloodletting of the previous week. The Germans had finally determined that the Elsenborn Ridge simply could not be carried, and the Americans were simply too exhausted and too disorganized to mount a counterattack. On 23 December, Monty visited V Corps headquarters and learned that the four assigned divisions were short a total of some 7,000 soldiers, mostly infantrymen, and that the 5th AD, in corps reserve, was at 60 percent strength.[145] The distinct lack of offensive inclinations at V Corps and First Army resulting from these manpower deficiencies was evident on the next day, when Huebner went to First Army headquarters. There he held a long conference with Hodges to develop a plan for the withdrawal of the V Corps units' heavy equipment "in order that, if it becomes necessary for these troops to withdraw, the roads would not be clogged with this heavy material and it would [not] be necessary to hand it over to the enemy."[146]

In the meantime, Model was desperate to pull all the troops he could away from the V Corps sector, while maintaining a modicum of defense.[147] He thus cast his eyes covetously upon the significant angle in the lines at Wirtzfeld, on the southeast corner of the Elsenborn Ridge, and directed General Hitzfeld, still commanding the LXVII Corps, to conduct a map maneuver to determine if the line should be straightened. The exercise, conducted on 26 December, concluded affirmatively. But it is important to note that there were no grandiose ideas of breakthrough here. The attack was merely a minor tactical maneuver to shorten a defensive line. Originally, Hitzfeld was to have four divisions for the task. But he was later told to make bricks without straw. The final assault force consisted of two battalions from the 246th VGD and three from the 12th VGD. They attacked on 28 December but were shredded by American artillery. The Sixth SS Panzer Army's attack against the Elsenborn Ridge was now clinically dead. With Bastogne and the drive on the Meuse absorbing more resources than Model had to spare, he simply did not have the forces to conduct even minor offensive operations successfully anywhere else. Hitzfeld's corps was reduced to three emaciated divisions and told to hold on as best it could.

Gerow's letter of instructions issued the same day as these abortive German attacks had all the hallmarks of defensive intent.[148] Units were told to improve their positions, establish outposts to deny enemy observation of the front lines, patrol aggressively, and maintain contact with the Germans. It also included something of a moral fillip, telling the V Corps soldiers that they held "the key sector on the Northern flank of the breakthrough" and that "the splendid efforts of the men and officers that have established our present lines and inflicted heavy losses on the enemy are recognized and appreciated." Over the next five days, the corps continued to hold on and recover as best it could. Its role in the First Army offensive of 3 January was limited to a demonstration. The V Corps order of 1 January provided merely that the 1st, 2nd, 9th, and 99th IDs would patrol in sufficient strength "to lead the enemy to believe an attack in force is underway or in prospect."[149] Despite this relatively passive role during the period of transition in the Bulge, the continued defense gave V Corps a firm base from which to launch an attack when it regained its offensive capability.

SOME CLOSING OBSERVATIONS

XVIII (Airborne) and VII Corps played the principal roles in the transition phase of the Ardennes campaign on the northern front. Ridgway's soldiers halted the II SS Panzer Corps and prevented it from gaining the Marche plateau. They did so against long odds and under extremely difficult circumstances. The defense of the 82nd Airborne Division against multiple armored attacks was particularly commendable.[150] The various defenders of St. Vith, most of whom were ordered to pick themselves up and fight again almost immediately after withdrawing from six days of harrowing combat, also deserve commendation. With the exception of his initial hesitation about the withdrawal of the forces in the St. Vith salient, Ridgway's leadership of the XVIII (Airborne) Corps had been firm, decisive, and effective. Collins's soldiers had halted the new German Schwerpunkt, the 5th Panzer Army's drive on the Meuse. In doing so, they were aided by the defense and relief of Bastogne, by the northern shoulder's holding firm, by the buffering effect of the XVIII (Airborne) Corps defense, by the tyranny of terrain and logistics that steadily sapped the strength from Manteuffel's armored spearheads, and by the cumulative effects of Allied airpower. Nevertheless, the staunchness of the 84th ID in the stationary defense and the alacrity of the 2nd AD in a more active defense were both commendable. Although Collins had an easier task than Ridgway, his generalship can hardly be faulted. It was thorough, clearheaded, and decisive. Both corps made the successful transition from defense to offense. This, coupled with the fact that the Germans had, by 4 January, lost all initiative in the south, meant that Collins, Ridgway, and later Huebner (who would assume command of V Corps on 15 January) would be able to keep the pressure on from the northern flank in the coming final phase of the campaign—the eradication of the Bulge.

PHASE III: AMERICAN INITIATIVE IN ACTION

13

Closing the Bulge: More Tension in the Allied Camp

I employed the whole available power of the British Group of Armies; this power was brought into play very gradually and in such a way that it would not interfere with the American lines of communication. Finally it was put into battle with a bang, and today British divisions are fighting hard on the right flank of First US Army.[1]   *Bernard L. Montgomery, 7 January 1945*

Nevertheless you must know after what has happened I cannot serve under Montgomery. If he is to be put in command of all ground forces, you must send me home, for if Montgomery goes in over me, I will have lost the confidence of my command.[2]   *Omar Bradley, 8 January 1945*

THE FINAL PHASE OF THE BULGE is clearly the most neglected.[3] This neglect stems from the fact that it was, at first glance, a fairly straightforward operation: twin drives by the First and Third Armies to join hands at Houffalize, followed by a push to the east to eradicate the remainder of the German penetration. But a closer look reveals two underlying complexities. First, the significant disagreements over future Allied strategy in the ETO that had apparently been resolved in Montgomery's "devoted subordinate" letter to Eisenhower of 31 December 1944 still festered beneath the surface and continued to affect current operations. Second, questions of timing and direction influenced how the corps on both the northern and southern wings of the penetration would be employed. Thus, despite its somewhat anticlimactic nature, the closing of the Bulge provides an interesting leadership study in both coalition warfare and how the various corps commanders dealt with the very tough realities of having to attack through the Ardennes in winter.

CLOSING THE BULGE

Every major decision Eisenhower made in the closing phase of the campaign had to take as its starting point how it would be perceived by Bradley and Montgomery. This state of affairs was due in no small part to an ill-fated press conference held by Montgomery on 7 January, to Bradley's great indignation over several things said there, and to Montgomery's persistent determination to make a powerful drive north of the Ruhr the main element of European strategy.

Realizing that feelings had been hurt by the recent brouhaha over the command issue and aware of Fleet Street's "sniping at Eisenhower," Montgomery petitioned Churchill for authority to hold a press conference for both British and American correspondents, in which he would "put in a strong plea for Allied solidarity."[4] Churchill approved, and the fateful die was cast. In many ways, Monty was graciousness personified. He opined that Rundstedt had been defeated "by the good fighting qualities of the American soldier and by the team-work of the Allies."[5] He praised the GI as "a brave fighting man, steady under fire, and with that tenacity in battle which stamps the first class soldier." He proclaimed his loyalty to Eisenhower: "The captain of the team is Eisenhower. I am absolutely devoted to Ike." Had he left it here, all would have been well. But the damage came in his description of the battle and his participation therein. His statement cited at the beginning of the chapter was misleading and factually inaccurate. The phrase "whole available power of the British Group of Armies" implied a force much larger than a single corps; the word "divisions" belied the fact that the units of XXX Corps committed to the battle on 7 January consisted only of the 29th Armoured Brigade, two battalions of the 6th Airborne Division, and the 53rd Welsh Division.[6] Worst of all, his observation—"the battle has been most interesting; I think one of the most interesting and tricky battles I have ever handled"—was far too self-congratulatory for the occasion and bound to feel like salt on an open wound, particularly at 12th Army Group.[7]

To understand the reaction at Bradley's headquarters, we must go back to 5 January. Bradley was at something of a loss as to how to respond to a congratulatory letter just received from Marshall on his handling of the Bulge. He wanted to give the chief an accurate accounting of the situation. But he confided to Hansen, "At the same time I don't want to apologize for what has happened."[8] Later that day he informed his aide that the general tenor of his response to the chief had been: "I do not blame my commanders, my staff or myself for the situation that result[ed]. We have taken a calculated risk and the German hit us harder than we had anticipated he could."[9] Having to explain the distinction between calculation and miscalculation to Marshall was obviously a sensitive matter. This sensitivity was also evident in Bradley's reaction to SHAEF's release of an official statement concerning the change of command arrangements precipitated by the German offensive.

The short announcement read as follows: "When the German penetration through the Ardennes created two fronts, one substantially facing south and the other north, by instant agreement of all concerned, that portion of the front facing south was placed under command of Montgomery and that facing north under command of Bradley."[10]

Bradley felt that this announcement was deficient in two particulars.[11] It did not specify when the shift had taken place; much more importantly, it did not specify that the arrangement was temporary. The first played into the British press's intimation that Montgomery's help had been necessary from the inception of the battle; the second fed an interpretation that Bradley could be condemned merely to commanding the Third Army for the indefinite future.

Feelings at 12th AG were badly hurt. On 6 January, Hansen composed a six-page, typed, double-spaced lament in his diary under the heading "MISCELLANY: 'Monty Takes Command.'"[12] It was a litany of woes. First Army had lost its American identity while under Montgomery's operational control. Montgomery was the champion of the British cause; Eisenhower was the champion of the Allied cause; no one was there to champion the American cause. What news stories there were about Bradley inferred that the German attack had succeeded because of his negligence. Perhaps the conniving British field marshal might just engineer an end run around Marshall through Churchill to get appointed as Ike's land deputy.[13] All these dire thoughts led Hansen to one, inescapable conclusion: Bradley and the 12th AG should "crow the Yankee Doodle Dandy."

With suspicions running rampant, Bradley's headquarters "exploded with indignation" when the transcript of Montgomery's conference reached Luxembourg on 8 January, and Bradley "got all-out, right-down-to-his-toes mad."[14] Hansen and New York publicist Lieutenant Colonel Ralph Ingersoll urged Bradley to go public with his version of the events.[15] Bradley was initially cool to the idea; but, egged on by Ingersoll, he acquiesced. The result was a press conference on the 9th, in which Bradley articulated his "calculated-risk" argument, stipulated that the command change had taken place on 20 December, and repeatedly used the word "temporary" to describe it. In a prepared statement, Bradley indicated that both Ninth and First Armies would be coming back under his command when the present arrangement came to an end. This was a clear effort to pressure Eisenhower to give him back both armies, even though he knew Ike had already decided that Simpson's army would remain under Montgomery's operational control after the joining of First and Third Armies at Houffalize. Ike did not buckle. But the attempt to make him do so was an egregious act of disloyalty on Bradley's part, and he is quite fortunate that Eisenhower not only forgave him but also argued insistently with Marshall for his promotion to four-star rank.[16]

Churchill, to his everlasting credit, set the record straight on just whose battle the Bulge was. His speech to Parliament on 18 January included the following remarks:

> I have seen it suggested that the terrific battle which has been proceeding since 16th December on the American front is an Anglo-American battle. In fact, however, the United States troops have done almost all the fighting and have suffered almost all the losses. They have suffered losses almost equal to those on both sides at the battle of Gettysburg. Only one British Army Corps has been engaged in this action. All the rest of the 30 or more divisions, which have been fighting continuously for the last month, are United States troops. The Americans have engaged 30 or 40 men for every one we have engaged, and they have lost 60 to 80 men for every one of ours. That is a point I wish to make. Care must be taken in telling our proud tale not to claim for the British Army an undue share of what is undoubtedly the greatest American battle of the war, and will, I believe, be regarded as an ever famous American victory.[17]

But there remained one area of significant contention between Montgomery and Bradley that revolved around three closely interrelated questions. Would Eisenhower stick to his decision to leave Ninth Army under Montgomery's control? If so, how strong would Simpson's army be? And finally, would Bradley be allowed to eradicate the Bulge completely, or would he have to desist from this effort in order to begin transferring divisions to Ninth Army before the penetration was completely closed. All three issues were complicated by continued German activity in southern France. In the face of these assaults, Eisenhower was willing to surrender Strasbourg temporarily in order to economize his commitments on that front; but De Gaulle would not countenance such action.[18] This caused troops to be dispatched to the tertiary area of operations in the ETO and, with both the British and the American armies running out of manpower, exacerbated the problem of allocating forces between Montgomery's efforts to close to the west bank of the Rhine in the north and Bradley's to do so in the center.[19]

By 14 January, Montgomery had become sufficiently alarmed by all this to conclude that Eisenhower must set ruthless priorities in his favor.[20] He felt sure that First and Third Armies would be unable to penetrate the Siegfried Line and drive on to Bonn. "We must," he told Brooke, "therefore make a new plan and allot sufficient resources to the main effort to make absolutely certain of success. Elsewhere we must be defensive with ample reserves suitably positioned to give complete balance and security in all areas whatever the enemy may do."[21] The upshot of all this was that Bradley's drive was to be halted, Ninth Army was to be given four corps with thirteen divisions, and another American corps was to be committed to Second British Army. This was a return to the old argument for a single drive into Germany and a repudiation of Eisenhower's broad front strategy. Eisenhower summoned Bradley to Versailles for a conference on 16 January, the date First and Third Armies linked up at Houffalize.[22] Disappointing Bradley, he reaffirmed his decision to make Montgomery's northern effort the theater priority and leave Simpson under 21st AG command. But in his subsequently issued directive, he trimmed out several divisions from Montgomery's proposal; disregarded the request for an additional American corps to Second Army; and, most pointedly, did not veto Bradley's offensive into the Rhineland. However, as additional nods in Montgomery's direction, he insisted that First Army's axis of advance be sufficiently northward to cooperate with Ninth Army and stipulated that Bradley move his headquarters to Namur.

On 19 January, with Bradley, now in command of both First and Third Armies, deeply involved in eradicating the Bulge and planning his follow-on offensive into the Rhineland, Montgomery wrote Eisenhower suggesting that "you may consider it desirable to close down in the Ardennes shortly, so that we can get on with preparations for GRENADE."[23] Operation Grenade was the southern complement to Veritable, a northeast attack by Ninth U.S. Army to link up with the First Canadian Army west of the Rhine. Eisenhower found early cessation of operations in the Ardennes undesirable. On operational grounds, it made no sense to leave the Germans with a penetration into the Allied lines. But the morale considerations were equally compelling. The German offensive had damaged the U.S. Army's psyche as well as its body, and all of its territorial gains simply had to be recovered to assuage the wound. Thus, Eisenhower gave Bradley leave to complete this task, which was accomplished by 28 January. This decision might have represented a slight genuflection on Ike's part toward American sensibilities, but it was also an understandable act of humanity.

THE GERMAN WITHDRAWAL

The Germans were in a purely reactive mode, but Hitler imposed his will on how the retirement would be effected. His two operative principles were to give ground as grudgingly as possible and to spare the SS units the rigors of this debilitating task. In implementing this design, he was materially aided by Model and Manteuffel, who fought a skillful delay for just over three weeks.

Hitler's first reprieve came on 8 January, when he authorized a withdrawal from the tip of the Bulge to a line running from Dochamps, about five miles north-northeast of La Roche, to Longchamps, just over two miles northwest of Bastogne.[24] This was accompanied by orders to withdraw the Sixth SS Panzer Army to assembly areas northeast of St. Vith for Dietrich's forces in the north and to the east of Wiltz for the SS units in the south. On 12 January, the long-anticipated Russian offensive began in the east.[25] This, combined with steady pressure from VII, XVIII (Airborne), VIII, and III Corps, precipitated several directives, issued in rapid succession. On 14 January, Hitler authorized further withdrawal to a line running from just east of Houffalize to Noville. Rundstedt and Model wanted to use the occasion to begin a phased withdrawal to the Rhine, but Hitler would surrender neither the small remaining buffer in the Ardennes nor the Rhineland without a fight.[26] On the 15th, I and II Panzer Corps were ordered to rest and refit in the OB West's rear area, completely disengaging them from the ongoing battle in the Ardennes. On 20 January, the entire Sixth SS Panzer Army and a number of supporting units were ordered to the east to meet the oncoming Soviet masses, providing the definitive indicator that Hitler's desperate attempt to gain a strategic victory in the west had failed.[27] The last directive came on 23 January, authorizing Rundstedt to pull his forces back to the West Wall.[28] From the German perspective, the Ardennes offensive was now officially dead.

ACTION IN THE AIR

With one major exception, Allied air action did little to interfere with the German withdrawal. From 6–9 January, fog and snowstorms, which severely limited both operating ceilings and visibility, prevented the Ninth Air Force TACs from getting off a single sortie.[29] And while it was possible for planes to fly above the storms, the nearly blinding conditions on the ground made close air support all but impossible. This meant that the bulk of the air effort was devoted to interdiction. On 14 January, XIX TAC hit Houffalize and St. Vith with 600 aircraft; on the 15th it reached out to Mainz, Bad Kreuznach, and Wiesbaden in a much deeper interdiction pattern, filling in for the heavies that had reverted to their strategic strikes.[30]

The linkup at Houffalize set the stage for the final air-ground engagement of the campaign.[31] On 22 January, the weather broke again, producing a bright sun on new-fallen snow. Four groups of P-47s from XIX TAC quickly got airborne to support Eddy's XII Corps. They found the roads below thick with German soldiers, trucks, armored cars, tanks, and horse-drawn transport. Some of the units involved were elements of Fifth Panzer Army moving east toward Dasburg; others were from the LIII Corps of Brandenberger's Seventh Panzer Army withdrawing to the northeast in a frantic effort to beat XII Corps to the crossing sites at Vianden; and still others were elements of the 2nd Panzer and Panzer Lehr Divisions cutting against the grain of the withdrawal to help the Seventh Army stave off defeat. This confluence of cross purposes and movements created a monumental traffic jam, which B-26s of IX Bomber Division compounded by dropping ninety-six tons of bombs around the bridge at Dasburg, damaging the approaches sufficiently to bottle up the eastward flow. Twenty-five squadrons of the XIX TAC flew over six hundred sorties against the chaos below, inflicting one last, punishing lick on the withdrawing German forces.[32]

SOME CLOSING OBSERVATIONS

It is difficult not to admire the German soldiers in this phase of the campaign. Their great hopes were dashed. They knew the war was over. All they could do was delay the inevitable. Yet they kept fighting, and they kept fighting well. According to the U.S. Army's official history, during the period 2–28 January, they inflicted 39,672 battle casualties on the advancing Americans, only slightly less than the 41,315 of the period 16 December–1 January.[33] When one considers that casualties in the first two weeks included the roughly 7,000 who were captured in the battle of the Schnee Eifel, it forces a realization of the tenacity of the German defense in the final phase of the campaign. This tenacity was aided by atrocious weather that made any offensive movement extremely difficult and, for the most part, inhibited American air action. But as the epic saga of the Bulge draws to an end, we shall also discover that the raw bravery of the GIs who pressed the attack in these deplorable conditions was likewise much to be admired, as were the guiding hands of their corps commanders.

14

VII, XVIII (Airborne), and V Corps Close the Bulge from the North

Co. moved by truck and foot at 0400 to Petite Tailles, Belgium, and jumped off in attack at 1015. Majority of men exhausted and scarcely fit for combat.[1]

Morning Report, Company K, 333rd Infantry, 13 January 1945

By MID-JANUARY, the freezing temperatures, deep snow, rugged hills, and thick forests of the Ardennes, combined with determined German resistance, had exacted a wearing, grinding toll on the American soldiers in the Bulge. Infantrymen exhausted themselves just to get basic protection: it took two hours of hard digging merely to penetrate the frozen surface, five hours to reach a depth of three feet, and an entire day to prepare a five-foot-deep foxhole.[2] At least two divisions issued their soldiers explosives to speed the process.[3] The tankers had it a bit easier but not a lot. Icy roads and deep snow made their movement agonizingly slow; and the frigid, wet weather frequently locked up traversing mechanisms, which led either to lost opportunities or death. In these circumstances, Collins, Ridgway, and (from 15 January on) Huebner had to determine how to eradicate the Bulge while conserving the fighting capability of their formations. These considerations were often in direct conflict, for the seizure of terrain entailed an inevitable cost in life and limb. There was one additional imperative. All senior commanders were poignantly aware that the return of First Army to Bradley's command would not take place until it had linked up with Third Army at Houffalize. This "event-driven" condition created an ever-present force, impelling the corps commanders forward.

VII CORPS ATTACKS TO HOUFFALIZE AND BEYOND

VII Corps represented First Army's main effort in Montgomery's and Hodges's plan to close the Bulge from the north. With two armored divisions (Harmon's 2nd and Rose's 3rd), two infantry divisions (Major General Robert C. Macon's 83rd and Bolling's 84th), and a relatively narrow sector, Collins had sufficient force to maintain a relatively sustained offensive. Nevertheless, it was far from a cakewalk; the VII Corps commander had to exercise firm, yet judicious direction to keep the advance moving forward at an acceptable cost. The terrain over which VII Corps attacked was largely uninhabited, stretching from the vital Salmchâteau–La Roche road, southeast toward the Ourthe River.[4] The zone is dominated by the Plateau de Tailles, a broad area of densely forested terrain, with heights running to just over 500 meters. In this large expanse of woodland, all the advantages of terrain lay with the defender. Accordingly, Collins's initial scheme was to lead with his two armored divisions, each reinforced by an infantry regiment, with the two infantry divisions following behind.[5] The 3rd AD, followed by the 83rd ID, attacked on the left adjacent to the XVIII (Airborne) Corps, while the 2nd AD, followed by the 84th ID, attacked on the right. The 4th Cavalry Group screened the corps' right flank along the east bank of the Ourthe.

Breaking through the German Crust, 5–10 January

With its attack zone narrowed to the roughly fifteen miles between Hotton in the west and Lierneux (still in German hands) in the east, VII Corps was facing three German divisions when it continued its attack on the morning of 5 January. They were, from west to east, the 2nd SS Panzer Division, the 560th VGD, and the 12th VGD.[6] These divisions were conducting an active defense. They would aggressively counterattack whenever the opportunity arose and withdraw when pushed back by superior force but always look for the opportunity to attack again. So it went on 5 January. In the area of the 3rd AD, the 12th VGD launched a regimental attack, supported by tanks of the 2nd SS Panzer Division. It was beaten off, and the Germans fell back to guarding the approaches to Lierneux. The defense along the corps front was supported by a significant volume of mortar and nebelwerfer fire against the American frontline troops. The Germans also harassed the GIs' advance by placing explosives with time-delay fuses in abandoned dwellings as they withdrew.

Results were mixed against this stiff resistance.[7] Although Rose's soldiers repelled the attack by the 12th VGD, they found the subsequent going very difficult. By the evening of the 5th, they had pushed to within visual firing range of Lierneux but had not been able to mount an assault on the village itself. Things fared slightly better in the west. CCB of Harmon's 2nd AD enveloped the village of Odeigne, just over two miles south of Manhay, and by the end of the day had secured it in the face of intense small arms and

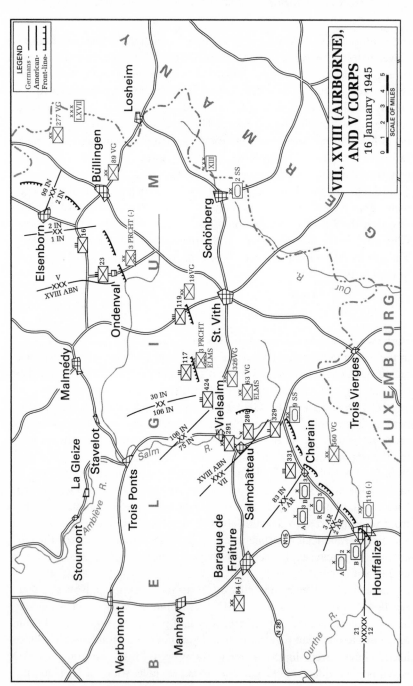

Map 8. VII, XVIII (Airborne), and V Corps, 16 January 1945

artillery fire. Meanwhile, the 84th ID followed in the 2nd AD's wake, mopping up bypassed pockets of resistance and generally facilitating the tankers' advance.

Over the next three days, VII Corps moved slowly forward, with the Germans contesting each small advance.[8] On the 6th, more snow fell, further complicating the attack. Additionally, the 12th VGD was reinforced by elements of the 326th VGD. On the other side of the ledger, German artillery fire began to slacken. The 3rd AD captured Lierneux, and the 2nd AD closed in on Dochamps, a key village on the route to the vital N-28 highway. On the next day, German artillery fire continued to abate. On the corps' left, the 3rd AD set up a roadblock at Parker's crossroads. In the evening, the 2nd AD entered Dochamps, but the Germans defending the village were still putting up a stiff fight. Late that night, another heavy snowfall came down. The 3rd AD cleared the village of Hebronval, just north of the N-28 and about three miles east of Parker's crossroads. Rose's tankers were now also up against the reconnaissance battalion and two panzergrenadier regiments of the 9th SS Panzer Division, which was committed to the fight to hold open the eastern edge of the northern flank of the Bulge. In the west, the 2nd AD finally got control of Dochamps.

To this point, things had proceeded fairly well on the corps' left flank but somewhat disappointingly on the right. The 3rd AD had closed on the N-28, but the 2nd AD was still about two miles to its north. After recounting the difficulties encountered in this phase of the attack, Collins noted that "for the first and only time I had to put some pressure on my good friend and great fighter Ernie Harmon to keep his 'Hell on Wheels' Division moving."[9] He ordered Harmon to attack on the 9th to seize Samrée, the northern edge of which abuts the southern side of the La Roche–Salmchâteau highway, and simultaneously instructed Macon to pass through the 3rd AD on the same day and continue the attack to the south.[10] Additionally, Collins's orders for the day reflected First Army's instructions to transfer the 75th ID (minus the 290th Infantry), which had essentially been in a holding position on the boundary with XVIII (Airborne) Corps, to Ridgway's control.

Samrée was a tough nut to crack. It rests atop an 1,800-foot hill, and the GIs had to attack over almost a mile of undulating terrain in knee-deep snow to get to it.[11] Furthermore, just south of the highway, the Germans emplaced an imposing roadblock.[12] Collins's G-2 had a realistic appreciation of the difficulties. In his periodic report for 9 January, he noted that the enemy was quite capable of defending strong points and "there is no reason to believe resistance will decrease noticeably on our front, especially not in the next 48 hours."[13] Unlike the Germans, the American gunners received an abundant

supply of ammunition. On the night of 8/9 January, the 2nd AD Artillery
fired over 12,000 rounds on Samrée. On the morning of the 9th, CCB attacked from the east and gained the roadblock. The obstacle was neutralized just before dusk, when Colonel Hinds, now commanding TFR of CCB,
decided that discretion was the better part of valor and halted the attack
for the day. That night, Harmon gathered White and Collier for a planning
session. The ensuing orders called for White to continue his attack from the
east and south, while Collier's men came in from the west. TFR's attacking
strength reflected the battle of attrition being waged in the Ardennes—the
tank battalion had three tanks, and the infantry battalion assaulted with
forty-eight effectives. Nevertheless, augmented by an engineer company with
a bulldozer, they fought their way into the town. The approach of CCA from
the west caught the defenders by surprise. By the afternoon of 10 January,
Samrée was in American hands, and with it solid access to the western end
of the N-28 in the VII Corps sector.

The Hell on Wheels soldiers had just been through hell and were clearly
exhausted. Weary GIs took refuge in the buildings they had just captured,
and Harmon rushed warming tents to the front to offer additional succor.[14]
In light of the steady wastage of men from exposure to the elements, the
division commander also established an informal rest camp to treat minor
cold-weather injuries and to give his men a brief respite from the rigors of
frontline combat. A similar convalescent center was set up by the 84th ID.[15]
These unauthorized facilities kept the men in their units, rather than forcing
them into hospitalization and the theater replacement pool.[16] Collins could
afford to give Harmon's men only a short breather. On the 10th, with the
capture of Samrée clearly in the offing, he ordered the 2nd AD to attack
toward Houffalize on the 12th.[17]

The 83rd ID now came into action. It had been activated in late 1942, arriving in the ETO on 19 June and almost constantly in the line thereafter.[18]
Macon was a 1912 Virginia Polytechnic Institute alumnus who had earned
an advanced degree in engineering, also from VPI, the following year. Commissioned in the infantry in 1916, he served in China and Panama, graduating from CGSS in 1931 and the Army War College in 1934. He commanded
a regiment in North Africa and assumed command of the Thunderbolt Division in January 1944.[19] Collins referred to the 83rd as "a slow-moving
division."[20] Macon's soldiers, having passed through the 3rd AD on 9 January, found the small village of Bihain in the eastern end of the corps zone
almost as tough as Harmon's men found Samrée.[21] Bihain occupies a road
junction a little over two miles southeast of Parker's crossroads, which gave
it some tactical importance in the eastern portion of the VII Corps sector. By

midnight on the 9th, the 1st Battalion, 330th Infantry, reached Bihain's out-skirts, which it found staunchly defended. On the 10th, the resistance from the 9th SS Panzer troops grew even more intense; it took a full day of bitter, house-to-house fighting for Bihain to fall to the Thunderbolt soldiers.

With Bihain in American hands in the east and Samrée secure in the west, Collins had firm control of the N-28 highway. In some excruciatingly tough going, Collins's soldiers had broken through the initial crust of enemy resis-tance and were now ready to advance on the corps, army, and army group main objective—Houffalize.

The Attack toward Houffalize, 11–16 January

The next five days would still be marked by tough fighting. But a pattern began to develop that the Germans were resisting most mightily in the east and gradually putting up less of a fight in the west. This would eventually allow Harmon's 2nd AD to punch through to Houffalize, while Macon's 83rd ID and Rose's 3rd AD pushed against the staunchest portion of the defense. Bolling's 84th ID also played an important supporting role on the right flank until the 15th, when Collins no longer required a division in the far western portion of the corps sector.

Over the next three days, the superiority of VII Corps' combat power vis-à-vis the now five defending German divisions began to overcome the advantages of terrain and weather enjoyed by the defenders and to be re-flected in a steady rate of advance.[22] On 11 January, Collins gave everyone a rest, except for the 83rd ID, which had just passed through the 3rd AD two days earlier. Macon's men reached the northwest edge of the small village of Langlir, some two miles southeast of Bihain. The next day, the Thunderbolt soldiers took both Langlir and its sister village, Petite Langlir, about a mile to the northeast. Additionally, the 2nd AD seized Petite Tailles, another tiny habitation about two miles due south of Parker's crossroads.[23] In making this attack, the tankers again had to fight bitter cold and icy roads as well as determined German resistance. The 13th of January was something of a breakthrough day, though not in the literal sense of the word. VII Corps units were subjected to fairly heavy artillery and nebelwerfer fire as the Ger-mans were being driven back on their supply lines, but the GIs could answer in more than fair measure. During the day, the four divisions fired some 18,000 rounds, while corps artillery added another 3,500. As the corps G-2 accurately noted, "Our offensive pressure increased rather than the enemy's defensive pressure weakening."[24] Collins put all four divisions on line. The 83rd ID advanced to gain a line of departure for the 3rd AD to attack through its right flank. Rose's tankers sliced to the south, pushing through heavy woods. On the east side of the division zone, CCB fought through minefields and booby-trapped trees to secure the small village of Lomre. Meanwhile, on Rose's right flank, CCR cut the road leading from Houffalize to St. Vith, just southwest of Cherrain. Severing this artery complicated the German withdrawal of those units still west of Houffalize. Meanwhile, CCB, 2nd AD, captured the hamlet of Pissorette against a stiff German rearguard action, while the 4th Cavalry Reconnaissance Squadron, attached to the 84th ID, pushed into that portion of La Roche east of the Ourthe River. Although the battle was far from over, one could sense that Houffalize was now within VII Corps' grasp.

On the 14th, the steady drive to the southeast continued.[25] The 83rd ID attacked to the east out of Langlir with the 331st IR and sent the 329th IR to capture the high ground northwest of Bovigny, which it secured late in the afternoon. To the west, CCB, 3rd AD, fought its way into the northern edges of Cherrain, which controls the junction between the Houffalize–St. Vith road and a fork leading north to Salmchâteau. The best news of the day was that CCA, 2nd AD, muscled its way through dense woods, dug-in tanks well guarded by infantry, and heavy antitank fire to capture Wibrin, about three miles northwest of Houffalize. On the far left flank, the 84th ID captured Nadrin, Grand Mormont, and Petite Mormont. Furthermore, the division discovered three abandoned 150-mm guns, all in excellent condition. These were sure indicators of the weakening ability of the German command to defend the western reaches of the salient. On the next day, the 83rd ID advanced to the outskirts of Bovigny but was driven back by a murderous hail of mortar, machine-gun, 20-mm antiaircraft, and antitank fire. CCB, 3rd AD, ran into a similar hornet's nest at Sterpigny and could not penetrate beyond the village's western outskirts. Harmon's soldiers had an easier go—by 2230, they pushed patrols into Houffalize and reported it largely unoccupied. And on the corps' right flank, with virtually no enemy contact, Collins pulled the 84th ID out of the line.[26]

The same pattern continued on 16 January.[27] In the east, the 83rd ID tried gamely to capture Bovigny; but every approach to the village was met with a hail of small arms, mortar, and heavy weapons fire. After losing five of their supporting tanks, the division resorted to securing portions of the surrounding woods. In the center, the 3rd AD was just barely able to capture and consolidate its holds on Cherrain and Sterpigny after very tough fights at both locations. But in the west, all was well. Early in the morning, Staff Sergeant Douglas Wood, a combat cameraman assigned to the 165th Signal Photo Company, made his way to Wibrin in search of a scoop.[28] From there, he was directed to the 2nd AD's 82nd Reconnaissance Battalion, commanded by Lieutenant Colonel Hugh O'Farrell. From the battalion's elevated vantage point, he could gaze down on Houffalize. O'Farrell told him not to expect linkup with the Third Army anytime soon, but Wood remained in the area taking shots of GIs from the 41st AIB. At 0905, a few soldiers emerged from the woods, identifying themselves as members of the 41st Armored Reconnaissance Squadron, 11th AD, operating under Middleton's VIII Corps. The long-awaited juncture of First and Third Armies had occurred, and Wood got both his photograph and his scoop. Later in the day, 2nd AD units pushed into Houffalize in greater strength, rooting out snipers from that portion of the town north of the Ourthe. Collins had accomplished his most important mission in the closing phase of the Bulge.

VII Corps Is "Pinched Out," 17–24 January

With XVIII (Airborne) Corps attacking from the Salm and Malmédy toward St. Vith, VIII Corps advancing from west of Bastogne toward Houffalize, and III Corps coming up from the east side of Bastogne toward Clerf, Bradley simply did not have the maneuver space to keep VII Corps in the fight for very much longer. Accordingly, as Collins's divisions moved to the east, they were progressively withdrawn from the lines until the entire corps was taken out of action or, in military jargon, "pinched out."

On 17 January, the 3rd AD attacked out of Cherrain and Sterpigny.[29] Collins had reported to Hodges that his divisions were "greatly fatigued and depleted" and said he would have to hold on his present line.[30] But he obviously had second thoughts. On the 18th, both the 83rd ID and the 3rd AD advanced as the former pushed patrols toward Bovigny and the latter advanced slowly along the Sterpigny-Gouvy road. Then things on the German side began to unravel. On 19 January, the Thunderbolt soldiers found their wary entry into Bovigny unopposed, and the 3rd AD took Brisy against faltering resistance. On the 20th, the Germans were quiescent except for a few desultory artillery rounds directed at Bovigny. The 83rd ID took Cierreux, again without opposition, and Collins pulled the 3rd AD back into assembly areas. He then swung Bolling's now-rested division around to the east and placed it behind Macon's infantry and Rose's armor. On the 22nd, the 84th ID attacked through both the 83rd ID and the 3rd AD, capturing Gouvy and Beho, the latter only seven miles southwest of St. Vith. In this advance, it encountered only sporadic resistance from isolated pockets of German armor. On the next day, the division captured Ourthe and took the high ground south of Beho. On the 24th at 1800, Bolling's division was transferred to XVIII (Airborne) Corps, officially ending Collins's participation in the Battle of the Bulge.

The corps headquarters was withdrawn from action on 25 January (D+133) and dispatched to Ochain, Belgium, about twenty miles east of Namur. The corps after-action report noted: "This is the first time since prior to the invasion of Europe that the Command Post of VII Corps was chosen with regard to the comforts and accommodations of the personnel of the Corps Headquarters Company, well to the rear of any front lines."[31]

Assessment

There is little direct evidence with which to evaluate Collins's generalship in the final phase of the Bulge. The major parameters of the attack were dictated by Montgomery. But Collins had a choice in picking the precise axis of advance, and he chose well. The Ourthe River, with some help from elements of the British XXX Corps, secured his right flank. And although the dense woods, steep hills, icy roads, and deep snow made the going very tough for his two armored divisions, he was correct in leading with them to give extra impetus to the initial push. It also made good sense to attach to each of them an entire infantry regiment. As the attack progressed, he showed a deft sense of timing, passing the infantry divisions through the armored units when the latter began to tire and later putting all four divisions on line when the German resistance showed definite signs of slackening. These sound tactics, combined with a little extra pressure on Harmon when it was needed, demonstrated a nice sense of balance between capturing Houffalize and preserving the strength of the fighting force. The deck was stacked in VII Corps' favor, with its being assigned four maneuver divisions, a cavalry group, and clear priority on army artillery; but Collins played his strong hand well.

XVIII (AIRBORNE) CORPS RECAPTURES ST. VITH

Ridgway's role in closing the Bulge on the northern flank was secondary but important—to retake St. Vith. Playing second fiddle, he had to make do with bits and pieces of combat power and to extract from such formations as were allotted to him all that was humanly possible. He was also restrained by the fact that Montgomery and Hodges, who, wary of a significant German counterattack, kept him on a short leash. The terrain between the Salm and St. Vith was the same wooded area over which the 7th AD had delayed the German advance in the third week of December—thickly forested and offering few roads for advance. A more promising approach lay southward from Malmédy and Waimes. The approach from Waimes is, for the Ardennes, particularly well suited for armor because of a large expanse of open ground northeast of Born. But access to this area is controlled by a gap between a north-south segment of the Amblève River and a forested area to its east, which became known as the Ondenval defile. Ridgway's corps was opposed by Corps Group Felber, commanded by General of the Infantry Hans G. Felber.[32] This formation, which was redesignated XIII Corps on 13 January, commanded the 18th, 62nd, and 326th VGDs and, from 8 January on, the remnants of Kampfgruppe Peiper for use as a mobile reserve. Within the VGDs, the infantry regiments were down to a strength of 750 to 1,000 men, but the artillery units were at nearly full complement. However, the only artillery under Felber's direct control was an assault gun brigade with eight cannons and two howitzers. The corps' major logistical challenge was a severe shortage of fuel.

Regaining the Salm, 5–12 January

Before any attack could be launched on St. Vith, Ridgway had to secure the west bank of the Salm. This task devolved to Gavin's 82nd Airborne, both by virtue of its position and by virtue of the fact that Ridgway could count on the airborne soldiers to do difficult work under tough circumstances. Gavin's men did not let him down.[33] On 5 January, the 517th PIR repulsed several strong counterattacks, the 504th seized the heights west of Grand-Halleux, the 504th captured Arbrefontaine, and the 325th GIR got on the high ground farther west. The next day, the division was held up waiting for an advance by the 3rd AD. On the 7th, the 504th and the 505th gained the west bank of the Salm between Grand-Halleux and Vielsalm, while the 508th PIR passed through the 325th and took positions on the Thier du Mont against very stiff German resistance. Over the next two days, the division consolidated its hold on the west bank of the Salm from Trois Ponts, south to Salmchâteau, then west to Grand-Sart. But the offensive had taken a toll. The 82nd had received no replacements during the heavy fighting in December; in the first four days of the January advance alone, it lost 138 killed in action, 647 wounded, and 44 missing.[34] Accordingly, Ridgway moved the 82nd into corps reserve, replacing it with Prickett's 75th ID on 10 January. The new unit remained relatively static for the next four days.[35]

Meanwhile, Ridgway finally secured permission from Hodges for a limited objective attack by the 30th ID at the hinge between Gavin's and Hobbs's divisions. On the morning of 5 January, he called Hobbs to the corps command post for a conference at which he outlined a plan for an attack to the south by the 112th Infantry (not yet returned to the 28th ID) on Hobbs's right flank, to be followed by the attachment of the 424th Infantry (the only remaining regiment of the 106th ID) to Hobbs for occupation of the zone between and south of Trois Ponts and Stavelot.[36] On the 6th, the 112th made modest gains on Hobbs's right flank.[37] On the 7th, the regiment advanced across the Amblève south of Stavelot and on the 8th penetrated as far south as Wanne, about three miles southeast of Trois Ponts.[38] Having been alerted of the required return of the 112th Infantry to Cota's and Middleton's eagerly awaiting hands, Ridgway effected its relief by the afternoon of 9 January.[39] Two days later, the 106th ID reassumed command of the 424th Infantry and with it the western portion of the 30th ID's zone.[40] Thus, by the evening of 12 January, XVIII (Airborne) Corps was arrayed as follows: Hobbs's 30th occupied a line from Waimes, west through Malmédy, then southwest toward Wanne. Perrin's 106th, buttressed to two regiments by Ridgway's attachment to it of the 517th PIR, held the hinge on either side of Wanne. And Prickett's 75th held the west bank of the Salm from Trois Ponts to Salmchâteau, with a small bubble on the east side of the river at Grand-Halleux.

Advance toward St. Vith, 13–19 January

Ever since he had begun thinking seriously about resuming the offensive, Ridgway had viewed St. Vith as the decisive objective on the northern flank of the Bulge. Thus, on 6 January when Montgomery asked the XVIII (Airborne) Corps commander to outline his intentions for the next few days, he had a ready answer.[41] Ridgway's idea was to use the 82nd to attack along the Vielsalm-Poteau-Recht road, while a small task force moved south from Stavelot, the 30th ID attacked toward Recht from Malmédy, and the 7th AD followed in corps reserve to exploit toward St. Vith when the opportunity arose. Montgomery approved the overall concept but warned Ridgway: "We must be careful to see that we did not expose ourselves piecemeal, while the enemy still was capable of launching powerful counterattacks." Although the details of this concept would change over the next several days, the essential structure would remain intact. The first change was that the green 75th ID would be substituted for the tested but tired 82nd Airborne. Then, in the early afternoon of 8 January, Hodges called Ridgway with instructions to plan an attack in the general direction Malmédy–St. Vith, employing the 30th ID and the 7th AD, whose flank would be protected by a southward attack of the 1st ID.[42] Although it was not clear at this juncture whether the 1st ID would be under Ridgway's control or that of V Corps, the addition of a third division on the critical corps left flank gave the project noticeably greater prospects for success.

The next afternoon, Hodges arrived to hear Ridgway's plan.[43] He approved Ridgway's scheme of maneuver but stipulated that "the attack should wait until the gap [between First and Third Armies] had been closed." Hodges and Montgomery were now equally apprehensive about German counterattack capabilities and, in Hodges's articulation of Montgomery's sentiments, did not want to become "unbalanced." Ridgway disagreed. He protested that the Germans had insufficient strength to attack Third Army, VII Corps, and XVIII (Airborne) Corps; that if he occupied the high ground north of St. Vith, he could not be knocked off of it; and that this ridge line "would deny them [the Germans] the use of ST. VITH to such an extent that he felt it was an opportunity for decisive action in the west from which the German Army could not recover in this war." Hodges had nothing of Ridgway's visions of glory. He replied that he did not want to launch the attack before the juncture at Houffalize because until then he would have no reserves and he "did not want to be caught by the Germans without any reserves." As it turned out, Hodges and Ridgway were both wrong. The Germans clearly lacked the means to attack in anything approaching the corps strength that Hodges apprehended.[44] On the other side of the coin, even if Hodges had authorized the attack to be made before the junction at Houffalize was effected, the inherent advantages of the defense would have impeded the American advance to the extent that no decisive entrapment of large German formations would have taken place. Nevertheless, Ridgway was correct that an earlier attack was preferable to a later attack.

Shortly after noon on 10 December, Kean called Ridgway to inform him that Hodges had approved his plan but insisted it be implemented in phases.[45] Phase I would be a limited objective attack by the 30th ID to gain the Amblève River in the western portion of its sector. Phase II would be an attack by the 1st ID, under V Corps control, to seize the Ondenval defile, followed by an exploitation by the 7th AD through the defile to capture St. Vith. Later on the 10th, Hodges, convinced that the linkup between First and Third armies was imminent, authorized the attack to begin on 13 January. On the 11th, Ridgway called the division commanders together and delivered a peroration about the coming attack:

Now, we can certainly expect the old German tactics of counter attack and penetration in this difficult country by groups of varying size. I would like you to imbue your commands with the idea that there's nothing to worry about in those little penetrations. We've got 85,000 men in the Corps with an overwhelming superiority in all weapons, and it's absolutely impossible for this German to put on any offensive effort against the forces now being brought to bear against him. . . . Now, we must get that down to the brains of every man that when these damn little forces penetrate, we'll destroy them. We don't intend to go in solid lines; we'll destroy him after he gets in. Let him get in, penetrate, we'll get him.

Reconnaissance, reconnaissance, reconnaissance, eternal reconnaissance! Every single major error I've seen in this Corps in the short time I've had it has been attributed to failure to reconnoiter, every single one. It's nothing but Indian scout stuff. The minute the doughboy uncovers these people, he's got this powerful support behind him. We know we're outgunned by the German tanks. We can't stick it out on open ground. We've got to locate him first, and then work it out in smoke or woods or fog; then we can get him; with your tank destroyers we can certainly get him.

Much emphasis must be placed on the employment of our artillery. . . . Our air is dependent on weather during daylight, but artillery we can use all the time. Artillery is valued in proportion to the emphasis placed on forward observers and liaison parties.[46]

Ridgway's remarks were notable in several respects. First, he had an acute understanding of the Germans' superiority in tank penetrating power and of their propensity for counterattack. Second, he grasped the importance of both clever tactics and psychology in dealing with these phenomena. And, finally, he saw the proper and ubiquitous employment of artillery as the great equalizer of this otherwise un-level playing field.

The 30th ID's attack kicked off on the morning of 13 January and progressed only about 3,000 yards as the day wore on, or only about to the depth of its previous patrol line.[47] Although the army plan called for a much deeper advance before commitment of the 1st ID, Ridgway petitioned Hodges, through Kean, to order it forward anyway.[48] After due consideration, Hodges demurred.[49] Ridgway was incensed. He could not get to St. Vith without the 7th AD; he could not commit the 7th AD until the 1st ID seized the Ondenval defile; and Hodges, not wanting to become "unbalanced," would not commit the 1st ID until more ground was gained by the 30th ID. Ten minutes after Hodges called, he phoned Hobbs and told him he was "thoroughly dissatisfied" with the lack of results and instructed him not to issue any orders for the next day until they had met face-to-face.[50] He then drove to the 30th ID command post and, in the presence of General

Harrison, Colonel Matthewson, and the division chief of staff, gave Hobbs a blistering tongue lashing.[51] The lack of progress of the 119th Infantry was the most significant bone of contention. Hobbs was unwilling to relieve the regimental commander, who was seeing his first combat action. Ridgway was unimpressed with this excuse and told Hobbs to press the attack the next day and that "no obstacles could be considered." Harrison later said, "I've never heard one general talk to another like Ridgway told off Hobbs."[52]

Meanwhile, a patrol from the 120th Infantry had reached the Baugnez crossroads, scene of the Malmédy massacre. By the morning of the 14th, graves registration personnel, accompanied by engineers, photographers, and a medical officer, began the grisly task of recovering and identifying the frozen, snow-covered bodies.[53] The long, difficult work of bringing the perpetrators to justice had finally begun.[54]

On the 14th, the 30th ID made sufficient general progress for Hodges to order commitment of the 1st ID on the following day.[55] Early in the evening, Ridgway gathered his division commanders together to work out details for the second phase of the corps attack, a meeting also attended by a representative from the 1st ID, whose capture of the Ondenval defile was key to commitment of the 7th AD.[56] That representative stated that the 23rd IR, attached from the 2nd ID, by attacking continuously through the night, hoped to be in the village of Ondenval before daylight on the 16th. With Perrin's reinforced 106th ID having, like Hobbs, attained its Phase I objectives and Hasbrouck thoroughly prepared to commit his division on two axes once the Ondenval defile had been seized, all seemed in readiness to move forward.

But friction intervened. A supporting part of Ridgway's plan was for the 75th ID to advance across the Salm against Recht.[57] Ideally, this would trap some Germans in the scissors between Prickett's west-east drive and Hasbrouck's north-south effort. At a minimum, it would force Felber to fight in two directions at once and thus dilute his strength. On the 16th, disturbed by the lack of progress of the 75th ID, Ridgway went forward to one of the division's regimental command posts to visit with Prickett.[58] Here, the two commanders reviewed the current situation and Ridgway asked Prickett to outline his intentions for the next twenty-four hours. At the conclusion of the session, Ridgway asked Prickett the normal question—was there anything the corps could do to help him. Prickett replied, "Nothing, just pray for me." Ridgway took this request to be an indication of weakness on Prickett's part; he asked the division commander to step outside, where he counseled him pointedly on the lack of confidence implicit in this remark. On the 18th, he sent Hodges a two-page request for Prickett's relief, stating that while the division had performed "in a satisfactory, though not highly creditable, manner, I feel potentially, and under proper leadership, the division could improve rapidly in battle efficiency." Hodges, who had his own reservations about Prickett, delayed action for five days.[59] On 23 January, he notified Ridgway that Prickett would be relieved and superseded by Major General Ray E. Porter.[60] In the meantime, Ridgway changed the 75th ID's axis of advance from the east to the southeast, apparently reckoning that the desired entrapment was beyond the division's ability.[61]

The 1st ID kicked off its attack on the morning of 15 January. As promised, the 23rd IR had troops into the northern edge of Ondenval by the morning of the 16th, while the 16th IR had also seized Faymonville, a larger village about a mile southeast of Waimes.[62] By the evening of the 17th, the 23rd IR had seized the high ground east of the Ondenval defile.[63] But on the next day, German resistance stiffened appreciably with a strong attack by Kampfgruppe Peiper at the Ondenval defile. The 1st ID commander, Brigadier General Clift Andrus, committed a battalion from the 16th IR to reinforce the 23rd, which the 30th ID chief of staff reported to Eaton as "pretty badly shaken up."[64] Hodges's aide noted of the action that "the heaviest kind of hand-to-hand fighting went on all through the day."[65] Despite the ferocity of the engagement, Peiper did not have the wherewithal to impose more than a temporary check.[66] And, having committed his corps reserve and not prevailed, there was little else Felber could do to stem the tide. On the 19th, Ridgway's troops advanced all along the front. By that evening, the 1st ID occupied the ground south of the Ondenval defile from near Eibertingen to Montenau, the 30th ID seized Recht, and the left flank of the 75th ID had patrols link up with the right flank of the Old Hickory advance.[67] In mid-afternoon, as reports of these encouraging developments filtered into the command post, Ridgway ordered Hasbrouck to attack on the 20th.[68]

As Ridgway was pushing his corps forward against a skillfully conducted German defense, he received a cordial note from Montgomery, dated 17 January:

My dear Matt

First Army passes from my command tonight and returns to 12 Army Group. It has been a great pleasure to work with you and your Corps, and it has been a very great honour for me. I hope we shall work together again and bring about the final destruction of the Germans. Good luck to you and I hope you will get to ST. VITH.

Yrs. sincerely

B. L. Montgomery

Field-Marshal [69]

The Recapture of St. Vith, 20–23 January 1945

Ridgway helped ensure the success of Hasbrouck's attack by giving him two parachute infantry battalions to beef up his combat commands and the entire 508th PIR to use as a mop-up and consolidation force.[70] Hasbrouck's plan for the attack was simple. He organized Triplet's CCA and Clarke's CCB identically, each having a battalion of tanks, a battalion of armored infantry, and a battalion of airborne infantry, augmented by tank destroyers and engineers. The attack would be made on two axes, with CCA on the left and CCB on the right, advancing by bounds. Clarke was being medicated with painkillers for a severe case of gallstones, but he refused medical evacuation so he could be in on the seizure of the town he had so skillfully defended for six critical days in December.[71]

Ridgway was at the front early on the 20th, visiting the CCA, 7th AD, command post and from there, finding "little evidence of progress on the part of the attack," moving on to the division headquarters in Waimes to express his displeasure to Hasbrouck.[72] Born, a good-sized village four miles north of St. Vith, was the most significant intermediate objective in Hasbrouck's attack; it was assigned to CCB.[73] Clarke's plan was to attack from two directions—one task force approaching from Montenau in the north, the other from the 30th ID sector in the west. The two task forces assaulted the village shortly before midnight. The Germans wanted Born as much as Clarke did and put up a tremendous fight. The last house was not cleared of enemy resistance until early evening of the 21st. The men of CCB took heavy casualties but captured 165 prisoners, 8 self-propelled guns, and 4 tanks.[74] Perhaps feeling that Born should have been taken on the 20th, Ridgway was still not pleased with the 7th AD's performance.[75]

For a while, Ridgway considered having 7th AD stop short of St. Vith and ordering the 30th ID to attack into the town. Whether this was out of a doctrinal preference for infantry, rather than armor, to conduct combat in cities or a psychological goad to impel Hasbrouck's men forward is not clear.[76] Clarke's men battered their way south, consolidating their hold on Hunnange, just one mile northwest of St. Vith, by the early evening of 22 January.[77] Ridgway ordered Hasbrouck to seize St. Vith on the 23rd, and Hasbrouck passed the assignment to Clarke.

As 7th AD was moving slowly but inexorably southward, Felber sent several requests up through channels for permission to abandon St. Vith, which he saw as "now nothing but a heap of rubble."[78] But to each entreaty, either Model or one of his staff officers responded with an implacable "*Nein!*" Thus, the corps commander was compelled to leave 250 soldiers of the 326th VGD as a rear guard to deny the Americans seizure of the town. The attack kicked off on the 23rd, shortly after noon; by early evening, CCB had subdued what little resistance it encountered, harassed mostly by XIII Corps artillery.[79] A month and a day after the men of the 7th AD had been driven from St. Vith, they returned to reclaim it. And, therewith, they accomplished the most important task of XVIII (Airborne) Corps in the final phase of the Bulge.

Assessment

Ridgway was a particularly demanding, perhaps even unreasonable, superior in the final phase of the campaign. His pressure on Hasbrouck, his dressing down of Hobbs, and his relief of Prickett all portray a man driven by the desire to recover lost ground quickly and kill as many Germans as possible before they were able to retreat behind the fortified positions of the West Wall. Gavin also suspected that personal ambition had much to do with the corps commander's behavior, particularly his refusal to release the 82nd to prepare for future airborne operations.[80] But Gavin admitted that he was probably "browned out" and needed a leave. And the hard fact was that the opportunities for future airborne operations looked slim, while the need for infantry in the line was compelling on many levels. But whatever the extent of Ridgway's personal ambition, it was harnessed to the accomplishment of a difficult mission that demanded determined commanders. As Ridgway and Gavin both knew, a few understrength German regiments were forcing an entire corps to conduct a slow, methodical advance, while the operational parameters of the attack literally cried out for speed.[81] The rugged terrain and atrocious weather, aided by enemy tactical skill and a firm determination to make the Americans pay dearly for every yard of ground gained, made such speed either impossible or extremely difficult. Clausewitz captured this situation perfectly:

> So long as a unit fights cheerfully, with spirit and élan, great strength of will is rarely needed; but once conditions become difficult, as they must when much is at stake, things no longer run like a well-oiled machine. The machine itself begins to resist, and the commander needs tremendous willpower to overcome this resistance.[82]

The final phase of the Bulge was a tough time, and Ridgway was a tough commander. But he was not unthinkingly bullheaded. Admittedly, he would have taken greater risks if he had served under commanders less worried than Montgomery and Hodges about what the enemy was going to do to them. But he waited until the Ondenval defile was secure before he launched the 7th AD into the attack; he made sure Hasbrouck had plenty of extra infantry to maintain the momentum of his advance; and he placed proper emphasis on the use of artillery as the GI's great equalizer. In short, his toughness did not cause him to set aside the requirement for sound tactical judgment. He demonstrated in the final phase of the Bulge that his pugilistic instincts remained relevant and that he had matured quickly as a corps commander.

V CORPS HELPS OUT

The role of V Corps in the final phase of the Bulge was limited. Its main mission was to continue to hold the Elsenborn Ridge as a secure base for the forthcoming attack into the West Wall. Both Hodges's and Huebner's concerns with making absolutely sure that that mission was fulfilled delayed offensive activity until 15 January. During the ten days preceding the attack, the corps engaged in a war of posts. Various units patrolled to maintain contact with the German 3rd Parachute Division, conducted raids to take prisoners, and delivered harassment and interdiction fires against known and suspected German positions.[83] Huebner assumed command of V Corps at 0900 on 15 January.

The attack of the 1st ID, augmented by the 23rd IR of the 2nd ID, to secure the Ondenval defile has already been sketched; but it remains to flesh out a few tactical details of its conduct.[84] The 23rd IR, attacking on the Big Red One's right flank, had as its initial objectives two hamlets just to the north and northeast of Ondenval. Both were staunchly defended but fell by the end of the day on 15 January to aggressive infantry assaults, supported by tanks. Ondenval itself was but lightly held and was in American hands early on the next day, with the GI assault sweeping on to the high ground southeast of the village. On the 18th, Peiper's counterattack struck in full fury. Here, in bitter hand-to-hand fighting, the gritty infantrymen of the 23rd established an improvised foxhole line and beat the SS soldiers to a standstill. On the 19th, the regiment, aided by the 1st Battalion, 18th Infantry, moved into Montenau and widened its hold on the defile two miles to the east by capturing Eibertingen. With Faymonville also in friendly hands, the way was now clear for commitment of the 7th AD. Memories of this attack are grim. The deep snow limited medical evacuation. And in the frigid temperatures, men who would otherwise have survived their relatively minor

wounds perished from shock and exposure. Over the next several days, the
1st ID consolidated its positions and made minor adjustments to the line. On
the 26th, it was attached in place to XVIII (Airborne) Corps, in preparation
for the attack on the Siegfried Line.[85]

Thus, V Corps' offensive activities in the closing phase of the Bulge were
little more than an appendage to those of XVIII (Airborne) Corps. And
the fact that the seizure of the Ondenval defile was a necessary condition
for commitment of Hasbrouck's division suggests strongly that the 1st ID
should have been placed under Ridgway's command. Why Hodges ordered
the 1st ID to attack under V Corps control remains something of a mystery.
The gallantry of its soldiers and of the men of the attached 23rd IR cannot
be gainsaid. No matter which corps they fought under, their seizure of the
Ondenval defile and their retention of it in the face of an aggressive counterattack by one of the Waffen-SS's most ruthless and determined leaders was a
vital task leading to the recapture of St. Vith. But Hodges's failure to adhere
to the principle of unity of command made the higher-level direction of their
efforts more complicated than it should have been.[86]

SOME CLOSING OBSERVATIONS

In the final phase of the campaign, XVIII (Airborne) Corps and VII Corps
again had the lead roles on the northern flank, while that of V Corps was
supporting. But unlike the second phase, in which Collins's blunting of
the German penetration at the Meuse had been dependent on Ridgway's
halting of the II SS Panzer Corps, Ridgway's seizure of St. Vith was now
dependent on Collins's closing the gap at Houffalize. During this phase,
there emerged some interesting similarities and differences between the two
commanders. Both wanted to recover lost ground quickly and both were
frustrated by Montgomery's and Hodges's caution. Collins seems to have
taken it somewhat more philosophically than Ridgway, though Ridgway
carefully avoided any hint of insubordination. In comparing and contrast-
ing their styles of command during these trying days, we are hampered by
the fact that much more documentary evidence has survived about Ridgway
than about Collins. We have the allusion in Collins's memoirs to his leaning
on Harmon when the 2nd AD was not making satisfactory progress. We
have much more complete information concerning Ridgway's severe dressing down of Hobbs and much lighter pressure on Hasbrouck. The reasoning
behind Ridgway's recommendation for Prickett's relief is also clearly documented.[87] The overall picture that emerges is that both Collins and Ridgway

pressured their subordinates when such pressure was required. Collins was smoother than Ridgway. Although Ridgway could be as charming as a diplomat when the occasion demanded, he was as rough as a cob whenever he sensed insufficient vigor in those around him. At least some of the difference in style may also be attributable to circumstance. With two armored divisions, two infantry divisions, and clear priority in army supporting assets, Collins had a closer match of resources to mission than did Ridgway. Issues of operational design were beyond the responsibilities of both men. Given the tactical tasks they were assigned, the circumstances of enemy, terrain, and weather under which they had to carry them out, and the forces at their disposal, each performed quite competently, successfully balancing mission accomplishment and force preservation. The grim realities of attacking in the Ardennes in January made these noteworthy achievements.

15

VIII, III, and XII Corps Close the Bulge from the South

We have to push people beyond endurance in order to bring this war to an end, because we are forced to fight it with inadequate means.[1]

George S. Patton Jr., 6 January 1945

MONTGOMERY AND PATTON BOTH FACED THE REALITY that even the "Germany First" strategy could not give Allied commanders in the European theater the wherewithal to maintain unrelenting pressure on the Wehrmacht.[2] But the problem of closing the southern flank of the Bulge was much more difficult than that of closing it from the north. In the VIII Corps zone, with Bastogne the locus of German main effort since late December, the density of enemy units arrayed between Middleton and Houffalize was noticeably greater than it was against Collins. In the III Corps area, Millikin had to deal with similar German densities on the northeast face of Bastogne and the fact that Model clearly recognized the Harlange Pocket to be a thorn in Patton's flesh. In the XII Corps sector, Eddy had to cross the Sûre River before he could make any meaningful advance. These circumstances meant that the various corps of Third Army would find it more difficult than did those of First Army to effect the junction at Houffalize and eradicate the Bulge.

VIII CORPS ATTACKS TO HOUFFALIZE AND THE OUR RIVER

Middleton's corps experienced some of its heaviest fighting during the last phase of the Bulge. Manteuffel and Model had to keep the Bastogne-Houffalize road open to prevent the entrapment of German formations in the western reaches of the salient, and they put up a tremendous fight to do so. Thus, as tough as the VIII Corps' defensive battles had been, its offensive ones would be even tougher.

Expanding the Bastogne Perimeter, 5–12 January

Expanding the Bastogne perimeter imposed two tasks on Middleton.[3] The most immediate was to push north-northeast toward Houffalize on the N-15 highway. Along this road were two intermediate objectives, which had figured prominently in the defense of Bastogne on 19 and 20 December: Foy, three miles north of Bastogne, and the somewhat larger village of Noville, another two miles distant. The latter was particularly significant because it controlled the junction between the N-15 and the road leading east to Clerf. Immediately to the east of the highway between Bastogne and Noville is the Bois Jacques. Middleton's second task, to the west of Bastogne, was to gain the line of the Ourthe River, running northeast from Ortheuville to Houffalize. The river is paralleled by a road some two miles to the southeast that runs from Amberloup, skirting Bertogne, to Houffalize. Roughly two miles south of Amberloup is the village of Tillet, the last habitation one encounters before reaching the road paralleling the Ourthe. The tiny villages of Flamierge and Flamizoulle, three and four miles, respectively, east of Amberloup, were typical examples of isolated habitations in the Ardennes whose importance stemmed merely from the fact that they offered a modicum of shelter to small units. The ground over which VIII Corps had to operate was undulating, with an irregular pattern of woods and open fields that provided excellent fields of fire for well-concealed German defenders.

Middleton was faced by a formidable, if depleted, array of Wehrmacht and SS units, most densely concentrated in the eastern portion of the corps zone.[4] The 9th and 12th SS Panzer Divisions, reinforced by the 26th VGD, straddled the Bastogne-Houffalize highway. The 3rd and 15th Panzergrenadier Divisions, buttressed by the FEB, occupied the center of the sector, northwest of Sibret. Bayerlein's Panzer Lehr, which had been instructed to "hold to the last cartridge," occupied the western third of the corps line of contact.[5] Bayerlein's orders notwithstanding, the German defense was clearly designed to increase in strength as it progressed to the east. And with this much force lined up against him, Middleton could not hope for a clean breakthrough. The best he could do would be to shove in a series of crowbars and worry them back and forth, until he finally developed a significant crack somewhere along the line.[6]

On 5 January, his instruments for this pulling and shoving were, from left to right, Culin's 87th ID, Miley's 17th Airborne, and Taylor's 101st Airborne. Kilburn's battered 11th AD was held in corps reserve. With the 101st still rebuilding from its defense of Bastogne and the 17th Airborne recovering from

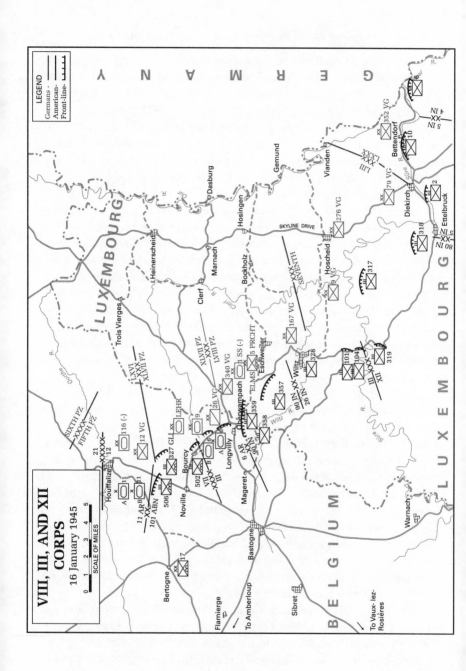

VIII, III, AND XII
CORPS
16 January 1945

SCALE OF MILES
0 1 2 3 4 5

LEGEND
Germans
American
Front-line

GERMANY

LUXEMBOURG

LUXEMBOURG

BELGIUM

Ourthe R.
Sûr R.
Clerf R.
Wiltz R.
Sûre R.
Our R.

Trois Vierges
Heinerscheid
Dasburg
Hosingen
Gemund
Vianden
Bettendorf
Diekirch
Ettelbruck
Clerf
Marnach
Bockholz
Hoscheid
SKYLINE DRIVE
Eschweiler
Wiltz
Wahlhausen
Longvilly
Mageret
Bourcy
Noville
Bastogne
Bertogne
Flamierge
Sibret
Warnach
To Amberloup
To Vaux-lez-
Rosières

SIXTH PZ
XXXXX
FIFTH PZ

XLVII PZ
XXX
LVIII PZ

XVI
XXX
XLVII PZ

XXX
SEVENTH

LIII
XXX

21
XXXXX
12

116 (-)
xx

12 VG
xx

340 VG
xx

26 VG
xx

LEHR
xx

9
xx

5 PRCHT
xx

1 SS (-)
xx

167 VG
xx

276 VG
xx

79 VG
xx

352 VG
xx

9 VG
xx

317
xx

328
xx

357
xx

359
xx

358
xx

ELMS

327 GLI
xxx

502

506

101 ABN
xxxx

11 AR
x

A
x

B
x

11
x

A
x

11
x

VII
xxx

B
x

III
xxx

6 AR
xx

90
xx

80 IN
xx

90 IN
xxx
26 IN

IX
III
319

101
104
xx

318
xx

80 IN
xx

2
xx

5 IN
xx
4 IN
10
xx

17
xx

its bloodletting of the day before, the only offensive activity for the 5th was made by the 87th ID, which, after beating off a spirited counterattack by Panzer Lehr near Bonnerue, cleared the woods east of Pironpré.[7] The following day was similarly quiet, the Golden Acorn Division again making the only gains. However, its report that Tillet was in friendly hands was premature.[8] A similar report at noon on the 7th that operations were continuing to "clear out" Tillet again proved overly optimistic, as Bayerlein's soldiers were taking literally the instructions given to their commander.[9] By the evening of the 7th, the true picture was in. Tillet was being held by well-emplaced infantry, supported by tanks, and the defenders were putting up "heavy resistance."[10] Miley's soldiers experienced similar problems. An attack by the 513th PIR toward Flamierge, along what the airborne soldiers called "Dead Man's Ridge," reached the outskirts of the village but was driven off by enemy armor.[11] The 513th regrouped and secured the village by the end of the day.[12] In the face of this tenacious holding action, Middleton issued instructions on the afternoon of the 7th for Miley to consolidate his present positions on the 8th, while Culin was to continue to advance, both in preparation for a coordinated corps attack on the 9th.[13]

This was to be part of an even larger Third Army attack by both III Corps and VIII Corps to break the Bastogne-Harlange logjam.[14] For extra punch, Patton gave Middleton the 4th AD; but it would take more than a day to move Gaffey's troops into position. Thus, Middleton had to do the best he could on the 9th.[15] He ordered the 87th ID to block Bayerlein's units around St. Hubert, "capture, or bypass and contain" Tillet, and continue its advance to the north. He instructed the 17th Airborne to gain the line of the Ourthe River. And he told the 101st to "stage a strong demonstration" toward Recogne, a hamlet one mile northwest of Foy.

Taylor's demonstration toward Recogne was actually an attack.[16] The 501st PIR secured the hamlet by late afternoon, while the 506th PIR and the 327th GIR assaulted into the Fazone Woods to the northwest, making gains of up to a mile. By the end of the day, the Screaming Eagles held a sawtooth-shaped piece of high ground on the western side of the Bastogne-Houffalize highway, threatening Foy from the northwest. On the 10th, with Gaffey's troops now in position, the plan was for them to attack through the 6th AD to support the attack of the 501st PIR across the Foy-Mageret road and into the Bois Jacques.[17] This would give VIII Corps the high ground on three sides of Foy. The 501st moved across the Foy-Mageret road; but as it advanced further, it received heavy fire from the railway running northeast from Bastogne. German resistance stiffened. Large quantities of artillery and mortar fire rained down on Taylor's airborne troopers, and the capture of several hundred prisoners indicated that the direct approach from Bastogne to Houffalize was being reinforced.[18]

At this juncture, events well beyond Bastogne impinged on VIII Corps, as Hitler's diversion to the south began to bear fruit.[19] Eisenhower ordered Patton, through Bradley, to position one armored division where it could respond to a possible German attack in the Saar. Patton selected the 4th AD and ordered its immediate withdrawal from Bastogne. He also called directly to Taylor and ordered the 101st to halt its attack. With no armor to support his extended gains, Taylor ordered his regimental commanders to return to the lines occupied on the morning of the 9th.[20] Thus, the high ground around Foy was surrendered voluntarily.

Meanwhile, almost nothing went well further west. Attacks on 9 January by the 87th ID gained no ground at all; the division reported by noon that it was "containing" the enemy in Tillet.[21] The 17th Airborne lost contact with the 3rd Battalion of the 513th PIR in Flamierge, thanks to a violent German counterattack from Flamizoulle.[22] On the 10th, the 87th ID finally captured Tillet, four days after the initial report of having done so.[23] Culin then decided to consolidate his gains.[24]

This was in consonance with Middleton's general inclinations. Having lost the 4th AD, he put the corps into a defensive posture on the evening of the 10th.[25] But the sands of time were running out for the Germans. On the next day, St. Hubert, Bonnerue, and Pironpré were evacuated and occupied by the 87th ID.[26] Middleton then began to shift his thinking back to the attack. In the evening of the 11th, he instructed all division commanders to "be prepared for offensive action on short notice."[27] On the 12th, he issued orders for resumption of the offensive the next day.[28] Middleton's plan was to insert Kilburn's 11th AD between the 17th and 101st Airborne Divisions. This move significantly increased the troop density immediately west of the N-15 highway and promised to provide the Screaming Eagles the armored assistance they required to pry open the road to Houffalize.

The Drive to Houffalize, 13–16 January

Though pulling back in the west, the Germans seemed determined to hold on to Foy for the duration of the war. The 2nd Battalion, 506th PIR, seized Foy on the 13th.[29] The regimental commander, Colonel Sink, reinforced the village, and a weak German counterattack was beaten off during the night. Then things deteriorated quickly.[30] A tank-infantry attack at 0415 on the 14th was repulsed; but a heavier attack about two hours later, featuring over a dozen tanks and around a battalion of infantry, forced the paratroopers

out. Sink, who had prudently positioned his regimental reserve south of
Foy, quickly organized a response to the German counterattack. At 0900,
a heavy artillery barrage cascaded down on the German defenders; within
another thirty minutes, Foy was back in American hands to stay. But the
tenacity of the German defense is indicated by the fact that over two weeks
after VIII Corps had launched its initial attack to regain the initiative around
Bastogne, it had progressed only three miles along the road to Houffalize.
Nevertheless, the 101st's capture and *recapture* of Foy signaled a tipping
point in the VIII Corps battle. The Germans had thrown in all their chips
and not been able to hold on.

As the two-day, seesaw battle for Foy raged on, the rest of Taylor's airborne troopers made marginal progress against similarly stiff resistance.
The 327th GIR pushed into the Bois Jacques but had a tough time fighting
against enemy units infiltrating between it and the 502nd PIR to its right,
while the 502nd was unable to gain Bourcy.[31] In the center, the 11th AD
flanked Bertogne, thus cutting the road paralleling the Ourthe River.[32] Farther west, the 17th Airborne reached the Ourthe and captured Bertogne.[33]
In the far west, the 87th ID also closed on the Ourthe, joining hands with
the British XXX Corps. With its mission accomplished, it was transferred
to Eddy's XII Corps.[34]

The next two days brought fairly rapid advances west of the N-15 highway, while resistance east of it remained strong. On the 15th, CCA, 11th
AD, captured the village of Rastadt, putting the division's lead elements just
five miles from Houffalize.[35] Meanwhile, Sink's workhorse 506th PIR captured Noville, and the 327th GIR and 502nd PIR moved leading elements
to the northern edge of the Bois Jacques.[36] Patton, anxious to link up with
First Army, dispatched orders for Kilburn to make a dash for Houffalize.[37]
Thus, on the evening of the 15th, Brigadier General Willard A. Holbrook,
Jr., commanding CCA, 11th AD, ordered Major Michael Greene, executive
officer of the 41st Armored Reconnaissance Squadron, to lead a task force
north to Houffalize. After pushing through dark woods all night, Greene's
men made contact with the 2nd AD. On the same day, CCB, operating on
the 11th AD's eastern flank, captured Vaux, with material assistance from
the 506th PIR.[38] The rest of the 101st made moderate gains to the east, with
the 327th GIR capturing Hardigny, a hamlet some two miles northeast of
Noville, and the 502nd PIR virtually surrounding Bourcy.[39] By the evening
of the 16th, the 11th AD had secured most of the ground west of the highway, while the 101st had bitten off a triangle northeast of Noville. Linkup
with VII Corps had been effected, but VIII Corps would have to reorganize
before it could drive to the east.

Reorganizing and Consolidating, 17–20 January

The first major change was the withdrawal of the 101st Airborne.[40] Middleton went to Bastogne to commemorate the division's departure with a formal review. Taylor playfully demanded he sign a receipt for return of the town. It read: "Received from the 101st Airborne Division the town of Bastogne, Luxembourg Province, Belgium. Condition: Used but serviceable, Kraut disinfected."[41] Middleton duly signed, ending the most storied tale in the 101st's proud history.

To accommodate the departure of the 101st, Middleton brought Miley's 17th Airborne up to relieve Kilburn's 11th AD and slipped the tankers south to take over from Taylor's paratroopers. On the 20th, the German vacuum to the corps front allowed the 17th Airborne to advance to Tavigny, some two miles east of the N-15, while CCR, 11th AD, picked up similar gains.[42] The new VIII Corps zone, oriented to the northeast, had as its northern boundary the Ourthe River from La Roche, through Houffalize and Ourthe to Thommen, which lies near the river's headwaters, some twelve miles northeast of Houffalize and about five miles south of St. Vith. The southern boundary followed the rail line northeast from Bastogne and then angled across to Thommen. The clear intent of this zone was to pinch out VIII Corps in an advance toward St. Vith. Middleton's attack plan was simple: the 17th Airborne and the 11th AD would advance abreast to the northeast to bring territory under their control and defeat enemy units in the zone.[43] Neither task was expected to be particularly difficult, as the four enemy divisions facing VIII Corps (Panzer Lehr, 9th Panzergrenadier, and the 26th and 340th VGDs) had all withdrawn from contact, leaving in their wake mined roads, destroyed bridges, and obstacles of various sorts.[44]

Attacking to the Our River, 21–28 January

After the bitter fighting around Bastogne, it was gratifying to measure daily progress in terms of miles rather than yards. Both divisions advanced against token resistance.[45] On 21 January, the First Army–Third Army boundary was shifted to the north to narrow Hodges's sector for his impending attack on the Siegfried Line. This brought the VIII Corps left flank to the southern outskirts of St. Vith.[46] From 24 to 26 January, a wholesale shuffling of corps boundaries at 12th Army Group brought the 6th AD, positioned on the III Corps left flank, under VIII Corps control.[47] It was subsequently relieved by the 90th ID. This change widened the corps front by some twelve miles to the south. As these adjustments were taking effect, Middleton became dissatisfied with the rate of advance of the 17th Airborne. He thereupon penned a letter to Miley, which read in part: "I find that there has been little forward progress by your troops since the day before yesterday. . . . Please push your leading units—if you need help, ask for it. We have much support in rear of you."[48] Middleton certainly had a softer touch than Ridgway! But he still had his eye on the prize. On the 25th, he ordered the 87th ID, rejoined from XII Corps, and the 90th ID, which became attached from III Corps on the next day, to secure the high ground west of the Our River.[49] This was accomplished by dusk on 28 January.[50] With the seizure of the Skyline Drive, VIII Corps now held a small segment of the eighty-five-mile front it had occupied on 16 December. Its mission in the Bulge was complete. Having the Oak Leaf Cluster to the Distinguished Service Medal for his role in the capture of Brest presented by Patton four days earlier, Middleton also had official indication of his accomplishments as a corps commander.[51]

Assessment

Middleton conducted a well-balanced operation in the closing phase of the Bulge. With the deck stacked against him along the Bastogne-Houffalize highway, he concentrated his effort in the west and center until sufficient combat power could be brought to bear in the east to make meaningful progress. It appeared that would be on 10 January, with commitment of the 4th AD. When Gaffey's tankers were taken away from his command, he waited to make an assault along the highway until Kilburn's 11th AD could be brought up. By keeping the 87th ID and the 17th Airborne reasonably active in the west and center, Middleton applied the pressure that, coupled with the advance of VII Corps toward Houffalize from the northwest, forced the Germans to give ground. When it became necessary to commit the 11th AD, he sensibly put it into the line just west of the N-15, where it would flank the main strength of the German defenses and provide support to the 101st for cracking the tough nuts at Foy and Noville. His letter to Miley indicates he kept appropriate pressure on his subordinates to maintain the momentum of the attack. When higher headquarters expanded his zone to include the Our River and shuffled his task organization, he wasted no time in giving his new divisions explicit instructions to capture the Skyline Drive. In short, Middleton performed just as competently in the offensive phase of the Bulge as he had in the defensive phase. And the fact that in breaking out of Bastogne, he had one of the most difficult assignments of the entire campaign has long been underappreciated.

III CORPS REDUCES THE HARLANGE POCKET AND ADVANCES TO THE OUR

III Corps also faced a heavy concentration of German formations. And, like VIII Corps, two of its divisions had been roughly handled—the 35th ID by the attack of the 1st SS Panzer Division on 30 December and the 6th AD by the assault of the 12th SS Panzer Division on 4 January. Before Millikin could make substantial progress, he would require an infusion of fresh legs.

Preparing to Attack, 5–8 January

On 5 January, III Corps was disposed in a large arc that began on the northeast face of Bastogne; ran southwest, then south along a line some two miles east of the Arlon-Bastogne road; then almost due east on a line that skirted just south of Harlange and terminated at the boundary with XII Corps, about a mile south of Wiltz.[52] The 6th AD was in Bastogne, the 35th ID along the arc west and south of Harlange, and the 26th ID south of the Wiltz River in the east. The German position south of the Wiltz River and east and north of the line of contact was referred to as the Harlange Pocket. Bradley and Patton both recognized that this enclave "must be eliminated before we can attack Houffalize."[53] There were, however, multiple problems. On paper, the enclave could have been cut off by an attack from the 6th AD southeast along the northern bank of the Wiltz. But this scheme of maneuver would have to deal with the ease of defense on the eastern side of Bastogne; furthermore, such a plan would hold reduction of the pocket hostage to the success of a single axis of advance. Thus, the preferred solution was to close it from both the northwest and the south, forcing the Germans to fight in two directions. But the 35th ID was still licking its wounds, and the 26th ID did not have the punch required to make rapid headway in the rough, cross-compartmented terrain south of the river. Finally, there were substantial German forces in the area.[54] Elements of the 9th and 12th SS Panzer Divisions sat astride the VIII Corps/III Corps boundary. The 340th VGD was near Bourcy. One of Bayerlein's panzergrenadier regiments was still in Neffe. The 167th VGD was deployed from Wardin to Bras. The 1st SS Panzer Division occupied positions from Wardin to Longvilly. The 5th Parachute Division defended from Villers-la-Bonne-Eau to Harlange, and the FGB extended east from Harlange to Berlé.

Under these circumstances, more force was clearly required. Bradley decided to pull in the 90th ID, which was positioned to the south in the Saar. The 90th, whose soldiers styled themselves as the Tough Hombres, had an uneven combat record. Activated in March 1942, it arrived in England in March 1944 and in France on D+2.[55] Collins had relieved its commander when it stubbed its toe badly during the Cherbourg operation and placed Brigadier General Eugene Lundrum in command. But Lundrum proved unable to turn the division around, and in August Eisenhower replaced him with Brigadier General Raymond S. McLain.[56] McLain, a National Guard officer, shaped the division up quickly and so impressed everyone in the chain of command that he was soon promoted and given command of XIX Corps.[57] The officer selected to take his place was Brigadier General James A. Van Fleet, assistant division commander of the 1st ID.[58] A West Point classmate and football teammate of Bradley's and Eisenhower's, he had served in World War I, commanding a machine-gun battalion in the St. Mihiel and Meuse-Argonne offensives. In June 1941, he assumed command of the 8th Infantry Regiment of the 4th ID, which he commanded at D-Day and until promoted to flag rank in August 1944. Van Fleet attended neither CGSS nor the Army War College, merely completing the former by correspondence. Despite this lack of formal schooling, he was a favorite of Bradley's, who referred to him as "another Ridgway, an absolutely superb soldier and leader."[59] He led the 90th across the Moselle with distinction, earning a promotion to major general shortly thereafter.[60]

Millikin and Van Fleet met with Patton on 6 January. The resulting plan called for insertion of the 90th along the boundary between Baade's 35th ID and Paul's 26th. Van Fleet's soldiers would attack to seize the high ground south of the Wiltz, with their right flank protected by the 26th ID. This thrust was to be complemented by a converging attack to the southeast out of Bastogne by the 6th AD, with a complementary push by the 35th ID on its southern flank.[61] The next day, Millikin added the additional, practical proviso that his 26th Cavalry Group be inserted on the 90th's left flank, in order to narrow Van Fleet's and Baade's attack zones and to provide a force for mopping up the pocket after the trap was closed.[62] Patton ordered Van Fleet's division to observe strict radio silence until contact was gained with the enemy.[63] By the evening of the 8th, the 90th was assembled south of Nothum, a village some three miles southwest of Wiltz.[64] Hopes were high that Van Fleet and his Tough Hombres would deliver in a manner fitting with their self-assigned appellation.

Collapsing the Harlange Pocket, 9–12 January

They did, but it took a while and there were a few anxious moments. The division's linkup point with the 35th ID and 6th AD was the village of

Bras, roughly halfway along the Bastogne-Wiltz road. The intersection two miles east of Bras, where a secondary road from Harlange to Oberwampach crosses the road from Bastogne to Wiltz, was an important intermediate objective. Whoever held this crossroads, about a mile northeast of Doncols, controlled both east-west and north-south movement in the pocket. The attack was aided by the fact that the 1st SS Panzer Division had been pulled out of the line farther to the west and the main force facing the 90th ID was the worn-out and over-extended 5th Parachute Division.[65] But given the terrain and weather, it would still be a tough fight.

Van Fleet's soldiers attacked with the 359th and 357th Infantry Regiments in the lead, from right to left, and the 358th in reserve. The first day was rough. By late afternoon, the division G-3 reported to III Corps that the 357th had hit strong resistance in the open ground surrounding Berlé and the 359th had encountered two strong points in its movement toward Trentelhof.[66] Both villages were taken by the end of the day, giving the division an advance of almost a mile.[67] Van Fleet called Millikin late in the afternoon and told him that despite these gains, there was a "pretty firm crust" that had not been penetrated and that Berlé had caused him "considerable trouble."[68] Nevertheless, he was prepared to attack early on the next morning. Elsewhere along the corps front, the other divisions made only marginal gains. Millikin's mood reflected these glass half-empty, glass half-full results. To Gay, he confided that "the thing has been a little disappointing," while to Patton, he opined, "I think Van did pretty well."[69]

On the next morning, Millikin and Gay had another revealing conversation:

> Gay: How does it look to you?
> Millikin: Your guess is as good as mine. We are all optimistic.
> Gay: I think Van is going to get through.
> Millikin: I do too. He said last night that he didn't think we were through their main defensive [*sic*] yet. He said he thought the main difficulty would be at the crossroads. If he can smash through that I think the rest is easy.[70]

When Patton visited the 90th ID command post on the 10th, he was informed by a division staff officer that the crossroads had been secured.[71] But the report turned out to be erroneous. The mistake in communication was particularly galling because of both the centrality of the intersection in the whole III Corps effort to reduce the Harlange Pocket and the personage to whom it had been made. Van Fleet learned of the incident when he returned to the command post after Patton's departure and was determined to capture the crossroads, thus rendering the report accurate. He immediately ordered the commander of the 359th IR, Colonel Raymond E. Bell, whose staff had tendered the erroneous information to division headquarters, to plan a night attack to that end.

Bell went forward to meet with the commanders of the regiment's 2nd and 3rd Battalions, Lieutenant Colonels Robert Booth and J. F. Smith, respectively, and instructed them to make it happen. The two battalion commanders developed an ingenious and daring plan. They decided to put the two units, each in single file, on either side of the road toward Doncols, with a tank destroyer, which made considerably less noise than a Sherman, backing up the infantrymen. The soldiers of the 5th Parachute Division, who had resisted mightily throughout the previous day, were asleep at the switch; and Booth's and Smith's men penetrated some three miles to the high ground commanding Doncols. The road junction fell soon thereafter, and the trapped Germans were roughly handled. This attack brought the coup de grace to the struggling 5th Parachute Division.[72] Many of the parachutists streamed north across the Wiltz; the antitank battalion commander, headquartered in Doncols, surrendered without resistance; the mortar battalion lost all its weapons; and the 15th Parachute Regiment was never heard from again.[73] But the cost to the 90th had been heavy as well. During three days of fighting, the 1st Battalion, 359th Infantry, lost twenty of the twenty-one officers assigned to its frontline units, leaving two companies to be commanded by staff sergeants. Total division battle casualties were over 500.[74]

With the evisceration of the 5th Parachute Division, the Harlange Pocket collapsed.[75] The 90th ID secured Bras by mid-afternoon on 12 January; and the 35th ID, moving through the woods to the west and southwest, linked up there with the Tough Hombres. The 6th AD attacked to the east, capturing Wardin and pressing on to within several hundred yards of Bras. The first phase of Millikin's attack was complete.

Expanding the Bastogne Perimeter, 13–17 January

Over the next five days, Millikin set the sensible, but limited, goal of expanding the perimeter of Bastogne some six miles to the northeast and east. The 6th AD was given an objective running along the road from Bourcy to Longvilly, while the 90th ID was told to attack across the Wiltz River to seize the twin villages of Niederwampach and Oberwampach.[76] German resistance was fierce, and accomplishing even this modest task proved to be excruciatingly difficult.

Millikin used the 13th to reorganize the corps. He pulled the 35th ID back into reserve for rehabilitation and moved the 26th Cavalry Group behind the corps' right flank for maintenance and refitting.[77] Meanwhile, the 6th AD and 90th ID made marginal gains. The right flank of Van Fleet's advance was pummeled by heavy nebelwerfer fire from east of Wiltz.[78] The 26th ID, bereft of infantry replacements, was assigned a heavily wooded sector south of Wiltz that required commitment of all three regiments.[79]

On the 14th, the 6th AD gained roughly a half mile, clearing Mageret before noon and securing Benonchamps by nightfall.[80] The German determination to hold ground was indicated by the Luftwaffe's air attack against the 358th Infantry, which, coordinated with a ground counterattack, stopped the 90th ID for the day.[81] On the 15th, Grow's soldiers continued their steady move to the east, capturing Arloncourt.[82] This little village rests halfway between Mageret and Longvilly on a secondary road that runs north-south from Bourcy to the Mageret-Longvilly road; its seizure gave III Corps a stepping stone toward Clerf. News from Van Fleet was mixed. His right flank, which had borne the brunt of the previous day's air attack, was forced back some 500 yards by heavy machine-gun, mortar, and artillery fire.[83] This fierce resistance, which the 90th ID described as "the heaviest concentration of AW [automatic weapons] fire yet received by the division," came from several units, including elements of the 1st SS Panzer Division that were thrown back into the line after the collapse of the 5th Parachute Division.[84] On the left flank, the 358th Infantry pulled off a major coup. Having crossed the Wiltz and advanced on Niederwampach, it came under fire from tanks, assault guns, and small arms in the village. A simultaneously delivered, four-teen-battalion concentration of artillery fire so stunned the trapped defenders that the GIs took the village and several hundred prisoners with minimal casualties.[85] Encouraged by this development and news from VIII Corps that the 101st Airborne would advance on Bourcy the next day, Millikin ordered Grow to continue the attack early in the morning to capture Michamps, roughly equidistant between Bourcy and Arloncourt, and press on to the Bourcy-Longvilly road.[86]

The next two days brought III Corps continued small victories and an intense German reaction. In a nifty example of combined arms cooperation, a 6th AD TF took Longvilly.[87] Millikin was content to wait before pushing much farther. Late on the afternoon of the 16th, he told Grow to secure the rest of the Bourcy-Longvilly road and patrol to maintain contact, but to await corps orders before continuing the attack.[88] On the 16th, Van Fleet committed his division reserve, the 359th Infantry, to capture Oberwam-pach.[89] On the 17th, the Germans attempted to retake it with five assaults of ever-mounting intensity, but all were repulsed. Why did the Germans fight so ferociously to eject the Americans from this seemingly insignificant

Belgian village? A glance at the map tells all: Oberwampach is on the direct route from Bastogne, through Eschweiler and Buchholz, to Hosingen on the Skyline Drive—the Panzer Lehr route of 16–19 December in reverse!

While the soldiers of the 359th Infantry were fending off the efforts of various German units to reoccupy Oberwampach, Patton came to Arlon to confer with Middleton and Millikin. With the linkup at Houffalize now solid and the perimeter east of Bastogne sufficiently expanded, he began to take the long view. He told both corps commanders to begin resting one-third of their units and allowing them to warm up because "we are going to attack until this war is over."[90] He also congratulated Middleton and Millikin for both doing "exceptionally well."[91]

Consolidating and Advancing Rapidly, 18–23 January

Millikin consolidated his gains from 18 to 20 January and then advanced rapidly against the retreating Germans.[92] During the period of relative rest, he carved out a zone for the 6th Cavalry Group on the 26th ID's right flank, thus narrowing Paul's zone and allowing him to advance to the south bank of the Wiltz. The 6th AD and 90th ID both made modest gains while attempting to maintain contact with the retreating Germans. The 35th ID was released for attachment to Walker's XX Corps.

The III Corps axis of attack was generally northeast astride the Bastogne–St. Vith highway, with the 6th AD to the left of the road, the 90th ID to its right, and the 26th ID and 6th Cavalry Group filling in between the Tough Hombres and the Clerf River.[93] Resistance throughout the period was generally light and scattered. On the 21st, the 26th ID and 6th Cavalry Group entered Wiltz from the northwest and southwest, respectively; the 6th AD advanced five miles to Hachiville, while the 90th ID almost kept pace by capturing Boevange. With III Corps pulling away from the 80th ID on Eddy's western boundary, Millikin ordered the 6th Cavalry Group to screen the open right flank. The next day was similarly productive. Grow's tankers pushed another four miles to Basbellain, while Van Fleet's infantrymen made three miles to Asselborn. Paul's foot soldiers were having a more difficult time in the tough terrain north of Wiltz, but the 6th Cavalry Group broke through to Eschweiler.[94] Moderate resistance was encountered on the 23rd. The 6th AD captured Trois Vierges, while the 90th ID penetrated as far east as Binsfeld. Simultaneously, the 6th Cavalry Group made contact with enemy forces in Clerf. Thus, in just three days, III Corps had advanced from the eastern side of Bastogne to the west bank of the Clerf River. On the afternoon of the 3rd day, Millikin received orders to change the direction of his attack from northeast to east.[95]

Wheeling East to the Our, 24–28 January

Resistance stiffened marginally over the next several days as the Germans attempted to mount a last-ditch defense along the Clerf River.[96] Millikin was now attacking with three divisions and an armored cavalry group in only a slightly larger zone than the sector originally defended by two battalions of Colonel Fuller's 110th IR. On 24 January, the 6th AD took Wilwerdange and Holler, bringing it to the northwestern corner of the Skyline Drive; the 90th ID forced a crossing of the Clerf River north of Clerf; and the 26th ID did likewise near Drauffelt. By the 25th, both Grow's and Van Fleet's divisions had their leading elements along the Skyline Drive, despite encountering much stiffer defenses; and Paul's soldiers had cleared Clerf. On the 26th and 27th, III Corps was caught up in 12th AG's shuffling of units and boundaries in preparation for the attack into the Rhineland. By 28 December, Millikin's corps, now consisting of the 6th AD, 17th Airborne Division, and 6th Cavalry Group, was arrayed along the Skyline Drive from roughly Heinerscheid in the north to Hosingen in the south, completing III Corps' contribution to the eradication of the Bulge.

Assessment

Millikin's actions in the closing phase of the Ardennes campaign revealed a steady, competent approach to command. Because the decision on how to employ the 90th ID was made collectively among Patton, Millikin, and Van Fleet, we cannot judge the corps commander's role therein. But the decision to insert the 6th Cavalry Group on van Fleet's left flank was Millikin's alone, and it demonstrated a deft understanding of the use of cavalry in economy-of-force roles. After the Harlange Pocket gave way, Millikin did all that he had to do—no more, no less. Obtaining breathing room on the eastern side of Bastogne was essential for the logistical support of an advance to the northeast. He managed the expansion of the perimeter judiciously, urging Grow forward when opportunity knocked but not allowing him to advance in a way that would bring about another recoil as had happened on 4 January. In the final advance to the Our, he kept his divisions on course and employed his cavalry well on the open right flank. Millikin was still a rookie. But when he stepped to the plate for the second time in his big-league career, he swung the bat just a bit more confidently than he had the first time—and he got another hit.

XII CORPS CROSSES THE SÛRE AND ROLLS UP
THE SKYLINE DRIVE

Patton was clearly aware that he could not launch XII Corps on a variation of his plan to cut the Bulge off at the base until VIII Corps and III Corps had attacked through the main enemy forces around Bastogne and unhinged the German defenses. By 15 January, that process was sufficiently advanced for him to give Eddy the green light for the 18th.[97]

Preparing to Attack, 5–17 January

Eddy's line of contact in early January began just southeast of Wiltz, ran generally southeast to just south of Ettelbruck, then went due east along the south bank of the Sûre to Echternach, finally bending south along the Sauer to Wasserbillig.[98] On 5 January, McBride's 80th ID occupied the western portion sector, Irwin's 5th ID was in the center facing the Sûre, and Blakely's 4th ID defended along the Sauer. Eddy required more troops to be able to mount an offensive, and he got them. Patton's initial instinct was to put the 87th ID, coming over from VIII Corps, into the line immediately; but Eddy asked for it to receive a few extra days to "rest up, train, and get in good condition."[99] Eddy's request was accepted, and Culin's soldiers were fed into the line to replace the 4th ID along the Sauer from 15 to 17 January.[100] This allowed Eddy to slip the 4th ID into the eastern third of the 5th ID's sector, thus narrowing the zone for Irwin's forthcoming attack, and to place the 12th Infantry from the 4th ID in corps reserve.

The general scheme for the operation had some interesting antecedents. Although Eddy had, at Patton's direction, dutifully drafted "Attack Plan A" that envisioned an attack to the east across the Sauer, followed by a wheel to the north into the Siegfried Line, he felt it far too risky. On New Year's Day, he told the Third Army commander that he believed it would be far better to attack north across the Sûre and up the Skyline Drive to the west of the Our.[101] Eddy fleshed out the concept with his division commanders and presented it the next day.[102] Patton bought the idea, and XII Corps published an implementing field order on 3 January, for execution at a later date.[103] Identities of divisions and detailed tasks were assigned in an operational directive of 16 January.[104] The plan would be implemented in two phases. Initially, the 4th ID would attack with one regiment into the angle formed by the Our and the Sûre; the 5th ID would cross the Sûre with two regiments, one on either side of Diekirch; and the 80th ID would conduct a demonstration. On corps order, when Eddy was reasonably assured that the bridgehead was well in hand, the 80th ID would attack to the northeast between Wiltz and Ettelbruck, generally toward Hosingen, while the 5th ID would advance to the northwest to gain the southern end of the Skyline Drive. With only two regiments at its disposal and limited maneuver room along the Skyline Drive, the role of the 4th ID in the final advance would be limited.

Eddy had assembled all the engineer support needed to make the crossing.[105] Each of the three assaulting infantry regiments was supported by a combat engineer battalion. The two infantry assault battalions of the 4th ID's 8th IR had thirty-eight three-man boats, thirty-two five-man boats, and twelve M-12 assault boats. The small craft were to be rowed across by infantry and then pulled back to the near bank by the engineers with ropes. The reserve battalion would cross on a footbridge, and a larger treadway bridge would be built for the wheeled vehicles. Additional support for follow-on echelons included several Bailey bridges and a seventy-foot timber trestle bridge.

Brandenberger anticipated that the next heavy blow would originate between Wiltz and Ettelbruck, rather than along the Sûre between Ettelbruck and the confluence of the Sûre and the Our.[106] Thus, for the area between Wiltz and Ettelbruck, he allocated to his LIII Corps commander, General Edwin Graf Rothkirch und Trach, three VGDs, while for the stretch of the Sûre east of Ettelbruck, he gave his LXXX Corps commander, General Franz Beyer, only a single VGD. Unlike other patterns of German dispositions observed in this phase of the campaign, Brandenberger's was stronger in the west than it was in the east. This was perplexing because the Germans had but five bridges over the Our, and three of them were at or south of Vianden. Perhaps the Seventh Army commander was counting on the obstacle value of the Sûre to protect these vital crossings. If so, it was a notion of which he would soon find himself rather painfully disabused.

Crossing the Sûre, 18–20 January

The "London fog" that covered the Ardennes in the early morning hours of 18 January helped the XII Corps attack.[107] Limited visibility favors the attacker, particularly in a river crossing, where the defender must identify the location and strength of the main effort before the attacker can establish a solid bridgehead.

The 5th ID's plan called for the 2nd Infantry to attack west of Diekirch, while the 10th Infantry assaulted downstream between Diekirch and Bettendorf, with the 11th Infantry held in reserve.[108] Five hours after the first boats had silently pushed off from the near bank, the 10th Infantry had consolidated its positions in the enemy rear and begun patrolling to the east to link up with the 4th ID's 8th Infantry. On the left flank, the surprise was not as complete. One battalion of the 2nd Infantry had to blast its way across the river in the face of determined opposition. But the regiment achieved a commanding position northwest of Diekirch. By nightfall, Irwin's soldiers had carved out an initial bridgehead just over a mile deep and nearly five miles wide. Thanks to efficient engineer support, tanks and tank destroyers were on the north bank to provide help in the event of an armored counterattack. Downstream, the 8th Infantry achieved similar results on a narrower front, moving against Bettendorf from the east and generally consolidating positions on the high ground north of the river.[109]

XII Corps' unanticipated grab forced a quick reappraisal by Brandenberger and Model.[110] The former shifted his artillery and other supporting assets from Rothkirch's corps to Beyer's and ordered a division from the LIII Corps back to the Skyline Drive to protect the Vianden crossings. Model ordered Manteuffel to release Lüttwitz's XLVIII Panzer Corps, consisting of Bayerlein's Panzer Lehr and Lauchert's 2nd Panzer, to Brandenberger's control. The units that had made the dash toward Bastogne in the heady days of mid-December were now being employed as the fire brigade to save the German Seventh Army from destruction. In the meantime, German engineers worked furiously to construct another bridge over the Our, located farther to the north in Manteuffel's rear area.

Over the next two days, the 4th and 5th IDs moved steadily northward, despite a howling snowstorm that produced drifts up to six-feet deep.[111] On the 19th, Eddy released the 12th Infantry from corps reserve; Blakely committed it through the 10th Infantry, which had come into his zone when Eddy shifted the 4th ID's boundary to the west. By noon on the 20th, the First Battalion, 12th Infantry, had secured the village of Longsdorf, two miles north of the river. In the meantime, the 5th ID cleared the last Germans out of Diekirch and advanced to the high ground north and west of Bastendorf, expanding the corps' depth to almost three miles in the western portion of Irwin's zone. This expanded toehold gave XII Corps a platform from which to bring artillery fire to bear on the German bridges south of Vianden.[112] The 80th ID also advanced to the Wiltz River without launching a major offensive. On the afternoon of the 20th, Eddy met with McBride and told him that the time had come to attack.[113]

Rolling up the Skyline Drive, 21–28 January

For the first and only time in the Bulge, the Germans were in precipitous retreat. The east-west roads over which they had to move were not as

robust as the north-south roads along which the 5th ID could press its attack; and the 80th ID's advance, coupled with the attack out of the Sûre
River bridgehead, added a threatening factor that could not be ignored.
These movements were rendered even more potent by the weather. On 21
and 22 January, the skies again cleared, bringing the American Jagbos into
the fight. The 21st passed as a day of almost-missed opportunity. At noon,
a report came into corps headquarters from the 5th ID of so many trucks
and tanks heading for Vianden that it "looks like a large-scale withdrawal
along the front."[114] XII Corps immediately alerted Weyland's airmen of the
inviting target of opportunity. But XIX TAC's runways were clogged by
snow and ice; and, despite the generally clear skies, a ground haze gave the
retreating Germans respite from the few planes that finally struggled into
the air.[115] But the next day was picture-perfect for the American airmen:
the runways were trafficable, visibility was virtually unlimited, and the Germans were heading pell-mell toward the bridges at Vianden. The result was
the already described, large-scale destruction of man, horse, and machine.
Brandenberger noted ruefully that 22 January 1945 was the only day in the
Ardennes campaign that "the situation in the air was similar to that which
had prevailed in Normandy."[116]

In the meantime, XII Corps pressed forward on the ground. The best
advances were made by the soldiers of the 5th ID.[117] By noon on the 22nd,
Irwin had committed the 11th Infantry, sending it toward Hoscheid, a small
but important village on the road from Wiltz to Vianden. South of Hoscheid, German resistance stiffened. The 11th Infantry reached its outskirts
on the night of the 23rd and was forced to mount a predawn attack on
the 24th to have it cleared by that evening. The 10th Infantry then pushed
east toward Putscheid, a hamlet about a mile to the east, to consolidate the
division's hold on the erstwhile escape route. Here, the Germans fought a
sharp rearguard action, holding on until the afternoon of the 28th. As this
encounter raged on, Irwin set his sights on the parallel road about two miles
to the north that ran from Wiltz to Gemund, locus of another bridge over
the Our. He dispatched his division reconnaissance troop northwest toward
Consthum, which is just south of the road, roughly two miles northwest of
Hoscheid. It reached the high ground overlooking this village by noon on
the 27th and cleared it on the 28th. By the end of the day on the 28th, the
11th Infantry also controlled Walhausen, which reposes at the eastern edge
of the ridge line dominating the final approach to Gemund.

Meanwhile, the 80th ID was responding to Eddy's order of 22 January
to attack on the Wilwerwiltz-Hosingen axis.[118] This move was intended to
flush the German LIII Corps to the east and position McBride's division

between the northern terminus of the 5th ID and the boundary between XII Corps and III Corps, which now ran just south of Hosingen. It was a frustrating and at times thankless mission because the Blue Ridge soldiers had farther to go than did their brethren moving up the Skyline Drive and because the terrain and road network were much less hospitable to the offensive. They performed well despite the adverse circumstances.[119] On the 21st, the division fought its way into Burden and Bourscheid, both northwest of Ettelbruck. Over the next two days, it cleared Bourscheid and shifted the 318th Infantry west to Wiltz. By noon on the 24th, the 317th Infantry was on the west bank of the Clerf at Wilwerwiltz. After being pummeled by fire from artillery, mortars, tanks, and small arms, the regiment attacked at 0400 on the 25th and by noon had cleared the village and seized a bridge across the Clerf intact. Demonstrating that no good deed goes unpunished, a staff officer at Third Army G-3 called XII Corps four hours later and chastised the regiment for "holding up the whole war."[120] The 317th pressed on, securing Pintsch, about a mile east of Wilwerwiltz. After three more days of hard fighting up the western face of the Skyline Drive, the 317th and 318th held the high ground near Hosingen, where they joined hands with the 17th Airborne Division in III Corps. The role of XII Corps in the Bulge was complete.

Assessment

Eddy's most significant contribution to the final phase of the campaign was convincing Patton to attack north across the Sûre, rather than east across the Sauer and north into the Siegfried Line. The results of Eddy's plan speak for themselves. It maneuvered Brandenberger's Seventh Army out of the Bulge and avoided the dangers of conducting an attack on German soil east of the Sauer and Our Rivers. Furthermore, by forcing the LIII Corps into a hasty retreat and compelling Model to dispatch the XLVII Panzer Corps to the rescue of Seventh Army, it set up the extremely destructive air-ground engagement of 22 January, which demonstrated the great value of combining ground maneuver on a large scale with a lethal and responsive air arm. Eddy also fared well in execution. He paid close attention to the details required to effect a major river crossing and set up the tactical dynamics to achieve surprise. Although some might question his waiting until the bridgehead was established before ordering the 80th ID into the fray, it was prudent and perhaps the only feasible way to ensure the success of the secondary attack.[121] The slight delay that resulted in arrival of the Blue Ridge soldiers atop the Skyline Drive did little to prejudice the overall result. In short,

Eddy's contribution to XII Corps' final operation in the Bulge was sound in concept and competent in action. Patton presented Eddy a Distinguished Service Medal for XII Corps' role in the dash across central France and crossing of the Moselle in the same ceremony in which Middleton received his award.[122] Given Patton's previous concern with his nerves, Eddy could not hold back a slight smile when the officer reading the citation mentioned his having protected Third Army's southern flank.[123] He had come a long way in a little over five months.

SOME CLOSING OBSERVATIONS

The picture that emerges from the study of VIII, III, and XII Corps in the closing phase of the campaign is one of three officers who dealt well with significant challenges. Middleton had the hardest task. The road from Bastogne to Houffalize was tenaciously defended. Middleton's approach was to make haste slowly. When he had sufficient force at his disposal to begin to increase the pace of the advance, he employed it sensibly. It appears that Patton provided the impetus for the 11th AD to send a task force to Houffalize in a daring night patrol to make contact with First Army (and so avoid the indignity of having Hodges's staff ask, "Where's Third Army?"), but Middleton's more cautious methods established the conditions that allowed this dash to be made. Millikin's challenge was to reduce the Harlange Pocket *and* deal with the rather thick crust of German units remaining east of Bastogne. For the former, he was fortunate to obtain the infusion of the relatively fresh 90th ID, led by the strong-willed and capable Van Fleet. But Millikin's success was also due to his deft use of the 6th Cavalry Group in critical economy-of-force roles and to his steady persistence in clawing through the German formations defending along Bastogne's eastern face. Eddy, too, played his hand well. In persuading Patton not to attack east across the Sauer, he demonstrated both a penchant for higher-level tactics and a significant degree of acceptance from a demanding commander. In turn, Patton was fortunate to have three such capable men as corps commanders.

The final note on closing the Bulge came from Hobart Gay, who penned in his diary on 27 January the prophecy that "final defeat of the German army is now within the offing."[124]

EPILOGUE

16

Conclusions and Epilogue

Strategy includes the working out of its consequences. The ranks of martial authority from multiple star to modest chevron correspond to an ordering of reality in which plans produce orders, orders produce actions, and actions produce isolated episodes of swirling fury where the issue hangs or falls on the skill and fortitude of individual human beings, under conditions of indescribable repulsiveness and stress.[1]   *Eric Larrabee*

THE REQUIREMENT FOR ORGANIC UNITY between high-level strategy and the most minor of minor tactics contains an imperative for the mid-level direction of war to keep the two poles in consonance with one another. This study has focused on a particular slice of that middle echelon—the U.S. Army corps as it was constituted in the Second World War—and the six men who commanded the various corps in a single campaign of that war. The stage has been set, the characters introduced, the events unfolded, and the curtain rung down. Two tasks remain: to ponder the meaning of the drama and to trace the fortunes of the protagonists after their exits from the stage.

CONCLUSIONS

The Campaign

The losses on both sides were horrendous. Given the intensity of the fighting and the intermingling of forces, SHAEF's initial tally of American casualties in the Bulge fighting from 16 December 1944 to 31 January 1945, collated on 2 February 1945, was reasonably accurate.[2] It listed 75,572 casualties, with 8,407 killed, 46,260 wounded, and 20,905 missing (most presumably captured). In 1954, when the numbers of captured and killed had been more accurately determined, Forrest Pogue's *Supreme Command* updated these estimates with data from the adjutant general's Strength Authorization Branch.[3] This compilation combined figures from the Ardennes and Alsace campaigns, without a separate listing for the Bulge. It cited 104,944 casualties: 15,982 killed, 62,372 wounded, 23,554 captured, 2,802 returned from missing, and 234 dead while missing. Cole's official history, published in 1965, neglected the subject, presumably because Pogue had already dealt with it. MacDonald's 1985 *A Time for Trumpets* reckoned the total American casualties in the Bulge to have been roughly 81,000, with 19,000 killed, 47,000 wounded, and 15,000 captured.[4] Estimates of German casualties range from the lowest German figure of 81,834 to the highest American figure of 103,900.[5] Again according to MacDonald, both sides lost about 800 tanks.[6] But in a war of attrition, the big difference was that, despite their continuing problems with infantry replacements, the Americans could make good their losses in both personnel and equipment with much greater ease than could the Germans, who had staked all on the Ardennes offensive and lost.

The strategic consequences of the campaign were unambiguous, almost perfectly fulfilling Hobart Gay's prophecy. With the Wehrmacht eviscerated and the Waffen-SS withdrawn from the field in the west, the Allied armies marched from strength to strength.[7] In mid-January, Eisenhower gave Devers the resources with which to close the Colmar Pocket, and by early February the last German forces had been driven from Alsace. There followed a number of major attacks to close on the west bank of the Rhine. In the north, Montgomery launched his long-desired Veritable-Grenade pincer, the former an assault by Crerar's First Canadian Army southeast from Nijmegen, the latter a drive to the northeast from Jülich by Simpson's Ninth Army. Bradley's operation, called Lumberjack, had Hodges's First Army attacking across the Roer River and Patton's Third Army moving north of the Moselle. Patch's Seventh Army, under Devers, attacked from northern Lorraine into the Saar in Operation Undertone. All these attacks reached the Rhine by mid-March. By the end of March, viable enclaves had been established east of the river—by Montgomery beyond Wesel, by Hodges beyond Remagen, and by Patton beyond Oppenheim. There soon followed the encirclement of the Ruhr industrial area, Montgomery's drive to the Baltic, Bradley's attack across central and southern Germany, and Devers's advance to the Alps. The official surrender was signed at Eisenhower's forward command post in Rheims early in the morning of 7 May 1945.

Given the rapidity of this collapse, was it a mistake for the Germans to have launched the Ardennes offensive? This question cannot be answered without first considering the ends. If the objective was to delay for as long as possible the defeat of the German armed forces, the answer is in the affirmative. A grudging defense to the Rhine, followed by an even more hard-fought defense along the Rhine would have most likely delayed the crossing of Germany's mystical barrier in the west until several months beyond March

1945. And at least some of the forces used for the audacious but ill-fated drive on Antwerp might also have been used to impede the remorseless advance of the Red Army. However, if the objective was not to stave off ultimate defeat but to turn the tide of battle so dramatically as to bring about the possibility of a negotiated peace, as Hitler's clearly was, then the daring but improbable offensive through the Ardennes in the winter of 1944 begins to look much more rational. And even Jodl and Keitel, the two condemned men whom Cole accurately described as "the artisans but not the architects of this venture," could not bring themselves to declare that Hitler had been wrong, leaving the criticism that the forces devoted to the Ardennes could have been better employed in the east "to the judgment of history."[8]

The quality of senior leadership on the German side varied radically. Accepting the strategic rationale of Hitler's bold gamble, his biggest mistake was to trust the main effort to Dietrich. Dietrich's clumsy assembly of Sixth SS Panzer Army prior to the start date and his inflexible pounding against the Elsenborn Ridge both depict a man out of his league in the handling of large formations. This is one of the penalties that dictatorships invariably pay when loyalty to the regime becomes the overriding consideration in the assignment of military tasks. Rundstedt, the Old Prussian aristocrat, played so small a role in the direction of the campaign that little can be said. Model was clearly the man caught in the middle between the Führer's grandiose ambition and the inadequacy of available means. Nevertheless, he gave the effort his all, moving well forward on the battlefield, even to the point of recklessness, exhorting subordinate commanders in both offense and defense, making cogent recommendations to OKW, and keeping German forces in the fight when the battle was clearly lost. Manteuffel also performed extremely well. His plan to encircle the Schnee Eifel was brilliant in concept and executed to perfection. And it is no accident that the offensive's high water mark at Celles came in the sector of the 5th Panzer Army, originally designated to make the secondary attack.

Senior leadership on the Allied side also varied, though not nearly as radically. Eisenhower was central to Allied victory in the Bulge. He recognized the nature of the attack far earlier than Hitler and the German generals anticipated. He also acted on that intuition, ordering the 7th and 10th ADs into the Ardennes before the attack was twenty-four-hours old and committing the theater's slim strategic reserve within less than two days. He outlined a sound concept to contain the offensive and developed a feasible plan to eliminate it. His most controversial decision, to appoint Montgomery the battle captain of the northern flank, was clearly vindicated by results. As Collins acutely observed a quarter century later, "The Battle of the Bulge was the turning point not only in sealing Allied victory in the west but in confirming Eisenhower's military competence and ability to command. It was Eisenhower, not Montgomery or Bradley or Patton, who dominated the conduct of this battle."[9] Nevertheless, Montgomery performed his assigned role well. His instinct to recoil in the face of German strength in the initial phase of the campaign was operationally sound, despite the fact that his penchant for describing it as "tidying up the battlefield" infuriated some of his American subordinates. He also brought a necessary tonic of moral vigor to First Army when Hodges needed it. He was several days late in launching the offensive on the northern wing. But given the inherent advantages of the defense and the atrocious conditions of attacking in the Ardennes in winter, this indiscretion had little serious consequence. Bradley, much like Rundstedt, was essentially a nonplayer by virtue of his and his staff's passivity in the initial days of the campaign and Ike's decision to give the northern half of the Bulge to Monty. Patton was a mixed blessing. His willingness to listen to his G-2 and his adroit contingency planning before the German attack enabled Third Army to come to the battle much earlier than would have otherwise been the case. His decision to assault the southern flank of the penetration on 22 December with only three divisions placed a heavy load on Millikin's shoulders, but he was clearly correct that the risks of waiting for additional forces outweighed the risks of early commitment. In the transition phase of the campaign, however, Patton's impetuosity got the better of him. Making exactly the opposite mistake of Montgomery, his premature order to Middleton to attack on 30 December failed to exploit the advantages of the defense in the face of a determined German attack. After repeating the mistake on 4 January, again with inauspicious results, Patton began to take the longer view. He realized that there was no quick solution to eradicating the Bulge and that saving American lives was as important as killing Germans. And his acceptance of Eddy's counsel to attack north across the Sûre, rather than east across the Sauer, represented the *mentalité* of a mature army commander.

It is appropriate to close this retrospective with a short reconsideration of why the Allies were surprised by the German offensive. A number of answers have already been brought forward, including poor weather for aerial reconnaissance, draconian measures to enforce secrecy during the planning process, an artfully conceived cover story, superb operational security on the part of German forces assembling in the Eifel, and a noticeable tendency toward "mirror imaging" on the part of Allied commanders and intelligence analysts. But there was a more subtle, psychological factor operating as well. As in the case of the attack by the Japanese against American forces at Pearl

Harbor and the attack by Al-Qaeda against the World Trade Center, there was a failure of imagination that did not appreciate the daring, inventiveness, and skill of a determined foe. Like the attacks of 7 December 1941 and 11 September 2001, that of 16 December 1944 raises a disturbing issue. Attacks of this scale and ambition lay so far outside the parameters of accepted wisdom that those possessed of sufficient imagination to penetrate with reasonable accuracy the minds and intentions of such a resourceful adversary are seldom given a full hearing. Thus, despite the best efforts of intelligence agencies to the contrary, human nature being what it is, strategic surprise remains a phenomenon with a reasonably bright future.

The Corps Commanders

The immediate task is to examine how these six men met or failed to meet the interwar command desiderata laid down at the CGSS and Army War College.

With one minor exception, all six were willing to take full responsibility for the performance of their commands. Collins, who knowingly violated the spirit, if not the letter, of instructions from Montgomery and Hodges not to engage in offensive operations when he ordered Harmon to attack on 25 December, is probably the most dramatic exemplar of this canon. Ridgway is a close second with his insistence that he, and he alone, would make all of the major (as well as some of the minor) decisions regarding XVIII (Airborne) Corps' tactical dispositions. Gerow, Millikin, and Eddy also showed themselves willing to make the tough calls and to be held accountable for the results. Middleton did likewise, particularly with regard to his most important determination—that Bastogne could and should be held. The one exception was his unwillingness to accept responsibility for the decision not to withdraw the 422nd and 423rd IRs from the Schnee Eifel. Middleton's delegation of that authority to Jones made him judicially correct; but with both more knowledge of the area and greater tactical expertise than the 106th ID commander, the moral responsibility was his.

All six demonstrated strength of will, though some had more opportunity to do so than others. Ridgway's desire to retain forces in the St. Vith salient pushed willpower to the limits of sensibility, but his implacable determination to hold ground proved to be of great utility in the recapture of Manhay. Middleton likewise showed great determination in saving all that he could from the debacle of having his extended frontage penetrated at multiple points and in chipping away west of Bastogne until he finally got an opening to Houffalize. Gerow was absolutely unyielding in his defense of the

Elsenborn Ridge. Millikin was strong in the dark days of late December, when the task of relieving Bastogne began to look like mission very difficult, if not mission impossible. He was similarly determined in reducing the Harlange Pocket after absorbing the body blow of the 1st SS Panzer Division's nearly successful attempt to sever the Arlon-Bastogne highway. Collins showed persistent determination in the VII Corps drive to Houffalize. Eddy was not challenged as strongly as his brethren, but his advance to the Sauer with marginally adequate resources demonstrated that he, too, had inner steel.

With minor exceptions, all six demonstrated keen mental acuity and celerity of action. Like his Leavenworth study partner Eisenhower, Gerow instantly understood the German attack to be significant; and he was willing to risk Hodges's ire for authority to pull the 2nd ID back from its attack on Wahlerscheid. He further recognized the vital importance of the Elsenborn Ridge and quickly developed a plan to secure it in the face of extremely adverse odds. Collins was swift to sense that the tipping point had come at the western extremity of the German advance and acted appropriately and without hesitation on this crucial insight. Middleton's ability to sense, almost instinctively, that delaying XLVII Panzer Corps' attack at the tiny road junctions east and northeast of Bastogne was the key to retention of that vital town is the stuff of legend, and properly so. As each increment of force arrived to help him to put into place his plan for the defense of Bastogne, the clarity and precision of his orders indicated the clarity and rapidity of his thought processes. He was also more insightful than Patton in sensing that the Germans still had too much strength around Bastogne in late December to justify VIII Corps' resumption of the offensive. His one failure was the lack of a timely order to withdraw the forces on the Schnee Eifel. Ridgway quickly arrived at the appreciation that containing Peiper was his most important task and developed a workable plan to do so; he also sensed, much more accurately than either Montgomery or Hodges, when the time had come for the transition to the offense. His one lapse was the delay in accurately appreciating the situation in the St. Vith salient—that the forces had to get out and that Jones had to be relieved. Fortunately, he recognized both these realities in time to prevent major harm. Millikin realized early in the III Corps attack that the relief of Bastogne would have to come from the southwest and gave Gaffey the forces and narrower sector that allowed him to stage CCR's attack from that direction. Eddy had the good tactical sense to recognize that an attack to the north across the Sûre was preferable to an attack east across the Sauer, and he persuaded Patton this was so well before the attack had to be made.

All demonstrated keen appreciation of terrain. Gerow did so at the Elsenborn Ridge; Middleton in the defense of Bastogne; Ridgway in the attack to St. Vith; Millikin in the relief of Bastogne; Collins in the advance on Houffalize; and Eddy in crossing the Sûre.

Care for subordinates is difficult to determine. If the best measure of this is good decisions that accomplish the mission with the least cost in blood, the criterion has to be subsumed under other headings. But even there it gets tricky. Middleton's decision not to authorize the withdrawal of TF Rose from its defense of an important road junction on 18 December clearly did not have the welfare of Rose and his men as its top priority. But one has to ask how many more lives might have been lost if Rose and his men had been spared. If this standard is best indicated by attempts to dissuade superiors from ill-considered decisions, be they successful or unsuccessful, then Gerow, Middleton, Eddy, Collins, and Ridgway all fare well. If the best indicator is apparent empathy, Eddy probably scores at the top. But the operative adjective here is "apparent." In sum, this book has failed to uncover sufficient evidence to make meaningful judgments in this area.

Regarding the ability to endure privation, Ridgway, whose corps headquarters was thrust into the Bulge with no warning and who prowled the front lines with reckless abandon, is probably the greatest exemplar. Collins, too, had to cover an extended corps front in atrocious weather to keep tabs on a fluid situation. Millikin had similar challenges on the southern flank. All three men bore up well, with no signs of fatigue apparently impairing their decision-making skills. Comments from Hobart Gay indicate that by late December Middleton was beginning to show the strain of the heavy load he had borne for some two weeks; but by early January, he seemed to have gained his second wind. Given that Eddy's corps headquarters was nicely ensconced in Luxembourg City and relatively close to the divisional headquarters under his command and that Gerow's active participation in the campaign was limited to the first phase, each had little opportunity to demonstrate this trait.

The above assessments should also be examined in light of the difficulty of the tasks assigned. Here, Middleton clearly deserves the greatest respect. Holding a front of sixty miles against an attack by five corps was manifestly impossible; delaying this assault sufficiently to hold Bastogne for the entire campaign and St. Vith for six days was a Herculean feat. With VIII Corps being given the toughest assignment in collapsing the Bulge, Middleton fully paid his dues. Next was Ridgway. By dint of circumstance, XVIII (Airborne) Corps was required to do everything on the fly. It also had to contain Peiper's attack, manage the withdrawal from St. Vith, stop the II SS Panzer Corps, and then retake St. Vith. Millikin's attack into the south flank was made, for good and sufficient reason, with inadequate force. The reduction of the Harlange Pocket involved very tough fighting and careful management of a concentric advance. The breakthrough on the eastern face of Bastogne came in the face of some of the most vicious German counterattacks of the entire campaign. The chief difficulty of VII Corps' initial task was timing the counterstroke; the challenging northern drive to Houffalize was aided by the provision of adequate resources. Gerow had a very tough task in the defense of the Elsenborn Ridge against Dietrich's Sixth SS Panzer Army, but V Corps' relative quiescence thereafter lowers his overall index of difficulty. Even the simplest of things in war is difficult, but the manner in which the campaign unfolded assigned to Eddy the least difficult of tasks in the Bulge.

The sequence changes somewhat when we consider importance. Clearly Gerow had the central task—stopping the German main effort. If Dietrich had been able to roll over V Corps in the first twenty-four to thirty-six hours of the attack, the damage to the entire Allied front would have been very grave and might have proven catastrophic. Middleton was next. Although Manteuffel's attack was secondary, it was integral to the plan to get to Antwerp. VIII Corps' delay was just enough to frustrate this important element of the OKW design. Ridgway and Millikin followed close behind. The commitment of XVIII (Airborne) Corps was the first tangible step taken to fill the gaping hole in the middle of the penetration; and the III Corps attack from the south was the first indication that the Germans might eventually have to dance to the American piper. Collins's attack at the tip sealed the fate of the Wehrmacht's westward expansion, while Eddy's crossing of the Sûre delivered the coup de grace to the remaining German forces in the Bulge.

If we ask how they performed relative to expectations, Millikin clearly tops the list. He came into the Bulge a novice; he left a competent and steadily maturing corps commander. Gerow rates second. By his cool, effective actions and orders in the Bulge, he partially erased the taint of his uninspired performance in the Hürtgen. Ridgway was known to be a fine division commander, but no one knew for certain if he could command a corps. By the recapture of St. Vith, there was no longer any doubt on that score. Expectations of Middleton's ability to handle a crisis were high before the Bulge; they were even higher afterward. By mid-December, Eddy had become regarded as a steady, effective corps commander; he did nothing to disappoint. Collins was almost universally acclaimed as the most effective corps commander in the ETO. If there was an ever-so-slight smirch on his reputation lingering from the Hürtgen, it was erased by his fine performance in the Ardennes.

Taken as a whole, these commanders made important and constructive contributions to the ultimate American victory in the Battle of the Bulge. When the Germans were on the offensive, Gerow held firm on the axis of main effort; Middleton took the steam out of the strong secondary attack; and Ridgway began to fill the yawning gap between the two. In the transition phase, while Gerow and Eddy held on to the northern and southern shoulders, Millikin competently directed the assault against the southern flank of the penetration, Ridgway stopped the II SS Panzer Corps, and Collins masterfully timed the strike against the tip of the offensive. In the collapse of the Bulge, Middleton and Millikin patiently and persistently cut through the thick crust of German forces surrounding Bastogne, Collins drove steadily toward Houffalize, Ridgway attacked with determination to recapture St. Vith, and Eddy crafted a surprise crossing of the Sûre, all done in terrible conditions of weather and terrain against a determined and skillful defender. Mistakes were minimal. Middleton erred in not ordering Jones to withdraw from the Schnee Eifel and in not assigning a single commander at St. Vith. He also bears some responsibility for the surprise in the Bulge. More active patrolling in early December might have provided a few more indicators of the impending offensive. Ridgway delayed for about a day in ordering the withdrawal from the St. Vith salient and in relieving Jones of command of the 106th ID. But none of these errors materially affected the overall outcome. In light of the widespread confusion induced by the strength, unexpectedness, and ferocity of the German offensive, they were remarkably few in number. It was fortunate that six men of such generally high competence were in command at the corps level in what was arguably the U.S. Army's most desperate struggle of the Second World War.

The Corps Structure

The structure and role of the U.S. corps was also a major contributor to victory. It allowed army and army group commanders to focus the right kinds of combat power in appropriate places, for appropriate periods in response to the ever-evolving requirements of a dynamic battlefield. A brief reprise of the units assigned to V Corps and III Corps demonstrates the point. When the battle broke out, V Corps had assigned, from north to south, the 8th and 78th IDs, the 102nd Cavalry Group, and the 2nd and 99th IDs. The attack east of the Elsenborn Ridge fell in the sector of the 2nd and 99th IDs. On 17 December, First Army assigned the 1st ID, which Gerow would use to defend the southern face of the Elsenborn Ridge, and the 30th ID, which he employed to contain Kampfgruppe Peiper. On the next day, First Army transferred control of the 8th and 78th IDs to VII Corps, thus freeing Gerow from concern for the territory north of Monschau. It also gave him the 9th ID, which he used to stiffen his northern flank, and the 82nd Airborne Division to begin to fill the gap between V Corps and VIII Corps. But with the continued pounding against the Elsenborn Ridge and Peiper still threatening to push toward the Meuse, this clearly stretched V Corps too far to the west and south; and on 19 December, the 82nd Airborne and a regiment of the 30th ID were transferred to the just-arrived XVIII (Airborne) Corps, with the rest of Hobbs's division following on the 20th. Thus, by the afternoon of 20 December, Gerow had four infantry divisions and a cavalry group, backed up by ample artillery, densely concentrated in an arc covering the eastern and southern approaches to the Elsenborn Ridge. It proved to be adequate. On 16 December, III Corps was located near Metz, preparing for Third Army's impending Saar offensive, with the 6th AD, 6th Cavalry Group, and 26th ID assigned. Four days later, it was in Arlon, preparing plans to attack into the southern flank of the penetration, with the 26th and 80th IDs and the 4th AD assigned. As the attack moved northward, Patton recognized that the corps was inadequately resourced. He reassigned the 6th Cavalry Group on 23 December and on 26 December gave Millikin the 35th ID, which the corps commander inserted in the troublesome gap between the 4th AD and 26th ID. To narrow Millikin's focus to the difficult problems around Bastogne, Patton also transferred the 80th ID to Eddy's XII Corps. When it became necessary to reduce the Harlange Pocket, the army commander gave Millikin the 90th ID, which was inserted on an extremely narrow front between the 35th and 26th IDs. This concentration of combat power, combined with an attack by the recently assigned 6th AD, allowed the III Corps commander to break the logjam on the southeastern face of Bastogne. Thus, in both defense and offense, the modular corps structure proved to be a vital contributor to tactical flexibility in the Bulge.

The Role of Airpower

Like a "fleet in being," the vast Allied air armada exercised a powerful influence over the campaign even when not directly engaged.[10] It set the terms of the German attack, forcing Hitler to choose the suboptimal location of the Ardennes based primarily on ability to conceal the strategic concentration in the Eifel region. The punishing blows on Germany's rail system throughout the autumn of 1944 significantly hampered the assembly of the attacking formations, delaying the attack some three to four weeks. This, in turn, reduced the period of poor visibility during which the attacking spearheads would be free from direct air attack. In the first phase of the campaign, things worked largely as the Germans had anticipated; both Bradley and Hodges were much distraught by the lack of air support. Nevertheless, a few interdiction attacks against rail facilities in the Rhineland provided an earnest of things to come. With only a brief period of clear weather, airpower contributed significantly to turning the tide of battle. The strikes against the 2nd Panzer Division at Celles were only the most visible manifestations of this contribution. Interdiction attacks against rail facilities and the Rhine River bridges continued apace, seriously hampering German supply efforts; C-47s in abundance dropped vital ammunition and medical supplies to the defenders of Bastogne; an entire airborne division was flown to France; and lifesaving medical evacuation sped wounded soldiers to England. The weather in the final phase of the campaign again generally precluded air operations. But one clear day on 22 January, combined with Eddy's flushing attack across the Sûre, provided a fully exploited opportunity for significant damage to the retreating German formations. Thus, although weather frequently impeded the effectiveness of air operations, as the German planners had hoped it would, Allied air superiority and a wide range of air capabilities exerted a far greater effect than they had anticipated and contributed materially to their defeat.

Summary

As in any campaign, there was no single ingredient of success or failure in the Bulge. The German offensive of 16 December 1944 was a desperate affair that flowed from desperate circumstances. The odds were against it, and the odds prevailed. Mistakes in execution on the German side and many fewer mistakes in execution on the American side helped make this so. Nevertheless, there were very anxious moments for the Americans as well. Eisenhower would not have placed two U.S. field armies under Montgomery's command had there not been. Victory owed a great deal to the grit of numerous small bands of GIs, led by courageous, competent leaders, who fought to hold their ground or take it back from a determined foe at the tiny road junctions, small villages, and bleak hilltops dotting the Ardennes. The high command was spotty; but Eisenhower, Montgomery, and Patton made up for the insufficiencies of Bradley and Hodges. The professional skill and determination of Gerow, Middleton, Ridgway, Millikin, Eddy, and Collins helped ensure that the sacrifices made by the men at the bottom were meaningfully linked to the strategic and operational designs crafted by the men at the top.

EPILOGUE

Leonard T. Gerow

Gerow continued in command of Fifteenth Army until October 1945, preparing newly arrived units for combat and assuming occupation responsibilities east of the Rhine as the American forces advanced into Germany.[11] Hodges recommended him for award of a second Oak Leaf Cluster to the DSM for his service as V Corps commander after D-Day, inclusive of the Bulge period.[12] The award was downgraded based on a policy established by Eisenhower to award no more than one DSM for service in the ETO; but when the policy was reversed after the war, the award was subsequently approved. Bradley variously rated Gerow as 4th out of 197 general officers assigned to his command and as 2nd of 9 lieutenant generals, noting in the latter appraisal that he was a "fine planner, particularly well qualified for long range planning."[13] In December 1945, Gerow was called upon to testify publicly before the Joint Congressional Pearl Harbor Commission. In the warm light of victory, he abandoned the evasiveness of his previous year's testimony before the Army Pearl Harbor Board and forthrightly declared, "If there was any responsibility to be attached to the War Department for any failure to send an inquiry to General Short, the responsibility must rest on the War Plans Division, and I accept that responsibility as Chief of War Plans."[14]

Before being called to testify in Washington, Gerow had been sent to Fort Leavenworth to become commandant of the newly redesignated Command and General Staff College (CGSC). It was a perfect match of man and mission. Gerow put his long experience as a staff officer together with his insights as a combat commander and offered his charges succinct and well-reasoned counsel. His remarks at the May 1946 graduation of the last general staff class to have been convened during the war were particularly apt. Regretting the paucity of attention the curriculum devoted to instruction in command, he noted that "the commander and his staff are one team and that neither staff nor command can be adequately presented as separate principles."[15] He specifically rejected the idea of a school solution and charged the graduates to be forward looking:

> I gather in talking to some students and listening in on your conferences
> that there is not universal agreement with some of our techniques. That
> is quite all right. We have merely tried to put across one way of doing
> the job, based on thorough study by the instructional staff of the methods and techniques employed in all Theaters. There are many ways of

winning battles and any officer who leaves this School with the idea it can be done by one method only has wasted his time. Follow adopted procedures as a general rule but do not hesitate to abandon them when conditions warrant. Be flexible in your thinking. Study the trends of future warfare. Adapt your thinking to the possible weapons and thinking of the next war, and not to those you used in the last one.[16]

And he provided some remarkably unprejudiced observations about air and ground operations: "Ground Forces will seldom fight in future wars without the assistance of the Air. Air Forces will at time[s] fight alone but before they can engage in combat, the Ground must secure and protect bases."[17] To help rectify the deficiency in command instruction, Gerow enlisted the services of fellow Virginian Douglas Southall Freeman as a guest lecturer, a useful addition to the curriculum that continued for at least five years.[18]

His duties were not limited to the college. In November 1945 he was appointed to chair the board established to design the army's postwar education system.[19] The resulting "Gerow Report," issued in February 1946, was a remarkably comprehensive and forward-looking blueprint. It proposed the educational establishment that served the army well throughout the Cold War. Reflecting awareness that a unified department of defense would soon be created, it also called for an "Armed Forces College" for the joint education of officers from all services at roughly the same level as the Army War College.[20] And, perhaps most far-reaching, it called for establishment of a "National Security University" that would comprise separate colleges for the study of war, diplomacy, industrial mobilization, administration, and intelligence. Not all these proposals were implemented. But the creation of the National Defense University as an outgrowth of the Goldwater-Nichols Defense Reform Act of 1986 demonstrates just how prescient was Gerow's vision of the nation's requirements for military education.

Gerow left Fort Leavenworth to assume command of the Second Army in 1948 and retired to his hometown of Petersburg, Virginia, on 31 July 1950.[21] In retirement, he maintained his close association with Eisenhower, serving as the chair of Ike's Virginia election campaign in 1952, as one of three grand marshals for the first inaugural parade, and as chair of the Virginia reelection campaign in 1956.[22] Attending a private dinner with Winston Churchill that Eisenhower hosted at the White House was another benefit derived from his close friendship with the president. Gerow was promoted to four-star rank in 1954, along with ten other lieutenant generals who had commanded field armies or similar formations in World War II.[23] He died at Fort Lee, Virginia, on 12 October 1972.[24]

Troy H. Middleton

Middleton remained in command of VIII Corps until shortly after V-E Day. Patton recommended him for another award of the DSM for his actions in the Bulge, calling his tactics "masterful" and his decision to hold Bastogne "the turning point of this offensive."[25] But because Middleton had received a previous DSM in the theater, it was downgraded to a Legion of Merit.[26] Meanwhile, he led VIII Corps through the Rhineland to the capture of Coblenz, across the Rhine at the Lorelei, and then across the Fulda River to the Czech border.[27] With his fighting done, he requested release from active service.[28] Bradley rated him 9th of 197 in the special general officer appraisal.[29] Eisenhower ranked him fourth among all corps commanders in the ETO for promotion to lieutenant general, noting that during the Ardennes offensive "he calmly retained control of his retiring forces and so conducted his operations as to impede and limit the extent of the German advance."[30] He also told Marshall he would have ranked him higher had Middleton not had a break in service. [31] Middleton was promoted in June, but the third star was rather immaterial.[32] Marshall told him he could remain in command of VIII Corps, which was being prepared for transfer to the Pacific theater; but the chief doubted the corps would again see combat.[33] Middleton chose to return to Louisiana State University, reverting to retired status in August.[34] As he was retired when the policy to allow no more than one DSM for service in the ETO was changed, the Legion of Merit for his role in saving Bastogne was never upgraded, a lapse constituting a patent injustice.

In Baton Rouge, Middleton was soon caught up in the postwar expansion of higher education in the era of the GI Bill, and he became involved in the important business of funding campus expansion to handle the steadily mounting enrollment.[35] He also performed the typical duties of an army elder statesman, offering advice to the authorities at West Point on curriculum design and serving on the board of investigation after the infamous cheating scandal of 1951.[36] His stature steadily grew in the eyes of the university's board of supervisors, who elected him president in late 1951.[37] Middleton aggressively expanded LSU's curriculum offerings and physical plant and was awarded an honorary doctor of law degree when he reverted to emeritus status in 1962.[38] He died in Baton Rouge on 9 October 1976.[39] Eleven years earlier, his biographer had traveled to Gettysburg to interview Eisenhower. In the course of the ensuing discussion, Ike noted that "Troy Middleton never got stampeded."[40] It would have made a fitting epitaph.

But as distinguished as it was, Middleton's career also raises an intriguing question. What would have happened if he had taken Eisenhower's advice in 1937 and not retired from the army? Any answer is speculative; but within the bounds of reasonableness, an alternative scenario might be advanced. We must start from the knowledge that Middleton, Hodges, and Patton were among the very few senior commanders in World War II to have commanded regiments or equivalent formations in World War I. Marshall was well aware of this and also aware that, perhaps next to himself, Middleton was the most highly regarded infantryman of the interwar era. Had he not retired, he almost assuredly would have commanded a larger formation than a corps. One can make a good argument that Middleton would have been a leading candidate, if not *the* leading candidate, to command First Army in the Normandy invasion. He had far better credentials than Bradley and far more balance than Patton. Had he done so, he would almost assuredly have risen to command of 12th Army Group, with Bradley perhaps stepping in to command First Army. And a command triumvirate under Eisenhower of Middleton as army group commander with Patton and Bradley as his principal lieutenants inspires much more confidence than the trio of Bradley, Patton, and Hodges. It is difficult, for example, to envision Middleton allowing the First Army staff to neglect the challenges of fighting in the bocage prior to the Normandy invasion or becoming nervous about closing the trap on the German Seventh Panzer Army at Falaise. There are dangers in pushing this line of thinking too far. But pausing to consider it does raise a question that will confront military professionals for as long as their particular expertise is necessary to society: "What will the consequences be if I leave the service?" This question is viewed most often in terms of the fate of the individual asking it, but Middleton's career argues that it might have more wide-ranging ramifications as well.

Matthew B. Ridgway

Ridgway continued in command of XVIII (Airborne) Corps until the end of the war.[41] On 28 January, the corps attacked across eastern Belgium and into the Rhineland, but it was soon pulled out of First Army for the airborne drop in support of Monty's crossing of the Rhine. It then went back to Hodges for the encirclement of the Ruhr. Finally, Eisenhower, desiring to put some hurry-up into Montgomery's drive to the Baltic, reattached XVIII (Airborne) Corps to 21st Army Group, this time in a ground role. The corps covered over 300 miles in 9 days, linking up with the Russians at Wismar. It then redeployed to the United States for further transfer to the Pacific. But Ridgway and a small advance party were the only ones who made it to Tokyo, arriving in the immediate aftermath of the Japanese surrender.[42] Bradley ranked him 8th of 197, one slot ahead of Middleton, in the postwar special rating.[43] When in late May Marshall asked Eisenhower for a second round of recommendations of corps commanders for promotion to lieutenant general, Eisenhower replied that his top pick was Ridgway, a man who had "never undertaken a job that he has not performed in a soldierly and even brilliant way" and who was "definitely a fighting leader."[44] Marshall acted on this recommendation quickly, awarding Ridgway his third star before the end of June.[45] Based on the recommendation of Hodges and others, he received an Oak Leaf Cluster to his DSM for his command of XVIII (Airborne) Corps from the Bulge to V-E Day.[46]

Over the next five years, Ridgway served in a number of sensitive and significant appointments, including Deputy Supreme Allied Commander, Mediterranean Theater; Chairman of the United Nations Military Staff Committee; Commander-in-Chief, Caribbean Command; and Deputy Chief of Staff for Operations on the Army Staff.[47] In the last position, he found himself working for his friend and West Point classmate J. Lawton Collins, who had been appointed chief of staff in August 1949, a month before Ridgway's arrival. Given Ridgway's intensely competitive nature, this pairing may have had its awkward moments. But Ridgway had the good sense and decorum to set aside whatever personal disappointment he may have felt. When the news that Lieutenant General Walton H. Walker had been killed in a jeep accident reached Washington on the evening of 22 December 1950, Ridgway was immediately selected as the new Eighth Army commander and dispatched forthwith to Korea. As he left, Collins graciously wrote, "One of the penalties of great ability is that it inexorably draws to itself great responsibilities."[48]

Collins was right—the man and the moment were made for each other.[49] Eighth Army was reeling from punishing attacks inflicted by the Chinese People's Army, which had come into the war after MacArthur's imprudent advance to the Yalu River. The combination of a frigid winter, a series of surprise assaults by an aggressive enemy, virtual collapse of the Republic of Korea's fledgling army, and the obvious inability to mount another amphibious operation on the scale of the Inchon invasion cast a pall of doom over the American soldiers fighting on the forlorn peninsula. Ridgway quickly turned things around. He inspected the front lines by every conveyance at his disposal and frequently on foot. He stressed the time-tested fundamentals of maintaining contact with the enemy, taking the high ground, tying in the flanks, counterattacking when opportunity beckoned, and using firepower and maneuver to kill the enemy and save friendly lives. He railed at his subordinates when he found them violating these precepts and artfully shuffled out or closely supervised those who responded with insufficient alacrity.

Although forced to withdraw behind the Han River and surrender Seoul, he stabilized the Eighth Army about fifteen miles to the south. After a transition period of ever-more-powerful patrols to the north and a desperate defensive stand, he took the offensive in late March 1951. Ridgway had, through the raw power of a driving personality and consummate professionalism, resurrected the Eighth Army and prevented the real possibility of either a calamitous defeat or an American resort to nuclear weapons.[50]

When President Harry S. Truman relieved General Douglas MacArthur as the Far East commander in April 1951, Ridgway was named as his replacement. He remained in that capacity for a year and was then transferred to Paris, where he became Supreme Allied Commander, Europe. One of the more interesting aspects of this assignment was having Montgomery serve as his deputy. In August 1953, he was appointed army chief of staff. During Ridgway's tenure as the army's professional head, he was instrumental in keeping America out of a war to support the French in Indochina, a contribution to the weal of the Republic arguably as great as his leadership in Korea.[51] He also crossed swords directly with the secretary of defense, Charles E. Wilson, and indirectly with the president over the Eisenhower administration's "New Look" strategy, which significantly reduced conventional forces in favor of nuclear deterrence on a massive scale. Ridgway struggled to articulate his strongly held objections to this strategy in a responsible manner, but his stance of loyal opposition within the administration sorely tested the president's patience.[52] As a result, Eisenhower declined to appoint him for a second two-year period. He retired in August 1955.

Ridgway moved to Pittsburgh and served for five years as director of the Mellon Industrial Research Institute. During the Vietnam War, he sought to influence the Johnson administration to limit the American involvement commensurate with his view of the national interest.[53] He died in Fox Chapel, Pennsylvania, on 26 July 1993.[54]

John Millikin

Millikin continued in command of III Corps until 17 March 1945. Patton recommended him for an Oak Leaf Cluster to the DSM for his role in the Bulge, noting that he had "inflicted great losses upon the enemy and succeeded in driving through their defenses to relieve the besieged forces defending the surrounded city of Bastogne" and offering similarly glowing comments in two efficiency reports.[55] But when Bradley told the Third Army commander in mid-February that he had to give up a corps to Hodges, Patton could not bear to part with Middleton, whose VIII Corps was on

First Army's south flank, so Millikin's III Corps was detached instead.[56] Hodges and Millikin did not mesh well from the beginning.[57] Hodges wanted an infantry regiment from Louis Craig's 9th ID attached to Leonard's 9th AD; Millikin instead attached a regiment from a different division. Hodges wanted the 1st ID sent against Bonn; but his intent in this regard was not made clear to Millikin, with the result that the corps order for the 1st ID, rather than the 9th ID, to seize Bonn was given too late to suit Hodges. The relationship began to deteriorate rapidly after 7 March, when Hoge's CCB, 9th AD, seized the partially demolished Ludendorff Bridge spanning the Rhine at Remagen.

Both First Army and III Corps had been desirous of seizing a Rhine bridge intact, even though all concerned realized it was a long shot.[58] Nevertheless, Millikin had his eyes set specifically on Remagen. As the corps moved rapidly toward the river on 6 and 7 March, he requested the bridge not be bombed, directed the artillery to use nothing but air-bursting shells against it, and told Leonard to take it intact if he could. Thanks to command disorganization on the German side and detonating wires that may have been damaged by American artillery, the bridge was still standing when Hoge's lead elements reached its western approaches.[59] Quick action by junior officers produced its capture. SHAEF directed expansion of the bridgehead sufficiently to be held by five divisions, but no further. A number of problems ensued. The Germans attacked the bridge with Luftwaffe strikes, V-2s launched from Holland, SS frogmen, and heavy concentrations from artillery on the east bank. The 11th Panzer Division also launched stiff counterattacks. Nevertheless, within twenty-four hours, some 8,000 troops were across the bridge; and within another day, the maneuver elements of two divisions were on the east bank. Millikin then ordered a series of phased advances, which by 16 March cut the critical Cologne-Frankfurt Autobahn.[60]

But Hodges was not happy. He complained about disorganization on both the near and far banks and blamed it on Millikin.[61] In doing so, he neglected to take into account the difficulties of constantly shifting German threats on the east side; the severely restricted road network leading to Remagen on the west side; and, perhaps most significantly, the fact that rear area traffic control was predominantly a field army function, rather than a corps responsibility.[62] Most of all, he and the rest of the First Army staff wished ardently that the accident of Remagen had happened in Collins's sector, rather than in Millikin's.[63] Hodges finally lost patience with Millikin and relieved him of command. There is some evidence that Millikin was not entirely blameless—the 9th ID chief of staff complained pointedly to Hodges's aide on 11 March that Millikin had not been forward frequently enough to keep the confusion on the east bank under control.[64] Nevertheless, one cannot avoid the conclusion that he was relieved largely because he was an outsider to the First Army "family" who found himself in the wrong place at the wrong time.[65]

Millikin took it like a man. He let it be known that if he could not command a corps he was more than willing to command a division. Thus, in mid-April, he was given command of the 13th AD, ironically under Hodges's First Army.[66] Later transferred to Patton's Third Army, he handled the division with aggressiveness and dash on the drive across Bavaria to the Austrian border.[67] In so doing, he became the only corps commander in the war who had been relieved for cause and subsequently granted a combat command.

Following the war, he was posted to Fort Sill, Oklahoma, where he served variously as commander and (after reverting to the rank of brigadier general) deputy commander of the Field Artillery Center. There are two ironic twists to the end of this tale. While at Fort Sill, Millikin was awarded the Silver Star for inspirational leadership in crossing the Ludendorff Bridge under fire, the recommendation having been submitted by Patton.[68] And after the Oak Leaf Cluster to the DSM for III Corps' actions in the Bulge had been twice turned down by Eisenhower, once in his capacity as European theater commander and again in his office as army chief of staff, it was finally approved when the secretary of war, Robert P. Patterson, overrode Eisenhower's objections.[69] Millikin retired from the service in 1948 and died in Washington, D.C., on 6 November 1970.[70]

Manton S. Eddy

Eddy remained in command of XII Corps until 19 April 1945. Patton's efficiency report for the period ending 31 December 1944 observed that "General Eddy has had very extensive combat experience and has been invariably successful. His tactical concepts are sound and well executed. He is better in offensive operations than defensive operations and is an outstanding soldier."[71] After the Bulge, XII Corps crossed the Sauer, seized Bitburg, and cleared Trier.[72] Shortly thereafter, Patton's competitiveness again kicked in. He and Eddy devised a scheme to cross the Rhine prior to Montgomery's Operation Varsity, which was scheduled for 24 March. Their plan called for XII Corps to make a series of feints along the west bank, north of Oppenheim. On 21 March, when Eddy met Patton to brief him on the corps' progress, the Third Army commander greeted him as "the Prince of the Rhine" and bade him conquer his fiefdom.[73] And so he did. At Oppenheim, Eddy and his trusted lieutenant, "Red" Irwin, pushed the 5th ID across the river on the night of 22/23 March, catching the German defenders on the east bank largely by surprise and giving Patton and Bradley the bragging rights they so deeply coveted. Eddy then found himself involved in Patton's ill-considered and abortive attack on the Hammelburg prison camp.[74] The army commander directed a raid to free American prisoners, among whom was strongly suspected to be his son-in-law. Eddy and William Hoge, now commander of the 4th AD, attempted to dissuade him, to no avail. Eddy stipulated that the assault be made by a small task force numbering about 300, rather than a full armored combat command as Patton wanted. The raiding party reached the prison and temporarily liberated the prisoners but could not fight its way back to friendly lines. The fault lies primarily with Patton for demanding that the raid be conducted, but Eddy assumes a portion of the blame for sending too small a force.

On 17 April, Eddy began experiencing symptoms of dangerously high blood pressure.[75] Two days later, when it had failed to subside, Patton directed his relief for medical reasons and ordered him home. He was then hospitalized for several months and took an extended leave. Ignoring his own policy of not granting two DSMs for service in the ETO, Eisenhower recommended Eddy for an Oak Leaf Cluster to the first medal; Marshall approved the award and presented it in a small, personal ceremony in his office.[76] Eddy's blood pressure subsided sufficiently to allow him to return to duty in early 1946. He briefly commanded the 3rd Service Command and served as deputy commander, Second Army, both headquartered in Baltimore, before becoming the army's chief of information in July 1947.[77] He apparently drew the assignment based on the cordial and constructive working relations he had established with the press during the war.[78] In a time of rapid demobilization, it was a particularly important billet; but Eddy, always too active to be a good desk man, was never really at ease in Washington. Thus, he was both relieved and gratified when six months later he was posted to succeed Gerow as commandant, CGSC, with promotion to lieutenant general.

Eddy used his bully pulpit to impart the wisdom gained from his active soldiering. He set an offensive problem that was based on 9th ID operations in Tunisia and gave a lecture on the capture of Nancy.[79] In the latter, he took particular pains to emphasize the role of intangibles: the character of one's immediate superior who "can worry you to death, or can be most helpful in his attitudes and suggestions" and the capabilities and limitations of one's subordinates. All these, Eddy said, could come to be known only through frequent, personal contact. Like Gerow, Eddy was also charged with chairing a board on army education.[80] Its chief contribution was the recommendation that the Army War College be reestablished, which was implemented in 1950. After two years at Leavenworth, Eddy was ordered to Germany to command the just-activated U.S. Seventh Army.[81] He served there for just under three years, instilling high standards of training and readiness that became a hallmark of that formation throughout the Cold War. Eddy retired on 31 March 1953 and moved to his wife's hometown of Columbus, Georgia. He died at Fort Benning on 10 April 1962.[82]

J. Lawton Collins

Collins continued in command of VII Corps until V-E Day, making him the only corps commander to serve in that capacity throughout the entire campaign in Northwest Europe. On 23 February, the corps attacked across the Roer, closing on the Rhine and capturing Bonn on 8 March.[83] It then encircled the Ruhr, regrouped, and drove across the Weser. On 26 April, it joined hands with the Red Army on the Elbe. Bradley ranked Collins 7th out of 197, one ahead of Ridgway, in the special general's rating and noted, "His outstanding quality is aggressiveness."[84] Eisenhower formally recommended him for promotion to lieutenant general on 11 April with the cachet, "He is a master of tactics and is a dynamic leader."[85] Collins was promoted five days later.[86]

After the war, Collins was assigned as chief of staff, Army Ground Forces; but his actual duties were serving as Marshall's point man for unification of the armed services.[87] He was then groomed by Eisenhower, now army chief of staff, who appointed him chief of army information, then deputy chief of staff, a position that later became vice chief of staff. Collins tried as hard as he dared to talk Ike out of giving him the public affairs position but later realized that the experience gained in the office was invaluable. His education continued unabated in his next position as he argued unsuccessfully with Congress for the establishment of universal military training. Thus, when Bradley, who served as army chief of staff from February 1948 to August 1949, stepped up to become the first chairman of the Joint Chiefs of Staff, Collins was well prepared to become the army's chief.

He did so in turbulent times.[88] He was directly involved in legislation related to the statutory powers of his own office and the racial integration of the armed services. But from June 1950 forward, his most pressing challenge was the Korean War. As the Joint Chiefs of Staff executive agent for that war, he was the principal liaison between MacArthur and the Department of Defense. Thus, he was called upon to pass judgment on MacArthur's bold but risky amphibious attack on Inchon, the authorization for MacArthur to attack north of the 38th Parallel, and ultimately MacArthur's fitness to continue in command. These were all weighty matters, and the nation was fortunate that Eisenhower had groomed Collins, rather than Ridgway, as his successor (one removed from Bradley) as army chief of staff. For this arrangement allowed Collins to manage the army's participation in the Korean War from Washington, where his well-developed political sensitivities and adroit bureaucratic skills were put effectively to work, while Ridgway resuscitated the Eighth Army in Korea and staved off disaster. Given that both men were fine commanders *and* competent administrators, it might have worked out the other way as well; but one can never be sure.

Collins left the chief's office in August 1953 and became the president's representative to NATO.[89] With the military and political situation in Indochina deteriorating after the French defeat at Dien Bien Phu, Eisenhower sent Collins to Vietnam in November 1954 as his special representative, with the rank of ambassador. Collins's mission was to help ensure the viability of a noncommunist South Vietnam, though American policy at the time specified that this be done by supporting the regime of Premier Ngo Dinh Diem. Over time, Collins developed grave concerns about Diem's ability to govern but was unable to alter the Eisenhower administration's policy of supporting him and returned to the United States in May 1955. Despite his special representative's manifest frustration, Eisenhower judged that Collins had "performed duties of the greatest difficulty and delicacy, and did so effectively and expeditiously."[90]

Collins retired from the army on 31 March 1956, but he remained unofficially active in military affairs.[91] Men become widely respected for their words as well as for their deeds. Collins, a prolific reader and clear thinker for his entire adult life, was a man of well-chosen words. In 1964, he gave an address at Utah Beach to commemorate the twentieth anniversary of D-Day. His remarks had all the eloquence and inspiration of President Ronald Reagan's "The Boys of Pointe du Hoc" speech two decades later:

> Before we came in June of 1944, this lovely countryside lay peaceful and relatively untouched by the war. Cattle grazed placidly, the orchards wore their mantles of blossoms in quiet beauty, and farmers stolidly plowed their fields as their fathers did before them. But beneath this outward show of complacency, these freedom-loving Normans seethed inwardly under the yoke of Nazi occupation. They longed for freedom, biding their time till help could come from overseas. . . . So the people of Normandy stoically accepted the seemingly endless bombing of their towns, the inescapable slaughter of their fine cattle by artillery fire, the churning up of freshly planted fields by tanks and skirmishing men. And their Free-French Resistance groups succored our widely scattered paratroopers, helped destroy enemy communications, and eagerly gave

information to our soldiers. . . . Did these men die in vain? Was all the toil and sacrifice of our soldiers, sailors and airmen . . . to no avail? . . . . We have our answer today as we see lovely Normandy, with the scars of war removed, and in fact all of la Belle France once again strong, confident and at peace with a Germany that we hope has renounced for all time the trappings of Prussian and Nazi aggression.[92]

Clearly, Collins saw military service not simply as a profession to be mastered but as a calling to help humanity. He died in Washington, D.C., on 12 September 1987.[93]

A FINAL THOUGHT

A comparison of how these six men performed in the Bulge with what happened in their subsequent careers reveals both congruities and incongruities. Collins and Ridgway were outstanding in the Bulge, were recognized by their superiors as having been so, and were advanced to the very upper reaches of the army, where their considerable talents were fully exploited. Middleton was similarly outstanding in the Bulge but stuck to his decision to return to civilian life as soon as hostilities ceased. His capacity for greater service was, however, recognized by the authorities at Louisiana State University, who elected him university president. Eddy never had the opportunity to demonstrate his full capacity in the Bulge, and his career was certainly affected by his ill health; nevertheless, he rose to positions of significant responsibility commensurate with his ability. Gerow and Millikin are outliers, though of slightly different sorts. Gerow was clearly the right man to serve as the first postwar commandant at CGSC and to lay down the design for the army's postwar education system, and the subsequent posting as commander of Second Army was entirely appropriate. But one cannot avoid the impression that the honorific fourth star awarded in retirement was largely a product of his close relationship with Eisenhower. After Millikin's unexpectedly strong performance in the Bulge, he deserved much better than he received. Had he remained assigned to Patton's Third Army, it is very unlikely that he would have been relieved, and it is possible that another promotion might have come his way. Instead, he retired quietly from the service.

The lives and fortunes of Gerow, Middleton, Ridgway, Millikin, Eddy, and Collins thus leave us with an important truth. Although personal connections and the accidents of timing can indeed affect an officer's career, the underlying ingredient of successful command is a harmonious blend of intelligence, character, and energy.

Gerow, Commanding General, Fifteenth Army, strolling down a hallway with Eisenhower at his headquarters in Dinant, France, 3 March 1945. Gerow's easy familiarity with Ike is evident in his position on the SHAEF commander's right, which is customarily the place of the senior officer. Courtesy Dwight D. Eisenhower Library.

Gerow, Commanding General, Second Army, receiving from President Eisenhower on 3 June 1954 a torch to be lighted at the tenth D-Day anniversary celebration in Normandy. Eddy, who would also participate in the ceremony, looks on. Associated Press.

Middleton, on the occasion of being advanced to the grade of lieutenant general on the retired list, in 1948. At this time, he was serving as comptroller of Louisiana State University. He became the university's president in 1951. National Personnel Records Center.

Ridgway, commanding American and United Nations forces in the Far East after President Harry S. Truman's relief of General Douglas MacArthur in April 1951. The steel helmet, web gear, and accoutrements were intended to convey Ridgway's command persona. National Personnel Records Center.

Millikin, Commanding General, 13th Armored Division, ca. summer 1945. Millikin, relieved at the Remagen bridgehead by General Courtney H. Hodges under questionable circumstances, was the only corps commander in World War II to have been removed for cause and granted a subsequent combat command. Courtesy Millikin family.

Millikin, Commanding General, U.S. Army Field Artillery Center, Fort Sill, Oklahoma, ca. 1945/1946, being congratulated by General Jacob L. Devers, Commanding General, Army Ground Forces, upon receipt of the Silver Star for inspirational leadership at the Remagen bridgehead. The award, recommended by Patton, perhaps represented some modest vindication for Millikin as a corps commander. Courtesy Millikin family.

On 21 March 1945, Patton hailed Eddy as "the Prince of the Rhine" and bade him conquer his fiefdom. Within two days, XII Corps had crossed the Rhine. On the third day, Patton decorated Eddy for having done so. Bad Kreuznach, Germany, 24 March 1945. National Archives.

Eddy posing in his office in Heidelberg, Germany, as the first Commanding General, U.S. Army, Europe, ca. 1951. National Personnel Records Center.

Collins's official photo as
Chief of Staff, U.S. Army, ca.
1949. National Personnel
Records Center.

NOTES

Preface

1. Eric Larrabee, *Commander-in-Chief: Franklin Delano Roosevelt, His Lieutenants, and Their War* (New York: Harper and Row, 1987), 6.

2. Henry Gerard Phillips, *The Making of a Professional: Manton S. Eddy, USA* (Westport, Conn.: Greenwood, 2000).

3. David W. Hogan, Jr., *A Command Post at War: First Army Headquarters in Europe, 1943–1945* (Washington, D.C.: USACMH, 2000).

1. Introduction

1. The account of Task Force Rose on 18 December 1944 is based on Hugh M. Cole, *The Ardennes: Battle of the Bulge* (Washington, D.C.: OCMH, 1965), 295–96; and Walter E. Reichelt, *Phantom Nine: The 9th Armored (Remagen) Division, 1942–1945* (Austin: Presidial Press, 1987), 131–34.

2. The U.S. Army official designation of the campaign is "Ardennes-Alsace," because it incorporates the American-French response to the German Nordwind offensive of January 1945 in southern France as well as the fighting in the Ardennes. This study, however, is limited to the fighting in the Ardennes. The British XXX Corps, commanded by Lieutenant General Brian Horrocks, also participated in the campaign. But its participation, while important, did not equal in magnitude that of any of the six American corps and is beyond the scope of this study.

3. Gerow's V Corps and Middleton's VIII Corps were both attacked on 16 December. For reasons that will become apparent as the story unfolds, V Corps will be treated first. Ridgway's XVIII (Airborne) Corps, Millikin's III Corps, Eddy's XII Corps, and Collins's VII Corps were committed on 19, 20, 21, and 23 December, respectively.

4. Close air support is that which takes place in such proximity to friendly troops that intimate coordination is required between the air and ground units involved. Interdiction entails halting or impeding the movement of enemy troops, equipment, and supplies to the battlefield. The tactical air commands were equipped mainly with the P-47, whose primary role was close air support but which could also be used in an interdiction role at limited ranges. Deeper interdiction was performed by the medium bombers assigned to the Ninth Air Force and by medium and heavy bombers of the strategic air forces based in England.

5. The two most noteworthy published accounts of air operations in the Ardennes are David G. Rempel's chapter, "Battle of the Bulge," in Wesley Frank Craven and James Lea Cate, eds., *Europe: Argument to V-E Day, January 1944 to May 1945*, vol. 3 in *The Army Air Forces in World War II* (Washington, D.C.: OAFH, 1983), 672–711; and Danny S. Parker, *To Win the Winter Sky: The Air War over the Ardennes, 1944–1945* (Conshohocken, Pa.: Combined Books, 1994). Each is filled with statistics of sorties flown and estimates of ground damage caused, but

neither discusses in detail the tactical or operational effects of these air missions. Patrick Delaforce's very readable account, *The Battle of the Bulge: Hitler's Final Gamble* (Harlow, England: Pearson Education, 2004), breaks new ground by devoting three of the thirty-seven chapters to the air war. Unfortunately, this otherwise quite useful and nicely illustrated study contains no documentation.

6. Gerald Astor, *A Blood-Dimmed Tide: The Battle of the Bulge by the Men Who Fought It* (New York: Donald I. Fine, 1992); Roscoe C. Blunt, Jr., *Inside the Battle of the Bulge: A Private Comes of Age* (Westport, Conn.: Praeger, 1994); William C. Cavanagh, *Krinkelt-Rocherath: The Battle for the Twin Villages* (Norwell, Mass.: Christopher Publishing House, 1986); Janice Holt Giles, *The Damned Engineers*, 2nd ed. (Washington, D.C.: Office of the Chief of Engineers, 1985); S. L. A. Marshall, *Bastogne: The Story of the First Eight Days in Which the 101st Airborne Division Was Closed within the Ring of German Forces* (Washington, D.C.: Infantry Journal Press, 1946); George W. Neill, *Infantry Soldier: Holding the Line at the Battle of the Bulge* (Norman: University of Oklahoma Press, 2000); Robert F. Phillips, *To Save Bastogne* (New York: Stein and Day, 1983); Michael Frank Reynolds, *The Devil's Adjutant: Jochen Peiper, Panzer Leader* (New York: Sarpedon, 1995); Stephen M. Rusiecki, *The Key to the Bulge: The Battle for Losheimergraben* (Westport, Conn.: Praeger, 1996).

7. David Irving, *The War between the Generals* (New York: Congdon and Lattes, 1981); David Eisenhower, *Eisenhower: At War, 1943–1945* (London: Collins, 1986); Nigel Hamilton, *Monty: Final Years of the Field Marshal, 1944–1976* (New York: McGraw-Hill, 1987); Carlo D'Este, *Patton: A Genius for War* (New York: Harper Collins, 1995); Omar Bradley and Clay Blair, *A General's Life: An Autobiography by General of the Army Omar N. Bradley and Clay Blair* (New York: Simon and Schuster, 1983).

8. Cole, *Ardennes*; Trevor N. Dupuy, David L. Bongard, and Richard C. Anderson, Jr., *Hitler's Last Gamble: The Battle of the Bulge, December 1944–January 1945* (New York: Harper Collins, 1994); John S. D. Eisenhower, *The Bitter Woods: The Dramatic Story, Told at All Echelons—from Supreme Commander to Squad Leader—of the Crisis That Shook the Western Coalition: Hitler's Surprise Ardennes Offensive* (New York: G. P. Putnam's, 1969; New York: Da Capo Press, 1995); George Forty, *The Reich's Last Gamble: The Ardennes Offensive, December 1944* (London: Cassell, 2000); Charles B. MacDonald, *A Time for Trumpets: The Untold Story of the Battle of the Bulge* (New York: William Morrow, 1985); Robert Merriam, *Dark December: The Full Account of the Battle of the Bulge* (New York: Ziff-Davis, 1947); John Toland, *Battle: The Story of the Bulge* (New York: Random House, 1959; Lincoln: University of Nebraska Press, 1999).

9. J. D. Morelock, *Generals of the Ardennes: American Leadership in the Battle of the Bulge* (Washington, D.C.: NDU Press, 1994).

10. Russell F. Weigley, *Eisenhower's Lieutenants: The Campaigns in France and Germany, 1944–1945* (Bloomington: Indiana University Press, 1981).

11. Michael Howard, "Leadership in the British Army in the Second World War: Some Personal Observations," in *Leadership and Command: The Anglo-American Military Experience since 1861*, ed. G. D. Sheffield (London: Brassey's, 1997), 120.

12. Charles R. Cawthon, *Other Men's Clay: A Remembrance of the World War II Infantry* (Niwot: University Press of Colorado, 1990), 78.

13. John W. Leonard, Jr., and George Ruhlen, "John W. Leonard, '15: A Star in the Class the Stars Fell On," *Assembly* 61 (March/April 2003): 48.

14. Stephen Ambrose, *Citizen Soldiers: The U.S. Army from the Normandy Beaches to the Bulge to the Surrender of Germany, June 7, 1944–May 7, 1945* (New York: Simon and Schuster, 1997), 218.

15. This was not always so. Before World War I, the corps had been a fixed organization. However, the early European experience of "wastage suffered by divisions in the line" led to the practice of withdrawing divisions for rest, refitting, and recuperation and inserting new divisions into the line. Thus, "a division could not remain in the same army, much less the same corps." This organizational scheme was "forced on the American Expeditionary Forces" and retained after the war. School of the Line, General Service Schools, *General Tactical Functions of Larger Units* (Fort Leavenworth, Kans.: General Service Schools Press, 1922), 19–20.

16. War Department, *Field Service Regulations: Larger Units* (Washington, D.C.: Government Printing Office, 1942), 56–57.

17. Matthew B. Ridgway, as told to Harold H. Martin, *Soldier: The Memoirs of Matthew B. Ridgway* (New York: Harper and Brothers, 1956), 18.

18. Determining such criteria was one of the most vexing methodological problems in writing this book. My first instinct was to survey the classical theorists on the subject of command and to synthesize a "command ideal" from this survey. But I could not demonstrate that such a synthesis would have any applicability to the subjects of the study. Several other approaches were contemplated with equally unsatisfactory results. Although one can argue that the method adopted is clearly imperfect, it does have the singular advantage that all six protagonists can be reasonably expected to have been familiar with the general canons of what was taught about command in the army school system.

19. This periodization of the Bulge is distinct from the norm, which tends either to conclude the story on or about 26 December 1944 when the 4th Armored Division broke through to the 82nd Airborne Division at Bastogne, or to divide it into two periods, a period of German initiative from 16 to 26 December and a period of American initiative from 27 December to 31 January. The more complex reality reflects a period of contested initiative in the middle, though one can legitimately argue about precisely where the dividing points should be.

20. J. Lawton Collins, *Lightning Joe: An Autobiography* (Baton Rouge: Louisiana State University Press, 1979; Novato, Calif.: Presidio Press, 1994); and Ridgway, *Soldier*.

21. Clay Blair, *Ridgway's Paratroopers: The American Airborne in World War II* (New York: Doubleday, 1985).

22. Frank James Price, *Troy H. Middleton: A Biography* (Baton Rouge: Louisiana State University Press, 1974).

23. Phillips, *Making of a Professional.*

24. "Gen. John Millikin: Commander of Cavalry Units, 82," *Washington Post,* 7 Nov. 1970, B-9; and R. Manning Ancell with Christine M. Miller, *The Biographical Dictionary of World War II Generals and Flag Officers: The U.S. Armed Forces* (Westport, Conn.: Greenwood, 1996), 228–29.

2. Toward an American Philosophy of Command

1. Joseph L. Fant III and Robert Ashley, eds., *Faulkner at West Point* (New York: Random House, 1964), 75. Faulkner's observation was made in response to a cadet's question concerning the extent to which political and military leaders were responsible for the horrors of war.

2. War Department, *Field Service Regulations, United States Army, 1923* (Washington, D.C.: Government Printing Office, 1924), 4.

3. For an intelligent and well-documented analysis of this transformation, see David E. Johnson, *Fast Tanks and Heavy Bombers: Innovation in the U.S. Army, 1917–1945* (Ithaca, N.Y.: Cornell University Press, 1998).

4. What follows is based on Timothy K. Nenninger, *The Leavenworth Schools and the Old Army: Education, Professionalism, and the Officer Corps of the United States Army, 1881–1918* (Westport, Conn.: Greenwood, 1978), 53–133.

5. What follows is based on Edward M. Coffman, "The American Military Generation Gap in World War I: The Leavenworth Clique and the AEF," in *Command and Commanders in Modern Warfare: Proceedings of the Second Military History Symposium, U.S. Air Force Academy, 2–3 May 1968*, ed. William Geffen (USAF, December 1969), 39–48.

6. The General Staff College was renamed the Command and General Staff School in 1923 (see below). The War Department order is cited in Harry P. Ball, *Of Responsible Command: A History of the U.S. Army War College* (Carlisle Barracks, Pa.: Alumni Association of USAWC, 1983), 171.

7. What follows is based on a War Department Board of Officers Report of 1922 and Army Regulations 350-5, cited in CGSS, *Instructional Circular No. 1, Series 1932–1933* (Fort Leavenworth, Kans.: CGSS Press, 1932), 7–8.

8. The remainder of this paragraph is from Timothy K. Nenninger, "Leavenworth and Its Critics: The U.S. Army Command and General Staff School, 1920–1940," *Journal of Military History* 58 (April 1994): 201.

9. This is slightly higher than the average for all World War II corps commanders of roughly 2.7 years. Thirty-three of the thirty-four officers who commanded corps during the war attended Leavenworth, James A. Van Fleet being the sole exception. Raymond S. McLain attended a special three-month National Guard course. The reason for the relatively high average is that fourteen of these officers served on the faculty. The author's calculations are derived from data in Robert H. Berlin, "United States Army World War II Corps Commanders: A Composite Biography," *Journal of Military History* 53 (April 1989): 156–57.

10. Curriculum content from CGSS Schedule for 1923–1924, CARL.

11. What follows is based on Timothy K. Nenninger, "Creating Officers: The Leavenworth Experience, 1920–1940," *Military Review* 69 (November 1989): 62–63.

12. The following two paragraphs are based on War Department, *Field Service Regulations, United States Army, 1923*, 4–5.

13. This schema for systematically assessing a combat situation in order to make a sound decision became known as "The Estimate of the Situation." The provisions of the *Field Service Regulations* precisely paralleled those developed at Leavenworth about a decade before America's entry into World War I by the army's preeminent tactical instructor, then Major John F. Morrison. For Morrison's teaching on the es-

timate, see Boyd L. Dastrup, *The U.S. Army Command and General Staff College: A Centennial History* (Manhattan, Kans.: Sunflower University Press, 1982), 56. This general format remains operative in contemporary U.S. Army doctrine and instruction. For an insightful survey of Morrison's broader contributions at Leavenworth from 1906 to 1912, see Nenninger, *The Leavenworth Schools and the Old Army*, 89–93.

14. The regulations also pointedly advised that such conferences could not be used to criticize or question the plans and orders of higher authority.

15. What follows is based on War Department, *Field Service Regulations, United States Army, 1923*, 6–7.

16. This paragraph is based on H. A. Smith, *Address at Opening Exercises of the Command and General Staff School, Fort Leavenworth, Kansas, September 10, 1923* (Fort Leavenworth, Kans.: General Service Schools Press, 1923), 5–7. Biographical details on Smith from *Who Was Who in American History: The Military* (Chicago: Marquis Who's Who, 1975), 536.

17. Lucian K. Truscott, Jr., *The Twilight of the U.S. Cavalry: Life in the Old Army, 1917–1942* (Lawrence: University Press of Kansas, 1989), 148.

18. The remainder of this paragraph is drawn from Edward L. King, *Command: Lecture to the Command and General Staff School, September 11, 1925* (Fort Leavenworth, Kans.: General Service Schools Press, 1925), 3–7. Biographical details on King from USMA, *Register of Graduates and Former Cadets, 1802–1947* (West Point, N.Y., 1947), 185.

19. This remark closely parallels Clausewitz's observation that genius "*rises above all rules*" (italics in original). Carl von Clausewitz, *On War*, ed. and trans. Michael Howard and Peter Paret (Princeton: Princeton University Press, 1976), 136.

20. This paragraph from King, *Command*, 9–17.

21. King's language paralleled in several respects the following passage from *On War*: "An army that maintains its cohesion under the most murderous fire; that cannot be shaken by imaginary threats and resists well-founded ones with all its might; that proud of its victories, will not lose the strength to obey orders and its respect and trust for its officers even in defeat; whose physical power, like the muscles of an athlete, has been steeled by training in privation and effort; a force that regards such efforts as a means to victory rather than a curse on its cause; that is mindful of all these duties and qualities by virtue of the single powerful idea of the honor of its arms—such an army is imbued with the military spirit." Clausewitz, *On War*, 187–88.

22. CGSS, *Instructional Circular No. 1, Series 1932–1933*, 15.

23. For an extended analysis of this point, see T. R. Phillips, "Solving the Tactical Equation: The Logical Foundation of the Estimate of the Situation," *Command and General Staff School Quarterly Review of Military Literature* 17 (September 1937): 5–51.

24. Lord Moran, *The Anatomy of Courage*, 2nd ed. (London: Constable, 1966), 180.

25. Eddy, it will be remembered, did not attend the Army War College.

26. George Pappas, *Prudens Futuri: The US Army War College, 1901–1967* (Carlisle Barracks, Pa.: Alumni Association of the USAWC, [1967]), 37. The Army War College Board, formed by Root to establish the particulars of the college, was formed in 1901; the college itself did not begin operations until 1903.

27. For testimony to the Army War College graduates' contribution to World War I from General Hugh Scott, Army Chief of Staff, and General John Pershing, AEF commander, see ibid., 87–88.

28. What follows is based on ibid., 89–101. Biographical detail on McAndrew from Nenninger, *The Leavenworth Schools*, 136.

29. Clausewitz, *On War*, 127.

30. McGlachlin's directive is cited in Pappas, *Prudens Futuri*, 109. Biographical detail on McGlachlin from Ball, *Of Responsible Command*, 176.

31. Biographical detail on DeWitt from J. L. DeWitt file, Biographical Reference Files, Library, MHI, Carlisle Barracks, Pa.

32. John L. DeWitt, "Orientation: The Army War College Course, 1928–1929," Lecture at the Army War College, 4 September 1928, 1, MHI.

33. The interplay of intellectual and temperamental qualities of the commander is covered exquisitely in Clausewitz, *On War*, 100–116.

34. DeWitt, "Orientation: The Army War College Course, 1928–1929," 10.

35. Biographical detail on Herr from USMA, *Register of Graduates*, 1947, 192.

36. John K. Herr, "General Allenby's Campaign in Palestine," Lecture at the Army War College, 12 April 1929, 18, MHI. Colonel Herr's excellent insight into Allenby's character was, not surprisingly, accompanied by the additional argument that the Palestine campaign demonstrated the continuing viability of cavalry as a force on the modern battlefield.

37. Cited material is from Nicholas Golovine, "The Galician Battle, 1914," Lecture at the Army War College, 4 and 8 December 1930, 30, MHI. The year after he lectured the War College students, Golovine's *The Russian Army in the World War* was published (New Haven: Yale University Press, 1931); and in 1933, his significant work on Tannenberg, *The Russian Campaign of 1914: The Beginning of the War and Operations in East Prussia*, was published (Fort Leavenworth, Kans.: CGSS Press, 1933).

38. What follows is based on Army War College, "Course at the Army War College, 1930–1931, Analytical Studies, Orientation, Outline of the Course," 2–25 February 1931, 1–6, MHI.

39. The rationale behind the Analytical Studies course is outlined in some detail in Ball, *Of Responsible Command*, 214–15. Biographical detail on Connor from ibid., 209.

40. This and what follows is drawn from Army War College, "Course at the Army War College, 1930–1931, Conduct of War, Orientation (First to Fourth Periods), February 26–June 26, 1931," 2–3, MHI.

41. Biographical detail on Rehkopf from USMA, *Register of Graduates,* 1947, 192. What follows is drawn from Ned Rehkopf, "Orientation: Course at the Army War College, 1936–1937, Conduct of War Course, Analytical Studies," Lecture at the Army War College, 28 January 1937, 1–3, MHI.

42. Arthur L. Conger, *The Rise of U.S. Grant* (New York: Century, 1931). Da Capo Press issued a reprint in 1996. For details of Conger's extensive contributions to army education, see Carol Reardon, *Soldiers and Scholars: The U.S. Army and the Uses of Military History, 1865–1920* (Lawrence: University Press of Kansas, 1990), 69–75, 78, 126–27, 177–79, 206, and 208.

43. What follows is based on A. L. Conger, "Grant as a Leader," Lecture at the Army War College, 5 February 1937, MHI.

44. These qualities are drawn directly from Clausewitz, *On War*, 100–116.

45. What follows is based on Douglas S. Freeman, "Lee as a Leader," Lecture at the Army War College, 11 February 1937, MHI. The text is identical to that found in Douglas Southall Freeman, *Douglas Southall Freeman on Military Leadership*, ed. Stuart W. Smith (Shippensburg, Pa.: White Mane Publishing, 1993), 134–46. The latter, however, contains a synopsis of the lecture as well as several helpful explanatory notes.

46. On Spaulding's work, see Reardon, *Soldiers and Scholars*, 195–97, 201–2, and 208–9.

47. What follows is based on Oliver L. Spaulding, "Washington and Grant as Leaders: A Comparison," Lecture at the Army War College, 8 February 1938, MHI.

48. Ibid., 14.

49. What follows is based on Freeman, "Lee as a Leader," Lecture at the Army War College, 10 February 1938, MHI. The published version, which includes a transcript of the discussion period as well, can be found in Freeman, *Douglas Southall Freeman on Military Leadership*, 148–63.

50. Clausewitz, *On War*, 101.

51. Clausewitz was explicit on this point: "Of all the passions that inspire man in battle, none, we have to admit, is so powerful and so constant as the hunger for honor and renown." Clausewitz, *On War*, 105.

52. Spaulding, "Washington and Grant," 14.

53. On Pershing's belief in the superiority of American methods to those of his European allies, see Frank Vandiver, *Black Jack: The Life and Times of John J. Pershing*, 2 vols. (College Station: Texas A&M University Press, 1977), 2:771–72.

3. The Making of Six Corps Commanders

1. W. G. F. Jackson, *Alexander of Tunis as Military Commander* (London: B. T. Batsford, 1971), 3.

2. Gerow entered VMI as a "state cadet," i.e., with tuition paid in return for service to the state or to the federal government following graduation. L. T. Gerow to Colonel E. V. Nichols, Acting Superintendent, VMI , 20 June 1907, VMI archives.

3. *Virginia Military Institute Official Register, 1911–1912* (Lexington, Va.: VMI, 1912), 60, 67–68; and *The Bomb* (Lexington, Va.: VMI, 1911), 32.

4. What follows is primarily based on the following documents among Gerow's papers in the VMI archives: extract of Gerow's official service record; a biographical sketch printed during his command of Second Army after World War II; and a 2 January 1920 letter from Gerow to Colonel Joseph Anderson of Lee, Virginia, summarizing his service up to that time.

5. The citation for the American decoration, the Distinguished Service Medal, is contained in a War Department memorandum of 10 November 1922, Gerow file, NPRC. Gerow was also appointed a Chevalier of the Legion of Honor.

6. Gerow's overall rating for the course was "Superior," and the commandant, Brigadier General B. H. Wells, noted that "his academic rating is of the highest order." Efficiency report for 15 September 1924–29 May 1925. In a subsequent report, Colonel D. L. Stone stated that he had known Gerow at Benning and that "he was an outstanding man and stood No.1 in his class on graduation." Efficiency report for 15 August 1926–30 June 1927, Gerow file, NPRC.

7. In a letter from Eisenhower to Gerow of 10 July 1950, shortly before Gerow's retirement, Eisenhower placed the date of their meeting as "on or about September 10, 1915." Gerow papers, VMI archives.

8. Details of Gerow and Eisenhower at Leavenworth from Dwight D. Eisenhower, *At Ease: Stories I Tell to Friends* (Garden City, N.Y.: Doubleday, 1967), 202–3. The two-man study team was something of a departure from the norm among CGSS students, who tended to assemble in larger groups for their collective deliberations.

9. Eisenhower modestly states that he and Gerow "both graduated with high marks, separated from each other by something like two-tenths of one per cent." Eisenhower, *At Ease*, 203. This statement is apparently what led Carlo D'Este mistakenly to infer that Gerow graduated second in his class, immediately behind Eisenhower. D'Este, *Patton*, 870n. Eisenhower's and Gerow's class standings from untitled document attached to letter from Major General Garrison H. Davidson to General Lyman L. Lemnitzer, 14 March 1955, 1, 6, Document no. N13423.98, CARL.

10. Efficiency report for 25 December 1931 to 30 June 1932, Gerow file, NPRC.

11. Gerow to Lejeune, 26 December 1934, Gerow papers, VMI archives.

12. Efficiency reports for 1 July 1937–30 June 1938 and 6 July–15 October 1938 by Krueger and Marshall, respectively, Gerow file, NPRC.

13. Marshall quote is from a *Time* magazine description of Gerow's assumption of duties at WPD in its "National Defense" section. The piece was titled "Brother Rat," to emphasize the VMI connection between Marshall and Gerow. *Time* 37 (6 January 1941): 15, copy in Gerow papers, VMI archives. Marshall was very sensitive about accusations that he favored VMI officers over West Point graduates, but in Gerow's case it seems that the *Time* piece was accurate when it stated that Gerow had "acquitted himself with the cold efficiency that George Marshall likes."

14. Gerow to Eisenhower, 18 November 1940, Gerow papers, VMI archives. Eisenhower cites the cable in full in *At Ease*, 238.

15. Eisenhower to Gerow, 18 November 1940, Eisenhower Pre-Presidential papers, Box 46, Gerow File, DDEL.

16. Gerow to Eisenhower, 2 January 1941, Gerow papers, VMI archives.

17. Eisenhower to Gerow, 9 January 1941, ibid.

18. There is no direct evidence that Gerow was responsible for Marshall's summons of Eisenhower to report to WPD. However, the evidence of Gerow's previous attempts to obtain Eisenhower's services and his close relationship with Marshall suggest fairly strongly that he played at least some role here.

19. Eisenhower's account of his preemptory transfer to WPD and first briefing from Marshall is found in Dwight D. Eisenhower, *Crusade in Europe* (Garden City, N.Y.: Doubleday, 1948), 14–18.

20. For details, see Eisenhower to Marshall, 19 September 1942, Alfred D. Chandler, Jr., et al., eds., *The Papers of Dwight David Eisenhower: The War Years*, 5 vols. (Baltimore: Johns Hopkins University Press, 1970), 565–67, 567n; and Marshall to Eisenhower, 28 September 1942, Larry I. Bland and Sharon Ritenour Stevens, eds., *The Papers of George Catlett Marshall*, vols. 1–5 (Baltimore: Johns Hopkins University Press, 1981–2003), 3:368, 368n.

21. Gerow to Eisenhower, 15 February 1943, Gerow papers, VMI archives. Eisenhower to Gerow, 24 February 1943, Chandler et al., *Eisenhower Papers*, 985–

87. Eisenhower's letter did not explicitly mention Kasserine Pass, but the tone made the reference unnecessary.

22. Description of the fighting at Omaha Beach is drawn from Gordon A. Harrison, *Cross Channel Attack* (Washington, D.C.: OCMH, 1951), 321–28.

23. Weigley, *Eisenhower's Lieutenants*, 79.

24. Charles B. MacDonald, *The Mighty Endeavor: American Armed Forces in the European Theater in World War II* (New York: Oxford University Press, 1969), 294.

25. On Gerow's problems in the liberation of Paris, see Weigley, *Eisenhower's Lieutenants*, 250–52. Extract of the Silver Star citation is in Gerow's service record, Gerow papers, VMI archives.

26. The standard account of the campaign as a whole remains Charles B. MacDonald, *The Siegfried Line Campaign* (Washington, D.C.: OCMH, 1963).

27. What follows is based on Joint Committee on the Investigation of the Pearl Harbor Attack, 76th Cong., 1st sess., pt. 29, Proceedings of the Army Pearl Harbor Board, 2188–91.

28. Weigley offers a particularly good analysis of the operational and higher tactical aspects of the Hürtgen battles in *Eisenhower's Lieutenants*, 412–20. A more comprehensive and very evenhanded account is found in Edward G. Miller, *A Dark and Bloody Ground: The Hürtgen Forest and the Roer River Dams, 1944–1945* (College Station: Texas A&M University Press, 1995).

29. What follows is based on Charles B. MacDonald, "Objective Schmidt: The Story of the 112th Infantry Regiment of the 28th Infantry Division in the Battle for Schmidt, Germany," in Charles B. MacDonald and Sidney T. Mathews, *Three Battles: Arnaville, Altuzzo, and Schmidt* (Washington, D.C.: OCMH, 1952), 251–417; Miller, *Dark and Bloody Ground*, 47–92; and the author's personal reconnaissance of the Schmidt battlefield. See also the trenchant critique of Schmidt by Cecil B. Currey in *Follow Me and Die: The Destruction of an American Division in World War II* (New York: Stein and Day, 1984).

30. On 8 November 1944, a day after the failure of the Schmidt attack, when Hodges stingingly rebuked Cota in Gerow's presence, Gerow provided Cota no support. Robert A. Miller, *Division Commander: A Biography of Major General Norman D. Cota* (Spartanburg, S.C.: Reprint Company, 1989), 129. Additionally, a special V Corps study of the battle ordered by Gerow concluded that the tactical planning had been sound. MacDonald, "Objective Schmidt," in MacDonald and Mathews, *Three Battles*, 416. Major General James Gavin, whose 82nd Airborne Division attacked across the same area in February 1945, provides an interesting commentary on the episode. Gavin described the scene as reminiscent of the lower reaches of Dante's *Inferno*: decayed bodies, abandoned equipment, and the general flotsam and jetsam of death and destruction. The next day when he asked a V Corps staff officer why First Army had attacked through the Hürtgen to begin with and why, given that it did, a more trafficable avenue of approach into Schmidt had not been used, his questions were brushed off with the distinct impression that these issues were off-limits to further discussion. James M. Gavin, *On to Berlin: Battles of an Airborne Commander, 1943–1946* (New York: Viking, 1978), 263–66.

31. In a 27 November 1944 letter to Marshall, Eisenhower informed the chief that because Lieutenant General Lucian K. Truscott, his first choice for Fifteenth Army command, would definitely command Fifth Army in Italy instead, he would

"probably" designate Gerow for the position. Chandler et al., *Eisenhower Papers*, 2321–22. Gerow had, however, been among three "possible" candidates for the Fifteenth Army position from as early as late July, the other two being Truscott and McNair. McNair was tragically killed while observing operations in Normandy by American bombs that fell short. In assessing Gerow's capability to command an army, Eisenhower said he had "shown all the qualities of vigor, determination, reliability and skill we [Eisenhower and Bradley] are looking for." Eisenhower to Marshall, 23 July 1944, Chandler et al., *Eisenhower Papers*, 2023.

32. After the war, when it appeared that Gerow would be appointed as commandant of the Army War College, a post coveted by Patton, the latter fulminated in his diary, "This is too bad, as he [Gerow] was one of the leading mediocre corps commanders in Europe and only got the Fifteenth Army because he was General Eisenhower's personal friend." Writing to his wife the next day about the prospective appointment, he went further, calling Gerow "the poorest corps commander in France." Martin Blumenson, ed., *The Patton Papers: 1940–1945* (Boston: Houghton Mifflin, 1972–1974), 739–40. Notwithstanding Patton's sour grapes over the War College, his perception of a link between the Gerow-Eisenhower relationship and Gerow's selection for command of Fifteenth Army is on very solid ground. The author is indebted to Dr. Edgar Raines for these references.

33. On Huebner's personality, see the interesting portrait by Omar Bradley in *A Soldier's Story* (New York: Henry Holt, 1951), 156–57.

34. Cole, *Ardennes*, 53–54.

35. This paragraph is based on Price, *Middleton*, 4–38.

36. This paragraph is based on ibid., 59–70.

37. Details of Middleton's actions are found in the recommendations for the award made by commanding general, 7th Infantry Brigade, 26 December 1918, for the Distinguished Service Cross and amended on 21 May 1919 to an award of the Distinguished Service Medal. Middleton file, NPRC. The quote is from Brigadier General B. A. Poore's amended recommendation of 21 May 1919.

38. This paragraph is based on Price, *Middleton*, 76–84.

39. Farnsworth's invitation from ibid., 86. Text of the lecture from Troy H. Middleton, "Infantry and Its Weapons," Lecture at Army War College, 7 March 1923, MHI.

40. Price, *Middleton*, 87.

41. There is a certain amount of confusion concerning the number of graduates in the CGSS class of 1924. Berlin's study lists Middleton as 8/240 and his classmate John P. Lucas as 78/247. Berlin, "World War II Corps Commanders," 187. A 1955 compilation of the class standings of various general officers lists graduating numbers of 240, 247, and 249. Untitled document attached to letter from Major General Garrison H. Davidson to General Lyman L. Lemnitzer, 14 March 1955, passim, Document no. N13423.98, CARL. The author's count of the actual list of graduates indicated the total was 248. This corresponds with the entry in Middleton's personnel file and what was reported in the *Leavenworth Times* of 20 June 1924, cited in D'Este, *Patton*, 870–71. The number is of mild historical interest because if the graduating class had contained only 240 members, as indicated in some sources, Patton, at 25th, would not have achieved the distinction he sought as an honor graduate. On this, see Price, *Middleton*, 89. Middleton's recollection, however, is slightly inaccurate.

The CGSS practice at the time was to designate the top 10 (not 25) percent as honor graduates and the next 15 (not 25) percent as distinguished graduates.

42. This list taken from the graduating classes of 1925 to 1928. The corps commanders were John Anderson, XVI Corps; Gilbert Cook, XII Corps; Willis Crittenberger, IV Corps; Ernest Dawley, VI Corps; Oscar Griswold, XIV Corps; Wade Haislip, XV Corps; Clarence Huebner, V Corps; Geoffrey Keyes, II Corps; John Millikin, III Corps; and Walton Walker, XX Corps. Price's biography asserts that at one time every corps commander in Europe had been a student under Middleton at Leavenworth (Price, *Middleton*, 91). The only time I have been able to substantiate this claim was during the Salerno operation when Dawley's VI corps was the only American corps "in Europe." During the campaigns in Northwest Europe, Collins was one of the first two American corps commanders to arrive; he served until V-E Day, and he was clearly not one of Middleton's students. This appears to be another example in which Middleton's generally excellent memory while dictating material for Price proved to be slightly faulty.

43. Price, *Middleton*, 91.

44. In the opening lecture, the assistant commandant, Colonel J. L. DeWitt, alluded to a distinction between the academic *geists* at Leavenworth and the War College when he informed the students that there was "no place in this College for academic competition, or for the blind acceptance of a principle or idea expressed by any member of the faculty." DeWitt, "Orientation: The Army War College Course, 1928–1929," 2, MHI.

45. This paragraph is based on Price, *Middleton*, 97–122.

46. This awareness is reflected in several places, most notably 1942, Chief of Staff correspondence files, RG 165, Box 48, NAII.

47. The army official historians of the Sicily campaign opined that the 45th was "probably one of the best trained divisions in the American Army when it sailed from the United States in June 1943." Albert N. Garland and Howard McGaw Smyth, *Sicily and the Surrender of Italy* (Washington, D.C.: OCMH, 1965), 95. Marshall's inspector general reported that the division's embarkation and movement was "meritorious in every respect." Virgil L. Peterson, Memorandum for the Deputy Chief of Staff, 8 June 1943, Marshall papers, Box 76, Folder 51, GCML. Marshall passed on these remarks as well as his own favorable observations of the division made while Middleton was in North Africa planning for the Sicily invasion. Marshall to Middleton, 14 July 1943, Marshall papers, Box 76, Folder 51, GCML.

48. Bradley's reservations are recorded in Bradley and Blair, *General's Life*, 171. The boundary change involved the now almost-infamous transfer of the Vizzini-Caltagirone road from Patton's to Montgomery's sector. For details, see Carlo D'Este, *Bitter Victory: The Battle for Sicily, 1943* (Glasgow: Collins, 1988), 321–33. This move forced Middleton to move the 45th from Bradley's right flank, behind the 1st Division, to the corps' left. Middleton performed this task with alacrity and continued the attack well before Bradley thought he would be capable of doing so. Bradley, *Soldier's Story*, 136–40.

49. The 45th's training in night operations figures prominently in Middleton to Marshall, 5 August 1943, Marshall papers, Box 76, Folder 51, GCML. See also Price, *Middleton*, 153–55.

50. Eisenhower's endorsement of Middleton's initial combat efficiency report in World War II, written on 22 July 1943, just as the 45th was approaching Sicily's

northern coast reads as follows: "General Middleton's performance to date in active operations as Commanding General of the 45th Division has been superior. He is apparently living up to the fine reputation he has always had as a combat commander." Efficiency report for 15–30 June 1943, Middleton file, NPRC.

51. Chandler et al., *Eisenhower Papers*, 1354. The other two were Lucian Truscott, who went on to command VI Corps and Fifth Army, and Ernest Dawley, who commanded VI Corps at Salerno but was relieved by Mark Clark.

52. Price, *Middleton*, 165, 169.

53. Ibid., 168.

54. The actual medical evaluation is contained in the 14 February 1944 record of proceedings of Middleton's medical board found in the Middleton file, NPRC. Marshall's awareness of the board's report is evident in a Memorandum for Record re: Middleton's knee evaluation in Chief of Staff's correspondence file, RG 165, Box 165, NAII.

55. Eisenhower to Marshall, 24 February 1944, and Marshall to Eisenhower, 25 February 1944, Verifax 1284, GCML.

56. Eisenhower to Marshall, 26 February 1944, and Marshall to Eisenhower, 28 February 1944, Verifax 1284, GCML. There have grown up some rather hoary legends about Middleton's knee. The first is based on a statement in Bradley's memoirs that when Marshall was originally informed about Middleton's imminent return to the United States, he replied: "I would rather have a man with arthritis in the knee than one with arthritis in the head. Keep him there." Bradley, *Soldier's Story*, 30. I have been unable to verify this quotation, and it is doubtful that if Marshall had so directed, Middleton would have returned to the United States. The second is contained in a statement Eisenhower made to Middleton's biographer in a 1965 interview to the effect that when Marshall informed him of Middleton's condition, he replied: "I don't give a damn about his knees; I want his head and his heart. And I'll take him into battle on a litter if we have to." Price, *Middleton*, 171. These might have been Eisenhower's thoughts, but they were not his words. His simple statement that he was "quite willing" to take a chance on Middleton's physical condition was all that was necessary.

57. Price, *Middleton*, 171.

58. Although Patton's Third Army headquarters was not officially activated until 1 August, Bradley authorized Patton to take tactical control of VIII Corps on 27 July. Blumenson, *Patton Papers: 1940–1945*, 489–90.

59. Middleton's command and control challenges during the Brittany campaign are described in Price, *Middleton*, 189; and Martin Blumenson, *Breakout and Pursuit* (Washington, D.C.: OCMH, 1961), 351–56.

60. Patton's relations with Middleton during the siege of Brest can be followed in Blumenson, *Patton Papers: 1940–1945*, 525, 532. See also Blumenson, *Breakout and Pursuit*, 635–36, 639–40, 656. Third Army headquarters significantly reduced Middleton's initial and very accurate forecast of the ammunition and forces that would be required to penetrate the Brest defenses.

61. Bradley, *Soldier's Story*, 435–37. Bradley presciently anticipated that Montgomery would "wangle" an army headquarters out of Eisenhower, and he wanted it to be Simpson's relatively inexperienced Ninth rather than Hodges's First. He admits, however, that Ninth Army soon became "a first-rate fighting unit."

62. Ridgway, *Soldier*, 18.

63. *The Howitzer* (West Point, N.Y.: USMA, 1917), 149.

64. Details on Ridgway's tour at West Point from Ridgway, *Soldier*, 33–34.

65. Efficiency report for 1 November 1921–30 June 1922, Ridgway file, NPRC. It is unclear what led MacArthur to give this assignment to Ridgway; but as a former football manager himself and one who followed Army athletics closely all his life, MacArthur was presumably aware of Daly's high opinion of Ridgway's work as football manager. And even though MacArthur had only recently returned to West Point, he also noted in this report that he had known Ridgway for "many years" and "very well."

66. Bradley states that assignments to schools were not normal from instructor duty and that Ridgway used "high connections in the War Department" to get to Benning, but that his posting established a precedent that others were able to follow. Bradley and Blair, *General's Life*, 53. What follows is based on Ridgway, *Soldier*, 35–44.

67. McCoy's appreciation of Ridgway's service is noted in his 27 September 1929 letter to the secretary of war; see also Díaz's 28 December 1928 letter to Ambassador Charles E. Eberhardt, Ridgway file, NPRC.

68. Efficiency report for 17 September 1929–10 June 1930, Ridgway file, NPRC. Marshall's general estimate of Ridgway was "clearly superior in efficiency, initiative, appearance, manners."

69. Untitled document attached to letter from Major General Garrison H. Davidson to General Lyman L. Lemnitzer, 14 March 1955, 12, Document no. N13423.98, CARL.

70. For details of how this relationship was strengthened, see Ridgway, *Soldier*, 43; Blair, *Ridgway's Paratroopers*, 10–11; and Bland and Stevens, *Marshall Papers* 1:505.

71. Army War College, Information copy of message from CG Ninth Corps Area and Fourth Army to the Adjutant General, 18 December 1937 [1936], MHI.

72. On Ridgway's duties at Fourth Army, see Ridgway, *Soldier*, 46–47. Ridgway's continuing closeness with Marshall is evident in Marshall's letter to Ridgway's second wife, Peggy, of 19 August 1938, expressing appreciation for her hospitality shown during his visit to San Francisco. Marshall papers, Box 83, Folder 3, GCML.

73. Description of Ridgway's participation in Marshall's Brazilian mission is based on Ridgway, *Soldier*, 47–48; Marshall's letter from Rio de Janeiro of 26 May 1939 to Army Chief of Staff Malin Craig, in which Ridgway is mentioned by name, Bland and Stevens, *Marshall Papers* 1:716–17; Forrest C. Pogue, *George C. Marshall: Education of a General, 1880–1939* (New York, Viking, 1963), 338–42; and Blair, *Ridgway's Paratroopers*, 12.

74. Ridgway, *Soldier*, 49–50.

75. On Bradley and Ridgway's early days at the 82nd, see Bradley and Blair, *General's Life*, 104–8; and Blair, *Ridgway's Paratroopers*, 19–28.

76. Bradley felt that Ridgway was "the best possible choice." Bradley and Blair, *General's Life*, 108. This sentiment was confirmed in the report written when Bradley departed to assume command of the 28th: "He possesses a very high degree of leadership; has fine judgment; has strong convictions; and has high ideals of training standards." Efficiency report for 25 February–23 June 1942, Ridgway file, NPRC.

77. Description of the conversion of the 82nd into an airborne division is drawn from Blair, *Ridgway's Paratroopers*, 29–54.

78. Ibid., 67.

79. The story of the 505th at Sicily is told in Gavin, *On to Berlin*, 14–50.

80. The engagement of the 504th by friendly fire is described in Blair, *Ridgway's Paratroopers*, 119–20; and Garland and Smyth, *Sicily*, 175–84.

81. Bradley and Blair, *General's Life*, 184.

82. Ridgway service record, Ridgway file, NPRC.

83. What follows is based on Eisenhower, *Crusade in Europe*, 245–47; Bradley and Blair, *General's Life*, 227; and Ridgway, *Soldier*, 101.

84. The difficult and costly attack across the Merderet causeway is described in Gavin, *On to Berlin*, 115–17; Harrison, *Cross Channel Attack*, 396–400; and Blair, *Ridgway's Paratroopers*, 322–23. I have stood at the eastern end of the causeway and marveled at the incredible bravery it took for men to storm across this long and very narrow route over the flooded river in the face of withering German fire. Blair correctly calls it "the stuff of instant legend."

85. What follows is based on Blair, *Ridgway's Paratroopers*, 361–413; Ridgway, *Soldier*, 105–11; and Gavin, *On to Berlin*, 133–92.

86. Notably, Blair in *Ridgway's Paratroopers*, 407; and Weigley in *Eisenhower's Lieutenants*, 318.

87. Ridgway's extreme frustration is evident in *Soldier*, 108 and 111. It is also evident in correspondence between Ridgway and Cornelius Ryan when the latter was conducting research for his history of Market-Garden, *A Bridge Too Far* (New York: Simon and Schuster, 1974). Ryan to Ridgway, 19 June 1973, and Ridgway's response of 24 June 1973, Ridgway papers, MHI.

88. What follows is based on Blair, *Ridgway's Paratroopers*, 412.

89. Ridgway to Marshall, 5 October and 1 November 1944, Marshall papers, Box 83, Folder 3, GCML.

90. Ridgway to Marshall, 4 December 1944, Marshall papers, Box 83, Folder 3, GCML. Despite Ridgway's frustration with Army Ground Forces headquarters, he was ultimately able to obtain some 4,000 more men for the European airborne divisions. See Kent R. Greenfield, Robert R. Palmer, and Bell I. Wiley, *The Organization of Ground Combat Troops* (Washington, D.C.: Historical Division, Department of the Army, 1947), 349.

91. Discussions with Millikin's grandson, Dr. John P. Millikin, of Scottsdale, Arizona, on 17 November 1997.

92. Millikin's entry in the 1910 *Howitzer*, 73; USMA class standing from Millikin file, NPRC.

93. Date of wedding from Millikin family papers.

94. Efficiency report for 12 February 1918–1 June 1918, Millikin file, NPRC.

95. Efficiency report for 12 January–3 June 1919, Millikin file, NPRC.

96. Commendation letter signed by Brigadier General H. H. Bandholtz, 19 May 1919, and approved DSM citation, 2 July 1920, Millikin file, NPRC.

97. Efficiency reports for the periods 12 June–31 December 1919, 20 July–31 December 1919, and 1 September–31 December 1919 cover Millikin's multiple duties, Millikin file, NPRC.

98. For details of these disturbances, see Constance McLaughlin Green, *Washington, D.C.: Capital City, 1879–1950* (Princeton: Princeton University Press, 1963), 260–67.

99. Correspondence, Commissioner Brownlow to Secretary Baker, 31 December 1919, and Major General W. G. Haan to Adjutant General, 9 September 1919; efficiency reports rendered by Baker and March for periods 12 June–31 December 1919, Millikin file, NPRC.

100. Details of March's inspection trip to Europe are in Edward M. Coffman, *The Hilt of the Sword: The Career of Peyton C. March* (Madison: University of Wisconsin Press, 1966), 212–16. War Department orders for other trips on which Millikin accompanied March are found in Millikin file, NPRC. The Millikin family papers contain a newspaper account of Mrs. Millikin's participation in the launch of the *Argonne*. Clearly at ease in these circles, she artfully opined on the dreary mixture of rain and snow that accompanied the event: "It's very appropriate to have bad weather on this occasion. They had plenty of it in the Argonne, our boys say."

101. For details, see Coffman, *Hilt of the Sword*, 212–30.

102. Efficiency report for 9 September 1924–30 June 1925, Millikin file, NPRC.

103. Separate report on student officer, 17 September 1925, Millikin file, NPRC.

104. Untitled attachment to letter from Major General Garrison H. Davidson to General Lyman Lemnitzer, 14 March 1955, 7, Document no. N13423.98, CARL.

105. What follows is based on a list of classes taught by Millikin kindly provided to the author on 17 December 1996 by Elaine McConnell, curator, Archives, Rare Books, and Special Collections, CARL.

106. This and the following sentence are based on the efficiency report for 14 August 1930–30 June 1931, Millikin file, NPRC.

107. Wainwright's obituary, *Assembly* 12 (January 1954): 53–55. For Wainwright's tactical views at the time, see Jonathan M. Wainwright, "Mobility," *Cavalry Journal* 44 (September–October 1935): 20.

108. George Grunert, "Cavalry in Future War," *Cavalry Journal* 42 (May–June 1933): 5–10; George S. Patton, Jr., "Mechanized Forces," *Cavalry Journal* 42 (September–October 1933): 5–8; and Alexander D. Surles, "The Cavalry and Mechanization, 1936," *Cavalry Journal* 45 (January–February 1936): 6–7. Interestingly, in the mid-1930s stage of his development, Patton, like many other cavalrymen, called for the continued use of horse cavalry units to conduct close tactical reconnaissance while mechanized units conducted distant reconnaissance.

109. Description and analysis of these exercises is based on "The Cavalry Maneuvers at Fort Riley, Kansas, 1934," *Cavalry Journal* 43 (July–August 1934): 5–14.

110. There is no correspondence in Millikin's file indicating that Wainwright requested that Millikin continue to serve under him at Fort Myer. But given their long association at Fort Riley and Wainwright's consistently positive comments on Millikin's performance, the strong probability of such a request is clearly a logical inference.

111. Efficiency report for 1 August 1936–30 June 1937, Millikin file, NPRC.

112. Efficiency report for 7 September 1937–30 June 1938, Millikin file, NPRC.

113. Efficiency report for 1 July 1938–29 November 1938, Millikin file, NPRC.

114. Provisional Corps Certificate of Commendation, 26 August 1939, Millikin file, NPRC.

115. The 7th Cavalry Brigade's role in these exercises is described in detail in Adna R. Chaffee, "The Seventh Cavalry Brigade in the First Army Maneuvers," *Cavalry Journal* 48 (November–December 1939): 450–61; and also assessed in T. J. Heavey,

"An Observer at the First Army Maneuvers," *Cavalry Journal* 48 (November–December 1939): 461–63.

116. The importance of these exercises to the army as a whole and their overall design is set out in William M. Grimes, "The 1940 Spring Maneuvers," *Cavalry Journal* 49 (March–April 1940): 98–114. In the initial movement, a combined mechanized force consisting of the 7th Cavalry Brigade (Mechanized), commanded by Brigadier General Adna Chaffee, and the 6th Cavalry Regiment would oppose the 1st Cavalry Division. Patton, a close friend of the 1st Cavalry Division commander, Major General Kenyon A. Joyce, provided Joyce with some information and advice on the upcoming maneuvers that he hoped would help Joyce "steal another march on Chaffee, Millikin and Company." Blumenson, *Patton Papers: 1940–1945*, 948.

117. Van Horn letter to Major General John Herr, 13 May 1940, Millikin file, NPRC.

118. Efficiency report for 12 April–27 May 1940, Millikin file, NPRC.

119. Short letter to Marshall, 6 June 1940, Millikin file, NPRC.

120. Efficiency report for 19 January–4 June 1941, Millikin file, NPRC.

121. Truscott, *Twilight of the U.S. Cavalry*, xx.

122. Between his departure from the 2nd Cavalry Division in May 1942 and his assumption of command of the 33rd Infantry Division in August 1942, Millikin was temporarily designated as commander of the 83rd Infantry Division and sent to a division commander's course at Fort Leavenworth. War Department orders of 12 May and 6 August 1942, Millikin family papers.

123. War Department orders of 30 September 1943, Millikin file, NPRC.

124. Efficiency report for 10 September–31 December 1942, 25 January 1943, Millikin file, NPRC.

125. The following memorandum for record appears at the bottom of Millikin's orders to assume command of III Corps: "General McNair recommended the above action. Chief of Staff approved 27 September 1943." Millikin file, NPRC.

126. The challenges of preparing units for overseas movement are described in Robert R. Palmer, Bell I. Wiley, and William R. Keast, *The Procurement and Training of Army Ground Combat Troops* (Washington, D.C.: Department of the Army, 1948), 596–604.

127. Efficiency report for 19 January–30 June 1944.

128. What follows is based on III Corps AAR, December 1944, 1, RG 407, Box 3262, NAII.

129. Details of Eddy's early life are taken from Phillips, *Making of a Professional*, 15–22.

130. What follows is based on Fort Benning, Georgia, Infantry School Library, M. S. Eddy, "Machine Gun Company, 39th Infantry (4th Division) in the Aisne-Marne Offensive (July 18–August 5, 1918)," Infantry School Officer's Advanced Course, 1929–1930 (hereafter Eddy, "Machine Gun Company"), 1–33.

131. Eddy, "Machine Gun Company," 33.

132. Following is based on Phillips, *Making of a Professional*, 29–32.

133. Efficiency report for 1 January–30 June 1921, Eddy file, NPRC.

134. Correspondence from mayor of Gainesville and president of Gainesville Chamber of Commerce to Eddy and letter from Superintendent, Riverside Military Academy, to Army Chief of Staff, Eddy file, NPRC.

135. What follows is based on Eddy, "Machine Gun Company," passim.

136. Phillips, *Making of a Professional*, 56.

137. Efficiency report for 17 September 1929–30 June 1930, Eddy file, NPRC.

138. Efficiency report for 1 July 1931–14 April 1932, Eddy file, NPRC.

139. Eddy's class standing from untitled document attached to letter from Major General Garrison Davidson to General Lyman Lemnitzer, 14 March 1955, 11, Document no. N13423.98, CARL. Comment is based on efficiency report for 1 July 1933–30 June 1934, Eddy file, NPRC.

140. I was very kindly furnished with a list of courses Eddy taught in an email message of 19 July 2002 from Pamela Bennett, chief, Public Services, CARL.

141. Efficiency reports for 24 September 1938–30 June 1940, Eddy file, NPRC.

142. This and the following sentence are based on material contained in Eddy's medical evaluation of 17 December 1945, which diagnosed "hypertensive cardio-vascular disease, moderate. Improved." Hypertension was first noted in 1930 and tracked annually thereafter. In the spring of 1939, his blood pressure rose to 170/100. It came down to 134/80 after an unspecified period of rest. Eddy file, NPRC.

143. Efficiency reports for 20 July 1940–2 October 1941, Eddy file, NPRC.

144. Efficiency report, signed by Drum, for 1 November–1 December 1941 and efficiency report for 12 December 1941–1 March 1942, Eddy file, NPRC.

145. Ernie Pyle, *Brave Men* (1944; reprint, Lincoln: University of Nebraska Press, 2001), 419.

146. Marshall's faith in Eddy received early confirmation when a War Department inspection team visited Fort Bragg and reported back to Marshall very favorable impressions of its visit. The team's comments were cited in a letter from Marshall to Eddy of 14 July 1942, Marshall papers, Box 66, Folder 38, GCML.

147. Details of the 9th Infantry's fight at El Guettar can be found in Phillips, *Making of a Professional*, 94–99; George F. Howe, *Northwest Africa: Seizing the Initiative in the West* (Washington, D.C.: OCMH, 1957), 563–77; and Rick Atkinson, *An Army at Dawn: The War in North Africa, 1942–1943* (New York: Henry Holt, 2002), 453–59.

148. What follows is based on Phillips, *Making of a Professional*, 108–12. See also Atkinson, *Army at Dawn*, 502–3, 520–21.

149. The 9th Infantry's operations in Sicily are described in Garland and Smyth, *Sicily*, 331–47 and 374–87.

150. Chandler et al., *Eisenhower Papers*, 2073.

151. Blumenson, *Patton Papers: 1940–1945*, 522. Patton, who was fond of exaggerating both his subordinates' timidity and his own audacity, wrote in his letter to his wife of 20 August 1944, which described the encounter: "He has been thinking [that] a mile a day [was] good going. I told him to go fifty and he turned pale."

152. The story of Patton's artful coordination of ground maneuver, airpower, and Ultra information in the August 1944 campaign is authoritatively and convincingly reconstructed in Bradford J. ("BJ") Shwedo, *XIX Tactical Command and ULTRA: Patton's Force Enhancers in the 1944 Campaign in France* (Maxwell AFB, Ala.: Air University Press, 2001).

153. The capture of Nancy is described in Phillips, *Making of a Professional*, 166–67; and Hugh M. Cole, *The Lorraine Campaign* (Washington, D.C.: U.S. Army Historical Division, 1950), 68–96.

154. This incident is described in Phillips, *Making of a Professional*, 169–71; Blumenson, *Patton Papers: 1940–1945*, 559–60; and Cole, *Lorraine Campaign*, 251–53.

155. The basis of the award and proposed citation are found in a Third Army letter of 21 October 1944, Eddy file, NPRC.

156. "P" was not Wood's middle initial but a nickname given him for his frequent tutoring of his West Point classmates. In cadet vernacular, "P" stood for "professor."

157. The former judgment is that of Caleb Carr, whose highly complimentary assessment of Wood appears in "The American Rommel," *Military History Quarterly* (Summer 1992): 77–85; the latter judgment is from Russell Weigley in *Eisenhower's Lieutenants*, 438. Both authors attribute some of the sentiment behind Wood's relief to his criticism of the entire American high command for its decision to persist in the capture of the Breton ports after the breakout at Avranches rather than exploiting immediately into the French interior. But Weigley admits that Eddy had no cause for resentment over this issue, and he appears to have some sympathy with the corps commander's reservations about Wood's irritability.

158. Blumenson, *Patton Papers: 1940–1945*, 575–76. Patton also informed Eddy that if Wood were relieved, Gaffey, another experienced armor officer and Patton confidant, would be his replacement.

159. The proximate cause of Eddy's decision to call in Patton's promise was Wood's belligerent response to Eddy's insistence that the 4th AD move with greater speed in returning to the XII Corps sector after having operated in the XV Corps sector for six days. The executive officer of CCA, 4th AD, who was present at the encounter, later recorded Wood's reaction as follows: "[Expletive] Matt, my boys have bought every foot of this ground with their blood, they have done everything humanly possible and I will not ask any more of them. We will get out as fast as we can but no faster." Wood then departed abruptly. A. Harding Ganz, "Patton's Relief of General Wood," *Journal of Military History* 53 (July 1989): 271.

160. Patton was distraught over what he saw as a painful but necessary decision. He wrote numerous letters to attempt to soften the impact of the relief. But he indicated the fundamental consideration of the whole affair in a letter to his wife of 1 December: "I got P sent home on a 60 day detached service. . . . He is too hard to handle." Blumenson, *Patton Papers: 1940–1945*, 586.

161. Details on Collins's early life are found in Collins, *Lightning Joe*, 1–6.

162. Collins's yearbook entry humorously described his rapid preparation for a formation and noted: "This little incident is thoroughly typical of Joe's cadet life—first, concentration and decision, second, rapid and hearty action." *The Howitzer*, 1917, 70.

163. What follows is based on Collins, *Lightning Joe*, 8–27.

164. Four successive reports spanning the period 26 August 1921–30 June 1925 are uniformly glowing on Collins as an instructor. Collins file, NPRC.

165. Collins to the Adjutant General, 8 August 1923, Collins file, NPRC.

166. Efficiency report for 18 September 1925–30 June 1926, Collins file, NPRC.

167. Efficiency report for 1 July 1928–30 June 1929, Collins file, NPRC.

168. Collins, *Lightning Joe*, 51–52.

169. Untitled document attached to letter from Major General Garrison H. Davidson to General Lyman L. Lemnitzer, 14 March 1955, 1, Document no. NN13423.98, CARL.

170. Collins's service in the Philippines is described in *Lightning Joe*, 60–85.

171. Ibid., 86.

172. Course at the Army War College, 1937–1938, Command Post Exercise assignment roster, MHI.

173. Efficiency report for 16 August 1937–30 June 1938, Collins file, NPRC.

174. J. Lawton Collins, "The Concentration of Large Units," Lecture Delivered at the Army War College, 28 February 1939; and "The Army and Large Units in Offensive Combat," Lecture Delivered at the Army War College, 8 March 1939, MHI.

175. Marshall's notation on Collins's efficiency report for 1 July 1940–2 January 1941, Collins file, NPRC. Collins's release from War Department duty is described in Collins, *Lightning Joe*, 97–99.

176. Ridgway to Collins, 14 January 1941, Collins papers, DDEL. The note read in part: "That's fine work—the first of the class to wear the Eagles. . . . I hope I may soon be able to write a similar note when you receive the star." Collins's similarly gracious reply said, "I am confident that it won't be too long before you get an equal break." Collins to Ridgway, 17 January 1941, Collins papers, DDEL.

177. What follows is based on Collins, *Lightning Joe*, 115–17.

178. What follows is based on ibid., 119–43.

179. Adjutant General Memorandum, 8 December 1942, Citation for Publication in War Department General Orders, 1942, Collins file, NPRC, contains the citation for this award.

180. Analysis of the 25th's combat action on Guadalcanal comes from Richard B. Frank, *Guadalcanal* (New York: Random House, 1990), 550–72; and Collins, *Lightning Joe*, 144–67.

181. Frank says that Collins "demanded and got a degree of logistical legerdemain achieved at no other time during the campaign so deep into Guadalcanal's interior." Frank, *Guadalcanal*, 552.

182. Headquarters, 25th Infantry Division, Informal Report on Combat Operations, 27 March 1943, Collins papers, DDEL.

183. Collins to Marshall, 26 January 1943, Marshall papers, Xerox 2297, GCML.

184. Marshall, Memorandum for the President, 11 March 1943, Marshall papers, Xerox 2297, GCML.

185. Patch's recommendation for Collins's Distinguished Service Medal and related correspondence is found in RG 165, Box 43, NAII.

186. Efficiency report for 1 January–25 April 1943, Collins file, NPRC.

187. Efficiency report for 1 July–4 November 1943, Collins file, NPRC.

188. Collins, *Lightning Joe*, 172–74. Toward the end of the New Georgia campaign, Collins had told Harmon that, having been away from his family for two years, it would be nice to go back to Washington. In the memoirs, the matter is treated quite lightly. But given the tension between Collins and Griswold, one has to wonder whether Collins had additional motives.

189. Ibid., 176.

190. Eisenhower's first choice for VII Corps was Major General Lucian C. Truscott, who had performed admirably as commander of the 3rd ID in Sicily; but the Mediterranean Theater commander, General Jacob Devers, would not release Truscott. Eisenhower's thinking about the critical selection of the VII Corps commander can be traced in Eisenhower to Marshall, 18 January 1944, 28 January 1944, 29

January 1944, and 9 February 1944, Chandler et al., *Eisenhower Papers*, 1664–65, 1694–95, and 1715–16. Collins's account of his interview with Eisenhower and Bradley is found in *Lightning Joe*, 179.

191. What follows is based on Collins, *Lightning Joe*, 180–97.

192. This sobriquet was originally derived from the 25th Infantry Division's switchboard name, "Lightning," but it was also indicative of Collins's propensity for rapid movement. Collins's account of its origins is found in *Lightning Joe*, 157. Eisenhower states that Collins's rapid capture of Cherbourg justified the nickname. Eisenhower, *Crusade in Europe*, 260.

193. The genesis of Operation Cobra is described in Blumenson, *Breakout and Pursuit*, 146–88; and Bradley, *Soldier's Story*, 315–32.

194. Bradley, *Soldier's Story*, 332.

195. Collins's refinements to Bradley's original concept are described in Blumenson, *Breakout and Pursuit*, 213–23.

196. What follows is based on Blumenson, *Breakout and Pursuit*, 229–46; and Collins, *Lightning Joe*, 239–42.

197. What follows is based on Blumenson, *Breakout and Pursuit*, 247–335.

198. The official history of the fighting in the Hürtgen questions the judgment of the First Army commander, Lieutenant General Courtney Hodges, as well as both Collins and Gerow for continuously feeding American units into the fight for, at best, negligible gains. See MacDonald, *Siegfried Line Campaign*, 492–93. Collins's reply to this criticism is noticeably defensive. See Collins, *Lightning Joe*, 278–79. He was similarly defensive in his responses to questions on the same subject received from students and faculty of the CGSC in a seminar held in 1983 when he was inducted into the Leavenworth Hall of Fame. See CSI Report no. 5, "Conversations with General J. Lawton Collins," transcribed by Major Gary Wade (Fort Leavenworth, Kans.: Combat Studies Institute, CGSC, [1983]), 9–10.

199. What follows is based on information obtained from the Middleton, Gerow, Ridgway, Millikin, Eddy, and Collins files, NPRC.

200. All CGSS class standings and sizes taken from the untitled attachment to letter from Major General Garrison H. Davidson to General Lyman Lemnitzer, 14 March 1955, 7, Document no. N13423.98, CARL. However, Middleton's class size is per note 41 above.

201. These officers are listed in Berlin, "United States Army World War II Corps Commanders: A Composite Biography," 164–65. Commissioning branches are from Ancell, *Biographical Dictionary of World War II Generals*.

202. I am indebted to Dr. Roger Cirillo for the Gerow-Meade analogy.

203. Eddy's December 1945 medical evaluation states: "Beginning in December 1944, while on duty in Europe, he developed some nervousness with occasional insomnia which he relieved with sodium amytal [*sic*] or a couple of high balls." Eddy file, NPRC.

204. Marshall to SGS, 13 October 1944, WDCSA 201 (Middleton, Troy H.), Reel 54, Item 1881; and Middleton to Marshall, 24 November 1944, Marshall papers, Box 76, Folder 51, GCML.

205. As a former aide to MacArthur and a consummate people person in his own right, Eisenhower was fastidious about getting names right. The misspelling in question occurs in Eisenhower's cable to Marshall of 19 January 1945, Chandler et al., *Eisenhower Papers*, 2443.

4. The Coming of the Bulge

1. Clausewitz, *On War*, 203.

2. For extended treatments of the run-up to the Bulge, see Eisenhower, *Bitter Woods*, 36–176; MacDonald, *Time for Trumpets*, 17–97; and Cole, *Ardennes*, 1–74.

3. For a concise description of the very thorough planning for and skillful execution of Operation Bagration, see David M. Glantz and Jonathan M. House, *When Titans Clashed: How the Red Army Stopped Hitler* (Lawrence: University Press of Kansas, 1995), 195–215.

4. Magna E. Bauer, "The Idea for the German Offensive of 1944: An Attempt to Determine the Authorship of the Idea and Its Historical Development" (Washington, D.C.: Office of the Chief of Military History, 1952), 22–23, RG 549, NAII. The transcript of this rambling discourse, dominated by Hitler, can be found in Helmut Heiber and David M. Glantz, eds., *Hitler and His Generals: Military Conferences, 1942–1945* (New York: Enigma, 2002–2003), 444–63. A concise analysis of the German thinking behind the attack can be found in Charles V. P. von Luttichau, "The German Counteroffensive in the Ardennes," in Kent R. Greenfield, ed., *Command Decisions* (Washington, D.C.: OCMH, 1960), 443–59.

5. Bauer, "The Idea for the German Offensive," 24, RG 549, NAII. The rationale for selecting November comes from Walter Warlimont, *Inside Hitler's Headquarters, 1939–1945*, trans. R. H. Barry (1964; reprint, Novato, Calif.: Presidio Press, [1991]), 457.

6. The most common date cited for Hitler's "momentous decision" to attack through the Ardennes is 16 September 1944. See, among others, Cole, *Ardennes*, 1; and Dupuy, Bongard, and Anderson, *Hitler's Last Gamble*, 1–2. However, both Bauer and the keeper of the OKW war diary, Major Percy Schramm, argue that the exact date is much less certain. Bauer, "The Idea for the German Offensive," 24a, RG 549, NAII; and Percy Ernst Schramm, "The Preparations for the German Offensive in the Ardennes," in *The Battle of the Bulge, the German View: Perspectives from Hitler's High Command*, ed. Danny S. Parker (Mechanicsburg, Pa.: Stackpole Books, 1999), 38.

7. What follows is based on Schramm, "Preparations for Offensive in the Ardennes," in Parker, *Battle of the Bulge, the German View*, 45–56.

8. The term OB West can refer either to the commander or to the command. It will be used here, as it is in German, interchangeably.

9. Blumenson, *Patton Papers: 1940–1945*, 625. For several tantalizing alternate scenarios about the Bulge that portray much more significant German success than that actually achieved, see Peter G. Tsouras, ed., *Battle of the Bulge: Hitler's Alternate Scenarios* (London: Greenhill Books, 2004).

10. This little-noted aspect of Hitler's strategy is described in Gerhard Weinberg, *A World at Arms: A Global History of World War II* (New York: Cambridge University Press, 1994), 720–21.

11. This paragraph is drawn from Cole, *Ardennes*, 21–22.

12. Except as otherwise indicated, this paragraph is based on Schramm, "Preparations for Offensive in the Ardennes," in Parker, *Battle of the Bulge, the German View*, 63–73.

13. Carlo D'Este, "Model," in *Hitler's Generals*, ed. Correlli Barnett (New York: Grove Weidenfeld, 1989), 319.

14. The case for oil as a target is outlined in Richard G. Davis, *Carl A. Spaatz and the Air War in Europe* (Washington, D.C.: CAFH, 1993), 490–500. Tedder, while arguing for attacks against the transportation net, admitted after the war that "the oil plants and the communication system were not alternative but complementary targets." Arthur Tedder, *With Prejudice: The War Memoirs of Marshal of the Royal Air Force Lord Tedder G.C.B.* (London: Cassell, 1966), 614. However, as David Mets sagely observes, by this time in the war there was so much airpower available to the Allies that arguments over "priorities" were virtually moot. David Mets, *Master of Airpower: General Carl A. Spaatz* (Novato, Calif.: Presidio Press, 1988), 259.

15. Major General Fritz Kraemer, "Sixth Panzer Army Operations in the Ardennes, 1944–45," 58, FMS A-924, RG 319, NAII.

16. The extraordinary efforts taken to keep the German rail system functioning in the period of November 1944–January 1945 and the continuing deterioration of rail throughout despite these efforts is examined in detail in Alfred C. Mierzejewski, *The Collapse of the German War Economy, 1944–1945: Allied Air Power and the German National Railway* (Chapel Hill: University of North Carolina Press, 1988), 132–35.

17. General Hasso von Manteuffel, "Fifth Panzer Army (Ardennes Offensive Preparations)," 99, FMS B-151, RG 319, NAII.

18. Manteuffel's description of this friction is particularly vivid: "The greatest efforts were made to keep strategic railroad lines and the most important stations open, and actually amazing results were achieved. But it could not be prevented that the wheels of the German war-machine turned slower than they used to." Manteuffel, "Fifth Panzer Army (Ardennes Offensive Preparations)," 99, FMS B-151, RG 319, NAII.

19. Adverse flying weather was a critical ingredient in the German plan. Hitler had instructed the OKW meteorologists to determine an attack date that would ensure "at least ten days of continuous bad weather." Their response was 25 November. Cole, *Ardennes*, 22.

20. What follows is based on Schramm, "Preparations for Offensive in the Ardennes," in Parker, *Battle of the Bulge, the German View*, 87–89.

21. Dupuy, Bongard, and Anderson, *Hitler's Last Gamble*, 19.

22. Cole, *Ardennes*, 71.

23. Kraemer, "Sixth Panzer Army in the Ardennes," 4, FMS A-924, RG 319, NAII.

24. Schramm, "Preparations for Offensive in the Ardennes," in Parker, *Battle of the Bulge, the German View*, 66.

25. The description of security measures is based on Schramm, "Preparations for Offensive in the Ardennes," in Parker, *Battle of the Bulge, the German View*, 127–31.

26. Montgomery's position is articulated in Bernard Law Montgomery, *The Memoirs of Field-Marshal the Viscount Montgomery of Alamein, K.G.* (Cleveland: World Publishing, 1958), 15–251. See also Hamilton, *Monty: 1944–1976*, 3–7. But one should also note Hamilton's subsequent statement that his official three-volume biography of Montgomery was intended to "re-balance military historiography . . . without concealing Monty's many warts." Nigel Hamilton, *The Full Monty: Montgomery of Alamein, 1887–1942* (London: Allen Lane, 2001), xv. For a comprehen-

sive review of the historiographical debate, which favors the Eisenhower approach, see G. E. Patrick Murray, *Eisenhower versus Montgomery: The Continuing Debate* (Westport, Conn.: Praeger, 1996).

27. See especially Carlo D'Este, *Eisenhower: A Soldier's Life* (New York: Henry Holt, 2002), 603.

28. For a more extended treatment of my views on the efficacy of Eisenhower's broad front strategy, see the entry on the subject in Dennis Showalter, ed., *World War II, 1944–1945*, vol. 5 of *History in Dispute* (Detroit: St. James, 2000), 20–22.

29. Eisenhower, *Crusade in Europe*, 291–93.

30. Eisenhower's grandson sums this all up quite nicely: "The 'broad front' was a flexible but cautious concept, aimed at clearing all of France and forgoing the advantages of concentration in attack. . . . In short, Eisenhower intended to proceed methodically, not boldly. SHAEF strategy would serve the dual purpose of pursuit and survival." David Eisenhower, *Eisenhower: At War*, 214–15.

31. See, for example, Timothy Naftali's review of D'Este, *Eisenhower*, in *New York Times Book Review*, 28 July 2002, 8.

32. Although the last reason alone was sufficient for the superior Allied force to reject Montgomery's plan, Eisenhower may also have been subliminally influenced by the realization that pitting the operational maneuver skills of Montgomery, or even Montgomery and Bradley, against those of commanders such as Rundstedt, Model, and Manteuffel was not a very good bet.

33. What follows is based on Forrest C. Pogue, *The Supreme Command* (Washington, D.C.: OCMH, 1954), 215–17, 244–60. For a detailed account of the frantic efforts of the supply services to keep up with the pursuing American armies, see Roland G. Ruppenthal, *May 1941–September 1944*, vol. 1 of *The Logistical Support of the Armies* (Washington, D.C.: OCMH, 1953), 488–583. For a stinging indictment of the "pusillanimous" logistical planning for the Northwest European campaign, see Martin van Creveld, *Supplying War* (Cambridge: Cambridge University Press, 1977), 202–30. Van Creveld's analysis insufficiently accounts for the multifarious and pervasive unknowns faced by logistical planners. It does, however, nicely portray the command challenges that arise when the assumptions upon which logistical plans and, thus, operational and strategic plans are based turn out to be invalid.

34. Pogue, *Supreme Command*, 255.

35. Details of Market-Garden can be found in Charles B. MacDonald, "The Decision to Launch Operation Market-Garden," in Greenfield, *Command Decisions*, 429–59; MacDonald, *Mighty Endeavor*, 338–46; Ryan, *A Bridge Too Far*, passim; and Blair, *Ridgway's Paratroopers*, 365–413.

36. MacDonald, *Mighty Endeavor*, 348.

37. The remainder of this paragraph is based on Jeffrey J. Clarke and Robert Ross Smith, *Riviera to the Rhine* (Washington, D.C.: CMH, 1993), 223–491.

38. In fact, both Britain and the United States were the only two belligerents of World War II pursuing a "general" or comprehensive air strategy consisting of four elements: air defense, strategic attack, naval aviation, and support to ground formations. Richard Overy, *The Air War, 1939–1945* (New York: Stein and Day, 1980), 204.

39. Eisenhower's side of this dispute is told in Eisenhower, *Crusade in Europe*, 221–23; and Pogue, *Supreme Command*, 123–25. The air side is told in John E. Fagg, "Plan for OVERLORD," in Craven and Cate, *Army Air Forces* 3:79–83. Arnold had

no objections to the American bombers being placed under Eisenhower's command, but the RAF leadership and Churchill objected strenuously to the possibility of the heavies being placed under Leigh-Mallory, thus giving them a purely "tactical" focus. Eisenhower's stipulation that he would direct all air operations through Tedder, thus keeping the strategic air forces out of Leigh-Mallory's control, was apparently a key concession that helped resolve this situation.

40. What follows concerning air support on D-Day is based primarily on Robert H. George, "Normandy," in Craven and Cate, *Army Air Forces* 3:186–96.

41. Phillip S. Meilinger, *Hoyt S. Vandenberg: The Life of a General* (1989; reprint, Washington, D.C.: Air Force History and Museums Program, 2000), 50.

42. Vincent Orange, *Coningham: A Biography of Air Marshal Sir Arthur Coningham* (1990; reprint, Washington, D.C.: CAFH, 1992), 208. For details of the American side of this operation, with some mention of the British, see Robert H. George, "The Battle of France," in Craven and Cate, *Army Air Forces* 3:253–58.

43. Eisenhower, *Crusade in Europe*, 307–8.

44. Pogue, *Supreme Command*, 274–75, contains a very circumspect account of this reorganization. For the tangled politics behind the disestablishment of AEAF and the concomitant removal of Leigh-Mallory from the European air chain of command, see Orange, *Coningham*, 202–10.

45. The most authoritative treatment of air support for Third Army is David N. Spires, *Air Power for Patton's Army: The XIX Tactical Air Command in the Second World War* (Washington, D.C.: Air Force History and Museums Program, 2002). For the integration of Ultra information as well as airpower into Patton's operational style during the August pursuit, see Shwedo, *XIX Tactical Air Command*.

46. A sampling of the published literature includes Ralph Bennett, *Ultra in the West: The Normandy Campaign, 1944–45* (New York: Scribner's, 1979), 187–204; Cole, *Ardennes*, 56–63; Eisenhower, *Bitter Woods*, 162–78; F. H. Hinsley et al., *British Intelligence in the Second World War: Its Influence on Strategy and Operations*, vol. 3, pt. 2 (New York: Cambridge University Press, 1988), 401–50; MacDonald, *Time for Trumpets*, 62–79; Pogue, *Supreme Command*, 361–72; and F. W. Winterbotham, *The Ultra Secret* (New York: Harper and Row, 1974), 177–80. See also Adolph G. Rosengarten, Memorandum for Colonel [Telford] Taylor [chief American Ultra representative at Bletchley Park, the British deciphering station], Subject: "Report on Ultra Intelligence at First U.S. Army," 21 May 1945, 5, SRH-023, "Reports by U.S. Army ULTRA Representatives in the European Theater of Operations," RG 457, Box 9, NAII.

47. The first portion of this sentence is a paraphrase of Clausewitz: "War is the realm of uncertainty; three quarters of the factors on which action in war are based are wrapped in a fog of greater or lesser uncertainty." *On War*, 101.

48. Bennett, *Ultra in the West*, 192; and Hinsley et al., *British Intelligence*, vol. 3, pt. 2, 421.

49. For details of American aerial reconnaissance, see David G. Rempel, "Battle of the Bulge," in Craven and Cate, *Army Air Forces* 3:673–83; Ultra information is from Bennett, *Ultra in the West*, 194–96.

50. Bennett, *Ultra in the West*, 178–80, 189; and Hinsley et al., *British Intelligence*, vol. 3, pt. 2, 423–24.

51. Hinsley et al., *British Intelligence*, vol. 3, pt. 2, 430n.

52. Pogue, *Supreme Command*, 365.

53. Cole, *Ardennes*, 59–60.

54. See especially Pogue, *Supreme Command*, 371–72; and Cole, *Ardennes*, 63.

55. This account is based on a letter from Strong to Pogue of 31 August 1945 found in Pogue, *Supreme Command*, 365n20.

56. Eisenhower, *Bitter Woods*, 172–73.

57. Hinsley et al., *British Intelligence*, vol. 3, pt. 2, 426–27. The misunderstanding of Rundstedt's operational freedom was also reflected in the G-2 portion of the daily briefing given to Bradley on 8 December, which began, "Gen VON RUNDSTEDT is running all operations on the Western front. He has fought a more intelligent campaign since the loss of France." 12th AG Commanding General's Daily Briefing, 8 December 1944, RG 331, Box 1764, NAII.

58. What follows is based on Eisenhower, *Bitter Woods*, 169–72; Pogue, *Supreme Command*, 366–70; and Hogan, *Command Post*, 205–7. For Dickson's apologia, see Benjamin A. Dickson, "G-2 Journal: Algiers to the Elbe," 170–81, Dickson papers, MHI.

59. Dickson's uneasy relations with Hodges, Kean, and Sibert are alluded to in Pogue, *Supreme Command*, 366, but dealt with more explicitly in Hogan, *Command Post*, 122, 123, and 208.

60. Cited from Eisenhower, *Bitter Woods*, 171.

61. There is a detailed analysis of the locations of Dickson's targets in Pogue, *Supreme Command*, 367n10. In Dickson's defense, twenty-four of the forty-eight targets were in the Eifel; but Pogue points out that twenty-six of the thirty-six first priority targets were further north, indicating that the Roer region was the main locus of Dickson's concern.

62. Dickson, "G-2 Journal," 181, Dickson papers, MHI.

63. What follows is based on Oscar W. Koch, with Robert G. Hays, *G-2: Intelligence for Patton* (Philadelphia: Whitmore, 1971), 78–90.

64. Unlike First Army, at which the G-2 was treated as something of a worrisome outsider, the Third Army G-2 was a valued member of Patton's inner circle. Koch attributed his success as a G-2 to the strong command support he received from Patton. Koch, *G-2: Intelligence for Patton*, 165–67. That this also applied to the Ultra representative is evident in Captain George C. Church, Memorandum for Colonel Taylor, "Ultra and the Third Army," 28 May 1945, 3, SRH 023, RG 457, Box 9, NAII.

65. This interpretation is most notably advanced in Winterbotham, *Ultra Secret*, 178.

66. This was particularly the view of the British vice chief of the Imperial General Staff. See Hinsley et al., *British Intelligence*, vol. 3, pt. 2, 429.

67. This point is strongly emphasized in Bennett, *Ultra in the West*, 203.

68. This point is a cardinal element of deception theory. See Donald C. Daniel and Katherine L. Herbig, "Propositions on Military Deception," in *Strategic Military Deception*, ed. Donald C. Daniel and Katherine L. Herbig (New York: Pergamon, 1982), 23.

69. Cole, *Ardennes*, 63.

70. What follows is based on Eisenhower, *Crusade in Europe*, 338–41; Bradley, *Soldier's Story*, 453–60; and Eisenhower, *Bitter Woods*, 100–101.

71. To Eisenhower's credit, he assumed full responsibility for the failure: "This plan [to continue the offensive] gave the German opportunity to launch his attack

against a weak position of our lines. If giving him that chance is to be condemned by historians, their condemnation should be directed at me alone." *Crusade in Europe*, 341. This is typical Eisenhower and reminiscent of his draft message accepting responsibility should the Normandy landings have failed. But it may have also been designed to shield Bradley from criticism. In this regard, it does not wash.

72. For a critique of Bradley's calculated-risk argument, see Morelock, *Generals of the Ardennes*, 120–21. In Bradley's partial defense, he admits that he underestimated both the potential size and intention of the German attack. Bradley, *Soldier's Story*, 459–60.

73. What follows is based primarily on Michael Doubler's very insightful work, *Closing with the Enemy: How GIs Fought the War in Europe, 1944–1945* (Lawrence: University Press of Kansas, 1994), passim. For the tale of the American army's adaptation from the beginning of World War II through the end of the Normandy campaign, see Russell A. Hart's equally astute *Clash of Arms: How the Allies Won in Normandy* (Boulder, Colo.: Lynne Rienner, 2001), 69–100, 271–302.

74. McNair's strong role in formulating the army's organizational philosophy is described in Greenfield, Palmer, and Wiley, *Organization of Ground Combat Troops*, 271–76.

75. McNair's stipulation was based on the presumption that "the division is part of a larger force from which it can obtain prompt combat and logistical support." Ibid., 277.

76. Artillery strengths from Shelby L. Stanton, *World War II Order of Battle* (New York: Galahad Books, 1984), 9.

77. Letter, Walter F. Winton, Jr., to author, 27 January 2004; and Blair, *Ridgway's Paratroopers*, 48–49. According to Blair, the short-barreled 105 had a range of only 8,000 yards, some 2,000 fewer than the standard 105. For this reason, about a dozen regular 105s were put into the division "tail" to augment some of the short-barreled models (presumably those in general support) when linkup with the ground forces was effected.

78. Roland G. Ruppenthal, *September 1944–May 1945*, vol. 2 of *The Logistical Support of the Armies* (Washington, D.C.: OCMH, 1959), 263–69.

79. Weigley, *Eisenhower's Lieutenants*, 22–24.

80. The story of the progressive reduction in the estimates of army divisions required for World War II is told most concisely in Maurice Matloff, "The 90-Division Gamble," in Greenfield, *Command Decisions*, 365–81. For Wedemeyer's role in the original estimate, see Albert C. Wedemeyer, *Wedemeyer Reports!* (New York: Henry Holt, 1958), 63–76. Despite several self-confessed "glaring" misprognostications, Wedemeyer's work to determine the broad outlines of a concept for victory in World War II remains one of the most remarkable pieces of strategic thinking to be produced by a relatively junior officer in the annals of American military history.

81. The figure of forty-four is from Ruppenthal, *Logistical Support of the Armies* 2:281. One of these, the 17th Airborne Division, was in England, available for deployment to the continent; two others, the 75th and 94th Infantry Divisions, had deployed to the continent but were not yet committed. Dupuy, Bongard, and Anderson, *Hitler's Last Gamble*, 34.

82. A great deal of attention has been given to the army's individual replacement system, most of it negative. Its detractors criticize the cold cruelty with which men were thrown into the line with virtually no opportunity provided to bond with their

new comrades. These include historians as diverse as Stephen Ambrose, Martin van Creveld, and Russell Weigley. See Ambrose, *Citizen Soldiers*, 273–89; Weigley, *Eisenhower's Lieutenants*, 729; and Martin van Creveld, *Fighting Power: German and U.S. Army Performance, 1939–1945* (Westport, Conn.: Greenwood, 1982), 74–79. A recent defender makes three counterarguments: that despite its drawbacks, the individual replacement system did keep American divisions much more nearly at full strength than were their German counterparts; that its adverse effects were ameliorated by those division commanders who established their own in-theater training and orientation centers; and that given the lack of divisions in the ETO, there was simply no other choice. See Peter R. Mansoor, *The GI Offensive in Europe: The Triumph of American Infantry Divisions, 1941–1945* (Lawrence: University Press of Kansas, 1999), 250–56. Mansoor makes arguable points; but I believe that had he been processed through the "Repple Depples" and found himself thrust into an infantry squad in combat with no prior opportunity to bond with the men already there, he would not wish to repeat the experience.

83. Mansoor, *GI Offensive in Europe*, 252.

84. The rising pitch of the manpower crisis of the autumn and early winter of 1944 is convincingly described in Ruppenthal, *Logistical Support of the Armies* 2:304–25.

85. Even the latter was insufficient to match the German Tiger tank with its 88-mm main gun and up to 100 mm of armor. The Americans did not field a tank that could match the Tiger until the M26 Pershing, equipped with a 90-mm gun and up to 112.5 mm of armor, arrived in Europe in January 1945. Peter Chamberlain and Chris Ellis, *British and American Tanks of World War II* (New York: Arco, 1969), 114–17; George Forty, *German Tanks of World War II "in Action"* (London: Blandford, 1988), 135–36.

86. On the pros and cons of tank destroyer doctrine and design, see Christopher R. Gabel, *Seek, Strike, and Destroy: U.S. Army Tank Destroyer Doctrine in World War II* (Fort Leavenworth, Kans.: CGSC, 1985).

87. The early development of the American artillery's centralized fire direction is described in Boyd L. Dastrup, *King of Battle: A Branch History of the U.S. Army's Field Artillery* (Fort Monroe, Va.: United States Army Training and Doctrine Command, 1992), 197–98. Its effectiveness in the ETO from Normandy to the eve of the Bulge is assessed in ibid., 217–23.

88. Van Creveld is particularly complimentary of the efforts by Major General Ira T. Wyche, commander of the 79th ID, to integrate replacements into his organization; see van Creveld, *Fighting Power*, 78.

89. What follows is based on Edmund L. Blandford, *Hitler's Second Army: The Waffen SS* (Osceola, Wis.: Motorbooks International, 1994), passim; and Brend Wegner, "SS," in *The Oxford Companion to World War II*, ed. I. C. B. Dear and M. R. D. Foot (Oxford: Oxford University Press, 1995), 1044–50.

90. Material in quotation marks from Blaine Taylor, "A Combat History of the 1st SS Panzer Division," in Editors of *Command Magazine*, *Hitler's Army: The Evolution and Structure of German Armed Forces, 1933–1945* (Conshohocken, Pa.: Combined Books, 1996), 115.

91. Complete order of battle for Sixth SS Panzer Army is found in Dupuy, Bongard, and Anderson, *Hitler's Last Gamble*, 442–43.

92. Schramm, "Preparations for Offensive in the Ardennes," in Parker, *Battle of the Bulge, the German View*, 131–33. To preserve the fiction that the overall

strategy was defensive, the offensive operations for which the army trained were always set in the scenario of countering an Allied breakthrough. For additional details, see Michael Reynolds, *Men of Steel: I SS Panzer Corps, the Ardennes and Eastern Front, 1944–45* (New York: Sarpedon, 1999), 35–41.

93. A very detailed description of the panzer and panzergrenadier divisional organizations can be found it Dupuy, Bongard, and Anderson, *Hitler's Last Gamble*, 410–11.

94. Ibid., 416–19.

95. R. L. DiNardo, *Mechanized Juggernaut or Military Anachronism? Horses and the German Army of World War II* (New York: Greenwood, 1991), 101.

96. What follows concerning the human component of the VGDs is based largely on MacDonald, *Time for Trumpets*, 43–44. The concluding assessment of unevenness is, however, my own.

97. MacDonald, *Time for Trumpets*, 65; again, the latter inference is mine.

98. Dupuy, Bongard, and Anderson, *Hitler's Last Gamble*, 411–13.

99. Ibid.

100. What follows is based on Eisenhower, *Bitter Woods*, 123–24 and 137–39.

101. In his comprehensive history of the Prussian, later German, General Staff, Walter Görlitz was later to comment ruefully on the Hitler-Skorzeny relationship: "Skorzeny was an apostle of Tito's brand of partisan warfare which always made a strong appeal to Hitler, and so a man after Hitler's own heart. It had been a long way—and a shameful one—from Moltke to Skorzeny." Walter Görlitz, *History of the German General Staff, 1657–1945*, tr. Brian Battershaw (New York: Praeger, 1959), 484.

102. Eisenhower, *Bitter Woods*, 123.

103. Alistair Horne, *To Lose a Battle: France 1940* (Boston: Little Brown, 1969), 204.

104. For the effects of rationalized production practices on German war industry, including an analysis of the economic effects of the Allied strategic bombing campaign, see Richard Overy, *War and Economy in the Third Reich* (Oxford: Clarendon, 1994), 342–75.

105. What follows is based on Schramm, "Preparations for Offensive in the Ardennes," in Parker, *Battle of the Bulge, the German View*, 133–37.

106. The standard history is Görlitz, *German General Staff*. Görlitz recognizes the general staff's operational acumen but chastises its undermining of political authority.

107. For a detailed examination of von Seeckt's reforming role, see James S. Corum, *The Roots of Blitzkrieg: Hans von Seeckt and German Military Reform* (Lawrence: University Press of Kansas, 1992); Hitler's conquest of the general staff is outlined in Görlitz, *German General Staff*, 340–409.

108. A description of how the general staff coped with the high casualties of World War II can be found in van Creveld, *Fighting Power*, 148–49.

109. This paragraph is based on van Creveld, *Fighting Power*, 43, 75–76.

110. This paragraph is drawn heavily from the very complete description of German weapons found in Dupuy, Bongard, and Anderson, *Hitler's Last Gamble*, 413–22. Additional technical details are from Peter Chamberlain and Hilary L. Doyle, *An Encyclopedia of German Tanks of World War Two* (New York: Arco, 1978), 98–136.

111. Weigley, *Eisenhower's Lieutenants*, 28–31.

112. This conclusion is at variance with previous assessments by Dupuy, van Creveld, and, to some extent, even Weigley. The scholarship of Doubler, Mansoor, and Hart cited above has forced a reconsideration of the whole picture and more or less evened the scales.

113. USSBS, *European War Report Number 61, Air Force Rate of Operations* (Washington, D.C.: USSBS, 1947), Exhibits 1 and 2.

114. Technical description of the P-47 from W. A. Jacobs, "The Battle for France," in *Case Studies in the Development of Close Air Support*, ed. Benjamin Cooling (Washington, D.C.: OAFH, 1990), 250.

115. 2nd TAF strength figures from Parker, *To Win the Winter Sky*, 54.

116. Davis, *Carl A. Spaatz*, 624–25.

117. Parker, *To Win the Winter Sky*, 59.

118. Mets, *Master of Airpower*, 193.

119. Details of regrouping east of the Rhine from Alfred Price, *The Last Year of the Luftwaffe, May 1944 to May 1945* (Osceola, Wis.: Motorbooks International, 1991), 97–99.

120. Adolf Galland, *The First and the Last: The Rise and Fall of the German Fighter Forces, 1938–1945*, trans. Mervyn Savill (New York: Henry Holt, 1954), 288–89; Great Britain, Air Ministry, *The Rise and Fall of the German Air Force, 1933–1945* (1948; reprint, New York: St. Martin's, 1983), 365–74.

121. Galland, *First and Last*, 309–10.

122. For representative pilot losses in November 1944, see Werner Girbig, *Six Months to Oblivion: The Defeat of the Luftwaffe Fighter Force over the Western Front*, trans. David Johnston and Richard Simpkin (West Chester, Pa.: Schiffer Military History, 1991), 28, 34, 38. In January 1945, a delegation of fighter commanders sought an audience with Göring and openly expressed their profound reservations concerning the Reich Marshal's policies, leadership style, and advisors. This incident became known as the "mutiny of the fighter pilots." For Galland's version of the events, see Galland, *First and Last*, 315–17.

123. The description of the Ardennes region that follows in this and the following paragraph has been adapted from that of Charles B. MacDonald in *Time for Trumpets*, 25–27.

124. This analysis is based on that of the Sixth SS Panzer Army's topographical officer, which is found in James Lucas, *The Last Year of the German Army, May 1944–May 1945* (London: Arms and Armour, 1994), 162–64.

125. Cole, *Ardennes*, 47.

126. Rempel, "Battle of the Bulge," in Craven and Cate, *Army Air Forces* 3:675.

127. Cole, *Ardennes*, 47.

128. Marvin Kays, *Weather Effects during the Battle of the Bulge and the Normandy Invasion* (White Sands Missile Range, N. Mex.: U.S. Army Electronics Research and Development Command Atmospheric Sciences Laboratory, 1982), 13.

5. The Germans Attack, the Allies React

1. Eisenhower, *Bitter Woods*, 179–80.

2. The historical appropriateness of Spa as a military headquarters is engagingly described in Weigley, *Eisenhower's Lieutenants*, 493.

3. Hogan, *Command Post*, 205.

4. D'Este, *Eisenhower*, 639.

5. Montgomery, *Memoirs*, 275. Montgomery's request for Christmas leave is contained in a handwritten note of 15 December 1944, Dwight D. Eisenhower Pre-Presidential Papers, Box 83, Montgomery file, DDEL.

6. D'Este, *Eisenhower*, 639.

7. What follows is based on Eisenhower, *Crusade in Europe*, 342–44; Eisenhower, *Bitter Woods*, 215; and D'Este, *Eisenhower*, 640. The SHAEF commander charitably gave full credit in his memoirs to Bradley for a mutual determination of the attack's significance; however, his son ferreted out the reality of the diverse assessments.

8. Eisenhower, *Bitter Woods*, 215.

9. Ibid.

10. Bradley, *Soldier's Story*, 465. The tenor of this treatment indicates it was all Bradley's decision, not Eisenhower's.

11. D'Este, *Eisenhower*, 642; Lieutenant Colonel Chester Hansen diary, 16 December 1944, Hansen papers, MHI.

12. What follows is based on D. K. R. Crosswell, *Chief of Staff: The Military Career of General Walter Bedell Smith* (New York: Greenwood, 1991), 283–84.

13. The SHAEF order placing XVIII (Airborne) Corps under 12th Army Group command and directing its concentration at Bastogne was released at 172255 December, SHAEF G-3 Battle of the Ardennes records, RG 331, NAII.

14. Eisenhower, *Crusade in Europe*, 344. For example, First Allied Airborne Army was directed to move the 17th Airborne Division from England to Rheims by air "as soon as possible." SHAEF message, 181949 December 1944, SHAEF G-3 Battle of the Ardennes records, RG 331, NAII.

15. Hansen diary, 17 December 1944, Hansen papers, MHI.

16. Ibid. Bradley later offered an additional rationale for not moving his headquarters: concern for the safety of the Luxembourgers.

17. Ibid.

18. Ibid., 18 December 1944.

19. What follows is based on Hogan, *Command Post*, 209–15.

20. Ibid., 212.

21. Ibid.

22. Ibid.

23. D'Este, *Eisenhower*, 644.

24. Ibid.

25. Eisenhower, *Crusade in Europe*, 345.

26. Weigley accurately refers to it as "the Doctrinal Response." Weigley, *Eisenhower's Lieutenants*, 465–90.

27. What follows is based on D'Este, *Eisenhower*, 644–45; Eisenhower, *Bitter Woods*, 256–57; Weigley, *Eisenhower's Lieutenants*, 499–501; and Blumenson, *Patton Papers: 1940–1945*, 599–600.

28. Blumenson called it "the sublime moment of his [Patton's] career." Blumenson, *Patton Papers: 1940–1945*, 599; Ike's retort from Eisenhower, *Bitter Woods*, 257.

29. Eisenhower, *Bitter Woods*, 256.

30. Details of security over the Meuse in various areas are contained in a memo of 21 December 1944 from Major General Robert W. Crawford, SHAEF G-4, to the SHAEF G-3. Meuse bridges from Liège, through Namur, to Givet were secured with

engineer forces; from Givet south, the bridges were secured with a combination of
four engineer regiments, four French battalions of unspecified composition, and either a battery or a battalion of (presumably French) 75-mm artillery. SHAEF Memo,
ACof S, G-4, to ACof S, G-3, Subject: COM ZONE DISPOSITIONS, 21 December
1944. Additionally, SHAEF message, 211938 December 1944, specified coordination
measures to be taken between the army groups and communications zone personnel
for defense and, if required, demolition of the bridges. RG 331, SHAEF G-3 Battle
of the Ardennes records, NAII.

31. SHAEF message, 192030 December 1944, Dwight D. Eisenhower Pre-
Presidential papers, Box 13, Bradley file, DDEL. Bradley's treatment of this message
in his memoirs is very disingenuous: "Although Eisenhower had evidenced no sign
of uneasiness during the conference at Verdun on December 19, his staff at SHAEF
had shown symptoms of what we at Group diagnosed as an acute case of the shakes.
. . . The first evidence of SHAEF's anxiety came in a TWX cautioning us to make
certain that no bridge over the Meuse fell into the enemy's hands. 'What the devil
do they think we're doing,' Lev Allen complained, 'starting back for the beaches?'"
Bradley, *Soldier's Story*, 476.

32. The treatment of Eisenhower's decision to give Montgomery command of
Ninth and First Armies is based on the following sources: Crosswell, *Chief of Staff*,
285–87; D'Este, *Eisenhower*, 647–48; Bradley, *Soldier's Story*, 476–77; and Hamilton, *Monty: 1944–1976*, 201–6. Monty, not being content with his demarche to
Whiteley, also cabled the British CIGS, Field Marshal Alanbrooke, on the evening
of the 19th, suggesting that Eisenhower be given a direct order, presumably by the
Combined Chiefs of Staff, of which Alanbrooke was a member, to put him in charge
of the northern half of the Bulge. Ibid., 197–98.

33. Forrest C. Pogue interview with Smith of 5 August 1947, cited in Hamilton,
Monty: 1944–1976, 206.

34. Crosswell, *Chief of Staff*, 286.

35. Montgomery's biographer points out that his desire for command over American troops went back to late September 1944. Hamilton, *Monty: 1944–1976*, 210.
But the issue was even larger. Montgomery never reconciled himself to the fact that
after the Normandy breakout he would no longer command all the ground troops in
Europe. His long disputes over strategy with Eisenhower were both substantive, in
their disagreement over the best course of action to pursue to defeat the Wehrmacht,
and personal, to fulfill a vision of himself as the most competent general of the war.
This long-standing tension with Montgomery over who would call the shots in Europe made Eisenhower's decision even more difficult than it would have been with
a more self-effacing commander and, in the final analysis, even more of a tribute to
him as a great commander.

36. Patton, for example, interpreted the move as a sign of weakness, noting caus-
tically in his diary, "Eisenhower is either unwilling or unable to command Montgomery." Blumenson, *Patton Papers, 1940–1945*, 601.

37. Hamilton, *Monty: 1944–1976*, 213.

38. Francis de Guingand, *Operation Victory* (New York: Scribner's, 1947),
429–30.

39. Hogan, *Command Post*, 219.

40. Crosswell, *Chief of Staff*, 287. The date of this communication is not given;
it was apparently on either the 20th or the 21st.

41. SHAEF message from Eisenhower to Montgomery, 221345 December 1944, Dwight D. Eisenhower Pre-Presidential papers, Box 83, Montgomery file, DDEL. Eisenhower also wrote Hodges telling him that now that he had been placed under Monty's operational command, "the slogan is 'chins up.'" SHAEF message from Eisenhower to Hodges, 221400 December, copy in diary of Hodges's aide-de-camp, Major William C. Sylvan, 143, CMH.

42. Incoming SHAEF message from Montgomery to Eisenhower, 222155 December 1944, Dwight D. Eisenhower Pre-Presidential papers, Box 83, Montgomery file, DDEL.

43. This modus operandi is suggested in Hogan, *Command Post*, 220.

44. What follows is based on Blumenson, *Patton Papers: 1940–1945*, 600–604.

45. Blumenson, *Patton Papers: 1940–1945*, 604.

46. USSTAF A-2 (Air Intelligence), "Allied Airpower and the Ardennes Offensive," daily summaries for 16–18 December 1944, USAFHRA File 519.601C(S). All material in this file has been declassified.

47. Ibid., daily summaries for 19–21 December.

48. Ibid., Statistical Annex.

49. The precise results of these attacks are the subject of some dispute. In a letter of 7 January 1945, Spaatz told Arnold that the attack had destroyed "fifty to sixty tanks." Mets, *Master of Airpower*, 265. The official air force history credits the attack with the destruction of thirty-two armored and fifty-six motor vehicles. Craven and Cate, *Army Air Forces* 3:688. The army official history says that the attack on the German forces at Stavelot "crippled a few enemy vehicles and drove the balance to cover." Cole, *Ardennes*, 337. Peiper's account reads as follows: "In the afternoon of 18 Dec 44 we had a bad break when the weather cleared and American fighter bombers came over. We lost two to three tanks and five armored half-tracks. The tanks blew up in the road, and the road was too narrow to by-pass them, thus causing additional delay." "Interview with Colonel Joachim Peiper, 1st SS Panzer Regiment in the Ardennes (11–24 December 1944)," FMS ETHINT-10, 29, RG 319, NAII.

50. USSTAF A-2, "Ardennes Offensive," Statistical Annex, USAFHRA File 519.601C(S). All material in this file has been declassified.

51. Craven and Cate, *Army Air Forces* 3:686.

52. Orange, *Coningham*, 226.

53. Tedder, *With Prejudice*, 627.

54. Mets, *Master of Airpower*, 264; Craven and Cate, *Army Air Forces* 3:691.

55. Eisenhower, *Crusade in Europe*, 345.

56. Hansen diary, 19 December 1944, Hansen papers, MHI. Reflecting Bradley's despondency over the lack of air support, Hansen ended his entry for the 19th with a long peroration on the air situation and its adverse implications for the 12th Army Group: "Moreover, weather is once again our undoing. Had the weather been suitable for proper Tac R[econnaissance] it might have been possible for us to detect his large scale movements of troops and supplies to the concentration areas for his jumpoff. Our air effort today has been negligible. Fighter bombers were either closed on their fields or compelled to attack enemy ground installations almost without a ceiling. Heavy enemy motor movements would have given him bumper to bumper targets for many miles along the road. The mediums bombed but without observed

results and there is no evidence they obtained any. Meanwhile he [the enemy] is re-
deploying his strength to exploit this attack while we have moved to ctontain [*sic*] it,
possibly prepare a dmaging [*sic*] counterblow."

57. Ibid., 20 December 1944.

58. Sylvan diary, 21 December 1944, 145, CMH.

59. Cole, *Ardennes*, Map VII.

6. V Corps Halts the German *Schwerpunkt*

1. Eisenhower, *Bitter Woods*, 224.

2. *Table of Organization and Equipment No. 100-2, Headquarters Company,
Corps* (Washington, D.C.: War Department, 15 July 1943), 2.

3. What follows is based on Ancell, *Biographical Dictionary of World War II
Generals*, 158–59.

4. Like Damon, Huebner was an up-from-the-ranks infantryman and a son
of the Nebraska plains. For elaboration on the Damon model, see Sidney B. Berry,
"No Time for Glory in the Infantry: The Letters of Anton Myrer, Author of *Once an
Eagle*," *Assembly* 56 (March/April 1988): 44. The book is Anton Myrer, *Once an
Eagle* (New York: Holt, Rinehart, and Winston, 1968).

5. Except as otherwise noted, this paragraph is based on Cole, *Ardennes*, Map
II, augmented by my personal observation of the terrain.

6. MacDonald, *Time for Trumpets*, 371.

7. This trail, described in Reynolds, *Men of Steel*, 56, does not appear on Map
II of Cole, *Ardennes*.

8. Information on Wahlerscheid from Dupuy, Bongard, and Anderson, *Hitler's
Last Gamble*, 30.

9. Walter E. Lauer, *Battle Babies: The Story of the 99th Infantry Division in
World War II* (Baton Rouge: Military Press of Louisiana, 1951), 5.

10. Biographical information on Lauer from Dupuy, Bongard, and Anderson,
Hitler's Last Gamble, 53; and Ancell, *Biographical Dictionary of World War II
Generals*, 183.

11. 99th ID's dispositions from Dupuy, Bongard, and Anderson, *Hitler's Last
Gamble*, 55.

12. Weigley, *Eisenhower's Lieutenants*, 109, 140–41, and 283–84.

13. Ancell, *Biographical Dictionary of World War II Generals*, 275.

14. 2nd ID's dispositions from Dupuy, Bongard, and Anderson, *Hitler's Last
Gamble*, 30–31.

15. Sixth SS Panzer Army dispositions and plans from Cole, *Ardennes*, 76–77.

16. Biographical sketch on Priess from Mark C. Yerger, *Waffen-SS Commanders:
The Army, Corps, and Divisional Commanders of a Legend*, 2 vols. (Atglen, Pa.:
Schiffer Military History, 1999), 2:162–64.

17. Cole, *Ardennes*, 76–77.

18. Reynolds, *Devil's Adjutant*, 32.

19. Reynolds, *Men of Steel*, 49.

20. The description of the *Rollbahnen* is based on MacDonald, *Time for Trumpets*, 162; and Reynolds, *Men of Steel*, Map 10.

21. Eisenhower, *Bitter Woods*, 161.

22. This is, in fact, the interpretation found in Eisenhower, *Bitter Woods*, 190.

23. What follows is based on excerpts of the interviews in Reynolds, *Men of Steel*, 48.

24. This paragraph is based on Dupuy, Bongard, and Anderson, *Hitler's Last Gamble*, 46.

25. Cole cites Model as the authority on this decision, noting that his staff speculated that the field marshal wished to spare the picturesque, wood-latticed homes that adorned this popular German resort. Cole, *Ardennes*, 86n. Dupuy, Bongard, and Anderson cite Hitzfeld's memoirs, published sometime after 1980, in which the corps commander states that the determination was his but that it was supported by Model. Dupuy, Bongard, and Anderson, *Hitler's Last Gamble*, 509n.

26. MacDonald, *Time for Trumpets*, 172.

27. Lauer, *Battle Babies*, 16. The translation Lauer cites is slightly different from the one found in Eisenhower's *Bitter Woods*, 179–80, but the essential meaning is the same.

28. This classic, and in hindsight critical, small-unit defense was of insufficient magnitude to find inclusion in the official history. It was covered in some depth by John S. D. Eisenhower in *Bitter Woods*, 183–92. For an engaging and even more detailed treatment, see Rusiecki, *Key to the Bulge*, 83–107. The platoon leader, Lieutenant Lyle J. Brouck, was awarded the Silver Star in 1945; but after a 1977 public relations campaign and testimony before the House Armed Services Committee, he and three other platoon members were awarded the DSC, while five additional soldiers were awarded Silver Stars. The platoon was awarded a Presidential Unit Citation. Rusiecki, *Key to the Bulge*, 155–56, 166–68. See also Alex Kershaw, *The Longest Winter: The Battle of the Bulge and the Epic Story of World War II's Most Decorated Platoon* (Cambridge, Mass.: Da Capo, 2004). Kershaw's work adds little tactical detail to Rusiecki's, but it contains an evocative account of the time Lieutenant Brouck and many of his men spent in German captivity.

29. What follows is based on MacDonald, *Time for Trumpets*, 167–69.

30. This paragraph is based on Dupuy, Bongard, and Anderson, *Hitler's Last Gamble*, 49–52.

31. For an engaging infantryman's view of the 3rd Battalion, 95th Infantry's defense of Höfen, see Neill, *Infantry Soldier*, 230–48.

32. The depiction of the Robertson-Lauer meeting that follows is based on MacDonald, *Time for Trumpets*, 179–80. It is also found in Dupuy, Bongard, and Anderson, *Hitler's last Gamble*, 53–54. Neither provides references.

33. Hogan, *Command Post*, 209.

34. The FUSA message reassigning CCB, 9th AD, from V Corps to VIII Corps is dated 161130 December. CCB was actually still in the VIII Corps sector at the time of its reassignment. V Corps G-3 files, RG 407, Box 3539, NAII.

35. V Corps Sitrep as of 161200 December, V Corps G-3 files, RG 407, Box 3539, NAII.

36. What follows is based on MacDonald, *Time for Trumpets*, 180; Lauer, *Battle Babies*, 20–21; and G-3 journal for 16 December, V Corps G-3 files, RG 407, Box 3539, NAII.

37. The Huebner-Robertson meeting is mentioned in Cole, *Ardennes*, 103; and MacDonald, *Time for Trumpets*, 180; as well as in several other sources. The general tenor of the meeting is clear: Huebner warned Robertson not to be wedded to a

continuation of the attack and to be well prepared for an order to withdraw. What follows adds some informed speculation as to the specifics of that discussion.

38. MacDonald, *Time for Trumpets*, 180.

39. FUSA message, 162232 December, V Corps G-3 files, RG 407, Box 3539, NAII.

40. Lauer, *Battle Babies*, 25n.

41. Ibid., 16. Lauer writes: "It became clear that the Germans, after making a reconnaissance in force, had launched an *all-out* effort on a large scale. This was definitely confirmed later during the day [16 December] when a copy of the 'Von Rundstedt Order' was captured by Company A 394th Infantry which sat astride the Losheim-Büllingen road."

42. This paragraph is based primarily on Reynolds, *Devil's Adjutant*, 70–81; and Reynolds, *Men of Steel*, 61–62. See also Cole, *Ardennes*, 90–91.

43. Strangely, there are no records of the Hodges-Gerow conversation in the V Corps files. This account is based on Cole, *Ardennes*, 104; and Hogan, *Command Post*, 211–12.

44. What follows is based on MacDonald, *Time for Trumpets*, 181, 372–74; and Cole, *Ardennes*, 103–4, 107–9.

45. This paragraph is based on Cole, *Ardennes*, 92–95; and Lauer, *Battle Babies*, 27–28, 37.

46. This paragraph is based on MacDonald, *Time for Trumpets*, 376–80.

47. As a note of some historical interest, Charles B. MacDonald, who later became an official army historian and one of the finest chroniclers of the Bulge, earned a Silver Star for his efforts to hold the lines while commanding Company I, 23rd Infantry. The tale of his soldiers' gallant but ultimately futile attempts to stem the German tide in that lonely forest is compellingly related in Charles B. MacDonald, *Company Commander* (1947; reprint, New York: Ballantine, 1961), 99–111.

48. Except as otherwise noted, this paragraph is based on Dupuy, Bongard, and Anderson, *Hitler's Last Gamble*, 60–64; and MacDonald, *Time for Trumpets*, 372–74, 380–81.

49. Cole, *Ardennes*, 101–2.

50. MacDonald, *Time for Trumpets*, 394; and Cole, *Ardennes*, 112.

51. An unsigned memorandum of this conversation with Gerow's initials typed at the bottom is in the V Corps G-3 files, RG 407, Box 3540, NAII. V Corps had also received a Sitrep from VIII Corps at 171500 December, stating that the front lines of the 106th ID were "not stabilized," which may have prompted the conversation.

52. The attachment message from FUSA indicated the 30th ID came with a battalion each of tanks, tank destroyers, and antiaircraft artillery. V Corps G-3 files, RG 407, Box 3540, NAII. On Simpson's underappreciated role in the Bulge, see Morelock, *Generals of the Ardennes*, 153–227.

53. V Corps LOI, 172200 December, V Corps G-3 files, RG 407, Box 3540, NAII.

54. Description of the German airborne operation is based on Eisenhower, *Bitter Woods*, 180–81, 224–25, and 280–81.

55. G-3 journal entry, 172255 December, V Corps G-3 files, RG 407, Box 3540, NAII.

56. What follows is based primarily on Reynolds, *Devil's Adjutant*, 88–97. See John M. Bauserman, *The Malmédy Massacre* (Shippensburg, Pa.: White Mane Publishing, 1995), for additional details.

57. This paragraph is based on Cole, *Ardennes*, 105–6.

58. Dupuy, Bongard, and Anderson, *Hitler's Last Gamble*, 55.

59. Cole, *Ardennes*, 115.

60. Except as otherwise noted, this paragraph is based on Cavanagh, *Krinkelt-Rocherath*, 108–26. Cavanagh has penned a fine tactical study and made a concerted effort over the years to make the details of this battle accessible to veterans and students alike.

61. MacDonald says the number was 217, in *Time for Trumpets*, 397; Cavanagh, whose count does not list the headquarters and headquarters company, gives it as 144. Cavanagh, *Krinkelt-Rocherath*, 111. The official history renders it as "approximately 240." Cole, *Ardennes*, 116.

62. Cole, *Ardennes*, 117; MacDonald, *Time for Trumpets*, 397.

63. Joseph R. Reeves, "Artillery in the Ardennes," *Field Artillery Journal* 36 (March 1946): 178.

64. Cole, *Ardennes*, 125.

65. G-3 journal, 181810 December, V Corps G-3 files, RG 407, Box 3540, NAII.

66. Except as otherwise noted, this paragraph is based on Cole, *Ardennes*, 119.

67. Reeves, "Artillery in the Ardennes," 174.

68. Peiper's activities on the 18th from Reynolds, *Devil's Adjutant*, 117–25. On the defense of Trois Ponts, see MacDonald, *Time for Trumpets*, 238–40. For a detailed account of the latter, see Giles, *Damned Engineers*, 239–46.

69. Ancell, *Biographical Dictionary of World War II Generals*, 153.

70. MacDonald, *Time for Trumpets*, 433.

71. What follows is based on Cole, *Ardennes*, 337–38.

72. V Corps Sitrep, 181200–182400 December, lists the 82nd Airborne Division's attachment to V Corps effective 181750. A FUSA message lists the time of attachment as 182145. V Corps G-3 files, RG 407, Box 3540, NAII.

73. V Corps Sitrep, 181200–182400 December, V Corps G-3 files, RG 407, Box 3540, NAII.

74. V Corps Sitrep, 181200–182400 December, and FUSA message, 181729 December, V Corps G-3 files, RG 407, Box 3540, NAII.

75. What follows is based on Reynolds, *Men of Steel*, 87–88.

76. Biographical details on Bittrich from Yerger, *Waffen-SS Commanders* 1:78–82.

77. Cavanagh, *Krinkelt-Rocherath*, 126; Reynolds, *Men of Steel*, 89–90.

78. What follows is based on "Plan of Withdrawal," a half-page typescript annotated in pencil, "2nd & 99th Div plan," V Corps G-3 files, RG 407, Box 3540, NAII.

79. Cavanagh, *Krinkelt-Rocherath*, 128–29.

80. G-3 journal, 191455 December, V Corps G-3 files, RG 407, Box 3540, NAII.

81. Cole, *Ardennes*, 338–39.

82. See Reynolds, *Men of Steel*, 84, 87–88, for how this affected the Sixth SS Panzer Army attack. The story of Manteuffel's consternation with traffic congestion is told below in the description of the battle for St. Vith.

83. MacDonald, *Time for Trumpets*, 404.

84. Reynolds gives an objective account of these actions in *Men of Steel*, 91–92. A 211220 December entry in the G-3 journal speaks of an attack by "15 tanks and

one Bn of Inf." V Corps G-3 files, RG 407, Box 3540, NAII. However, it was foggy that morning and American soldiers commonly misidentified assault guns as tanks.

85. V Corps Sitrep, 190001–191200 December, V Corps G-3 files, RG 407, Box 3540, NAII.

86. Biographical detail on Kraas from Yerger, *Waffen-SS Commanders*, 1:318–25.

87. The next two sentences are based on Cole, *Ardennes*, Map II.

88. Reynolds, *Men of Steel*, Map 9.

89. MacDonald, *Time for Trumpets*, 390.

90. Dupuy, Anderson, and Bongard, *Hitler's Last Gamble*, 168. This figure may be slightly exaggerated because one battalion of the 99th ID Artillery had lost all but five of its howitzers. Nevertheless, the available artillery on the Elsenborn Ridge by 20 December was indeed formidable.

91. Reynolds, *Men of Steel*, 108–10. See also Cole, *Ardennes*, 130–31; and MacDonald, *Time for Trumpets*, 404–5.

92. This and the following quotations are from V Corps LOI, 201300A December 1944, V Corps G-3 files, RG 407, Box 3540, NAII.

93. Except as otherwise noted, the description of the battle for the Dom B on 21 December is drawn from Reynolds, *Men of Steel*, 110–14; and MacDonald, *Time for Trumpets*, 405–7.

94. MacDonald gives the figure at twelve battalions; the G-3 journal indicates the number was nine. G-3 journal, 211001 December, V Corps G-3 files, RG 407, Box 3541, NAII.

95. Reynolds, *Men of Steel*, 114.

96. MacDonald, *Time for Trumpets*, 407.

97. There is an interesting historiographic note to this assessment. When Eisenhower published his war memoirs in 1948, he used the following language to describe the initial fighting in the V Corps sector: "In Gerow's corps the veteran 2nd Division under General Robertson and the new 99th Division under Major General Walter W. Lauer were initially struck by the German attack. The 99th was rapidly forced back in confusion." Dwight D. Eisenhower, *Crusade in Europe* (New York: Doubleday, 1948), 347. Lauer protested that the characterization was not justified by the division's actual performance, and Eisenhower uncharacteristically relented. Lauer, *Battle Babies*, 89–90. The revised version of *Crusade in Europe* changed the offending sentence to read: "Our lines were forced back by superior numbers." Eisenhower, *Crusade in Europe*, 347.

98. John S. D. Eisenhower has compared this plan with Robert E. Lee's defense of Marye's Heights during the battle of Fredericksburg (*Bitter Woods*, 221). It is an apt comparison in several respects. Both commanders used a dominating piece of ground to establish an integrated infantry-artillery (or, perhaps, artillery-infantry) defense. And both commanders successfully repulsed multiple, heavy assaults. Furthermore, as Eisenhower points out, Gerow, a Virginian and a VMI graduate to boot, had stories of the American Civil War coursing through his consciousness from a very early age. But the comparison breaks down at the margins. First, Lee, having received very firm indications of Burnside's intention to attack at Fredericksburg, had three weeks to establish his defense. Gerow had to put his in place in less than three days. Second, Lee appears to have deliberately refrained from strengthening Marye's Heights as much as he could have for fear that such action might induce

Burnside not to attack there. Gerow had no such apprehensions. For details on Lee's plan for the Battle of Fredericksburg, see Douglas Southall Freeman, *R. E. Lee: A Biography*, 4 vols. (1934–1935; reprint, New York: Scribner's, 1962), 2:432–42.

7. VIII Corps Slows the Flood

1. Price, *Middleton*, 243.

2. This discussion of the VIII Corps sector is based on Cole, *Ardennes*, 238, Maps I, III, IV, and V. None of these maps depicts the entire sector because the German attack was limited to the northern sixty miles thereof. However, the description of the 4th ID sector (southernmost of VIII Corps) allows a reasonably accurate determination of the total width. The same description of the corps' southern boundary is found in VIII Corps, "Report of the VIII Corps After Action with Enemy Forces in France, Belgium, Luxembourg, and Germany for the Period 1–31 December 1944," 6 April 1945, 1, RG 407, Box 3959, NAII. Middleton describes the front as being eighty-eight miles in length. Phillips describes its length as "approximately 85 miles." Phillips, *To Save Bastogne*, 18.

3. See Cole, *Ardennes*, 42, for a detailed description of the course of the Ourthe; Manteuffel's appreciation of its obstacle value is found in Hasso von Manteuffel, "Fifth Panzer Army (Ardennes Offensive Preparations)," 112, FMS B-151, RG 319, NAII.

4. R. Ernest Dupuy, *St. Vith Lion in the Way: The 106th Infantry Division in World War II* (Washington, D.C.: Infantry Journal Press), 6–7. Dupuy opined as follows on the effects of this turbulence: "One cannot say that these men [who replaced the 1943 losses] were of inferior quality. One can say—and this writer here says it—that one cannot take more than fifty per cent of a trained unit's complement away, fill it up with other men and expect the unit to be fit to enter battle as a combat team. It just can't be done, no matter how good the replacements, or the cadre, are. The spark of team play gained by rigorous training, the patina of *esprit de corps*, the pride of organization, are missing."

5. Cota's nickname came from his methodical and deliberate personality. Eisenhower, *Bitter Woods*, 305.

6. Phillips, *To Save Bastogne*, 20–21.

7. Cole, *Ardennes*, 238–39.

8. Phillips, *To Save Bastogne*, 18–19.

9. Manteuffel's background from Franz Kurkowski, "Dietrich and Manteuffel," in Barnett, *Hitler's Generals*, 422–30.

10. Eisenhower, *Bitter Woods*, 140.

11. Manteuffel, "Fifth Panzer Army (Ardennes Offensive Preparations)," 66–67, FMS B-151, RG 319, NAII.

12. What follows is based on ibid., 73–79, FMS B-151, RG 319, NAII. See also Cole, *Ardennes*, 173–75.

13. Hasso von Manteuffel, "Fifth Panzer Army—Mission (November 1944–January 1945)," 10, FMS ETHINT-46, RG 319, NAII.

14. What follows is based on Manteuffel, "Fifth Panzer Army (Ardennes Offensive Preparations)," 80–83, FMS B-151, RG 319, NAII.

15. For a complete troop list of the corps subordinate to Fifth Panzer Army, see Dupuy, Bongard, and Anderson, *Hitler's Last Gamble*, 444–45.

16. Manteuffel, "Fifth Panzer Army (Ardennes Offensive Preparations)," 137–38, FMS B-151, RG 319, NAII. Lucht's age from Dupuy, Bongard, and Anderson, *Hitler's Last Gamble*, 76.

17. What follows, including the Fifth Panzer Army timetable for the offensive, is based on Manteuffel, "Fifth Panzer Army (Ardennes Offensive Preparations)," 83–84, 98, 107–9, FMS B-151, RG 319, NAII.

18. Seventh Army plan based on Cole, *Ardennes*, 212–13.

19. Except as otherwise noted, what follows is based on Cole, *Ardennes*, 140 and Map III; MacDonald, *Time for Trumpets*, 112–18; and Dupuy, Bongard, and Anderson, *Hitler's Last Gamble*, 79–81.

20. Middleton's views on the advisability of holding the Schnee Eifel evolved noticeably after the campaign. In an interview of 19 January 1945, he indicated that he had felt the position "unsound" and had been denied authority to withdraw from it by the "High Command." Notes of interview of Middleton by Captain L. B. Clark, 19 January 1945, 1, Combat Interviews, RG 407, Box 24115, NAII. The VIII Corps AAR for December 1944 stated the rationale for retaining the position as if it were Middleton's. VIII Corps AAR, 1–31 December 1944, 6, RG 407, Box 3959, NAII. In a letter to the ETO historian of 30 July 1945 responding to a query on this point, he said, "Army did not want the bulge held by the 106th Division through the Siegfried Line [the Schnee Eifel] given up. A stronger position would have been one running generally northeast through St. Vith. However, to have voluntarily given up the large area in and through the Siegfried Line and have gone back several miles to the [stronger] position would have been foolish." Questions Answered by Lieutenant General Troy H. Middleton in a Letter to Theater Historian, 30 July 1945, 4, Combat Interviews, RG 407, Box 24115, NAII.

21. What follows is based on MacDonald, *Time for Trumpets*, 103–11; Dupuy, *St. Vith Lion in the Way*, 22; and Gregory Fontenot, "The Lucky Seventh in the Bulge: A Case Study in AirLand Battle" (Fort Leavenworth, Kans.: USACGSC, 1985), 37.

22. This and the following two sentences are based on MacDonald, *Time for Trumpets*, 117–21.

23. Morelock, *Generals of the Ardennes*, 275–78.

24. For Jones's actions and orders on 16 December, see Dupuy, *St. Vith Lion in the Way*, 22–23; and MacDonald, *Time for Trumpets*, 118, 122–25. MacDonald is more critical of Jones in the early hours of the battle than am I.

25. There is a bit of confusion as to the composition of the division reserve. MacDonald and Dupuy indicate that Jones also considered as a divisional reserve the 424th Infantry's reserve, its 1st Battalion, stationed near Steinbrück. MacDonald, *Time for Trumpets*, 120; and Dupuy, *St. Vith Lion in the Way*, 14. However, Dupuy also states that the regimental commander, Colonel Reid, was unaware of this "string" being attached to his reserve. The confusion caused some delay in committing the battalion when the 18th VGD pressed on Eigelscheid.

26. MacDonald unearthed a story suggesting that the telephone switchboard operator connecting Middleton and Jones may have disconnected their call in mid-sentence after Middleton's statement, "You know how things are up there better than I do," but during his qualification, "but I agree it would be wise to withdraw them." MacDonald, *Time for Trumpets*, 127–29. As an exercise in historical investigation and imaginative reconstruction it is absolutely fascinating, but I find it just a bit too

speculative. The more prosaic and well-documented explanation is that Middleton simply left the judgment to Jones as the man on the ground.

27. This and the following sentence are based on Dupuy, *St. Vith Lion in the Way*, 23–25.

28. The corps order attaching CCB of the 9th AD to the 106th was issued at 1120. VIII Corps message, 161120 December, VIII Corps G-3 files, RG 407, Box 4029, NAII.

29. Jones also considered a third alternative for CCB, 9th AD: attacking in the sector of the 14th Cavalry Group. In fact, this was Jones's initial task for Hoge, but it was revoked in favor of the Winterspelt attack later in the evening. MacDonald, *Time for Trumpets*, 126–27.

30. Virtually all sources treat this decision as Jones's. See, among others, Dupuy, *St. Vith Lion in the Way*, 23; MacDonald, *Time for Trumpets*, 126; and Fontenot, "Lucky Seventh," 41. However, in the interview with Captain Clark on 19 January 1945, previously cited, Middleton indicated that he gave the order for Hoge's unit to be used in the southeast, rather than in the east. He defended this commitment by noting that the major consideration was maintaining contact between the 106th and the 28th IDs. Notes of interview of Middleton by Captain L. B. Clark, 19 January 1945, 2, Combat Interviews, RG 407, Box 24115, NAII. Because Dupuy had access to all the divisional records and because there is no documentation in the VIII Corps files substantiating Middleton's claim to have stipulated this particular employment of CCB, 9th AD, I treat the decision as having been made by Jones. Middleton's comments to Captain Clark may have indicated that there was a corps-level rationale for the decision as well.

31. What follows is based on VIII Corps G-3 message text, 162045 December, VIII Corps G-3 files, RG 407, Box 4029, NAII. A pencil notation at the bottom indicates the message was released from the G-3 section at 162120 December. Dupuy indicates it was received and entered into the 28th ID G-3 log at 170036 December. Dupuy, *St. Vith Lion in the Way*, 64.

32. What follows is based on MacDonald, *Time for Trumpets*, 310–20; Cole, *Ardennes*, 161–66; and Dupuy, *St. Vith Lion in the Way*, 79–95.

33. Dupuy, *St. Vith Lion in the Way*, 91.

34. Based on subsequent orders from the 423rd, Dupuy infers that this conditional withdrawal order was received by that regiment at about 171500 December, though there is no documentation to establish the precise time of receipt. Dupuy, *St. Vith Lion in the Way*, 101n.

35. Except as otherwise indicated, this paragraph is based on MacDonald, *Time for Trumpets*, 322–29; Cole, *Ardennes*, 273–80; and Eisenhower, *Bitter Woods*, 227–35.

36. Hogan, the most knowledgeable authority on First Army headquarters in World War II, investigated in some depth the charge that the 7th AD's departure was delayed by inaction on the part of Hodges's staff and concluded that responsibility for the delay was "hard to pinpoint from the existing records." Hogan, *Command Post*, 213. See also the lengthy note on p. 233.

37. Jones's son's assignment from MacDonald, *Time for Trumpets*, 125. Hoge said Jones was "jittery and nervous," while Clarke commented that he was "out on his feet." Fontenot, "Lucky Seventh," 41.

38. Eisenhower, *Bitter Woods*, 229.

39. As an indication of the latter, two days later VIII Corps received information that the 106th Division Artillery S-2, S-3, signal officer, 450 men, and eleven guns were in Namur, nearly sixty miles west of St. Vith. VIII Corps G-3 memo, 191430 December, VIII Corps G-3 files, RG 407, Box 4030, NAII. Mildly to their credit, these officers requested instructions as to how to rejoin the division. The main element of this group was apparently from the 592nd Field Artillery Battalion. The battalion commander found his stray souls some fifteen miles west of Dinant and reunited them with the division on the evening of the 20th. Dupuy, *St. Vith Lion in the Way*, 159–60.

40. The Model-Manteuffel dialogue is drawn from Eisenhower, *Bitter Woods*, 239.

41. The author is indebted to Colonel (then Major) Gregory Fontenot for pointing out during a 1985 staff ride in the Ardennes the remarkable similarity of Model's and Manteuffel's command sensitivities that brought them both to the area east of St. Vith on the night of 17 December.

42. Cole, *Ardennes*, Maps IV and V.

43. Description of Cota's career up to his assumption of command of the 28th ID is based on Miller, *Division Commander*, 19–95.

44. For a scathing indictment of both Cota and Gerow in the Battle of Schmidt, the iconic symbol of the entire Hürtgen debacle, see Currey, *Follow Me and Die*, 262–63.

45. This paragraph is based on MacDonald, *Time for Trumpets*, 130–34; and Eisenhower, *Bitter Woods*, 208.

46. Fuller's background is drawn from Eisenhower, *Bitter Woods*, 205; and MacDonald, *Time for Trumpets*, 134–35.

47. What follows is based on Cole, *Ardennes*, Map IV; MacDonald, *Time for Trumpets*, 135–36; and the author's reconnaissance of the route from Dasburg, through Marnach and Clervaux, to Bastogne.

48. This paragraph is based on MacDonald, *Time for Trumpets*, 134–45; and Phillips, *To Save Bastogne*, 33–74.

49. For details of the attack on Pointe du Hoc, see JoAnna MacDonald, *The Liberation of Pointe du Hoc: The 2nd U.S. Rangers at Normandy* (Redondo Beach, Calif.: Rank and File Publications, 2000).

50. The remainder of this paragraph is based on MacDonald, *Time for Trumpets*, 147–52; and Eisenhower, *Bitter Woods*, 208.

51. Regarding the early optimistic reporting, a 1415 telephone call to the VIII Corps G-3 ended with the observation, "The situation for the Division is well in hand." Report of 28th ID telephonic message, 161415 December, VIII Corps G-3 files, RG 407, Box 4029, NAII.

52. This paragraph is based on Cole, *Ardennes*, 199–204; and MacDonald, *Time for Trumpets*, 265–67.

53. As the 3rd Battalion approached Ouren on the night of 17/18 December, the commander, Major Walden F. Woodward, sent a patrol forward to reconnoiter. Learning the village was occupied by Germans, Woodward led his men to a ford further south and thence to safety. Later that night the 1st Battalion approached the village from the north and similarly sent a patrol forward. When he learned that the bridge was guarded by only a half dozen men, the battalion commander, Lieutenant Colonel William H. Allen, decided to bluff his way though. Detailing an officer who

spoke German to issue all the commands, Allen formed his men up and marched them across the bridge without a shot being fired. Cole, *Ardennes*, 203; and MacDonald, *Time for Trumpets*, 267.

54. There is an apparent discrepancy between MacDonald, who says the bridges themselves would not allow a Mark V to cross, and Cole, who maintains that the problem was in the approaches. MacDonald, *Time for Trumpets*, 267; and Cole, *Ardennes*, 204. It is, of course, possible that both the bridges and the approaches were inadequate.

55. Except as otherwise noted, this and the following paragraph are based on Phillips, *To Save Bastogne*, 75–144; MacDonald, *Time for Trumpets*, 268–78; and Cole, *Ardennes*, 188–93.

56. Manteuffel had received permission from Hitler to select his panzer division commanders, and he chose Lauchert, whom he referred to as "an experienced commander from the east," to command the 2nd Panzer Division. Lauchert's subsequent performance justified Manteuffel's faith in him and was made all the more remarkable by the fact that he did not join the division until two days before the offensive began. Manteuffel, "Fifth Panzer Army (Ardennes Offensive Preparations)," 138, FMS B-151, RG 319, NAII.

57. Manteuffel's timetable had been to be across the Clerf by the evening of the 16th. Thus, in the center of his sector, Fuller had delayed the advance by twenty-four hours. In the south at Hosingen, where Company K held out along the top of the Skyline Drive until past midnight of 17/18 December, the delay was at least thirty-six hours. An interesting sequel indicates Middleton's appreciation for the actions of the 110th. After Fuller was freed from captivity in April 1945, Middleton wrote him as follows: "I went over the ground where your unit fought it out with the Krauts, and left with sufficient data to leave no doubt in my mind that your unit did a magnificent job. Had not your boys done the job they did, the 101st Airborne could not have reached Bastogne in time." Price, *Middleton*, 222.

58. This paragraph is based on MacDonald, *Time for Trumpets*, 358–61.

59. Middleton message to CG, 9th AD, 171630 December, confirming verbal orders issued at 1535, VIII Corps G-3 files, RG 407, Box 4209, NAII.

60. Telephonic message from 28th ID G-3 to VIII Corps G-3, 171950 December, VIII Corps G-3 files, RG 407, Box 4209, NAII; Miller, *Division Commander*, 144. Cota's headquarters had "real-time" information of the capture of Fuller's command post. As German tanks were shelling the Hotel Claravallis, the regimental commander was on the phone to Cota's chief of staff, Colonel Jesse L. Gibney, vainly requesting authorization to withdraw. As the conversation continued, three tank shells went off in the ground floor of the hotel, just below Fuller. When Gibney inquired as to the source of the noise, Fuller emphatically informed him and abruptly hung up the phone. MacDonald, *Time for Trumpets*, 276–77.

61. Middleton to CG, CCR, 9th AD, 172140 December, VIII Corps G-3 files, RG 407, Box 4029, NAII.

62. VIII Corps G-2 Periodic Report for period 162400–172400 December, VIII Corps G-2 files, RG 407, Box 3965, NAII. The VIII Corps AAR states that Middleton divined the German intention "by the night of the 16th and the morning of the 17th." But it goes on to say that the defensive plan for dealing with the offensive was predicated on use of the airborne divisions, a fact of which he was unaware until midnight on the 17th. Given the time it takes to prepare a G-2 periodic report, it is

most likely that Middleton's appreciation of the magnitude of the offensive began to develop late on the 17th, as the defenses of the 110th Infantry collapsed, and matured over the night of the 17th/18th, as the reports and captured documents mentioned in the AAR were analyzed. Despite this generally accurate appreciation, Middleton still did not grasp the enormity of Hitler's ambition, thinking that the objectives were "Liège and possibly Namur." VIII Corps AAR, 1–31 December 1944, 8, RG 407, Box 3959, NAII.

63. Hasbrouck had been elevated to division command in early November upon the relief of Major General Lindsay M. Silvester. Bradley informed Eisenhower that the basis of relief had been a general loss of confidence and that "my whole general impression of the division is that it has not done as well as it should." Bradley to Eisenhower, 2 November 1944, Dwight D. Eisenhower Pre-Presidential Papers, Box 13 (Bradley file), DDEL.

64. Except as otherwise indicated, this paragraph is based on Fontenot, "Lucky Seventh," 45–52; and Cole, *Ardennes*, 281–87. See also Dupuy, *St. Vith Lion in the Way*, 103–32.

65. Cole, *Ardennes*, 293.

66. The sad story of the abortive effort to resupply the 422nd and 423rd Infantry by air is told in Royce Thompson, "Air Supply to Isolated Units, Ardennes Campaign, 16 December 1944–27 January 1945" (Washington, D.C.: OCMH, 1951), 2–32, 2–37, RG 549, NAII; copy also available at AUL File M-U 44112-1. See also Cole, *Ardennes*, 171–72; and Hogan, *Command Post*, 218. Jones's last-gasp effort to save his two regiments was transmitted by radio at 1415. It read as follows: "Panzer regimental combat team on Eimerscheid–Schönberg–St. Vith road, head near St. Vith. Your mission is to destroy by fire from dug-in positions south of Schönberg–St. Vith road. Ammunition, food and water will be dropped. When mission accomplished, move to area St. Vith–Wallerode–Weppeler, organize and move west." Dupuy, *St. Vith Lion in the Way*, 104.

67. Dispositions of CCR, 9th AD, on the morning of 18 December are taken from Reichelt, *Phantom Nine*, 131–32.

68. Except as otherwise noted, the description of CCR, 9th AD's fight on 18 December is based on Dupuy, Bongard, and Anderson, *Hitler's last Gamble*, 181–83; Reichelt, *Phantom Nine*, 132–40; and Phillips, *To Save Bastogne*, 175–78.

69. Report of telephonic message from CCR, 9th AD, to VIII Corps G-3, 181405 December, VIII Corps G-3 files, RG 407, Box 4030, NAII.

70. Report of telephonic messages from CO, CCR, 9th AD, and XO, CCR, 9th AD, to VIII Corps G-3, 181430 December and 181525 December, respectively, VIII Corps G-3 files, RG 407, Box 4030, NAII. Though unknown at the time, several tanks from Rose's task force evaded the German net and broke out toward Houffalize.

71. Report of telephonic message from First Army G-3 to VIII Corps G-3, 180100 December, VIII Corps G-3 files, RG 407, Box 4030, NAII.

72. Reichelt, *Phantom Nine*, 137.

73. Report from Liaison Officer, CCB, 10th AD, to VIII Corps G-3, 181845 December, VIII Corps G-3 files, RG 407, Box 4030, NAII.

74. Report from Liaison Officer, CCB, 10th AD, to VIII Corps G-3, 181930 December, VIII Corps G-3 files, RG 407, Box 4030, NAII.

75. Bayerlein had served as Rommel's chief of staff in North Africa and commanded the 3rd Panzer Division in Russia before being given command of Panzer

Lehr in January 1944. Wounded in August, he returned to command of the division in October. P. A. Spayd, *Bayerlein: From Afrikakorps to Panzer Lehr* (Atglen, Pa.: Schiffer Military History, 2003), 60–174. After the war, Bayerlein was bitterly criticized by both Lüttwitz and Manteuffel for this decision because of the delay it imposed on the attack on the 19th. Bayerlein justified the call by arguing that his advance elements reported the chosen route suitable (if true, this is an indictment of his reconnaissance battalion), and these reports were confirmed by locals (here, there is the suggestion of conscious deception). He also thought the attack along the Mageret-Bastogne road would be less expected. For a summary of Lüttwitz's and Manteuffel's criticisms and Bayerlein's rejoinder, see Spayd, *Bayerlein*, 181–82.

76. Except where otherwise indicated, this paragraph is based on MacDonald, *Time for Trumpets*, 354–63.

77. VIII Corps Sitrep for period 172400 to 181200 December and record of telephonic message from 4th ID to VIII Corps G-3, 180940 December, VIII Corps G-3 files, RG 407, Box 4030, NAII.

78. This paragraph is based on Cole, *Ardennes*, 289–93; and Dupuy, *St. Vith Lion in the Way*, 133–57.

79. Hanson W. Baldwin, *Battles Lost and Won: Great Campaigns of World War II* (New York: Harper and Row, 1966), 338.

80. Message CG, 7th AD, to CG, VIII Corps, 19 December, VIII Corps G-3 files, RG 407, Box 4030, NAII. The time of origin of this message is uncertain. The overlay was dated as of 182100 December; Hasbrouck's handwritten message was dated merely 19/12/44. The Corps G-3 journal indicates that the time dated was 181430, but this was in all probability a typographical error. The most likely time of dispatch was 191430, but this is conjecture.

81. Message, CG, VIII Corps, to CG, 7th AD, 191810 December, VIII Corps G-3 files, RG 407, Box 4030, NAII.

82. VIII Corps Message to 106th ID (to be passed to 7th AD), 191830 December, VIII Corps G-3 files, RG 407, Box 4030, NAII.

83. Dupuy, *St. Vith Lion in the Way*, 155–56. Dupuy indicates that the initiative for the attachment came from Jones; message traffic in the VIII Corps files suggests it may have come from Cota, with Middleton's concurrence. Message from CG, 28th ID, to VIII Corps (to be passed to CG, 106th ID), 19 December, VIII Corps G-3 files, RG 407, Box 4030, NAII. The message has no time of dispatch, but it was logged into the Corps G-3 at 192020 December.

84. This paragraph is based on Phillips, *To Save Bastogne*, 217–31; and MacDonald, *Time for Trumpets*, 298–309.

85. McAuliffe's G-3, Lieutenant Colonel Harry W. O. Kinnard, found Middleton's orientation sketchy. There was, however, little Middleton could tell the 101st commander, other than the facts that three German divisions were advancing on Bastogne and that he had dispatched three teams of CCB, 10th AD, to give him as much breathing room as possible to organize his defense. Kinnard admits getting fairly complete logistical information and a very slim supply of maps—all the corps map section had left. Marshall, *Bastogne*, 15–16. It is a testimony to Middleton's imperturbability that he remained in Bastogne as long as he did.

86. Cole, *Ardennes*, 307, 444.

87. For a brief description of the transportation efforts, see Marshall, *Bastogne*, 15.

88. Disposition of 26th VGD on the 18th from General Freiherr v. Lüttwitz, "The Commitment of the XXXXVII Panzer Corps in the Ardennes, 1944–1945," 6, FMS A-939, RG 319, NAII.

89. Orders to and condition of the 26th VGD on the morning of the 19th from Cole, *Ardennes*, 449–50.

90. The 2nd Panzer Division's route lay north along the Bastogne-Houffalize road, then west toward the Ourthe River; but the lack of off-road trafficability dictated the capture of Noville for this route to be followed. Except as otherwise indicated, this paragraph is based on "Early Defense of Bastogne," interview with LTG William R. Desobry, USA (Ret.) by LTC Ted S. Chesney, USAWC, 8 September 1977, MHI; and Cole, *Ardennes*, 452–54. See also Phillips, *To Save Bastogne*, 201–8.

91. Price, *Middleton*, 243.

92. This paragraph is based on Phillips, *To Save Bastogne*, 183–94; Marshall, *Bastogne*, 22–29; and Cole, *Ardennes*, 448–49.

93. This paragraph is based on Marshall, *Bastogne*, 40–48.

94. Middleton's employment of his engineers is examined in detail in Cole, *Ardennes*, 310–29. This investigation concludes that Middleton's frequent decisions to use engineers in their secondary role as infantry contributed significantly to the delay of the Germans in reaching Bastogne, but it ends by noting that such use is not always the most efficient use of these trained assets.

95. See especially Morelock, *Generals of the Ardennes*, 251–53.

96. This assertion came in the context of Clausewitz's discussion of the practical value of theory. "It will be sufficient if it helps the commander acquire those insights that, once absorbed into his way of thinking, will smooth and protect his progress, and will never force him to abandon his convictions for the sake of any objective fact." Clausewitz, *On War*, 147.

97. Morelock argues that Middleton's calm demeanor was his *most* significant attribute; see *Generals of the Ardennes*, 249–51. My slight disagreement as to the relative importance of this quality is a matter of personal interpretation.

98. This and the following sentence are based on Eisenhower, *Bitter Woods*, 310–11.

99. VIII Corps LOI, 19 December, VIII Corps G-3 files, RG 407, Box 4030, NAII. The Corps G-3 log has this LOI listed as "Out" 200800 December. If this is accurate, the instructions were even more unrealistic than if the letter was issued, as dated, on the 19th. Dupuy indicates that it was logged into the 7th AD G-3 journal at 200855 December. *St. Vith Lion in the Way*, 162 and 164n.

100. 109th Infantry situation on 19 December from Cole, *Ardennes*, 225–26; and MacDonald, *Time for Trumpets*, 354–55.

101. 9th AD situation on 19th from Cole, *Ardennes*, 235–36; see also MacDonald, *Time for Trumpets*, 358.

102. 10th AD Sitrep, received 191730 December, VIII Corps G-3 files, RG 407, Box 4030, NAII.

103. Cole, *Ardennes*, 255.

104. Effective time of boundary change from VIII Corps AAR, 1–31 December 1944, 18, RG 407, Box 3959, NAII.

105. Message, 211515 December, 7th AD, to VIII Corps, VIII Corps G-3 files, RG 407, Box 4030, NAII.

106. Memorandum from Middleton to General Hasbrouke [*sic*], 20 December,

VIII Corps G-3 files, RG 407, Box 4030, NAII. The memo itself does not have a time of dispatch indicated, but the G-3 log indicates it was dated at 0945 and logged out at 0955.

107. Dupuy, *St. Vith Lion in the Way*, 162.

108. Ibid., 161.

109. Ibid., 162. The FUSA radio message was dated 201230 December, but it was not received by the 7th AD until 202230 December.

110. What follows is based on Lüttwitz, "XXXXVII Panzer Corps in the Ardennes," 3, 7–8, FMS A-939, RG 319, NAII; and Spayd, *Bayerlein*, 182–84.

111. The most complete list of units in Bastogne other than the 101st is in Marshall, *Bastogne*, xi–xiii; see also Ralph M. Mitchell, *The 101st Airborne Division's Defense of Bastogne* (Fort Leavenworth, Kans.: USACGSC, 1986), 9–12, for a concise appraisal of the relative balance of forces.

112. According to Price, Middleton's words to McAuliffe were along the lines, "Now Tony, you're going to be surrounded here before long. But don't worry; help is on the way from Patton. You've got fine men. There's a lot of artillery backing you up. It can put plenty of fire at any point about Bastogne." Price, *Middleton*, 234. There might have been some telescoping of Middleton's memory on relating this conversation as having been on the 19th rather than the 20th when he and McAuliffe subsequently met at Neufchâteau. Patton's attack from the north was not approved until the afternoon of the 19th at the Verdun conference. Notwithstanding this apparent discrepancy, Middleton was relatively optimistic about the 101st's ability to hold out; he communicated this to McAuliffe.

113. The order attaching CCB, 10th AD, and CCR, 9th AD, was dated 201230 December; the order attaching the 705th TD Battalion was dated 201345 December; the G-3 journal indicates they were logged out at 201230 and 201355, respectively. VIII Corps G-3 files, RG 407, Box 4030, NAII. Marshall mistakenly states that these attachments were not made until the 21st. Marshall, *Bastogne*, xi, xiii.

114. The standard accounts of the Bastogne defense from 19–26 December are Marshall, *Bastogne*, which focuses on events within and immediately outside the perimeter; and Cole, *Ardennes*, 445–81, which covers these events in some detail but also puts them into the context of the campaign as a whole. See Cole's note on p. 445 for elaboration of the two approaches. Mitchell's short study, *The 101st Airborne Division's Defense of Bastogne*, is particularly valuable for its tactical insights. Eisenhower; MacDonald; and Dupuy, Bongard, and Anderson all render good accounts in *Bitter Woods*, 316–29 and 345; *Time for Trumpets*, 491–513, 525–29, and 532–33; and *Hitler's Last Gamble*, 186–97 and 216–17, respectively. For small unit perspectives, see Stephen E. Ambrose, *Band of Brothers: E Company, 506th Regiment, 101st Airborne, from Normandy to Hitler's Eagle's Nest* (New York: Simon and Schuster, 2001), 179–90; Robert M. Bowen, *Fighting with the Screaming Eagles: With the 101st Airborne from Normandy to Bastogne* (London: Greenhill Books, 2001), 163–97; and Donald R. Burgett, *Seven Roads to Hell: A Screaming Eagle at Bastogne* (Novato, Calif.: Presidio Press, 1999), 44–176.

115. Cole, *Ardennes*, 460–61.

116. This paragraph is based on Cole, *Ardennes*, 454–54; and MacDonald, *Time for Trumpets*, 496–500. See also Marshall, *Bastogne*, 86–98, which contains, on p. 91, a particularly good diagram of the closely intertwined and at times much confused action.

117. Cole, *Ardennes*, 456.

118. This sentence and the remainder of the paragraph are based on Cole, *Ardennes*, 456–57; and MacDonald, *Time for Trumpets*, 501–2.

119. The following Patton-Middleton dialogue is from Eisenhower, *Bitter Woods*, 333.

120. Middleton's position on the issue evolved the further removed he became from the battle. In an interview of 19 January 1945, he opined that the weight of the entire III Corps attack should have been made from the southwest, rather than from the south. At the end of July, when responding to queries on the matter by the ETO historian, he reversed his field, noting, "I was in accord with the direction of the attack made by the Third Army. I suggested if more troops were available that another attack be made along the Neufchateau-Bastogne highway. Troops were not available." Questions answered by Middleton to ETO historian, 30 July 1945, 1, Combat Interviews, RG 407, Box 24115, NAII.

121. Radio message, CG, VIII Corps, to CG, 101st Airborne Division, 201515 December, VIII Corps G-3 files, RG 407, Box 4030, NAII.

122. Except as otherwise indicated, direct quotations in this paragraph are taken from Marshall, *Bastogne*, 107, which is based on Marshall's interview with McAuliffe conducted in Bastogne in January 1945.

123. As it turned out, this warning was unnecessary—the 116th Panzer Division would continue its attack to the west and not become involved in the Bastogne fight. Nevertheless, it was a prudent caution. At this juncture, it was clearly best for Middleton not to withhold potentially bad news from McAuliffe.

124. Eisenhower, *Bitter Woods*, 320.

125. Ibid. Marshall's citation is nearly identical but omits the "Tony."

126. Price, *Middleton*, 251; and VIII Corps G-3 journal entry, 211330 December, VIII Corps G-3 files, RG 407, Box 4030, NAII.

127. The remainder of the paragraph is based on Cole, *Ardennes*, 463–64; and Marshall, *Bastogne*, 112–14.

128. To hedge against having to rely on insecure communications, Middleton and McAuliffe prudently developed a series of code words at their meeting on the afternoon of the 20th to allow them to converse about various contingencies. Eisenhower, *Bitter Woods*, 320.

129. CG, VIII Corps message, 211645 December, VIII Corps G-3 files, RG 407, Box 4030, NAII.

130. VIII Corps AAR, 1–31 December 1944, 8, VIII Corps G-3 files, RG 407, Box 3959, NAII.

131. One such was the action of "Task Force Navaho," an odd band of stragglers collected by First Lieutenant Joe V. "Navaho" Whiteman, Executive Officer, Company B, 23rd AIB. On 17 December, Whiteman found himself at Petit Their, a hamlet between Vielsalm and Poteau. With troops of the 1st SS Panzer Division threatening his position, Whiteman reasoned, "If Jerry was going to be stopped, he'd have to be stopped some place, and it might as well be right here." He subsequently stopped several disoriented units that drifted into Petit Their and organized an effective defense of the road junction that materially helped Hasbrouck and his subordinates secure the important lifeline between Vielsalm and St. Vith. Fontenot, "Lucky Seventh," 49–51.

132. In response to a question from Colonel Marshall on this issue, Middleton answered as follows: "When the German attack got underway on the 16th I advised

General Jones that I thought it best to withdraw to the rear position. Jones did not consider a withdrawal proper. He felt that he could hold. He was on the ground, I was not. As it turned out he made a mistake. It was an honest one. I think he is a good Commander. He had a fighting heart. I did not order Jones to withdraw at that time for I felt that he knew more about local conditions than I did. In fact he did. As it developed it just happened that my hunch was right. When Jones decided to withdraw his left it was too late." Questions answered by Middleton to ETO historian, 30 July 1945, 4, Combat Interviews, RG 407, Box 24115, NAII. In my judgment, Middleton's attitude reflected in this correspondence did him little credit.

133. Eddy War Log, 2 January 1945, Fort Benning, Georgia, National Infantry Museum.

8. *XVIII (Airborne) Corps Stands in the Breach*

1. Ridgway, *Soldier*, 113. The quotation conveys Ridgway's recollections concerning his thoughts as he was passing through Rheims, en route from England to Werbomont to establish the XVIII (Airborne) Corps headquarters in the Bulge.

2. Ridgway was notified of the commitment at "about 0215 December 18." Blair, *Ridgway's Paratroopers*, 431.

3. The latter included the G-1, Colonel Frederick M. Schellhammer; the G-2, Colonel Whitfield Jack; and the G-4, Colonel Frank W. Moorman. Ridgway, *Soldier*, 118; and Blair, *Ridgway's Paratroopers*, 438 and 603.

4. Surles would later opine: "I had never been in combat before. At first it didn't seem all that bad, but it soon became so. I wasn't wise enough in the ways of combat to know how bad it really was." Blair, *Ridgway's Paratroopers*, 438. Nevertheless, Ridgway valued Surles's competence and promoted him to colonel during the course of the campaign. XVIII (Airborne) Corps G-3 journal entry, 041000 January 1945, RG 407, Box 4974, NAII.

5. Price, *Middleton*, 228.

6. Ridgway later attributed this choice to "God's guidance." Ridgway, *Soldier*, 115.

7. Blair, *Ridgway's Paratroopers*, 427. The reason that Anderson's corps was initially considered for this assignment is unclear. Blair speculates that Bradley may have wanted a corps that, though untested like Ridgway's, was designed for sustained ground operations. Hodges, however, would have none of it and insisted on getting the XVIII (Airborne) Corps.

8. What follows is based on First Army LOI, 19 December 1944, found in VIII Corps G-3 files, RG 407, Box 4030, NAII.

9. There is an internal inconsistency in this portion of the First Army order, for the assigned XVIII (Airborne) Corps sector embraced almost the entire zone of action of the 30th ID, even though only the 119th RCT was under its control.

10. The measurement of this line is exclusive of the St. Vith salient.

11. This paragraph is based on Cole, *Ardennes*, 339–42; and MacDonald, *Time for Trumpets*, 438–43.

12. With the exception of the last sentence, this entire paragraph describing the 82nd Airborne Division's deployments on 19 December is paraphrased from a similar paragraph in Blair, *Ridgway's Paratroopers*, 439. Cole, *Ardennes*, 435, states that the 3rd Battalion, 325th GIR, was sent to Hotton, rather than Barvaux. Given the

distance involved, this is unlikely; and the corps AAR clearly supports Blair (XVIII [Airborne] Corps, Summary of Operations, 18 December 1944–13 February 1945, 1 March 1945, Plate 2, Ridgway papers, MHI), as does Gavin's AAR, "The Story of the 82nd Airborne Division in the Battle of the Belgian Bulge in the Siegfried Line and on the Roer River," Section II, 2, MHI.

13. There is no published map showing the entire dispositions of the XVIII (Airborne) Corps on 20 December. The distance cited has been determined by plotting the frontline trace on Cole, *Ardennes*, Map I. The identical figure is used in Cole, *Ardennes*, 400.

14. The note, dated 211010 December, read, "Dear Leland, Delighted to have your CT 119. Know how you feel about detachments. Meanwhile we will take best of care of them, and I know they will deliver the goods. Warm regards, Matt." Ridgway papers, MHI. Text also in Eisenhower, *Bitter Woods*, 271.

15. Blair, *Ridgway's Paratroopers*, 441.

16. In a conversation with Kean on the night of 22 December, Ridgway lamented, "I'm going to put more stuff up behind Leland's area in the morning. I want to get more infantry up to him. It's the only thing he lacks. He's got everything else in the world, a list of attachments as long as your arm. More stuff than any other division, and yet he's always crying for more." XVIII (Airborne) Corps headquarters diary entry of conversation with General Kean, 222210 December, Ridgway papers, MHI. Ridgway remembered this trait of Hobbs's for a long time. In December 1971, he commented to an army interviewer, "They had one division commander in the Ardennes—my God, he had about twice as much artillery as any other division, and he was crying for more all the time." When pressed to identify the unit, Ridgway would only say, "It was a fine division." Senior Officers Debriefing Program, General Matthew B. Ridgway, USA, Ret., Vol. I, Section Two, 85, MHI.

17. Cited from XVIII (Airborne) Corps headquarters diary entry, 20 December 1944, Ridgway papers, MHI.

18. This paragraph is based on Cole, *Ardennes*, 348–49; and MacDonald, *Time for Trumpets*, 443–45.

19. Description of Stoumont's defenses based on author's personal reconnaissance and Cole, *Ardennes*, 349.

20. The account of the fighting in and west of Stoumont on 20 December is based on Cole, *Ardennes*, 349–50; and MacDonald, *Time for Trumpets*, 445–47. One of the priests in the basement of the sanatorium described the moment of liberation as follows: "What joy, what relief! The Sister Superior recited a dozen rosaries for the eternal rest of the soldiers killed in the battle . . . while the Americans set up their guns on the first floor and, in the kitchen, made hot water for tea, coffee, and chocolate. Our liberators were as happy as we were." MacDonald, *Time for Trumpets*, 446.

21. Except as otherwise indicated, this paragraph is based on Blair, *Ridgway's Paratroopers*, 439; Gavin, *On to Berlin*, 223–25; and MacDonald, *Time for Trumpets*, 448–49.

22. In describing the seizure of the bridge near Cheneux, Gavin used this word twice in the same paragraph. See his AAR, "The Story of the 82nd Airborne Division in the Battle of the Belgian Bulge in the Siegfried Line and on the Roer River," Section II, 2–3, MHI.

23. Gavin would later comment with classic understatement, "It had been costly; the Germans were well equipped and had given us a good fight." Gavin, *On to*

Berlin, 225. MacDonald would more critically classify the action as "ill-conceived and senseless." MacDonald, *Time for Trumpets*, 449. Given what we know now about Peiper's fuel-starved lack of mobility, MacDonald's judgment that Tucker should have waited for more advantageous conditions to launch the attack is clearly correct. However, without such perfect knowledge and with the ominous consequences of an armored spearhead's arriving at Werbomont, the 504th PIR commander must be given the benefit of the doubt; and whatever one thinks of his tactical reasoning, one cannot but admire the incredible courage of the troopers who carried out his orders in the face of such overwhelming odds.

24. Cole, *Ardennes*, 394–95.

25. Ibid., 395.

26. It is, of course, unclear whether the initiative for the appointment of Hasbrouck as the single St. Vith commander came from Hodges, Kean, or perhaps even Thorson. But if Hodges receives criticism for the bad decisions made at First Army in the early days of the Bulge, he should also receive credit for the good decisions.

27. The German abbreviation for this unit was FBB, for Führer Begleit Brigade.

28. Cole, *Ardennes*, 396, offers a sketch of this action; but much interesting tactical detail on how it was both planned and executed is found in Fontenot, "Lucky Seventh," 64–65.

29. The reader will recall that on the night of 17 December Model had indicated to Manteuffel that he would have the FEB for employment on the 18th. The delay of three days to get Remer's entire unit to St. Vith is a reflection of the tremendous congestion and horrible road conditions in the Losheim Gap and the area immediately west of the town. Well, indeed, might Model be directing traffic there!

30. Cole, *Ardennes*, 396.

31. Except where otherwise indicated, background on Rose is from Steven L. Ossad and Don R. Marsh, *Major General Maurice Rose: World War II's Greatest Forgotten Commander* (Lanham, Md.: Taylor Trade Publishing, 2003), xi–192.

32. Chandler et al., *Eisenhower Papers*, 2099.

33. Ridgway, *Soldier*, 115.

34. Although definitive identifications were not made of the German units, their designations were correctly divined by the 3rd AD G-2. Cole, *Ardennes*, 352–54.

35. XVIII (Airborne) Corps headquarters diary entry for 20 December, Ridgway papers, MHI. For details of the division's arrival at Marche on the night of 20/21 December, see Theodore Draper, *The 84th Infantry Division in the Battle of Germany: November 1944–May 1945* (1946; reprint, Nashville: Battery Press, 1985), 87–90.

36. This paragraph is based on Cole, *Ardennes*, 361–63; Eisenhower, *Bitter Woods*, 353; and a very brief account of the battle by Skorzeny himself in Otto Skorzeny, *My Commando Operations: The Memoirs of Hitler's Most Daring Commando*, trans. David Johnston (Atglen, Pa.: Schiffer Military History, 1995), 341–42.

37. Background on General Harrison from D. Bruce Lockerbie, *A Man under Orders: Lieutenant General William K. Harrison, Jr.* (New York: Harper and Row, 1979), 115–17. As further light on the situation at Stoumont, Lockerbie states that Harrison had previously asked Hobbs to relieve Colonel Sutherland, the regimental commander; but Hobbs demurred and instead put Harrison in direct supervision of the action. Lockerbie, *Man under Orders*, 120. This was not an uncommon role for assistant division commanders.

38. Description of the action west of Stoumont on 21 December is drawn from Cole, *Ardennes*, 364–65; and MacDonald, *Time for Trumpets*, 445, 455–57.

39. Description of the fight at Cheneux on 21 December is drawn from Gavin, "The Story of the 82nd Airborne Division in the Battle of the Belgian Bulge in the Siegfried Line and on the Roer River," Section II, 3–4, MHI; Cole, *Ardennes*, 367; and MacDonald, *Time for Trumpets*, 448–49.

40. For an engaging sketch of Vandervoort, see Michel de Trez, *Colonel Ben Vandervoort "Vandy" 0-22715: Commanding Officer, 2nd Battalion, 505th Parachute Infantry Regiment, 82nd Airborne Division* (Wezembeek-Oppem, Belgium: D-Day Publishing, 2004).

41. This sentence and the remainder of the paragraph (except as otherwise noted) are based on Gavin, *On to Berlin*, 228.

42. Gavin, "The Story of the 82nd Airborne Division in the Battle of the Belgian Bulge in the Siegfried Line and on the Roer River," Section II, 4, MHI.

43. Description of the German capture of St. Vith is based on Cole, *Ardennes*, 401–6; and Fontenot, "Lucky Seventh," 83–84.

44. For a detailed tactical analysis of the action, heartily endorsed by Clarke, see "The Battle at St. Vith, Belgium, 17–23 December 1944: An Historical Example of Armor in the Defense" (3rd printing, Fort Knox, Ky.: U.S. Army Armor School, [1966]).

45. The chief of staff of the 18th VGD noted, "Not only had the enemy safely withdrawn, but he had taken along his weapons and equipment, a remarkable achievement under the circumstances." Fontenot, "Lucky Seventh," 84.

46. XVIII (Airborne) Corps G-3 journal, 211145 December, XVIII (Airborne) Corps G-3 files, RG 407, Box 4974, NAII. See also Dupuy, *St. Vith Lion in the Way*, 168; and Cole, *Ardennes*, 401. The latter misleadingly states that Ridgway's order separating the commands "clarified" the command arrangements.

47. Hasbrouck expressed his preference for working alongside Jones rather than being in overall command, in a letter to Ridgway of 21 December and in a letter to Kean, annotated in hand, "Copy for General Ridgeway [*sic*]," of the same date. The former ended as follows: "Major General Alan Jones, the Commanding General [of the 106th ID] and his Division headquarters are in VIELSALM . . . with my Tactical Headquarters. He is a Major General, I am a Brigadier so it is probably not legal to attach him to me. Possibly Army didn't realize he and his Headquarters are present. I most definitely do *not* want to be attached to him and suggest he be directed to cooperate with me in holding our present positions which I know he will do. We have been getting along on that basis alright." There is no time indicated on either of the letters. The latter is reproduced in its entirety in Eisenhower, *Bitter Woods*, 295. It included a P.S. to Jones indicating it had been dispatched at 1230.

48. XVIII (Airborne) Corps headquarters diary entry, 212237 December, Ridgway papers, MHI.

49. The remainder of the paragraph, including the direct quotation, is drawn from the memorandum of Ridgway's 212350 December conversation with Kean, XVIII (Airborne) Corps headquarters diary, Ridgway papers, MHI.

50. Parker's unit had, in Dupuy's words, been "commandeered" by Colonel Herbert W. Kruger, commander of the 174th FA Group, VIII Corps artillery, to assist the latter's withdrawal from the St. Vith salient. Dupuy, *St. Vith Lion in the Way*,

183. This account of the action at Parker's Crossroads on 21 December is based on Dupuy, *St. Vith Lion in the Way*, 187–88; and Fontenot, "Lucky Seventh," 66–68.

51. Description of the action at Hotton on 21 December is based on Cole, *Ardennes*, 378–80; see also Ossad and Marsh, *Major General Maurice Rose*, 265–68.

52. Draper, *84th Infantry Division*, 90.

53. Cole, *Ardennes*, 382.

54. Distribution of the five battalions from Blair, *Ridgway's Paratroopers*, 442.

55. Ridgway to Hobbs, 212245 December, Ridgway papers, MHI.

56. Ridgway to Brereton, 212140 December 1944, Ridgway papers, MHI. Parks-Ridgway relationship from Blair, *Ridgway's Paratroopers*, 354.

9. III, XII, and VII Corps Prepare for Battle

1. Clausewitz, *On War*, 118.

2. George S. Patton, Jr., *War as I Knew It* (Boston: Houghton Mifflin, 1947), 188.

3. Martin Blumenson, *Patton: The Man behind the Legend* (New York: William Morrow, 1985), 246.

4. The remainder of the paragraph is based on Blumenson, *Patton Papers: 1940–1945*, 596–97.

5. Ibid., 597.

6. III Corps AAR, 8–31 December 1944, n.d., 8, RG 407, Box 3262, NAII.

7. Cole, *Ardennes*, 487.

8. III Corps AAR, 8–31 December 1944, n.d., 8, RG 407, Box 3262, NAII.

9. Given that III Corps was already in the general area of the penetration and XII Corps was far to the south in Lorraine, it clearly made much more sense to use Millikin's corps to make the attack toward Bastogne and Eddy's to buttress the southern shoulder than vice versa.

10. Hansen diary, 19 December 1944, Hansen papers, MHI. Like many others in the ETO to whom Millikin was a complete stranger, Hansen misspelled the III Corps commander's name as "Milliken."

11. Blumenson, *Patton Papers: 1940–1945*, 602.

12. This paragraph is based on Cole, *Ardennes*, 510–11.

13. Description of the III Corps order of 21 December is based on III Corps AAR, 8–31 December 1944, n.d., 9, RG 407, Box 3262, NAII.

14. Patton, *War as I Knew It*, 188.

15. What follows is based primarily on Eddy War Log, 19 December 1944, Fort Benning, Georgia, National Infantry Museum; and Phillips, *Making of a Professional*, 176. The latter incorrectly identifies Culin as a major general and adds some imaginative dialogue but is accurate in the essentials of its presentation.

16. Culin recovered from this close call, commanding the 87th ID throughout the European campaign and being promoted to major general in March 1945. Ancell, *Biographical Dictionary of World War II Generals*, 72.

17. Except as otherwise noted, this paragraph is based on Eddy War Log, 20 December 1944, Fort Benning, Georgia, National Infantry Museum.

18. Cole, *Ardennes*, 488. This is also the source of the observation concerning the 35th ID's extended time in the front lines noted in the previous sentence.

19. Except as otherwise noted, this entire paragraph is based on Eddy War Log, 21 December 1944, Fort Benning, Georgia, National Infantry Museum.

20. Ibid.

21. For a graphic account of the movement of the advance echelon of Eddy's CP to Luxembourg, see George Dyer, *XII Corps: Spearhead of Patton's Third Army* (n.p.: XII U.S. Army Corps, n.d.), 284–88. A copy of this rather obscure publication can be found in the XII Corps history files, RG 407, Box 4261, NAII.

22. History of VII Corps for the period 1–31 December 1944, Incl (Report after action against the enemy), 9 January 1945, Appendix 1, 54, RG 407, Box 3827, NAII.

23. VII Corps AAR, 1–31 December 1944, Appendix 1, 56–57, RG 407, Box 3827, NAII.

24. Hamilton, *Monty: 1944–1976*, 214. Hamilton mentions Monty's admiration of Collins in the Cherbourg operation but does not comment on the close eye Monty also kept on Collins in the Cobra breakout.

25. The description of Collins's actions on 20–21 December is drawn from Collins, *Lightning Joe*, 282–84.

10. The Struggle for Initiative

1. Montgomery to Brooke, 22 December 1944, cited in Hamilton, *Monty: 1944–1976*, 223.

2. Patton diary, 27 December 1944, in Blumenson, *Patton Papers: 1940–1945*, 608.

3. Magna E. Bauer and Charles von Luettichau [*sic*], "Key Dates during the Ardennes Offensive 1944/5: An Attempt to Show When Hitler and the German Commanders Realized the Failure of Their Offensive, 16 December 1944—28 January 1945" (Washington, D.C.: OCMH, 1952), 64, RG 549, NAII.

4. Cole, *Ardennes*, 611.

5. For an accurate reflection of Monty's state of mind during this period, see Hamilton, *Monty: 1944–1976*, 227–37.

6. For Bradley's outlook at this juncture in the campaign, see Bradley and Blair, *General's Life*, 369–73; and Hansen diary, 22–27 December 1944, Hansen papers, MHI.

7. D'Este, *Eisenhower*, 655.

8. Brooke letter to Montgomery, 21 December 1944, cited in Arthur Bryant, *Triumph in the West: A History of the War Years Based on the Diaries of Field-Marshal Lord Alanbrooke, Chief of the Imperial General Staff* (New York: Doubleday, 1959), 278.

9. Montgomery letter to Brooke, 25 December 1944, cited in ibid., 278.

10. Bradley made no record of this conversation, but remarks made to Hansen shortly thereafter indicate that he had been singularly unable to accelerate Montgomery's plans to mount a counter to the German offensive, the same sentiment that is reflected in his memoirs. Hansen diary, 25 December 1944, Hansen papers, MHI; Bradley, *Soldier's Story*, 481.

11. Bradley and Blair, *General's Life*, 369–70.

12. Hamilton argues that this meeting, more than Monty's 7 January press conference, was the true cause of the resentment between Montgomery and Bradley. Hamilton, *Monty: 1944–1976*, 249. He is correct to a point. Bradley was humiliated at this meeting and may have even regretted not telling Monty off. But it was

private. The press conference, to be discussed in Chapter 13, did infinitely more damage.

13. The account of Bradley's 27 December presentation to Eisenhower is based on Bradley and Blair, *General's Life*, 372–73.

14. Ibid., 373.

15. Monty's concerns about increasing German strength from Hamilton, *Monty: 1944–1976*, 230; description of Operation "Veritable" from Montgomery, *Memoirs*, 289.

16. Eisenhower, *Crusade in Europe*, 361.

17. Montgomery to Brooke, 28 December 1944, cited in Hamilton, *Monty: 1944–1976*, 262.

18. Monty's offer to serve under Bradley from General Frank Simpson's memo to Brooke of 31 December 1944, cited in ibid., 264.

19. Ibid., 261–62, 264.

20. D'Este, *Eisenhower*, 655.

21. Brooke's diary entry for 23–30 December 1944, cited from Alex Danchev and Daniel Todman, eds., *War Diaries, 1939–1945: Field Marshal Lord Alanbrooke* (Berkeley: University of California Press, 2001), 638.

22. Eisenhower, *Bitter Woods*, 381.

23. Ibid., 382.

24. Bland and Stevens, *Marshall Papers* 4:721.

25. What follows is based on Francis de Guingand, *Generals at War* (London: Hodder and Stoughton, 1964), 106–12; and Hamilton, *Monty: 1944–1976*, 271–79. Parallel narratives in D'Este, *Eisenhower*, 656–57, and Eisenhower, *Bitter Woods*, 382–84, appear to be based on the de Guingand account. All agree in the essentials. But de Guingand relates that he was alerted to the proposed Eisenhower-Marshall cable on 30 December before he left Brussels. Hamilton reconstructs a more credible time line: de Guingand left Brussels on the 30th to deliver Montgomery's letter to Eisenhower, remained at SHAEF overnight for a chiefs of staff conference, learned of Ike's proposed message to Marshall during his stay, requested and received a twenty-four-hour reprieve, left Versailles on the 31st, and met Montgomery in Zonhoven that afternoon.

26. Hamilton, *Monty: 1944–1976*, 276.

27. Montgomery's attitude toward Alexander is reprised in ibid., 278.

28. Montgomery message to Eisenhower, 31 December 1944, cited from ibid., 279, which is based on the copy in Montgomery's papers. The same message cited in de Guingand, *Generals at War*, 112, has only minor textual differences.

29. Eisenhower's reply to Montgomery is found in Eisenhower, *Bitter Woods*, 385–86; his reply to Marshall of 1 January 1945 is found in Chandler et al., *Eisenhower Papers*, 2390–91.

30. Hamilton, *Monty: 1944–1976*, 279.

31. Patton confided to his diary on 27 December: "If Ike will put Bradley back in command of First and Ninth Armies, we can bag the whole German army. . . . If I could get three more divisions, I could win this war now." Blumenson, *Patton Papers: 1940–1945*, 608. See Dupuy, Bongard, and Anderson, *Hitler's Last Gamble*, 326, for support of the Patton solution. For my detailed critique of that argument, see my review of the book in *Parameters* 25 (Winter 1995/1996): 157–59.

32. Hasso von Manteuffel, "Fifth Panzer Army (Ardennes Offensive)," 57, FMS B-151a, RG 319, NAII; see also Cole, *Ardennes*, 613.

33. Manteuffel, "Fifth Panzer Army (Ardennes Offensive)," 97, FMS B-151a, RG 319, NAII.

34. Ibid., 98. Manteuffel's report does not provide the precise date Decker's corps was assigned to Fifth Panzer Army. Over Lüttwitz's objections, Manteuffel further subordinated Decker's corps to his corps commander on the scene, creating, for a short while, Army Groups Lüttwitz. Cole, *Ardennes*, 614. Manteuffel considered such action normal and provided a detailed justification in Manteuffel, "Fifth Panzer Army (Ardennes Offensive)," 98–99, FMS B-151a, RG 319, NAII.

35. P. E. Schramm, "The Course of Events of the German Offensive in the Ardennes," 10, FMS 858, RG 319, NAII.

36. Ibid., 11.

37. The German Alsace offensive, which was launched on 31 December 1944, is beyond the scope of this study. A basic account can be found in Pogue, *Supreme Command*, 397–404. For additional details, see Clarke and Smith, *Riviera to the Rhine*, 492–512.

38. Schramm, "The Course of Events of the German Offensive in the Ardennes," 12–16, FMS 858, RG 319, NAII.

39. Craven and Cate, *Army Air Forces* 3:689.

40. Except as otherwise noted, what follows is based on Thompson, "Air Supply," 64–138, RG 549, NAII.

41. It is rather ironic that these planes were loaded with supplies originally intended for the two surrounded regiments of the 106th ID.

42. The battalion low on small arms ammunition, which was probably typical for the division, was 2nd Battalion, 506th PIR. Its executive officer, Captain Richard Winters, noted with a bit of typical infantry humor, "This keeps up, we can challenge the Germans to a Christmas Day snowball fight. That's all we'll have." Larry Alexander, *Biggest Brother: The Life of Major Dick Winters, the Man Who Led the Band of Brothers* (New York: NAL Caliber, 2005), 143.

43. Lewis Sorley, *Thunderbolt: General Creighton Abrams and the Army of His Times* (New York: Simon and Schuster, 1992), 76–81.

44. This paragraph is from USSTAF A-2, "Ardennes Offensive," Statistical Annex, USAFHRA File 519.601C(S). All material in this file has been declassified.

45. Craven and Cate, *Army Air Forces* 3:687.

46. Lieutenant General Richard Wirtz, "Army Group B Engineers (January 1–25, 1945)," FMS B-172, 8, RG 319, NAII.

47. Mierzejewski, *Collapse of the German War Economy, 1944–1945*, 131–32. Mierzejewski argues that these attacks also degraded the Reichsbahn's ability to deliver coal to German industry. Thus, the Allies were achieving a dual effect: their concentration on the German rail net south of the Ruhr and immediately east of the Rhine was not only helping Eisenhower halt the German offensive but it was also abetting the strategic bombing effort. To the extent that it was done by design, it represented sophisticated targeting on the part of the Allied air leaders.

48. USSTAF A-2, "Ardennes Offensive," 47, USAFHRA File 519.601C(S). All material in this file has been declassified.

49. USSTAF A-2, "Ardennes Offensive," Statistical Annex, USAFHRA File 519.601C(S); all material in this file has been declassified. Craven and Cate, *Army Air Forces* 3:693–94.

50. General Erich Brandenberger, "Comments on Lieutenant General Richard Wirtz, 'Army Group B Engineers (January 1–25, 1945),'" FMS B-172a, 2, RG 319, NAII.

51. Details of attacks on St. Vith and Houffalize from USSTAF A-2, "Ardennes Offensive," 53–54, USAFHRA File 519.601C(S); all material in this file has been declassified. Also Arthur Harris, *Bomber Offensive* (New York: Macmillan, 1947), 253–54; and Martin Middlebrook and Chris Everitt, eds., *The Bomber Command War Diaries: An Operational Reference Book, 1939–1945* (London: Penguin, 1990), 637, 640, and 648.

52. The adjective "apocalyptic" comes from an account of the bombing by John Toland based on a description given him by Private Hans Ulrich Leske, a member of the rocket-launcher battalion of the Hitler Youth Division, who was about a mile from St. Vith when the attack occurred: "Three hundred British Lancasters and Halifaxes dumped their loads. The ground shook, like an earthquake. Fir trees toppled down. To Leske's horror St. Vith seemed to rise in the air to meet the planes. . . . Leske shakily got to his feet. A vast red cloud was drifting westward from St. Vith, a cloud of dust lit by the dying rays of the setting sun. He was transfixed. It was apocalyptic." Toland, *Battle*, 286–87.

53. General Hasso von Manteuffel, "Comments on Lieutenant General Richard Wirtz, 'Army Group B Engineers (January 1–25, 1945),'" FMS B-172b, 2, RG 319, NAII.

54. Field Marshal Wilhelm Keitel and Colonel General Alfred Jodl, "Answers to the Questionnaire on the Ardennes Offensive," 3, FMS A-928, RG 319, NAII.

55. Manteuffel, "Fifth Panzer Army (Ardennes Offensive)," FMS B-151a, 125, RG 319, NAII.

56. Lieutenant General Karl Tholte, "Army Group B Artillery (Ardennes)," FMS B-311, 6–11, RG 319, NAII.

57. This account of the action at Celles is based on MacDonald, *Time for Trumpets*, 582–83.

58. Air operations described in this paragraph from USSTAF, Battlefield Studies World War II, "Air Resupply Ardennes Counter-Offensive, 16 December 1944–16 January 1945," n.d., 5–6, USAFHRA File 519.042. This very brief synopsis, with little documentation, is not to be confused with the earlier-referenced USSTAF A-2 analysis of airpower in the Bulge.

59. This account based on Royce Thompson, "Malmedy, Belgium, Mistaken Bombing, 23 and 25 December 1944" (Washington, D.C.: OCMH, 1952), passim, RG 549, NAII; copy also at AUL, File M-U 44112-2. Thompson's study includes typed extracts of the IX Bomber Division summaries of the missions flown on 23 and 25 December. I verified the accuracy of these extracts against the actual mission summaries found in USAFHRA File 534.333. The operative statements were "6 a/c bombed the town of Malmedy, 1/2 mile W of bombline, due to misidentification of target" (23 December) and "the leader of one flight misidentified primary. This a/c plus 3 others dropped 64x250 GP at Malmedy-friendly territory" (25 December).

60. Cole, *Ardennes*, 377.

61. What follows is based on Girbig, *Six Months to Oblivion*, 107–67. Girbig's painstaking research provides a very detailed account of Operation *Bodenplatte*. Another extended account is offered in Parker, *To Win the Winter Sky*, 373–449. A concise summary can be found in Great Britain, Air Ministry, *Rise and Fall*, 379–81.

62. USSTAF A-2, "Ardennes Offensive," daily summary for 3 January 1945, USAFHRA File 519.601C(S). All material in this file has been declassified.

11. III, VIII, and XII Corps Fight for Initiative in the South

1. Patton letter to his wife, 29 December 1944, Blumenson, *Patton Papers: 1940–1945*, 608.

2. Patton's guidance on division formations and Millikin's reaction thereto are based on III Corps G-3 memorandum for record, 211345 December 1944, III Corps G-3 files, RG 407, Box 3302, NAII. See also Cole, *Ardennes*, 515; and Weigley, *Eisenhower's Lieutenants*, 521.

3. Cole, who posits the left flank of III Corps at Neufchâteau, describes the III Corps front as being thirty miles wide. Cole, *Ardennes*, 510. This is technically correct. However, except during a road march to reposition CCR, 4th AD, on the night of 24/25 December, III Corps never had units that far west. I take the westernmost point of the III Corps advance as roughly Vaux-lez-Rosières, where CCR began to encounter German resistance on 25 December. This gave III Corps an actual attack frontage of approximately twenty-five miles.

4. Background on General Gaffey is from Ancell, *Biographical Dictionary of World War II Generals*, 110; and Blumenson, *Patton Papers: 1940–1945*, 419–20, 422.

5. Background on General Paul is from Ancell, *Biographical Dictionary of World War II Generals*, 252; and Chandler et al., *Eisenhower Papers*, 1696.

6. Background on General McBride is from Ancell, *Biographical Dictionary of World War II Generals*, 210–11; and Blumenson, *Patton Papers: 1940–1945*, 515–16, 563–64.

7. Account of the 4th AD's attack on 22 December is based on an ETO historical manuscript, ca. 1946, "The Intervention of the Third Army: III Corps in the Attack, 22 December–28 December, 1944," pt. II, chap. 1, 14–21, 8-3.1 AR, CMH; and Cole, *Ardennes*, 525–26.

8. III Corps Message to VIII Corps, received 221500 December 1944, VIII Corps G-3 files, RG 407, Box 4030, NAII.

9. Account of the attack of the 26th ID on 22 December is based on "Intervention of the Third Army: III Corps in the Attack," pt. II, chap. 1, 7–14, 8-3.1 AR, CMH; and Cole, *Ardennes*, 520–22.

10. The FGB was a demi-armored division with a panzer battalion, a panzergrenadier regiment, an artillery battalion, and various supporting units. Dupuy, Bongard, and Anderson, *Hitler's Last Gamble*, 524n.

11. Morale in the FGB "suffered a significant decline" when the commander, Colonel Hans Joachim-Kahler, was killed. Dupuy, Bongard, and Anderson, *Hitler's Last Gamble*, 219. Given the breadth of the III Corps attack and Seventh Army's mission of protecting Manteuffel's southern flank, there was little else Brandenberger could do with this formation.

12. Description of the 80th ID's attack on 22 December is based on "The Intervention of the Third Army: III Corps in the Attack, 22 December–28 December 1944," pt. II, chap. 1, 1–5, 8-3.1 AR, CMH; and Cole, *Ardennes*, 515–16.

13. CG, III Corps, to CG, 80th ID, 222135 December 1944, III Corps G-3 files, RG 407, Box 3302, NAII.

14. III Corps chief of staff memorandum, 22 December 1944, III Corps G-3 files, RG 407, Box 3302, NAII. Colonel Phillips's numerous, succinct memoranda in the III Corps files kept Millikin and his staff fully informed of the developing situation. They also constitute a very valuable resource to the historian.

15. III Corps memorandum, conference with General Patton—attended by General Gaffey and General Millikin, 221604 December 1944, III Corps G-3 files, RG 407, Box 3302, NAII. See also Cole, *Ardennes*, 525. Cole implies that this guidance was issued before the attack, but the III Corps log makes it evident that Patton's reverie on armored warfare was delivered late on the afternoon of 22 December.

16. Patton's account of this conversation is contained in his letter to his wife of 22 December, cited in Blumenson, *Patton Papers: 1940–1945*, 604. As the only known face-to-face meeting between Patton and Millikin occurred in the late afternoon when the Third Army commander came to the III Corps CP to discuss armored tactics with Gaffey and Millikin, it stands to reason that this advice was proffered at the same time, though perhaps privately.

17. Blumenson, *Patton Papers: 1940–1945*, 604.

18. Eisenhower, *Bitter Woods*, 322.

19. Lüttwitz, "Commitment of the XXXXVII Panzer Corps in the Ardennes," 9, FMS A-939, RG 319, NAII.

20. The 101st's side of the story is told in Marshall, *Bastogne*, 118; and Eisenhower, *Bitter Woods*, 322–23. The latter contains most of the text of Lüttwitz's note demanding surrender.

21. The characterization of McAuliffe's reply as laconic is drawn from the description of Bastogne in the 1963 *Michelin Guide* for the Benelux countries: *"Bastogne, réputée pour son fameux jambon d'Ardenne, a été célèbre par l'héroïque résistance des troupes américaines encerclées par von Rundstedt, en décembre 1944. Invité à se rendre, le général Mac Auliffe* [sic] *fit cette réponse laconique et péremptoire: <Nuts> (litteralement: <des noix>)."* Cited from Weigley, *Eisenhower's Lieutenants*, 514. The division G-2, Lieutenant Colonel Paul A. Danahy, also knew good copy when he saw it and inserted the following entry in his periodic report for 22 December: "The Commanding General's answer was, with a sarcastic air of humorous tolerance, emphatically negative. The catastrophic carnage of human lives resulting from the artillery barrage of astronomic proportions failed to materialize." Marshall, *Bastogne*, 118. Once the news of McAuliffe's reply got out through VIII Corps, it spread like wildfire. The "Battered Bastards" appellation apparently originated in a *Stars and Stripes* story of 4 January 1945, which noted, "It was one of the 101st's own wounded men who described his comrades as the 'battered bastards of the bastion of Bastogne.'" Cited from John Brawley, *Anyway, We Won: A Civilian Soldier from the Ozarks Spends Five Years in the Army* (Marceline, Mo.: Walsworth, 1988), 259n. Brawley served as the assistant VII Corps signal officer and participated in the Ardennes campaign.

22. Description of III Corps fighting on 23 December from "The Intervention of the Third Army: III Corps in the Attack," pt. II, chap. 2, 1–13, 8-3.1 AR, CMH; and Cole, *Ardennes*, 516–23, 526–30.

23. III Corps chief of staff memorandum for record of conversation with Third Army commander at 231100 December 1944, III Corps G-3 files, RG 407, Box 3302, NAII.

24. III Corps chief of staff memorandum for record of Millikin's conversation with Paul at 26th ID command post, 231645 December 1944, III Corps G-3 files, RG 407, Box 3302, NAII; see also Cole, *Ardennes*, 523.

25. 101st Airborne Division message to VIII Corps, 230855 December 1944, VIII Corps G-3 files, RG 407, Box 4031, NAII. Middleton had previously requested that 4th AD provide VIII Corps with hourly updates, and III Corps headquarters had consented to this arrangement. CG, VIII Corps, message to 4th AD (Attn: G-3 Operations), 220945 December 1944, VIII Corps G-3 files, RG 407, Box 4030, NAII. It is not clear why, nearly twenty-four hours later, the 101st initiated another request for hourly updates. But the second request does indicate that the 101st was definitely interested in the 4th AD's progress.

26. Message from VIII Corps LNO, 231900 December 1944, III Corps G-3 files, RG 407, Box 3302, NAII.

27. Description of the 23 December fight at Marvie from Marshall, *Bastogne*, 119–30.

28. Cole, *Ardennes*, 472.

29. Ibid., 531.

30. "The Intervention of the Third Army: III Corps in the Attack," pt. II, chap. 3, 1, 8-3.1 AR, CMH.

31. Description of missions given to 6th Cavalry Group is based on III Corps message to CO, 6th Cavalry Group, 242330 December 1944, III Corps G-3 files, RG 407, Box 3302, NAII. According to a G-3 journal entry for 241400 December, Millikin had earlier ordered General Paul's 26th ID to take over from CCR, 4th AD, in the area of Bigonville. The insertion of a cavalry squadron between 26th ID and 4th AD offered slightly greater assurance that the gap between the two divisions would not become a source of trouble, but it was still a temporary fix.

32. "The Intervention of the Third Army: III Corps in the Attack," pt. II, chap. 5, 2, 8-3.1 AR, CMH.

33. Ibid., pt. II, chap. 5, 3, 8-3.1 AR, CMH.

34. Description of the fighting of the 26th ID on 24 December is drawn from ibid., pt. II, chap. 4, 1–5, 8-3.1 AR, CMH.

35. Description of the 80th ID combat on 24 December is drawn from ibid., pt. II, chap. 3, 1–3, 8-3.1 AR, CMH.

36. This and the following two sentences are based on Cole, *Ardennes*, 472–74.

37. With the glidermen of the 327th holding one end of the village and the panzergrenadiers of the 901st holding the other, an American air attack against Marvie was called in on the 24th. Cole, *Ardennes*, 474.

38. Cole, *Ardennes*, 475.

39. Description of the German air attack against Bastogne on Christmas Eve is from Eisenhower, *Bitter Woods*, 327.

40. First Lieutenant Edward P. Hyduke, who had commanded Colonel Cherry's advance guard at Longvilly and miraculously made it back to Bastogne after being cut off on the 19th, was killed in this raid. Eisenhower, *Bitter Woods*, 327.

41. Marshall, *Bastogne*, 155–56.

42. Price, *Middleton*, 259.

43. III Corps Operations Directive no. 2, 24 December 1944, III Corps G-3 files, RG 407, Box 3302, NAII.

44. Blumenson, *Patton Papers: 1940–1945*, 605.

45. The account of TF Abrams's advance on 25 December is based on "The Intervention of the Third Army: III Corps in the Attack," pt. II, chap. 7, 3–4, 8-3.1 AR, CMH.

46. Description of CCB's and CCA's attacks on 25 December from ibid., pt. II, chap. 5, 4–5, 8-3.1 AR, CMH.

47. Account of the fighting in the 26th ID sector on 25 December is from ibid., pt. II, chap. 4, 5–7, 8-3.1 AR, CMH.

48. Ibid., pt. II, chap. 3, 4–5, 8-3.1 AR, CMH.

49. III Corps G-3 message of phone conversation with Third Army G-3, 250845 December 1944, III Corps G-3 files, RG 407, Box 3302, NAII.

50. Details of the 35th ID's assignment to III Corps and 80th ID's assignment to XII Corps, both effective 26 December, are from III Corps chief of staff memorandum for record of conversation with Third Army G-3, 251045 December 1944, III Corps G-3 files, RG 407, Box 3303, NAII.

51. The Gay-Patton dialogue on commitment of the 35th ID is drawn from "The Intervention of the Third Army: III Corps in the Attack," pt. II, chap. 5, 1, 8-3.1 AR, CMH. The official history credits Gay with delaying the deployment of the 35th until "other Third Army divisions in better condition had been committed." Cole, *Ardennes*, 606n.

52. Description of the 25 December fight at Bastogne is based on Marshall, *Bastogne*, 157–69; and Cole, *Ardennes*, 478–79.

53. The story of Colonel Abrams's dramatic breakthrough to Bastogne is drawn from "The Intervention of the Third Army: III Corps in the Attack," pt. II, chap. 7, 8–13; Sorley, *Thunderbolt*, 68–81; and Eisenhower, *Bitter Woods*, 343–45.

54. Sorley, *Thunderbolt*, 77. Abrams's gutsy call has been dramatized in a painting by the noted military artist Don Stiver, titled simply "Let's Go."

55. Dwight-McAuliffe dialogue from Eisenhower, *Bitter Woods*, 345.

56. The transfer was effective 262000 December 1944. XII Corps G-3 Journal, 26 December 1944, RG 407, Box 4366, NAII.

57. Initial actions to secure the Bastogne corridor based on "The Intervention of the Third Army: III Corps in the Attack," pt. II, chap. 7, 14–16, 8-3.1 AR, CMH.

58. What follows is based on Maxwell D. Taylor, *Swords and Plowshares* (New York: W. W. Norton, 1972), 102; and Eisenhower, *Bitter Woods*, 407–9. Gaffey had offered Taylor a tank for the run to Bastogne, but Taylor demurred.

59. Taylor records in his memoirs that McAuliffe and his men were "incredulous when I told them they were heroes and indignant when they learned that they had been 'rescued.' The attitude of the Division had been expressed the first day the German lines closed around the town—'They've got us surrounded, the poor bastards!'" Taylor, *Swords and Plowshares*, 102. McAuliffe explicitly rebutted the notion of having been rescued, telling the *Stars and Stripes*, "Anyone who says we were rescued, or who thinks we needed rescue, is all wrong." *Stars and Stripes*, 4 January 1945, cited in Brawley, *Anyway, We Won*, 259n. The Screaming Eagles' defense of Bastogne was truly heroic, and nothing can diminish their accomplishment. But the documentary record clearly indicates that they were, nevertheless, quite desirous of relief from Millikin's III Corps.

60. What follows is based on "The Intervention of the Third Army: III Corps in the Attack," pt. II, chap. 7, 19–21, 8-3.1 AR, CMH.

61. Background on General Baade is from Ancell, *Biographical Dictionary of World War II Generals*, 10; and Weigley, *Eisenhower's Lieutenants*, 141–42.

62. Cole, *Ardennes*, Map X.

63. *Presenting . . . The 35th Infantry Division in World War II, 1941–1945* (1946; reprint, Nashville: Battery Press, 1988), chap. 10, n.p.

64. Description of the 35th ID's fight on 27 December from "The Intervention of the Third Army: III Corps in the Attack," pt. II, chap. 8, 3–5, 8-3.1 AAR, NAII.

65. Description of the 26th ID's fight on 27 December is drawn from ibid., 1–2, 8-3.1 AR, CMH; and Cole, *Ardennes*, 546–47.

66. This paragraph is based on "The Intervention of the Third Army: III Corps in the Attack," pt. II, chap. 8, 5–9, 8-3.1 AR, CMH.

67. Dupuy, Bongard, and Anderson, *Hitler's Last Gamble*, 296.

68. Message, 4th AD G-3 to III Corps G-3, 291234 December 1944, III Corps G-3 files, RG 407, Box 3304, NAII.

69. *Presenting . . . The 35th Infantry Division*, chap. 10, n.p.

70. Cole, *Ardennes*, 624; and Reynolds, *Men of Steel*, 148–49.

71. Cole, *Ardennes*, 640.

72. Dupuy, Bongard, and Anderson, *Hitler's Last Gamble*, 296.

73. What follows is from Third Army Operational Directive, 28 December 1944, III Corps G-3 files, RG 407, Box 3304, NAII.

74. Cole, *Ardennes*, 612.

75. Unless otherwise noted, what follows is based on Reynolds, *Men of Steel*, 146–53; and Cole, *Ardennes*, 623–27.

76. At 300945 December 1944, the 35th ID staff informed III Corps headquarters that Baade had asked Gaffey for assistance. III Corps G-3 files, RG 407, Box 3304, NAII. The German advance to the Bastogne-Arlon road was halted at roughly 1600. Reynolds, *Men of Steel*, 152.

77. Telephonic message, 4th AD G-3 to III Corps G-3, 301515 December 1944, III Corps G-3 files, RG 407, Box 3304, NAII. It is not clear whether the sender of the message was the 4th AD G-3 himself or a member of his staff.

78. Background on General Grow from George F. Hofmann, *Cold War Casualty: The Court-Martial of Major General Robert W. Grow* (Kent, Ohio: Kent State University Press, 1991), 10–11. Grow became the center of an international cause célèbre in 1951 when he carelessly left his diary, which contained information about targets designated for attack in the Soviet Union, unattended in a guesthouse in Frankfurt, Germany. The diary was photographed by Soviet agents, and excerpts were exploited by Soviet propaganda. Grow was court-martialed for a breach of security and found guilty. Eisenhower, then president, approved the findings but remitted Grow's sentence. On Grow's pre-Bulge relationship with Patton, see also Blumenson, *Patton Papers: 1940–1945*, 425.

79. What follows is based on George F. Hofmann, *The Super Sixth: History of the Sixth Armored Division in World War II and Its Post-War Association* (Louisville: Sixth Armored Division Association), 275–76.

80. What follows is based on Cole, *Ardennes*, 628–29; and Hofmann, *Super Sixth*, 277.

81. Description of CCA, 6th AD's attack on 31 December from Cole, *Ardennes*, 629; and Hofmann, *Super Sixth*, 278–79.

82. This and the following sentence are based on Millikin's memorandum to Colonel Phillips outlining his discussions held at the 4th AD, 6th AD, and 35th ID command posts, 31 December 1944, III Corps G-3 files, RG 407, Box 3304, NAII. Support from the 101st was the subject of some acrimony on Grow's part. In his diary entry for 31 December, he castigated Taylor for failing to aid his attack. Hofmann, *Cold War Casualty*, 1. Taylor's memoirs are silent on the subject. The official history indicates that Middleton had granted permission for a single battalion of the 101st to be used in this capacity but later reversed the order. Cole, *Ardennes*, 629–30.

83. III Corps chief of staff memorandum for record of conversation with Third Army commander, 311225 December 1944, III Corps G-3 files, RG 407, Box 3304, NAII.

84. Cole, *Ardennes*, 629.

85. The tenuous supply situation of the 6th AD at this juncture was evident when the commander of the division trains called to inform III Corps headquarters that he had not been able to reach his division's front lines because of congestion along the roads into Bastogne and the continued presence of ice thereon. III Corps deputy chief of staff memorandum for record, 31 December 1944. On the following day, Gaffey was sufficiently concerned about the security of the Arlon-Bastogne road to inform Colonel Phillips that he found the infantry coverage between Villers-la-Bonne-Eau and Lutrebois to be too thin. III Corps chief of staff memorandum for record of discussion with CG, 4th AD, 1 January 1945. Both documents from III Corps G-3 files, RG 407, Box 3304, NAII.

86. Description of the fighting of the 6th AD on 1 January is based on Cole, *Ardennes*, 630–31; and Hofmann, *Super Sixth*, 282–83.

87. III Corps chief of staff memorandum for record of conversation with Third Army commander, 011305 January 1945, III Corps G-3 files, RG 407, Box 3305, NAII.

88. Phillips was entirely accurate here. III Corps Operational Directive no. 1, 1 January 1945, stipulated that 6th AD was to "make plans for encirclement of enemy in direction Bras [four miles north-northeast of Harlange] . . . in conjunction with 26th Inf Div." III Corps G-3 files, RG 407, Box 3304, NAII.

89. Millikin memorandum for record of instructions to division commanders for 2 January, 1 January 1945, III Corps G-3 files, RG 407, Box 3305, NAII.

90. Cole, *Ardennes*, 631–32.

91. Messages from 6th AD G-3 to III Corps G-3, 020020, 020125, and 020145 January 1945, III Corps G-3 files, RG 407, Box 3305, NAII; and Cole, *Ardennes*, 632.

92. Description of 6th AD fight on 2 January is based on Cole, *Ardennes*, 632–34; and Hofmann, *Super Sixth*, 282–88.

93. Charles B. MacDonald, *The Last Offensive* (Washington, D.C.: OCMH, 1973), 34.

94. There is an apparent error in the official histories concerning the date the I SS Panzer Corps attack kicked off. Both Cole, *Ardennes*, 632, and MacDonald, *Last Offensive*, 34, state that the date was 4 January. This date is apparently given based on a statement made in Priess's postwar report (FMS A-877) that Model approved a

delay until the 4th. But Reynolds, *Men of Steel*, 174n, points out that this throws the entire narrative off by twenty-four hours. It is also clear from message traffic received from 4th AD on 3 January that the division received a substantial counterattack on its left flank on 3 January, as described in Reynolds's narrative. Thus, I agree with Reynolds that the attack began on 3 January and continued on 4 January.

95. The account of the clash between the 6th AD and 1st SS Panzer Corps on 3 January is based on Reynolds, *Men of Steel*, 162–67, which is supported by messages of German attacks from 6th AD to III Corps at 031435 January 1945 and 032140 January 1945, III Corps G-3 files, RG 407, Box 3305, NAII.

96. The account of the 6th AD's fight on 4 January is based on Reynolds, *Men of Steel*, 167–70; and Hofmann, *Super Sixth*, 289–95.

97. Millikin's memorandum for record of conversations with commanders, 6th AD, 4th AD, and 35th ID, 4 January 1945 [conversation with Grow at 1745], III Corps G-3 files, RG 407, Box 3305, NAII.

98. Except as otherwise indicated, this paragraph is based on Cole, *Ardennes*, 635–37.

99. *Presenting . . . The 35th Infantry Division*, chap. 10, n.p.

100. Message from CG, III Corps, to CO, 6th Cavalry Group, 011410 January 1945, III Corps G-3 files, RG 407, Box 3305, NAII.

101. III Corps Sitrep, 030600–031200 January 1945, and III Corps chief of staff memorandum for record of conversation with Third Army chief of staff, 5 January 1945 [discussion of 26th ID related to activities on 4 January], III Corps G-3 files, RG 407, Box 3305, NAII.

102. Cole, *Ardennes*, Map X.

103. Phillips, *To Save Bastogne*, 266n.

104. Location of 109th Infantry Regiment from "The Intervention of the Third Army: III Corps in the Attack," pt. II, chap. 1, 2, 8-3.1 AR, CMH.

105. This and the following sentence are based on the 28th ID G-3 periodic report, 231200–241200 December 1944, VIII Corps G-3 files, RG 407, Box 4031, NAII.

106. 80th ID's relief of 109th Infantry Regiment from "The Intervention of the Third Army: III Corps in the Attack," pt. II, chap. 1, 2, 8-3.1 AR, CMH. VIII Corps' persistent entreaties to Third Army for return of the regiment are noted in Middleton's message to Patton of 231000 December 1944, a staff officer's phone call of 242145 December 1944, and another staff officer inquiry of 251010 December 1944. The reply to the last one: "Our chief has not yet made a decision. . . . but we have not overlooked them and will release them to you as soon as possible." The notice of the regiment's return the following day was received at 261520 December 1944. VIII Corps G-3 files, RG 407, Box 4031, NAII.

107. This formation consisted of three TD battalions and an AAA battalion. Its total complement consisted of twelve towed antitank guns, four of which did not have soldiers to man them; ten self-propelled antitank guns; and four quad-.50-caliber antiaircraft guns. Corps antitank officer memorandum to G-3, 26 December 1944. Attachment is indicated in Sitrep for period 271200–272400 December 1944, VIII Corps G-3 files, RG 407, Box 4031, NAII.

108. The plan for defense of the Meuse in the 12th AG sector is based on the Third Army operational directive of 23 December 1944 and information relayed from the Third Army G-3 to VIII Corps headquarters by an 11th AD liaison officer, 23 December 1944, VIII Corps G-3 files, RG 407, Box 4031, NAII.

109. The screening action of the 4th French Parachute Battalion is based on message, CG, VIII Corps, to CG, XVIII (Airborne) Corps, 241830 December 1944, VIII Corps G-3 files, RG 407, Box 4301, NAII.

110. Sketchy details of TF "W" are found in messages from it to VIII Corps headquarters of 261045 December 1944 and 291330 December 1944, VIII Corps G-3 files, RG 407, Boxes 4301 and 4302, respectively, NAII. Task Force W included elements from "2nd Tank Battalion, 52nd Armored Infantry Battalion, 89th Recon, Division Headquarters Rear Echelon, Headquarters CCR, Division Trains, 3rd Field Artillery Battalion, 16th Field Artillery Battalion, 28th Infantry Division, 811th Tank Destroyers, 10th Armored Division, and the 16th Field Artillery Observation Battalion." Reichelt, *Phantom Nine*, 159.

111. Cole, *Ardennes*, 433.

112. VIII Corps message to CG, First Army, 252230 December 1944, VIII Corps G-3 files, RG 407, Box 4301, NAII.

113. Cole, *Ardennes*, 613.

114. Except as otherwise noted, background on the 11th AD is from Berry Craig, *11th Armored Division Thunderbolts* (Paducah, Ky.: Turner Publishing, 1988), 1.

115. Memorandum for G-3, 27 December 1944, VIII Corps G-3 files, RG 407, Box 4031, NAII.

116. Background on Kilburn from Ancell, *Biographical Dictionary of World War II Generals*, 175.

117. Background on the 87th ID from *An Historical and Pictorial Record of the 87th Infantry Division in World War II, 1942–1945* (1946; reprint, n.p.: 87th Infantry Division Association, 1988), map insert; and Weigley, *Eisenhower's Lieutenants*, 440.

118. Background on Culin from Ancell, *Biographical Dictionary of World War II Generals*, 72.

119. Third Army operational directive, 28 December 1944, VIII Corps G-3 files, RG 407, Box 4032, NAII.

120. Patton's sympathies with Bradley are evident in a diary entry made on 27 December: "I wish Ike were more of a gambler, but he is certainly a lion compared to Montgomery, and Bradley is better than Ike as far as nerve is concerned." Blumenson, *Patton Papers: 1940–1945*, 608.

121. Details of the VIII Corps attack plan from Cole, *Ardennes*, 617–18, Map X. There is a minor discrepancy here. The map shows the 87th ID/4th AD boundary being split by the Bois de Haies de Magery, but the text makes it clear that one combat command of the 11th AD attacked west of the woods.

122. VIII Corps messages to CG 11th AD and CG 87th ID, 282330 December 1944, VIII Corps G-3 files, RG 407, Box 4302, NAII. Distances for the 11th AD and 87th ID road marches are from Cole, *Ardennes*, 617 and 643, respectively.

123. Cole, *Ardennes*, 617.

124. Middleton's request for a postponement is inferred here. Only Patton's end of the conversation is recorded: "He didn't care how Middleton made the attack, but he must make it, and he must secure the objective." Blumenson, *Patton Papers: 1940–1945*, 609.

125. Description of the 3rd PGD attack on 30 December from Cole, *Ardennes*, 619–20, Map X; and Manteuffel, "Fifth Panzer Army (Ardennes Offensive)," 100–101, FMS B-151a, RG 319, NAII.

126. LD time from VIII Corps AAR, 1–31 December 1944, 31, RG 407, Box 3959, NAII.

127. Description of the VIII Corps fight on 30 December is drawn from Cole, *Ardennes*, 620–22; and Dupuy, Bongard, and Anderson, *Hitler's Last Gamble*, 297–99.

128. Cole, *Ardennes*, 621.

129. Patton wrote his wife on December 31: "Yesterday my luck held out in a big way. I was launching two new divisions, but they were late in getting to the assembly area, and every one urged the attack be suspended. I insisted that they attack, if it was only with their advance guards. They did attack and ran right into the flank of a German attack. Had this not happened, things could have been critical. As it was, we stopped the attack in its tracks." Blumenson, *Patton Papers: 1940–1945*, 610. The next day, he took a similar line publicly at a press conference, calling the attack "a very fortunate piece of timing." Blumenson, *Patton Papers: 1940–1945*, 612.

130. Unless otherwise noted, this paragraph is based on Cole, *Ardennes*, 644–47.

131. Middleton said of Kilburn, whom he found on 1 January directing traffic, "I told him a PFC could do that. I told him to move on. He was very nervous and kept most of those around him nervous." Price, *Middleton*, 268. Patton relieved General Kilburn from command of the 11th AD in March 1945, during the Palatinate campaign. When he did so, he opined, "I should have relieved him in January." Blumenson, *Patton Papers: 1940–1945*, 653.

132. This paragraph is based on Cole, *Ardennes*, 643–44.

133. VIII Corps memorandum on the general situation, 1 January 1945, VIII Corps G-3 files, RG 407, Box 4033, NAII.

134. Background on the 17th Airborne Division from Don R. Pay, *Thunder from Heaven: Story of the 17th Airborne Division, 1943–1945* (1947; reprint, Nashville: Battery Press, [1980]), 17–20. The division also included the 550th Glider Battalion, which had participated in Operation Dragoon. Blair, *Ridgway's Paratroopers*, 488.

135. Telephone message, 17th Airborne Division to VIII Corps, 032005 January 1945, VIII Corps G-3 files, RG 407, Box 4033, NAII.

136. Background on Miley from Pay, *Thunder from Heaven*, 17–20.

137. VIII Corps field order number 1, 021830 January 1945, VIII Corps G-3 files, RG 407, Box 4033, NAII.

138. VIII Corps operational memorandum number 2, 3 January 1945, VIII Corps G-3 files, RG 407, Box 4033, NAII. The G-3 journal indicates an "out" time of 1700.

139. Manteuffel, "Fifth Panzer Army (Ardennes Offensive)," 103, FMS B-151a, RG 319, NAII.

140. Except as otherwise noted, the story of the 17th Airborne Division's abortive attack on 4 January is drawn from Blair, *Ridgway's Paratroopers*, 488–89.

141. All except the detail on artillery support to the 194th GIR is based on Blair's account; the artillery shift is noted in the diary of General Gay, who visited the division on 5 January. Gay Diary, 5 January 1945, Gay papers, MHI.

142. Gay Diary, 5 January 1945, Gay papers, MHI.

143. VIII Corps Sitrep, 041200–041800 January 1945, VIII Corps G-3 files, RG 407, Box 4033, NAII.

144. Patton diary, 4 January 1945, Blumenson, *Patton Papers: 1940–1945*, 615.

145. Gay recorded that Middleton was "quite depressed and felt that he could not attack and also questioned if he could hold out against the enemy's attacks." Gay Diary, 5 January 1945, Gay papers, MHI.

146. Manteuffel, "Fifth Panzer Army (Ardennes Offensive)," 104, FMS B-151a, RG 319, NAII.

147. This discussion of terrain on the southern shoulder is drawn generally from Cole, *Ardennes*, 507.

148. This problem became particularly acute in the XII Corps sector. Reports reached Eddy that on 31 January sixteen P-47s had bombed Echternach, five days after it had been captured by the 5th ID. An Army Air Forces officer later informed Eddy that the planes had been dropping from high altitude and were attempting to hit a bridge over the Sauer. Two days later, after learning of five separate incidents of his soldiers having been attacked by aircraft with clear American markings, Eddy, in a state of some frustration, mused, "I am inclined to believe that some of these planes are flown by German pilots." Eddy War Log, 31 December 1944 and 2 January 1945, Fort Benning, Georgia, National Infantry Museum.

149. Unless otherwise noted, the account of the 10th Infantry Regiment's attack on 22 and 23 December is drawn from Cole, *Ardennes*, 492–93.

150. Eddy War Log, 22 December 1944, Fort Benning, Georgia, National Infantry Museum.

151. Ibid., 23 December 1944.

152. Details on XII Corps attack plan for 24 December from Cole, *Ardennes*, 493–94.

153. Eddy War Log, 23 December 1944, Fort Benning, Georgia, National Infantry Museum.

154. On 29 December, Eddy noted in his diary that "Gen. McNair's statement that we would need 130 divisions is certainly being borne out." On 30 December, General McBride expressed his concern that "some very good platoon leaders and company commanders were breaking under combat" and suggested sending them back to the United States to teach in the school system. Eddy realized this was impractical but told McBride to send as many as possible to Paris and Luxembourg City for rest and recuperation. Eddy War Log, 29 and 30 December 1944, Fort Benning, Georgia, National Infantry Museum.

155. See, among others, Eddy War Log entries of 28 and 30 December 1944, Fort Benning, Georgia, National Infantry Museum.

156. Hugh Cole also noted this conservative streak in Eddy and perhaps Patton's grudging acceptance thereof. Commenting on Eddy's instructions to Irwin on the morning of 24 December to call off the attack if it became too costly, he noted wryly, "Caution, it may be said, had become less opprobrious in the Third Army since 16 December." Cole, *Ardennes*, 495.

157. Background on 5th ID from Stanton, *World War II Order of Battle*, 83–84.

158. Except as otherwise noted, background on Irwin from Ancell, *Biographical Dictionary of World War II Generals*, 163–64.

159. Date of Irwin's assumption of command from *The Fifth Infantry Division in the ETO* (1945; reprint, Nashville: Battery Press, 1997), n.p. Ancell, *Biographical Dictionary of World War II Generals*, 164, erroneously lists it as 1944.

160. Unless otherwise noted, the attack of the 5th ID on 24 December is drawn from Cole, *Ardennes*, 497–99.

161. There is an apparent contradiction in Cole's account. In his reference to the 1st Battalion, 10th Infantry's attack, he implies that it had been previously rebuffed on the same ground. But his account of the fighting on the 22nd and 23rd suggests

that the 2nd Battalion was on the east side on the first two days, an interpretation supported by the division history. See Cole, *Ardennes*, 492–93, 497; and *The Fifth Infantry Division in the ETO*, n.p.

162. Background on 10th AD from Lester M. Nichols, *Impact: The Battle Story of the 10th Armored Division* (New York: Bradbury, Sayles, O'Neill, 1954), 7–55.

163. Background on Morris from Ancell, *Biographical Dictionary of World War II Generals*, 233–34; and Nichols, *Impact*, 17–18, 56–57.

164. Cole, *Ardennes*, 501.

165. Account of the 10th AD attack on 24 December and its effect on the 276th VGD is based on Cole, *Ardennes*, 501.

166. Eddy War Log, 24 December 1944, Fort Benning, Georgia, National Infantry Museum.

167. Except as otherwise noted, attack of the 5th ID on 25 December from Cole, *Ardennes*, 501–3.

168. 2nd Infantry's surrounding of Waldbillig from XII Corps G-3 report, 241200–251200 December 1944, XII Corps G-3 files, RG 407, Box 4364, NAII.

169. Eddy War Log, 25 December 1944, Fort Benning, Georgia, National Infantry Museum.

170. Details of the 10th Infantry's attack on 26 December from Cole, *Ardennes*, 503–4.

171. Eddy War Log, 25 December 1944, Fort Benning, Georgia, National Infantry Museum.

172. Cole, *Ardennes*, 504.

173. XII Corps G-3 Journal, 281457 December 1944, XII Corps G-3 files, RG 407, Box 4366, NAII.

174. This feeling is powerfully expressed in *The Fifth Infantry Division in the ETO*, n.p.

175. Cole, *Ardennes*, 506–7.

176. Eddy War Log, 26 December 1944, Fort Benning, Georgia, National Infantry Museum; and Cole, *Ardennes*, 508.

177. Eddy War Log, 27 December 1944, Fort Benning, Georgia, National Infantry Museum.

178. Eisenhower to Marshall, 29 December 1944, Chandler et al., *Eisenhower Papers*, 2385. Barton took up duties as the army's head of infantry training in March 1945. Ancell, *Biographical Dictionary of World War II Generals*, 17.

179. Ancell, *Biographical Dictionary of World War II Generals*, 23.

180. Eddy War Log, 27 December 1944, Fort Benning, Georgia, National Infantry Museum.

181. XII Corps Operational Directive 61, 30 December 1944, XII Corps G-3 files, RG 407, Box 4263, NAII.

182. What follows is based on XII Corps Attack Plan "A," 1 January 1945, XII Corps G-3 files, RG 407, Box 4266, NAII.

183. XII Corps AAR for 1–31 January 1945, 8 February 1945, 8, RG 407, Box 4264, NAII.

184. The XII Corps AAR does not have a day-by-day breakout of battle casualties, but the totals for the month of December for the two divisions making the attack from 22–26 December were 5th ID: 78 KIA, 679 WIA, and 66 MIA during its eleven days of attachment to the corps; and 10th AD: 13 KIA, 50 WIA, and 20 MIA during

its five days of attachment to the corps. XII Corps AAR, 1–31 December 1944, 5 January 1945, 39, RG 407, Box 4263, NAII. The 5th ID's casualties were relatively light for infantry divisions in offensive operations in the Bulge, and the 10th AD's were extremely light for such operations.

12. XVIII (Airborne), VII, and V Corps Fight for Initiative in the North

1. Montgomery to Brooke, 23 December 1944, cited in Hamilton, *Monty: 1944–1976*, 232.

2. Citation from Montgomery to Brooke, 22 December 1944, from ibid., 229; for a detailed recapitulation and spirited justification of Montgomery's approach toward transitioning from the defensive to the offensive in the Bulge, see ibid., 230–72.

3. Eisenhower, *Crusade in Europe*, 360.

4. For the disparaging of Montgomery's lack of offensive inclinations, particularly in the Bulge, see, among others, Bradley, *Soldier's Story*, 482; Bradley and Blair, *General's Life*, 374, 376; Blumenson, *Patton Papers: 1940–1945*, 608, 620, and 628; Price, *Middleton*, 391; and Dupuy, Bongard, and Anderson, *Hitler's Last Gamble*, 365.

5. This analysis is drawn from Cole, *Ardennes*, 578–79.

6. Eisenhower, apparently drawing mostly on Clarke's perspective, places great emphasis on Ridgway's reluctance to withdraw from St. Vith, in *Bitter Woods*, 299–301. Clarke's almost hagiographic biographers do likewise. See William Donohue Ellis and Thomas J. Cunningham, Jr., *Clarke of St. Vith: The Sergeants' General* (Cleveland: Dillon/Liederbach, 1974), 127–29. But even as objective an observer as Cole paints Ridgway as being "sanguine" about the ability of the St. Vith defenders to hold out east of the Salm. Cole, *Ardennes*, 413. Ridgway's 212350 December discussion with Kean indicates otherwise.

7. In an impassioned pre-Christmas message to the soldiers of XVIII (Airborne) Corps, released coincidentally with the beginning of the Ardennes offensive on 16 December 1944, Ridgway referred to the Wehrmacht as "the beast we must slay" and, alluding to a quotation from Thomas Jefferson, predicted that the flames of liberty the Germans "seek to extinguish will consume them and their works." Ridgway, *Soldier*, 124.

8. Dupuy, *St. Vith Lion in the Way*, 173.

9. Ibid.

10. It was not, however, as erroneously characterized by Chester Wilmot and later by Gavin, a relief of Hasbrouck. Wilmot's charge is found in Chester Wilmot, *The Struggle for Europe* (New York: Harper and Brothers, 1952), 596; Gavin's is in *On to Berlin*, 232. When the latter was published, Gavin sent a copy to Ridgway with a letter correctly anticipating that his old boss would not be happy about his criticism. Gavin to Ridgway, 1 September 1978, Ridgway papers, MHI. This set off a long series of correspondences involving Ridgway, Gavin, and Hasbrouck, which is thoroughly summarized in Blair, *Ridgway's Paratroopers*, 635n. The gist of Ridgway's thoroughly documented refutation was that Gavin was just as mistaken as Wilmot had been. Ridgway's intention at the time was merely to put both divisions in the salient under a single commander, not to relieve Hasbrouck. Hasbrouck's grateful response correctly characterized the allegation of his having been relieved as "nonsense." Hasbrouck to Ridgway, 18 October 1978, Ridgway papers, MHI.

11. There is a photograph in Eisenhower, *Bitter Woods*, n.p., of what is purported to be a map diagram of the "fortified goose egg" proposed by XVIII (Airborne) Corps. However, close inspection reveals that this diagram contains the three routes that Hasbrouck developed for the withdrawal after Ridgway's approval thereof. Thus, while it does represent the last positions held by the units in the salient, it does not necessarily depict the positions outlined in Ridgway's proposal. I was unable to locate a graphic depiction of the proposal in the XVIII (Airborne) Corps files.

12. Much of this is drawn from Clarke's critique of the "fortified goose egg" proposal, which is reprised in Cole, *Ardennes*, 407; and Eisenhower, *Bitter Woods*, 299.

13. Eisenhower, *Bitter Woods*, 299.

14. Ibid. See also Ellis and Cunningham, *Clarke of St. Vith*, 127–29.

15. Unless otherwise noted, the description of the battle east of the Salm on 22 December is based on Cole, *Ardennes*, 409–10.

16. Toland, *Battle*, 215.

17. Fontenot, "Lucky Seventh," 84.

18. Hasbrouck to Ridgway, 22 December 1944, XVIII (Airborne) Corps headquarters diary, Ridgway papers, MHI.

19. Ridgway by radio to CG, 106th ID, 221225 December 1944, XVIII (Airborne) Corps headquarters diary, Ridgway papers, MHI.

20. Ridgway memo of phone conversation with Kean, 221400 December 1944, XVIII (Airborne) Corps headquarters diary, Ridgway papers, MHI.

21. Montgomery's tribute from Cole, *Ardennes*, 413. That the decision was his, rather than Hodges's, is indicated in his 22 December nightly cable to Brooke, which stated, "I was at HQ First US Army at the time and I gave orders at once that the whole party [in the St. Vith salient] was to be withdrawn at once into reserve in the BRA area 5793 [a map reference] and this is being done." Hamilton, *Monty: 1944–1976*, 227.

22. Transcript of Ridgway's phone conversation with Kean, 222110 December 1944, XVIII (Airborne) Corps headquarters diary, Ridgway papers, MHI; Ridgway's characterization of Hoge from Ridgway, *Soldier*, 119.

23. The account of the Ridgway-Hoge meeting, including the quoted dialogue, is drawn from Ridgway, *Soldier*, 119–20.

24. Details of Jones's relief are found in Ridgway's memorandum thereof, 221850 December 1944, XVIII (Airborne) Corps headquarters diary, Ridgway papers, MHI. See also Ridgway, *Soldier*, 120. The suggestion that Hoge may have said something about Jones is speculation on my part. Ridgway, by now, probably had enough of his own assessment of Jones to make the call unaided. See Ridgway, *Soldier*, 120. Nevertheless Hoge's low opinion of Jones's leadership, Ridgway's high opinion of Hoge's judgment, and the timing of the relief almost immediately after the Ridgway-Hoge meeting suggest that Hoge might have given Ridgway cause to scrutinize Jones more closely than he would have otherwise. In *On to Berlin*, 232–33, Gavin criticized this relief as well. Here, he was factually accurate: Ridgway did indeed relieve Jones. But Gavin was also erroneous in his judgment. If any criticism can be legitimately leveled against Ridgway, it was for waiting too long to relieve Jones, who had virtually abdicated his command on 17 December when he turned the battle for St. Vith over to Clarke.

25. This sad drama had an almost Shakespearian ending. Before the night was out, Major General Alan Jones, erstwhile commander of the 106th ID, the Golden

Lions, collapsed on the floor of his office from a heart attack and was evacuated through medical channels. Dupuy, *St. Vith Lion in the Way*, 174. See also Blair, *Ridgway's Paratroopers*, 460–61.

26. Details of Hasbrouck's withdrawal plan from Fontenot, "Lucky Seventh," 90.

27. Cole, *Ardennes*, 410–11.

28. The following description of the withdrawal from the St. Vith salient is based on ibid., 415–21; for additional detail, see Fontenot, "Lucky Seventh," 91–97.

29. Gavin's redispositions on 22 December from Gavin, "The Story of the 82nd Airborne Division in the Battle of the Belgian Bulge in the Siegfried Line and on the Roer River," Section II, 5–6, MHI; and Cole, *Ardennes*, 390. Gavin's read of the constantly shifting enemy situation over the next four critical days demonstrated remarkable prescience and good intelligence support.

30. This paragraph is based on MacDonald, *Time for Trumpets,* 544–45; and Cole, *Ardennes*, 390–91.

31. Cole says that forty-four of Captain Woodruff's men returned to friendly lines; MacDonald claims that the number was forty-five.

32. MacDonald, *Time for Trumpets*, 548. The effective time of the transfer was 231630 December 1944. XVIII (Airborne) Corps G-3 Journal, XVIII (Airborne) Corps G-3 files, RG 407, Box 4974, NAII. This entry was logged in at 232045 December, but the headquarters diary indicates the corps was notified at 231520 December. Blair, *Ridgway's Paratroopers*, 666n.

33. The following account of Gavin's reaction to the loss of Baraque de Fraiture is based on Blair, *Ridgway's Paratroopers*, 465.

34. Gavin relates that, after learning of the loss of the crossroads, "I went at once to Corps Headquarters to explain the situation to them and to obtain some assistance in holding the main highway from Fraiture to Manhay. . . . To my amazement, the Corps Chief of Staff showed no reaction whatever. I asked him what I should do, and he told me that it was up to me. I asked him if he could commit more troops, particularly armor, in the area, and he told me that they had none." Gavin, *On to Berlin*, 235. Blair suggests that this confrontation may have been influenced by a perception on Eaton's part that Gavin was becoming something of a publicity hound who was "not sufficiently beholden to Ridgway." Blair, *Ridgway's Paratroopers*, 465. For John Eisenhower's criticism of Ridgway on this score, see *Bitter Woods*, 300.

35. Ridgway's memorandum of phone conversation with Gavin, 241812 December 1944, XVIII (Airborne) Corps headquarters diary, Ridgway papers, MHI.

36. XVIII (Airborne) Corps headquarters diary, 231845 and 231850 December 1944, Ridgway papers, MHI.

37. Ridgway's memorandum of conversation with Gavin, XVIII (Airborne) Corps headquarters diary, 240652 December 1944, Ridgway papers, MHI.

38. Cole, *Ardennes*, 585.

39. For an excellent account of Hasbrouck's efforts to reorganize the 7th AD after the withdrawal of 23 December and the strain on the soldiers of the division caused by having to reenter the fray the very next day, see Fontenot, "Lucky Seventh," 97–99.

40. Memorandum of Ridgway's conversation with First Army G-3, 240610 December 1944, XVIII (Airborne) Corps headquarters diary, Ridgway papers, MHI.

41. Memorandum of CG XVIII (Airborne) Corps phone call to CGs 106th ID, 7th AD, and 30th ID, 240645 December 1944, XVIII (Airborne) Corps headquarters diary, Ridgway papers, MHI.

42. Memorandum of Ridgway phone conversation with Kean, 240900 December 1944, XVIII (Airborne) Corps headquarters diary, Ridgway papers, MHI.

43. Blair, *Ridgway's Paratroopers*, 467–68.

44. Description of the redisposition of the XVIII (Airborne) Corps from Blair, *Ridgway's Paratroopers*, 468; and Cole, *Ardennes*, 587.

45. Memorandum of conversation between Ridgway and Kean, 241300 December 1944, XVIII (Airborne) Corps headquarters diary, Ridgway papers, MHI.

46. Ridgway's 1971 Senior Officers Debriefing Program interview, cited in Blair, *Ridgway's Paratroopers*, 468.

47. Ridgway's memoirs are silent on the subject; but in his Senior Officers Debriefing Program interview, he stated that the soldiers of the 82nd Airborne "hated like hell the order to give it [the high ground they had captured east of Werbomont] up." Blair, *Ridgway's Paratroopers*, 468. Gavin's AAR is even more explicit: "The troops willingly and promptly carried into execution all the withdrawal plans, although they openly and frankly criticized it and failed to understand the necessity for it." Gavin, "The Story of the 82nd Airborne Division in the Battle of the Belgian Bulge in the Siegfried Line and on the Roer River," Section II, 8, MHI. Nevertheless, Gavin later noted that in terms of its tactical sense Montgomery's order to pull back "was very much in order." Gavin, *On to Berlin*, 238.

48. The account of the battle at Manhay on 24/25 December is based on Cole, *Ardennes*, 583–90; and Fontenot, "Lucky Seventh," 99–104.

49. Cole, *Ardennes*, 590. Ridgway displaced the corps CP to Harzé, located some five miles north of Werbomont, at 2000 on Christmas Eve. XVIII (Airborne) Corps G-3 journal entry, 242000 December 1944, XVIII (Airborne) Corps G-3 files, RG 407, Box 4974, NAII. Hodges's aide described the setting as being in "the old and beautiful chateau d'Herze." Sylvan diary, 9 January 1945, 163, CMH. The new venue was certainly a more fitting location for a corps command post than the farmhouse at Werbomont. But with the 2nd SS Panzer Division driving toward Manhay, security may have also been a consideration.

50. Letter from Chief of Staff of XVIII (Airborne) Corps to Commanding General, 7th AD, 251330 December 1944, XVIII (Airborne) Corps War Diary, Ridgway papers, MHI. The original order to retake Manhay was dictated by Ridgway to the 7th AD chief of staff at 0825 on the 25th in the corps CP and confirmed in writing at 0925.

51. Blair, *Ridgway's Paratroopers*, 472.

52. Fontenot, "Lucky Seventh," 104. The following details of 7th AD's attempt to recapture Manhay on 25 December 1944 are drawn from Fontenot, "Lucky Seventh," 104–11. Cole, *Ardennes*, 593, indicates the abatis was put in by the retreating forces of CCA, 7th AD; Clarke believed it had been put in by the 3rd AD.

53. Account of Ridgway's actions near Manhay on 25 December from Ridgway, *Soldier*, 121–22.

54. Recapture of Manhay from Blair, *Ridgway's Paratroopers*, 474; and Cole, *Ardennes*, 598.

55. All details of the Ridgway-Clarke confrontation on 24 December, including the quoted dialogue, are drawn from Ellis and Cunningham, *Clarke of St. Vith*, 136–37.

56. Ridgway, *Soldier*, 118. General Buechler is not mentioned by name in this reference, only by position. Blair identifies him in *Ridgway's Paratroopers*, 495.

57. Ridgway, *Soldier*, 118. Ridgway's impatience with General Buechler was evident in an undated conversation from about 24 December 1944 in which he said, "Now this is the spot where we want a concentration. . . . we want to clean that up and clear all this area out. We don't want any more fiddling around in here. We've got to get rid of it, and so I want to concentrate some big stuff in here. I don't want a little, but really want to pound them with all we've got. It's a vital spot and we've got to get control of it. . . . Is that clear[?]" Notes of conversation between Ridgway and Buechler, XVIII (Airborne) Corps diary, n.d., Ridgway papers, MHI.

58. Ridgway, *Soldier*, 118. Ridgway and Matthewson had a long association. Both were Spanish linguists, and Matthewson had replaced Ridgway as chief of the Latin American section of WPD. Ridgway had earlier tried to get Matthewson assigned to the 82nd Airborne but to no avail. Blair, *Ridgway's Paratroopers*, 495.

59. Ridgway memorandum of 270700 December 1944, Ridgway papers, MHI. A notation appears at the bottom, "Appd by ARMY Comdr in personal phone call at 0800."

60. Unless otherwise noted, the account of the 82nd Airborne's withdrawal on 24/25 December is drawn from Gavin, "The Story of the 82nd Airborne Division in the Battle of the Belgian Bulge in the Siegfried Line and on the Roer River," Section II, 7–8, MHI.

61. Ibid., 8–9, MHI.

62. The account of the 82nd Airborne's defensive stand from 25 to 28 December is based on ibid., 9; and Cole, *Ardennes*, 600–601.

63. Memorandum of Ridgway phone conversation with Kean, 240900 December 1944, XVIII (Airborne) Corps headquarters diary, Ridgway papers, MHI.

64. What follows, including direct quotations, is based on Ridgway's memorandum of the conference, which lasted from 291245 to 291400 December, found in the XVIII (Airborne) Corps headquarters diary, Ridgway papers, MHI.

65. What follows, including direct quotations, is based on ibid., 301030 to 301150 December 1944.

66. Ridgway to Gavin, 012130 January 1945, Ridgway papers, MHI.

67. Cable message, Brereton to Ridgway, 221655 December 1944, in ibid.

68. Blair, *Ridgway's Paratroopers*, 495–96.

69. Triplet's 1984 correspondence with Clay Blair cited in Blair, *Ridgway's Paratroopers*, 471.

70. Ridgway to Brereton, 28 December 1944, Ridgway papers, MHI.

71. Ridgway to McAuliffe, 28 December 1944, in ibid.

72. Ridgway to Taylor, 30 December 1944, in ibid.

73. Ridgway to Clark, 28 December 1944, in ibid.

74. Ridgway to all units and staff sections, XVIII (Airborne) Corps, 2 January 1945, in ibid.

75. This paragraph is based on XVIII (Airborne) Corps Summary of Operations, 18 December 1944–13 February 1945, 1 March 1945, 6, in ibid.

76. This description of Hodges's attack plan, which was probably the best that could be developed within the constraints of Montgomery's guidance, is drawn from Gavin, *On to Berlin*, 249.

77. XVIII (Airborne) Corps G-2 Estimate of the Situation no. 3, 022245 January 1945, RG 407, Box 4793, NAII. The remainder of the paragraph is also based on this document.

78. Gavin's claim to have encountered elements of the 9th SS Panzer Division on 4 January in *On to Berlin*, 249, contradicts this estimate. But the Corps G-2, Colonel Whitfield Jack, is supported by the postwar report of General Kraemer, Chief of Staff, Sixth SS Panzer Army, who stated that by the night of 3/4 January, the 9th SS Panzer Division had been withdrawn to support the Bastogne operation and that the only mobile unit available to the army was 2nd SS Panzer Division. Kraemer, "Sixth Panzer Army Operations in the Ardennes, 1944–45," 54, FMS A-924, RG 319, NAII.

79. Gavin, "The Story of the 82nd Airborne Division in the Battle of the Belgian Bulge in the Siegfried Line and on the Roer River," Section II, 9, MHI. Except as otherwise noted, the remainder of this paragraph is based on the same document, Section III, Part 2, 1–2.

80. Gavin, *On to Berlin*, 250.

81. XVIII (Airborne) Corps Summary of Operations, 18 December 1944–13 February 1945, 1 March 1945, 6, Ridgway papers, MHI.

82. Gavin, *On to Berlin*, 249. The frustration is also palpable in Gavin's AAR. As early as 3 January, the narrative for the attack of the 325th GIR, which was on the right flank and thus directly on the XVIII (Airborne)/VII Corps boundary, notes, "Further advance limited to patrolling pending advance of VII Corps units." Gavin, "The Story of the 82nd Airborne Division in the Battle of the Belgian Bulge in the Siegfried Line and on the Roer River," Section III, Part 2, 1, MHI.

83. Sylvan diary, 4 January 1945, 159, CMH.

84. "There can be no question that the place for the general in battle is where he can see the battle and get the odor of it in his nostrils." Gavin, *On to Berlin*, 252.

85. This paragraph is based on Manteuffel, "Fifth Panzer Army (Ardennes Offensive)," 53–55, FMS B-151a, RG 319, NAII.

86. Manteuffel, "Fifth Panzer Army (Ardennes Offensive)," 54, FMS B-151a, RG 319, NAII.

87. Unless otherwise indicated, this paragraph is based on Collins, *Lightning Joe*, 282–83. Details of Collins's interactions with Hodges on 22–23 December are confirmed by Major Sylvan's diary entries for those dates, 146–48, CMH.

88. Collins, *Lightning Joe*, 284.

89. The 84th ID was, in fact, involved in some heavy fighting. Bolling dispatched two battalions of the 335th Infantry south and west of Marche on two different axes, extending beyond Rochefort to the hamlets of Wellin, Tellin, and Grupont. But the main garrison was that of the 3rd Battalion in Rochefort. On the 23rd, it delivered a stunning rebuke to Bayerlein's Panzer Lehr. Although forced to evacuate the next morning, it gained valuable time for assembly of the 2nd AD and provided Collins with early warning of the drive toward the Meuse. See Cole, *Ardennes*, 435–37; and Draper, *84th Infantry Division*, 92–95.

90. Harmon was picked by Patton to command the 1st AD in North Africa when Bradley relieved Major General Orlando Ward. Bradley and Blair, *General's Life*, 149. Subsequent details of Harmon's World War II career from Chandler et al., *Eisenhower Papers*, 2073, 2074n. The 2nd AD was open because its erstwhile

commander, Major General Edward H. Brooks, was elevated to command of VI Corps.

91. Gavin, *On to Berlin*, 248.

92. VII Corps AAR, 1–31 December 1944, 9 January 1945, 78, VII Corps History Files, RG 407, Box 3827, NAII.

93. Sylvan diary, 22 December 1944, 146, CMH.

94. What follows is based on Cole, *Ardennes*, 437–38.

95. Except as otherwise noted, this paragraph is based on Collins, *Lightning Joe*, 285; and Cole, *Ardennes*, 434.

96. E. N. Harmon with Milton MacKaye and William Ross MacKaye, *Combat Commander: Autobiography of a Soldier* (Englewood Cliffs, N.J.: Prentice-Hall, 1970), 234–35.

97. This paragraph is based on Collins, *Lightning Joe*, 286.

98. Montgomery's reasoning for wanting Collins to give ground rather than to attack is reconstructed in Hamilton, *Monty: 1944–1976*, 234. That Montgomery's inclinations for VII Corps on 24 December were defensive is also reflected in Hodges's aide's contemporaneous note: "The VII Corps, instead of proceeding to the offensive as planned, has now to assume a completely defensive attitude." Sylvan diary, 24 December 1944, 149, CMH.

99. Harmon, *Combat Commander*, 235.

100. What follows is based on an interview with General Palmer, by Lieutenant Colonel H. L. Hunter, 12 February 1972, 73–74, MHI.

101. Enclosure to VII Corps AAR, 1–31 December 1944, 9 January 1945, VII Corps History Files, RG 407, Box 3827, NAII. Palmer's note is also reproduced with minor textual differences in Eisenhower, *Bitter Woods*, 369.

102. Palmer interview, 74, MHI.

103. Palmer, of course, still did not have things exactly right: The "H" to which Kean referred was Hotton, not Huy. But he now accurately comprehended the general direction of the desired move, and this was sufficient to galvanize him into sending a corrective missive to Collins.

104. Palmer interview, 75, MHI.

105. Enclosure to VII Corps AAR, 1–31 December 1944, 9 January 1945, VII Corps History Files, RG 407, Box 3827, NAII.

106. What follows is based on Collins, *Lightning Joe*, 287–89.

107. Enclosure to VII Corps AAR, 1–31 December 1944, 9 January 1945, VII Corps History Files, RG 407, Box 3827, NAII. There is a typed note at the bottom that reads as follows: "The above instructions were typed personally by Colonel R. F. Akers, Jr. at Headquarters VII Corps, Mean [*sic*], Belgium, the evening of 24 December 1944. Colonel Akers had been sent by CG, First Army to deliver these instructions orally to CG, VII Corps. JLC." The letter itself is also reproduced in Collins, *Lightning Joe*, 290.

108. This paragraph is based on Collins, *Lightning Joe*, 289–90. Although Collins's account of the First Battle of the Marne is essentially correct, he misidentifies von Kluck as von Kluge.

109. Collins later recounted the parallels between his situation and von Kluck's at some length. See General J. Lawton Collins, Senior Officers Oral History Program interview of 11 January 1972, conducted by Lieutenant Colonel Charles C. Sperow, 132–36, MHI.

110. In the words of the VII Corps AAR's narrative for 25 December, "The Corps Commander chose to accomplish his mission by resorting to active defense tactics and launched a series of limited objective attacks to prevent a dangerous concentration of enemy strength at any single point." VII Corps AAR, 1–31 December 1944, 9 January 1945, 85, VII Corps History Files, RG 407, Box 3827, NAII.

111. Baldwin, *Battles Lost and Won*, 348.

112. Account of the action at Verdenne on 24 December is based on Draper, *84th Infantry Division*, 95–97; and Cole, *Ardennes*, 441–42.

113. Details of the action at Rochefort on 24 December can be found in Draper, *84th Infantry Division*, 94; and Cole, *Ardennes*, 438–40. Without taking anything at all away from the courage of the men of the 333rd Infantry, who held out at Rochefort for two full days against greatly superior forces, the action was not on the same scale as Bastogne and thus should not be compared in terms of significance.

114. Cole, *Ardennes*, 441.

115. Harmon, *Combat Commander*, 235.

116. Unless otherwise noted, this paragraph is based on Cole, *Ardennes*, 567–70. For additional, small-unit detail, see Donald E. Houston, *Hell on Wheels: The Second Armored Division* (San Rafael, Calif.: Presidio Press, 1977), 342–47.

117. Sylvan diary, 25 December 1944, 151, CMH.

118. Houston, *Hell on Wheels*, 347.

119. This paragraph is based on Cole, *Ardennes*, 570–73.

120. This paragraph is drawn from ibid., 574.

121. Even before this dénouement, Lüttwitz's spirits were low. As he noted after the war, "Christmas Eve was rather melancholy for the Corps. Its members knew that the decisive moment for the success or failure of the offensive had come. . . . For the Commanding General, who had been Commander of the 2d Pz Division, the situation took the same turn as at AVRANCHES. As at that time the Division was isolated and far in advance before the front and would probably be destroyed unless our air force screened the spearhead. But nobody reckoned any longer with its support." Lüttwitz, "XXXXVII Panzer Corps in the Ardennes," 14, FMS A-939, RG 319, NAII.

122. Details of this attack, a microcosm of the 84th ID's defense of the Marche-Hotton road, are related in Harold P. Leinbaugh and John D. Campbell, *The Men of Company K: The Autobiography of a World War II Rifle Company* (New York: William Morrow, 1985), 134–41, supplemented by Draper, *84th Infantry Division*, 97–100. See also Cole, *Ardennes*, 574–76; but the official history misidentifies Leinbaugh's unit as Company K, 334th Infantry.

123. Bradley and Blair, *General's Life*, 371.

124. The phrase "aggressive spirit" is Montgomery's biographer's, not his own; but Monty had on numerous occasions expressed his admiration for this trait of Collins. Indeed, this was why he had specifically instructed Hodges to pull VII Corps out of the line to blunt the penetration. Nevertheless, shortly before midnight on Christmas Eve, he telegraphed Brooke expressing mild disappointment: "I had hoped that 7 Corps would be able to remain concentrated and available for [subsequent] offensive action but it is now getting involved with 5 Panzer Army." Montgomery to Brooke, 242225 December 1944, cited in Hamilton, *Monty: 1944–1976*, 235.

125. Collins's account implies that having Palmer stay at the corps headquarters and act as his deputy was fairly habitual. Collins, *Lightning Joe*, 286. Palmer

indicates that this role was reserved for particular occasions. Palmer interview, 72–73, MHI.

126. Clausewitz, *On War*, 107.

127. With the battalion already loaned to the 3rd AD the previous day, this left Prickett with only two infantry battalions under his command.

128. Details of Prickett's prior service from Ancell, *Biographical Dictionary of World War II Generals*, 263–64.

129. Stanton, *World War II Order of Battle*, 141.

130. Collins, *Lightning Joe*, 286.

131. See Cole, *Ardennes*, Map VIII.

132. Defense of Amonines on 24 December from *Spearhead in the West, 1941–1945: The Third Armored Division* (1945; reprint, Nashville: Battery Press, 1980), 112.

133. Fighting in and around Grandménil on 25 December from Cole, *Ardennes*, 591–92.

134. Fighting around Sadzot on 28–29 December from Cole, *Ardennes*, 601–3. See also *Spearhead in the West*, 112–14.

135. This paragraph, including all direct quotations, is based on Collins's letter to Hodges, Subject: Plans for Offensive Operations, 27 December 1944, VII Corps G-3 files, RG 407, Box 3838, NAII.

136. Sylvan diary, 27 December 1944, 154, CMH.

137. Ibid., 28 December 1944.

138. This and the two following direct quotations are cited from Collins, *Lightning Joe*, 293.

139. This paragraph, including all direct quotations, is based on Collins, memorandum to Hodges, 30 December 1944, Collins papers, Box 3, DDEL.

140. On Dickson's estimate of German capabilities in late December 1944, see Hogan, *Command Post*, 225.

141. This and the following two sentences from Hogan, *Command Post*, 228.

142. Hamilton, *Monty: 1944–1976*, 279.

143. This paragraph is based on the historical narrative section, VII Corps AAR for 1–31 January 1945, 7–8, 10, VII Corps history files, RG 407, Box 3826, NAII. For Montgomery's expectations of the difficult fighting that lay ahead, see Hamilton, *Monty: 1944–1976*, 288–90.

144. Description of enemy action on the V Corps front on 22 December is drawn from *V Corps Operations in the ETO, 6 January 1942–9 May 1945* (n.p., n.d.), 356; and "Intelligence Operations of the V U.S. Corps in Europe," 78, MHI. A copy of the former, somewhat obscure, publication can be found in the V Corps historical files, RG 407, Box 3408, NAII.

145. Hamilton, *Monty: 1944–1976*, 232–33.

146. Sylvan diary, 24 December 1944, 150, CMH.

147. Description of the German attacks against V Corps on 28 December is derived from Cole, *Ardennes*, 604.

148. What follows, including the direct quotation, is from V Corps LOI of 28 December 1944, reproduced in *V Corps Operations in the ETO*, 358.

149. V Corps LOI of 1 January 1945, reproduced in ibid., 360.

150. Ridgway felt, with good reason, that the 82nd's performance was "equally meritorious" to that of the 101st at Bastogne but could not prevail upon Eisenhower

to recommend the entire division for a Presidential Unit Citation, as he did for the Screaming Eagles. Blair, *Ridgway's Paratroopers*, 481.

13. Closing the Bulge

1. From complete text of Montgomery's notes used for his 7 January 1945 press conference, reproduced in Montgomery, *Memoirs*, 279.

2. Bradley, *Soldier's Story*, 487, contains the substance of his comment to Eisenhower; the date is drawn from Hansen diary, 8 January 1945, Hansen papers, MHI.

3. Hugh Cole's official history of the Ardennes ignored it entirely, leaving coverage to MacDonald's sequel, which devoted one chapter of thirty-three pages to the campaign's end. MacDonald, *Last Offensive*, 22–54. MacDonald's commercially published *Time for Trumpets* gave a skimpy sixteen pages to the subject, while Eisenhower's *Bitter Woods* provided only ten more. MacDonald, *Time for Trumpets*, 604–19; Eisenhower, *Bitter Woods*, 405–30. Coverage by John Toland in *Battle* and Dupuy, Bongard, and Anderson in *Hitler's Last Gamble* is a more credible forty-five and forty-seven pages, respectively; but none of these works comprehensively addresses the final operations of all six corps. Toland, *Battle*, 333–77; Dupuy, Bongard, and Anderson, *Hitler's Last Gamble*, 312–58.

4. Montgomery, *Memoirs*, 278. For additional details on the prelude to the press conference, see Hamilton, *Monty: 1944–1976*, 294–99.

5. Montgomery, *Memoirs*, 280. The citations in the remainder of the paragraph are drawn from ibid., 280–81.

6. British units committed on 7 January 1945 from MacDonald, *Time for Trumpets*, 278.

7. De Guingand, who was not present, noted Montgomery's demeanor at the conference: "From all accounts he was rather 'naughty,' or human enough to adopt the 'what a good boy am I' attitude." De Guingand, *Operation Victory*, 434.

8. Hansen diary, 5 January 1945, Hansen papers, MHI.

9. Ibid.

10. Bradley, *Soldier's Story*, 484.

11. Bradley's critique of the SHAEF announcement is found in *Soldier's Story*, 486–87.

12. This paragraph, including the direct quotation, is drawn from the Hansen diary, 6 January 1945, Hansen papers, MHI.

13. "Brad assured me today that Ike would resist this move [appointment of Montgomery as a land deputy]—that Marshall would resist it with everything in his control. The only person who might force the issue would be the president who would respond, in that case, to heat from the PM."

14. Bradley, *Soldier's Story*, 485; and Ralph Ingersoll, *Top Secret* (New York: Harcourt, Brace, 1946), 279. There is an interesting twist on this story. Chester Wilmot believed that the 12th AG headquarters actually heard a twisted version of Montgomery's remarks, reported by a German disinformation broadcast from Arnhem. Wilmot, *Struggle for Europe*, 611n. However, Forrest Pogue's research indicates that this incident occurred several days later. Pogue, *Supreme Command*, 388. Ingersoll's account clearly states that Bradley and his staff reacted to a transcript received on 8 January, not the bogus German broadcast.

15. What follows is based on Bradley, *Soldier's Story*, 485–87; Bradley and Blair, *General's Life*, 382–84; and Hansen diary, 8–9 December 1945, Hansen papers, MHI.

16. D'Este, *Eisenhower*, 668. Bradley's promotion was confirmed by the Senate Military Affairs Committee at the end of March. Bradley, *Soldier's Story*, 528.

17. Robert Rhoades James, ed., *Winston S. Churchill: His Complete Speeches* (New York: Chelsea House, 1974), 7:7095–96.

18. For an insightful analysis of the political and strategic tensions caused by this offensive, see Franklin Louis Gurley, "Policy versus Strategy: The Defense of Strasbourg in Winter 1944–1945," *Journal of Military History* 58 (July 1994): 481–514.

19. For a concise summary of the Allied manpower difficulties at the time, see Pogue, *Supreme Command*, 391–93. For details of the German offensives in southern France throughout January 1945 and the eventual reduction of the Colmar Pocket, see Clarke and Smith, *Riviera to the Rhine*, 513–60.

20. What follows is based on Hamilton, *Monty: 1944–1976*, 319–26.

21. Montgomery's cable to Brooke of 14 January 1945, cited from ibid., 325.

22. What follows is based on Bradley and Blair, *General's Life*, 386–87.

23. Montgomery to Eisenhower, 19 January 1945, cited in Hamilton, *Monty: 1944–1976*, 335.

24. Unless otherwise indicated, this paragraph is based on Schramm, "The Course of Events of the German Offensive in the Ardennes," 18–20, FMS 858, RG 319, NAII.

25. Schramm gives the date for the beginning of the Soviet offensive as 13 January 1945. It actually started on 12 January when Marshal I. S. Konev's 1st Ukrainian Front penetrated to a depth of some twenty kilometers in the opening assault of the Vistula-Oder Operation. Glantz and House, *When Titans Clashed*, 242.

26. MacDonald, *Last Offensive*, 43.

27. Magna E. Bauer, "The German Withdrawal from the Ardennes (15 January–31 January 1945)" (Washington, D.C.: OCMH, May 1955), 1, RG 549, NAII. For additional details, see Magna E. Bauer, "Sixth Panzer Army Transfer from the West to the East in 1945" (Washington, D.C.: OCMH, 1951), RG 549, NAII.

28. Bauer, "German Withdrawal from the Ardennes," 64, RG 549, NAII.

29. USSTAF A-2, "Ardennes," Statistical Annex, USAFHRA File 519.601C(S). All material in this file has been declassified.

30. Ibid.

31. What follows is based on MacDonald, *Last Offensive*, 51; and USSTAF, "Battlefield Studies World War II: Air Force Participation in the Battle of the Ardennes, 16 December 1944–16 January 1945," n.d., USAFHRA File no. 519.042.

32. The undocumented USSTAF study referred to above listed claims for the air as destruction or damage of thirty-six armored vehicles, fifty-nine horse-drawn vehicles, and over seventeen hundred motor vehicles. This level of claims led the army official historian to comment, "For various reasons, claims of enemy losses from air action were almost always high." MacDonald, *Last Offensive*, 51n. The statement by the U.S. Air Force official historian that the damage "far surpassed destruction in the Falaise Gap of August 1944" (Craven and Cate, *Army Air Forces* 3:705) is manifestly inaccurate even if one accepts the figures of the USSTAF study referenced above. In this sense, it is unfortunate that the very detailed and well-documented

USSTAF A-2 study of March 1945 does not extend beyond 16 January 1945. Bauer's report on the withdrawal, which is based on a close reading of the records of the German units involved, states only that the Germans "were easy targets for the Allied air forces which inflicted heavy losses in personnel and materiel and caused numerous vehicles to burn out," thus confirming the general story without providing any statistical detail. Bauer, "German Withdrawal from the Ardennes," 59, RG 549, NAII.

33. MacDonald, *Last Offensive*, 53.

14. *VII, XVIII (Airborne), and V Corps Close the Bulge from the North*

1. Leinbaugh and Campbell, *The Men of Company K*, 181.

2. Draper, *84th Infantry Division*, 113.

3. H. R. Knickerbocker et al., *Danger Forward: The Story of the First Division in World War II* (Washington, D.C.: Society of the First Division, 1947), 350. See also the picture captioned "Blasting foxholes in the frozen ground at Elsenborn," in *Combat History of the Second Infantry Division in World War II* (1946; reprint, Nashville: Battery Press, 1979), 109.

4. This and what follows is based on MacDonald, *Last Offensive*, Map III.

5. The remainder of this paragraph is based on entries for 5–25 January 1945 taken from "The War Diary of VII Corps, 2 June 1944–1 April 1945," MHI. Attachment of infantry regiments to each armored division is drawn from 5 January entry in VII Corps AAR for 1–31 January 1945, 15, VII Corps history files, RG 407, Box 3826, NAII.

6. This and the remainder of the paragraph are based on VII Corps G-2 periodic report for 5 January, Incl. 7 to VII Corps AAR, 1–31 January 1945, VII Corps history files, RG 407, Box 3828, NAII.

7. This paragraph is based on the 5 January entry in VII Corps AAR for 1–31 January 1945, 16–18, VII Corps history files, RG 407, Box 3826, NAII.

8. This paragraph is based on VII Corps G-2 periodic reports for 6–8 January, Incl. 7 to VII Corps AAR, 1–31 January 1945, VII Corps history files, RG 407, Box 3828, NAII; and the 6–8 January entries in the VII Corps AAR for 1–31 January 1945, 19–31, VII Corps history files, RG 407, Box 3826, NAII.

9. Collins, *Lightning Joe*, 294.

10. This and the following sentence are based on VII Corps Operations Memorandum 147, 8 January 1945, Orlando C. Troxel papers, MHI.

11. Draper, *84th Infantry Division*, 114. The 2nd AD's attack on Samrée is included in Draper's history based on the attachment of the 335th IR to Harmon's division.

12. Unless otherwise indicated, the story of the capture of Samrée is based on Houston, *Hell on Wheels*, 365–69.

13. VII Corps G-2 periodic report for 9 January, Incl. 7 to VII Corps AAR for 1–31 January 1945, VII Corps history files, RG 407, Box 3828, NAII.

14. This and the following sentence are drawn from Houston, *Hell on Wheels*, 368–69.

15. For details of the 84th ID's approach to the problem of short-term convalescence, which employed members of the division band who were given a crash course in medical assistance, see Draper, *84th Infantry Division*, 112.

16. Houston relates that a staff officer at SHAEF headquarters ordered Harmon to close the center but that he conveniently ignored the directive until after the Bulge had run its course. Houston, *Hell on Wheels*, 369.

17. VII Corps Operations Memorandum 149, 10 January 1945, Troxel papers, MHI.

18. Background on 83rd ID from Stanton, *World War II Order of Battle*, 154–55.

19. Background on Macon from Ancell, *Biographical Dictionary of World War II Generals*, 198–99.

20. This characterization was made at a command conference that Collins attended at Ridgway's headquarters on 9 January. The issue was whether or not Collins would require help from the 75th ID to secure Bovigny, some five miles east-southeast of Bihain. Hodges thought he might; but Collins felt that the approach to Bovigny from the north around Salmchâteau, where the 75th ID was to be positioned after it relieved the 82nd Airborne, would be too difficult. The memorandum of the conversation incorrectly identifies the 83rd ID as the 84th ID, which is clearly in error based on the latter's position on the VII Corps west flank. Summary of conference at XVIII (Airborne) Corps headquarters, 091400 January 1945, XVIII (Airborne) Corps headquarters diary, Ridgway papers, MHI.

21. The story of the 83rd ID's fight to capture Bihain is based on the entries for 9 and 10 January in the VII Corps AAR for 1–31 January 1945, 31–38, VII Corps history files, RG 407, Box 3826, NAII.

22. Unless otherwise indicated, the paragraph is based on VII Corps G-2 periodic reports for 11–13 January, Incl. 7 to VII Corps AAR, 1–31 January 1945, VII Corps history files, RG 407, Box 3828, NAII; and the 11–13 January entries in the VII Corps AAR for 1–31 January 1945, 39–53, VII Corps history files, RG 407, Box 3826, NAII.

23. Houston, *Hell on Wheels*, 370. By this time in the battle, the 116th Panzer Division, which had previously been deployed primarily in the British XXX Corps zone, was now aligned with the bulk of its strength against VII Corps.

24. VII Corps G-2 periodic report, 13 January, Incl. 7 to VII Corps AAR, 1–31 January 1945, VII Corps history files, RG 407, Box 3828, NAII.

25. Unless otherwise indicated, this paragraph is based on the 14–15 January entries in the VII Corps AAR for 1–31 January 1945, 54–63, VII Corps history files, RG 407, Box 3826, NAII.

26. VII Corps Operations Memorandum 151, 15 January 1945, Troxel papers, MHI.

27. Unless otherwise indicated, this paragraph is based on the 16 January entry in the VII Corps AAR for 1–31 January 1945, 64–67, VII Corps history files, RG 407, Box 3826, NAII.

28. The story of the linkup between VII Corps and VIII Corps at Houffalize is based primarily on Houston, *Hell on Wheels*, 372–73; the time of 0905 is taken from the VII Corps G-2 periodic report for 16 January, Incl. 7 to VII Corps AAR, 1–31 January 1945, VII Corps history files, RG 407, Box 3828, NAII.

29. This paragraph is based on the 17–24 January entries in the VII Corps AAR for 1–31 January 1945, 68–87, VII Corps history files, RG 407, Box 3826, NAII.

30. This citation is from Hodges's recounting of Collins's statement in a conversation with Ridgway on 17 January. Summary of conversation 171300 to 171500 January 1945, XVIII (Airborne) Corps headquarters diary, Ridgway papers, MHI.

31. 25 January entry in the VII Corps AAR for 1–31 January 1945, 87, VII Corps history files, RG 407, Box 3826, NAII.

32. What follows on the German XIII Corps is based predominantly on General of the Infantry Hans G. Felber, "Report on the Ardennes Campaign, Part II, 1–25 January 1945," 1–3, FMS B-039, RG 319, NAII; supplemented by XVIII (Airborne) Corps G-2 Periodic Report no. 28, 15 December 1945, Galbraith papers, MHI. The latter also indicated there were also elements of the 3rd Parachute Division facing XVIII (Airborne) Corps.

33. Details of the 82nd Airborne Division's advance to the Salm are based on Gavin, "The Story of the 82nd Airborne Division in the Battle of the Belgian Bulge in the Siegfried Line and on the Roer River," Section III, Part 2, 2–3, MHI.

34. Dupuy, Bongard, and Anderson, *Hitler's Last Gamble*, 322.

35. *The 75th Infantry Division in Combat: The Battle in the Ardennes, 23 Dec 1944–27 Jan 1945; The Colmar Pocket Battle, 30 Jan 1945–9 Feb 1945; The Battle for the Ruhr, 31 Mar 1945–15 Apr 1945* (n.p., n.d.), 9.

36. XVIII (Airborne) Corps headquarters diary, 051000 January 1945, Ridgway papers, MHI.

37. XVIII (Airborne) Corps Sitrep as of 062400 January 1945, XVIII (Airborne) Corps G-3 files, RG 407, Box 4976, NAII.

38. XVIII (Airborne) Corps Sitreps as of 071200 and 081200 January 1945, XVIII (Airborne) Corps G-3 files, RG 407, Box 4976, NAII.

39. XVIII (Airborne) Corps Sitrep as of 092400 January 1945, XVIII (Airborne) Corps G-3 files, RG 407, Box 4976, NAII.

40. XVIII (Airborne) Corps Sitrep as of 112400 January 1945, XVIII (Airborne) Corps G-3 files, RG 407, Box 4976, NAII.

41. What follows, including the direct quotation, is drawn from Ridgway's memorandum of a command conference with Montgomery and Collins, 061330–061430 January 1945, XVIII (Airborne) Corps headquarters diary, Ridgway papers, MHI.

42. Ridgway summary of conversation with Hodges, 081210 January 1945, XVIII (Airborne) Corps headquarters diary, Ridgway papers, MHI.

43. This paragraph, including all direct quotations, is drawn from the memorandum of the 091400 command conference between Ridgway and Hodges, with appropriate staff officers also present, XVIII (Airborne) Corps headquarters diary, Ridgway papers, MHI.

44. Hodges's uneasiness may have been partially based on the fact that as late as 7 January, Dickson still believed that "we may expect or at least should be on the lookout for a counterattack by a Corps consisting of at least two or three divisions." Sylvan diary, 7 January 1945, 161, CMH.

45. Ridgway's memorandum of conversation with Kean, 101205 January 1945, XVIII (Airborne) Corps headquarters diary, Ridgway papers, MHI.

46. Report of Division Commanders' Conference Held at Call of Corps Commander at XVIII Corps CP at Time Stated Above [110930 January 1945], XVIII (Airborne) Corps headquarters diary, Ridgway papers, MHI.

47. Depth of attack from Blair, *Ridgway's Paratroopers*, 500; the statement that the attack progressed only to its previous patrol line from Hodges, as recorded in the Sylvan diary, 13 January 1945, 166, CMH.

48. Memorandum of Ridgway's discussion with Kean, 131215 January 1945, XVIII (Airborne) Corps headquarters diary, Ridgway papers, MHI.

49. Memorandum of Ridgway's discussion with Hodges, 131715 January 1945, XVIII (Airborne) Corps headquarters diary, ibid.

50. Memorandum of Ridgway's discussion with Hobbs, 131725 January 1945, XVIII (Airborne) Corps headquarters diary, ibid.

51. What follows is based on Colonel Matthewson's memorandum of the Ridgway-Hobbs session, 13 January 1945, XVIII (Airborne) Corps headquarters diary, ibid.

52. Lockerbie, *Man under Orders*, 122. There may have been more to the 30th ID's stumbling on 13 January than simply the breakdown of a single regiment. Harrison, whose professional opinion of Hobbs's tactical competence was low, was sick as the attack was being planned. He later blamed himself for not rising from his sickbed and participating therein. Lockerbie, *Man under Orders*, 121–22. Hobbs admitted the next day that he should have attacked with three regiments abreast, rather than with two regiments forward and one in reserve. Had he done so, he said, "it would have been a much simpler proposition." Report of Division Commanders' Conference Held at Call of Corps Commander at XVIII Corps CP at Time Stated Above [141800 January 1945], XVIII (Airborne) Corps headquarters diary, Ridgway papers, MHI.

53. Bauserman, *Malmédy Massacre*, 84–85.

54. The results of this effort were dissatisfying on many levels. Generals Dietrich, Kraemer, Priess, and Peiper and seventy men of Kampfgruppe Peiper were tried at Dachau in May 1946 for a number of atrocities committed during the Bulge, including the murders at the Baugnez crossroads. Major evidentiary problems arose, including the inability of all but one of the survivors to identify who opened fire and confessions obtained under considerable duress. Peiper, among several others, was convicted and given the death sentence. After a series of reviews reaching all the way to the U.S. Senate, all death sentences were commuted and most terms of imprisonment significantly reduced. Peiper was released from prison in December 1956 and died in France in July 1976 when his house was destroyed by arson. Reynolds, *Devil's Adjutant*, 252–69. For a fascinating portrait of the military defense attorney in the case, see James J. Weingartner, *A Peculiar Crusade: Willis M. Everett and the Malmedy Massacre* (New York: New York University Press, 2000).

55. Ridgway's memorandum of discussion with Hodges, 141605 January 1945, XVIII (Airborne) Corps headquarters diary, Ridgway papers, MHI.

56. The remainder of this paragraph is based on Report of Division Commanders' Conference Held at Call of Corps Commander at XVIII Corps CP at Time Stated Above [141800 January 1945], XVIII (Airborne) Corps headquarters diary, Ridgway papers, MHI.

57. XVIII (Airborne) Corps, Field Order 2, 112000 January 1945, XVIII (Airborne) Corps G-3 files, RG 407, Box 4974, NAII.

58. What follows, including the direct quotations, is based on Ridgway's letter to Hodges of 18 January 1945, Subject, Leadership, 75th Infantry Division, Ridgway correspondence file, Ridgway papers, MHI. See also Ridgway's treatment of the incident in *A Soldier Reports*, 120–21. The description in the latter account is slightly inaccurate in that Ridgway actually *recommended* Prickett's relief to Hodges, rather than *ordering* the relief, as he had done in the case of Archer Jones. The lack of progress on the part of the 75th ID is reflected in Sylvan diary, 16 January 1945, 168, CMH.

59. Hodges's reservations concerning the 75th ID are reflected in the following notation in his aide's diary: "The 75th Div likewise continued to scrap against the enemy across the [Salm] river but made very slow progress. General Hodges believes that offensively the 75th is through for the time being, tired out and exhausted. It appears the 75th is not going to be one of First Army's better divisions." Sylvan diary, 16 January 1945, 168, CMH.

60. Ridgway's memorandum of phone conversation with Hodges, 231610 January 1945. Porter, who until late December 1944 had headed the organization and training division of the Army G-3, was sent to Europe specifically so Eisenhower would have a pool of capable division commanders in the event that what Marshall called "the vicissitudes of fighting" generated a requirement for replacements. Chandler et al., *Eisenhower Papers*, 2371.

61. The rationale for the change in direction is unstated in the XVIII (Airborne) Corps papers, and this presumption represents some speculation on my part.

62. V Corps G-3 journal entry, 160830 January 1945, V Corps G-3 files, RG 407, Box 3546, NAII.

63. Assistant G-3 memorandum to chief of staff, 172001 January 1945, V Corps G-3 files, RG 407, Box 3546, NAII.

64. Andrus had assumed command of the division when Huebner was elevated to deputy V Corps commander in December 1944. Commissioned in the field artillery in 1912, he graduated from CGSS in 1930, the Army War College in 1934, and the Naval War College in 1935. After serving in the Hawaiian department in the opening months of the war, he became commander of the 1st Division Artillery in May 1942 and held that position until appointed to division command. Ancell, *Biographical Dictionary of World War II Generals*, 7. The V Corps Sitrep, 180001–181200 January 1945, V Corps G-3 files, RG 407, Box 3546, NAII, is the source for the commitment of a battalion of the 16th IR to support the 23rd IR. The "pretty badly shaken up" comment comes from Eaton's memorandum of his phone conversation with the 30th ID chief of staff, 181440 January 1945, Ridgway papers, MHI.

65. Sylvan diary, 18 January 1945, 170, CMH.

66. The terrain and weather were also factors. Felber opined that "the counterattack by combat team 'Peiper' was not entirely effective because of the pathless woodland, deep in snow, in which it took place." Felber, "Report on the Ardennes Campaign, Part II, 1–25 January 1945," 13, FMS B-039, RG 319, NAII.

67. The XVIII (Airborne) Corps advance on 19 January is described in Felber, "Report on the Ardennes Campaign, Part II, 1–25 January 1945," 13, FMS B-039, RG 319, NAII; and Sylvan diary, 19 January 1945, 171, CMH.

68. XVIII (Airborne) Corps G-3 journal, 191445 January 1945, XVIII (Airborne) Corps G-3 files, RG 407, Box 4974, NAII.

69. Montgomery to Ridgway, 17 January 1945, Ridgway correspondence file, Ridgway papers, MHI.

70. The description of the 7th AD plan for the recapture of St. Vith is based on Hasbrouck's comments found in Report of Division Commanders' Conference Held at Call of Corps Commander at XVIII Corps CP at Time Stated Above [141800 January 1945], 6–7, XVIII (Airborne) Corps headquarters diary, Ridgway papers, MHI; and Fontenot, "Lucky Seventh," 138.

71. Blair, *Ridgway's Paratroopers*, 502.

72. Ridgway's memorandum of his activities on 20 January 1945, XVIII (Airborne) Corps headquarters diary, Ridgway papers, MHI.

73. Description of CCB, 7th AD's attack on Born is drawn from Fontenot, "Lucky Seventh," 142–48.

74. Sylvan diary, 21 January 1945, 172, CMH.

75. Ibid., 173.

76. Fontenot suggests the former interpretation in "Lucky Seventh," 149; Blair suggests the latter in *Ridgway's Paratroopers*, 502.

77. Fontenot, "Lucky Seventh," 152.

78. This and the following two sentences are based on Felber, "Report on the Ardennes Campaign, Part II, 1–25 January 1945," 16, FMS B-039, RG 319, NAII.

79. Description of CCB, 7th AD's seizure of St. Vith is based on Fontenot, "Lucky Seventh," 153–54; and Felber, "Report on the Ardennes Campaign, Part II, 1–25 January 1945," 17, FMS B-039, RG 319, NAII.

80. This and the following sentence are based on entries in Gavin's diary for 18 and 24 January 1945, Gavin papers, MHI.

81. Ridgway's memorandum of a conversation with Hodges held the afternoon of 15 January includes the observation that "all intelligence had convinced me that there was only a shell of second class infantry between me and ST. VITH." Ridgway's summary of conversation with Hodges, 171300 to 171500 January 1945, XVIII (Airborne) Corps headquarters diary, MHI. Gavin expressed similar sentiments in his diary entry for 18 January 1945, Gavin diary, Gavin papers, MHI.

82. Clausewitz, *On War*, 104.

83. V Corps G-2 section, "Intelligence Operations of the V U.S. Corps in Europe," 79–81, MHI.

84. Unless otherwise indicated, this paragraph is based on *Combat History of the Second Infantry Division in World War II*, 108–12; and Knickerbocker et al., *Danger Forward*, 326–29.

85. XVIII (Airborne) Corps Sitrep as of 262400 January 1945, XVIII (Airborne) Corps G-3 files, RG 407, Box 4976, NAII.

86. As early as 11 January, one day after receipt of the First Army order for the attack, Ridgway identified to Hodges the complete dependence on V Corps' seizure of the Ondenval defile for accomplishment of the XVIII (Airborne) Corps mission. He did not, however, mention the obvious solution. On the first day of the attack, he had to go through Hodges and Huebner to have orders given for the 1st ID to advance toward the line Eibertingen-Montenau; he did not receive notification that these instructions were issued until twenty-one hours later. And on the 17th, Huebner called Ridgway to request his concurrence in a change to the corps boundary, which Ridgway did not grant until contacted by Hodges. Ridgway letter to Hodges, 111215 January 1945, Ridgway memoranda of conversations with Hodges of 151400 and 161100 January 1945, and Ridgway memoranda of conversation with Huebner and Hodges, respectively, 171600 and 171615 January 1945, XVIII (Airborne) Corps headquarters diary, Ridgway papers, MHI. All this would have been obviated had the 1st ID been placed under control of XVIII (Airborne) Corps.

87. This still raises the question: Was Ridgway's recommendation for relief of Prickett justified? It was certainly not as clear a case as the relief of Archer Jones, who had clearly lost his ability to command. There was, however, evidence in support of recommendation. The 75th ID had, since its commitment, performed below

expectations; Prickett's confidence in his own ability to improve the capabilities of his subordinates was low; and, as indicated in a long conversation he had with Eaton on 22 January, he tended to pass his problems up the chain of command, rather than fix them himself. Eaton memorandum for Ridgway of conversation with Prickett on combat status of 290th IR, 22 January 1945, XVIII (Airborne) Corps headquarters diary, Ridgway papers, MHI. On the other side of the ledger, there were mitigating circumstances and considerations: Collins's initial decision to commit two regiments of the 75th ID under the command of other divisions inhibited Prickett's ability to command; and the division's first combat action came under extremely difficult conditions. Finally, there was the chance, as there always is, that Prickett could have turned things around, as did other commanders who had stumbled early on. Thus, it came down to Ridgway's best judgment. The letter to Hodges indicated that his major considerations were that the men of the 75th ID deserved better leadership than they were getting from Prickett and that, although it was possible things could get better, the exigencies of combat demanded a higher degree of assurance that they would get better. Thus, while Ridgway's recommendation for relief may have been unfair to Prickett, it appears to have been justified because it gave the benefit of the doubt to his soldiers.

15. VIII, III, and XII Corps Close the Bulge from the South

1. Patton diary entry, 6 January 1945, Blumenson, *Patton Papers: 1940–1945*, 616.

2. For an enlightened analysis of the inadequate means problem, particularly as it applied to infantry replacements and ammunition, see Weigley, *Eisenhower's Lieutenants*, 567–74.

3. This paragraph is based on Cole, *Ardennes*, Maps IV and VI.

4. Unless otherwise noted, this paragraph is based on VIII Corps G-2 Periodic Report no. 202, 052000 January 1945, VIII Corps G-2 files, RG 407, Box 3965, NAII.

5. "Hold to the last cartridge" is from Spayd, *Bayerlein*, 191.

6. This bore a distinct resemblance to Montgomery's attack at El Alamein, which he referred to as "crumbling" operations. Montgomery, *Memoirs*, 109–10. There is no inference here that Middleton took any inspiration from Montgomery, merely that the two commanders' methods were similar.

7. VIII Corps AAR, 1–31 January 1945, 25 April 1945, 6, VIII Corps G-3 files, RG 407, Box 3959, NAII.

8. The VIII Corps Sitrep for 061200–061800 January 1945 reported that Tillet had been captured at 1700. VIII Corps G-3 files, RG 407, Box 4033, NAII; this erroneous report was corrected in the Sitrep for 062400–071200 January 1945, VIII Corps G-3 files, RG 407, Box 4034, NAII.

9. VIII Corps Sitrep, 070600–071200 January 1945, VIII Corps G-3 files, RG 407, Box 4034, NAII.

10. VIII Corps Sitrep, 071200–071800 January 1945, VIII Corps G-3 files, RG 407, Box 4034, NAII.

11. 17th Airborne Division Sitrep for 071100–071800 January 1945, VIII Corps G-3 files, RG 407, Box 4034, NAII. "Dead Man's Ridge" from Pay, *Thunder from Heaven*, 19–28.

12. Flamierge's recapture by 513th PIR on 7 January from corps AAR, 1–31 January 1945, 25 April 1945, 7, VIII Corps G-3 files, RG 407, Box 3959, NAII.

13. VIII Corps messages to 17th Airborne and 87th Infantry Divisions, 071645 January 1945, VIII Corps G-3 files, RG 407, Box 4034, NAII.

14. What follows is drawn from Third Army Operational Directive (confirmation of verbal orders), 8 January 1945, VIII Corps G-3 files, RG 407, Box 4034, NAII.

15. What follows, including the direct quotations, is based on VIII Corps Field Order 2, 081200 January 1945, VIII Corps G-3 files, RG 407, Box 4034, NAII.

16. Description of the 101st Airborne's attack on 9 January 1945 from Leonard Rapport and Arthur Northwood, Jr., *Rendezvous with Destiny: A History of the 101st Airborne Division* (1948; reprint, Nashville: Battery Press, 2000), 637–38.

17. Description of the 101st's attack on 10 January from Rapport and Northwood, *Rendezvous with Destiny*, 641–42.

18. VIII Corps AAR, 1–31 January 1945, 25 April 1945, 9, VIII Corps G-3 files, RG 407, Box 3959, NAII.

19. What follows is based on Blumenson, *Patton Papers: 1940–1945*, 621.

20. Rapport and Northwood, *Rendezvous with Destiny*, 642–43.

21. VIII Corps AAR, 1–31 January 1945, 25 April 1945, 8, VIII Corps G-3 files, RG 407, Box 3959, NAII; "containing" is from VIII Corps Sitrep, 090600–091200 January 1945, VIII Corps G-3 files, RG 407, Box 4034, NAII.

22. VIII Corps AAR, 1–31 January 1945, 25 April 1945, 7–8, VIII Corps G-3 files, RG 407, Box 3959, NAII.

23. VIII Corps Sitrep, 101200–101800 January 1945, VIII Corps G-3 files, RG 407, Box 4034, NAII.

24. VIII Corps AAR, 1–31 January 1945, 25 April 1945, 9, VIII Corps G-3 files, RG 407, Box 3959, NAII.

25. VIII Corps Operations Memorandum 8, 10 January 1945, VIII Corps G-3 files, RG 407, Box 4034, NAII.

26. VIII Corps AAR, 1–31 January 1945, 25 April 1945, 10, VIII Corps G-3 files, RG 407, Box 3959, NAII.

27. VIII Corps Operations Memorandum 9, 11 January 1945, annotated "out at 111745A," VIII Corps G-3 files, RG 407, Box 4034, NAII.

28. VIII Corps Field Order 3, 121100 January 1945, annotated "out 121300A," VIII Corps G-3 files, RG 407, Box 4034, NAII.

29. This action is described in some detail in Ambrose, *Band of Brothers*, 205–12.

30. Account of the fighting at Foy after its initial capture is based on VIII Corps AAR, 1–31 January 1945, 25 April 1945, 11, VIII Corps G-3 files, RG 407, Box 3959, NAII; and Rapport and Northwood, *Rendezvous with Destiny*, 650, 653.

31. Rapport and Northwood, *Rendezvous with Destiny*, 647–55.

32. VIII Corps AAR, 1–31 January 1945, 25 April 1945, 10–11, VIII Corps G-3 files, RG 407, Box 3959, NAII.

33. VIII Corps Sitrep, 140600–141200 January 1945, VIII Corps G-3 files, RG 407, Box 4035, NAII.

34. Third Army Troop Assignment Letter, A-90, 17 January 1945, VIII Corps G-3 files, RG 407, Box 4036, NAII. The assignment of the 87th ID to XII Corps was effective 14 January.

35. VIII Corps General Situation Memorandum, 15 January 1945, VIII Corps G-3 files, RG 407, Box 4035, NAII.

36. Rapport and Northwood, *Rendezvous with Destiny*, 655–57.

37. The story of the 11th AD's end of the linkup at Houffalize is drawn from Toland, *Battle*, 360–64.

38. VIII Corps AAR, 1–31 January 1945, 25 April 1945, 13, VIII Corps G-3 files, RG 407, Box 3959, NAII.

39. Rapport and Northwood, *Rendezvous with Destiny*, 657–61.

40. What follows is based on ibid., 662–65.

41. Ibid., 665.

42. VIII Corps activities on 20 January and description of its attack zone are based on VIII Corps AAR, 1–31 January 1945, 25 April 1945, 14, VIII Corps G-3 files, RG 407, Box 3959, NAII.

43. VIII Corps Field Order 6, 181000 January 1945, VIII Corps G-3 files, RG 407, Box 4036, NAII.

44. VIII Corps G-2 Periodic Report no. 217, 202000 January 1945, VIII Corps G-2 files, RG 407, Box 3965, NAII.

45. VIII Corps Sitrep, 231200–231800 January 1945, VIII Corps G-3 files, RG 407, Box 4036, NAII.

46. Third Army Amendment to Operational Directive, Register no. TUSA 1729, dated 19 January 1945, 21 January 1945, VIII Corps G-3 files, RG 407, Box 4036, NAII.

47. Changes in VIII Corps boundaries and task organization from 24–26 January from VIII Corps AAR, 1–31 January 1945, 25 April 1945, 14, VIII Corps G-3 files, RG 407, Box 3959, NAII. The primary rationale for the change was that Patton wanted Middleton, who, though tired, was already familiar with the terrain around St. Vith, involved in that portion of the upcoming offensive. Patton, *War as I Knew It,* 224–25. See Gay diary, 697, Gay papers, MHI, for additional details of early planning for the VIII Corps' role in this attack.

48. Middleton to Miley, 24 January 1945, VIII Corps G-3 files, RG 407, Box 4036, NAII.

49. VIII Corps Operations Memoranda 16 and 17, 25 January 1945, RG 407, Box 4037, NAII.

50. VIII Corps Sitrep for 281200–281800 January 1945, VIII Corps G-3 files, RG 407, Box 4037, NAII.

51. Simpson's efficiency report on Middleton for 5 September–24 October 1944, Middleton file, NPRC, mentions the Ninth Army commander's recommendation for the award. Given Patton's ambivalence about the Brest operation, there is some distinct irony in his serving as the presenting official. The presentation of the award is mentioned in both Gay's diary entry for 24 January 1945, 698, Gay papers, MHI, and Eddy's activity log for the same date, Eddy War Log, Fort Benning, Georgia, National Infantry Museum.

52. Disposition of III Corps units on 5 January from Annex 1a to III Corps, Action against Enemy, Report After [1–31 January 1945], 1 February 1945, III Corps History Files, RG 407, Box 3262, NAII.

53. Patton diary entry for 5 January 1945, Blumenson, *Patton Papers: 1940–1945,* 616.

54. Enemy dispositions in III Corps zone on 5 January, from III Corps G-2 Periodic Report no. 28, 5 January 1945, III Corps G-2 files, RG 407, Box 3267, NAII.

55. Stanton, *World War II Order of Battle*, 164.

56. Bradley and Blair, *General's Life*, 262; and Chandler et al., *Eisenhower Papers*, 2080.

57. Chandler et al., *Eisenhower Papers*, 2080, 2234n.

58. Biographical background on Van Fleet from Paul F. Braim, *The Will to Win: The Life of General James A. Van Fleet* (Annapolis: Naval Institute Press, 2001), 10–99.

59. Bradley and Blair, *General's Life*, 263. Bradley spins an interesting yarn here about the reason Van Fleet had been held back from promotion to general officer, when many of his USMA classmates (most notably Bradley himself and Eisenhower) had progressed much more quickly. In this story, Marshall had confused him with another Van Fleet, who was thought to have a problem with alcohol. Van Fleet, however, discounted the interpretation and said that Marshall, whom he knew well, was distinctly aware that he was a teetotaler. Van Fleet's biographer believes the more likely cause was his lack of military education and particularly the fact that, having been selected to attend CGSS following the advanced course, he chose instead to go back to the University of Florida for a repeat assignment as professor of military science. Marshall, then assistant commandant at the Infantry School, was aware of this decision. Braim, *Will to Win*, 93–94.

60. Braim, *Will to Win*, 95–115.

61. Gay diary entry for 6 January 1945, 656, Gay papers, MHI. See also MacDonald, *Last Offensive*, 40.

62. III Corps Field Order 3, 7 January 1945, III Corps G-3 files, RG 407, Box 3306, NAII.

63. III Corps G-3 memorandum of instructions received telephonically from Third Army G-3, 061550 January 1945, III Corps G-3 files, RG 407, Box 3306, NAII.

64. Braim, *Will to Win*, 128.

65. Heilmann, "5th Parachute Division (1 December 1944–12 January 1945)," 48, FMS B-023, RG 319, NAII.

66. III Corps G-3 memorandum of conversation with G-3, 90th ID, 091630 January 1945, III Corps G-3 files, RG 407, Box 3306, NAII.

67. III Corps Sitrep, 091200–091800 January 1945, III Corps G-3 files, RG 407, Box 3306, NAII.

68. This and the two following sentences are based on Millikin's "Notes on Today's Activities," 9 January 1945, III Corps G-3 files, RG 407, Box 3306, NAII.

69. Millikin's memoranda of telephone conversations with Gay and Patton, respectively, 091930 and 091940 January 1945, III Corps G-3 files, RG 407, Box 3306, NAII.

70. Millikin's memorandum of conversation with Gay, 101010 January 1945, III Corps G-3 files, RG 407, Box 3306, NAII.

71. The account of the erroneous report rendered to Patton and the subsequent attack of the 359th IR is based on John Colby, *War from the Ground Up: The 90th Division in WWII* (Austin: Nortex, 1991), 365–79.

72. What follows is based on Ludwig Heilmann, "5th Parachute Division," 30–49, FMS B-023, RG 319, NAII.

73. Heilmann, "5th Parachute Division," 49, FMS B-023, RG 319, NAII.

74. The starting figure of twenty-one officers, when normally only six officers were assigned to a rifle company, derives from the fact that one extra officer had been brought into each company in anticipation of casualties. Colby, *War from the Ground Up*, 365. The fact that two companies were being commanded by staff ser-

geants is from Millikin's memorandum of his conversation with Van Fleet, 122000 January 1945, III Corps G-3 files, RG 407, Box 3307, NAII. Battle casualties for the 90th ID were around 100 KIA, 320 WIA, and 130 MIA. Dupuy, Bongard, and Anderson, *Hitler's Last Gamble*, 335.

75. This paragraph is based on III Corps, Action against Enemy, Report After [1–31 January 1945], 1 February 1945, 11, III Corps History Files, RG 407, Box 3262, NAII.

76. These objectives have been reconstructed from III Corps, Action against Enemy, Report After [1–31 January 1945], 1 February 1945, 15, III Corps History Files, RG 407, Box 3262, NAII.

77. This and the two following sentences are based on III Corps, Action against Enemy, Report After [1–31 January 1945], 1 February 1945, 12, III Corps History Files, RG 407, Box 3262, NAII.

78. Memorandum of 26th ID telephonic report to III Corps, 131330 January 1945, III Corps G-3 files, RG 407, Box 3307, NAII.

79. The multiple challenges facing the 26th ID are described in a memorandum of a liaison visit by the III Corps assistant G-3 to the unit and his discussion with the division's chief of staff, 13 January 1945, III Corps G-3 files, RG 407, Box 3307, NAII.

80. 6th AD telephonic report to III Corps, 141130 January 1945, and III Corps Sitrep for 141200–141800 January 1945, III Corps G-3 files, RG 407, Box 3307, NAII.

81. 90th ID telephonic report to III Corps, 141515 January 1945, III Corps G-3 files, RG 407, Box 3307, NAII.

82. III Corps Sitrep, 151200–151800 January 1945, III Corps G-3 files, RG 407, Box 3307, NAII.

83. III Corps Sitrep, 151200–151800 January 1945, III Corps G-3 files, RG 407, Box 3307, NAII.

84. The direct quotation and the identity of the 1st SS Panzer Division are from III Corps, G-2 Periodic Report no. 38, 15 January 1945, III Corps G-2 files, RG 407, Box 3267, NAII.

85. Braim, *Will to Win*, 130.

86. Millikin message to Grow, 152100 January 1945, III Corps G-3 files, RG 407, Box 3307, NAII.

87. An interesting human portrait of the action was captured by Richard Stokes of the *St. Louis Post-Dispatch*, who wrote that the Germans were "fighting with the desperation of men convinced that in their hands lies the salvation or downfall of their country for generations to come." The scribe also accurately captured the GI mentality: "The Yanks are driving forward on a relentless will, because they are persuaded . . . that every step toward BERLIN is a step toward Kokomo or Oshkosh or New York or St. Louis." Hofmann, *Super Sixth*, 301.

88. Millikin to Grow, 161720 January 1945, III Corps G-3 files, RG 407, Box 3307, NAII.

89. 90th ID telephonic report to III Corps, 162140 January 1945, III Corps G-3 files, RG 407, Box 3307, NAII, gives the contemporaneous report of Oberwampach's capture; the regimental identification is indicated in III Corps AAR, 1–31 January 1945, 1 February 1945, RG 407, Box 3362, NAII.

90. Blumenson, *Patton Papers: 1940–1945*, 626.

91. Ibid., 625.

92. III Corps Field Order 3, 18 January 1945, III Corps G-3 files, RG 407, Box 3308, NAII, ordered subordinated units to complete seizure of previously assigned objectives, consolidate positions, and maintain contact with the enemy. Description of remainder of III Corps activities from 18–20 January is drawn from III Corps, Action against Enemy, Report After [1–31 January 1945], 1 February 1945, 16–18, III Corps History Files, RG 407, Box 3262, NAII.

93. Except as otherwise indicated, this paragraph is based on III Corps, Action against Enemy, Report After [1–31 January 1945], 1 February 1945, 18–22, III Corps History Files, RG 407, Box 3262, NAII.

94. The capture of Eschweiler by the 6th Cavalry Group drew attention to the relatively slow progress of the 80th ID, evident in the comments of the Third Army chief of staff, who noted that the division had not yet crossed the Wiltz River. Gay diary entry for 22 January 1945, 695, Gay papers, MHI.

95. MacDonald, *Last Offensive*, 52–53.

96. This paragraph is based on III Corps, Action against Enemy, Report After [1–31 January 1945], 1 February 1945, 22–26, III Corps History Files, RG 407, Box 3262, NAII; and MacDonald, *Last Offensive*, 53.

97. Gay diary, 15 January 1945, 679, Gay papers, MHI.

98. This and the following sentence are based on XII Corps G-3 periodic reports, 7–14 January 1945, XII Corps G-3 files, RG 407, Box 4365, NAII. There were minor movements of the corps' front line during this period, mostly in the sector of the 80th ID, but otherwise it remained relatively stationary.

99. Eddy War Log, 13 January 1945, Fort Benning, Georgia, National Infantry Museum.

100. This and the following sentence are based on XII Corps Operational Directive 67, 15 January 1945, XII Corps G-3 files, RG 407, Box 4263, NAII, which contains a detailed timetable for precisely how the various regiments of the 87th ID would relieve those of the 4th ID and how specific regiments of the 4th ID would relieve the 11th IR, which was located in the eastern third of the 5th ID's sector. It was a very carefully choreographed operation.

101. Eddy War Log, 1 January 1945, Fort Benning, Georgia, National Infantry Museum.

102. Ibid., 2 January 1945.

103. XII Corps Field Order 13, 3 January 1945, XII Corps G-3 files, RG 407, Box 4236, NAII.

104. XII Corps Operational Directive 68, 16 January 1945, RG 407, Box 4236, NAII.

105. Description of bridging preparations is drawn from "Plan for Crossing of the SURE River," 16 January 1945, and XII Corps Engineer Section memorandum, 18 January 1945, XII Corps G-3 files, RG 407, Box 4433, NAII.

106. This paragraph is based on MacDonald, *Last Offensive*, 48; and Dupuy, Bongard, and Anderson, *Hitler's Last Gamble*, 348–49.

107. The phrase "London fog" is from Patton's description of the weather in his diary entry for 19 January 1945, Blumenson, *Patton Papers: 1940–1945*, 626.

108. Description of the 5th ID's crossing of the Sûre on 18 January 1945 is drawn from *The Fifth Infantry Division in the ETO*, n.p.

109. XII Corps G-3 periodic reports from 171200–181200 and 181200–191200 January 1945, XII Corps G-3 files, RG 407, Box 4365, NAII.

110. This paragraph is based on MacDonald, *Last Offensive*, 50; and Dupuy, Bongard, and Anderson, *Hitler's Last Gamble*, 349.

111. Description of the advances of the 4th and 5th IDs on 19 and 20 January from XII Corps G-3 periodic reports for 181200–191200 and 191200–201200 January 1945, XII Corps G-3 files, RG 407, Box 4365, NAII. Details of snowstorm from Dupuy, Bongard, and Anderson, *Hitler's Last Gamble*, 350.

112. MacDonald, *Last Offensive*, 49. MacDonald credits this condition as having obtained by the evening of the 18th; but he erroneously refers to the bridgehead at this time as being "two miles deep," when in reality it was only just over a mile.

113. Eddy War Log, 20 January 1945, Fort Benning, Georgia, National Infantry Museum.

114. Memorandum of telephonic report from 5th ID, XII Corps G-3 files, RG 407, Box 4435, NAII.

115. MacDonald, *Last Offensive*, 51.

116. Dupuy, Bongard, and Anderson, *Hitler's Last Gamble*, 350.

117. This paragraph is based on the daily XII Corps G-3 periodic reports for the periods ranging from 211200 January 1945 to 281200 January 1945, XII Corps G-3 files, RG 407, Box 4365, NAII.

118. XII Corps Operational Directive 71, 22 January 1945, XII Corps G-3 files, RG 407, Box 4263, NAII.

119. Unless otherwise noted, the remainder of the paragraph is based on XII Corps G-3 periodic reports for the periods ranging from 211200 January 1945 to 281200 January 1945, XII Corps G-3 files, RG 407, Box 4365, NAII.

120. XII Corps G-3 memorandum of telephone message from Third Army operations section, 251600 January 1945, RG 407, Box 4436, NAII.

121. I have been unable to discover any recorded rationale for Eddy's decision in this matter. It seems, however, to have derived from three considerations: the understrength condition of the 80th ID, the strength of the German forces opposing it, and the rugged terrain over which it would have to attack. Under these circumstances, the judgment to wait until the bridgehead was secure and the German LIII Corps had begun displacing to the east before giving Mc Bride the go-ahead was eminently sensible.

122. Eddy War Log, 24 January 1945, Fort Benning, Georgia, National Infantry Museum. The recommendation for the award was signed by Patton on 21 October 1944, Eddy file, NPRC.

123. Eddy War Log, 24 January 1945, Fort Benning, Georgia, National Infantry Museum.

124. Gay diary, 27 January 1945, 704, Gay papers, MHI.

16. Conclusions and Epilogue

1. Larrabee, *Commander-in-Chief*, 6.

2. Appendix "A," ARDENNES Battle Casualties to SHAEF, Memorandum/17100/12/1, Statistics—Battle of the ARDENNES, 2 February 1945, SHAEF papers, RG 331, NAII. Also cited in Pogue, *Supreme Command*, 396. The figures

given here exclude the estimated 1,408 British casualties: 200 KIA, 969 WIA, and 239 MIA.

3. Pogue, *Supreme Command*, 402.

4. MacDonald, *Time for Trumpets*, 618.

5. Pogue, *Supreme Command*, 396.

6. MacDonald, *Time for Trumpets*, 618.

7. This paragraph is based on Eisenhower, *Bitter Woods*, 431–56.

8. Cole, *Ardennes*, 676.

9. Collins's review of Stephen E. Ambrose, *The Supreme Commander: The War Years of Dwight D. Eisenhower*, in *Washington Post*, 5 October 1970.

10. For an insightful elaboration of the "fleet in being" concept in naval theory and practice, see Julian S. Corbett, *Some Principles of Maritime Strategy* (1911; reprint, Annapolis: Naval Institute Press, 1988), 209–27.

11. Excerpt from Gerow's record of service, 2 June 1950, Gerow file, NPRC.

12. ETO Amendment to Distinguished Service Medal Policy, 10 August 1946, and First Army Recommendation for Award, 27 March 1947, Gerow file, NPRC.

13. The former ranking was contained in Bradley's War Department–directed special rating of general officers, 1 June 1945, Gerow file, NPRC. The latter was contained in Bradley's efficiency report rendered on Gerow, 30 June 1945, Gerow file, NPRC. The number two ranking is somewhat curious because Fifteenth Army had few operational responsibilities in the closing months of the war. One cannot avoid the suspicion that Bradley was at least partially influenced here by his awareness of Eisenhower's high opinion of Gerow.

14. Gerow's testimony cited from Ray S. Cline, *Washington Command Post: The Operations Division* (Washington, D.C.: OCMH, 1951), 78. A *Washington Post* reporter, obviously unaware of the general's previous testimony, commended Gerow for "the forthright manner in which he took it on the chin." "General Gerow's Courage," *Washington Post*, 7 December 1945.

15. Graduation, 27th General Staff Class, 31 May 1946, addresses given by Lieutenant General Leonard T. Gerow during the period he served as commandant, CGSC, November 1945–January 1948, 62, CARL.

16. Graduation, 31 May 1946, Gerow addresses, 62, CARL.

17. Ibid., 61.

18. The unnamed individual introducing Freeman in 1951 stated it was his fifth year, indicating that the first time had been in 1947 during Gerow's tenure as CGSC commandant. "Leadership," lecture at CGSC by Dr. Douglas Southall Freeman, 23 March 1951, CARL.

19. What follows is based on "Gerow Board," in William E. Simons, ed., *Professional Military Education in the United States: A Historical Dictionary* (Westport, Conn.: Greenwood, 2000), 147–49.

20. This was arguably the one deficiency of the Gerow report, for the concomitant assumption was that with an "Armed Forces College" established, the army would no longer require its own war college. This mistake was not rectified until 1950 with the reestablishment of the Army War College, temporarily at Fort Leavenworth, Kansas, until it moved to Carlisle Barracks, Pennsylvania, in 1951.

21. Gerow service record, Gerow file, NPRC.

22. This and the following sentence are based on correspondence between Gerow and Eisenhower found in the Gerow papers, VMI archives.

23. Gerow was notified of the promotion in a letter from the adjutant general dated 4 August 1954. Gerow papers, VMI archives. The other officers, whose names appear in an unsourced newspaper clipping of 6 July 1954 located in the same file, were Lesley J. McNair, Simon B. Buckner, Alexander M. Patch, William H. Simpson, Ben Lear, Lucian Truscott, Jr., Robert C. Richardson, Robert L. Eichelberger, Albert C. Wedemeyer, and John L. DeWitt.

24. Report of Casualty, 18 October 1972, Gerow file, NPRC; and *Petersburg Progress-Index* obituary, 13 October 1972, Gerow papers, VMI archives.

25. Third Army, Recommendation for Award of Distinguished Service Medal (Oak-Leaf Cluster), 1 February 1945, Middleton file, NPRC.

26. ETO indorsement to Patton's recommendation, 19 May 1945; and reply from Adjutant General of 25 July 1945, Middleton file, NPRC.

27. Price, *Middleton*, 275–92.

28. Middleton wrote Bradley in May 1945 stating his desire to return to Louisiana State University. Ibid., 293–94.

29. Special Rating of General Officers, 1 June 1945, Middleton file, NPRC.

30. Eisenhower to Marshall, 11 April 1945, Chandler et al., *Eisenhower Papers*, 2599.

31. Eisenhower to Marshall, 9 April 1945, in ibid., 2595.

32. Ibid., 2600n.

33. Price, *Middleton*, 296.

34. Middleton's formal letter of request for relief from active duty came on 27 July 1945, Middleton file, NPRC. His retirement orders were received in about mid-August. Ibid., 297.

35. Ibid., 298–305.

36. Note of correspondence, 18 February 1946; and letter from Secretary of the Army Frank Pace to Middleton, 4 August 1951, Middleton file, NPRC.

37. Price, *Middleton*, 306.

38. Ibid., 306–68.

39. Report of Casualty, 24 November 1976, Middleton file, NPRC.

40. Price, *Middleton*, 370.

41. Unless otherwise indicated, this paragraph is based on Blair, *Ridgway's Paratroopers*, 505–93.

42. Author's personal knowledge. Blair ends his story with Ridgway and the advance party taking off from San Francisco shortly before announcement of the Japanese surrender. The author's father was a member of the XVIII (Airborne) Corps advance party.

43. Special Rating of General Officers, 1 June 1945, Ridgway file, NPRC.

44. Eisenhower to Marshall, 21 May 1945, Marshall papers, GCML.

45. Chandler et al., *Eisenhower Papers*, 2617n, states that Ridgway was promoted to lieutenant general on 4 June; Ridgway's service record indicates the promotion was made on 28 June with date of rank 4 June. Ridgway file, NPRC.

46. Report of the Decorations Board, 5 May 1947, Ridgway file, NPRC.

47. Ridgway service record, Ridgway file, NPRC. The position was actually titled deputy chief of staff for administration, but the duties were those of an operations deputy. See Collins, *Lightning Joe*, 347.

48. Collins letter to Ridgway, 23 December 1950, Collins papers, Box 17, DDEL.

49. Unless otherwise indicated, this paragraph is based on James F. Schnabel, "Ridgway in Korea," *Military Review* 44 (March 1964): 3–13; and Clay Blair, *The Forgotten War: America in Korea, 1950–1953* (New York: Times Books, 1987), 564–780.

50. This judgment is the author's.

51. Ridgway's brief account of this episode is found in *Soldier*, 275–78; a more comprehensive treatment is found in Jonathan M. Soffer, *General Matthew B. Ridgway: From Progressivism to Reaganism, 1895–1993* (Westport, Conn.: Praeger, 1998), 93–202.

52. Andrew M. Mueller, "Challenging Policy: Confronting the Military Professional's Dilemma" (Maxwell AFB, Ala.: SAASS, June 1999), argues that Ridgway felt torn between the requirement to inform the American public of the country's defense needs and the subordination of military to civilian authority and felt that his definition of the proper role of the soldier in society allowed him to challenge a policy with which he disagreed, as long as he ultimately followed orders. A. J. Bacevich, "The Paradox of Professionalism: Eisenhower, Ridgway, and the Challenge of Civilian Control, 1953–1955," *Journal of Military History* 61 (April 1997): 303–33, argues that Ridgway went too far in his challenge to the Eisenhower administration. Although these interpretations are not mutually exclusive, I find the former more compelling than the latter.

53. Soffer, *Matthew B. Ridgway*, 203–13.

54. Ridgway's obituary is in *Assembly* 54 (March 1994): 148.

55. Third Army, Recommendation for Award of Distinguished Service Medal (Oak Leaf Cluster), 30 January 1945; and Patton's efficiency reports on Millikin of 28 January and 1 March 1945, Millikin file, NPRC.

56. Patton felt so strongly about not losing Middleton that he went over Bradley's head to Ike on the matter. Blumenson, *Patton Papers: 1940–1945*, 635–36. But on the occasion of the transfer, Millikin received a very cordial note from Hobart Gay noting that "the cheerful and cooperative spirit exhibited by the entire staff of the III Corps, during its months under Third U.S. Army, was so outstanding and effective that I cannot refrain from commending them." Gay to Millikin, 12 February 1945, Millikin file, NPRC.

57. What follows is based on Hodges's relief-for-cause letter attached to his efficiency report on Millikin rendered for the period 11 February–20 March 1945, dated 7 May 1945, and for Millikin's rebuttal thereto dated 5 June 1945, Millikin file, NPRC.

58. This and the following sentence are based on the Sylvan diary for 7 March, which indicates Kean's interest, and Millikin's rebuttal to Hodges's letter of relief, which outlines the specific steps he took to facilitate the Remagen Bridge's capture.

59. What follows is based primarily on Weigley's account of the seizure, in *Eisenhower's Lieutenants*, 626–30.

60. Date of interdiction of the Autobahn from Sylvan diary, 16 March 1945, CMH.

61. Hodges's letter of relief, 7 May 1945, Millikin file, NPRC; and Sylvan diary entry for 15 March 1945, CMH. Hodges also points the finger at Millikin in a manuscript titled, "Remagen: The Bridge That Changed the War," Governor's Island, New York, January 1949, Hodges papers, Box 21, DDEL.

62. All the extenuating circumstances except the traffic control function are addressed in Weigley, *Eisenhower's Lieutenants*, 631–32. This detail was brought to the author's attention in a conversation with Dr. David Hogan of the CMH on 18 October 1996.

63. This sentiment was evident immediately. Two days after the bridge's capture, Sylvan noted that "there is no attempt to hide the fact that everybody here wishes the bridge command had fallen to General Collins." Sylvan diary, 9 March 1945, CMH.

64. The 9th ID chief of staff, Colonel William C. Westmoreland, used his previous acquaintance with Sylvan to relay to Hodges his dissatisfaction with Millikin's leadership, which he "feared a commander as loyal as [Major General Louis A.] Craig would fail to do." William C. Westmoreland, *A Soldier Reports* (New York: Doubleday, 1976), 25. There is no record of this conversation in the Sylvan diary and thus no certainty as to whether Westmoreland's remarks did, in fact, reach Hodges.

65. This judgment is shared by a number of other students of the incident. See Weigley, *Eisenhower's Lieutenants*, 630–32; Reichelt, *Phantom Nine*, 229; Martin Blumenson, "Relieved of Command," *Army* 21 (August 1971): 35–36; and Daniel P. Bolger, "Zero Defects: Command Climate in First US Army, 1944–1945," *Military Review* 71 (May 1991): 72. Hogan evenhandedly reviews both Hodges's frustrations with Millikin and the extenuating circumstances in Millikin's defense but comes essentially to the same conclusion. Hogan, *Command Post*, 253–54. Hodges's distance from Millikin is perhaps unconsciously indicated in the fact that his relief-for-cause report consistently misspelled the erstwhile III Corps commander's name as "Milliken." Bradley's endorsement was also curious. He stated flatly, "I am not prepared to state that Major General Millikin 'failed' as a corps commander." He then justified the relief as follows: "I have always operated on the principle that our soldiers are entitled to the best commanders available in the Theater. In this case, I felt that General Van Fleet (and probably several other veteran division commanders) was better qualified to command the corps than General Millikin with his limited experience." The 9th ID historian draws attention to the fact that Van Fleet was "a West Point classmate whom he [Bradley] had advanced from regimental to corps command in nine months." Reichelt, *Phantom Nine*, 229. This observation does not indicate that Bradley engineered Millikin's relief in order to give Van Fleet a corps. It does, however, suggest that with an extremely competent division commander waiting in the wings who was a much more known quantity to Bradley than was Millikin, Bradley had neither hesitation nor qualms in acceding to Hodges's request for a new corps commander. Van Fleet went on to command III Corps with distinction and did likewise with Eighth Army in Korea. Braim, *Will to Win*, 132–50 and 237–312. But he was afforded the first opportunity by army and army group commanders who were arguably a bit too quick to pull the trigger on his predecessor.

66. Millikin assumed command of the 13th AD after Major General John B. Wogan was seriously wounded while trying to push forward the division's attack in the Ruhr. Weigley, *Eisenhower's Lieutenants*, 679.

67. MacDonald, *Last Offensive*, 437, for final operations of 13th AD. Walker's efficiency report, rendered shortly after V-E Day, called Millikin an "alert, aggressive leader. Eminently qualified to command either an infantry or armored division in the field." Efficiency report for 21 April–19 May 1945, dated 19 May 1945, Millikin file, NPRC.

68. Third Army General Orders 297, 15 October 1945, Millikin file, NPRC.

69. Bradley recommended approval of the award on 1 March; but Eisenhower turned it down on 31 March, based on Millikin's subsequent relief. Indorsements by 12th AG and ETO, Millikin file, NPRC. Bradley went to bat for Millikin in 1947, requesting that Eisenhower review his previous consideration. Ike again refused but was overridden by the secretary of war, who approved a special review board's recommendation that the DSM be awarded. Memorandum, Subject: Distinguished Service Medal—Major General John Millikin, 25 February 1947, with subsequent indorsements, Millikin file, NPRC.

70. Report of Casualty, 24 November 1970; and *Washington Post* obituary, 7 November 1970.

71. Efficiency report for 19 August 1944–31 December 1944, Eddy file, NPRC.

72. MacDonald, *Last Offensive*, 101–15, 199.

73. Eddy War Log, 21 March 1945, Fort Benning, Georgia, National Infantry Museum. The author is indebted to Eddy's biographer, Colonel Henry G. Phillips, for providing this page from Eddy's log.

74. Précis of the Hammelburg raid is based on MacDonald, *Last Offensive*, 281–84. See also John Toland, *The Last 100 Days* (New York: Random House, 1966), 287–99; and Richard Baron, Abe Baum, and Richard Goldhurst, *Raid! The Untold Story of Patton's Secret Mission* (New York: Berkley Books, 1984).

75. Description of Eddy's hypertension and recuperation therefrom is based primarily on Phillips, *Making of a Professional*, 186–93. The medical history of Eddy's illness indicates his blood pressure was 200/150 when first treated. Report of medical condition, 17 December 1945, Eddy file, NPRC.

76. Memorandum for the Chief of Staff, Subject: Award of Distinguished Service Medal (OLC) to Major General Manton S. Eddy, 20 April 1945, Eddy file, NPRC; and Phillips, *Making of a Professional*, 192.

77. Eddy service record, Eddy file, NPRC.

78. This and the following two sentences are based on Phillips, *Making of a Professional*, 196.

79. This and the following two sentences are based on ibid., 202–3.

80. This and the following sentence are based on ibid., 199–201.

81. Eddy service record, Eddy file, NPRC; and Phillips, *Making of a Professional*, 204–5.

82. Eddy service record and Report of Casualty, 12 April 1962, Eddy file, NPRC.

83. VII Corps operations from 23 February to 26 April 1945 are drawn from *Mission Accomplished: The Story of the Campaigns of the VII Corps United States Army in the War against Germany, 1944–1945* (Leipzig: J. J. Weber, 1945), 52–69.

84. Special Rating of General Officers, 1 June 1945, Collins file, NPRC.

85. Eisenhower to Marshall, 11 April 1945, Chandler et al., *Eisenhower Papers*, 2599.

86. Chandler et al., *Eisenhower Papers*, 2600n.

87. This paragraph is based on Collins, *Lightning Joe*, 333–46.

88. This paragraph is based on ibid., 347–75.

89. Except as otherwise indicated, this paragraph is based on ibid., 376–411.

90. Eisenhower's indorsement of Collins's efficiency report for 1 June 1955–31 March 1956, Collins file, NPRC.

91. Record of service, Collins file, NPRC.

92. J. Lawton Collins, Speech at Utah Beach, 6 June 1964, Collins papers, Box 46, DDEL. The author is indebted to Valoise Armstrong of the DDEL for providing the text of this speech.

93. Report of Casualty, 2 December 1987, Collins file, NPRC; and *Washington Post* obituary, 13 September 1987.

BIBLIOGRAPHY

Unpublished Sources

Abilene, Kansas. Dwight D. Eisenhower Library (DDEL)
    J. Lawton Collins Papers, Dwight D. Eisenhower Papers
Carlisle Barracks, Pennsylvania. U.S. Army Military History Institute
    Manuscript Holdings and Biographical Reference
        Clay Blair, J. L. DeWitt, Benjamin A. Dickson, James M. Gavin, Hobart R.
        Gay, Chester B. Hansen, Matthew B. Ridgway, and Orlando C. Troxel
    Miscellaneous Documents
        War Diary of VII Corps, 2 June 1944–1 April 1945
    Oral Histories and Interviews
        J. Lawton Collins, William R. Desobry, Williston B. Palmer, and Matthew
        B. Ridgway
    U.S. Army War College Curriculum Archives, 1923–1940
College Park, Maryland. National Archives
    Record Group 165, Records of the War Department General and Special Staffs
    Record Group 319, Records of the Army Staff
    Record Group 331, Records of the Supreme Headquarters, Allied Expeditionary
        Forces
    Record Group 337, Records of the Headquarters, Army Ground Forces
    Record Group 407, Records of the Adjutant General
    Record Group 457, Records of the National Security Agency
    Record Group 549, Records of U.S. Army, Europe
Fort Benning, Georgia. Infantry School Library
    Eddy, M. S. "Machine Gun Company, 39th Infantry (4th Division) in the Aisne
        Marne Offensive (July 18–August 5, 1918)." Infantry School Officer's
        Advanced Course, 1929–1930.
Fort Benning, Georgia. National Infantry Museum
    Manton S. Eddy War Log, "Activities of General Eddy."
Fort Knox, Kentucky
    U.S. Army Armor School. "The Battle at St. Vith, Belgium, 17–23 December
        1944: An Historical Example of Armor in the Defense." 3rd printing. [1966].
Fort Leavenworth, Kansas. U.S. Army Combined Arms Research Library
    Archival Holdings
        Command and General Staff College Records, 1945–1948; Command and
        General Staff School Records, 1924–1936; Correspondence of
        Garrison H. Davidson; VIII Corps Records; First Army Records; VII
        Corps Records; Third Army Records

Research Works

CSI Report No. 5, "Conversations with General J. Lawton Collins." Transcribed by Major Gary Wade. Fort Leavenworth, Kans.: Combat Studies Institute, U.S. Army CGSC, n.d. [1983].

Fontenot, Gregory. "The Lucky Seventh in the Bulge." Fort Leavenworth, Kans.: U.S. Army CGSC, 1985.

Lexington, Virginia. George C. Marshall Library

George C. Marshall Papers

Lexington, Virginia. Virginia Military Institute Archives

Leonard T. Gerow Papers, Virginia Military Institute Records

Maxwell Air Force Base, Alabama. U.S. Air Force Historical Research Agency

IX Bomber Division Mission Summaries

United States Strategic Air Forces. Battlefield Studies World War II: Air Force Participation in the Battle of the Ardennes, 16 December 1944–16 January 1945

United States Strategic Air Forces, A-2. Allied Airpower and the Ardennes Offensive

Washington, D.C., Center for Military History Manuscripts and Documents

Diary of Major William C. Sylvan

"The Intervention of the Third Army: III Corps in the Attack, 22 December–28 December, 1944."

Published Sources

JOURNAL ARTICLES

Bacevich, A. J. "The Paradox of Professionalism: Eisenhower, Ridgway, and the Challenge of Civilian Control, 1953–1955." *Journal of Military History* 61 (April 1997): 303–33.

Berlin, Robert H. "United States Army World War II Corps Commanders: A Composite Biography." *Journal of Military History* 53 (April 1989): 147–67.

Berry, Sydney B. "No Time for Glory in the Infantry: The Letters of Anton Myrer, Author of Once an Eagle." *Assembly* 56 (March/April 1988): 43–46.

Blumenson, Martin. "Relieved of Command." *Army* 21 (August 1971): 30–37.

Bolger, Daniel P. "Zero Defects: Command Climate in First US Army, 1944–1945." *Military Review* 71 (May 1991): 61–73.

Carr, Caleb. "The American Rommel." *Military History Quarterly* (Summer 1992): 77–85.

"The Cavalry Maneuvers at Fort Riley, Kansas, 1934." *Cavalry Journal* 43 (July–August 1934): 5–14.

Chaffee, Adna R. "The Seventh Cavalry Brigade in the First Army Maneuvers." *Cavalry Journal* 48 (November–December 1939): 450–61.

Ganz, A. Harding. "Patton's Relief of General Wood." *Journal of Military History* 53 (July 1989): 257–73.

Grimes, William M. "The 1940 Spring Maneuvers." *Cavalry Journal* 49 (March–April 1940): 98–114.

Grunert, George. "Cavalry in Future War." *Cavalry Journal* 42 (May–June 1933): 5–10.

Gurley, Franklin Louis. "Policy versus Strategy: The Defense of Strasbourg in Winter 1944–1945." *Journal of Military History* 58 (July 1994): 481–514.

Heavey, T. J. "An Observer at the First Army Maneuvers." *Cavalry Journal* 48 (November–December 1939): 461–63.

Nenninger, Timothy K. "Creating Officers: The Leavenworth Experience, 1920–1940." *Military Review* 69 (November 1989): 58–68.

———. "Leavenworth and Its Critics: The U.S. Army Command and General Staff School, 1920–1940." *Journal of Military History* 58 (April 1994): 199–231.

Patton, George S., Jr. "Mechanized Forces." *Cavalry Journal* 42 (September–October 1933): 5–8.

Reeves, Joseph R. "Artillery in the Ardennes." *Field Artillery Journal* 36 (March 1946): 138–42, 173–84.

Schnabel, James F. "Ridgway in Korea." *Military Review* 44 (March 1964): 3–13.

Surles, Alexander D. "The Cavalry and Mechanization, 1936." *Cavalry Journal* 45 (January–February 1936): 6–7.

Wainwright, Jonathan M. "Mobility." *Cavalry Journal* 44 (September–October 1935): 20.

COMMAND AND GENERAL STAFF SCHOOL PUBLICATIONS

Command and General Staff School. *Instructional Circular No. 1, Series 1932–1933*. Fort Leavenworth, Kans.: CGSS Press, 1932.

King, Edward L. *Command: Lecture to the Command and General Staff School, September 11, 1925*. Fort Leavenworth, Kans.: General Service Schools Press, 1925.

Smith, H. A. *Address at Opening Exercises of the Command and General Staff School, Fort Leavenworth, Kansas, September 10, 1923*. Fort Leavenworth, Kans.: General Service Schools Press, 1923.

DOCTRINAL MANUALS AND RELATED PUBLICATIONS

School of the Line, General Service Schools. *General Tactical Functions of Larger Units*. Fort Leavenworth, Kans.: General Service Schools Press, 1922.

Table of Organization and Equipment No. 100-2, Headquarters Company, Corps. Washington, D.C.: War Department, 15 July 1943.

War Department. *Field Service Regulations: Larger Units*. Washington, D.C.: Government Printing Office, 1942.

———. *Field Service Regulations, United States Army, 1923*. Washington, D.C.: Government Printing Office, 1924.

GENERAL WORKS

Ball, Harry P. *Of Responsible Command: A History of the U.S. Army War College*. Carlisle Barracks, Pa.: Alumni Association of the USAWC, 1983.

Blair, Clay. *The Forgotten War: America in Korea, 1950–1953*. New York: Times Books, 1987.

Clausewitz, Carl von. *On War*. Edited and translated by Michael Howard and Peter Paret. Princeton: Princeton University Press, 1976.

Coffman, Edward M. "The American Military Generation Gap in World War I: The Leavenworth Clique and the AEF." In *Command and Commanders in Modern Warfare: Proceedings of the Second Military History Symposium, U.S. Air Force Academy, 2–3 May 1968*, edited by William Geffen, 39–48. USAF Academy, December 1969.

———. *The Hilt of the Sword: The Career of Peyton C. March*. Madison: University of Wisconsin Press, 1966.

Conger, Arthur L. *The Rise of U.S. Grant*. New York: Century, 1931. Reprint with new introduction by Brooks D. Simpson. New York: Da Capo, 1996.

Corbett, Julian S. *Some Principles of Maritime Strategy*. 1911. Reprint. Annapolis: Naval Institute Press, 1988.

Corum, James S. *The Roots of Blitzkrieg: Hans von Seeckt and German Military Reform*. Lawrence: University Press of Kansas, 1992.

Daniel, Donald C., and Katherine L. Herbig, eds. *Strategic Military Deception*. New York: Pergamon, 1982.

Dastrup, Boyd L. *King of Battle: A Branch History of the U.S. Army's Field Artillery*. Fort Monroe, Va.: United States Army Training and Doctrine Command, 1992.

———. *The U.S. Army Command and General Staff College: A Centennial History*. Manhattan, Kans.: Sunflower University Press, 1982.

Fant, Joseph L. III, and Robert Ashley, eds. *Faulkner at West Point*. New York: Random House, 1964.

Freeman, Douglas Southall. *Douglas Southall Freeman on Military Leadership*. Edited by Stuart W. Smith. Shippensburg, Pa.: White Mane Publishing, 1993.

———. *R. E. Lee: A Biography*. 4 vols. 1934–1935. Reprint, New York: Charles Scribner's, 1962.

Golovine, Nicholas N. *The Russian Army in the World War*. New Haven: Yale University Press, 1931.

———. *The Russian Campaign of 1914: The Beginning of the War and Operations in East Prussia*. Fort Leavenworth, Kans.: CGSS Press, 1933.

Görlitz, Walter. *History of the German General Staff*. Translated by Brian Battershaw. New York: Praeger, 1959.

Green, Constance McLaughlin. *Washington: Capital City, 1879–1950*. Princeton: Princeton University Press, 1963.

Johnson, David E. *Fast Tanks and Heavy Bombers: Innovation in the U.S. Army, 1917–1945*. Ithaca, N.Y.: Cornell University Press, 1998.

Moran, Lord. *The Anatomy of Courage*. 2nd ed. London: Constable, 1966.

Mueller, Andrew M. "Challenging Policy: Confronting the Military Professional's Dilemma." Maxwell AFB, Ala.: SAASS, June 1999.

Myrer, Anton. *Once an Eagle*. New York: Holt, Rinehart and Winston, 1968.

Nenninger, Timothy K. *The Leavenworth Schools and the Old Army: Education, Professionalism, and the Officer Corps of the United States Army, 1881–1918*. Westport, Conn.: Greenwood, 1978.

Pappas, George. *Prudens Futuri: The US Army War College, 1901–1967*. Carlisle Barracks, Pa.: Alumni Association of the USAWC, [1967].

Phillips, T. R. "Solving the Tactical Equation: The Logical Foundation of the Estimate of the Situation." *Command and General Staff School Quarterly Review of Military Literature* 17 (September 1937): 5–51.

Reardon, Carol. *Soldiers and Scholars: The U.S. Army and the Uses of Military History, 1865–1920*. Lawrence: University Press of Kansas, 1990.

Simons, William E., ed. *Professional Military Education in the United States: A Historical Dictionary*. Westport, Conn.: Greenwood, 2000.

Truscott, Lucian K., Jr. *The Twilight of the U.S. Cavalry: Life in the Old Army, 1917–1942*. Lawrence: University Press of Kansas, 1989.

van Creveld, Martin. *Supplying War*. Cambridge: Cambridge University Press, 1977.

Vandiver, Frank. *Black Jack: The Life and Times of John J. Pershing.* 2 vols. College Station: Texas A&M University Press, 1977.

WORKS ON WORLD WAR II

Ambrose, Stephen E. *Band of Brothers: E Company, 506th Regiment, 101st Airborne, from Normandy to Hitler's Eagle's Nest.* New York: Simon and Schuster, 2001.

———. *Citizen Soldiers: The U.S. Army from the Normandy Beaches to the Bulge to the Surrender of Germany, June 7, 1944–May 7, 1945.* New York: Simon and Schuster, 1997.

Atkinson, Rick. *An Army at Dawn: The War in North Africa, 1942–1943.* New York: Henry Holt, 2002.

Baldwin, Hanson W. *Battles Lost and Won.* New York: Harper and Row, 1966.

Baron, Richard, Abe Baum, and Richard Goldhurst. *Raid! The Untold Story of Patton's Secret Mission.* New York: Berkley Books, 1984.

Bennett, Ralph. *Ultra in the West: The Normandy Campaign, 1944–45.* New York: Scribner's, 1979.

Blandford, Edmund L. *Hitler's Second Army: The Waffen SS.* Osceola, Wis.: Motorbooks International, 1994.

Blumenson, Martin. *Breakout and Pursuit.* Washington, D.C.: OCMH, 1961.

Bryant, Arthur. *Triumph in the West: A History of the War Years Based on the Diaries of Field-Marshal Lord Alanbrooke, Chief of the Imperial General Staff.* New York: Doubleday, 1959.

Chamberlain, Peter, and Hilary L. Doyle. *An Encyclopedia of German Tanks in World War Two.* New York: Arco, 1978.

Chamberlain, Peter, and Chris Ellis. *British and American Tanks of World War II.* New York: Arco, 1969.

Clarke, Jeffrey J., and Robert Ross Smith. *Riviera to the Rhine.* Washington, D.C.: CMH, 1993.

Cline, Ray S. *Washington Command Post: The Operations Division.* Washington, D.C.: OCMH, 1951.

Cole, Hugh M. *The Lorraine Campaign.* Washington, D.C.: U.S. Army Historical Division, 1950.

Cooling, Benjamin, ed. *Case Studies in the Development of Close Air Support.* Washington, D.C.: OAFH, 1990.

Craven, Wesley Frank, and James Lea Cate, eds. *The Army Air Forces in World War II.* 6 vols. 1949. Reprint, Washington, D.C.: OAFH, 1983.

Currey, Cecil B. *Follow Me and Die: The Destruction of an American Division in World War II.* New York: Stein and Day, 1984.

Dear, I. C. B., and M. R. D. Foot, eds. *The Oxford Companion to World War II.* Oxford: Oxford University Press, 1995.

D'Este, Carlo. *Bitter Victory: The Battle for Sicily, 1943.* Glasgow: Collins, 1988.

———. *Fatal Decision: Anzio and the Battle for Rome.* New York: Harper Collins, 1991.

DiNardo, R. L. *Mechanized Juggernaut or Military Anachronism? Horses and the German Army of World War II.* New York: Greenwood, 1991.

Doubler, Michael D. *Closing with the Enemy: How GIs Fought the War in Europe, 1944–1945.* Lawrence: University Press of Kansas, 1994.

Editors of Command Magazine. *Hitler's Army: The Evolution and Structure of German Armed Forces, 1933–1945*. Conshohocken, Pa.: Combined Books, 1996.

Forty, George. *German Tanks of World War II "in Action."* London: Blandford, 1988.

Frank, Richard B. *Guadalcanal*. New York: Random House, 1990.

Gabel, Christopher R. *Seek and Destroy: U.S. Army Tank Destroyer Doctrine in World War II*. Fort Leavenworth, Kans.: U.S. Army CGSC, 1985.

Garland, Albert N., and Howard McGaw Smyth. *Sicily and the Surrender of Italy*. Washington, D.C.: OCMH, 1965.

Glantz, David, and Jonathan M. House. *When Titans Clashed: How the Red Army Stopped Hitler*. Lawrence: University Press of Kansas, 1995.

Great Britain, Air Ministry. *The Rise and Fall of the German Air Force, 1933–1945*. 1948. Reprint, New York: St. Martin's, 1983.

Greenfield, Kent R., ed. *Command Decisions*. Washington, D.C.: OCMH, 1960.

———, Robert R. Palmer, and Bell I. Wiley. *The Organization of Ground Combat Troops*. Washington, D.C.: Department of the Army, 1947.

Harrison, Gordon A. *Cross Channel Attack*. Washington, D.C.: OCMH, 1951.

Hart, Russell. *Clash of Arms: How the Allies Won in Normandy*. Boulder, Colo.: Lynne Rienner, 2001.

Heiber, Helmut, and David M. Glantz, eds. *Hitler and His Generals: Military Conferences, 1942–1945*. New York: Enigma, 2002–2003.

Hinsley, F. H., E. E. Thomas, C. A. G. Simkins, and C. F. G. Ranson. *British Intelligence in the Second World War: Its Influence on Strategy and Operations*. Vol. 3, pt. 2. New York: Cambridge University Press, 1988.

Hogan, David W., Jr. *A Command Post at War: First Army Headquarters in Europe, 1943–1945*. Washington, D.C.: U.S. Army CMH, 2000.

Horne, Alistair. *To Lose a Battle: France 1940*. Boston: Little Brown, 1969.

Howard, Michael. "Leadership in the British Army in the Second World War: Some Personal Observations." In *Leadership and Command: The Anglo-American Military Experience since 1861*, edited by G. D. Sheffield. London: Brassey's, 1997.

Howe, George F. *Northwest Africa: Seizing the Initiative in the West*. Washington, D.C.: OCMH, 1957.

Irving, David. *The War between the Generals*. New York: Congdon and Lattes, 1981.

Koch, Oscar W., with Robert G. Hays. *G-2: Intelligence for Patton*. Philadelphia: Whitmore, 1971.

Larrabee, Eric. *Commander-in-Chief: Franklin Delano Roosevelt, His Lieutenants, and Their War*. New York: Harper and Row, 1987.

Leinbaugh, Harold P., and John D. Campbell. *The Men of Company K: The Autobiography of a World War II Rifle Company*. New York: William Morrow, 1985.

MacDonald, Charles B. *The Mighty Endeavor: American Armed Forces in the European Theater in World War II*. New York: Oxford University Press, 1969.

———. *The Siegfried Line Campaign*. Washington, D.C.: OCMH, 1963.

———, and Sidney T. Mathews. *Three Battles: Arnaville, Altuzzo, and Schmidt*. Washington, D.C.: OCMH, 1952.

MacDonald, JoAnna. *The Liberation of Pointe du Hoc: The 2nd U.S. Rangers at Normandy*. Redondo Beach, Calif.: Rank and File Publications, 2000.

Mansoor, Peter. *The GI Offensive in Europe: The Triumph of American Infantry Divisions, 1941–1945*. Lawrence: University Press of Kansas, 1999.

Middlebrook, Martin, and Chris Everitt, eds. *The Bomber Command War Diaries: An Operational Reference Book, 1939–1945*. London: Penguin, 1990.

Mierzejewski, Alfred C. *The Collapse of the German War Economy, 1944–1945: Allied Air Power and the German National Railway*. Chapel Hill: University of North Carolina Press, 1988.

Miller, Edward G. *A Dark and Bloody Ground: The Hürtgen Forest and the Roer River Dams, 1944–1945*. College Station: Texas A&M University Press, 1995.

Murray, G. E. Patrick. *Eisenhower versus Montgomery: The Continuing Debate*. Westport, Conn.: Praeger, 1996.

Overy, Richard. *The Air War, 1939–1945*. New York: Stein and Day, 1980.

———. *War and Economy in the Third Reich*. Oxford: Clarendon, 1994.

———. *Why the Allies Won*. New York: W. W. Norton, 1995.

Palmer, Robert R., Bell I. Wiley, and William R. Keast. *The Procurement and Training of Army Ground Combat Troops*. Washington, D.C.: Department of the Army, 1948.

Pogue, Forrest C. *The Supreme Command*. Washington, D.C.: OCMH, 1954.

Price, Alfred. *The Last Year of the Luftwaffe, May 1944 to May 1945*. Osceola, Wis.: Motorbooks International, 1991.

Pyle, Ernie. *Brave Men*. 1944. Reprint, Lincoln: University of Nebraska Press, 2001.

Ruppenthal, Roland G. *Logistical Support of the Armies*. 2 vols. Washington, D.C.: OCMH, 1953–1959.

Ryan, Cornelius. *A Bridge Too Far*. New York: Simon and Schuster, 1974.

Showalter, Dennis, ed. *World War II, 1944–1945*. Vol. 5 of *History in Dispute*. Detroit: St. James, 2000.

Shwedo, Bradford J. *XIX Tactical Air Command and ULTRA: Patton's Force Enhancers in the 1944 Campaign in France*. Maxwell AFB, Ala.: Air University Press, 2002.

Spires, David N. *Air Power for Patton's Army: The XIX Tactical Air Command in the Second World War*. Washington, D.C.: Air Force History and Museums Program, 2002.

Stanton, Shelby L. *World War II Order of Battle*. New York: Galahad Books, 1984.

Toland, John. *The Last 100 Days*. New York: Random House, 1966.

United States Strategic Bombing Survey. *European War Report Number 61, Air Force Rate of Operations*. Washington, D.C.: USSBS, 1947.

van Creveld, Martin. *Fighting Power: German and U.S. Army Performance, 1939–1945*. Westport, Conn.: Greenwood, 1982.

Weigley, Russell F. *Eisenhower's Lieutenants: The Campaigns in France and Germany, 1944–1945*. Bloomington: Indiana University Press, 1981.

Weinberg, Gerhard. *A World at Arms: A Global History of World War II*. New York: Cambridge University Press, 1994.

Wilmot, Chester. *The Struggle for Europe*. New York: Harper and Brothers, 1952.

Winterbotham, F. W. *The Ultra Secret*. New York: Harper and Row, 1974.

WORKS ON THE BATTLE OF THE BULGE

Bauserman, John M. *The Malmédy Massacre*. Shippensburg, Pa.: White Mane Publishing, 1995.

Cavanagh, William C. C. *Krinkelt-Rocherath: The Battle for the Twin Villages*. Norwell, Mass.: Christopher Publishing House, 1986.

Delaforce, Patrick. *The Battle of the Bulge: Hitler's Final Gamble*. Harlow, England: Pearson Education, 2004.

Dupuy, Trevor N., David L. Bongard, and Richard C. Anderson, Jr. *Hitler's Last Gamble: The Battle of the Bulge, December 1944–January 1945*. New York: Harper Collins, 1994.

Eisenhower, John S. D. *The Bitter Woods: The Dramatic Story, Told at All Echelons—from Supreme Commander to Squad Leader—of the Crisis That Shook the Western Coalition: Hitler's Surprise Ardennes Offensive*. New York: G. P. Putnam's, 1969. Reprint, New York: Da Capo Press, 1995.

Forty, George. *The Reich's Last Gamble: The Ardennes Offensive, December 1944*. London: Cassell, 2000.

Giles, Janice Holt. *The Damned Engineers*. 2nd ed. Washington, D.C.: Office of the Chief of Engineers, 1985.

Kays, Marvin. *Weather Effects during the Battle of the Bulge and the Normandy Invasion*. White Sands Missile Range, N. Mex.: U.S. Army Electronics Research and Development Command Atmospheric Sciences Laboratory, 1982.

Kershaw, Alex. *The Longest Winter: The Battle of the Bulge and the Epic Story of World War II's Most Decorated Platoon*. Cambridge, Mass.: Da Capo, 2004.

MacDonald, Charles. *The Last Offensive*. Washington, D.C.: OCMH, 1973.

———. *A Time for Trumpets: The Untold Story of the Battle of the Bulge*. New York: William Morrow, 1985.

Marshall, S. L. A. *Bastogne: The Story of the First Eight Days in Which the 101st Airborne Division Was Closed within the Ring of German Forces*. Washington, D.C.: Infantry Journal Press, 1946.

Merriam, Robert. *Dark December: The Full Account of the Battle of the Bulge*. New York: Ziff-Davis, 1947.

Mitchell, Ralph M. *The 101st Airborne Division's Defense of Bastogne*. Fort Leavenworth, Kans.: U.S. Army CGSC, 1986.

Morelock, J. D. *Generals of the Ardennes: American Leadership in the Battle of the Bulge*. Washington, D.C.: NDU Press, 1994.

Neill, George W. *Infantry Soldier: Holding the Line at the Battle of the Bulge*. Norman: University of Oklahoma Press, 2000.

Pallud, Jean Paul. *Battle of the Bulge: Then and Now*. London: Battle of Britain Prints International, 1984.

Parker, Danny S. *To Win the Winter Sky: The Air War over the Ardennes, 1944–1945*. Conshohocken, Pa.: Combined Books, 1994.

———. ed. *The Battle of the Bulge, the German View: Perspectives from Hitler's High Command*. Mechanicsburg, Pa.: Stackpole Books, 1999.

Phillips, Robert F. *To Save Bastogne*. New York: Stein and Day, 1983.

Reynolds, Michael. *Men of Steel: I SS Panzer Corps, the Ardennes and Eastern Front, 1944–45*. New York: Sarpedon, 1999.

Rusiecki, Stephen M. *The Key to the Bulge: The Battle for Losheimergraben*. Westport, Conn.: Praeger, 1996.

Toland, John. *Battle: The Story of the Bulge.* 1959. Reprint, Lincoln: University of Nebraska Press, 2001.

BIOGRAPHICAL WORKS AND REFERENCES

Alexander, Larry. *Biggest Brother: The Life of Major Dick Winters, the Man Who Led the Band of Brothers.* New York: NAL Caliber, 2005.

Ancell, R. Manning, with Christine M. Miller. *The Biographical Dictionary of World War II Generals and Flag Officers: The U.S. Armed Forces.* Westport, Conn.: Greenwood, 1996.

Astor, Gerald. *Terrible Terry Allen, Combat General of World War II: The Life of an American Soldier.* New York: Ballantine, 2003.

Barnett, Correlli, ed. *Hitler's Generals.* New York: Grove Weidenfeld, 1989.

Blair, Clay. *Ridgway's Paratroopers: The American Airborne in World War II.* New York: Doubleday, 1985.

Bland, Larry I., and Sharon Ritenour Stevens, eds. *The Papers of George Catlett Marshall.* Vols. 1–5. Baltimore: Johns Hopkins University Press, 1981–2003.

Blumenson, Martin. *Patton: The Man behind the Legend.* New York: William Morrow, 1985.

———, ed. *The Patton Papers.* 2 vols. Boston: Houghton Mifflin, 1972–1974.

Blunt, Roscoe C., Jr. *Inside the Battle of the Bulge: A Private Comes of Age.* Westport, Conn.: Praeger, 1994.

The Bomb. Lexington, Va.: Virginia Military Institute, 1911.

Bowen, Robert M. *Fighting with the Screaming Eagles: With the 101st Airborne from Normandy to Bastogne.* London: Greenhill Books, 2001.

Bradley, Omar. *A Soldier's Story.* New York: Henry Holt, 1951.

———, and Clay Blair. *A General's Life: An Autobiography by General of the Army Omar N. Bradley and Clay Blair.* New York: Simon and Schuster, 1983.

Braim, Paul F. *The Will to Win: The Life of General James A. Van Fleet.* Annapolis: Naval Institute Press, 2001.

Brawley, John. *Anyway, We Won: A Civilian Soldier from the Ozarks Spends Five Years in the Army.* Marceline, Mo.: Walsworth, 1988.

Burgett, Donald. *Seven Roads to Hell: A Screaming Eagle at Bastogne.* Novato, Calif.: Presidio Press, 1999.

Cawthon, Charles R. *Other Men's Clay: A Remembrance of the World War II Infantry.* Niwot: University Press of Colorado, 1990.

Chandler, Alfred D., et al., eds. *The Papers of Dwight David Eisenhower: The War Years.* 5 vols. Baltimore: Johns Hopkins University Press, 1970.

Colby, John. *War from the Ground Up: The 90th Division in WWII.* Austin: Nortex, 1991.

Collins, J. Lawton. *Lightning Joe: An Autobiography.* 1979. Reprint, Novato, Calif.: Presidio Press, 1994.

Crosswell, D. K. R. *The Chief of Staff: The Military Career of General Walter Bedell Smith.* New York: Greenwood, 1991.

Danchev, Alex, and Daniel Todman, eds. *War Diaries, 1939–1945: Field Marshal Lord Alanbrooke.* Berkeley: University of California Press, 2001.

Davis, Richard G. *Carl A. Spaatz and the Air War in Europe.* Washington, D.C.: CAFH, 1993.

de Guingand, Francis. *Operation Victory.* New York: Scribner's, 1947.

D'Este, Carlo. *Eisenhower: A Soldier's Life*. New York: Henry Holt, 2002.

———. *Patton: A Genius for War*. New York: Harper Collins, 1995.

Eisenhower, David. *Eisenhower: At War 1943–1945*. London: Collins, 1986.

Eisenhower, Dwight D. *At Ease: Stories I Tell to Friends*. Garden City, N.Y.: Doubleday, 1967.

———. *Crusade in Europe*. Garden City, N.Y.: Doubleday, 1948.

Ellis, William Donohue, and Thomas J. Cunningham. *Clarke of St. Vith: The Sergeant's General*. Cleveland: Dillon/Liederbach, 1974.

Galland, Adolf. *The First and the Last: The Rise and Fall of the German Fighter Forces, 1938–1945*. Translated by Mervyn Savill. New York: Henry Holt, 1954.

Gavin, James M. *On to Berlin: Battles of an Airborne Commander, 1943–1946*. New York: Viking, 1978.

Girbig, Werner. *Six Months to Oblivion: The Defeat of the Luftwaffe Fighter Force over the Western Front*. Translated by David Johnston and Richard Simpkin. West Chester, Pa.: Schiffer Military History, 1991.

Hamilton, Nigel. *The Full Monty: Montgomery of Alamein, 1887–1942*. London: Allen Lane, 2001.

———. *Monty: Final Years of the Field-Marshal, 1944–1976*. New York: McGraw-Hill, 1987.

Harmon, E. N., with Milton MacKaye and William Ross MacKaye. *Combat Commander: Autobiography of a Soldier*. Englewood Cliffs, N.J.: Prentice-Hall, 1970.

Harris, Arthur. *Bomber Offensive*. New York: Macmillan, 1947.

Hofmann, George F. *Cold War Casualty: The Court-Martial of Major General Robert W. Grow*. Kent, Ohio: Kent State University Press, 1993.

The Howitzer. West Point, N.Y.: USMA, 1910 and 1917.

Jackson, W. G. F. *Alexander of Tunis as Military Commander*. London: B. T. Batsford, 1971.

James, Robert Rhoades., ed. *Winston S. Churchill: His Complete Speeches*. New York: Chelsea House, 1974.

Leonard, John W., Jr., and George Ruhlen. "John W. Leonard, '15: A Star in the Class the Stars Fell On." *Assembly* 61 (March/April 2003): 46–48.

Lockerbie, D. Bruce. *A Man under Orders: Lieutenant General William K. Harrison, Jr*. New York: Harper and Row, 1979.

Lucas, James. *The Last Year of the German Army, May 1944–May 1945*. London: Arms and Armour, 1994.

MacDonald, Charles B. *Company Commander*. 1947. Reprint, New York: Ballantine, 1961.

Meilinger, Phillip S. *Hoyt S. Vandenberg: The Life of a General*. Bloomington: Indiana University Press, 1989.

Mets, David. *Master of Airpower: General Carl A. Spaatz*. Novato, Calif.: Presidio Press, 1988.

Miller, Robert A. *Division Commander: A Biography of Major General Norman D. Cota*. Spartanburg, S.C.: Reprint Company, 1989.

Montgomery, Bernard. *The Memoirs of Field-Marshal the Viscount Montgomery of Alamein, K.G.* Cleveland: World Publishing, 1958.

Orange, Vincent. *Coningham: A Biography of Air Marshal Sir Arthur Coningham*. Washington, D.C.: CAFH, 1992.

Ossad, Steven L., and Don R. Marsh. *Major General Maurice Rose: World War II's Greatest Forgotten Commander*. Lanham, Md.: Taylor Trade Publishing, 2003.

Patton, George S., Jr. *War as I Knew It*. Boston: Houghton Mifflin, 1947.

Phillips, Henry Gerard. *The Making of a Professional: Manton S. Eddy, USA*. Westport, Conn.: Greenwood, 2000.

Pogue, Forrest C. *George C. Marshall: Education of a General, 1880–1939*. New York: Viking, 1963.

———. *George C. Marshall: Organizer of Victory, 1943–1945*. New York: Viking, 1973.

Price, Frank James. *Troy H. Middleton: A Biography*. Baton Rouge: Louisiana State University Press, 1974.

Reynolds, Michael Frank. *The Devil's Adjutant: Jochen Peiper, Panzer Leader*. New York: Sarpedon, 1995.

Ridgway, Matthew B. As Told to Harold H. Martin. *Soldier: The Memoirs of Matthew B. Ridgway*. New York: Harper and Brothers, 1956.

Skorzeny, Otto. *My Commando Operations: The Memoirs of Hitler's Most Daring Commando*. Translated by David Johnston. Atglen, Pa.: Schiffer Military History, 1995.

Soffer, Jonathan M. *General Matthew B. Ridgway: From Progressivism to Reaganism, 1895–1993*. Westport, Conn.: Praeger, 1998.

Sorley, Lewis. *Thunderbolt: General Creighton Abrams and the Army of His Times*. New York: Simon and Schuster, 1992.

Spayd, P. A. *Bayerlein: From Afrikakorps to Panzer Lehr*. Atglen, Pa.: Schiffer Military History, 2003.

Taylor, Matthew D. *Swords and Plowshares*. New York: W. W. Norton, 1972.

Tedder, Arthur. *With Prejudice: The War Memoirs of Marshal of the Royal Air Force Lord Tedder GCB*. London: Cassell, 1966.

Trez, Michel de. *Colonel Ben Vandervoort "Vandy" 0-22715: Commanding Officer, 2nd Battalion, 505th Parachute Infantry Regiment, 82nd Airborne Division*. Wezembeek-Oppem, Belgium: D-Day Publishing, 2004.

United States Military Academy. *Register of Graduates and Former Cadets, 1802–1947*. West Point, N.Y.: USMA, 1947.

Virginia Military Institute Official Register, 1911–1912. Lexington, Va.: VMI, 1912.

Warlimont, Walter. *Inside Hitler's Headquarters, 1939–1945*. Translated by R. H. Barry. 1964. Reprint, Novato, Calif.: Presidio Press [1991].

Wedemeyer, Albert C. *Wedemeyer Reports!* New York: Henry Holt, 1958.

Weingartner, James J. *A Peculiar Crusade: Willis M. Everett and the Malmedy Massacre*. New York: New York University Press 2000.

Westmoreland, William C. *A Soldier Reports*. New York: Doubleday, 1976.

Who Was Who in American History: The Military. Chicago: Marquis Who's Who, 1975.

Yerger, Mark C. *Waffen-SS Commanders: The Army, Corps, and Divisional Commanders of a Legend*. 2 vols. Atglen, Pa.: Schiffer Military History, 1999.

UNIT HISTORIES

Combat History of the Second Infantry Division in World War II. 1946. Reprint, Nashville: Battery Press, 1979.

Craig, Berry. *11th Armored Division Thunderbolts*. Paducah, Ky.: Turner Publishing, 1988.

Draper, Theodore. *The 84th Infantry Division in the Battle of Germany, November 1944–May 1945*. 1946. Reprint, Nashville: Battery Press, 1985.

Dupuy, R. Ernest. *St. Vith Lion in the Way: The 106th Infantry Division in World War II*. Washington, D.C.: Infantry Journal Press, 1949.

Dyer, George. *XII Corps: Spearhead of Patton's Third Army*. N.p.: XII U.S. Army Corps, n.d.

V Corps Operations in the ETO, 6 January 1942–9 May 1945. N.p., n.d.

The Fifth Infantry Division in the ETO. 1945. Reprint, Nashville: Battery Press, 1997.

An Historical and Pictorial Record of the 87th Infantry Division in World War II, 1942–1945. 1946. Reprint, n.p.: 87th Infantry Division Association, 1988.

Hofmann, George F. *The Super Sixth: History of the 6th Armored Division in World War II and Its Post-War Association*. Louisville: Sixth Armored Division Association, 1975.

Houston, Donald E. *Hell on Wheels: The Second Armored Division*. San Rafael, Calif.: Presidio Press, 1977.

Knickerbocker, H. R., et al. *Danger Forward: The Story of the First Division in World War II*. Washington, D.C.: Society of the First Division, 1947.

Lauer, Walter E. *Battle Babies: The Story of the 99th Infantry Division in World War II*. Baton Rouge: Military Press of Louisiana, 1951.

Mission Accomplished: The Story of the Campaigns of the VII Corps United States Army in the War against Germany, 1944–1945. Leipzig: J. J. Weber, 1945.

Nichols, Lester M. *Impact: The Battle Story of the Tenth Armored Division*. [New York]: Bradley, Sayles, O'Neill, 1954.

Pay, Don R. *Thunder from Heaven: Story of the 17th Airborne Division, 1943–1945*. 1947. Reprint, Nashville: Battery Press [1980].

Presenting . . . The 35th Infantry Division in World War II, 1941–1945. 1946. Reprint, Nashville: Battery Press, 1988.

Rapport, Leonard, and Arthur Norwood, Jr. *Rendezvous with Destiny: A History of the 101st Airborne Division*. 1948. Reprint, Nashville: Battery Press, 2000.

Reichelt, Walter E. *Phantom Nine: The 9th Armored (Remagen) Division, 1942–1945*. Austin: Presidial Press, 1987.

The 75th Infantry Division in Combat: The Battle in the Ardennes, 23 Dec 1944–27 Jan 1945; The Colmar Pocket Battle, 30 Jan 1945–9 Feb 1945; The Battle for the Ruhr, 31 Mar 1945–15 Apr 1945. N.p., n.d.

Spearhead in the West, 1941–1945: The Third Armored Division. 1945. Reprint, Nashville: Battery Press, 1980.

INDEX

Grow, Robert W. (*continued*)
    Bastogne and, 230
    Eisenhower and, 425n78
    Millikin and, 230
    Patton and, 229
    post-war court-martial of, 425n78
    Skyline Drive and, 328
Guadalcanal, 54–55, 60
Guderian, Heinz, 91, 97

Haislip, Wade H. "Ham," 190, 375n42
Halifaxes, 94, 212, 420n52
Hamilton, Nigel, 3, 386n26, 418n25
    on Montgomery/Bradley, 417–418n12
Hamilton, Paul, 223, 225
Hammelburg prison raid, 356, 460n74
Hansen, Chester, 101, 103, 288, 416–417n10
    air operations and, 110
    Montgomery and, 289
Hardigny, 319
Harkins, Paul D., 230
Harlange, 228, 229, 324
Harlange Pocket, 233, 314
    encirclement of, 231
    reduction of, 322–28, 334, 342, 344, 346
Harmon, Ernest N., 271, 274, 276, 341, 444n16
    1st AD and, 437n90
    2nd AD and, 213, 270, 280, 294, 295, 299
    Ninth Army and, 192
    335th Infantry Regiment and, 443n11
    attack by, 281
    Buissonville and, 270
    checkmate by, 275
    Collins and, 312, 383n188
    Houffalize and, 299, 300
    leadership of, 270
    Patton and, 437n90
    planning by, 272–73, 298
    Samrée and, 297
Harper, Robert S., 155
Harris, Arthur "Bomber," 94, 109–110
Harrison, Willard E., 178, 181
Harrison, William K., 181, 307, 414n37, 446n52
Harrold, Thomas L., 152
Hasbrouck, Robert W., 259, 261, 265, 308, 310, 311, 312
    7th AD and, 434n39
    Jones and, 154, 182, 415n47
    at La Roche, 158
    leadership of, 169
    letter to Kean from, 178–79
    Middleton and, 159, 178
    Ondenval defile and, 307
    Ridgway and, 179, 185, 432n10
    St. Vith and, 155, 164, 178–79, 183, 253, 256, 309
    at Vielsalm, 146

withdrawal and, 251, 253, 255, 256, 257, 433n11
Hasselt, 205, 206
Hawaiian Department, 54
Hawaiian Division, 45
Heinerscheid, 151, 152, 328
Heintzelman, Stuart, 50
Henderson, G. F. R., 19
Henry, Patrick, 24
Hermann Göring Division, 42
Herr, John K., 26, 27, 28
    on Allenby's leadership, 22, 23, 370n36
Hickey, Doyle, 258, 278, 281
Higgins, Gerald J., 160
Hightower, John M., 124, 128
Hindenburg, Paul von, 24, 27
Hinds, John H., 120, 133–34
Hinds, Sidney R., 276, 298
Hines, John L., Jr., 230
Hirschfelder, Chester J., 121, 123, 124
Hitler, Adolf, 74, 181, 204, 267, 318, 407n62
    150th Brigade and, 90–91
    Antwerp and, 105, 269
    Ardennes campaign and, 3, 69, 70, 81, 102, 112, 209, 339, 346
    assassination attempt on, 89
    determination of, 68, 72
    general staff and, 392n107
    Manteuffel and, 139, 141, 406n56
    Model and, 71, 117, 232
    OKW meteorologists and, 386n19
    political goal of, 107
    Skorzeny and, 90–91, 392n101
    small slam and, 117
    strategy and, 92, 385n10
    surprise by, 80
    two-front war and, 80
    western theater and, 69
    withdrawal from Ardennes and, 291–92
Hitler's Last Gamble (Dupuy, Bongard, and Anderson), 4
Hitler Youth Division, 420n52
Hitzfeld, Otto, 283, 398n25
    LXVII Corps and, 118, 119, 282
Hobbs, Leland S., 177, 184, 259, 303, 304, 306, 310, 346
    30th ID and, 130
    119th IR and, 307
    Hodges and, 130
    Ridgway and, 176
    tactical competence of, 446n52
Hodges, Courtney H., xii, 37, 77, 145, 156, 414n26
    First Army and, 4, 76, 101, 103, 376n61
    1st ID and, 312, 354
    7th AD and, 255
    XVIII (Airborne) Corps and, 412n7